MW01617123

IF YOU'RE
CRACKED
YOU'RE HAPPY

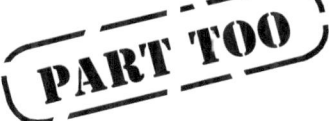

ALSO BY MARK ARNOLD:

The Best of The Harveyville Fun Times!

Created and Produced by Total TeleVision productions:
    The Story of Underdog, Tennessee Tuxedo and the Rest

IF YOU'RE

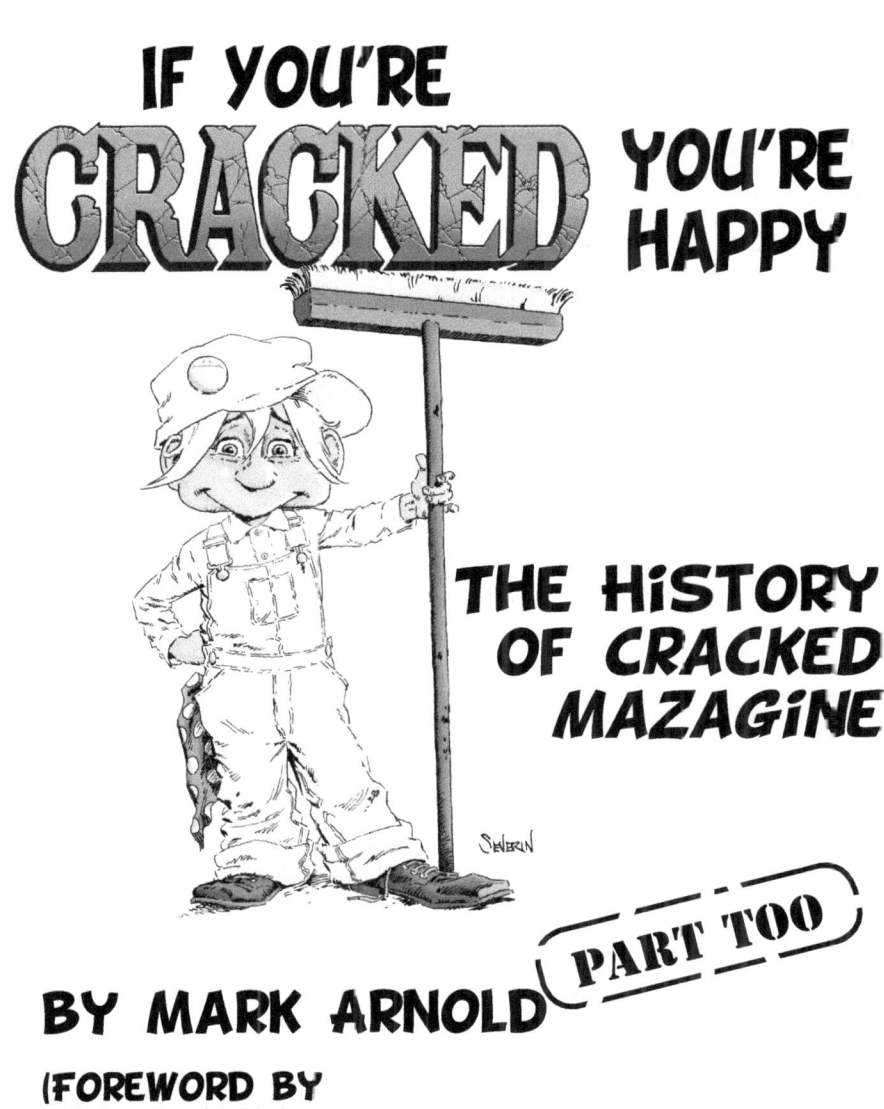

CRACKED YOU'RE HAPPY

THE HiSTORY OF CRACKED MAZAGiNE

BY MARK ARNOLD PART TOO

(FOREWORD BY PHiLiP FREY)

BearManor Media

2011

If You're Cracked, You're Happy: The History of Cracked Mazagine, Part II
©2011 Mark Arnold and Fun Ideas Productions.
All Rights Reserved.

Published in the USA by BearManor Media
1317 Edgewater Dr #110 • Orlando, FL 32804
www.bearmanormedia.com

Cover artwork by John Severin from the collection of Jerry Boyd. Color and additional layout by Mort Todd. Interior graphics courtesy of Mike Arnold, Greg Beda, Jerry Boyd, Dan Fiorella, Marten Jallad, John Severin, B.K. Taylor, Mort Todd, and from various issues of *Cracked* magazine and other sources. Typesetting and layout by John Teehan.

ISBN 978-1-62933-678-7

Printed in the United States of America.

TABLE OF CONTENTS

Iron-On detail from *Cracked* #123, March 1975.
Artwork by John Severin.

DEDiCATiON

This book is dedicated to the various people who believed in me during the past year and who put up with my devotion to completing this book in a reasonable amount of time, considering all of my other obligations. Your respect and loyalty is appreciated, and you are all acknowledged by name below...

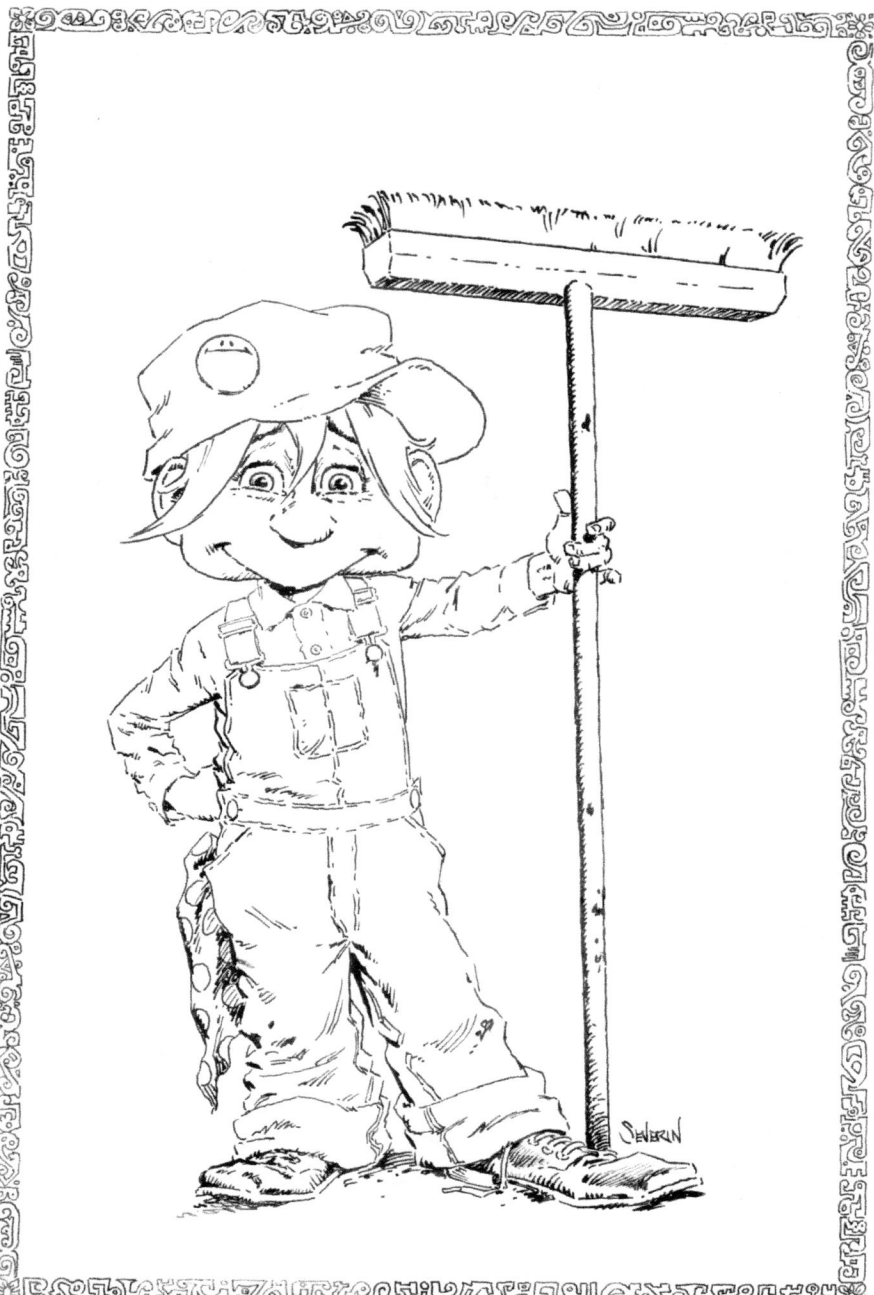

Sylvester Phooey Smythe (1925-   )

ACKNOWLEDGEMENTS

SPECIAL THANKS to Ellen Abramowitz, Jim Amash, Rick Altergott, Noel Anderson, Sergio Aragonés, Mike Arnold, Peter Bagge, Ron Barrett, Jerry Beck, Greg Beda, Bobbie Bender, Dave Berns, Ray Billingsley, Michael Ian Black, Luciano Blotta, Oskar Blotta, Bruce Bolinger, Jerry Boyd, Christie Brehm, Walter Brogan, Gary Brodsky, Roger Brown, Dan Budnick, Brian Buniak, Daryl Cagle, Joe Catalano, Dan Clowes, Ernie Colon, Terry Colon, Frank Cummings, Barbara Dale, Susan D'Antilio, Jack Davis, Michael Delle-Femine, Carson Demmans, Stephen De Stefano, Steve Ditko, Heather Durham, Barry Dutter, Don Edwing, Douglas Everett, Andrew Farago, Al Feldstein, Gary Fields, Bob Fingerman, Dan Fiorella, Pete Fitzgerald, Charles Foster, Kent Gamble, Grant Geissman, George Gladir, Stan Goldberg, Scott Gosar, Greg Grabianski, Murad Gumen, Charles E. Hall, Larry Hama, Russ Heath, Rich Hedden, Sam Henderson, Lee Hester, Troy Hickman, Todd Jackson, Al Jaffee, Marten Jallad, Eric Johnson, Oren Katzeff, Mike Kazaleh, Milton Knight, Dick Kulpa, Alan Kupperberg, Aron Laikin, Paul Laikin, Andy Lamberti, Kit Lively, Jay Lynch, Norma Martin, Nick Meglin, Grant Meihm, Cliff Mott, Rick Nielsen, Dan O'Brien, Ben Ohmart, Don Orehek, Rick Parker, Tom Richmond, Mike Ricigliano, Kevin Sacco, Jim Salicrup, Frank Santopadre, Warren Sattler, John Scrovack, J.J. Sedelmeier, John Severin, Dan Shahin, Scott Shaw!, Lou Silverstone, Andy Simmons, Joe Simon, Lenore Skenazy, Ricky Sprague, Bill Sproul, Howard Stern, Steve Strangio, Tony Tallarico, B.K. Taylor, Roy Thomas, Mort Todd, Angelo Torres, Rurik Tyler, Jim Vadeboncoeur, Sam Viviano, Jim Warren, Rob Weske, Samuel B. Whitehead, Marv Wolfman, Jeff Wong, Bill Wray. I apologize to anyone I didn't get into contact with for this book. Your work on *Cracked* does not go unappreciated or unnoticed.

Dedicated to the memories of Bernard Baily, Henry Boltinoff, Frank Borth, E. Nelson Bridwell, Bernie Brill, Sol Brodsky, Carl Burgos, Pete Costanza, Jerry De Fuccio, Bill Elder, Bill Everett, Sururi Gumen, Lennie Herman, Bill Hoest,

Joe Kiernan, Jack Kirby, Larry Levine, Lugoze, Joe Maneely, Don Martin, Vic Martin, Marian McMahon, Howard Nostrand, Jack O'Brien, Paul Reinman, Charles Rodrigues, Syd Shores, Jerry Siegel, Robert C. Sproul, Bob Stevens, Chic Stone, Bill Ward, Ed Winiarski, Basil Wolverton, Pete Wyma, Bob Zahn. There may be more, and I honor them, too.

Interviews conducted specifically by the author for this book were completed on the following dates:

Rick Altergott, February 28, 2010
Noel Anderson, April 27, 2009 and November 24, 2009
Mike Arnold, March 15, 2009
Ron Barrett, February 1, 2010
Ray Billingsley, April 17, 2009
Bruce Bolinger, November 24, 2009
Walter Brogan, March 10, 2009
Roger Brown, February 3, 2010
Dan Budnik, June 4, 2009
Brian Buniak, April 4, 2009
Daryl Cagle, March 9, 2009
Frank Cummings, November 24, 2009
Jack Davis, May 22, 2009
Carson Demmans, March 3, 2009
Barry Dutter, August 29, 2009
Michael Eury, November 14, 2009
Gary Fields, April 28, 2009
Bob Fingerman, March 11, 2009
Dan Fiorella, February 2, 2010
Pete Fitzgerald, February 28, 2009
Kent Gamble, March 10, 2009
George Gladir, March 21, 2009
Scott Gosar, March 23, 2009
Greg Grabianski, August 12-14, 2009
Murad Gumen, March 31, 2009
Charles E. Hall, March 2, 2010
Larry Hama, February 22, 2009
Russ Heath, March 8, 2009
Frank Jacobs, January 24, 2010
Al Jaffee, May 8-10, 2009
Milton Knight, April 26, 2009
Todd Jackson, February 3, 2010
Marten Jallad, March 8, 2009

Mike Kazaleh, July 28, 2009
Dick Kulpa, November 23, 2009
Alan Kupperberg, February 1, 2010
Aron Laikin, May 9, 2009
Paul Laikin, May 4, 2009
Andy Lamberti, March 10, 2009
Kit Lively, March 25, 2009
Jay Lynch, February 25, 2009 and November 22, 2009
Grant Meihm, March 5, 2009
Cliff Mott, April 2, 2009
Rick Nielsen, August 28, 2009
Don Orehek, March 10, 2009
Rick Parker, January 28, 2010
Steph Ramsay, February 3, 2010
Tom Richmond, May 7, 2009
Mike Ricigliano, February 19, 2009
Kevin Sacco, March 14, 2009
Warren Sattler, March 12, 2009
John Scrovak, February 23, 2009
Michelena Severin for John Severin, March 11, 2009
Lou Silverstone, March 14, 2009
Andy Simmons, March 3, 2009
Joe Simon, March 16, 2009
Ricky Sprague, February 2, 2010
Bill Sproul, January 20, 2010 and February 1, 2010
Steve Strangio, February 1, 2010
Terry Colon, February 3, 2010
Tony Tallarico, March 8, 2009
B.K. Taylor, December 9, 2009
Mort Todd, April 4, 2009
Angelo Torres, May 8, 2009
Marv Wolfman, February 27, 2008

FOREWORD

BY PHILIP FREY

WHY CRACKED?

That's the question I am often asked when I begin discussing my fandom of the "other" humor magazine. To most, *Mad* is pretty much the end-all and the be-all of humor magazines. But not to me. I always found more pure enjoyment from an issue of *Cracked*. But why? Why?

Part of it, no doubt, is the maverick streak in me against the popular choice. I seem to naturally gravitate towards the other guy. Pepsi, not Coke. Burger King, not McDonalds. And *Mad* may have started out tilting against the windmills of pop culture, but eventually it became as much a part of it as the subjects it skewered. *Cracked* was comfortably off most people's radar.

Part of it, of course, is thanks to *Cracked*'s premiere artist, John Severin. Among the seemingly hundreds of Mort Drucker imitators found in the pages of *Crazy*, *Sick* and even *Mad* itself, Severin's realistic art style in *Cracked* made his work stand out from the crowd.

Another major difference was that while all the comics-style humor magazines had mascots and several had recurring characters, only *Cracked* had a full-blown cast that actually interacted with each other (and the artists, editors, publishers, etc.).

But if there was one thing that set it apart for me, it was the comedic sensibility I found in the pages of *Cracked*. Every other *Mad* "rip-off" basically tried to "out-Mad" *Mad*. There was certainly some of that in the early days of *Cracked*, but in its heyday (and here I'm thinking around 1974–1985) it was a very different beast from the others. *Mad* was (and is) all about mockery, its humor based on making fun of the subjects it parodied. *Cracked*, on the other hand, *had* fun with them. Of course in this day and age, with most humor being of the sarcastic, smart-alecky variety, this approach has been criticized as "soft". It's been said that a "Barney Miller" parody, for instance, is hardly distinguishable from an actual episode of "Barney Miller". But, ultimately, that's what endeared *Cracked* to me. As a fan of "Star Wars" (and "M*A*S*H", "Mork & Mindy", "The Dukes of Hazzard", "The A-Team", you name it), I wasn't interested in articles that were going to mercilessly knock the stuff I loved. Calculated or not, *Cracked* parodies spoke to the fanboy in me. I *wanted* to see Luke Skywalker team up with Steve Austin or C-3PO and Chewbacca playing on the Bad News Bears baseball team.

And that's the *Cracked* that I remember and still enjoy to this day. A few years ago, I learned of the final demise of the magazine that had helped define my youth. Learning that there were precisely 365 issues of the magazine (one a day!) spurred a revived interest for me, a determination to have them all. Looking over the magazine's entire history, I can't say it always stuck to the formula that first drew me to it. In the early days, it did follow the *Mad* template much more closely and in the latter days it deteriorated into amateurish gross-out jokes and pandering to a Howard Stern-ish mentality. But even at the end, it was still *Cracked*, the one that outlived Bill Gaines and all the others. While it's fitting that *Mad*, Harvey Kurtzman's genre defining creation, should still be running, even in an era where the comics medium is barely a bump on the mass media road, *Cracked* more than earned its place as the "next-to-the-last man standing".

Why *Cracked*? Because they may not have been first, but to me they were the best.

CAPTURING A MAD MAN: DON MARTIN AT *CRACKED*

WALTER Brogan comments on the arrival of *Mad*'s Maddest Artist Don Martin coming over to *Cracked* in 1987: "Mort Todd: what he did which I thought was pretty good was to bring Don Martin over."

Roger Brown was the catalyst. "One thing that I had a hand in was Don Martin's move from *Mad* to *Cracked*. I had been sending material to Don for some other projects he was working on and mentioned to him that *Cracked* would love to have him onboard. I contacted *Cracked*'s editor Mike and gave him Don's phone number. Shortly after that a deal was made and Don started appearing in *Cracked*. It was great to see a childhood idol in the same magazine I was in."

Michelina Severin said, "The only thing I remember about her is that she thought she had a gold mine on her hands."

Bob Fingerman recalls, "I think Mort was working on that. I do remember Mort trying to sweet talk the wife. I remember Mort talking about how Don's wife was his business manager and it took a lot of time trying to win over her trust and all that. I don't remember any of his work, but everybody was just a huge Don Martin fan. Someone who says they like comics and then say that they don't like Don Martin, well then they don't really like comics."

Dan Clowes, in his interview by Mike Sacks, said, "There was some below-the-radar talk about lawsuits, but I don't think they had any real claim. They were furious. Don had been at *Mad* for more than thirty years.

"I remember *Cracked* throwing this big, fancy dinner for Don and Mrs. Martin in an attempt to woo them over to the other side. Don's wife was really a character. She acted as his agent and was furious about the way *Mad* had treated him. She thought they paid too little, and she was angry that they wouldn't allow Don to own the rights to his own work. Companies would call Don and ask, 'Can we make a calendar or t-shirts with your work?' And he'd have to say no.

"Both were very happy to jump ship. Don received a little more money per page—I think $100 more—and he retained the rights to his own work, which was more important to him. As far as I could tell, he was happy. He never seemed to notice that *Mad* was somewhat respected, while *Cracked* was thought of as the lowest rag imaginable."

Mort Todd reveals how he successfully lured Martin away from *Mad*, due to Martin's increasing dissatisfaction: "Charlotte Catling was painting super-sexy pin ups for *Cracked* with Elvira and Nanny Dickering as a Batwoman, cool color cheesecake stuff in the Ward manner. She has since designed all the Agent Provocateur lingerie stores and created all their way cool packaging. Charlotte's mother, the beloved Diane Wheeler-Nicholson, was a literary agent for a long time. She dealt with a lot of literary lawyers and agents. She was the one that told me about the lawyer handling the Martins and that they were really unhappy at *Mad* and all. I got the Martins' number from the lawyer and called them up and told them, 'We will give you the same page rate. We will give you your original art back and you'll own the copyright.'

"Ill will had obviously been brewing for years at *Mad*. Jack Davis became the first millionaire cartoonist only because he was banned from *Mad* and had to get *real* work by doing advertising, film and magazine covers. He did *Time* and *TV Guide* and had big clients, and that was good pay along with the animation – all kinds of stuff – because he wasn't allowed to work at *Mad* for a few years. So you have all of these artists like Mort Drucker and Don Martin that are toiling there for years for a good rate but not as good as Davis got on the 'outside.' Drucker did, like, only a few movie posters, most notably *American Graffiti*, and he should have done tons more. What it boils down to is that ad agencies would call *Mad* and wanted to get contact information for the artists and they wouldn't give it out to them. Drucker, Don Martin and who knows whom else, lost out on (you could say) millions of dollars because employers couldn't get in touch with them. A couple times, they did squire some advertising work. I recently saw an American Airlines ad that Don did from the '60s. If *Mad* artists got some extra work it had to be Gaines-approved.

"That was one of the problems the Martins had at *Mad*. And there was an animated TV pilot where they used Don's work without his involvement. Norma got a lot of grief about being the reason Don left, but she was, and is, a great guardian of Don and his work. They must've felt trapped to a degree at *Mad*. A thing about cartoonists that I have always envied are the ones where the wives handle the business. It can be daunting from an editorial viewpoint; you've got to get through the artist's wives, like Mickey and Norma, to get to the artists. I'll tell you, it's a cartoonist's dream. They field the calls and follow up on late checks and other grief, so you can sit in your studio and draw all the time. They care about their men and their family and that's an invaluable partner to have for an illustrator."

"For awhile Don had been legally blind. I was using two legally blind cartoonists at the time, he and Bill Ward. Don had had all kinds of revolutionary and groundbreaking cornea transplants back in the '60s, I think even in the '50s.

"It was butcher work where they actually stitched the cow corneas right onto your eyeballs. He had all kinds of heroic operations from the '60s and stuff, so what it boiled down to was like Ward, he had to draw close to the paper, or like James Thurber, draw giant. Here you've been at this magazine for 32 years doing legendary work for them, and making the company tons of money, and you still living solely on a page rate that's based on whether they want to give you two or four pages a month. The same with the treatment of artists like Steve Ditko and others, after decades in the industry. First of all, nobody wanted you 'because your style's old.' You created the industry for these new editors. And if you do get work, you've got to eke out a page rate. Any other industry you'd be getting royalties from reprints or reissues. Wow! It's just criminal.

"Growing up, there was that the Jerry Siegel and Joe Schuster action against the *Superman* movie and as a creator myself, I got familiar with rights issues and junk like that. At DC and Marvel you'd have to sign a voucher to get paid that has all this fine print on it about how you don't own nothing forever in this universe and in perpetuity in media known or not yet known. You know if I was a soulless company man, I would have said to the *Cracked* publishers, 'You know what LL and KB? We've got to draft up a work-for-hire contract, pronto, see?' It was just the opposite; I was, 'All right!' I just wouldn't mention it and all the people can own their own work which was appealing to some artists."

Mort Todd also promised to give the original art work back: "Who the hell needs it? First of all, you print it; you've got the film and you got the issues, in the medium it was created for. Who needs all this artwork sticking around? At Marvel, pages get stolen and then at *Mad*, Gaines auctioned it off before he died. I know he gave some money to some of the artists, but what about the dead ones?

"Interestingly, the *Mad* artists owned the rights to the paperbacks they did, and Don worked with *Mad* writers on the books. They owned the work but had to pay 25% of the royalties to use the *Mad* name and the logo. Therefore Don owned the art but not the story. After I left *Cracked*, Norma called me about rewriting some of these stories, because they had a pretty lucrative European market. I rewrote some of the books, and it was work-for-hire but I got to be a secret Martin co-creator! I approached the assignment like watching a foreign film without knowing the language or subtitles. You can come up with your own plot that is often radically different than the original. I had to figure what story I could whomp out of the pictures. We altered a slight amount of artwork, and when there was a giant spider, I came up with a different giant spider gag." (This material was used in *Don Martin's Droll Book*, published by Dark Horse, and also featured material that originally appeared in *Cracked*.)

Bruce Bolinger got his start at *Cracked* due to Don Martin, but as Todd remembers, "They kept that a secret. I found out about those things later. Norma was keeping their proprietary interests close to the vest, with the impression that it was all Don doing it all. I could tell by the line work that it other people were working on it. But what successful artist doesn't use assistants or ghosts?"

Bolinger comments on his involvement, "I became involved with *Cracked* through my association with Don Martin. Don and Norma Martin were looking for someone to ink Don's material because he was undergoing eye problems, which demanded his time and their development of a daily strip called *The Nutheads*. I submitted samples and was picked by the Martins to ink the *Cracked* articles for Don. Another inker was chosen to ink the daily strip. After working with the Martins for a time Don suggested that I try out for *Cracked* and he put me in direct contact with Andy Simmons at the magazine. I became a regular after a time and for a couple issues I had my own drawings in the magazine, running in the same issues that contained the articles I inked for Don. After about three years with Don he took back the duties, in apparent good health again.

"*Cracked* was my first choice and my only choice. When I connected with the Martins and the staff at *Cracked,* I settled right in. Every contact with *Cracked* staff at that time was great, friendly and comfortable. Andy Simmons was my main contact and he was exceptionally nice to work with.

"I felt that working for *Cracked* required my loyalty and full attention and I didn't think that working for the competition was wise. I never did submit material to *Mad* but I'm sure I would have fit in fine with their body of work. My style would have worked fine there also. I did work some with others who were or who had been with *Mad*, editor Lou Silverstone being one example."

Silverstone adds, "Kenneth Baratto. He was ok, because he agreed to pay Don Martin a lot of money, and he agreed to pay me a lot of money. Norma Martin should be flattered. He worked for *Cracked* for a couple of years, and they can't reprint the stuff because they had that in the contract. He drove a real hard bargain. They didn't want to turn it down."

Silverstone adds about payment at that time, "Once the Globe took over that never happened and I think with Kenny, they always paid on time. He was upfront.

"When Al Feldstein left *Mad* magazine, the editor of *Cracked,* Michael Delle-Femine, made the bold move to get Don Martin away from *Mad*, which was really a coup because Don was *Mad*'s most famous artist and writer, I think. He also went after Mort Drucker and myself. Now Mort stayed loyal, Don signed a contract with *Cracked* which was very good financially, and get to own his own artwork, which was a big deal."

Mort Todd comments on the *Mad* raid: "When we had Don Martin, I called Drucker and Davis and a bunch of people trying to get them, and Dave Berg called us!

"Gaines would take them on a trip only if they did a certain amount of pages a year, which they had no control over. Some of the wives told me that it would have been a lot nicer to get a bonus instead of going on a stupid trip and ditching the family. It was a write-off and not so sincere. I talked to Drucker and he is a super nice guy. Drucker had just had a quadruple bypass and Gaines paid for it, so he said he felt obligated to stay there. If these guys had health insurance, they wouldn't have to be obligated.

"We didn't do it for all the freelancers, but we had a package plan. They could have joined our health coverage, and done it cheap. They could have done a co-pay, and that was offered to all the writers and artists. Mainly, it was used by John Severin and Don Martin because you know, they were our big guys. So Drucker felt obligated because Gaines had just paid for this thing, and apparently that had happened a couple other times with other artists' emergencies.

"Sergio Aragonés is a sweetheart and a phenomenal genius! We were having a launch party for *Monsters Attack!* magazine and he started spitting like 'Ptui, ptui' at the despised competition. He's very warm-hearted and open and that's the way it should be, friendly rivals. How many humor magazines were there? Two. And, a lot of creators worked for both magazines. *Mad* was like 'We shouldn't socialize or communicate with them.' It was Stalinesque. Evidently that ruffled my feathers.

"When we put out a *Collectors' Edition* that focused on Jack Davis, I kinda wanted to get his permission to do the reprints and I even asked him if he wanted to do a new cover, matching his rate and everything. He declined but suggested, 'Well, I just did a postage stamp.' He gave me the contact information for the Post Office head honcho who commissioned it so we could get permission to use it. He was very friendly and said he had retired from *Mad*, but not officially, and at this late date, he didn't want to rock the boat.

"I even tried to get Harvey Kurtzman. That was before—I don't know if you remember in the 80s when he went back to *Mad*—I was trying to get him. He was a cranky guy and said, 'Aw, I have to get back in the mood to do all that.' I was thinking new Kurtzman and Severin stuff would be pretty interesting."

Gary Fields also got to work for the great Don Martin: "One of the coolest things I got to do was 'ghost' a Don Martin article on *Batman*. He had rough penciled out his work and then had cataract surgery or something, so Michael asked me to takes his pencils and finish them up. Don gave me a great pencil sketch thanking me for assisting him."

Mike Ricigliano offers his insights: "People who worked for *Cracked* at the time, it was my greatest day the idea that they had gotten Don Martin. I couldn't understand why we're doing it, but I was thrilled that Don Martin was going to be part of the magazine. He gave it instant credibility as a humor magazine. That was awesome and he did good stuff for them and like I said, I got to meet him at a couple reunions. He was a very, very nice guy too. John was great because he used to slip me into some of his artwork. I have a couple of his pages. He had never met me but he had photos of me and he had worked me into a few of the panels. I have a couple of those panels.

"We had a couple of reunions in there, which were great, so I got to meet Don Martin at one of those. There was a time in there where they used Don Martin for about three years. That was when Don had his falling out with *Mad* where they wouldn't give him reprint rights and all that. *Cracked* was willing to do that, so Don did the covers. I still keep in touch with his wife. I just sent her a Christmas card, but he's my all-time favorite. I always loved Don Martin."

Bolinger continues about Martin: "Don was easy to work with. He would do tight pencil roughs and send them up on the fax. I'd follow his instructions and notations on the roughs, then render them in ink. He and Norma would check the finals via fax and make minor changes. When some detail required a phone call we would have phone exchanges that involved work and non-work-related topics. He was quiet, full of humor and calm. The most animated conversation we ever had came over his boat trailer and boat coming loose on a Florida bridge and getting totaled. Most of my dealings were with Norma Martin, the studio boss. She kept everything running on schedule, doing all the business tasks that were required in running their considerable business. Together they formed a team that worked well.

"I know that leaving *Mad* was rough for Don. He really enjoyed the long relationships with the others there but when the time came that he and Norma wanted a bigger piece of the action *Mad* wouldn't give an inch when it came to ownership and intellectual property holdings. *Mad*, at the time, was run like a fiefdom and Bill Gaines was the king and Bill made all the rules. All the original art was owned by *Mad* and the vaults were filled with a grand fortune in originals."

Peter Bagge offers this story about meeting Don Martin: "I was attending *Cracked*'s 30th anniversary party in 1988, I think it was. I met Rick Altergott for the first time there. I also was introduced to Don Martin there, who was a big hero of mine—so much so that I was afraid to attempt a conversation with him. Later I was told he liked my work, so I wish I had spoke up!"

Don Martin appeared regularly in *Cracked* from 1987-1993, with one final cover appearance in 1995. He passed away in 2000, and was saluted with a tribute by Mike Ricigliano.

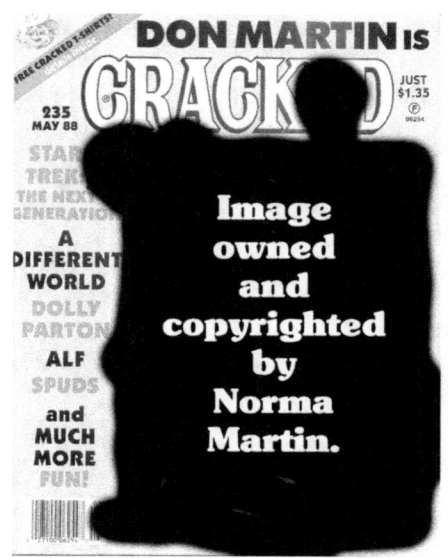

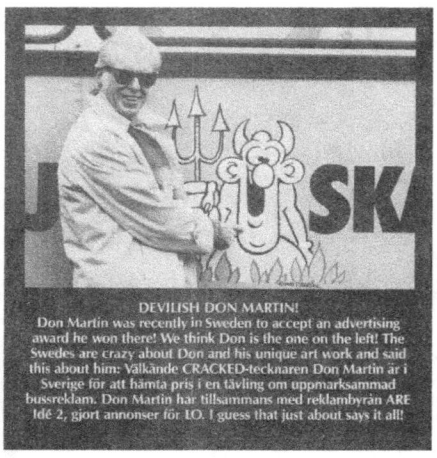

DEVILISH DON MARTIN!
Don Martin was recently in Sweden to accept an advertising award he won there! We think Don is the one on the left! The Swedes are crazy about Don and his unique art work and said this about him: Välkände CRACKED-tecknaren Don Martin är i Sverige för att hämta pris i en tävling om uppmärksammad bussreklam. Don Martin har tillsammans med reklambyrån ARE Idé 2, gjort annonser för LO. I guess that just about says it all!

Don Martin as he appeared in *Cracked* #263, July 1991.

Don Martin first appeared in *Cracked* #234, March 1988, but his first full front cover was *Cracked* #235. *Image not courtesy of Norma Martin.*

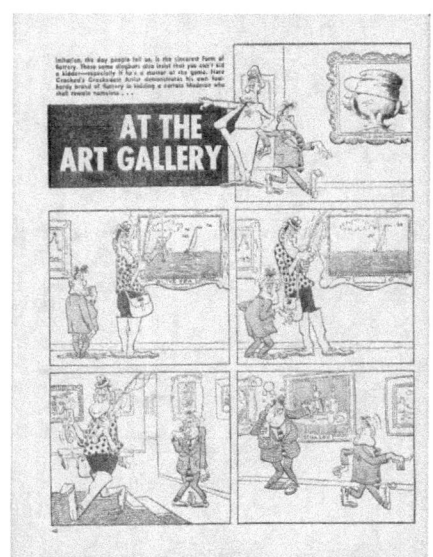

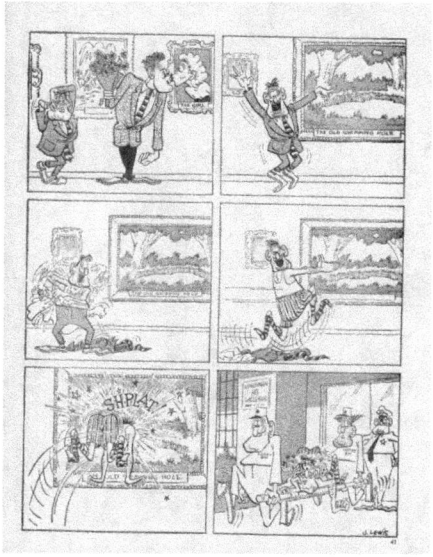

John Severin does his best Don Martin imitation in *Cracked* #27, November 1962, written by Jay Lynch.

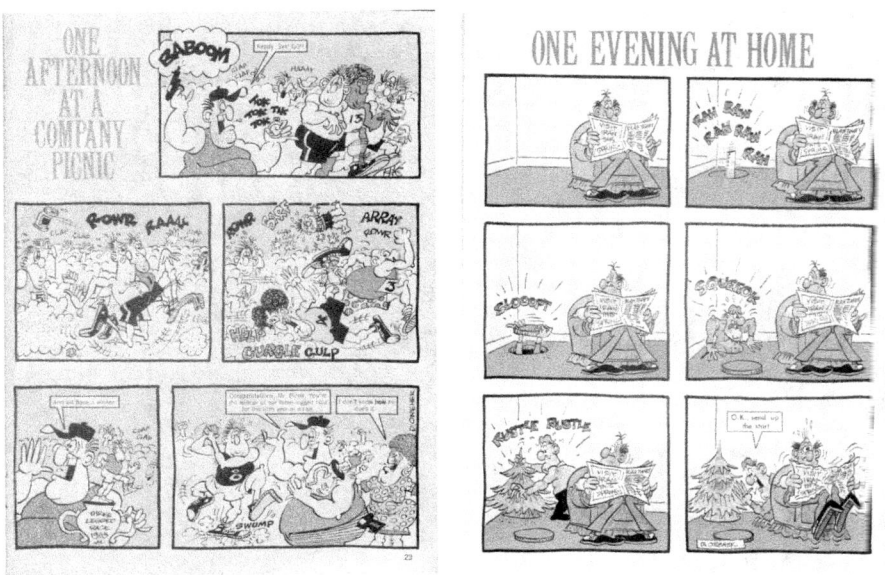

Don Orehek does his best Don Martin imitation in *Cracked* #202, March 1984.

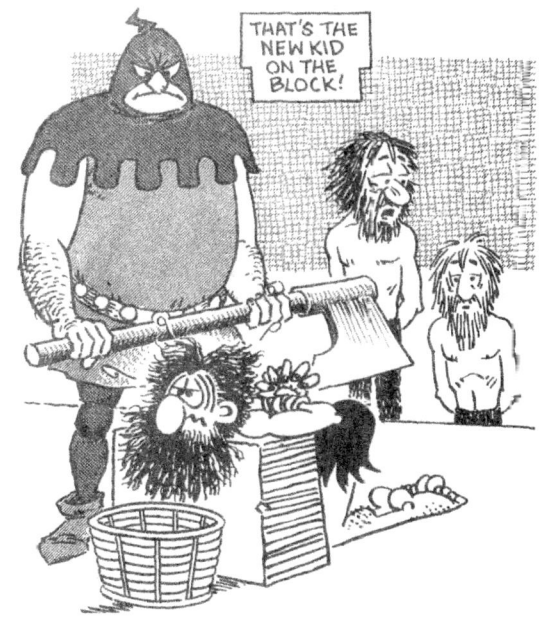

John Severin draws Don Martin in
Ye Hang Ups from *Cracked* #236,
July 1988.

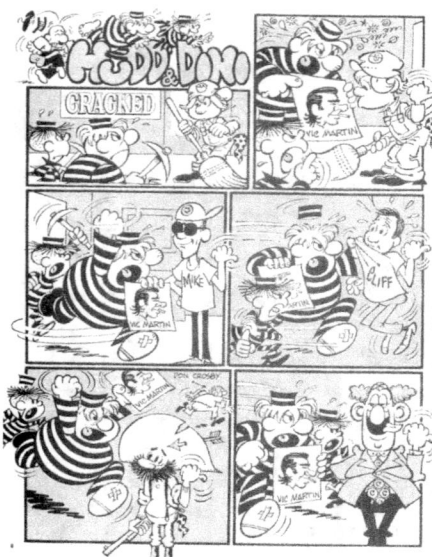
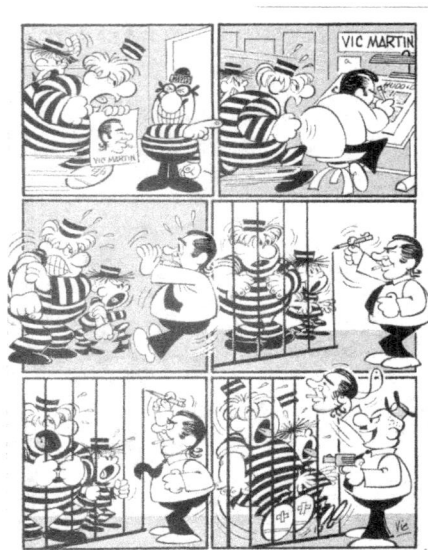

Vic Martin does his best Don Martin imitation in *Cracked* #250, December 1989.

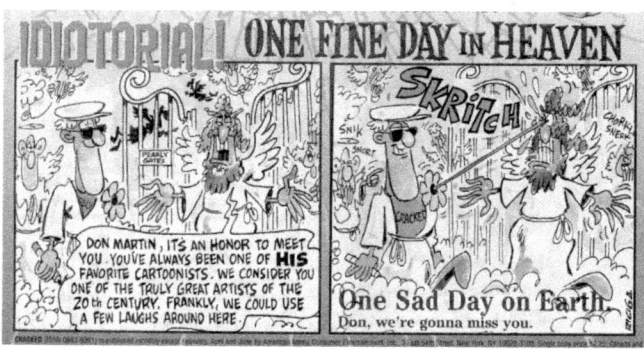

Mike Ricigliano pays tribute to Don Martin in *Cracked* #343, May 2000.

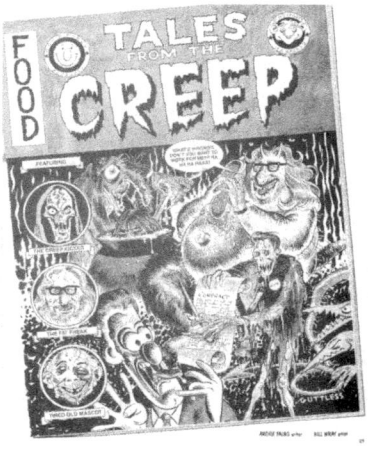

Bill Wray's final contribution to *Cracked*, featured a Don Martin imitation in "Tales from the Creep" from *Cracked* #250, December 1989.

MORT TODD'S PHOTO ALBUM

Images courtesy of Mort Todd. Captions by Mort Todd.

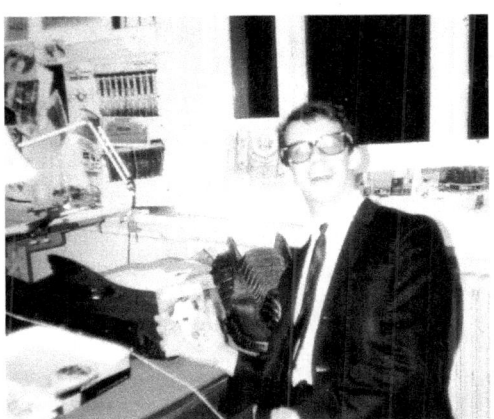

Mort Todd at Pinewood Studios in England during the shooting of the Tim Burton *Batman* film. Behind him are two Batmobile prototypes and production art and storyboards on the wall. Mort is holding *The Joker Jokebook* which had just been published.

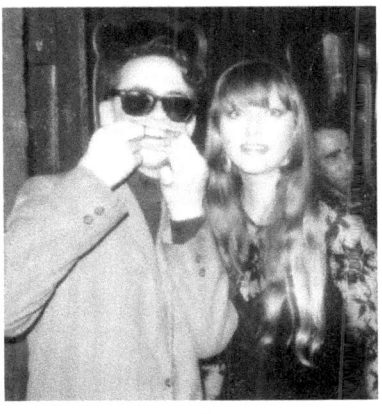

The *Cracked* 30th Anniversary Party at the Tunnel Club in NYC. Left to right: Mort Todd, Bebe Buell and Vic Martin and John Severin in the background. Bebe and her band the Gargoyles performed at the event.

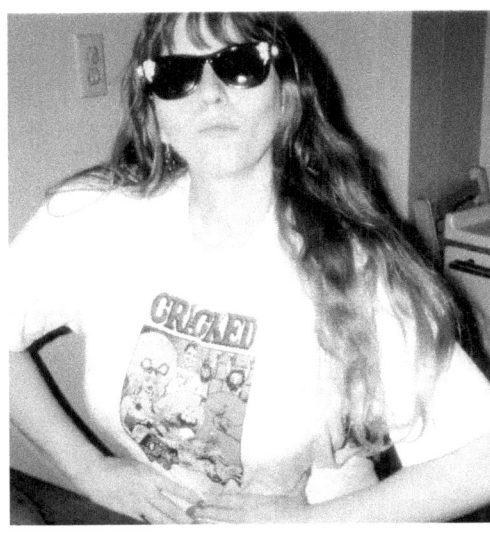

Bebe proudly sports her *Cracked* T-Shirt. The Severin art features Nanny Dickering, the character Bebe played in the *Cracked* photo comic.

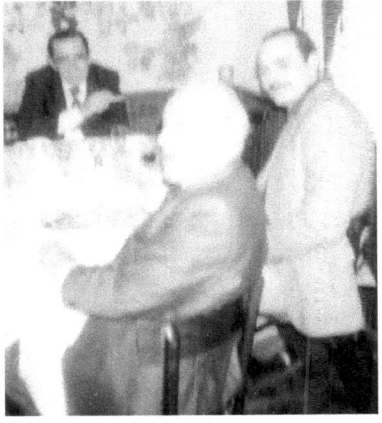

A *Cracked* holiday party at the Palm Restaurant in NYC. From back to front: Cartoonists Vic Martin, Walter Brogan and Henry Boltinoff. The Palm was popular with publishers and the walls were covered with cartoon by many *Cracked* contributors.

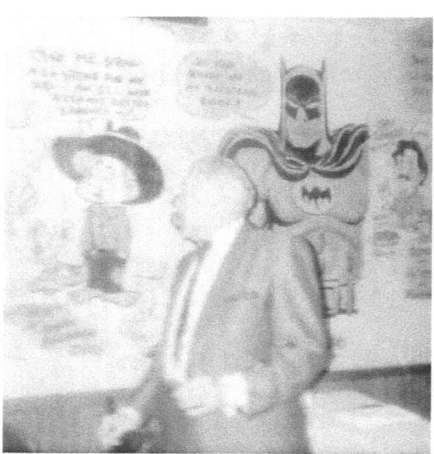

Legendary cartoonist Henry Boltinoff admires his wall painting of his comic strip character Nubbin. Next is a Carmine Infantino illustration of Batman saying "Get your hands off my Batsteak, buddy!" Following is a Don Orehek head and a bit of *Dondi* by Irwin Hasen.

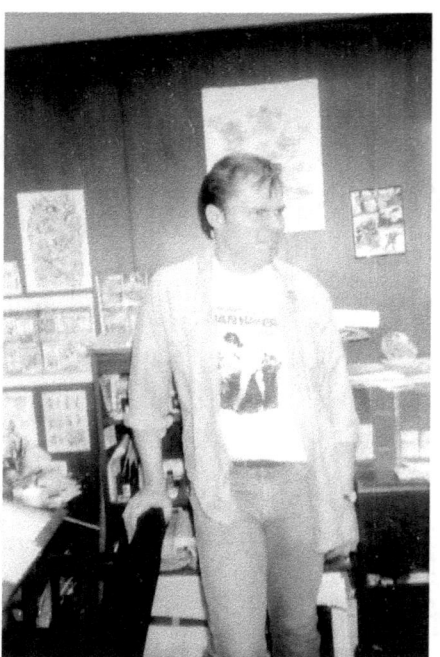

Cracked writer Charles E. Hall.

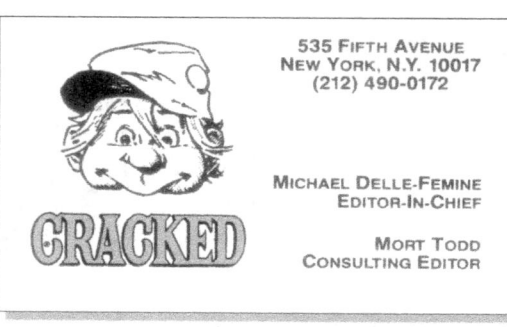

The *Cracked* business card, meticulously copied from the *Mad* business card.

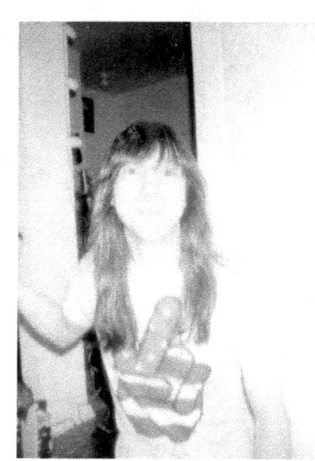

Cracked Art Director Cliff Mott pondering deadlines at the *Cracked* office.

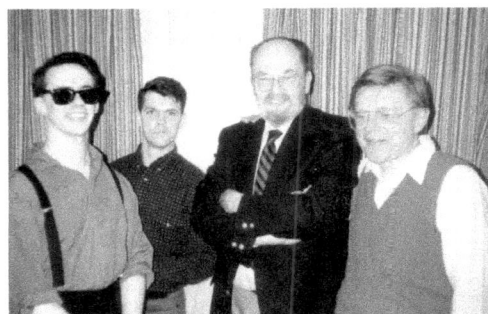

At a comic convention celebrating the *Cracked* 30th Anniversary. Left to right: Mort Todd, writer Peter Bagge, Artist John Severin and writer George Gladir.

Actor Al Lewis, Granpa from *The Munsters*, is horrified by an issue of *Cracked* presented by Mort.

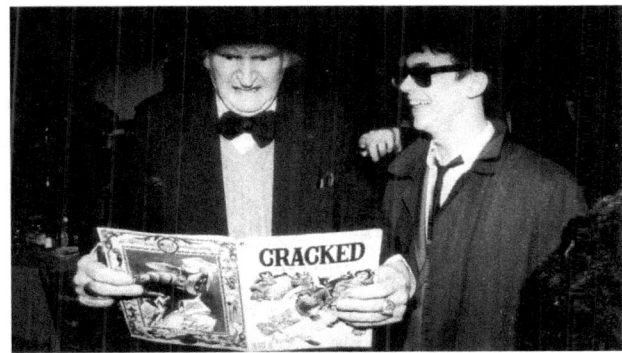

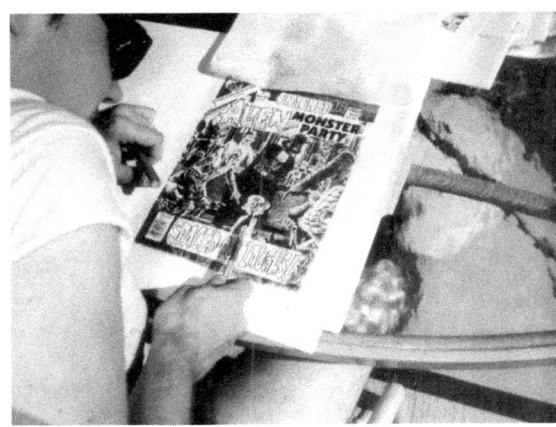

Cliff Mott pastes up the cover of *Cracked Monster Party* by a rooftop pool during a business trip to Hollywood.

At the Palm. Left to right: Cliff Mott, Mort Todd and Associate Editor Roger D. Crosby. Some Orehek heads peer from the wall.

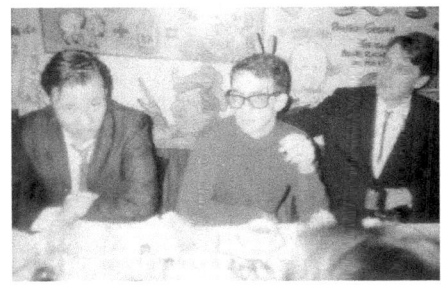

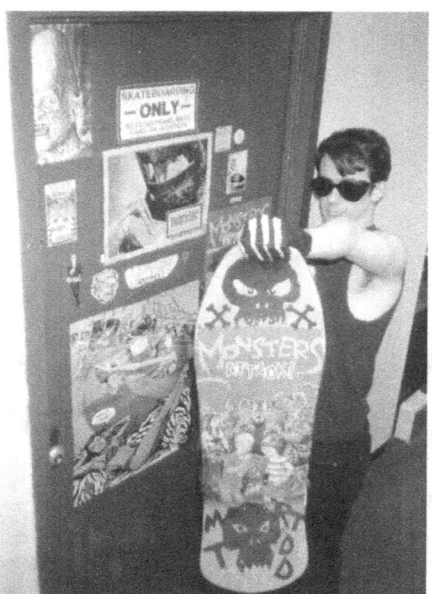

Mort Todd outside his *Cracked* office door showing off his customized *Monsters Attack!* skateboard.

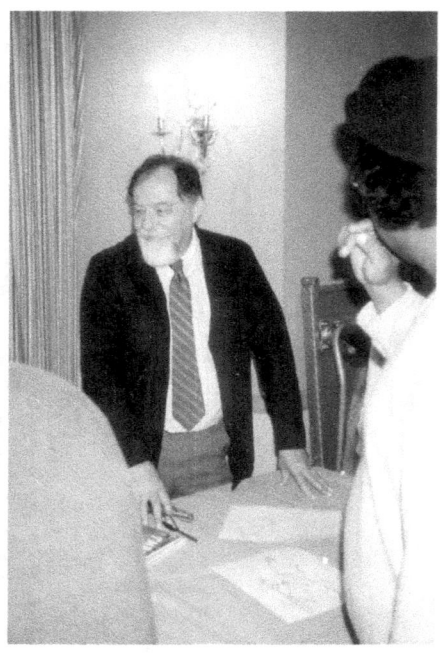

Don Orehek surrounded by *Shut Up* fans at the convention.

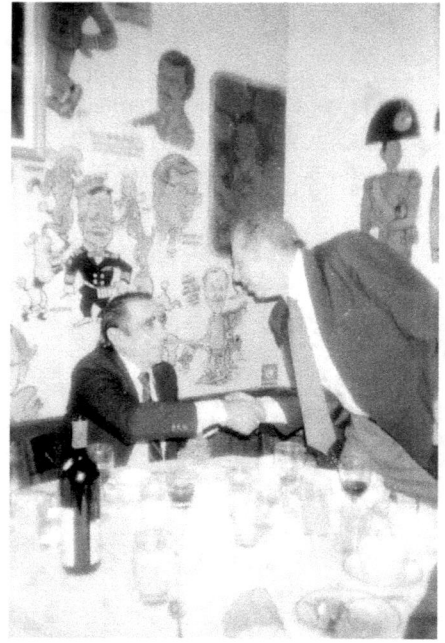

Cartoonist Al Scaduto (right) greets Vic Martin.

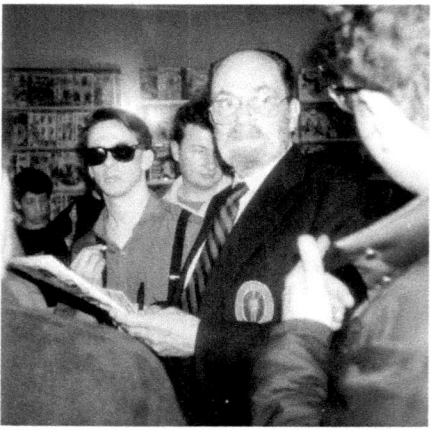

Mort and John Severin mobbed by Sev fans at the convention.

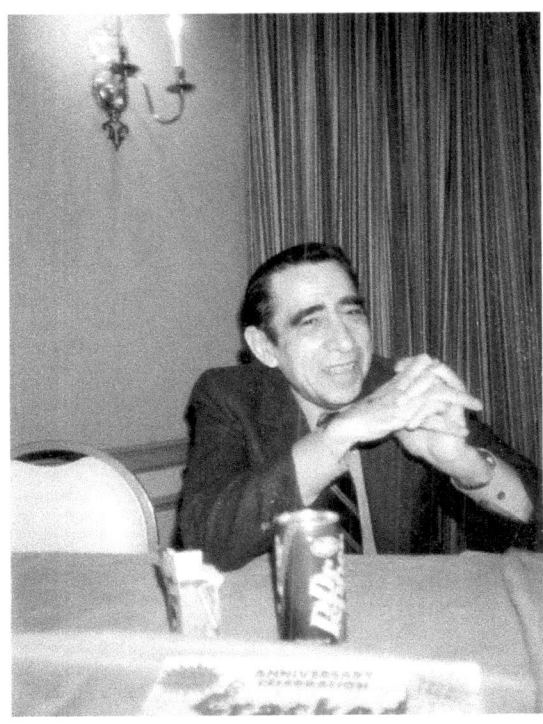

Cartoonist Vic Martin at the convention.

Mort shows *Batman* actor Adam West the splash page from the *Cracked Batman* parody by Charles E. Hall and Rick Altergott.

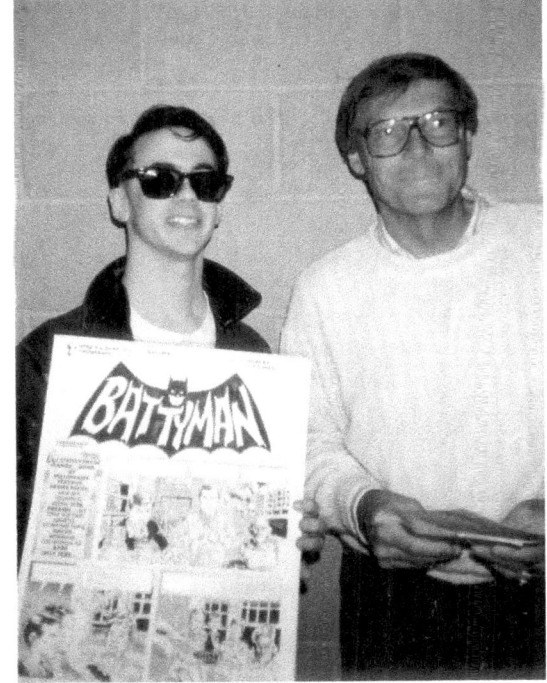

LOU SiLVERSTONE, JERRY DE FUCCiO AND ANDY SiMMONS

LOU Silverstone explains: "Michael Delle-Femine. I told him not to resign. He had something going with the publisher. I don't know what that was and he recommended me for the job. He turned the magazine around by hiring Don Martin. He didn't increase the sales by that much, but he made *Cracked* legitimate by getting artists and writers to work there who wouldn't work there before. My first move was trying to get Al Jaffee to move from *Mad* to *Cracked*, but he wouldn't. Then, they hired Andy Simmons as the co-editor. I wasn't too sure of that move, but it turned out fine because we were both low-key guys and neither one of us has big egos, so no problem there."

Prior to becoming co-editor of *Cracked* in 1990, Lou Silverstone moonlighted for both *Mad* and *Cracked*, until he was discovered. Silverstone explains, "When I was working with both ends of the scale, I used to go to the *Cracked* offices and I'd use the name Alfred E. Neuman. The receptionists would call on the loudspeaker and say, 'Michael, Mr. Neuman is here to see you.' I'd always mess up whenever I left *Mad* and I'd say, 'Well, I've got to get cracking now,' and they'd all look at me.

"I was interviewed for a book about *T.H.U.N.D.E.R. Agents*. It was another one that I couldn't use my own name. I didn't want to upset Gaines."

Mort Todd explains how Silverstone worked for *Cracked* at that time: "Undercover. He called me and said he was getting maybe a couple stories a year out of *Mad* and so I said, 'C'mon over!' He used a lot of pseudonyms in our mag and at times we'd hear the scuttlebutt from *Mad*.

Everything worked out well as Silverstone used pseudonyms while at *Cracked* until Bill Wray, who was trying to leave *Cracked* to get into *Mad* spilled the beans: "I used Tommy Yudo from *Kiss of Death*. It was Richard Widmark's character. I tried to work on both sides for *Mad* and *Cracked* without telling *Mad*, but one of the *Cracked* artists who was trying to get into *Mad*, he squealed on me. He's still there I think. Eventually, I had to admit it and I quit *Mad* and Gaines asked me to stay and I stayed for awhile, but things didn't get any better. I wasn't getting that much work, so *Cracked* made me an offer I couldn't refuse and it really was a good move for me, financially and it was a good move for me just for my career. I had my own magazine, practically. It was a lot of fun." Silverstone used other names while at *Cracked*, including Tony Frank, Vic Bianco and Rich Kriegel.

Silverstone continues, "Oh yeah. Nobody at *Mad* would talk to me. They said they were not allowed to talk to me. The art director Schneider, he left there and he talked to me and said, 'You were not allowed to laugh at *Cracked*.' The editor there had announced that it was not funny. The great thing that happened there and they all watched *Seinfeld* and they had a big discussion about the program the next day and when it was over, one thing that they used in *Seinfeld*, they used *Cracked*. I wish I could have been a fly on the wall in that office. We did a takeoff—I wrote it and Brogan drew it—on *Seinfeld* and they liked it very much. That's when they used it and they also invited us out there to see the show and the publisher went, naturally. So, he was a fan of *Cracked*, too."

The *Seinfeld* episode is one of the few latter day claims to fame for *Cracked*. The episode entitled "The Couch" originally aired on October 27, 1994, and was written by Larry David. Jerry Seinfeld (as well as Stephen King) have confessed to being *Cracked* fans. In the episode, George (portrayed by Jason Alexander) is supposed to be reading *Breakfast at Tiffany's* for his new book club, but procrastinates and at one point is shown reading an issue of *Cracked* magazine. Other plot elements are involved with Elaine (Julia Louis-Dreyfus) dating the man who drops off Jerry's new couch, and Kramer (Michael Richards) gets involved with a "make your own pizza" business.

Murad Gumen mentions another coup around this same time, the editorial staff of *Cracked* appearing on *Howard Stern*: "They appeared on Howard Stern's radio show; this was a period, probably beginning with Laikin's young successor—Mort Todd—where some efforts to plug the magazine took place. I think the magazine succeeded in getting planted during a scene of *The Cosby Show*, if I'm not mistaken. I remember I was impressed that someone had managed that small coup."

Stern appeared in comic form many times in *Cracked*, but the editorial staff of *Cracked* appeared at least two times on Stern's show. The first time was in 1992, when Lou Silverstone, Andy Simmons and Walter Brogan appeared with photos and a write-up about the event in issue #273. A semi-recurring feature started appearing with #332 called *Stuttering John's Historical Interviews*.

Later, when Dick Kulpa took over as Editor, another visit to Stern and another write-up appeared about Stern in #257 in 2001. This time, Kulpa appeared with Barry Dutter. Miss *Cracked* Debbie Rochon was supposed to appear, but a model named Leslie Ann appeared in her stead.

When asked why Silverstone didn't try to become *Mad*'s editor after Al Feldstein's retirement, Silverstone had this to say: "Jerry De Fuccio was the associate editor, and for some reason he was going to move to California and he called me to see if I was interested, but I wouldn't be able to write. They had a rule that editors couldn't write, so I'd rather be a writer than editor any day."

Walter Brogan agrees, "What I got was that Lou didn't really want it. I think Nick Meglin played a big part in that, because Lou was one hell of a writer. I mean, he was a much better writer than Nick Meglin. Who else could do a parody of a parody like *Batman*? You know what I'm saying?"

Brogan tended to do a lot of Disney parodies during the Lou Silverstone era: "That was his choice. I didn't mind doing them. I found them easy to do. They knew I could do it."

Around the same time of the transition of Mort Todd to Lou Silverstone and Jerry De Fuccio as editors, there was a transition of publishers as well as Larry Levine and Kenneth Baratto sold out their interests to Barry Rosenbloom in 1991. Mort Todd comments on the transaction: "There's a story behind that as well. I basically quadrupled the number of freelance artists. So instead of giving me a raise or hiring me assistants, they end up hiring two editors at full salary, and then they hire Andy Simmons, so they had three editors at full salary. Within six months or a year after I left, they sold their part of the magazine to Globe, totally. I'm under the impression now that they kind of wanted to squeeze me out so they could sell it saying that they got these numbers and this salary, so you got this sort of profit. When Globe took over they realized that one person cannot handle this and it took three people to do the work I was doing, and I don't think as well, if I may say so."

Brian Buniak came back to *Cracked* after working for *Mad* for a time. Buniak explains, "I really didn't have much of a choice on anything. The final time that I had there was a little bit better. When I got in, this was after I had worked for *Mad*, so I know that it improved. I didn't want to go back to *Cracked*, but I knew the work for *Mad* wasn't huge. I went to *Cracked* and I knew the rates were getting pretty low, but I recall that they said that they wanted quality and they were even saying how good it was. They were talking about doing more and getting more money for the art and I said, 'How about increasing it a little?' For something like $25 more a page, I would have done something. As an artist, you can always put in less work into what you're doing. If you want a salary increase, then you take one page more, but I didn't want to do that. I had certain standards and I decided to do less per page until I couldn't do it anymore.

"A lot of the bad stories come out, but ultimately I'm glad I worked for *Cracked*. It wasn't the best humor magazine, but it was cool. I was glad to have been a part of it. I'm glad you're doing this, because if you didn't, it probably would never be done.

"The last one I did it really stands out because I did with the intention of hitting them up for more dough. It put in a lot of stuff. It was a triumph and not just in the artwork, all these gags and everybody was all, 'Wow! That's really neat!' It's *Cracked*, but it looked like a *Mad* piece, which was my whole thing. Even though *Cracked* really tried to beat *Mad*, it really never was competition. I never found a single person who said, 'Gee, I could buy either *Mad* or *Cracked*, which one should I get?' They would either buy *Mad*, or buy *Mad* with *Cracked* as well. You were never just a *Cracked* reader. *Lampoon* was something that genuinely hurt *Mad*, but if you worked for *Cracked*, you couldn't work for *Mad*. *Mad*'s art director is Sam Viviano. Sam did tons of work for other publications. A guy who really was with their competitor is now convincing people that somebody who works there would never work for the competition. It throws you off."

Mike Ricigliano discusses the tenure of Silverstone and company: "I had such a great experience with Lou and Jerry there. I would actually go into the city and see those guys. They were there for a number of years, too, and of course, Lou would do all the TV satires for *Mad* for all those years and Jerry was the associate editor for *Mad* for a number of years, so they used to love telling me *Mad* stories and even though I never got into *Mad*, they had all the stories, Jerry in particular had all the stories. Jerry, he was like a 'Godfather' to me when I met him—a fellow Italian for one thing. Once he met me and we hit it off. He did some ideas where he would give me the concept and I would write them and then after Jerry passed away, then Lou and Andy Simmons were the co-editors. Andy was a great guy. I believe Andy works for *Reader's Digest*. I don't know if you've contacted Lou, but he'd be an awesome guy to talk to. Those guys were great. Out of all the editors, I think Lou kind of used me the best. They kind of knew whatever they needed if they asked me to do it, I'd come up with an article for it. He thought it was funny and he gave me many nice compliments at the time we worked together, so I always appreciated it.

Mike Ricigliano remembers, "Over the course of those 20 years, I was the jack-of-all-trades in the magazine. I would write a lot of stuff and after a while they realized that I could write well and funny, so they would let me go. Especially when Lou was there and Jerry, they would let me just write stuff, draw stuff, whatever I came up with. I did a lot of sports stuff, which predicates what I do now for a living. I would just come up with three and four page articles and for a while there were some one-pagers a la Don Martin type gags. I knew all the different styles from *Mad*, but I couldn't draw all the different styles from *Mad*. I could come up with concepts along those lines, so I would pitch them concepts and then they'd let me do some three-page articles, some four-page articles. I remember doing one on Super Soakers that the guy who invented Super Soakers called me up and flew me down to Florida and wanted me to write a show about Super Soakers. It was fascinating to go down there because this guy invented these water pistols and he told me his whole story and he had this amazing plant where he invented where basically he could just sit back and invent toys. That was his lifestyle right now and pretty impressive and pretty cool. I tried, but he wanted a more kind of action kid's morning type of show that wasn't really within my wheelhouse. It wasn't going to be funny; it was going to be more serious. I just couldn't write it. I wasn't very good at writing it. My writing range is narrowed to keep money.

"I did a lot of different sports ones over the years. Like I said, one of my favorites was the Super Soakers one, partially because it was a funny concept where we take a Super Soaker and make it 10,000 degrees more than what they were. I mean they were getting bigger and bigger in the article where they were just Super Soaker tanks and this guy was amused by this and then the contact and the meeting with him, that was very cool thing to do. Have you ever heard of *Cracked* coming back on some level on the old level? I would love to do the occasional piece for them again. I don't think it's ever gonna happen. I don't think we'll see that kind of stuff full bloom again in magazine form."

Pete Fitzgerald continued with *Cracked* during this era: "The second era was when *Mad*'s Lou Silverstone took over in 1990, with Jerry De Fuccio and Cliff Mott sticking around, joined a little later by Andy Simmons, when Jerry left / retired. Todd Jackson came in a little bit after that. The bulk of my *Cracked* days were with them, roughly a decade. They were very supportive, and encouraged me to add gags whenever I could.

"One thing I did they liked too much—I drew a video game-themed piece, and rendered the video portion of the imagery in low-res style, so it looked like something from an Atari or Nintendo screen. So, if something had a curved outline, I'd finish it with a stair-step line, using a straightedge and a Radiograph. They apparently really liked that, so they eventually gave me several video game pieces to do, including one in color. Those were murder to draw! Plus they looked too primitive compared to the disc-based video games kids were starting to use, like the Sega! I asked if I could just draw the stuff normal-style, since graphics were advancing, or if they could process my normal drawings into a 'digitized' look, but it was no use... they wanted my hand-drawn graphics! Ugh! But the other things they had me do were fun, like the color alien trading cards."

Silverstone claims that they didn't really hire too many new artists and writers during his tenure, but that claim doesn't completely ring true: "We didn't really hire more when we were running it. In fact, we tried to get rid of some of them. They were all mediocre. We went for the best that we could afford. I think with John Severin, we had the best. I think he and Mort Drucker were the best."

Silverstone did hire Frank Borth, Steve Strangio, Jed Vier, Rob Weske, Lenore Skenazy, Andy Simmons, Jeff Wong, Bruce Bolinger, Eric Goldberg and Mark Howard, Dan Birtcher, Tom Grimes, Terry Colon, Ron Barrett, P.C. Vey, Greg Grabianski, Barry Zeger, Todd James, Randy Jones, Ed Subitzky, Alan Kupperberg, Carson Demmans, Ricky Sprague, Todd Jackson, Gunnar Johnson, J. Kelly, Frank Cummings, R.J. Reiley, C.L. Walker, Barry Dutter, Mike Lotter, Kit Lively, Katey Dash, Dan Fiorella and Kent Kennedy. Many stayed on through the Dick Kulpa era.

Frank Borth was a writer who wrote for *Treasure Chest* and Quality Comics. He began at *Cracked* in 1990 and passed away in 2009 at age 91.

Steve Strangio has done various acting roles including stand-up comedy besides writing for *Cracked* during its final 15 years, beginning in 1991. He comments on his years there: "There were two magazines that fit this style of writing, *Cracked* and *Mad*. I submitted material to both magazines at the same time. After waiting a fair amount of time, I contacted both editorial offices by phone to see what they thought of my writing.

"*Mad* magazine said that it'd take about a minimum of six months before they could get back to me. Alright then.

"*Cracked* magazine was a little bit different.

"The person that picked up the phone that day was the legendary Lou Silverstone—ironically, a former writer for *Mad* and now current editor of *Cracked*. He was very nice, had a great way about him, and took the time to speak to me about my work.

"By the end of the phone call, I made my very first sale as a writer, and I was on my way to being published.

"Honestly, I'm not even sure if *Mad* even got back to me. Does that bother me? Hell no. They are a great publication and I will still pick up a *Mad* magazine every so often.

"However, I was now a regular contributor to *Cracked* magazine and that continued for 15 years.

"Barry Rosenbloom owned the joint, Lou Silverstone and Andy Simmons were the Editors, and Cliff Mott was the art director and associate editor.

"I was there from 1990 to 2005 ... and enjoyed every second of it.

"Lou and Andy had to endure sitting in this small office at Globe Communications in New York City. However, it always looked like they were having a great time. I would always drop by there whenever I was in the neighborhood and just free associate some ideas with them.

"When I first got the job, I thought I'd be thrown into a bullpen with other writers and that would be our 9 to 5 gig. Nah, didn't work that way. Lou and Andy controlled the *Cracked*verse from their office and all us mailed in our stuff to them.

"Honestly, I would have preferred working in an office making comedy all day, but this is the way it was. But we still got to hang out in the office and make each other laugh every once in a while.

"I really liked my 'L.A. Riot Trading Cards' article. I think that was my edgiest parody. I'm really proud of all of the pro wrestling and video game parodies. I also really enjoyed my series of 'Replacement Shows' television parodies. All of the 'Star Trek Newsletter' stuff was damn fun to write and I even think a little kid swiped one of my 'Vulcan Knock-Knock' jokes for one of the *America's Funniest Home Videos* or *America's Funniest People TV* shows. I didn't really mind that. Actually thought it was kinda cool and the kid did a great job with it.

"I wasn't a fan of my *Chucky* movie parody that came out in *Cracked Monster Party*. Couldn't done better with that. That was my first swipe at a movie parody and Lou Silverstone helped me get better with that style of parody.

"I did a *Blossom* parody and actually made the character of Six's tongue get tangled in her mouth due to high speed momentum… yeah… good times.

"My most surreal moment was when Don Orehek actually drew three caricatures of me and placed them into a parody I wrote about things you overhear in a comedy club. Pretty damn cool to be immortalized in cartoon form.

"One of my most commercial parodies was the 'ETWF—Extra Terrestrial Wrestling Federation.' *Cracked* actually printed up real trading cards and provided them as an insert and I got the cover for that issue. It was the *Cracked Collectors' Edition Sc-Fi Special* #90 from April 1992. I've always felt that would be a kick-ass cartoon show and video game. I still do."

Jed Vier began writing and drawing for *Cracked* in 1991.

Rob Weske has been a writer for various Cleveland, Ohio TV stations after his time writing for *Cracked*. He started at *Cracked* in 1992.

Lenore Skenazy is a syndicated columnist, author, and a very funny public speaker, and has had a few books published besides being a writer for *Cracked* beginning in 1992.

Andy Simmons started as a writer at *Cracked* in 1992, eventually replacing Jerry De Fuccio as co-editor with issue #273. He currently works for the *Reader's Digest*. When approached about being interviewed for this book, Simmons commented, "A book on *Cracked*; a sure-fire way to land you on the *New York Times* bestseller list!" His father, Matty Simmons, was an integral part of the original *National Lampoon* and as a result, Andy was able to bring over a few *Lampoon* regulars to *Cracked* as *Lampoon* stopped publishing a magazine in 1998.

Jeff Wong became a semi-replacement starting in 1992 for both Rob Orzechowski and John Severin on *Cracked* and is a master caricaturist, doing regular back cover posters and occasional front covers.

Bruce Bolinger became an artist on his own for *Cracked* in 1992 and after Don Martin stopped doing regular work in 1995: "Lou Silverstone and Andy Simmons were the editors in charge at the time I began, around 1989. I'm foggy about exact dates because of the overlapping with Don's work and my work. I'm not certain when my first stand-alone effort began but it was around that time."

Eric Goldberg and Mark Howard always wrote as a team while at *Cracked*, beginning in 1992.

Dan Birtcher also wrote for *Mad* before joining *Cracked* in 1992.

Tom Grimes is another artist for *Cracked*, starting in 1992.

Terry Colon has drawn for both *Mad* and *Cracked* among other things, starting in 1992 at *Cracked*. He speaks about his work: "About 1989 or so I came across a local Detroit humor/satire mag called *Fun*. I submitted some things to the editor and started getting published. They stopped publishing *Fun* about a year later and started a bi-weekly tabloid magazine called *Orbit* which I designed, wrote for, and did a regular cartoon feature called *OZ&NS*. After a couple years I gathered up the best cartoons and submitted them to *Cracked*. They bought some as a regular part of *Backwash*, which they had me hand-letter, illustrate and put together. They also bought some features I wrote and illustrated as well as illustrating some features others wrote.

"The editor I dealt with was Andy Simmons from about 1991 to 1998 or so. I don't remember the exact dates. I submitted things, they said yea or nay, I did them up. I worked at home via mail, phone, fax, e-mail. Not very glamorous, I admit. But then, *Cracked* and glamour aren't synonyms.

"*Cracked* was easy to work for, they let me do it my way pretty much. No deadlines for features. There wasn't that much give and take between us. No meetings, brainstorming, or any of that. They'd edit the initial ms, but no art revisions or the like.

"To be frank, *Mad* paid better and had more cache so I tried them first. As they didn't bite, *Cracked* got second crack.

"I've since worked for dozens of clients all on a freelance basis, some more demanding than others. Most of what I do is illustration, not cartooning or writing as I did for *Cracked*. In many ways there's no good comparison.

"Everything I did for *Cracked* was freelance. I work at home in my own studio. I don't think environment applies. I'm sort-of off in my own little world without anyone hovering over me breathing down my neck or anything.

"The only actual job I've had, as an employee, was working for Suck. com, a part of *Wired* magazine. But that was so different I don't know that there is a meaningful comparison.

"As far as my submissions, I liked them all, if not I wouldn't have submitted them. Though I'm sure if I reviewed them I'd think some were better than others, but nothing comes to mind.

"It was a nice outlet for my whimsies. A boost for both my ego and my bank account. What's better than being paid for something you enjoy, something amusing as well."

Ron Barrett wrote and drew *Politenessman* for *National Lampoon* for a number of years before joining *Cracked* in 1992. He also illustrated the book version of *Cloudy with a Chance of Meatballs*. Says Barrett of working at *Cracked*, "Andy Simmons is a sweet guy and a pleasure to work with. There's not much more to say. I was an occasional contributor."

Peter (P.C.) Vey has drawn for *National Lampoon*, *The New Yorker* and *Mad* as well as *Cracked*, which he started at in 1993.

Lou Silverstone comments about the hiring of Greg Grabianski: "He was the first we hired as an associate editor because he was so damn funny, but the publisher wanted an Ivy League person for some damn reason. We insisted upon getting Greg because he was truly funny. He's out in LA now. He went on to *Beavis and Butt-Head*, *The Wayans Brothers Show* and *Scary Movie*."

Grabianski adds, "I was an associate editor / writer at *Cracked* from about 1995 to about 1996, but then I was a freelance writer with them until about 1999 when the magazine was sold. Lou Silverstone and Andy Simmons were co head editors at the time. All three of us were crammed into one room, since the publisher used the rest of the entire floor for his bridal magazine. The arrangement was fine with me since I got to spend every day with an old-time *Mad* writer from their classic years, Silverstone. He became my comedy mentor and I learned a lot from him.

"Lou and Andy were cool. The publisher was kind of a tightwad and we clashed a few times because he didn't appreciate my casual attitude (strolling in late all the time, wearing shorts to work, feet up on the desk, etc.) Personally, I didn't like the structure of a 9-to-5 job, and after about 9 or 10 months I had enough and moved on to doing freelance for them.

"Naturally, at first I wanted to work at *Mad*, but what I learned first-hand while at *Mad* is that the creative process there is so stilted, so constipated that it wasn't fun. At *Cracked*, it was a loose, very "anything goes" attitude that I found really enjoyable. The editors at *Mad* told me how great I was, but never put their money where their mouth was. *Cracked* appreciated me and was very happy to have me work for them.

"My favorite was a parody we did of a high school yearbook. The editors and me all got in costumes and we did a photo shoot (I was in a fat suit, in drag—I forget which character I was). That was a lot of fun to do. Also I was lucky enough to have a lot of my TV parodies illustrated by the great John Severin. Those were always my favorite to do. It's so great working with an illustrator of that caliber because he takes the jokes and story to a whole other level."

Barry Zeger was a writer for *Cracked* starting in 1994. He also has written liner notes for Rhino Records.

Todd James was an artist for *Cracked* starting in 1994.

Randy Jones and Ed Subitzky both defected from *National Lampoon* when it was winding down. They began at *Cracked* in 1994.

Alan Kupperberg did a lot of work for Marvel and DC and then started working at *Cracked* in 1994. He also worked on Marvel's *Crazy*: "I had done a great deal of work for the *National Lampoon* from the early 1970s, on. So I knew Andy Simmons, the son of Matty Simmons, the publisher of the *Lampoon*. By 1993, the *Lampoon* was, for all intents and purposes, virtually defunct. Andy became an editor at *Cracked*, along with Lou Silverstone. In April 1993, I believe Andy called me and asked me if I were interested in doing work for *Cracked Monster Party*. I was. Very. Though the page rate was about half that the *Lampoon* had paid, the work was "broader" and an artist had more latitude to have fun. *Lampoon* scripts were very exacting, with literary allusions and such.

"I worked there from mid-1993 until the end, including reprints. I dealt with both Lou and Andy. Both were genial and pleasant men to work with. Lou wore large eyeglasses with thick lenses. When he would look at the artwork, his nose was about an inch and a half from the page. He had very bad eyesight. They always joked that they could identify my pages because they smelled like cigarette smoke. I don't smoke anymore.

"After the new folks took over they reprinted virtually every piece I did and didn't ever toss me a farthing. They were not obligated to, however it is done by Marvel and DC and it is appreciated. They could've given me some new assignments. But again, no obligation existed.

"I submitted stuff to Sproul's *Cracked* in the 1980s. They were on Fifth Avenue, like 46 Street. I don't think I even received the courtesy of a reply. I may have even submitted material to his *Web of Horror*. I was friends with all those guys, Jones, Kaluta, Wrightson, Reese, etc. In the early 1990s I submitted some stuff, scripts, to *Mad*. Got a weird rejection slip from them. But I was always too intimidated to show my art portfolio to *Mad*. They've got Mort Drucker. Forget it. No, I never felt good enough. And people who do work there have told me that if it weren't for the prestige, and maybe the bucks, they wouldn't put up the revisions and changes demanded. I've worked for just about every other humor magazine in my day: *Grin, Crazy, National Lampoon, Harpoon, Parody, Sick, Spy*... I'm probably forgetting some. And both Peter Kuper and Kyle Baker broke in as Howie Chaykin's assistants. So I met them when they were kids. They're both nice men and talented men.

"I met Mort Drucker about eight years ago and we were talking about Al Hirschfeld. Mort mentioned that he'd just seen the documentary *The Line King* about the caricaturist. And Mort said to me, 'I was watching Hirschfeld work, and do you know what I noticed?' And knowing how both men work, I knew. And I said, 'The way he builds his (ink) line,' because Drucker does it in one stroke. Al Hirschfeld builds up his line. Works with a stiffer pen. Mort Drucker and I both came up under the same guy at DC Comics, Jack Adler, in the Production Department.

"The only places that weren't pleasant were the ones that Jim Shooter ran (into the ground). Though I did have a bad experience with Tony Tallarico. He was editing a humor magazine, *Trash*, for Martin Goodman, whom I had worked for at Atlas/ Seaboard. I believe he wanted to squeeze me out to fit in some more of his cronies. At least I got to meet the great Jack Sparling in Goodman's waiting room.

"The least favorite was a satire of the *Mighty Morphing Power Rangers* movie. Gag, choke. My favorite was "'A Stiff Penalty,' which I have appended below. I did a couple of nice color back covers for them that I'm fairly pleased with."

Carson Demmans describes what selling his first script was like in 1994: "I wish I could say that the Heavens opened up and my brilliant script was bought. It wasn't. Instead, I got a very well thought out critique of it by Andy Simmons, the same Andy Simmons who was still famous from his run at *National Lampoon*, dissecting my script, sometimes on a line by line basis. He made some suggestions for formats of future submission, in particular funny lists that could be easily illustrated. I sent three more scripts, and one, in a heavily edited form, ended up in the *Backwash* section, 'Reasons why Disney never made sequels to these films.'

"Success! Ok, not the success I dreamed of as a kid. No high print run graphic novels, no fan mail, no acclaim. But there was my name in print and something I wrote as well, published in a magazine most people recognized the name of. I became a regular submitter to *Cracked*, if not a regular contributor. I sent in hundreds of ideas, but was only published six times by Simmons and another couple of times by Jallad, including my only cover featured piece, a Schwarzenegger parody. Simmons often gave commentary, and I even got to talk to him on the phone a couple of times. He gave me many tips, including some his bosses would probably have frowned on. I asked him once what I should use as reference material for writing funny one page gags, and he suggested back issues of *Mad* from the '70s. He also warned me about writing pieces that were too sexy. He said their readership was quite young, often pre-teen, and they got as many complaints about sex as *National Lampoon* did when it was critical of religion. 'If these people have no sense of humor, why do they read my magazines?' he asked. After Simmons came Kulpa, who didn't reply to any of my submissions, so I eventually stopped submitting, which only disappointed the guy hired to shred my material, who was promptly laid off. Later came Jallad, whom had published some of my stuff in his small press books *Thwak* and *Jokester*. I was back, at least briefly for two-page layouts.

"I was a minor contributor (writer) for a few pieces in the '90s and 2000s. I am also generally recognised as the biggest Warren Sattler fan in the known universe. Warren's also a great guy I enjoy getting a hold of every few years.

"Andy Simmons was the first editor to ever buy anything from me. Andy was a genuinely funny guy that I talked to on the phone a few times. He warned me to avoid submitting pieces about sex to *Cracked* because that brought almost as many protest letters to *Cracked* as doing pieces about religion brought protest letters when he edited *National Lampoon*. After a pause, he said, 'If these people don't have a sense of humor, why do they read my magazines?'"

Ricky Sprague is a writer who started at *Cracked* in 1994 writing *Awkward Moments for Limbs to Fall Off*. Later, his work started appearing in *Mad*. He commented on his work for *Cracked*: "Like most smartasses who came of age in the late '70s-early '80s, I'd read a lot of *Mad* magazine. I was aware of *Cracked*, but I didn't really take it seriously until Don Martin kerflunked over, in '88 or '89. By that time I was a regular reader of *National Lampoon*, which had the benefit of foul language and pictures of nude women. From then on, I mostly got my periodical humor fix from *NatLamp* (and, occasionally, *Spy*) although I did from time to time flip through *Cracked* to see if Martin was in it.

"In the early '90s, I decided I was clever enough to start writing professionally, and started sending article ideas to *Mad*. They rejected everything I sent them, but they were surprisingly sweet about it; I got some nice handwritten encouragement from their editors. Of course, encouragement was not scratch, nor did it count as a published credit. So I figured I'd send some stuff to *Cracked*.

"I was pretty amazed when I cracked open an issue, looking for a mailing address. The editors' names were two that I recognized—Lou Silverstone, from *Mad*, and Andy Simmons, from *NatLamp*. *Cracked* immediately rose in my estimation. These were two guys who'd had a lot of influence over my smartass development. Newly inspired, I wrote up a whole batch of stuff, stick-figure drawings with my fevered, chicken-scratch captions.

"I got a reply a couple of months after I'd sent my submissions, in August 1994. My confidence being what it was, I was sure it was a rejection. But it was a contract. The note from Lou read, 'Sign it and we're in business.' The following Monday I called the number on the contract and asked for Lou, who quickly said something like, 'Andy's the one you want to talk to' (I think he didn't like the sound of my voice).

"My first appearance in *Cracked* hit the newsstands on November 8, 1994, #296—*Star Trek: Generations* was on the cover. I remember the date well, because it was the day of what became known as 'The Republican Revolution,' when that political party took control of the House and Senate. It was all anyone talked about—all over the television news and papers. Meanwhile, it seemed like everyone was ignoring my national publishing debut. In a way, you could say I was the first victim of the Republican Revolution. Naturally, I was filled with resentment.

"And why wouldn't I be? The article, *Awkward Moments for Limbs to Fall Off* was as hilarious as it sounds, but even better than the writing was the fact that the great Gray Morrow illustrated it. Being a comics and SF fan, I was a huge fan of his work from *Heavy Metal* magazine, and Ace's SF paperback novels. I was pretty excited.

"I'd end up having my *Cracked* articles illustrated by some fantastically talented artists, including of course The Maestro John Severin, bold Bruce Bolinger, wily Walter Brogan, fantastic Frank Cummings, Terry "Total Package" Colon, mighty Mike Ricigliano, awesome Arnoldo Franchioni, bad Brian Buniak, and other fantastic artists for whom I am too lazy to attempt alliterative nicknames. They enabled all of the articles that I sold, and I am afraid that if I tried to pick a favorite from among those I'd end up alienating one of those very talented people. So I will alienate them all by choosing as my favorite of my *Cracked* works something called 'Guide to Handwriting Analysis' that appeared in #309—with *Third Rock from the Sun* on the cover. There was no artist credited on that one, just me analyzing 'handwriting.' Oh, it was funny. The joke was, the 'analysis' of the 'handwriting' totally missed the point of what was written on the page. Trust me, it was funny.

"I ended up appearing in over 30 issues of *Cracked*, sometimes only in the *Backwash* section at the front of the magazine, and sometimes with multiple articles. My primary association was with Andy, and I can say unequivocally that he was a rare gentleman and a fantastic editor. He was never too busy to take a call, always genuinely helpful and supportive of my work. He was the first person to ever commission me to write something (I think it was my article on Tiger Woods—how Woods managed to get all those women to sleep with him after the withering takedown he received in that article is beyond me; hats off to him!), and also the second (I think it was the article about the Madden Football game—for some reason, Andy thought I liked sports), which is a big ego boost for a young writer. He even took the time to read a very crummy screenplay (!) that I wrote around that time. Oh, Andy! Please accept my apology for that!

"In the years since my writing for *Cracked*, I've worked with several editors and agents. The relationship that I had with Andy was certainly one of the best I've ever had, and I'm grateful to him for the way he treated me. I want to make it clear that when I used the word 'relationship' in the previous sentence, I was speaking in purely professional terms. Andy and I never had anything other than a strictly professional relationship, not that he wasn't a good-looking guy. As you can see from his photograph in my article on celebrity cookbooks in #305, he was certainly a good-looking guy. So was Lou, even if he didn't like the sound of my voice.

"After about five years or so, around 1999, I decided to try my luck with *Mad*. Back then, *Mad* had a policy of not working with anyone who worked with *Cracked*, which always struck me as unnecessarily draconian. *Mad* always seemed to top *Cracked* in sales and in cache, anyway. As funny as *Cracked* was—and it was funny – it was never going to have the history of *Mad*. Also, *Mad* paid a heck of a lot more. I'm not entirely sure if I should reveal the page rates, but *Mad*'s was more than double *Cracked*'s. It was more than triple. It was not more than quintuple. Wait; what's the word that means 'five times'? Is that 'quintuple'? It wasn't that much. It was somewhere between triple and quintuple. If you're a linguist or a mathematician you can probably figure out how much it was.

"As it turned out, not long after I moved on and sold a couple of articles to *Mad*, *Cracked* was sold by Globe Communications to the people who published *National Enquirer*. Those people obviously knew funny, so the magazine was in great hands—that's why it's thriving to this day. Of course, all magazine publishing is experiencing a renaissance these days.

"It became increasingly difficult to find at the newsstands. A friend of mine made a sale to them after the *Enquirer* people took it over, so I did hunt down that issue. Lou and Andy's touch was long gone, sadly. It was a completely different magazine from the one that had stood with me against the Republican Revolution."

Todd Jackson conceived, coded and designed the original *Cracked* website back in 1994. Later, he became managing editor. He's also worked for Cartoon Network and developed their website as well. Jackson comments: "I moved to NYC a year after college because I wanted to be involved with magazine publishing. I knew how rare humor magazines were, so it was always a wistful idea that I might end up working for one again. But I was really focused on being a journalist / writer of some kind. I found the associate editor job in the *NY Times* classifieds while looking to break in and couldn't believe my luck. I was already interning at *Rolling Stone* at the time and doing production work on the *NY Press* for money, but this seems like too much of a good fit to let go. After a couple rounds of interviews, I was in.

"*Cracked* was a great gig. We put out a lot of stuff (21 issues a year counting all the specials) but I don't think it was ever so taxing that I hated doing any of it for too long. I actually brought home the box of resumes from people who applied for my gig and would look at every once in a while when I had a bad day to remind myself that a lot of people wanted to be doing what I was doing.

"The biggest change that happened when I was at *Cracked* was we began using Macs to create type for the magazine. When I got there, *Cracked* was still sending out to get type from typesetters. And that would take forever. My background in desktop publishing parody was leveraged pretty quickly, allowing Cliff Mott and myself to really help take the magazine to new spaces visually.

"The other was the addition of color to the magazine, something that just seemed like a necessity to attract kid's eyeballs considering all the changes in the culture. It was also a way to differentiate us from *Mad*.

"But *Cracked* was in what inevitably would be a downhill period I think; the competition for kids' attentions just got bigger and bigger, particularly with video games and the web becoming big industries. We did a lot of stories on that—I did a fair amount of them because I was young enough to enjoy them and get why they were popular.

"The other problem was parodying a fractured culture—the sandbox of what kids enjoyed was filled with niche hits. With the dominance of the three networks going and movies that were #1 at the box office for a week, you really couldn't count on anything being huge enough that it would generate sales for months on end.

"The only way to change the circumstances would have been to put a massive rebranding effort—similar to the one that's happened now with *Cracked* now only living on as a website for more 20 somethings. And I don't think that would have done much good if it was only a magazine. *Cracked*, as a magazine, was never going to last much longer. I had my disappointments there, but nothing traumatizing.

"I never even thought about *Mad*. The only humor magazine I tried out for before *Cracked* was *Spy*, which was going through a relaunch at the time. *Mad* and *Cracked* were not big parts of my childhood, despite being a heavy reader of comic books. So, I never really considered either as an option until I saw the help wanted ad in the paper.

"*Cracked* was, essentially, four mostly easy-going guys talking about silly things in a room. It wasn't like a lot of PC office environments—you could say a lot of things you could never say anywhere else, because that was our job. Being funny requires you to go strange places sometimes and say things that you wouldn't say in front of people. There were a lot of times, particularly during an interminable cover discussion, where I'd say, 'OK, this isn't the gag, but 'what if...' simply to get the joke out of my head so I could find the real joke. You have to have an environment like a lot of Improv classes, where you can 'Yes, and No' each other.

"I worked at a short-lived dot com humor start up that was a lot like this too, but then later, as an editorial director at Comedy Central, found it to be mostly like this. Though it's a hip company, it's a tighter environment because while everybody is working for something that pushes funny, most people jobs there are to make things function like any other cable network. You had to really concentrate this kind of talk to the folks in your own department, whose job it was to be funny while occasionally filthy.

"I really enjoyed parodying *Buffy the Vampire Slayer* and *King of the Hill*, which were both brilliant TV shows. I think there's a difference you can see in those parodies of mine, because when the person who's doing them actually really loves (or hates) the target, it makes for a much more interesting read. At the very least you make a lot of jokes that the people who also love (or hate) the show will enjoy immediately. Sometimes you have no attachment to what you're targeting. You can write funny jokes, but if you don't care a little, I think you're starting from a weak position. I did a couple like that I'm sure, but none of them stick out in my head.

"I loved it then, but it would be the wrong thing for me now. I probably did it for too long as it was—it was a very easy place to get comfortable in and just ride it out. It's not going to be perfect, but it's going be just good enough that you're enjoying yourself most days. After I saw *The Onion*, I knew things were going to the web and I really should have thought more about how to adapt."

Gunnar Johnson did a lot of Photoshopped articles for *Cracked* started in 1995.

J. Kelly started writing and drawing for *Cracked* in 1995.

Frank Cummings also was hired at this time: "I grew up being a fan of both *Mad* and *Cracked*. I was self-publishing a regional (southeast) humor mag and caught the eye of associate editor Todd Jackson. He and Andy Simmons (editor) contacted me and made me an offer I couldn't refuse. (Stop losing money on your own mag and come work for us!)

"I joined at the tail end of Globe's ownership. I've always suspected that I pushed them over the edge and prompted the sale to American Media / Dick Kulpa. Andy Simmons was the editor; Lou Silverstone was the head writer / God.

"I never actually worked in the NYC office. Visited a few times. Lou Silverstone made me feel like a bumpkin. Then, later I found out that I actually WAS a bumpkin and am now forever grateful to Lou for pointing it out.

"I loved my time there and most every assignment. Must say, my least favorite projects were movie parodies with little or no promo photos available. I'd wind up making up everything (costumes, settings, backgrounds) and it would never turn out anything like the actual move."

R.J. Reiley started writing for *Cracked* in 1996. He has also worked for Cartoon Network.

C.L. Walker also started writing for *Cracked* in 1996.

They also hired Barry Dutter. Dutter explains, "I started out at *Cracked* in 1996 doing some freelance writing for those guys. In the beginning they liked my stuff and they were using it a lot. As time went on, they didn't like my stuff as much. When Kulpa took over as the new editor of *Cracked*, he was someone that I had worked with before on something for Topps Comics. When he was put in charge of *Cracked*, he gave me a call. He told the New York guys, because he was in contact with them at the time, that he wanted to bring me aboard and their response was, 'Dutter! What do you want to hire him for? He's not funny!' Traditionally, all the editorial people who worked for *Cracked* hated all the other people who worked on the magazine. Everybody thinks that their version was the best version and everybody hates all the other versions. I would like to add here that I am a good friend with Mort Todd, even though I knew my version of *Cracked* was way funnier than his. Just kidding, Mort!"

Mike Lotter also started as a writer for *Cracked* in 1996.

Kit Lively discusses his time at *Cracked*, which began in 1997: "I loved *Cracked* as a kid and teen, but had dropped it when I discovered *National Lampoon*. When the *Lampoon* faltered and eventually stopped publishing the magazine, I took another look at *Cracked* (and *Mad*) and began to read both again, noticing that the former had brought aboard quite a few of the *Lampoon*'s old guard. In fact, *Cracked* had a more off-color, dark-humor sensibility than when I had left it years before and was almost like a *Lampoon, Jr*. It didn't initially occur to me that I should submit material, as the work I was doing for other magazines was either of the single-panel cartoon variety, or prose; neither of which *Cracked* used very much. After reading the magazine on a regular basis for several years, I decided to send them a batch of my single-panels. They were rejected, but the rejection came with a friendly note from assistant editor Todd Jackson, encouraging me to send in more material. I re-fashioned some of my single-panels into full-page comic strips and sent them in, and they bought two or three. After that, I was pretty much in and began selling to them regularly, rarely missing an issue for a three-year run at the magazine.

"My favorite would have to be either 'The Ice Cream Vendor' in #328, or 'The Wishing Well,' in #319. A lot of times jokes can get away from you and into a magazine before you realize that they're not as funny as you thought that they were, but these two seem okay. The real reason they've aged so well is due to the art by Don Orehek and Bruce Bolinger, respectively. As far as a least favorite…well, I can probably see areas for improvement in just about everything I write or draw.

"I did try *Mad* first, at a time that I wasn't sure either mag was a good fit for the type of stuff that I was doing. I sent copies of my self-published humor magazine to a *National Lampoon* writer that I liked, and he in return sent me a complimentary letter, encouraging me to send copies of my magazine to places like the *Lampoon* and *Mad*. I did so, and they just sent them back. I was naive at the time, and now realize that it was an odd sort of submission to make to a magazine. Years after *Cracked*, I did finally get into *Mad*, but have only sold them two things so far.

"I loved contributing to *Cracked*. Not only was it a kick to be published in a magazine that I had enjoyed as a kid, but also it seemed to be a much better magazine in the '90s, as well as a magazine that I was proud to be a part of. The material in the magazine as a whole was consistently strong and funny. Also, it was a big deal for me to have my written work illustrated by guys like Don Orehek, Bruce Bolinger, Mike Ricigliano and other guys whose work I had enjoyed and been a huge fan of for years. The guys at *Cracked* were always open to new stuff, so I got the chance to create and write several new recurring features for the mag, such as 'True Tales of Romantic Love,' 'Nursery Rhymes for Naughty Children' and 'Jane the Insensitive Friend' (the latter not entirely mine, as it was editor Andy Simmons' idea to turn my single-panel cartoon into a regular feature, and he came up with the title as well). The editorial staff, at the time, was a bunch of great guys. They were easy to get on the phone, or you'd typically get a callback within the hour. The fact that the editorial staff included personal humor-writing faves like Lou Silverstone and Andy Simmons didn't hurt. It really did feel like walking with giants, and it was quite a surreal and great experience."

Katey Dash began writing for *Cracked* in 1997.

Dan Fiorella is a writer, has done stand-up and has written for various TV and movie productions. He started at *Cracked* in 1997, and also served as their roving editor, and also worked on *Weekly World News*. He also co-founded *The Plague*, New York University's humor publication. Fiorella tells the story: "After years of irregular submissions to *Mad*, a friend pointed *Cracked* out to me. It's one of those things where I knew it was around, but never occurred to me to submit. It never would have occurred to me to submit to *Mad* if I hadn't seen the *NY Times* classified ad. So, I put together some of my rejected *Mad* bits and submitted it to them cold. A couple of months later I got call from them saying they liked my stuff and were going to use a bit and invited me to continue to submit.

"Back in 1997. This was prior to e-mail and such, so most of my transactions with them were via mail. The editor was Andy Simmons, I dealt with him and Todd Jackson. Funny, easy-going and supportive. They tried to get a 'team' feeling going, hosting a lunch or two for their regular contributors and trying spark some new life into the magazine. Lou Silverstone was an editor, but I didn't deal with him much. I live with a certain level of obviousness, so I didn't realize that these meetings were reaction to drops in circulation of *Cracked* and of published materials in general.

"Then it happened. The company that owned *Cracked* got sold to American Media, the folks that run the *National Enquirer*. All the editors were out. Then we heard that the *National Enquirer* people only wanted the

Globe tabloid and was ready to can *Cracked*. Then, one of their employees, Dick Kulpa, begged them to keep it going and basically got the mag. He was open to submissions from the old freelancers. He really was interested in keeping *Cracked* alive in its familiar form. It was a tough time. There were many conference calls and on-line meetings. I was dealing with Kulpa and Barry Dutter thru all of this. But as they explained it to me, *Cracked*'s distribution (which was an amazing set-up for the magazine, getting into places *Mad* never could) collapsed after the sale, so that one advantage was lost. Since American Media didn't care, Kulpa was fighting his own people to get the magazine out. In the end, they sold the magazine to Kulpa and he tried mightily, but he just couldn't keep it going. There were talks about TV, about a CD-rom of the entire 50-year history, but nothing ever happened.

"All at long distance...At one point Kulpa asked us if we could donate material for an issue, since he couldn't pay us. I simply dug out a bit from the trunk that had gotten a pass under the Simmons' regime and re-submitted to Dick and he was thrilled to get it. When he could pay, it was at a decreased rate.

"At one point, the issues were often 30% reprints of earlier bits, they were so desperate for material and so lacking funds. That's when I discovered that the old editors had used one of my bits, but with the sale, the records got lost and I never got paid. And I had to haunt them to get my money from Kulpa and co.

"At around this point, I played up the guilt to get myself named 'roving editor' to make up for the cut in pay. I'm listed as that in a couple of issues.

"Barry Dutter has the real horror stories. At some point he was the sole figure proofing and editing and doing it for free, because (as he put it) 'It's going out there with my name on it.'

"Once it got sold again, the new people made it pretty clear they didn't want any of us old-timers around. It was going to be hot and edgy now. Who knew assembling random lists and links to YouTube could be so hot and edgy?

"Okay, while technically not a 'horror' story, it was kind of goofy. During one of the longer Cracked droughts (2000-01), Kulpa was anxious to keep the writers happy, so he and Dutter got us various gigs on another American Media publication, *The Weekly World News*, the humor magazine that nobody knew was a humor magazine. It took me awhile to get my sea legs for that, but I soon spent a year or so as 'Dear Dottie' their advice columnist and was regularly submitting stories under the name Jerome Howard. Kulpa and Dutter went really out of their way on that, helping me with things until I got the rhythm of the paper. I slowly stepped away from 'Dear Dottie' to submit the Howard articles. I was doing okay so that even after Kulpa and Dutter departed the tabloid, I was getting published by *WWN* regularly, until

2005 when it got a new editor who had some 'new bold' ideas for a tabloid of made-up facts.

"I never really thought about writing for *Cracked* or *Mad*, I had my eyes on the movies but I considered myself a comedy writer and started to broaden my attempts, especially having toiled on the *Plague* for 2+ years.

"As I mentioned, *Mad* was my first attempt. And even after working for *Cracked*, I continued to submit to *Mad*, usually then submitting the same material to *Cracked* after *Mad* passed. *Mad* was a very hard nut to crack (pardon the pun). Andy Simmons even told me once how he heard that people might get one thing in *Mad* and never get published by them again. He knew a writer who had been a contributor and finally got a piece accepted by *Mad* and basically announced he was 'moving on and up.' A few months later, he was back submitting to *Cracked*."

Kent Kennedy was the last major contributor hired during the Lou Silverstone-Andy Simmons era. His artwork appeared in *Cracked* beginning in 1999.

B.K. Taylor comments on how he almost returned to *Cracked* during this period: "Around 1999 or thereabouts I was part of a company called Stunt Pilot Productions. It was a film and television development company, and we obtained the rights, with the help of editor Andy Simmons, to *Cracked* magazine. We also received an option from Sony television. Unfortunately, it never came to pass…but *Cracked* magazine almost became a TV show."

Mort Todd never got the opportunity to return with a byline, "I hope it wasn't just sour grapes, but it was hard for me to get excited about *Cracked* after I left. There was more 'toilet humor' than I would've used. Severin's work didn't seem as inspired, perhaps because of the subject matter of the scripts he got.

"I'm a different person than subsequent editors, so obviously I would've gone in a different direction. The artists didn't always seem to get paired with the best script to suit their strong points. But during the Lou/Jerry/Cliff/ Andy era the magazine looked great and continued to give *Mad* gas pains during *Cracked*'s last hurrah.

"Before I left, there was talking about me continuing to freelance for the magazine. I don't know if that was something with the publishers or if they wanted a clean break, but they just closed communications with me completely. I have remained great pals with Cliff and ghosted some plots, layout and inking on his *Cracked Monster Party Animal* strip."

Walter Brogan describes the office environment while at *Cracked* during the Silverstone years: "There were a couple of them. They were all right. It wasn't as big as the *Mad* office. Lou would always say that *Mad* was like the Disney stuff and we were like the Chuck Jones stuff.

"They had like four or five rooms, while *Cracked* only had two rooms. You had to clean out the closet and throw the *Cracked* guys in there. I enjoyed working with all the guys, go up, get the story and go out to lunch. We hung out together and had two hour lunches. I would say my favorite was Lou. We hit it off really well; right from the first time we met. We all got along really well at *Cracked*. I even got along with Don Orehek."

Brogan recalls one of his favorite assignments as well as the hazards of obtaining photographs in order to draw the movie parodies for *Cracked*: "Yeah, I liked *The Unforgiven*. That came out really good. *Matlock*, *The Godfather III* but with that one I wished I had even three more days. I would have to sit down and draw the caricature and most of the time it was the first one that I had to go with. I would do a sketch over and try to do it better. I just didn't have the luxury of time to do that. Sometimes they'd give you a photo, but most of the time I just took clippings from the newspaper."

John Severin would go into the movie theater and take a little flashlight and just draw looking at the screen in order to overcome the lack of photos at *Cracked*, but as Bill Sproul explains, this policy was not needed later on: "When we started getting current with the hot released movies we did all number of things to get it out on time. We wrote the *King Kong* parody using a copy of the script someone got their hands on. Some scenes we parodied were left on the editing room floor of the movie and didn't make any sense; but we are *Cracked*, so it was hardly noticed. One editor here in Florida set up accounts, as if we were an independent theater, with publicity houses, picture stills agencies and such. If we needed movie stills of any movie we got them. This was great and saved John Severin many trips to the movies. The writers and myself had to see every movie and stay current on all the things kids were into. I went to matinees so often for so many years; I still prefer seeing a good movie by myself. It seems easier to let the film carry you away, more like reading a book."

Brogan explains the difference in prestige *Mad* had over *Cracked*: "Jerry De Fuccio would get a stack of photo stills to work with, like 60 or 70 photo stills from the movie while at *Mad*. Not true for *Cracked*. I used to ask for one or two and I had to get my own, whatever I could get. I would go down to a place on 14th Street and I would buy the photos myself. I remember once I was trying to get a photo of Clint Eastwood from *Unforgiven* and I remember that they didn't have a photo from that movie at that point, so I would get Clint Eastwood from a different movie that he did five or six years ago. So I would do that from time to time to get some sort of reference or I would go see the movie. One time I went with a good friend of mine to see *Goodfellas* and I brought a camera in with me. I didn't know how to turn the flash off and I took a picture of it and lit the whole fuckin' theater up. You know that flash goes off and the usher and the manager come running down and said,

'What are you doing?' I said that I was working for *Cracked* and I needed a photo to use as a reference and I was escorted out of the movie theater. I did! It was an old 35mm camera and I thought I had turned the flash off. My wife at the time said, 'Man, you got so red. I thought you were going to bust,' and my friend said, 'Thanks, Walt, I was really looking forward to this movie.' We were all rejected. All four of us. We all got booted out. I said, 'Well, that killed that idea.' So then I started using clippings. I had this clipping that I cut out that was 2x2 or 1x1. It was so small; I almost went blind looking at it. I just went down and bought my own photos and they were pretty expensive. What I would do is to look through the photos and would get a front view and a side view of the actors. Basically, that's all I really needed. That was about it."

Brogan comments on publisher Barry Rosenbloom: "He was a really nice guy. We got along with him really well and he'd come out and we'd have lunch. I think he was a little sorry it folded, too. I don't think he wanted to sell it. I thought when Barry Rosenbloom had it; it was the best it ever looked. I don't know, from what Lou told me for a year or two, it may have outsold *Mad*."

Lou Silverstone reflects on the shake-up that led to Dick Kulpa taking over *Cracked* in 2000: "I think we did fairly well at *Cracked* the last few years. If not sales-wise, at least production-wise. We had the magazine going in a good direction, but then the Globe sold the whole thing to the *Enquirer*. I guess *Cracked* was a throw-in. The *Enquirer* wasn't that interested in running *Cracked*, so they sold it to the person they hired as the editor." That person was Dick Kulpa.

Don Orehek reflects on the various regimes he worked under while at *Cracked*: "They were all good guys. There was Lou Silverstone and there was Michael Delle-Femine, and they were great guys. Then the Italian kid Jerry De Fuccio went someplace else and then Lou continued and I did very well with these people. Then when they sold out, it started to go downhill for me and then they shipped it out to Florida. *National Enquirer* took over for awhile and then from there it really went to hell."

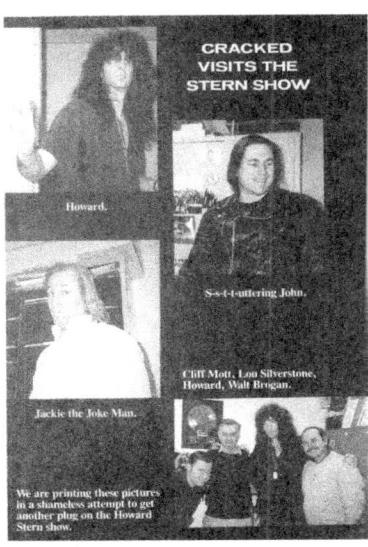

The *Cracked* staff appeared on *The Howard Stern Show* for the first time during the Lou Silverstone / Andy Simmons era. Here are photos from *Cracked* #273, August 1992, documenting the visit.

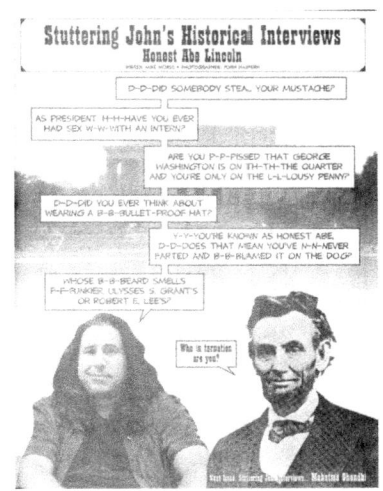

The *Stern Show* and *Cracked* were so taken with each other that eventually a regular feature started appearing called *Stuttering John's Interviews*. This is the first one from *Cracked* #332, January 1999, featuring John Melendez.

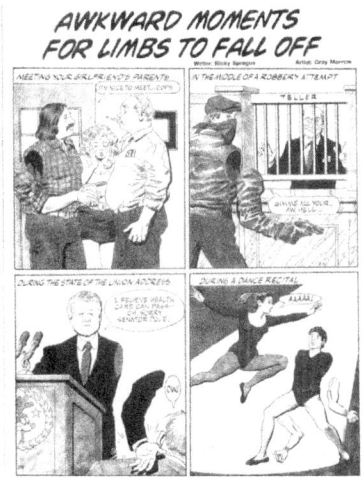

Ricky Sprague was thrilled when he discovered Gray Morrow was assigned to draw his *Awkward Moments for Limbs to Fall Off*. This is the first one from *Cracked* #296, January 1995.

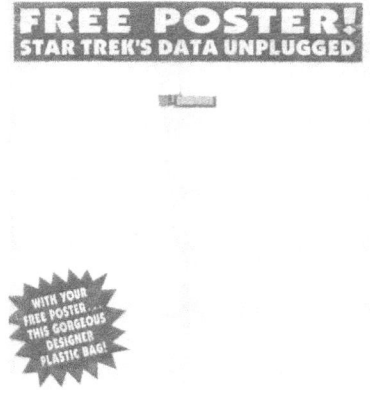

Three different issues of *Cracked* were polybagged with some nice bonus features. Here's the bag from *Cracked Sci-Fi Special Blockbuster* #8, Summer 1994, which featured a full-color oversized poster of Data from *Star Trek: The Next Generation*.

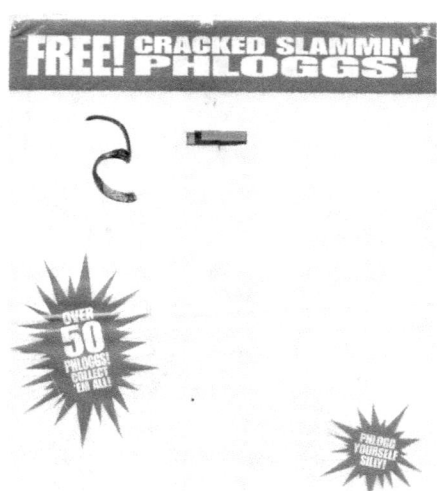

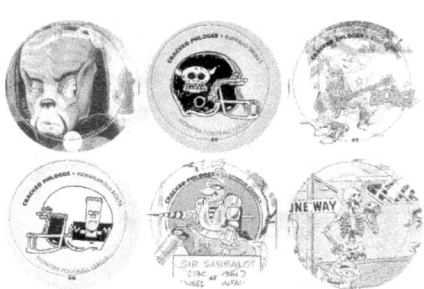

Here are the six Phloggs I received. Does anyone have the complete set of 50??

The second polybagged issue was *Cracked Blockbuster* #9, Summer 1995, which featured a set of *Cracked* Phloggs, which was *Cracked*'s take on the brief pog fad at the time.

FREE: CRACKED ISSUE #1

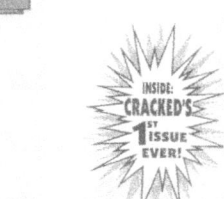

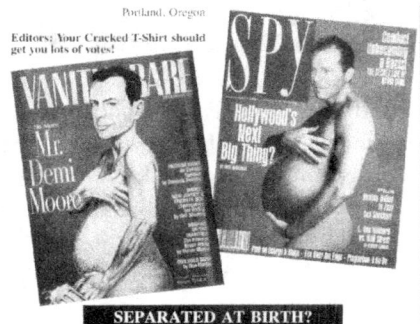

A TALE OF TWO HUMOR MAGAZINES

Editors: Here's proof that humor is a language, though we may speak different dialects. Rurik Tyler had just delivered our #268 back cover painting of Bruce Willis, in the "temporarily plump" mode of Demi Moore, Willis's expectant wife. Rurik was called to the satirical Spy Magazine to do an assignment. Once there, Rurik discovered that Spy was doing a near-duplicate of Rurik's cover for Cracked. Rurik quickly explained that we had "the same thing" in the works. We doff our Cracked caps to Spy and congratulate them for beating us to the newsstands.

Cracked's claim that they scooped *Spy* magazine with their pregnant Bruce Willis cover parody of the infamous Demi Moore *Vanity Fair* cover. Unfortunately, *Spy* carried it off with more class. The *Cracked* parody appeared on the back cover of #268, December 1991.

The final polybagged issue was *Cracked Collectors' Edition* #97, January 1994, which featured a full reprint of *Cracked* #1, March 1958, with some minor changes.

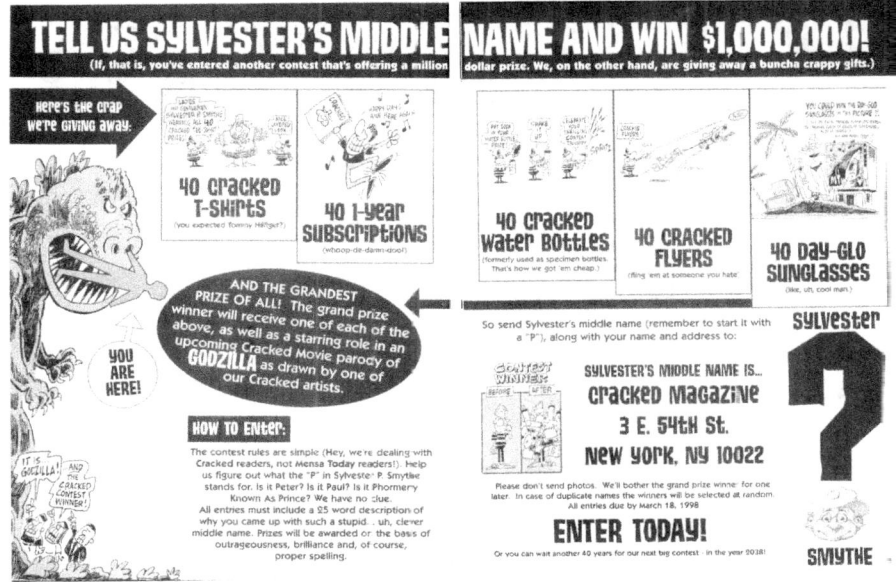

Cracked #325, May 1988, featured the Sylvester's Middle Name contest.
I was one of the winners.

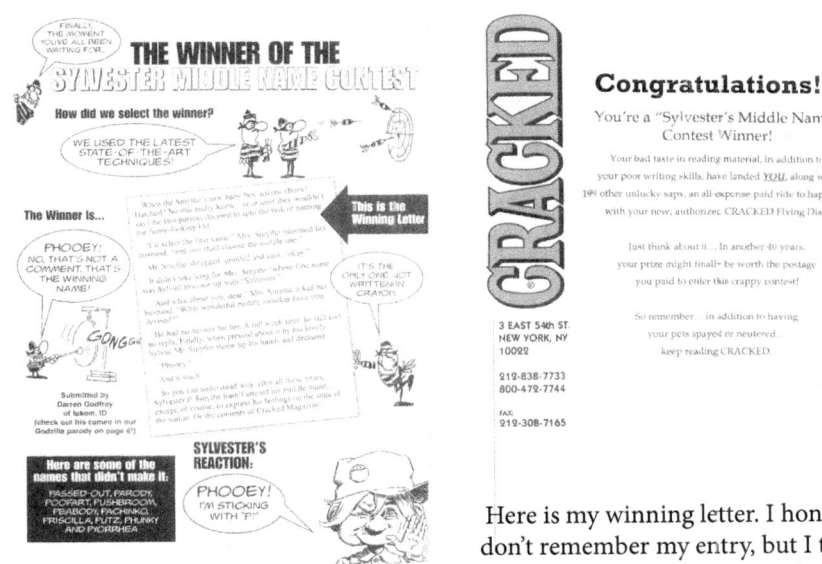

Here is my winning letter. I honestly
don't remember my entry, but I think
it was "Pneumonia." The actual winner
was "Phooey."

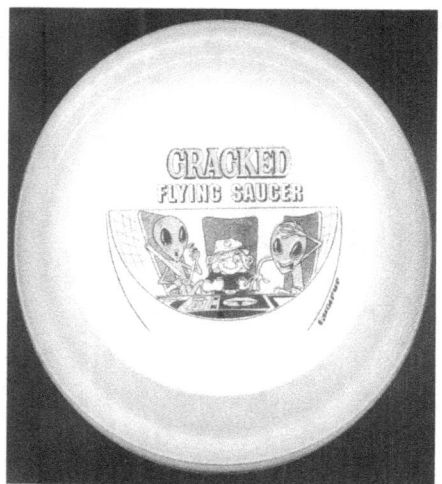

And here is my prize, the *Cracked* Flying Disc.

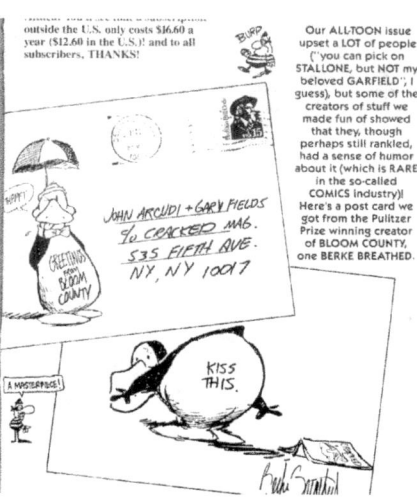

Berkeley Breathed of *Bloom County* and Opus contributed a letter, which appeared in *Cracked* #247, September 1989.

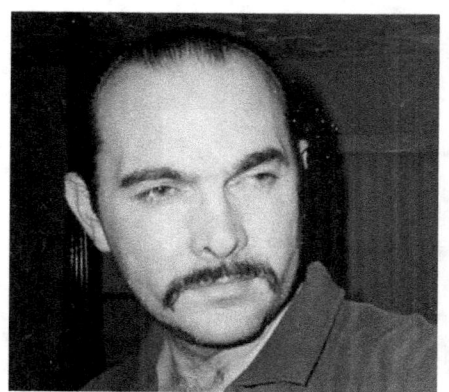

Walter Brogan appeared many times in *Cracked* in various photo assignments. He's the cop on the cover of *Cracked Collectors' Edition* #95, July 1993.

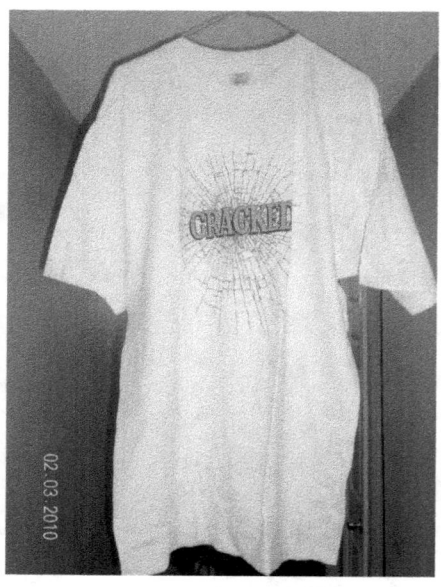

There was a black *Cracked* T-Shirt. Now here's the white *Cracked* T-Shirt. Image courtesy of Dan Fiorella.

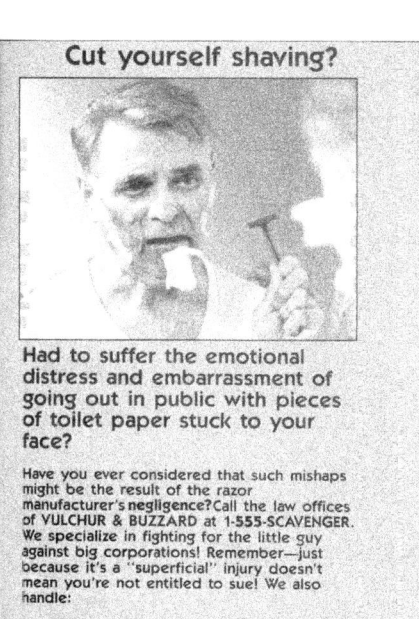

Cut yourself shaving?

Had to suffer the emotional distress and embarrassment of going out in public with pieces of toilet paper stuck to your face?

Have you ever considered that such mishaps might be the result of the razor manufacturer's negligence? Call the law offices of VULCHUR & BUZZARD at 1-555-SCAVENGER. We specialize in fighting for the little guy against big corporations! Remember—just because it's a "superficial" injury doesn't mean you're not entitled to sue! We also handle:

* Stubbed toes (furniture or door manufacturer's neligence)
* Mouth/tongue burns (pizza restaurant's negligence)
* Paper cuts (book publisher's negligence)

Cracked Editor Lou Silverstone also gets into the act. Here's his appearance from *Cracked* #290, July 1994.

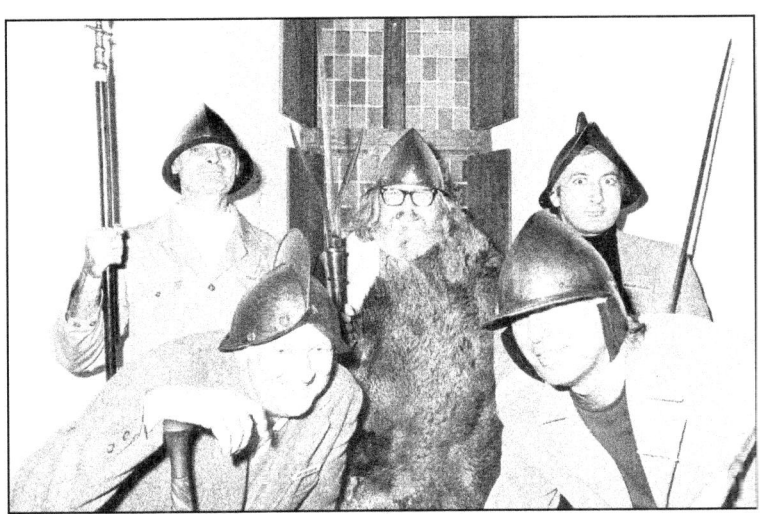

Defectors! Everyone in this picture (save for William M. Gaines) worked for *Cracked* at one point or another. Flanking Gaines are Lou Silverstone, Jack Davis, Don Martin and Jerry De Fuccio. *Image courtesy of Frank Jacobs from his book The Mad World of William M. Gaines, 1972.*

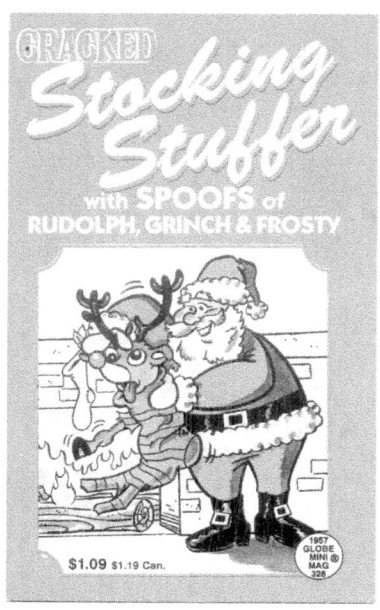

Probably the rarest *Cracked* issue of all is the *Cracked Stocking Stuffer* from 1999, due to its odd size (2"x3") and location for sale, which was at the supermarket checkout line with all the small astrology and game booklets. It is unknown whether any further Globe Mini-Mags featuring *Cracked* were produced.

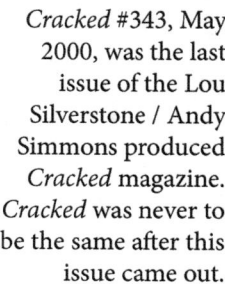

Cracked #343, May 2000, was the last issue of the Lou Silverstone / Andy Simmons produced *Cracked* magazine. *Cracked* was never to be the same after this issue came out.

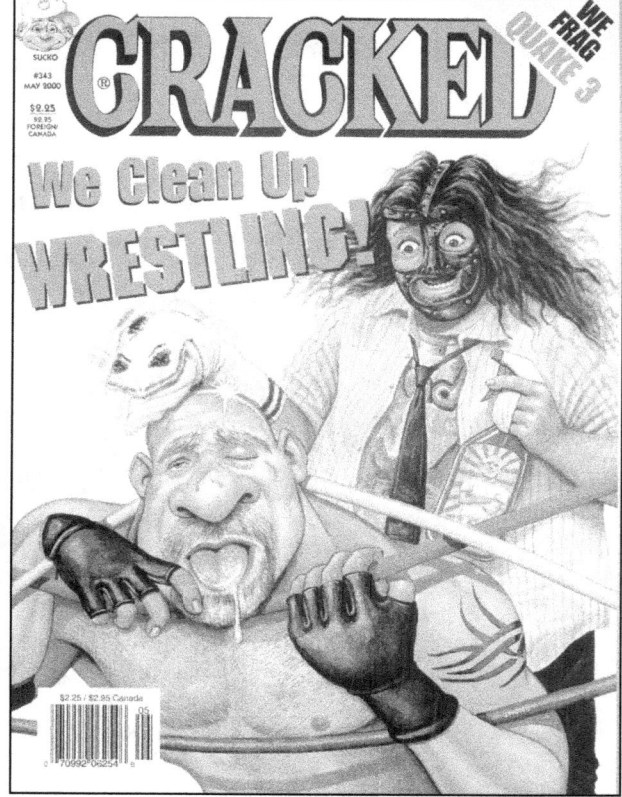

DiCK KULPA

BARRY Dutter explains what happened next: "There was a company called Globe Communications that published *Cracked* and they also published some tabloids. I think they might have had the *Star* or something like that and there was this other tabloid publisher called AMI—American Media International—that had the *National Enquirer*. AMI was the #1 tabloid publisher in America. One day they decided to buy the #2 tabloid publisher. They bought Globe and all of its holdings including *Cracked* magazine. So now you've got this huge magazine publisher, which suddenly owns *Cracked* magazine. The most important thing you have to understand is that they didn't want *Cracked* magazine. That wasn't their goal to own *Cracked* magazine. It's like if you go to a garage sale and you buy a box of stuff and you find something in the box and you say, 'Well, I don't know what this is, but we'll see what we can do with it.' One of the publications at AMI was the *Weekly World News*, which was their funny, goofy newspaper about UFO's and Batboy. One of the people working on it was Dick Kulpa. I don't remember what his specific title was at that time, if he was an Art Director or some kind of Editor. Anyway, so AMI gets *Cracked* and they say, 'Well, we got this guy who works for us—Dick Kulpa. He's a cartoonist. He's kind of wacky. Let's give him *Cracked*. He'll do it for a few months. If it doesn't work, we can just put him back on *Weekly World News*.' That was exactly how it happened. I wish there was some grand story behind it, but *Cracked* at this time was bleeding money. They were overspending so much so on every issue that there was no way it could make a profit.

"They were so overspending and one of the problems is that they were overpaying Severin. This is in no way intended to disrespect John Severin. He is a genius and incredibly talented, but he was getting a huge pay rate, higher than any other artist in the industry at one point. I know, because I was working for Marvel at one point and I know that Severin was making way more money per page than Marvel's top artists. My understanding was the budget for *Cracked* at

45

that time was some ridiculously high number. They were spending something like $50,000 to put out an issue of *Cracked* every month. That wasn't the exact number, but it was such a ridiculously high number that it was impossible to make a profit on. When AMI got the magazine, they gave Kulpa an edict you might say, to get the costs down, to not spend $50,000 per issue. They wanted to make the magazine profitable. Kulpa said, 'Well, I'm an artist. I can do the covers myself.' Over at AMI, they have this policy where they just hire a bunch of writers as staff and those writers write the magazine. That was the policy that worked for *Weekly World News* and various other publications. It worked pretty well for them so they figured they would try it with *Cracked*, too. I got a call from Kulpa—I guess it was late '99 or early 2000—and he said, 'Hey, Barry, how would you like to talk to the editor of *Cracked* magazine?' And I said, 'Oh, you've got Andy Simmons there?' And Kulpa said, 'No, no. It's me! I'm the new editor of *Cracked*!' and I said, 'Ok. Well, that's cool.' Kulpa was someone I got along well with. I was living in Florida at the time by coincidence where *Cracked* ended up. It ended up about 30 minutes away from my home. It was a happy coincidence. Kulpa said, "How would you like to come aboard as head writer?' And I said, 'Sure.' I did a little bit of soul searching because I kind of felt like *Cracked* was sort of the least-respected magazine in America. It just seems like anytime you mention *Cracked* to anyone; it was always, 'Oh, that's that rip-off of *Mad*.' That is the magazine's identity. That is what *Cracked* is known for, a rip-off of *Mad*. It didn't matter if you put the best artists in *Cracked*, or the best stories, it will always come up short in comparison to *Mad*. Over the years there have been many things that ripped off other things, and become very successful. Dick always liked to use the example of Ford and Chrysler. Ford invented the car, but when Chrysler came along and created their own car, nobody said, 'Well, they're just ripping off Ford.' But *Cracked* was never able to escape its stigma of being 'The magazine that is a rip-off of *Mad*.' So after much soul-searching, I decided to give it a go. It seemed like a fun opportunity to come aboard and take a turn as Head Writer for *Cracked*. A fellow by the name of Peet Janes was the editor. He was brought over from Dark Horse Comics."

Gary Fields explains his time during Dick Kulpa: "There was one issue; I think it was Kulpa's first issue as publisher, when he asked if we had any older stuff that hadn't been printed and could he print it for free? I had a couple pages I let him use to be a "team player" and also because I got to keep the copyrights on my printed work.

"Unfortunately, the only horror story I can think of was when my page rate got cut by a third. I guess Kulpa couldn't afford to pay everyone's higher rates and was trying to keep things going. I think it was supposed to be a temporary thing and I had a full time job at the time, so I stuck with it. I eventually left because it really seemed like a sinking ship and I'm still owed for a page of art. It just didn't seem like it was going to work."

Bruce Bolinger agrees, "I remained with the magazine until 2001 or so. The magazine had changed hands and the slow death of *Cracked* was obvious. Everyone's salary was cut; new artists were brought in for low wages, editorial changed hands and circulation faded. I quit about '01—'02 and when I left the magazine still owed me money."

Michelina Severin explains, "*Cracked* was sold to Globe and because Globe was owned by Barry Rosenbloom at the time and his father owned Globe. So, Barry was there when Globe sold the *Enquirer* to American Media. *Cracked* was in the sale, but Barry didn't know why, but he was sorry that they didn't leave it out. Even he thought about trying to buy it back. Then later on, nobody from *Cracked* wanted to come back. They asked Lou Silverstone and Cliff Mott who worked on *Cracked* if they would put it out and if they wanted to do it, but none of them wanted to move to Florida. So nobody was working on *Cracked*, and so they gave it to Dick Kulpa."

Lou Silverstone continues, "He was in way over his head. He got stung with this thing. They made restrictions on him financially. They asked me to come to Florida as a consultant. I'm glad I didn't go. That was a big problem."

Mike Ricigliano adds, "It wasn't for me. I can tell you that much. Dick wanted me to do it more digitally at the time and I didn't know how to do the digital stuff yet. He seemed like a nice enough guy, but…a lot of that is a blur to me because the writing seemed to be on the wall at that point and I was already looking for other options. I just think we were kinda doing what we could do there until the work finally ran out."

Pete Fitzgerald shares his views: "My final *Cracked* superior was Dick Kulpa, based in Boca Raton, Florida, a.k.a. 'National Enquirerville,' in late 1999/2000. Unlike my former New York-based bosses, I never had chance to meet Dick in person. From e-mails and phone conversations, he struck me as a wheeler-dealer type. Proud of his claim to fame: dreaming up the "Bat-Boy" for the cover of *The Weekly World News*. He always seemed to have plans that would never really pan out. E-mail contests for staff and freelancers to come up with *Cracked* slogan signs kids could put on their bedroom doors, upcoming appearances on *The Howard Stern Show*, etc.

"He wanted—and got—*Cracked* as his own independent magazine, which I can appreciate… especially since American Media had no interest in continuing *Cracked*, after absorbing its parent company, Globe Communications. However, I didn't have a lot of confidence in what I saw the magazine becoming, plus the difficulty in getting paid, so I dropped out.

"We (the freelance artists) were semi-jokingly told, at a certain point, that we were going to be 'dragged, kicking and screaming, into the digital age'—meaning that they supposedly weren't going to accept shipments of original artwork after such-and-such date, everything was going to have to be scanned and e-mailed to them. This was in 2000, and if we didn't already have them, we had to purchase scanners and zip-drives, on our own dime.

"I had access to a computer, and had slow-w-w-w dial-up Internet, but none of the accessories they were talking about, so I spent about $300 to get outfitted. It was all for naught, however, since the computer didn't have enough memory to even rotate a simple black-and-white line drawing I scanned in, much less compress and e-mail it to Florida. And I didn't have the money to spring for a new computer. Maybe it was all a bluff on their part, because all the subsequent work I did for them I was able to ship down to them the old-fashioned way, via FedEx.

"The other 'horror story,' if you could call it that, was later on, when there was some major foot-dragging on paying the freelancers. I was owed a few hundred dollars –nothing compared to what people like Mike Kazaleh were owed—and talked to Dick Kulpa on the phone about it. He gave me a story on how rough things was for him, trying to work on my sympathy. I forget the details of what he told me, but all that was missing was a violin playing 'Hearts and Flowers.' The thing is, I was having a tough time myself at that point, as some of the other companies I was working for were also taking their sweet time sending payment, my income was meager anyway, and I was in danger of missing my health insurance payment and losing coverage. I told him this, and so my story, which was entirely true, ended up being sadder than his! So I got paid the full amount!"

Rick Parker came back during this time and made some brief contributions: "I believe I did just two covers, 'Animation Wars' and 'When Pokemon Go Bad' (based on ideas by Barry Dutter). I don't think I was ever paid even a penny for that one in spite of the publisher's promises. Oh well, we all break promises, but I'd hate to be a publisher and have to break my promise to a freelancer who did a cover for me. I'm sure that Dick Kulpa had bigger problems to deal with than paying me. Toward the end, Barry talked me into donating a bunch of my original creative work to them to run without my even expecting any compensation. I'm afraid my experiences with them were rather disappointing overall. My own thought at the time was that Dick Kulpa should not have been using the magazine as a form of vanity press or as a forum for his own terrible drawings, which, in my opinion, were far below the lowest standards set by other more successful humor publications."

Since Kulpa was struggling most of the time he owned *Cracked* very few new talents were hired that had any sort of staying power. Most appeared in one issue, even those with impressive resumes. These include Keith Knight, Ernie Colon, John Lustig and Frank Kelly Freas. Those of note with longer tenures include Tom Richmond, Art Bouthillier, Rich Hedden, Mike Kazaleh, Grant Meihm, Daryl Cagle, Noel Anderson, Santiago Cornejo, Michael Eury, Dave Berns, Jay Lynch (on a return engagement), John Pound and Troy Hickman.

One of the major people who got his start during Kulpa's regime was Tom Richmond, who started in 1999. Originally, he went to *Mad* and they gave him the cold shoulder and then he went to *Cracked* and then after *Cracked* folded, he went back to *Mad* and they embraced him mainly because Drucker and Torres weren't doing as much and they needed somebody to do the parodies.

Richmond picks up the story: *Cracked*'s new editor Dick Kulpa put out the word on various internet message boards and forums that the magazine was looking for new talent. I had just finished a movie parody of the film *Godzilla* (the Matthew Broderick version) that I did to show to *Mad* magazine's art director, Sam Viviano, at an event he was the guest speaker for. He was not particularly impressed with that piece, but when I sent it to Dick he immediately offered to buy and publish it. Thus began my stint with *Cracked*.

"*Cracked* had just been purchased as part of a larger deal by American Media, and Dick had convinced them to give him the helm and try to revive the flagging magazine. This was 1999. Production of the magazine moved to American Media's Florida offices, and the entire staff changed over to Dick's crew. Many of the longtime artists for *Cracked* like John Severin and Wally Brogan apparently didn't want to work for the 'New' *Cracked*... that might have been a function of loyalty to the old staff or due to the severely cut pay rates, I do not know for certain. Certainly the page rate was now terribly low, regardless of the reason why they now needed new artists and writers willing to work for cheap. I was still struggling as a freelancer so it made sense to get some experience under my belt even if the money was bad. I only worked for them for four issues. I wrote the first two parodies I did, the *Godzilla* one and one of *The Sopranos* (with writing contributions from friend Jim Batts) and then worked with writer Barry Dutter on *X-Men* and *Gladiator*.

"Dick made some very questionable 'editorial decisions' that would often ruin the art or impact of the content in *Cracked*, like adding word balloons and text to Ed Steckley's *Mr. Precious*, which was supposed to be a pantomime cartoon. These things were done without consulting the artist. I was shocked upon receiving a copy of the issue with my first *Cracked* appearance (#344) to see that my *Godzilla* parody had several pages badly distorted in print. It seems Dick wanted to include 'marginals' ala *Mad* and since I did all the pages as full bleeds, he decided to squeeze the pages by about an inch to provide the blank margin areas. The problem was he only changed the width, not the height on some and the height not the width on others. As a result, the art and text on those pages were squeezed and either narrowed or fattened, and looked awful. Another example: my parody of *Gladiator* in #347 was to be in the color section, so I spent hours and hours coloring this elaborate splash page and the next few pages... I really put a lot of effort into the color work.

Then I got a call from Barry Dutter telling me the story had been bumped to the black and white section. Not only did I waste all that time coloring it, but also I had to go back and adjust the now grayscale version so the contrast worked in black and white. *Gladiator* proved to be my last piece in *Cracked*.

"I tried out for *Mad* first, and kept trying even as I worked for *Cracked*. It was obvious to me that *Cracked*'s days were numbered, and that the number was a small one, so I kept up my efforts to break into *Mad*.

"I did not work for the pre-Kulpa version of *Cracked*, which I am sure was run with a better understanding of humor publication and professionalism. I never worked for what I would consider the 'real' *Cracked*. Dick was full of enthusiasm and energy but several quarts low on experience and knowledge in how to handle a magazine like *Cracked*. In his defense, budget limitations and a tight leash by American Media, who expected immediate results, also hampered him. Nevertheless, in my brief experience, *Mad* is and was run in a far more competent and professional manner than the *Cracked* I worked for. Everything from the editorial to the art direction and production... the guys at *Mad* know what they are doing. One thing I noticed immediately was that with *Cracked*, and in particular when Dick was in charge, they had a very 'Us against *Mad*' mentality. Dick could not give an interview or publish an editorial in the magazine without bringing up *Mad* and how much he thought *Mad* hated *Cracked*. In fact that rivalry was entirely one sided. *Mad* paid zero attention to *Cracked*... no one on staff bothered to look at it or keep track of what was going on in it. They were entirely unaware the work I was sending them trying to break in to *Mad* was work published in *Cracked*... not until I told them. The only thing that concerned them about *Cracked* was that they did not want any of their artists and writers doing work for both magazines at the same time.

"I tried for about nine months to break into *Mad* before I got a chance with them. It was in the spring of 2000 and I was at the NCS Reuben awards being held in NYC that year. Sam Viviano was there and I was showing him my latest portfolio stuff, which included my *Gladiator* piece for *Cracked*. Sam and *Mad* editor Nick Meglin looked it over and Sam met up with me later in the day.

"We like what we see," Sam said. 'We'd consider giving you an assignment for *Mad*, but I can't promise when... and there is a complication.'

"'What's that?' I asked.

"'Well, you say you are doing work for *Cracked*,' Sam replied. 'We have a policy that we don't use artists whose work would appear in both magazines at the same time.'

"'That's not a problem,' I said. 'I no longer work for *Cracked*.'

"'Oh? When did that happen?' Sam asked.

"'Five seconds ago,' I replied."

Art Bouthillier is an artist who also worked for *The Saturday Evening Post* and *Hustler*. He began at *Cracked* in 2001.

Rich Hedden is an artist who also did work for *Teenage Mutant Ninja Turtles* and *Roachmill*.

Mike Kazaleh describes how he got involved with *Cracked*: "Whenever there was a regime change, I would send samples to *Cracked*. Eventually somebody wrote back. I worked for *Cracked* from 2000 to 2004. I'd contacted them after American Media bought the magazine. By the time my first assignment had seen print, Dick Kulpa had become editor. A short time later, Kulpa bought the magazine from American Media. Kulpa still owned *Cracked* when I stopped working for them.

"The fact that *Cracked* got onto rocky footing shortly after I got involved made the whole experience somewhat harrowing. First American Media cut the magazine's budget down to zero. Then Dick Kulpa bought the magazine. It never came out on a regular schedule after that. You were never sure if you were going to get paid, because Kulpa never really had an operating budget. He just printed the magazines whenever he collected enough money to pay the printer. He did the page paste-ups himself, too. I got along well with Barry Dutter and the other folks at *Cracked* during this time, but the unstable nature of the magazine could be very unsettling. Artists kept disappearing from the roster. Dick tried desperate ways of filling the pages as cheaply as possible, sometimes trolling the Internet to find free material. I was still owed money when I stopped working for *Cracked*, but I kept asking for my money, and every now and then Dick would send a small check for part of the money. One day, without my asking again, I received a check in the mail for the remaining amount. The following day, I had heard that *Cracked* had been purchased by a Kuwaiti investment company.

"Early in my cartooning career, I sent some of my comics to *Mad* in an attempt to get illustration work. I had enclosed a tongue in cheek cover letter telling them why they shouldn't hire me. I was expecting to get *Mad*'s famous form-rejection letter. What I got back instead was a note saying that *Mad* had all the artists they needed. The note went on to ask me if I was interested in writing. I wrote a bunch of gags and short articles and sent them in. *Mad* sent back a rejection slip."

Grant Meihm said of his brief *Cracked* tenure in 2000: "I was only lucky enough to do about three assignments for *Cracked*, about 10 years ago, just before the magazine was sold for the first time." Although Meihm's work was commissioned during the Silverstone-Simmons era, it did not appear in print until the Kulpa era.

Daryl Cagle who is known for his political cartoon website among other things and his artwork, claims, "I didn't have much to do with *Cracked*." He appeared in five issues around 2001.

Noel Anderson also had a brief tenure at *Cracked* during the end of its run: "I had submitted a few pieces to *Cracked* but had never heard back from them. Then in 2000, when Dick Kulpa took over the magazine, they had a far more active online presence. As a regular visitor to the *Cracked* message boards, I caught the attention of Mr. Kulpa and editor Barry Dutter and asked them to do an interview on the morning radio show I that hosted in Fargo, ND. I mentioned to them during the interview that I had tried getting material into *Cracked* for many years. A couple of days later they called me and told me they had seen some of my artwork that was still in the *Cracked* submission files and asked if I would illustrate a piece on Bill Clinton that Barry had written. I excitedly said yes and appeared in many issues after that. The first piece was called "New Jobs for Bill Clinton" and appeared in issue #353 in 2001.

"I illustrated for *Cracked* during the Dick Kulpa / Barry Dutter years up until November of 2004. Usually, somebody else wrote and I just got to draw the funny pictures. My shining moment, however, was issue #363 (July 2004) in which I not only illustrated two installments of *Shut-Ups*, but also actually wrote and illustrated a three-page 'Nanny Dickering Interviews' piece. To top it all off, that very same issue had a cover that was illustrated by none other than Kent Gamble, who had drawn for Marvel's *Crazy* magazine back in the '70s and '80s. To the average person this probably doesn't seem like that big of a deal, but to a humor magazine nerd like myself, it was as if all of the stars had aligned and God himself had looked down upon me and said, 'Your moment of glory has arrived, punk!' It never got that good again; although it was awfully cool being the regular *Shut-Ups* artist those last few issues until Dick Kulpa sold the magazine.

"Aside from a few issues of waiting to get paid things were pretty good! It was just exciting to be a part of that era of *Cracked*. Having spent much of my adolescence reading what was widely considered to be the *Mad* knockoffs, I usually thought of *Mad* as something that was utterly out of my reach. I hadn't submitted anything to *Mad* over the years but several pieces to *Cracked*.

"Although I live in Minnesota, I had quite a bit of interaction with the *Cracked* staff over the phone and through the *Cracked* online message boards. They were really embracing the online thing at that time. Most of the other mags I've illustrated for haven't had that kind of interaction with fellow staff and readers."

Barry Dutter explained that it was during this time that Dick Kulpa would scour foreign publications in order to get material for issues, usually without paying, and with the promise of US exposure. Artist Santiago Cornejo came in this way. Cornejo was from Buenos Aires. Cornejo also appeared in *Mad*, *MadKids* and *Thwak*.

Michael Eury, editor of *Back Issue* magazine, did one piece for *Cracked* for issue #355. He confirms his sole contribution: "That was me. 'Internet Dating Warning Signs' was the piece. I recently found that issue and re-read it, and still laughed despite the aging of some of the gags. My experiences with *Cracked* were very limited. I pitched a few ideas during a shaky editorial period for the magazine, and had hoped to contribute more features but that didn't occur."

Barry Dutter comments about Dave Berns: "The smartest thing Dick ever did was to bring aboard Dave Berns as art director of *Cracked*. Dave was a really talented, nice guy, just a really solid magazine design guy, and a good artist. He had a lot of friends who were artists that he had gone to school with who were all successful in their own right. It gave it a new edge and new blood. That allowed Dick to back off the creative side of the magazine somewhat and focus on the business side. Once Dave Berns came aboard, all of a sudden the magazine was looking better and especially the covers were looking better. There was one that we did—a Harry Potter cover. It was a really nice painting that Tom Fleming did. He did a nice cover with an attractive layout. The covers weren't so cluttered anymore. We had a product we were proud of and they looked better than the AMI issues. This is no knock against Dick, but Dick is an old school guy. He came up in the '60s and '70s and he had an old-fashioned look to layout and design. In some ways, I think *Cracked* suffered because of that, but Dick was smart enough to hire a talented young kid who was hungry to put out the best mag he could. When Berns came along, then the magazine looked younger and fresher and modern. It was a good thing. We did a half a dozen issues under Kulpa's ownership."

Dave Berns comments on his own involvement: "Well, I didn't take no for an answer. I contacted *Cracked*'s webmaster, Mark Van Woert, and he passed my info and links to my work along to the owner, Dick Kulpa. I was slim, trim (ok, less tubby and willing to leave the house) and ready to make things happen, and so was Dick, kinda, sorta.

"I was completely unaware of the magazine's recent history and naively assumed that given its long and illustrious history, which it had some scratch behind it, and I was pursuing a legitimate gig! To me, work with *Cracked* was potentially that much more promising than *Mad*, as it would give me a chance to prove myself by belly flopping right in the middle of the proverbial little pond, relatively speaking.

"Shot out of a cannon, I began creating anything I could for the magazine and quickly assumed the duties of art directing and editing much of the thing too (someone had to).

"The first issue I was involved in was #357, Dick Kulpa was the publisher and owner, Barry Dutter was the head writer and helped Dick edit the thing. It was the very beginning of 2002. Dick was attempting to run the magazine out of a one-room office in Boynton Beach… one of those 'office condos' where he basically rented a closet that shared a communal secretary, conference room and break room with 30 or so other dreamers also renting closets. What time he didn't spend outside of the building chain-smoking menthol 100's, he spent trying to finagle business relationships with folks who thought he ran a legitimate magazine. At this stage, you could call the operation a PINO (Publication In Name Only), as I don't believe he was working on the magazine itself, was avoiding dealing with legal issues and debt to the former owners (AMI) and was pretty close to folding the whole operation if schemes to secure outside funding didn't come through soon. Barry had been strung along following Dick's dreamer with barely a clue lead for a while and was frustrated with the whole relationship, and was already owed tens of thousands of dollars for previous work! He was basically tending bar and writing books, and agreed to hear out Dick's schemes one more time, even though he'd been burned enough to know better at this point.

"Barry and I hit it off creatively and my take is that that's the genesis of what made #357 come together, and essentially kept the magazine in sporadic print over the next couple of years. Who knows if Dick would cop to this, we haven't talked for some time, last we did, he wasn't big on conceding ego points. I wasn't credited for much, but if you look at the issue versus the previous few, you can see my fingerprints all over it. I wrote and drew two features in the issue, the first being a repackaging of some of my NewsJunkie comic strips as a two page feature and the second was titled "The King of All Wedgies," it was a lovingly violent tribute to my favorite radio show of all time, *The Howard Stern Show*, featuring Wedgie Boy, a character created by Steph Ramsay's (former *Cracked* art director and later co-worker of mine at *WWN*) son (who I would later find out, was supposed to be credited in name and money when the character appeared in the magazine, I don't believe that ever happened). Dick was uncomfortable with the near-lesbian kiss I drew in the first page and decided to completely screw the flow of the panels and dialogue up on it as a solution to his quandary. I didn't see this, or the mess-up of the laugh panel in the second page until it saw print. That was such a bummer to me, as I would have gladly made any requested changes, were they requested. This was my first work for a big-time comic book / humor magazine, it was a feature on my comedic hero who got me through every morning for nearly a decade at that point and to me, it had been bastardized. Ah well, I did give copies of it to Artie Lange at one point, and he seemed to still get a kick out of it! I also lettered, toned or colored, art corrected and laid out about half of that issue, drew *Cracked*'s main proprietary characters (Dick was trying like hell to establish other reoccurring characters than Sylvester to mine them for future licensing opportunities) dancing to the Silly CD's advertorial feature, redesigned the 'But *Cracked*' headline and mailbag and drew some spot illos for the letters column.

"Before work on the following issue commenced (I'm not 100% sure on the timeline here) Dick was called in by his former employers at AMI to have a go as editor-in-chief of the *Weekly World News*. He had a LONG run on the publication as its art director and, in my opinion; he was an absolute perfect fit for this position. His particular genius was as good as anyone else's ever was in that tabloid's (Klontzes included) history. AMI was (is probably still) just a brutal revolving door of borderline thank-you-sir-may-I-have-another hazing of its editorial staff, this went double for the redheaded stepchild of its publications, the *Weekly World News*. They didn't get the *Weekly World News*, it wasn't glossy or pretty, it didn't just comment on culture, it created it (ok, maybe subculture is more appropriate... point is it generated content, not just commentary on content), and the publication was perpetually hamstrung by bean counters and over-thinkers until its eventual demise as a print publication (sure it's more complicated than that, but this is my take on things). Dick did get it (the guy co-created their claim to fame besides Elvis sightings and alien political endorsements, the ubiquitous Bat-Boy), and was one of maybe three or four people alive who could make that paper come to life (none who followed in him could), so they brought him into the mix, despite his owing them 'less than five million dollars' (the non-figure Dick would quote when discussing *Cracked* in press releases and interviews). At this point, one could assume, they had written the 'sale' of *Cracked* off as a loss already, and just wanted to make their existing assets successful.

"So, soon after being brought in as EIC of *WWN*, Dick offered to bring Barry and I into the mix there, too. It was NEVER discussed, but I got the impression that he felt doing this was a favor (in some ways it was, but it always colored the experience with a lack of respect, IMO) to keep us afloat while the meager agreed upon rations for work on *Cracked* weren't being fulfilled with any regularity. This would have been true, had he arranged to pay us more than our time was worth, but in truth it was just a reasonable wage for work we were both more than qualified to do, and there was a standoffish undercurrent to our relationships with many of our new coworkers because, I believe, they shared this impression. I would cut my puny invoices for the next few issues of *Cracked* in half, just to insure collection of anything from Dick, as he was the walking, talking, chain-smoking definition of undercapitalized. This was a drag, as it was another blow to the ego, but I was working on two creatively fulfilling publications in so many exciting capacities at the same time, that it was ultimately worth it (for a while anyways)! I got to make so many of my friends and family infamous in the fake stories I worked on at the *Weekly World News*, it was just such a kick! My grandpa was an oldster busted doing panty raids in his nursing home... My dog was a mutant that ate a car... My cousin was heartbroken after being dumped by the world's smartest chimp... I smoked cow poop to get high! Fuggetaboutit, I had so much fun helping to make up the shit that YOU couldn't help chuckling at in the supermarket checkout line! I'm sad that I didn't take the chance to formally join the staff when it was presented, remaining a freelancer on day-rate and photographing, drawing and writing on the side for them when schedule allowed instead... I wanted to remain flexible for when *Cracked* inevitably 'took off' and was burning all of my midnight oil trying to help make that happen. Nothing I did for *WWN* was credited in my name, if at all. I used my pen name 'Bernie Soul' for most of the writing I did there (maybe ten or so articles). Since we were both considered 'his' people, when Dick was sacked from his editorial position there, it was only a matter of time (somewhere between one and two months) that Barry and I both followed. One of these days I'll get around to compiling a 'best of' to put on my website featuring all of my favorite stuff I did there, much of it was quite funny, and I had a number of great spot illustrations see print as well.

"With #358, I got masthead credits for editorial contributions to *Cracked*, which was a nice feather in my cap. It also marked the first one of my guys brought into the fold. My friend Troy Hickman (*Common Grounds, Witchblade, City of Heroes*) wrote the *Shut-Ups* that issue, which I drew, we used to trade mini-comics with each other when I was publishing them as a teenager, and he is one of the greatest comedy writing talents I know of. Seriously, if you need something funny written, please look him up and hire him, you're guaranteed at least one sale, as I will forever want to read the stuff he writes!

"Kulpa was having a rough go, financially speaking, his distributor was not paying him in a timely fashion and he was convinced that AMI was sabotaging *Cracked*'s distribution (which I'm not entirely convinced of otherwise, myself). As I remember things, somewhere along the way, he had it out with them over the debt for acquiring *Cracked*. I don't know if he'd made any payments to them as he'd agreed to, and they may have been monkey-wrenching his distribution efforts (being one of the top six newsstand publishers and owning the distribution company that racks all supermarket checkout lines gives them a bit of industry pull) making things harder than they already were for Dick (that does not sound right... people, if your name is Richard, please go by the Richard or Rich, Dick is just downright distracting... unless you're working in porn). Somehow or another, he believed that he had a legitimate claim (and convinced them he did as well) to the ownership of the Bat-Boy character, which at the time was enjoying a run as an award winning off-Broadway play and had nibbles from production companies about creating a movie based on the character (Tim Burton's company was rumored to be one of them). So as I understand it, after some tense negotiation, DK's debt to AMI was more-or-less considered a wash once he signed over all claims to Bat-Boy to AMI. Sweet deal for Dick, as he got the magazine for considerably less than 5 million in the end!

"I brought a few more of my friends from my small press and Joe Kubert School past in issue #359, including the amazing Derrick Wyatt (lead character designer for *Teen Titans* and *Transformers* animated, then an artist with John Kricfalusi's Spumco Studios) and his good friend, the also amazing, Ben Jones (*Batman: Brave & Bold* character designer, also with Spumco at that point). Kevin Tuma, political cartoonist for the libertarian think tank, The Cato Institute also joined us that issue, he's really come into his own since as an artist and a commentator! Dick was feeding us whatever cartoons he could get people to give him for free, and drawing some of his own, which usually looked like someone had done them for free.

"With issue #360, Barry and I just said screw it and more-or-less took over the reigns of most of the magazine. Dick still shoe-horned in a few pages of material, but we didn't let him stack the deck with as much crap this go around, because realistically, the future was looking bleak and we wanted a decent issue if it was to be our swan song. So there's a *Ghost Story Club* reprint, another Silly CDs advertorial (don't believe they ever paid for their spots, as they'd agreed to, either) and a reprint of a John Severin feature from the 50s (utmost respect to Severin, he made *Cracked* what it was for decades, but the guy was still alive, woulda been nice to throw him a new assignment and a few bucks), but otherwise it's a pretty solid issue. Maybe it wasn't up to the level of *Mad*, but *Mad* hasn't been as good as *Mad* consistently for some time either (kidding, Alfred, kidding, call me)! We added new talent including: Todd Casey (JKS buddy), Ray Morelli (Spumco), Andy Ristiaro (Spumco), Scott Dalrymple (*Fade from Blue*, JKS buddy) and Shawn Braley (*New England Illustrated*, JKS buddy)... Ben and Derrick also returned with stellar work and Barry convinced former *Cracked* contributors Chuck Frazier (Marvel), Tayyar Ozkan (*Caveman*), Rich Hedden (*Roachmill*), Mike Kazaleh (*TMNT*, Marvel) and Ed Steckley (Who's since done work for *Mad*) to pitch in again, despite many of them being burned in the past... stellar work all around wrapped in a beautiful Tom Fleming painted Harry Potter cover (that I did the layout of, so it wasn't cluttered with clunky type boxes and unfunny word balloons as DK was want to do)! I am very proud of the results, half dozen or so pages of reprints and relative junk, notwithstanding. We put a nice team together, Barry and I and this continued into the next issue.

"Issue #361 was to be my last in any editorial capacity. I added a few more talented and very dear friends to the mix including my high school friend turned playwright Travis Kramer (*Hey, It's Karate, Kid! the musical, Dial 'N' for Negress!*) who I'd made my first damn comics with and my Joe Kubert School roommate the mightily talented Chris Caldwell (Industrial designer of like half of the plastic bottles in your pantry and garage... he should be drawing *Spider-Man* for Marvel, though), both of whom were groomsmen in my wedding, in addition to the phenomenal Wil Branca (Spumco) and Jason

Robinson (*Spawn*). Also, I'm not sure who brought landed him, but this marked Jason Seiler's (*Mad*, *Village Voice*, etc) first issue as a contributor, that guy has since completely blown up and is arguably (if you feel like winning the argument) the greatest working caricature artist today, he also teaches through schoolism.com, anyone interested in cartooning as a career should definitely look into his courses.

"I was starting to hold DK's feet to the fire about paying up on back invoices at this point and as such was leery of doing much more work or bringing in any more of my friends to be burned without pay for their contributions. I had one more feature that hadn't run yet appear in #362, "Rapper Remakes" (which contained my favorite line I've ever written... uncredited, at that... The final panel had Eminem and Vanilla Ice as Luke Skywalker and Darth Vader, Vanilla Ice proceeds to say "Word to ya Mother, I am your father"), and that was it for me in the pages of *Cracked*. Scott Gosar was chomping at the bit to take over editorially, I seem to recall him trying to start some drama by shit-talking myself and Barry to Dick around this point as well, but can't remember what exactly was said. It didn't matter, I didn't care anymore, I think Barry was on the same page... we'd given all we had to give at that point. In our opinions, DK wasn't interested in putting out a quality mag. I recall making the observation at the time that he wanted to be the star artist, not by raising his own bar, but by lowering everyone else's.

"Thus began the Scott Gosar and Marten Jallad era (like how I say era when referring to less than dozen issues for my own and theirs, combined? I sure am blathering on about some insignificant shit here). They'd done a decent humor magazine of their own, *Thwak*, but, in my estimation, were really more interested in creating the magazine of the past they were reverential of, not the future. Kind of like those dudes that painstakingly restore cars to factory spec and then end up driving around with no A/C or adapter for their iPod as a result. Some of Barry and my friends remained on (why not, it's published credit, and fun work, regardless of how it's mishandled), but most new, or new-old blood was either more Kulpa freebie talent or derivative knock-off artists... Plus, the direction just wasn't there... features had two times the text necessary to tell their jokes, the layouts and lettering were awful throughout, and the covers, despite the AMAZING talent of Jason Seiler, had DK mucking them up with too much type, bad jokes and no defined concept and even more incorrect-corrections (Sylvester's face in the Seiler cover for #361, for instance) etc... not even Cheap Trick money was able to polish those turds!

"Barry had written a *Daredevil* movie parody for issue #361 that I got the green light on, then red light, then green, then finally red on orders to draw it from DK. In the eleventh hour, after repeated mixed messages, and informing me of intent to use another piece and not to bother, I was told to send in the, as yet, non-existent finished artwork. I busted it out over the course of two days and one night, and while it definitely showed, Dick proceeded to ham-fistedly 'correct' the art on the splash page making it considerably worse. He 'taught' me how to draw eyes properly, which consisted of drawing one poorly, copying it, flipping it and placing it on the other side of the face... as I recall, he did this with a mouse, not a Wacom tablet. The result of this and other corrections, most notably to the mouths of the characters on the splash page just broke my heart, I was already iffy on the feature, as I had to rush it through in record time and the likenesses and inks suffered as a result. Just before he sent it to the printer, I told Dick he could have those five pages of full color artwork for free if he'd only make one last minute change to the artwork, changing my name to an old pen name I used to use in the credits for it.

"I didn't formally try out there at *Mad*, though I did show caricature and cartoon samples and an Alfred E. Neuman toy design project I'd done while at the Joe Kubert School to one of their editors. I believe it was Nick Meglin, though I'm not certain. We took a class trip for portfolio reviews to the DC offices near the end of my last year at JKS. Whomever the editor, he was appreciative of my work, told me I'd drawn a nice Alfred even, but realistically, even now I'm not on that level consistently, though I feel some of my work could be passable there.

"There wasn't really an environment to *Cracked* when I worked on it. It was the same one as any other freelance work I've done, my own home office or wherever I feel like sitting with an art board if I'm drawing freehand. That suits me fine.

"I spent a number of years as art director at a couple of different marketing and advertising agencies. Occasionally, I'd get to work on a really fun project in those environments (the odd children's book or cover illustration for a marketing piece), but mostly I found I was just helping someone sell something that people don't want or need in the first place. Thinking about that just gets the old Bill Hicks 'If you work in marketing or advertising... please kill yourself' routine playing in my head. I love Bill Hicks, and as such, don't need him encouraging such thoughts in my head ad nauseum. Plus, I'm not a big fan of corporate environments or 9-5 (usually more like 9-7 or 8 at marketing companies) schedules, so I'm hoping to keep plugging away as a freelancer (I take requests... daveberns.com... hit me up) for as long as I can with reasonable success.

"My favorite piece was probably 'Bling Bling Ding-a-lings' from issue #361, which I feel had my most successful illustrations, plus I wrote it and still think it's pretty funny. It was a take-off on the ridiculous excesses rappers tend to go to when spending their money. I drew it entirely on board with ink, markers and inkwash... kicked it old school, like an old fool. A close second was the *Star Wars* parody Barry and I did in #358. 'Star Snores: Send in the Clones' was drawn entirely in the computer, I think it's pretty funny and I got to draw a bunch of my favorite characters in it. Quite a thrill. If the Howard Stern piece wouldn't have been altered, it would have probably been #1 for much the same reason. My least favorite feature was the *Daredevil* parody, 'Devildawg' from #361."

Jay Lynch (on a return engagement) and John Pound were the instigators behind the Silly CD's advertorial pages. They had previously worked on similar parodic card series for Topps.

Troy Hickman also started during the Dick Kulpa era: "I worked on some of the later issues of *Cracked* (no, I don't blame myself for its demise).

"I did a few movie and TV parodies (*Lord of the Rings*, *Ren & Stimpy*, a couple others…man, I don't even REMEMBER now).

"I do remember that they still owe me $175, though… ;)"

Barry Dutter opens up to what really happened while Dick Kulpa was in charge: "Kulpa put together a small staff. There were five or six of us altogether. I think I started in February of 2000 and the next issue of *Cracked* was due on the stands in March of 2000. You say, 'How come two months were in New York and then the next ones were in Florida?' The people in New York were offered the chance to come to Florida. I believe the editorial people, Andy Simmons and Lou Silverstone. My understanding is that they turned it down, moving to Florida. In retrospect, that was a smart idea because the mag wound up being canceled by AMI a few months later anyway. But I digress.

"Anyway, Kulpa hired me as a writer and he put together a good team. Bobbie Bender was brought aboard as another staff writer, and there was an art director. I started writing for them. Kulpa did the cover for the first issue and from my own standpoint; my biggest regret for *Cracked* is that I don't think we ever came up with a cover that was funny. That's the single hardest thing to do, I think. We should have reached out to the artists and writers and asked, 'Do you have good ideas for a cover?' But we never did that.

"Kulpa came from a tabloid background. Think of it that way. Think of it like the *Enquirer* or the *Star*. A lot of people said, 'Well, he's doing tabloid covers on a humor magazine.' You could say that was a different angle or a unique approach, or you could say it just didn't work and move on. We published three issues. We did a special where we wanted to reprint the funniest material that *Cracked* ever published. It was 40 years of the magazine at that point, and there wasn't really that much material that was really funny. If you talk to anyone who worked on *Cracked*, they'll usually tell you that the people who came before them or after them usually weren't as funny as when they were there. But we managed to come up with enough quality material to fill 48 pages. We put together a pretty solid special and it went to the printer and for whatever reason, it didn't have a cover price on it, so the suits in corporate flipped out and they took Peet Janes aside because he was the editor at the time, and they asked, 'Well, how comes there's no price on the cover?' and he said, 'I don't know.' It was one of those things that didn't work out; so then, a month or so later, another issue of *Cracked* was published without a cover price on it. At that point, let's just say Peet Janes was no longer with the company. So, that's probably why he won't talk about it. He was living where Dark Horse Comics was in Oregon. He and his girlfriend packed up and moved to Florida where he didn't know anyone. It didn't work out well, and the next thing, he's back home in Oregon. So, basically I stepped in and took over a lot of the editorial stuff. We really didn't have the budget to hire anyone else at that point.

"So we did three issues at AMI at which point AMI looked at the sales figures and said, 'We're used to selling a million copies a week of the *Star* and the *Enquirer*, and *Cracked* is selling around 30,000 copies a month.' It wasn't really profitable enough for them. If AMI didn't have these other tabloid mags that were selling so well, they might have held on to *Cracked*, but the fact was, they just didn't need it. So they pulled the plug. They announced that *Cracked* was canceled, and we were all very sad. We felt like, 'It was a fun thing to work for, we didn't want it to end,' and then a few days later, out of the blue, the boss comes in and says, 'We're going to do three more.' So, we were so excited. We were all, 'Yay!' At that point, the staff of *Cracked* was supposed to go work for different newspapers within the same company, but we knew we wouldn't have as much fun as we had working for *Cracked*. *Cracked* was the only comic book that AMI published, and I'm a comic book guy. I could work for a newspaper, but my first love is always going to be comics. I was supposed to go work for another newspaper called the *Sun*, and I was going to have an editorial position there, so I said, 'Well, let me finish up my last two weeks at *Cracked*, and then I'll come work for you guys,' and then *Cracked* got extended for three months, and then I told the editor of the *Sun*. I'm just going to stay and work on *Cracked* for three more months. And he said, 'Well, this job at the *Sun* is not going to be here for you in three months.' I said, 'I understand that, but I just want to do *Cracked*.' Even though I knew it wasn't going to last. I knew it was a short-term thing. I'll take three months of working for a humor mag anytime over working years at a boring newspaper. We got an extension. We got a few more months. There was no budget. We could hardly afford to pay anyone. I called up some of my old Marvel Comics buddies and they were kind enough to donate a page or two. We would do anything to fill up pages. Dick's idea was to reprint stuff that was recent—only a few months old. That was a policy that had worked for him on 'Weekly World News' so he tried to implement it at *Cracked*. I was strongly opposed to that idea. I have no objection to reprinting older stuff from 30 or 40 years ago, stuff that the current readers might not have seen. But I did not like the idea of reprinting an article from

3 months ago. That might work in a weekly newspaper, but not in a humor mag that only comes out once a month or less. I did not agree with all of Dick's ideas on how to run the magazine. One time we received a letter that said, 'Oh, the new *Cracked* isn't as good as the Lou Silverstone era.' Dick's reaction to that was to hire Lou Silverstone to write a parody for us. Dick was really reactive to what one fan letter might say. Dick hired Lou Silverstone and Walter Brogan to do a *Sopranos* parody for us, but we had just done a *Sopranos* parody the month before. As a longtime fan of humor mags, I don't think you should ever spoof the same show two issues in a row. Here's another example: before he started working for us, Tom Richmond sent us a *Godzilla* spoof he had done as a sample of his work. Dick went ahead and printed it, even though Tom had not intended it for publication, it was just meant as a sample of his work. This was in 2000; about five years after the big-budget *Godzilla* movie had come out. I did not like the idea of spoofing a movie five years after it came out. But Dick said we needed something to fill those pages, and here was a five-page job, finished and ready to print. Dick came up with a new ending where Godzilla takes off his mask and reveals himself to be Hillary Clinton. The joke here was that Hillary was about to become the Senator of New York, and she was going to do as much damage to the city as Godzilla would. I have never been a fan of parodies where a person takes off a mask at the end and reveals themselves to be someone else. Those kinds of things don't make a lot of sense to me, and they have been done in *Cracked* a lot. Dick and I had very similar senses of humor in some ways, but there definitely were times where he wanted to take things in a more old-fashioned direction. I always preferred edgier over cornier. I still don't understand how Hillary Clinton could put on a costume and become Godzilla, or why she would want to do that. Dick would say, 'Well, can you come up with a better ending?' And I would say, 'I don't see why we're running a spoof of a movie that came out five years ago, which *Cracked* already spoofed five years ago when the movie came out.' But Dick didn't see it that way. He was more focused on, 'We've got to fill these pages, here is a beautifully drawn story, let's use it.' This is in no way meant to be a knock on Tom Richmond, who I think was as surprised as anyone that the story was actually going to be printed.

"It was one of those things where we did a parody of *The Sopranos* in one issue, and then Dick hired Lou Silverstone to do another parody of *The Sopranos* in the next issue. And Dick promoted it on the cover, the fact that we had Lou Silverstone and Walter Brogan back. It is one of the few times in the history of *Cracked* that the creators were ever mentioned on the cover, and I don't think we sold a single additional copy because of it. This is not a knock against Lou Silverstone, I just don't think fans of *Cracked* care who writes the stories, they just want funny stuff.

"And I guess *Cracked* had a history of spoofing the same thing again, but usually not a full parody followed by a full parody. In the beginning Dick was kind of like, 'Yeah, let's get Andy Simmons to write a few things.' He wanted the New York guys to be involved, which they were in the beginning. Either they lost interest, or we stopped asking him, or a combination of both. I guess we did six or eight issues of *Cracked* at AMI with lower and lower budgets, more and more reprints and lower and lower pay for the artists. I would reach out and ask people in the industry, 'What do you have that we can run? We cannot afford to pay you, but it's for the magazine and you can own it.' Rick Parker and Chris Eliopoulos were kind enough to donate a couple of pages.

"In the beginning, we were paying everybody. Rick is one of the first guys I called, and we paid him for several jobs that he did for *Cracked*. He's one of my favorite cartoonists. After the first few issues came out, the budget for *Cracked* was slashed dramatically. I guess AMI figured that if they could produce this thing cheaply enough, they could keep it going, if the sales stayed at the same level. At that point, the sales sunk down to about 25,000. I think our final one was about 20,000. Kulpa was obsessed about the sales figures. He'd be a good person to ask about the sales. Another thing, I think *Cracked* was really overprinting in the New York days. They were printing hundreds of thousands of copies and selling maybe 50,000 copies. There were tons of copies being destroyed. That was back in the day. That was how magazines worked. This is going back about 10 years. I think there was a lot of waste going on. They were overspending, overprinting. *Cracked* was canceled I believe three times at AMI. I could be wrong about that, but maybe twice. It's been canceled at least four times in the last decade, two of them were AMI. So, AMI decided that they didn't want to do *Cracked* anymore and Kulpa got this idea into his head that we got a magazine that sold maybe 25,000 copies, it's got national distribution, it's cheap to produce, if you do it on a low budget. So, he started thinking that if he could start publishing the magazine himself, this could be a profitable thing. I guess he put an offer in and one way or another Dick winds up owning *Cracked*.

"At this point, Dick says to himself, 'Alright, this essentially is a brand new magazine.' Forget all the old stuff, forget all the overpaying. This is a new magazine. He used to say over and over again, 'This is a startup.' And he used to stress that we had no budget. He would say that if we all chipped in and we all worked for free, then we could turn this into something that would generate income for all of us. He was always trying to work deals with TV studios and movie studios. He was always trying to convince people to work for him by saying, 'You could generate other revenue. You could bring other projects in here.' One time when I started complaining about money, Dick asked, 'Well, why aren't you using *Cracked* to promote your books?' I had not thought of that. And so I started doing one ad per issue to promote my books.

That was the kind of thing Dick was talking about. I don't know if I sold any extra copies because of those ads, but they were fun to shoot. Dick tried to get everyone to understand that, okay, maybe *Cracked* was not paying much, but you could use the mag as a national platform to promote your other projects. He really had this old-fashioned mentality, like, 'My dad's got a barn, let's put on a show.' Only in this case it was, 'My Dad's got a printing press. Let's put out a humor mag.' I hope none of this sounds like I'm bashing Dick, because he really is a good guy. He just never really got anyone to come around to his way of thinking of how if we all work fort free today, it could lead to big dividends down the road. The only ones who were willing to work for free were artists who were not that good, guys who we used to reject in the early days as not being worthy of having their material in *Cracked*, suddenly these inferior artists were found to be good enough if they donated their work for free.

"The problem was that when *Cracked* made the transition from decent-paying mag with a big-time publisher to non-paying mag from a tiny publisher, it was never really made clear to freelancers that the arrangement had changed. Dick would say, 'Keep working for me,' and then people just wouldn't get paid, or they would get paid very very late. Dick would get so agitated when someone wanted to get paid for their work. I was coming from Marvel Comics and the earlier *Cracked* magazine. I was used to getting paid for everything I had ever done and I would assume that most of our creators were, too. When suddenly the freelancers began asking, 'Why aren't you guys paying us anymore?' Dick would get so angry and say, 'People just want money! People are greedy!' It was like, 'Wow!' Here you have a guy who was an artist and had been a freelancer at different times in his life, and yet he was getting mad at other freelancers for wanting to get paid. You would think a fellow artist would be a little more sympathetic. Dick worked very hard, getting the magazine off the ground and trying to make it successful, but he always wasn't as diplomatic as he could have been with the creators.

"I think we were working on an issue for AMI. I think everyone was paid for that issue. AMI's first *Cracked* came out in early 2000. Let's say we did eight issues or whatever and that took us to 2001. There was a gap. We were working on that one issue of *Cracked* that had the cover where all the American cartoon characters fight all the Japanese cartoon characters. When it came time a year later to do one more issue of *Cracked*, we already had the story done. The good thing about it is it was a timeless story. It wasn't tied into anything specific at the time. We got lucky in that sense. We already had the cover and the story. Then, we threw together whatever we had in the drawer.

"I actually went over to work for *Weekly World News* during that year off, one of the other publications. It was one of those things where they always had the door open for me to work for that other publication. I went over there and there was a brief period where I was working 9-5 at *Weekly* and then on my lunch hour and before and after work, I would go over and work on *Cracked*, cranking out the last couple issues of *Cracked*. It was always so much more fun working on *Cracked*. The editor of *Weekly World News* got furious about the time I spent on *Cracked*."

Michelina Severin recalls, "As far as Dick himself, he couldn't afford to pay John, but he was trying. At that time, he would put out more issues with John because he would put in an article about John with some pictures that John drew, and it would give him something to write about in the magazine. He couldn't afford to pay. He put on a mortgage on his house in order to do this. John tried, but he and I had issues with him, because he did a couple of reprints of John, but then he sold it. They sold it and they said, 'Oh, they can't do it without John,' and they called John. When they called, we asked, "What are you going to do with the magazine?" because they called John and we didn't like the direction they were going and they said, 'Oh no, we're going to do a different magazine.' Well, they simply did something that was unbelievable and completely different."

Barry Dutter explains his side of what happened that led to the end of Severin working on the magazine: "When we took over, Severin was still on board and he did an *X-Men* pin-up—a two-page pin-up that we had in one of our first issues. We were happy to use Severin, but we just couldn't afford to give him more than a page or two per issue. I don't think it was ever discussed that we would lower his rate. I don't think he was even asked. I'm pretty sure that I was the guy who got John Severin to quit *Cracked*. It's not something I'm proud of. At the time Regis Philbin had just saved the ABC-TV network because his show, *Who Wants to be a Millionaire?* was the hottest thing on TV. So I said, 'Why don't we do an article where we have him save a whole bunch of other shows?' and do a spoof of *Sex and the City*, but I called it 'Sex and the City with Regis.' The cartoon would show Regis in bed with the four girls. Severin was the artist and he was so disgusted to draw this horrible debauchery that he drew it, but he drew it in silhouette. Regis was in bed with the four girls from *Sex and the City*, but they were all drawn in silhouette. He really didn't want to draw it. That's when Severin said, 'Aw, the magazine is all sex. I don't want to be associated with that filth.' I was the guy who put the final nail in the coffin regarding Severin. It's not something I'm proud of. I love John Severin.

"There was a piece that I wrote after I came aboard. There was a two-page *X-Men* thing that had a whole bunch of funny gags coming out of the first one in 2000. It was a recent thing. *Who Wants to be a Millionaire?* was in 2000. That was all stuff that we commissioned from him. I don't remember if there were any other pieces besides those two. Oh yeah. We did *The Patriot*, the Mel Gibson movie. Severin drew that as a two-page spoof. It was a hell of a ride. It was a load of ups and downs. I'd like to think that we took the least-respected magazine of all time and dropped it down a couple of notches. That was our legacy. If you look at certain individual issues, there was stuff that we could be proud of, and there was stuff that shouldn't have ever been printed. I guess the key thing that I'd like to point out that the stuff that people thought sucked, we knew it sucked. There was stuff that we really didn't think should have gone into the magazine, so when people think, 'How could you produce such crap?' Well, sometimes we knew it was crap, but we had no choice. I guess my final thing about *Cracked*; I did a lot of soul searching before I came on board. It did seem like such a disrespected magazine. The more I thought about it, the more I realize that for a humor magazine, there's no limit on how good the stories can be and there's no limit on how the pictures can be, so if you do your best work, the magazine can be something you can be proud of. I'm very proud of all the movie spoofs that I did and a few other things here and there."

Walter Brogan comments, "I stayed at *Cracked* until 2001, I think. That's when the rates went down, but around '86, I had gotten a rep and I was working in advertising doing storyboards and I've been with this company called Famous Frames for about 15 years. They're in California. I enjoyed worked with Lou more. Nothing against Mort Todd, but Lou gave me a lot more freedom. Mort was ok, but I preferred working with Lou."

Mike Ricigliano remembers: "The horror stories all occurred at the end of the life of the magazine. It was rough to see the slow demise of a great magazine. After the corporation sold the package it was apparent the new management was struggling, trying new approach after new approach. Then the magazine was sold again, adding another layer to the top. Nothing they tried brought up the circulation and it bled out. If you looked at the table of contents toward the end you could see that we were carrying a huge financial burden in the form of management, former management, old investors, and Sylvester's groupies. The magazine's money all went to the vampires from the past. It was the same problem seen in every form of organizations that have a long history…management grows and grows while the people actually working support more and more load. I think that if 90% of the magazine's staff disappeared the magazine could have flourished."

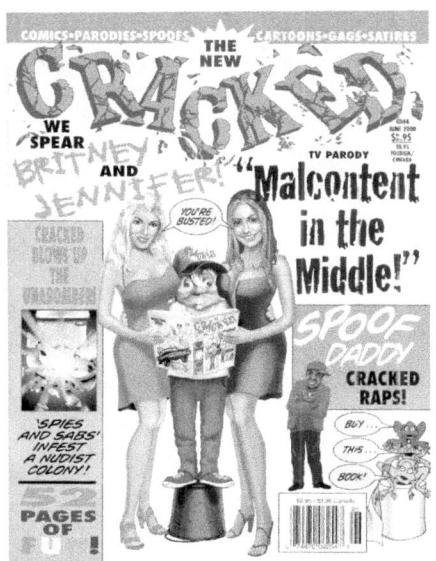

The first issue published after
Dick Kulpa took over, *Cracked* #344,
June 2000.

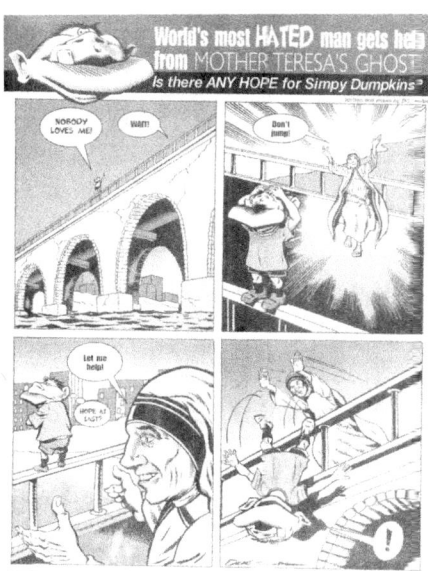

The first *Simpy Dumpkins, World's Most
Hated Man* from *Cracked* #346, August
2000, art by Dick Kulpa.

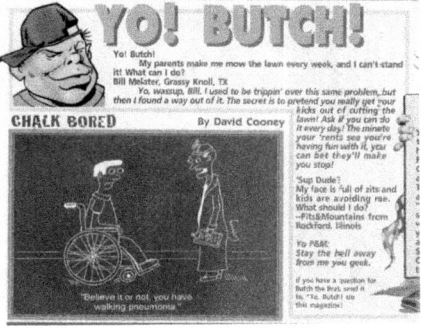

The first *Yo Butch* from *Cracked* #348,
October 2000, art by Dick Kulpa.

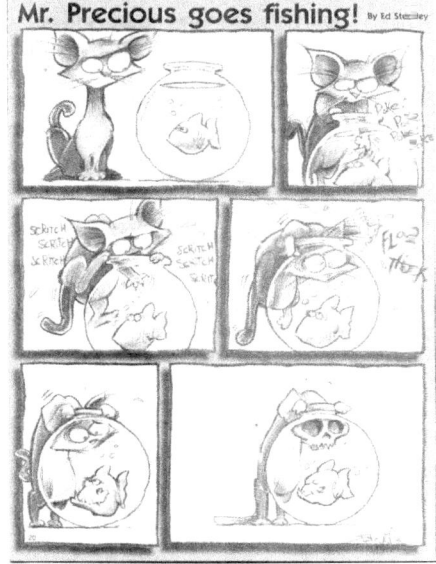

The first *Mr. Precious* from *Cracked*
#345, July 2000, art by Ed Steckley.

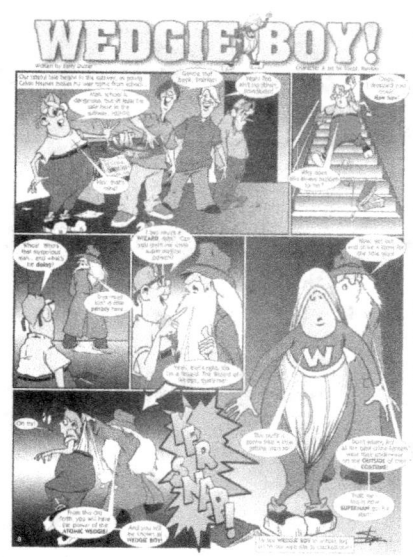

The first *Wedgie Boy* from *Cracked* #351, January 2001, art by Steph Ramsay.

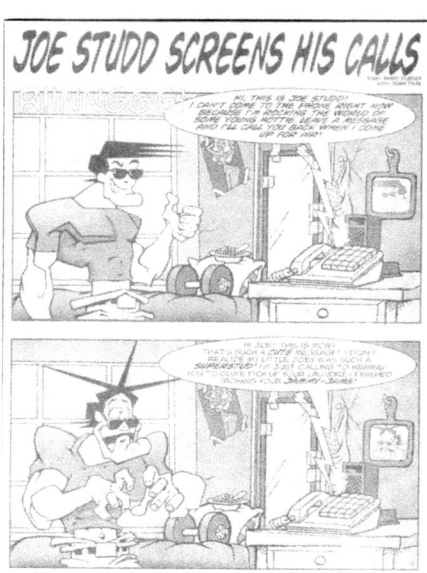

The first *Joe Studd* from *Cracked* #345, July 2000, art by Rurik Tyler.

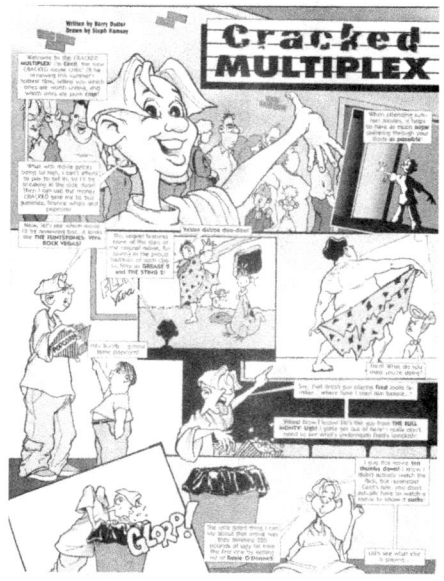

The first *Cecil, the Cracked Movie Critic* from *Cracked* #347, September 2000, art by Steph Ramsay.

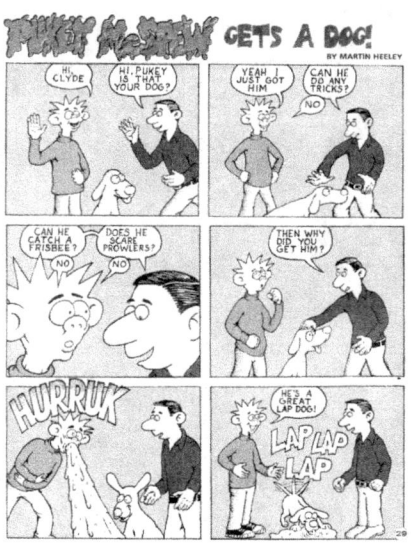

The first *Pukey McSpew* from *Cracked* #357, July 2002, art by Martin Heeley.

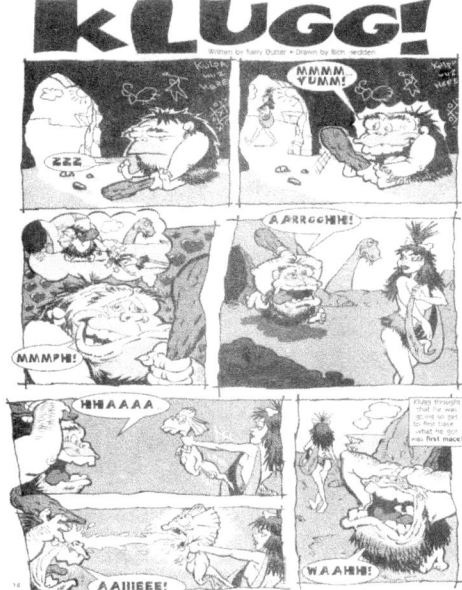

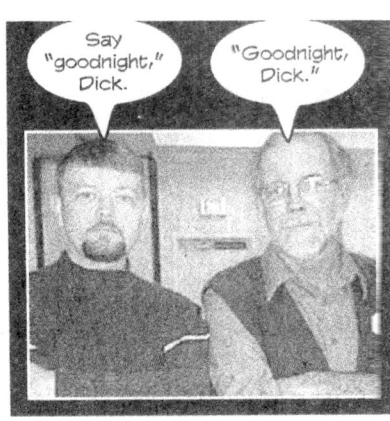

Dick Kulpa and Mark Van Woert
photo from *Cracked* #362,
April 2004.

The first *Klugg* from *Cracked* #352,
February 2001, art by Rich Hedden.

Mad and *Cracked* did similar
Harry Potter rip-offs, but
Cracked's came first, from
Cracked Collectors' Edition
#122 (Harry Pottey), April
2000. This fact was mentioned
in *Cracked* #345, July 2000,
that it beat *Mad* #391 to the
stands by two months.

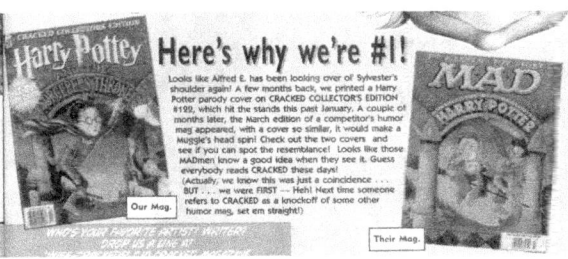

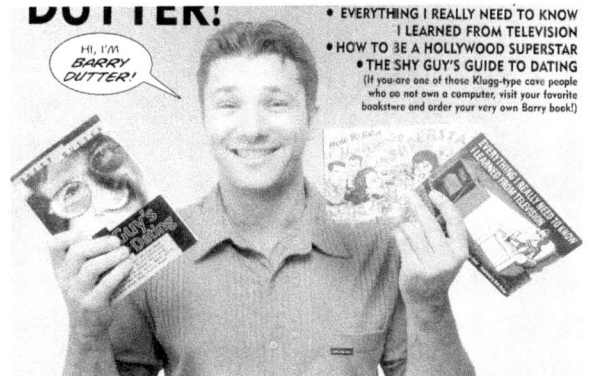

Barry Dutter photo from
Cracked #357, July 2002.

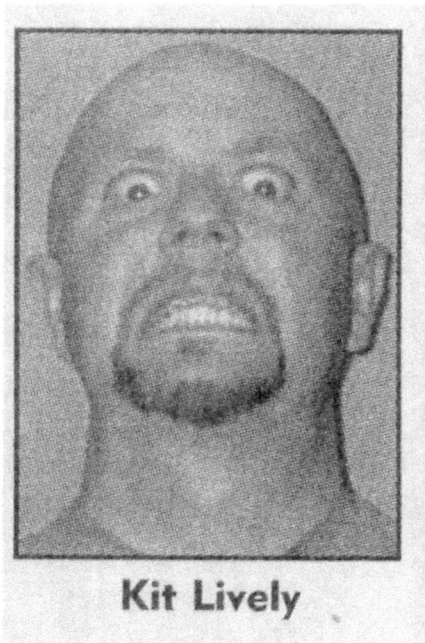

Kit Lively photo from *Cracked* #363,
July 2004.

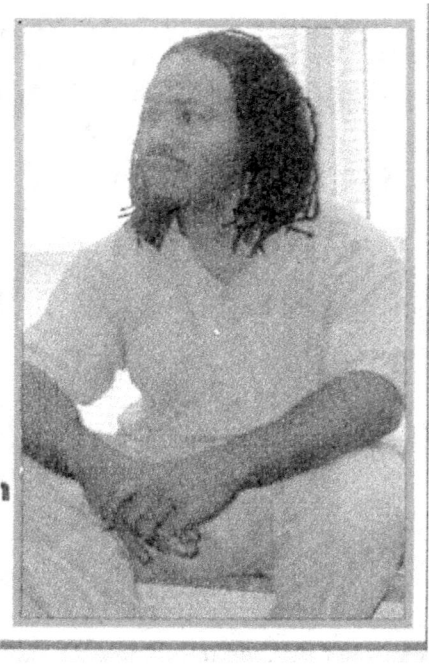

Rush Humphrey photo from *Cracked*
#363, July 2004.

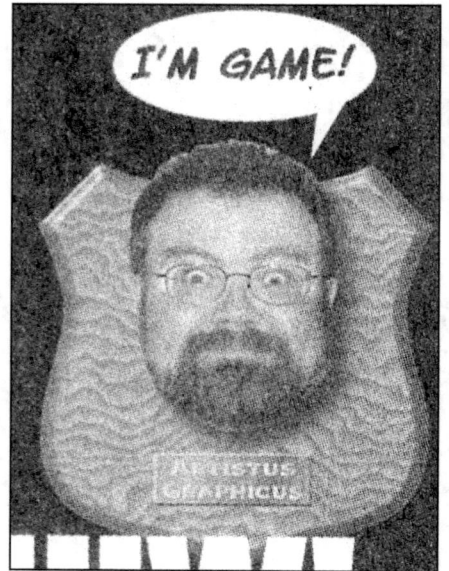

Huw Evans photo from *Cracked* #364,
September 2004.

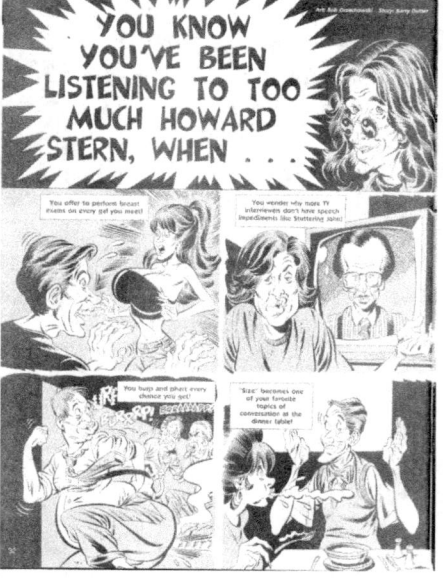

Howard Stern appears in *Cracked* #354,
April 2001.

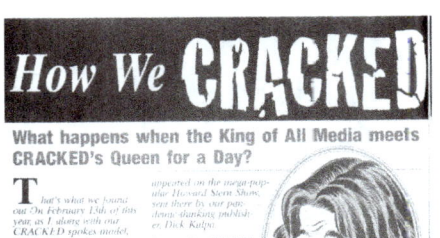

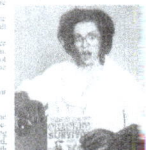

Howard Stern appears again in this write-up from *Cracked* #356, July 2001.

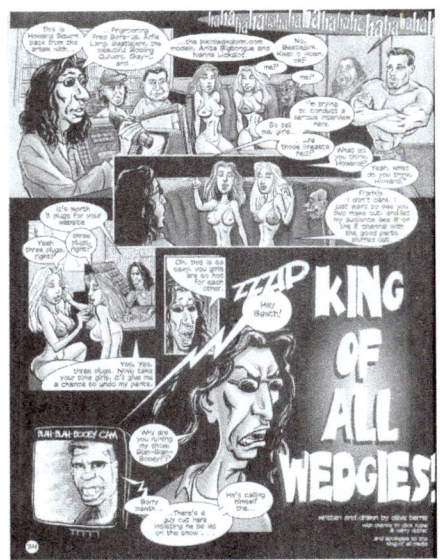

Yet another Howard Stern article from
Cracked #357, July 2002.

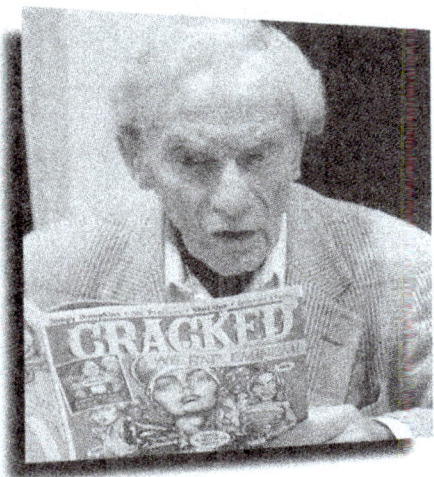

Jonathan Harris (*Lost in Space*) photo
from *Cracked* #356, July 2001.

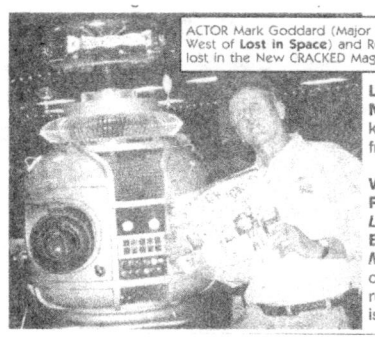

ACTOR Mark Goddard (Major Don West of **Lost in Space**) and Robot get lost in the New CRACKED Magazine!

Mark Goddard (*Lost in Space*) photo from *Cracked* #346, August 2000.

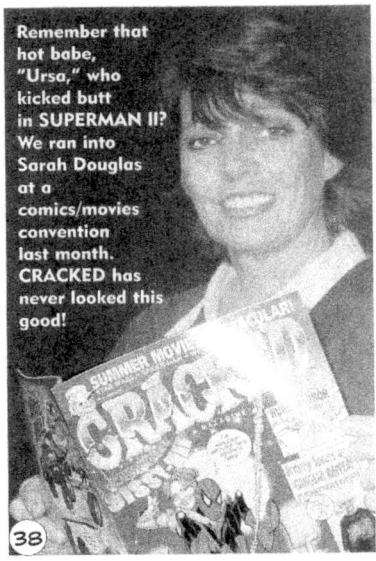

Remember that hot babe, "Ursa," who kicked butt in SUPERMAN II? We ran into Sarah Douglas at a comics/movies convention last month. CRACKED has never looked this good!

Sarah Douglas (*Superman*) photo from *Cracked* #359, February 2003.

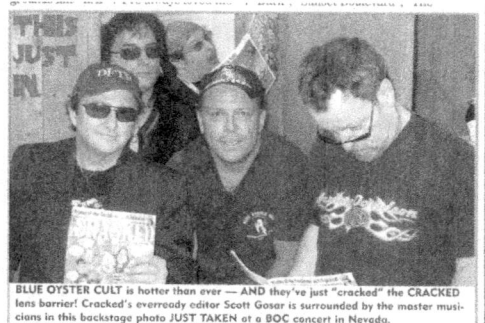

BLUE OYSTER CULT is hotter than ever — AND they've just "cracked" the CRACKED lens barrier! Cracked's everready editor Scott Gosar is surrounded by the master musicians in this backstage photo JUST TAKEN at a BOC concert in Nevada.

Blue Öyster Cult photo from *Cracked* #364, September 2004.

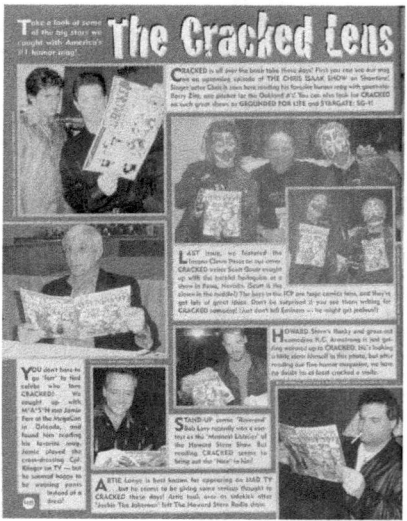

The Cracked Lens

Celebrity photos from *Cracked* #360, May 2003.

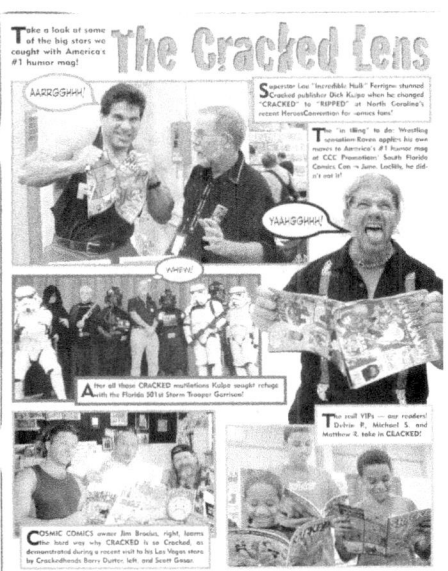

Celebrity photos from *Cracked* #361,
September 2003.

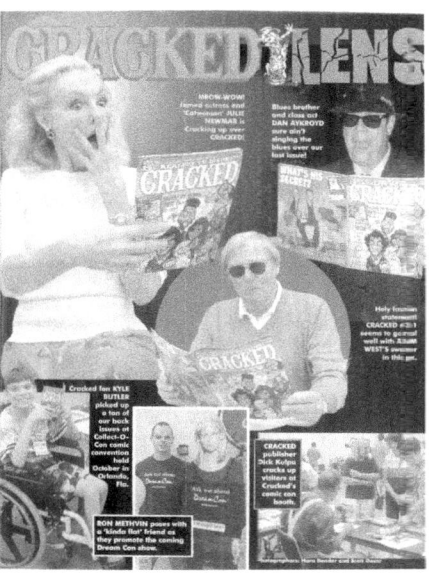

Celebrity photos from *Cracked* #362,
April 2004.

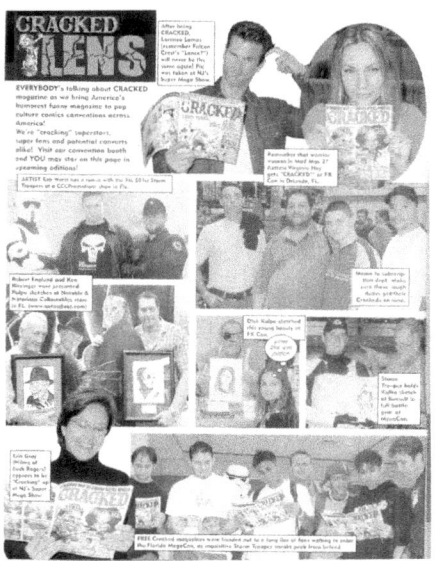

Celebrity photos from *Cracked* #363,
July 2004.

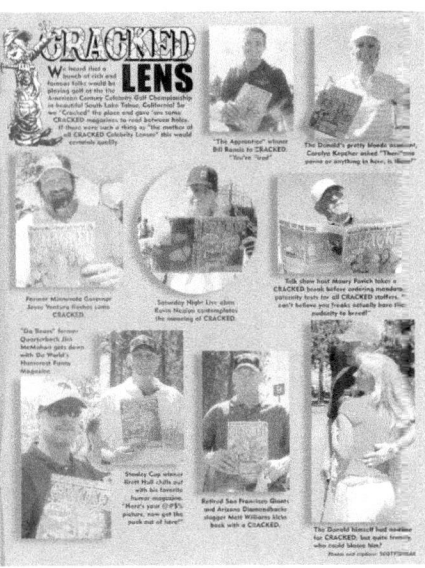

Celebrity photos from *Cracked* #365
November 2004.

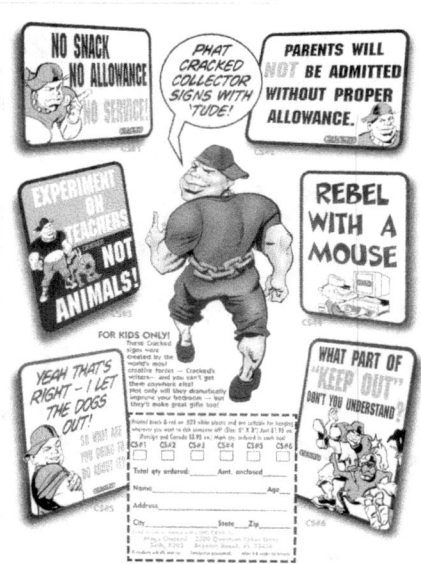

Cracked signs for sale in *Cracked* #355,
May 2001.

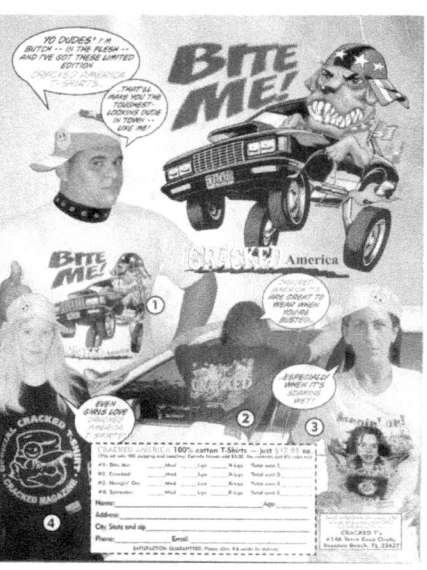

New *Cracked* merchandise as featured
in *Cracked* #358, September 2002.

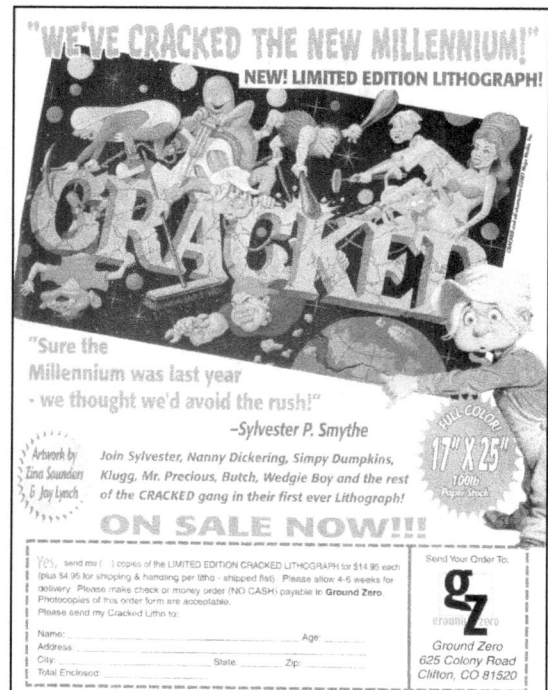

The Millenium Lithograph
from *Cracked* #357, July 2002.

ANTHRAX AND THE
END OF AN ERA

FROM Cracked.com: "According to words I read from former *Cracked* Editor Mort Todd in *The Comics Journal*, due to contamination, all of the film used to print the beautiful *Cracked* magazine from 1958 to 2000 had to be destroyed. That's right. We lost all of the original *Cracked* prints because some asshole went a little nutty with the anthrax." Apparently, the target was American Media, Inc. and the culprit was Bruce Ivins, a government scientist who committed suicide in August 2008 when fingers started pointing at him in the anthrax attack that killed five people in 2001.

Barry Dutter confirms the anthrax story: "We were in a different room in the same building. AMI, we were there during the anthrax scandal."

Dutter also confirms that the *Cracked* archives had to be destroyed as a result: "Yeah, I believe that's true. That's my recollection. There was an archive. Whenever we reprinted an article, I think we would just use a film. Then, after the anthrax incident, anything that was in that building had to be destroyed, which would have included the *Cracked* archives. That's my recollection, that all of that stuff was destroyed. So anyway, that was unfortunate. When AMI bought *Cracked*, they received all the films and all the magazines— everything that Globe had. That was a very scary time, the anthrax attack. It was about a month after 9/11, so it seemed like another terrorist attack. For one brief moment, the staff of AMI was at the center of the biggest news story in America. There were TV crews camped out around then building. No one knew what was going on. We were all questioned by the FBI. We all had to take an antibiotic called Cipro, because none of us knew if we had been infected by anthrax. We were told that if we were infected, we would be dead in two weeks. As it happened, only two members of the staff were infected. A photo editor who died, and a mail carrier, who was hospitalized but later recovered and went back to work. We never found out for sure, but the theory was that the mail carrier handed a piece of mail to the photo editor. They were the only two people who handled the letter, and they were the only two who got infected. The entire staff of AMI was moved to another building. The original building was sold to I believe it was Rudy Guliani's company, who planned to sterilize the building and turn it into a new building where their full-time job would be to sterilize buildings after chemical attacks. So, yes, it was a very scary time. But I did get a week off from work, so that was cool."

Dave Berns also comments on the anthrax story: "The great and very funny Bobbie Bender, also a contributor to *Cracked* Mazagine, the *Weekly World News* and the *Sun* tabloid was the guy who actually opened the anthrax envelope at AMI... the J. Lo letter info was based on his recounting of the incident. Small, cruel, freaky world we live in and our time on it is short!

"Bobbie's still alive and kicking as far as I know... he's in my Facebook friends if you want to reach out to him (he was also really close with Steph Ramsay). I'm pretty sure he's out of work, and the guy is a real character (kind of Rodney Dangerfield-ish). I haven't spoken to him about any of that stuff since I worked at AMI, so he could probably clarify quite a bit.

"The only death in Florida was of Bob Stevens, who was working as photo editor at the *Sun* tabloid. He'd recently been let go or reached retirement or something like that at the *Globe*. He almost took my old job with this model tank magazine, but was offered the *Sun* gig, which probably paid better and kept him in the company of his longtime friends and coworkers. Bobbie was pulling articles, fact checking, proof reading, writing sidebar articles and also opening the mail there. I can't remember if Bobbie was hired on originally as a writer for the *Weekly World News* or *Cracked*, but from what I recall, I want to say Eddie Klontz, but I'm not sure, anyway, someone who'd been with AMI for a while and had pull thought he was the funniest guy in the bar, and that as such, he'd make a great writer for one of those two publications. If you talk to him, maybe he could clarify. I hope that doesn't insult him in any way, as I really love Bobbie, he's a kind-hearted, very funny man, who's had to put up with a lot of shit in his life. I only wish the best for him! He also proof-read *Gag!* magazine for Barry and I.

"Everyone who worked in the building was immediately put onto a month or more cycle of the newly launched anti-biotic, Ciprofloxin (remember Tom Brokaw's famous "In Cipro We Trust" broadcast? You cannot buy advertising that powerful without cracking a few eggs). A woman I knew there casually from smoke breaks (wish I could remember her name to look her up and see how her story developed) had an allergic reaction to the drug that caused her tendons to pop off of her fucking bones around her ankles... nasty shit. She was wearing all sorts of progressively sturdier ankle braces and went from a cane to crutches while I was there. Ernesto Blanco, the mail guy at AMI actually caught the anthrax, but he was able to recover after intensive antibiotics and an extended hospitalization. He'd come back to work there from his recovery after I'd started working there, a real sweet old Cuban Guy. He was always in the news in the months before I started at AMI, and the first time I saw him wheeling the mail cart around, I was a little star struck. It was surreal. When I first got there, the place was full of people just beat the hell up by fate, experimental antibiotics, corporate bosses, the federal government, etc… they were very much bonded and I was an outsider on so many levels during my time there."

Steph Ramsay picks up the story: "I got involved with *Cracked* through a caricature artist's list serve e-mail system. The editor at the time, Dick Kulpa, had advertised on the list serve that he was looking for an art director.

"My time with *Cracked* was bittersweet from the very first day that I walked in the door. I started in 2000 and it was within months of the magazine being cut from the American Media publishing roster. Dick Kulpa, as I stated, was the editor at the time and the relationship that we had was dicey at best. I moved from PA to FL to take the position of art director and my family was following me down after the packing and sale of our home. In the midst of all of this AMI decided that they were going to drop the mag. Kulpa went off the deep end for a week and me and two others finished the 2000 'Back to School' edition even after we had essentially been fired by the publisher. Shortly after that, Kulpa decided that he was going to buy the mag and publish it himself from his living room/office. The following year was spent dividing my time between *Cracked* and the *Weekly World News* until the internal staff manipulations and Kulpa's management style ended my involvement with the publication.

"I worked for AMI after *Cracked*, the environment was most unusual in many ways. I have worked for a lot of companies in my life, but AMI was the first company that I ever had the experience of getting attacked by anthrax!

"My favorite piece was the 'Back to School' cover in Fall 2000. It was also the best selling issue that *Cracked* had had for nearly 10 years. My least favorite was the *Wedgie Boy* series. It was a creation of my son, Parker

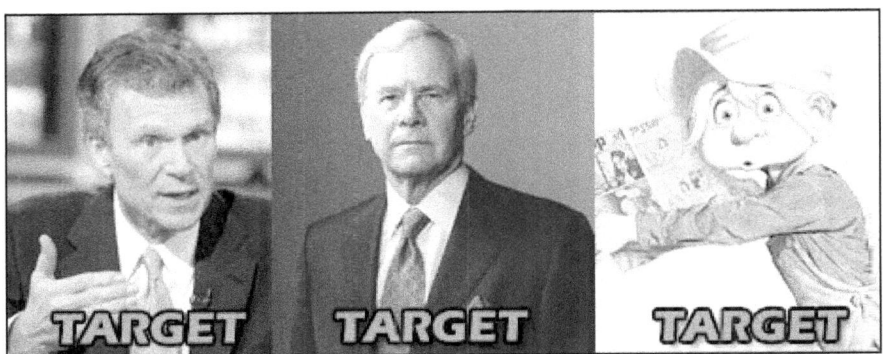

The various targets of the anthrax scare in 2001 from Cracked.com.

and myself, but too a many people had their hands into it and it wound up being a bastardization of what it was intended to be until Kulpa took over the character entirely and turned him into something that I did not even recognize.

"I miss the *Cracked* as it was when I started. You can't really count the last year or so of its existence as it became something surreal. *Cracked* had as much, if not more, potential as *Mad*….but it was never developed the way that it should have been due to the personalities involved in its management those last years."

CHEAP TRICK'S
RICK NIELSEN

NEAR the end of *Cracked*'s original run, Rick Nielsen took over as the publisher, hailed by much fanfare in the magazine. Barry Dutter explains as to why in the world would the guitarist from Cheap Trick be interested in a humor magazine: "I would say tax write-off. I can't think of any other reason. You got a magazine that's not very profitable and probably wasn't going to make a lot of money. I can't think of another reason other than a tax write-off.

"At various times, I stopped working for the magazine, because I got frustrated with the payment thing and then every now and then, Dick would find an influx of new cash and I'm sure he told you about when he convinced the guy from Cheap Trick—Rick Nielsen—and some other investors from Chicago—to put some money into *Cracked*. Dick was always a man on a mission. He was so determined that *Cracked* should survive. He was selling back issues, he was trying to do a website, sell t-shirts and other merchandise, whatever he could to get revenue to keep the magazine going. The problem was he wasn't really paying its freelancers. And that was just the thing. He'd say, 'Well if you guys just came aboard and worked for free for a while, this thing could go on forever and it would be a huge success.' A couple of times there were *Cracked* TV offers. Legitimate studios would come in and say, 'Oh, we're interested in turning this into a TV show.' And then I don't know if they ever paid an option or anything, but they would come in and work up some proposals and we'd meet with people. It always seemed like there was a chance that something would happen—it was a long shot—but it always seemed like something would happen. One company came in—it was NBM—and said, 'We want to do a book.' It was *The Cracked Guide to the Movies*. We said, 'Ok. Why not?' I don't know if there was a lot of money involved. *Cracked* has been around so long that there's always this kind of interest in outside companies asking, 'What can we do with this? I've got about 100 copies of the darn thing.'

"I don't think anyone put money into it not expecting a return. Dick had a skill for selling stuff. He would travel back to his old stomping grounds in Illinois and try to drum up investors for *Cracked*. I believe he knew Rick Nielsen from back in his college days—they had gone to school together or something like that. He was really skilled at getting people to do stuff and I think that he was able to convince people by saying, 'Hey, I've got this 50-year-old humor magazine, that's been successful over the years. It's ready for a big comeback and you're ready to come on board.' He probably mentioned it was going to be a TV show. There were many ways that you could sell it. I think it was probably more along those lines. I don't think anyone would invest in something that they didn't think would sell, but I don't know how the deal was structured.

"In the case of AMI, they owned it. When Dick was the publisher, he owned it. I don't think Rick Nielsen was ever an actual owner, more like a partner. When *Cracked* was finally sold for the final time, it was sold to Dick Kulpa. He was the one who benefited the most from that sale. He may have given up partial ownership, but I don't think he gave up full ownership. Yeah, I think he just had Rick Nielsen up there for publicity.

"Towards the end, I quit working on *Cracked*. Basically, I was tired of working for free. Every now and then Kulpa have a sudden influx of cash. He would call me and say, 'Hey! Would you like to write a spoof of *The Hulk* movie?' I said, 'Well, if you're going to pay, I'll do it.' I had no objection of working for pay. To this day, it's something I stick to. There was a period of a year to almost a year and a half where I did part-time work for free on *Cracked* because partly out of the love for the magazine, partly with the hope that it was going to pay down the line. One day I did ask Kulpa for pay and he said, 'Well, if I knew you were going to ask me for pay, I wouldn't have asked you to do all that work.' It was one of those things where seriously, it was hard to deal with. I left the magazine. I don't know specifically what year— 2002, 2003. At that point I moved on. Scott Gosar had been a freelancer for *Cracked*, was hired as an editor, along with Marten Jallad, who had done *Thwak* magazine. Scott told me that a lot of the time; he wouldn't even get to see the material before it was printed. Kulpa would just hire freelancers to do stuff without consulting with the editors. Dick was always trying to work a deal—like the 'Silly CD's thing. He had someone who was basically an advertiser who convinced Kulpa that they should be partners, so Kulpa goes and puts 'Silly CD's on the cover, basically putting an ad on the cover of the magazine. That was the kind of thing where you tear your hair out and say, 'How can you do this? How can you put an ad on the cover?' 'Silly CDs'—the year was 2001, 2002 or whatever and CDs were on the way out anyway. People were already moving over to downloaded music anyway. To come out with a spoof of CDs like 10 years too late didn't make a lot of sense to me and then to put it on the cover. That's just an example of one of those things where—the funny thing is I like Dick Kulpa—Dick and I get along well—but we've had our disagreements. Dick always said that everything he did was done for the survival of the magazine. He'd always say that he was trying to help everyone by getting *Cracked* to where we can all benefit by getting movies and TV and merchandising, at the end of the day, we weren't getting paid. That's something that he really misunderstood. People like to get paid for their work. If you ever asked for money, Dick would offer you a new job title, instead, like 'Assistant to the Executive in Charge of Production' or something like that. I tried to tell him that there's no point in having a fancy title if the job doesn't pay anything."

Kit Lively explains how he was called back to write at this time when Marten Jallad and Scott Gosar were placed as editors: "Years later, when I was asked back to *Cracked* by friend and then editor Marten Jallad, it was a much different experience entirely (albeit in no way due to Marten's involvement).

"During the early months of 2000, *Cracked* was sold to a new publisher, which moved the offices from New York to Florida. None of the staff at the time wanted to make the move, so a new staff was needed. Dick Kulpa worked for one or more of the tabloids that *Cracked*'s new owners published, and he requested the task of redesigning the magazine. I, of course, didn't know any of this at the time. I just knew that *Cracked* was changing hands and I hoped that I would still have a regular gig when the dust settled.

"After talking with Mr. Kulpa (to see if I would be right for a position on staff at the magazine), I was calmed by his enthusiasm for the magazine and for my work, as well. He even went so far as to say that, even if I didn't make the cut for a staff position, my work would be prominently featured in the magazine. Well, my admittedly fragile psyche didn't stay soothed for long, as his pep talk was followed by months of mostly no response to work that I sent in. When I next spoke with him, he told me that there wasn't currently room on staff for me, but that I was next on the list (another apparent lie).   Most of the material never received anything in the way of comment—it wasn't formally rejected, I just usually never heard back, and none of it was used. He continued to reprint my previous *Cracked* material in special and regular editions of the magazine, which, of course, meant that he didn't have to pay me. Now, I naturally realize that when magazines change hands, sometimes the new folks don't like your stuff like the previous staff did and that's just part of the business, but I just didn't like the way it had been handled. I felt like I had been tricked or at least misled. So, I just went elsewhere. I spent the next few years contributing cartoons to *National Lampoon*, SmartAlex (a greeting card company) the *Hustler* mags, *Thwak* and various other magazines.

"Then in 2003, I was contacted by my friend and editor at *Thwak*, Marten Jallad. He and another friend/fellow humor writer, Scott Gosar, had been hired as editors at *Cracked*, and he wanted me to come back to the magazine. I was a bit leery, as Dick was still seemingly in charge as publisher, and I definitely got the feeling that he didn't like my stuff. Still, I liked Marten and Scott, and they had some good ideas for the magazine. So I started sending stuff in again. The first thing I had published in the new *Cracked* was a page of single-panel cartoons titled *Cracked Gross Gags*, which was illustrated by my friend and sometimes *Hustler Humor* collaborator, Noel Anderson. Our names were left off of the article, but we did get a blurb on the cover ('GROSS GAGS!'). We were assured that a correction would be on the letter page of the next issue, but there wasn't. I knew the magazine was in a period of transition, though, and wanted to be patient and hope for the best. The next thing accepted by the guys was a three-page article titled 'Pick-Up Lines to Use on Chicks at a Rock Concert.' The artwork was completed by Jay Chuppe, without incident, and placed in the magazine. Not long before going to print, however, Dick saw the article (how had he not seen it previously?), and didn't like what he saw. Proclaiming it unfunny and offensive, he demanded that it be removed from the magazine. And again, this was after the article had been approved, sent to the artist—who then sent in roughs, which were approved, and then final art. Then it was killed at the last moment. Editor Scott Gosar argued on behalf of Jay and me, but to no avail. Neither Jay nor I received any sort of payment, not even a kill fee."

"The last thing I had published in *Cracked* was a full-page gag strip that was illustrated by editor Jallad. When he finished drawing the strip, he sent it to Dick with credits given as 'Written by Kit Lively, Illustrated by Marten Jallad.' Somehow, when the issue hit the stands, the entire page was 'By Marten Jallad.' Marten quickly contacted me, apologizing profusely (even though it obviously wasn't his fault), but I had just had it with how Dick ran things and I never sent anything into *Cracked* again. Oh, and I was never paid for that final page, either—I didn't have as much to complain about as other contributors at the time, however, many of whom went unpaid for dozens of pages.

"As a footnote, I have to mention that I did have contact with Dick Kulpa one more time. Several years ago, I noticed that he and I were both going to be at a comic convention in St. Louis, so I sent him an e-mail to see if he would mind me sitting at the *Cracked* table, along with him and any other writers/artists he had onboard. I guess I wanted to be able to say that I had sat at the *Cracked* table at a show before the mag finally went under. I did have a good time signing copies of the magazine and drawing stuff for con-goers. Dick did turn out to be nice and friendly in person, so I decided to let bygones be bygones. But regardless, the end result was a previously nice arrangement that got unpleasant very quickly. A lot of people got treated worse than they deserved, and the magazine wasn't what it could have been during that time period as a result."

Kent Gamble adds, "I was in the Marten Jallad and Scott Gosar on those latter issues of *Cracked* and I was paid for some, but not all."

Scott Gosar takes up the story expressing his views: "It was sometime in the summer of 2001. I was writing for Marten Jallad's *Thwak* magazine and running my website, TheMadStore.com. I was contacted by Mark Van Woert, who was *Cracked's* Webmaster at the time. My memories of how exactly my involvement with *Cracked* came about are a bit hazy, but I think he was looking for some back issues of *Mad* or *Cracked*, and I recognized his name from the current *Cracked* masthead. I asked him if he would forward something I wrote to *Cracked's* editor, Barry Dutter, and he said 'Sure. No problem.' I e-mailed Mark a scathingly funny script called 'In George W. Bush's America?' and not long after; Barry contacted me personally and said he wanted to run the piece in the next issue of *Cracked*. As luck would have it, this all happened about two weeks before the tragic attacks of September 11, 2001, and in the aftermath, Barry and I both agreed that the Bush piece would be inappropriate for publication. There were only two issues of *Cracked* published in 2002, and later in '02, I submitted a piece called 'Scenes We'll Never See On *The Anna Nicole Show*' that was supposed to run in #358, but the artist who was supposed to illustrate it flaked on us and it got bumped to the next issue. The Anna Nicole piece, along with another called 'Where The Hell Is Osama?' ran in my debut issue, *Cracked* #359, February 2003.

"I didn't have any 'time at *Cracked*,' per se. My *Cracked* experience was purely 21st-century style, with everything done over the phone and through the Internet, with e-mail being our primary form of communication. When Marten and I edited *Cracked*, we did it by bouncing Quark files of art and writing back and forth through e-mail. At present, the only *Cracked* colleague or alumni I have ever met in person has been Barry Dutter. We learned early on that we both share a passion for the casino game of Blackjack and, in 2002; we began collaborating on a book about the subject. The unfinished manuscript still sits on my hard drive to this day. Barry and I have met in Las Vegas, on two separate occasions, to play cards and chase bikinis at the Tropicana Hotel pool.

"By the middle of 2002, I was in constant contact with editor Barry Dutter and owner-publisher Dick Kulpa, who established an e-mail relationship with me after I managed to photograph the rap group Insane Clown Posse holding copies of *Cracked* #359, which was a rap-themed issue. Barry had landed me a freelance writing gig at the supermarket tabloid *Weekly World News*, at which he was a writer/editor and Kulpa was editor-in-chief. Under a variety of pseudonyms, I wrote feature stories, advice columns and even a few 'Ed Anger' editorials. Three of my stories became 'Page 1' cover stories, a record number for a new freelancer, according to Dutter. Not long after *Cracked* #361 hit the stands, Kulpa, Dutter and associate editor Dave Berns had a falling out (over 'creative differences,' as Dutter would later tell me), which resulted in Dutter and Berns leaving the magazine. When Kulpa told me this, over the phone, he was freaking out, and said that he had no choice but to end the magazine. I begged him to reconsider, offering myself up as his new editor. He said that he would think about it and get back to me. A few days later, I was the editor of *Cracked* magazine. 'Jesus Christ,' I thought, 'I've never edited a national magazine before, so, I'll need some help. Barry had a co-editor, so I'll bring one in myself, and maybe I won't look like such an idiot if I have someone with me who has actually edited and published something.' Marten Jallad was my first and only choice. He had self-published *Thwak* since 2000, and I figured that he knew something about layouts and the publishing industry in general things that I had never dealt with before. I knew that I had an eye for art and a way with words in a humorous context, but I didn't feel like a complete magazine editor, and Marten had given me my first break in *Thwak*, so he was in. We had the magazine for four issues and when Kulpa sold it in 2005; we were just beginning to find our voice, so to speak."

"My opinion of *Cracked*, throughout its history, was that it strived to be a younger kid's version of *Mad*. *Cracked* was rarely controversial and tended to be considerably less threatening than its rival. In the '70s and '80s, *Cracked* would latch on to a TV show or certain celebrities and just beat them to death in issue after issue. The Fonz, *Laverne and Shirley*, Mork, *Dukes of Hazzard* and the *Diff'rent Strokes* kids are prime examples of how *Cracked* would over-do things. There was a period during the 1990s that *Cracked* broke away from this mold and actually became more daring and original. A favorite of mine from the '90s was *The Simpson* cover of #295. My vision of a successful *Cracked* magazine was to grow it up a bit. Having been an avid collector of *National Lampoon* magazine throughout my teens and twenties, I wanted *Cracked* to walk that fine line between *Mad* and *National Lampoon*-type humor, but Kulpa wasn't going for it. I envisioned a magazine for teens and 20-somethings and Kulpa still saw *Cracked* as the wholesome children's magazine that it had always been.

"If there were a horror story to be told about *Cracked*, it would have to do with all of the glaring typographical errors that would find their way into the finished product and onto the newsstand, most prevalently during what I call 'The Kulpa Era.' I first noticed this in *Cracked* #359, in my 'Where The Hell Is Osama?' piece. In the panel where Osama and Saddam Hussein are sitting together in a fishing boat, the panel should have read 'Perhaps he's just spending some quality time with an old friend.' Instead, it read 'Perhaps he's just spending quality some time with an old friend.' In a piece I wrote for

Cracked #361 entitled 'What Is Rock n' Roll?' there is a panel where a guy is standing up in a convertible loaded with money, playing a guitar. The panel should have read 'Rock n' Roll: Where multi-millionaire performers rake in the big bucks by singing about being broke, starving and living on mean city streets.' Well, that panel probably would have worked better had the word 'streets' not been left out. Marten and I became *Cracked* editors starting with #362. We soon learned that our jobs began and ended with receiving and sorting through written submissions, selecting artists to illustrate scripts, and, in my case, writing my own material and re-writing other scripts that may have needed some fluffing up. Dick Kulpa built all of the pages and hastily rushed the Quark files off to Quebecor for printing, never allowing us to proofread them. His treatment was the final treatment and that was it. When the finished product of *Cracked* #362 got back to us, it was a bit of a shocker. There was a subscription ad stuck right at the end of an article, a 16-year-old Michael Jackson piece reprinted (and featured on the front cover, no less), and, worst of all, the word 'mazagine,' which had appeared in its correct form on decades of *Cracked* covers, was misspelled! I asked Dick if he would take the title of 'Executive Editor' starting on the masthead of *Cracked* #363, and he agreed. My reason was simple: That was MY name on that masthead, below the word 'Editor.' If the magazine was going to look like shit, and I couldn't control it, then I wanted it known that there was another editor, above Marten and myself, who was allowing it to hit the stands looking and reading the way it did.

"Just before #363 went to press, Marten, who lives a lot closer to Dick Kulpa than I do, was about to attend a comic convention that we knew Kulpa was going to be at. We arranged for Kulpa to bring a pre-publication copy of #363 that Quebecor sent to be proofread for errors that would be sent back with corrections noted before the main print run was to commence. Because Marten was given access to that copy, *Cracked* #363 remains our best looking, most thoroughly edited issue of our tenure. We were not given access to pre-pub copies of #362, #364 or our last issue, #365.

"Lest anyone gets the impression that I'm out to bash or demean Dick Kulpa in any way, I just want to say that while I'm grateful for the opportunities that Dick provided me with, I wished that he had cared a little bit more about the quality of *Cracked* toward the end. It was a crazy time for all of us. He had moved from Florida to Rockford, Illinois during that period and had just landed some new investors (including Cheap Trick guitarist Rick Nielsen) who he was trying to keep happy. He just wanted to crank out issues as quickly as possible to show the Rockford people that the magazine was still relevant and viable, and, in the process, the quality suffered because he had two good editors who were in it for the simple love of humor magazines, yet bypassed us time and again in a rush to get a new issue on the stands.

"The first humor magazine I ever read and bought at a newsstand was a copy of *Mad*. As a writer, I had a drawer full of rejection slips from *Mad* by the time Barry Dutter published the second and third scripts I had ever sent in to *Cracked*."

Marten Jallad was the "other half" of the editorial staff at this time, and he offers his perspectives of how he got involved with *Cracked* and what happened next: "I did in fact submit premises to both *Mad* and *Cracked* in the '90s with little luck, but then focused my energies on *Thwak*. I also stumbled across TheMadStore.com shortly after *Thwak* #1 had come out and found out that owner Scott Gosar was a writer and he started contributing to the magazine from then on. I believe that Scott was doing some work for *Weekly World News* and had written a couple of premises for *Cracked* when he found out that the previous editors were leaving *Cracked* and let me know that there was going to be some openings. In the meantime Dick Kulpa had met a couple of the *Thwak* contributors at various comic conventions that he was set up at and so he was familiar with what I had done with the magazine and the contacts I had built among many artist and writers. A few months after *Thwak* #5 come out in late summer of '03; I received a call from Dick Kulpa one day and was asked to be co-editor with Scott. Knowing that Scott and I had the same enthusiasm and commitment to creating great humor I was very excited about the possibilities.

"Our first big task upon taking over the editorial reigns was to put together issue #362 in less than a month (October 2003). We immediately jumped right into it and decided to do a California Gubernatorial themed issue as that whole incident with Arnold and other celebrities jockeying for position was in full swing. We had a great cover gag written, an artist picked out to render it, 15-plus pages of themed finished material, and just as we were about to send it to the printer we hit the first of many printing setbacks. It ended up rendering all but two pages irrelevant, as we didn't end up printing until a few months later (April 2004). Also, there was material slated for *Thwak* #6 in that issue as well as a reprint that appeared in *Thwak* #2. It was cool to see the issue finally hit the stands though, and naturally I had to go take a picture of the issue on the stands for posterity.

"With each subsequent issue I learned that we would have to expect the unexpected at every turn. It was frustrating to not actually see the finished product prior to getting it back from the printers only then to find out that there were a host of grammatical errors or silly spelling mistakes, or find unrelated back issue filler material be used instead of brand new fresh work. The only time that I did actually get to edit an issue was #363 when Dick and I just happened to be at the same convention.

"My main roll at *Cracked* was that of liaison/communicator between artist and writers, while editing and reviewing submissions, pairing artists and writers based on their styles, coming up with themes for issues and suggesting layout for each issue. I also did a fair bit of promotion, attending some comic conventions, having a newspaper article written, on line interviews and appearing on a still airing segment on PBS talking about *Cracked* magazine. Scott and I would spend many hrs discussing our strategies on the direction we wanted to take the book in. Prior to starting with *Cracked* I had noticed a dramatic decline in quality and consistency and my first goal was to raise the level back to the Silverstone / Simmons level (my favorite of any *Cracked* era). We desperately wanted to get away from the cluttered tabloid style cover that Dick had been putting out and concentrate on a single cover gag relating to the interior, which by issue #363 we had achieved! We also felt that what *Cracked* had always lacked was some clever writing. Not dumbed down material but stuff that you would actually have to think about in order to understand. Again I feel that this level of writing was also getting more exposure under our tenure.

"All in all I felt stifled and would have certainly liked to have had more control over the overall process like my prior experience with *Thwak* where I was solely responsible for the final product.

"I'm not sure what you will hear from others about their working relationships but the most difficult and frustrating part for me was that Dick Kulpa did not communicate well and allow us to put out the best possible product. I say this because Scott and I never saw the final product prior to it going to the printers. We were really unable to edit the book. He would lay out the book sometimes putting in his own illustrations on other artists' pages or slapping an ad in the middle of a page, which in both cases upset the artists as they felt that compromised their work. It was also more and more apparent that his heart wasn't really in it and that he just wanted product on the stands.

"I would like to share that although there were many discrepancies and inconsistencies during the Kulpa era of *Cracked*, I believe that Dick initially tried to rejuvenate the magazine using his editorial background in the Tabloid business."

Mike Arnold (no relation to the author) discusses his brief tenure being a contributor during the tail end of the publication: "It was a lot of fun for me. I was able to contribute about twelve pieces in the last few issues before they ceased publication. I had a ton of ideas and Marten and Scott liked a lot of them so they let me do almost all of them.

"I was always a huge *Cracked* fan so never considered submitting to *Mad*. It wasn't until I had a few things published in *Cracked* that I thought to try *Mad*. Then I found out that one of my instructors from SVA, Sam Viviano was the Art Director over at *Mad*, so I thought it would be easy, but that wasn't the case. It still took a year or so of submissions before I finally got into *Mad*.

"My favorite piece I did for *Cracked* never got published! I did a parody of those old Charles Atlas ads featuring Dubya getting sand kicked in his face by Sadaam titled 'The Insult That Made A Mess of Iraq' and I came up with it just a bit to late for the issue we were working on (#365) so it was pushed to the next issue which never got published.

"I did some work that never got to appear in *Cracked* because they ceased publication after issue #365 so Marten and I decided to contact the other artists whose work would not appear in the next issue and self publish our own cartoon humor magazine called *Jokester*. It contained a lot of the material that was slated for issue #366 as well as some new stuff. The original idea for the mag was to also include written jokes as well as cartoon humor but we decided not to include the jokes but kept the name. Marten had already self-published five issues of his own humor mag *Thwak* so his experience was extremely helpful getting that project off the ground."

Dick Kulpa discusses his side of the story of what exactly happened to *Cracked*: "My tenure at *Weekly World News* not only transformed me from wannabe national cartoonist into a formidable editorial powerhouse, it also acquainted me with other publishing facets, such as distribution, rack placement, sell-through, and so forth. When *Cracked* magazine emerged, I saw the chance to fully harness my 30 years of experience—and success – in the field I had originally aspired to. But *Cracked* had some major "issues"—no pun intended.

"Sales were in decline, and the previous staff's final issue inexplicably plunged nearly 20,000 in single copy sales. Some features were up to *WWN* standards, but many weren't. My *WWN* editor was opposed to my transfer, and did his damndest to 'monkey wrench' my assumption. (For instance, I was only allowed nine days to flesh out my first edition, a hodgepodge of original as well as procured works snagged from associates I knew through the Internet.)

"But it was 'damn those torpedoes, full speed ahead!' I began to implement format and qualitative improvements as we went—with a diminishing budget.

"Under me, one had to check his ego at the door. If an alleged 'caricature' failed to resemble the person satirized, it was adjusted—one way or another. If the artist failed to fix it, I did. If pages came in mis-proportioned, they were animorphically distorted to fit. If features appeared to 'steal' rather than satirize trademarked characters, they were killed. Stories deemed 'humorless' were killed. 'Silliness' was discouraged. Efforts to look like *Mad* magazine—overwhelming as they were—were also discouraged. Unclear panels were redrawn. Silly things like that. My *WWN* training was in full tilt and in high gear!

"*Cracked* was a dream come true. Imagine yourself, as a comic creator, suddenly facing a startling choice: Own *Cracked* magazine, or lose your home. I had the easy option of acquiring *Cracked* through a corporation—and if things went wrong—corporate bankruptcy was a viable escape. Easy choice. End of story. I wound up "buying" *Cracked* outright in November 2000, but publication of a glowing newspaper feature story (about me) would lead to actions, which suddenly transformed my efforts at "salvation" into "survival." The future looked bleak, but I refused to be manipulated into bankruptcy. Deliberately destroyed distribution records further hampered my efforts, as reports of skids of *Cracked* magazines going to wrong venues began to surface. Who knows where the hell the 250,000 copy draw was going—a number, incidentally, that was suddenly and without warning cut by 40% by the 'new' distributor. Anyone in the publication biz knows the old adage: 'Cut your draw, cut your throat.' SOMEONE cut my throat. (There is reference to this on Wordpress.com.)

"The 'new' system suddenly foisted upon me denied me 50% of expected upfront funding, something even the closest staffers failed to grasp. And while I secured alternative employment to the tune of tens of thousands of dollars to key people, that went unappreciated. 'Betrayal' was rampant. And as money diminished, I was forced to utilize more second-rate talent for the book than I cared to. Some of these folks were given a 'marvelous high point' in their careers, something they'd never have received otherwise. And at least two artists gained prominent footholds in the national arena, directly as a result of my *Cracked* stewardship. As they bask in their windfalls, I am left to struggle as a caricature artist—legally blind, I might add—but quite successful.

"Nonetheless, my four-year quest for support, investment and whatnot for *Cracked* led to the realization that I was viewed not as a 'golden goose,' but a 'turkey to be plucked,' in today's American business culture. A scene from the movie *GalaxyQuest*, featuring 'Bat Boy-like' aliens suddenly pouncing upon one of their own injured, aptly describes my experience.

"If a time machine suddenly emerged, and I could travel back to when the sabotage first occurred, I would immediately rent a truck and dump the entire *Cracked* inventory onto the 'seller's' doorstep. I must admit, I received an inkling as to what was to come when I saw the John Lithgow *Don Quixote* movie in 2000, as I was negotiating to buy *Cracked* in what appeared to be an 'all-too-easy' deal. As two blinded fools rode the wooden rocking horse to the amusement of the rich aristocrat, I turned to my then-girlfriend and asked… 'Could THIS be what is happening with me and *Cracked*?'

"There is much, much more to the story. A woman familiar with the situation once grabbed a competing magazine—published by a former staffer—out of my hands, ripping it to shreds. The anthrax attack on the AMI building resulted in the death of my direct counterpart, sitting yards from my office—during the height of my *Cracked* dispute with the company. I was not 'perfect' in my performance, and was criticized for not doing more drawing for the publication. In my defense, I can only say it this way: For me, drawing is like sex—only better. But if the gal looks like the northbound side of a southbound pig, forget it.

"*Cracked* was not a total tale of negatives. Comic convention organizers were extraordinarily supportive—providing free booth space for *Cracked*—when I tapped into that circuit in 2003-2004. *Mad* magazine attorneys—when I'd occasionally hear from them—were respectful and friendly—as was *Mad* icon Al Feldstein. Maybe they remembered the free *WWN* t-shirts I sent them when I took over *Cracked*. Who knows? It's not like I didn't try to build bridges. Celebrities such as Lou Ferrigno, Noel Neill, Julie Newmar and Sarah Douglas (from whom I got a kiss) made things easier to endure. And folks like Charles Cerrito and the comicconventions.com people—who declared me as best convention sketch artist in 2004—eased the pain.

"Numerous and growing letters and e-mails showed me we were headed the right way, and many of these writers compared us favorably to *Mad*! Few 'counter comparisons' ever emerged. By all counts, it appeared my emphasis on editorial over art was taking hold...particularly through increased product placement for *Cracked* on TV shows at the time, as well as measurable sales gains through each three-issue run.

"In retrospect, I now realize that this magazine was never meant to succeed. In the final words of our next-to-last Curtis Circulation distribution account exec, issued in 2004: 'What I don't get is, you're authorized to be in 62,000 racks...WHY are you only in 15,000???' He's asking ME this? That would be the last I'd ever hear from him.

"Legal recourse? Who's going to believe some tabloid editor who once donned superhero tights at demolition derbies over so-called upstanding 'suits'? They knew what they were doing.

"One key strategy in revitalizing a publication is to 'throw away current readership.' In its early days, *Weekly World News* 'struggled' with a 200,000 weekly base readership. New editors were brought in, and they switched *WWN* from a second-rate celeb tab to the superstar million-plus weekly circulation fantasy tab it became in the late '80s. *Cracked*, laden with dry humor, clutter, and seemingly pointless features, needed such a change. I converted the covers to a tabloid-style format, featuring headlined features, in an effort to attract new readers.

"Satire mags, *Mad* included, didn't fare well at comic conventions. *Cracked* was no exception. Tables featuring dozens of old 'collector' issues, in the old style and prominently displayed, generated two to three copy sales daily. The more defined color newer editions sold about 10—until I dropped that price to 'a buck a book' and ended up selling over 100. Observation: Price is everything.

"As publisher, I had to decide between 'edge' and 'good taste.' 'Sicko party jokes,' for instance, were killed. Though we experimented with some sexual innuendo, I slowly eliminated it. My 2003 aim was to get *Cracked* distributed in schools, and in order to accomplish this, it had to be cleaned up. While I had established direct connection with the Florida Department of Education, the Rockford business people failed to follow up on this.

"In 2004, I posted several bins full of *Cracked* magazines at stores as an experiment. All sold out.

"In 2003 / 2004 I logged over 29,000 miles—the circumference of Earth—pushing *Cracked* at comic conventions and in meetings with investors.

"I told one potential investor, a roofing billionaire—that with proper foundation, *Cracked* would go 'through the roof.' Two years later, he went 'through the roof' to his death, while fixing his private roof. He should have listened to me. (wink)

"I published three issues in Rockford, Illinois. The deal was, I would handle editorial, and they would handle the business side. Two of the three printer dates were not met, and in one particularly galling incident, promised sample copies featuring Donald Trump on the cover were never sent to the Invitational Golf Tournament he was hosting. Subscription mailings were handled by a 78-year-old woman licking envelopes. *Cracked* was delegated to a bathroom-sized office—with no phone.

"Nonetheless, the third issue was the charm, but the Rockford dunderheads lost interest. It became increasingly clear that I was actually recruited as a potential 'Pell Grant Magnet' and that *Cracked* was secondary to my being there. This was confirmed by an associate of mine who hobnobbed at the root level—with other employees of that operation. The last edition cover would feature Kelly Freas' final cover for any publication.

"Publication of a nearly full broadsheet newspaper article hailing my arrival may have also done me in there. After that article appeared we would not see the director for six weeks!

"The various contracts I signed during the *Cracked* debacle were bad enough. BUT—in every case, those contracts also were breached (and not by me). There also remain unresolved ethics issues, and technically, the *Cracked* sale was never fully closed.

"One outspoken staffer, disappointed when the sabotage emerged in January 2001, was so unhappy about 'not getting' the promised full-time *Cracked* position, that his chronic and constant complaints very likely sealed my doom early—in spite of the $40,000 yearly position I was able to land him—twice!

"I was once forced to modify a freelance artist's 'caricature,' so poorly done and unrecognizable that it was a 'must fix.' I was later told by another freelancer… 'I should not have done that.'"

In an article by Susan Port for *The Palm Beach Post* on January 24, 2004, she reported, "One day soon, there could be a Sylvester P. Smythe doll in toy stores. Never heard of him? Soon you might. The yellow-haired boy mascot of *Cracked* magazine is about to appear in a DVD and could show up in an animated TV series from DPS Film Roman. The Hollywood-based company produces *The Simpsons* and *King of the Hill*." Sadly, this television venture as with all attempted over the years with *Cracked* never saw the light.

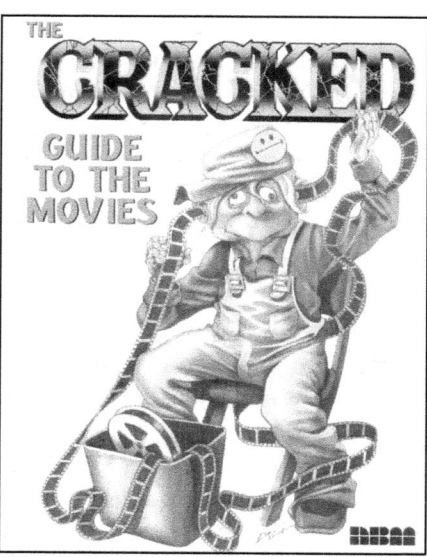

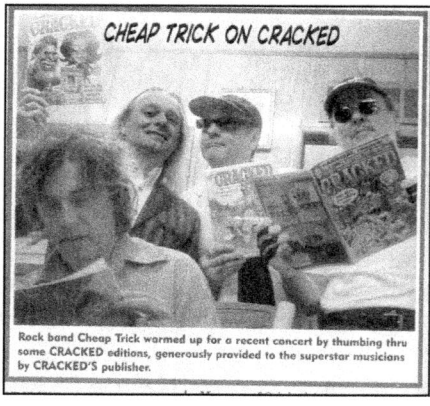

Cheap Trick photo from *Cracked* #363, July 2004.

Finally, after years of not trying, *Cracked* publishes its first oversized trade paperback called *The Cracked Guide to the Movies*, 2001.

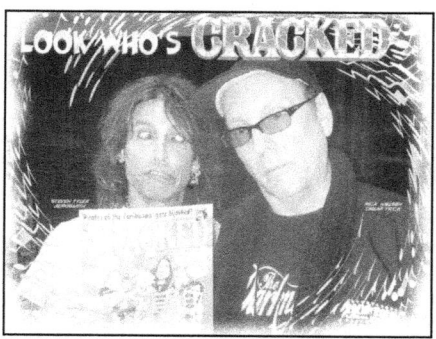

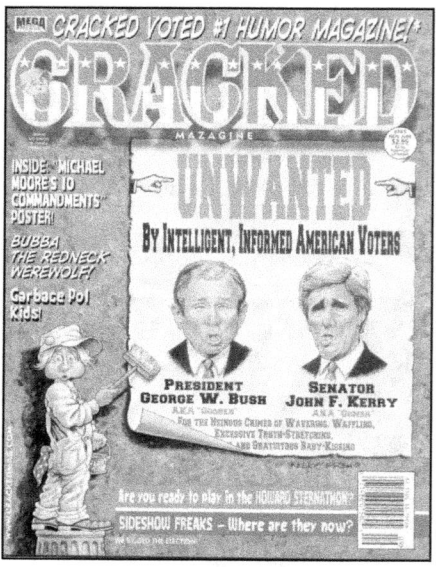

Steve Tyler and Rick Nielsen photo from *Cracked* #364, September 2004.

The very last issue of the original run, *Cracked* #365, November 2004, art by Frank Kelly Freas. Also, his very last cover.

SCOTT GOSAR'S PHOTO ALBUM

Images courtesy of Scott Gosar.

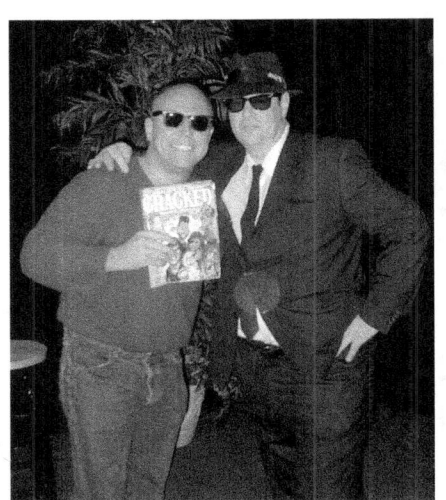

Dan Aykroyd with Scott Gosar.

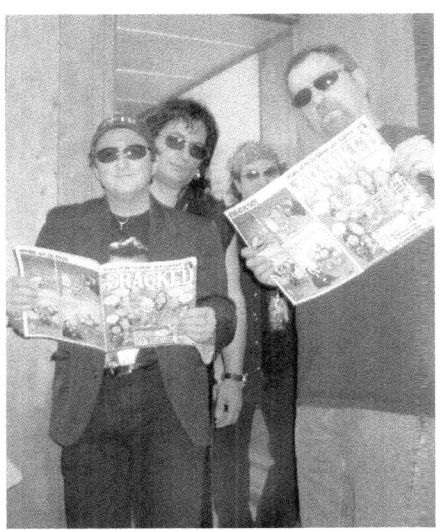

Blue Öyster Cult.

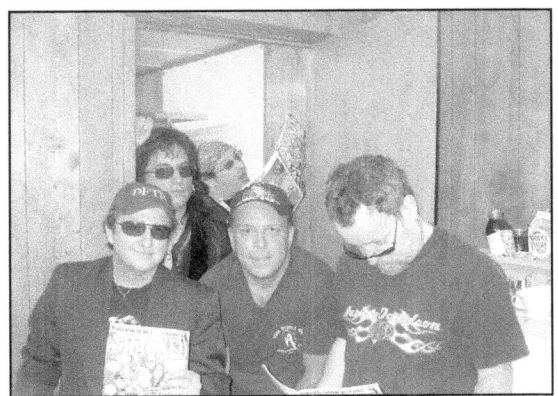

More Blue Öyster Cult.

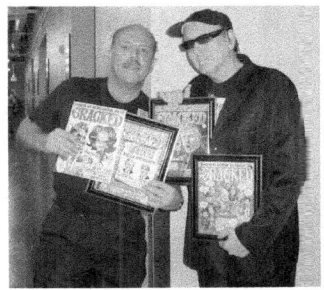

Scott Gosar with
Rick Nielsen.

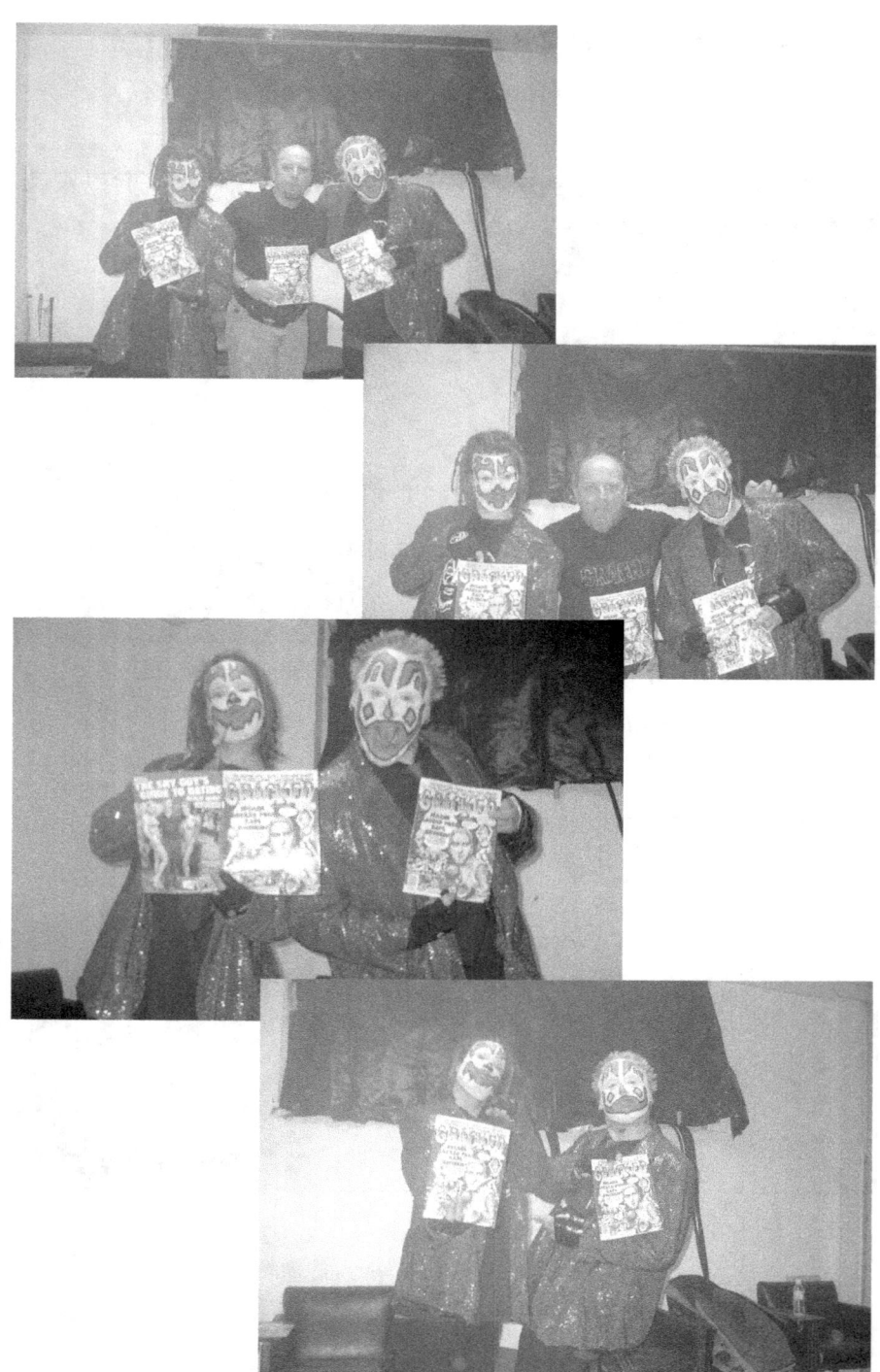

Insane Clown Posse with Scott Gosar.

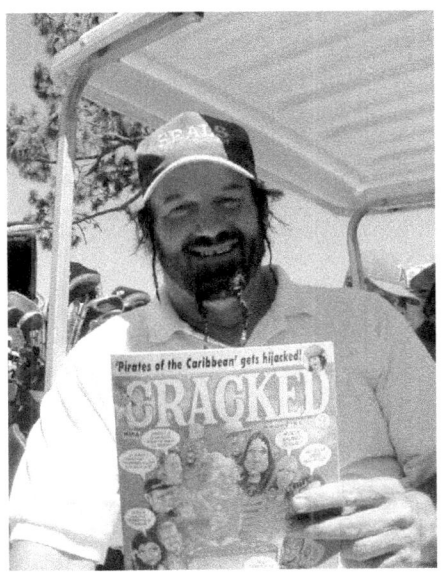

Jesse Ventura.

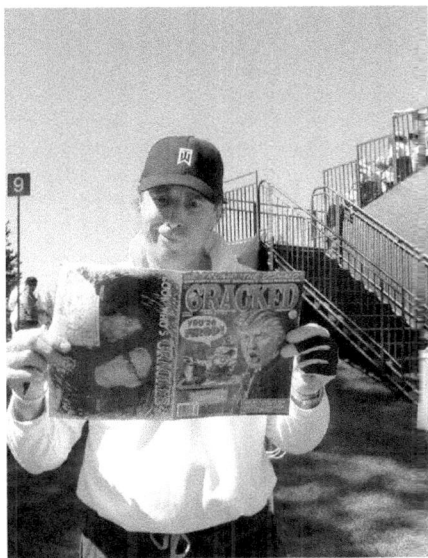

Kevin Nealon.

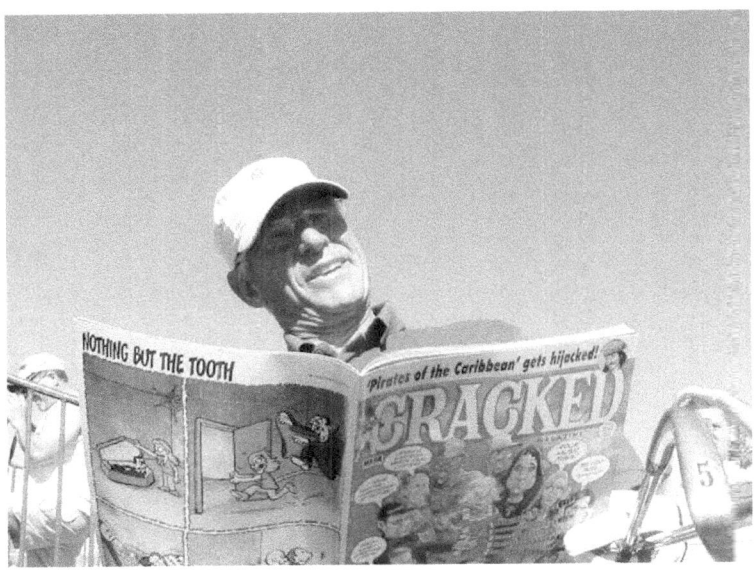

Maury Povich.

INTRODUCiNG MAXiM...
I MEAN, THE NEW
CRACKED

A press release introducing the "new" *Cracked* appeared on August 15, 2006 that read:

FOR IMMEDIATE RELEASE

***CRACKED* MAGAZINE RE-LAUNCHES**

48-year-old humor and parody magazine re-imagined; Hits
newsstands nationwide today

***

Comedian / Actor Michael Ian Black to serve as Editor-at-Large;

Magazine features writers from *The Daily Show*,
Saturday Night Live and *Chappelle's Show*

August 15, 2006 [New York, NY]—*Cracked* Magazine, the 48-year-old national publication, officially re-launches today as a general humor magazine for 18- to 34-year-olds. Popular actor/comedian Michael Ian Black (VH1's *I Love the ...* series; NBC's *Ed*) will serve as an Editor-at-Large.

The all-new *Cracked* leaves behind its illustrated past and debuts a new look, a new editorial direction and a roster of high-profile talent including author/satirist Neal Pollack and writers from such popular shows as *Saturday Night Live*, *The Daily Show* and *Chappelle's Show*.

Acquired in 2005 by entrepreneur Monty Sarhan, *Cracked* spent the last year-and-a-half on hiatus while undergoing a total re-design and "re-imagining" as a humor magazine for a new generation. The all-new *Cracked* features articles, parodies, magazine spoofs, pranks, recurring columns and a completely new section called *But Seriously...* with news, reviews and interviews covering the world of comedy.

The new *Cracked* has almost doubled in size—from 48 pages to 80 full-color pages on glossy paper. With a cover price of $3.99, the new *Cracked* will be available nationwide. It is being distributed by Curtis Circulation, the largest distributor of magazines in North America.

Sarhan, who serves as CEO and Editor-in-Chief, discussed the magazine's new look and its re-launch. "We're extremely happy to debut the all-new *Cracked*." And while the new *Cracked* is different than its previous incarnation in many ways, it is the same in one essential way: our mission continues to be parodying politics, pop culture and society. The way in which we go about fulfilling that mission is what is entirely new and different," said Sarhan. "The new *Cracked* is smart, relevant, sarcastic, clever and biting. Our goal is "intelligent irreverence," and we have evolved *Cracked* into a best-of-breed humor magazine."

"When *Cracked* was at its peak, it was relevant and funny. It held a mirror up to society and pop-culture. We are getting back to that mission, albeit in a fresh and interesting way, because the times we live in demand that kind of commentary and voice," adds Sarhan.

The first issue of the all-new *Cracked* features a spoof of ESPN's popular magazine, an article on celebrity idiots, a periodic table of the 80s and a variety of general humor pieces on pop culture, war and politics.

Along with the new *Cracked*'s humor section is coverage of headlines and headliners from the world of comedy—a section of news, reviews and interviews demonstrating the new *Cracked*'s commitment to be the *Rolling Stone* of comedy. The first issue also contains interviews with Rob Corddry and Ed Helms of *The Daily Show* and *South Park* creators Matt Stone and Trey Parker.

"In many ways, comedy is the new rock 'n' roll. It's the voice of a generation. We see comedians becoming respected political commentators, people getting their news from *The Daily Show* and publications like *Time*, *Newsweek* and *The New York Times* featuring more and more humor," said Sarhan. "All of these factors point to the need for a magazine covering comedy—and *Cracked* is that magazine."

Cracked fans have been getting a taste of the new editorial formula since Sarhan and his team re-launched their website, Cracked.com, late last year. The website features new content daily, including comics, videos, links, blogs and general humor pieces. In the eight months since its re-launch, Cracked.com has become one of the top destinations for original humor content on the Internet.

Cracked's new creative, editorial and business team includes experienced individuals from the publishing world from companies such as Universal Studios, Dennis Publishing, American Media, Marvel Entertainment, Wenner Media and National Lampoon. In addition to Sarhan, who serves as Editor-in-Chief and CEO, the new *Cracked* team includes Editors-At-Large Michael Ian Black and Neal Pollack, Chief Operating Officer Marc Liu, Publishing Director Larry Durocher, Jr., Editors Justin Droms, Jack O'Brien and Jay Pinkerton, and a business team that includes Darren Kane and Sebastian Nagy-Gyorgy.

About Cracked Entertainment, Inc.

Based in New York, *Cracked* Entertainment publishes *Cracked* magazine (www.Cracked.com), one of America's oldest and most well-known comedy magazines, both in print and online.

About *Cracked* Editor-at-Large, Michael Ian Black

Michael Ian Black is an actor, comedian, writer and director who is perhaps best known as the lead commentator on VH1's *I Love The* series and for his role as bowling alley manager Phil Stubbs for four years on NBC's hit comedy-drama *Ed*. He appears regularly to discuss current affairs on CNN. Black also co-founded two acclaimed sketch comedy groups (*The State* and *Stella*) both of which became the basis for television shows. In addition, he was a series regular on *You Wrote It, You Watch It*, and has guest starred on ABC's *NYPD Blue* and *Spin City*. He also executive produced, wrote and starred in the Comedy Central series *Viva Variety*. Most recently, Black wrote and directed the upcoming feature, *The Pleasure of Your Company*, starring Jason Biggs and Isla Fisher.

# # #

Then on March 2, 2007, the following press release appeared:

R.I.P. *Cracked* Magazine
By *Cracked* Staff March 2, 2007

Well, we gave it our best shot. That's right, folks: *Cracked* Magazine is, as of issue #3, no longer on newsstands. (Don't worry about the comedy going away, though. Cracked.com's alive and kicking, so keep on checking back.)

# # #

Barry Dutter comments, "Kulpa was very lucky to find a buyer for *Cracked* when he did, because I don't think that there were a lot of people offering. I don't know what they paid for it, but they got it and ran it for three issues. By the way, Jim Salicrup told me that he was instrumental in getting *Cracked* sold. I don't know if a lot of people know that, but Jim claims he played a huge part in making it happen.

"Yeah, they weren't really *Cracked* magazines. They had a few cartoons in there, but they didn't really have the content. I don't know why they bothered to acquire the rights to *Cracked* if they really weren't going to use any of it, other than the name of the magazine and the mascot. My time on *Cracked* was an interesting ride. It was a lot of fun. I'm proud of the good work we did and I'm ashamed and embarrassed of the bad work. It's very popular for people to bash the Kulpa *Cracked* and yes, there was some stuff in there that was as horrible as anything that has been done, but if you go back and look at the old *Cracked*, they're not that funny, most of them. I was a kid. I was eight years old and I would read *Cracked* and didn't think it was that funny, but there was something about it that I kind of liked. I just enjoyed it, but I never thought it was that funny."

Lou Silverstone recalls, "I don't know what happened to it after that. Some lawyer bought it last. He called me up one night and said he bought *Cracked*. He asked me if I would like to work and blah, blah, blah, but then I never heard from him again. The next thing I heard, he had hired a bunch of people from Marvel Comics to run the magazine. I don't know if they put one out or not. I don't know what *Cracked* is doing now. That is a sad ending. We worked hard to put out a good magazine and we were better than *Mad* at the end."

Murad Gumen comments, "The ambitious "Kuwaiti Korps" picked up the title from the cartoonist who somehow wound up with the rights, Dick Kulpa. I did meet with the Kuwait bunch, and their peculiar plan to go the "funny *Maxim*" route that must have fallen flat."

Paul Laikin adds, "You see that *Cracked* came out last year with those three issues? Incredible how they borrowed the name and you'd think that they'd take some of the tradition along. If they had come to me, maybe I would have contributed something."

Michelina Severin reflects: "So many people would call after John wasn't on *Cracked*, when it started to go downhill, and John wasn't on it. They had been fans for years, but now that John wasn't on it, they wouldn't read it. A lot people said they read it because of the covers by John. I know Kevin Eastman said that because John was on the cover, "I just went to the newsstand and John drew my turtles! He owns that cover. Like I said, there was a following that John had over there.

"They did ask me if John could modernize Sylvester for them and they kept talking to me about what they wanted, and I told them, "Maybe you could tell John to do Sylvester for them." And so John did do four drawings of Sylvester trying to get them what they wanted. These were full figures and I have the original art."

Mort Todd did briefly meet with the new *Cracked* owners: "I got in touch with the jokers at the new *Cracked* and actually worked as an Associate Editor for a couple of minutes. I sat down with the publisher and squeezed out of him that they paid about $5 million for it! Their immediate mission was to change the logo and change Sylvester, making him 'hipper' or something. So I'm saying, 'You paid $5 million for the magazine, you want to change the format, change the logo, change the character, you have no film to reprint anything?' and I told them, 'You realize that during the years I worked there, it's all creator-owned work, so you can't use any of that material without permission?' His face like hit the table. 'So what in hell did you buy for $5 million?' A lot of people were saying they probably would have done better doing a *Maxim*-type humor magazine without the *Cracked* name. Save their secret investors a couple million!

"They told me what they intended to do. For many years post-*Cracked* I had pitched a few publishers a different format humor magazine that would be part text and photos, so I'm open to change. As *Mad* evolved from a comic book to magazine, I felt it the time for the next level of humor mag was long due. They offered me an Associate Editor position, but it was kinda scammy. I would get paid based on stories I would bring in by other artists and writers, which was like 10% of the creators' rates. They were offering like $200 a page or something, less than a lot of artists were getting in the 80s. It was also work-for-hire. Despite reservations, I was thinking, "OK, let's try it out." I went to a couple meetings and saw what their direction was, their sense of humor and intended content, and it was like, "Uh-oh!" Wasn't my cup of hemlock. Since *MadKids* had just come out, they were thinking of doing reprints of the old stuff and calling it *Cracked Kids*. When you aim low to your audience, it's evident to readers and *Cracked Kids* would have been a lobotomy of the material. I thought it was really insulting to think like that about your audience. *The Comics Journal* called me about it and told them what I thought of the revamp. I remember Monty Sarhan, Publisher, got into a pissing war on the web about it, denying it was geared as a *Maxim* clone, and said, "Mort Todd is living in the past." Fortunately, the abomination only lasted three issues. It was abysmal and they thought they were so clever coming up with this the kind of junk we rejected offhand 20 years earlier."

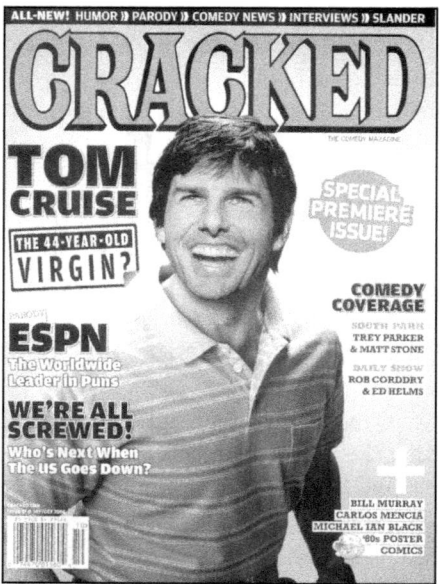

The cover of the new *Cracked* #01, September / October 2006, the first of the new format.

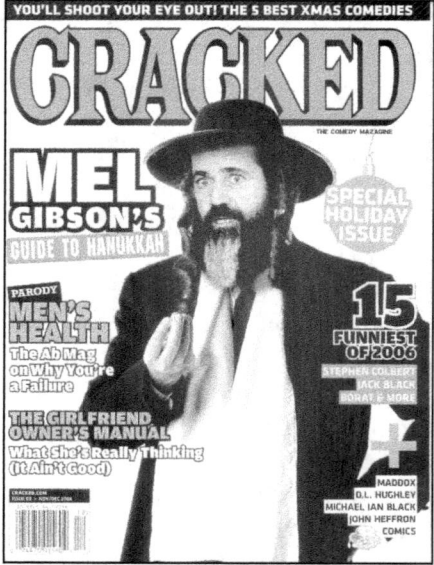

The cover of the new *Cracked* #02, November / December 2006.

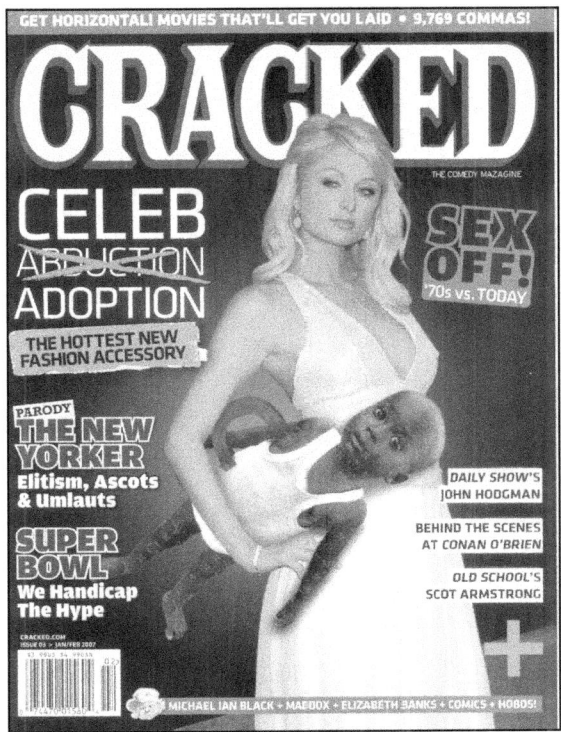

The cover of the new *Cracked* #03, January / February 2007, and the last one ever published to date.

John Severin contributed his final piece of artwork for *Cracked* in *Cracked* #03, January / February 2007.

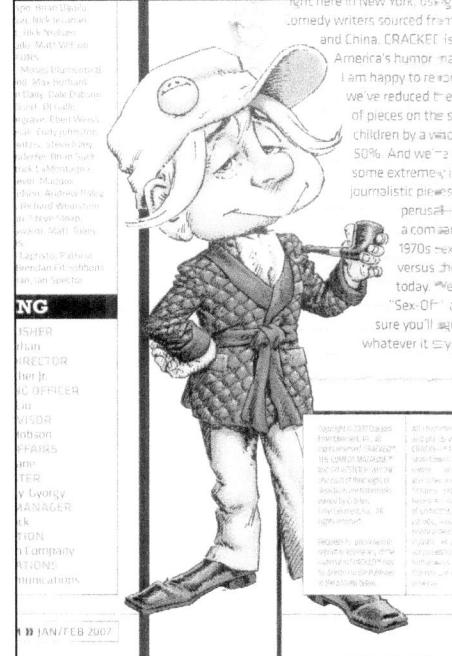

CRACKED.COM AND OTHER WEBSITES

CRACKED.com as a website had its origins with Todd Jackson back in 1994 (and even was called Crackedmag.com for a time), and then handled by Webmaster Mark Van Woert before Dick Kulpa's last issue. After *Cracked* ceased publication for good after its third *Maxim* issue, the current owners turned their attentions to beefing up the website as a major comedy rest stop on the web. This revised version made its online debut on October 1, 2006. Jack O'Brien is current Web Editor.

The website as it is today bears little resemblance to the former 1958-2004 publication, and even scant resemblance to the 2006-2007 version. It consists mainly of various "Top 10 Lists," though while funny, seem a bit belabored. A forum is also available for people to outright insult each other in their posts, and merchandise is sold, but all now bear the legend Cracked. com instead of just *Cracked*.

Dan O'Brien comments, "I'm the Assistant Editor here at Cracked. com. I'm interested in touching base with you and getting a little bit more information on this project."

Oren Katzeff adds, "I am the VP and GM of Cracked.com—I saw your forum post about the book you are planning on writing about the history of *Cracked*.

"As you can imagine, the brand is very important to us. We've spent the last few years really growing a passionate, dedicated online audience."

John Scrovak is a writer for the Cracked.com website: "Let me start off by saying John Scrovak is not my real name but rather, a pen name. I am a frequenter of the Cracked.com forums, and have two articles *Cracked* is set to publish within the coming months. I guess I would be described as a contributor. *Cracked* basically gave me the start I needed to begin writing humor online, and I am now published at three sites. If not for *Cracked*, I would not have been able to get in touch with the editor of *STDP7* or *The*

Deadbeat. Without either of those, I would not have gotten in contact with the editor of *Regretful Morning*."

No worries, men. This book focuses mainly on the extinct black-and-white print publication featuring artwork, and apart from a quick plug here for the website, there is really no connection between it and what I'm writing about.

During the writing of this book, Cracked.com made their first foray into print publishing with the book *You Might be a Zombie and other Bad News*, which borrows the idea from *National Lampoon's* old *True Facts* section. The book was issued at the tail end of 2010 and if proven successful, may pave the way for many more book collections.

One website not affiliated with *Cracked* or Cracked.com is http://www.satiregallery.com/cracked/index.html. Douglas Everett, who graciously helped out with some information needed from issues missing from my collection (mainly *For Monsters Only* and *Zany* issues) for the index in this book, has scanned and uploaded virtually every *Cracked* publication ever produced. Missing are the *Cracked Stocking Stuffer*, *The Cracked Guide to the Movies* and the three *Maxim Crackeds*.

Dan Budnik writes a blog about *Cracked* where he reviews various printed issues from the past. He comments, "I write the *Cracked* magazine review blog under the assumed name of "Pierre L." (The name of a guy I work with who would never read *Cracked*.) I will be first in line for the *Cracked* book. Although I enjoy the mystery behind "Where the heck did this come from?," I would like to know more about the magic that is *Cracked*.

"I have a small collection of *Cracked* magazines, from #108-212. I am slowly working back towards #1. I stopped at #212 because that is where, I believe, Mr. Sproul left the editorship of the magazine to others. So, it's a nice spot to stop. I have a few of the Specials and such but my main focus is on the regular issues. I do have the *Fonz for President Collectors' Edition* (I am not a nerd) and some monster stuff but how can anyone resists those? Whereas *Mad* always seemed to grab the more political and more adult stuff, I prefer the light-hearted charm of the pop culture threads that *Cracked* grabs on to.

"I just posted the review of Issue #161: Mork and Gary Coleman! Get outta here. And, on the upcoming #162, one of the rare non-Severin covers. I think the cover with hundreds of little Fonzies coming out of a UFO is possibly my favorite (#153)."

Budnik's blog can be found at http://crackedreviews.blogspot.com/.

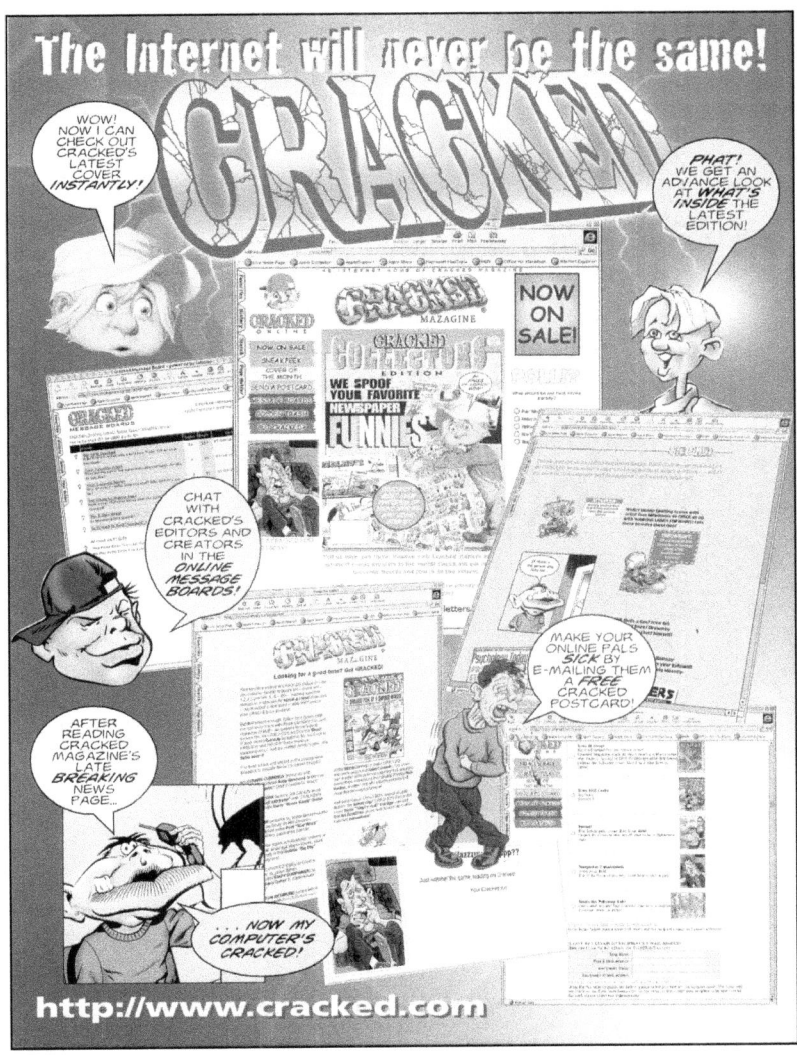

Cracked.com is all that's left, a website that got its start during the print run in 1994. Here is an ad for the site from *Cracked* #349, November 2000.

IS THERE A FUTURE FOR CRACKED? OR HUMOR MAGAZINES IN GENERAL...

HUMOR magazines traditionally have not had dramatically long lifetimes anyway, but in today's "instant gratification" market of Internet postings, the actual "need" for humor magazines has probably past.

Lou Silverstone comments on the fabled *Mad* voodoo doll, supposedly emblazed with pins of all the different competitors and by the end of it, there was only a pin for *Cracked*: "I know he had the voodoo doll, but I don't know if he did that. It was the *Mad* voodoo doll that they had in one of the specials."

Silverstone adds, "That's why Bill Gaines was successful. It was the writer's magazine. Hollywood followed suit, you can have all the actors and directors, but it all starts with the writing."

Frank Jacobs cleared the air about the *Mad* voodoo doll, in page 198 in his book, *The Mad World of William M. Gaines*: "Actually, it's hard putting out an imitation of *Mad*, even when it is not intended as a parody. About two dozen publishers have tried, most of them during *Mad*'s first decade. Their attempts were called *Frenzy, Loco, Crazy, Goofy*—names like that. One fast-moving publisher even put out a couple of issues of a humor magazine called *Panic*, having picked up the title after Gaines discarded it. Most of the imitations featured an Alfred E. Neuman-like character on the cover and borrowed liberally from *Mad*'s format and premises.

"Only two remain (though not mentioned in Jacobs' book by name, these were *Cracked* and *Sick* by 1972). The rest died painlessly at an early age. Gaines likes to feel he helped speed them on their way by means of a ceremony held in his office. He would print the name of each new competitor on a small slip of paper, then take a wooden darning needle and stick the paper into a voodoo doll that he got in Haiti. It is probably the only religious rite he ever observed."

Cracked was most certainly aware of this doll as the cover of #107 indicates. On it, Sylvester is pushing a pin into a voodoo doll that casts a shadow that looks remarkably like the silhouette of Alfred E. Neuman!

This wasn't Neuman's only cover appearance on *Cracked*. In fact it was one of many. All told, Alfred E. Neuman appeared on the cover of *Cracked* six times, on issues #99, 107, 177, 200, 202 and 341, and eight times in articles in issues #13, 21, 131, 141, 239, 249, 255 and 349.

Cracked wasn't immune from directly ripping off articles from *Mad*. Notable examples include:

Severin doing Don Martin in *Cracked* #27 and Don Orehek doing Don Martin in *Cracked* #202.

Cracked's "65-Man Klonkball" as a rip-off of *Mad*'s "43-Man Squamish."

"Television Roulette" and "Celebrity Wallets," both of which had been done in *Mad*, were both later in *Cracked*.

"*Cracked*'s Snappy Comebacks" ripping off Jaffee's "Snappy Answers to Stupid Questions."

Bill Ward's "*Cracked* Looks at Dating" which looks more than suspiciously like something Dave Berg would have done and Severin doing Berg in *Cracked* #202.

Even *Crazy* wasn't immune from *Cracked*'s copying ways. "Realistic Toys" in *Cracked* was originally done as the "Realistic Toy Catalog" in *Crazy* and the cover of *Cracked* #214 is cribbed from *Crazy* #41.

In one case, however, *Mad* ripped off *Cracked* when their cover of #69 ripped off the cover of *Cracked* #15, and *Mad* #155 was uncannily like *Cracked* #104, but both were ripping off *The Godfather* movie poster, so it was just a matter of who got to the stands first. A more recent example was with *Harry Potter*.

In fact, *Cracked* #202 may go down as the most *Mad* rip-offs to appear in one issue with Neuman on the cover and Severin and Orehek doing Dave Berg and Don Martin, respectively on the interior!

Mad is still going after 59 years, but is now limping along on a quarterly basis, though recently, thanks to an animated series on Cartoon Network, upped their frequency to six times a year. After being monthly for over a decade, *Mad* is the sole magazine issued; the other spin-offs canceled. Virtually all the classic "Usual Gang of Idiots" are now dead or retired save for Al Jaffee (who now just contributes his *Fold-In*) and Sergio Aragonés.

Mort Todd recently contacted *Mad* to offer some common sens≥ suggestions. "You heard *Mad* went quarterly, right? I wrote to Paul Levitz, th≥ publisher, because in comics, going quarterly is a death knell for a title. So, I sent him a real brief outline that we should hook up and I'd spill some ideas on how to cut overhead immediately (I mean, seven friggin' editors, really? and improve quality of content. I said I wasn't even interested in them hiring me; I just wanted to share thoughts from my experience. I got a one-line reply about a week later saying, 'We have no interest in talking to you.' And about seven years ago, I heard *Mad* was looking for an associate editor. I called John Ficarra and he hung up on me! I guess they were still angry that I dared compete with them. This thin-skinned attitude doesn't exist in man⸴ other industries that are concerned with making money.

"Now would be a great time to start a humor magazine. While I was at Marvel, we talked about re-launching *Crazy* but I was too busy to take action. And sure, I've done pitches for some publishers over the years, and printec up some dummy issues of a title called *Vex*. One thing I admired about *Mad*, the title was only three letters and brevity is the spice of life."

Cracked continues on as a website and although the possibility c⸗ another printed publication of any sort be it a book or special magazine has been bandied about since the 2007 end of the *Maxim Cracked*, the likelihooc is pretty limited since the films of the *Cracked* back issues were destroyed in 2001.

National Lampoon also continues on as a website, and occasionall⸴ appears on the covers of some trade paperbacks, CDs and movies, but th≥ name doesn't have the same meaning or impact as it once did. An actual magazine has not appeared since 1998, and legally, they can no longer publish a magazine after a renegotiated contract with *Harvard Lampoon*.

Harvard Lampoon continues on as the longest-running American humor magazine. Normally, such magazines would not be lumped in with the res⸗ except for the fact that *HL* has had regular national newsstand distribution with its various parody issues. Their *National Geographic* parody was their most recent example.

Crazy ran from 1973-1983. Post-*Crazy*, there was a one-shot featuring *Obnoxio the Clown vs. The X-Men* and Bob Foster compiled his *History cf Moosekind* into a book. Marvel Comics occasionally dabbles with variou⸱ humor books, usually parodying their superhero characters in a *Not Bran⅃ Echh* style. *What Th'* was a fairly long-running example and *Strange Tales* is the most recent example. A revival of *Crazy* in any form has yet to materialize, though one wishes for an archival edition.

Crazy did acknowledge the existence of *Cracked* with the *Cracked* log⊃ appearing on the cover of *Crazy* #1, and the inclusion of Sylvester P. Smythe in "The Nebbish" stories that appeared in *Crazy* #9-11. (As an aside, Smythe also appeared on the cover of *Thwak* #4 and *Wacko* #1 and in an issue of *LCD*, with Smythe getting reamed by Neuman.)

Sick ran from 1960-1980, with issues from the 1960s being the best period, with humor that truly rivaled *Mad*. Joe Simon still owns the rights even through the disastrous Charlton years from 1976-1980. Simon will license out Huckleberry Fink, but who would care?

Scholastic's *Bananas* magazine ran from 1975-1984, but with heavy emphasis on celebrity material, it is only a pseudo-*Mad* rip-off, though it contained many TV and movie parodies drawn by Sam Viviano and Samuel B. Whitehead. *Hustler Humor* is also only pseudo-*Mad*-like with its heavy reliance on dirty sexual humor.

Next on the totem pole as far as tenure was Harvey Kurtzman's *Help!* which ran from 1960-1965. Everything else is not worth mentioning or even remembered in most cases except for the hardest core collectors, as each title only lasted a handful of issues or sometimes a single issue.

Many artists and writers accustomed to this type of work have no other recourse than to try working for *Mad* or retiring to other ventures. Don Orehek recalls his reluctance to work for *Mad*: "No, I never did. I figured they wouldn't want me anyway, because I worked for *Cracked*. Recently, I sent them a thing to see if they were interested, but they never got back to me."

Kent Gamble tells of his many attempts to get into *Mad*: "I went up there. I called and made an appointment. I don't know who was on the phone, but I said, 'Hi, I'm Kent Gamble.' Like they're going to say, 'Oh, my God!' And they went, 'Yeah?' And I said, 'Well, I'm in town, I'm from Texas, and I'm going to be here for a few days. I really would like to show you my portfolio.' 'We're not looking for art!' 'Oh. I'd really like to show you my portfolio.' So, one day I put on my suit again and got my portfolio and I went to 485 Madison Avenue and they were on the 13th floor, of course. I started out and I waited in this tiny waiting room. This trip when we went it was colder than hell in January. I was in this little tiny waiting room and of course, they had the Christmas tree up year round. I didn't realize that. It was close enough to Christmas and I figured that they hadn't taken it down yet. It was there all the time. Anyway, Nick Meglin comes out and I'm, 'Hi. I'm Kent Gamble,' and he goes, 'hi.' He looks and me and says, 'Put your portfolio down. Have you been mugged yet?' 'No sir, not yet.' 'Ah, you will be.' 'Let me take you on a tour of the office.' So he kind of took me around. I was just kind of terrified, but it was just great. That was when all the original cover artwork was on the wall and lined the hallway. It was kind of messy, but it looked just like the way you'd expect *Mad* to look. We finally got all through and he took me in to see John Putnam, the art director at that point. Here's Nick Meglin and John Putnam looking at my stuff and they just went, 'Wow!' And I thought, 'Wow, I'm in.' And Meglin looks up and says, 'We have tons of Don Martin impersonators, we have tons of Jack Davis impersonators. We don't get many Mort Drucker impersonators.' And I asked, 'Well, is that good?' And they said, 'No, we've got him! What the hell would we want you for?' 'Oh, ok.' I mean, I was just a novelty. I was just the novelty of the day. They just laughed and listened. He and Putnam never had so much fun. I remember Meglin would go to the door, look up and down the hall and say, 'We don't want Gaines to see this.' I don't know why not. Anyway, they never had so much fun looking at my stuff. So finally they said, 'Well, we've got Mort and you need to kind of develop your own style.' I heard that about 10 billion times. So I said, 'Well ok, I'll work on it.' Of course, they figured that I would go and talk to Marvel and whoever else was publishing, but it really was fun.

Eventually, Gamble did get in *Mad*. Says Gamble, "I did a two-pager for Australian *Mad*, and that was via John Hett. His connections with the guy that edits or something and so I did a two-pager for Australian *Mad*. In my book, that counts as being in *Mad*."

Barry Dutter describes his attempts to get into *Mad*, after leaving *Cracked*: "*Mad* always had a policy that if you worked for *Cracked*, they didn't really want you. Ok yeah, there are exceptions. If don't know if Kulpa ever told you the story of Tom Richmond. Tom Richmond is a very talented artist and a great guy and he was trying to get into *Mad* for years. They always said, 'Well, we've already got Mort Drucker, what do we need you for because you draw kind of like Mort Drucker.' So we hired Tom Richmond and as soon as we hired him for *Cracked* and made him our star movie parody guy, suddenly he was good enough to work for *Mad*. At that point, I think Drucker was getting ready to retire and then *Mad* actually needed a new guy to come in. They stole him away from us. Tom was a great guy and it's every artist's dream to work for *Mad* instead of *Cracked*, so he left us and Kulpa felt betrayed. Everybody else kind of understood that that's what any other artist would have done. At the end of the day, it's just business. *Mad* is very willing to make exceptions if you are an exceptional talent. In my case, I did some freelance writing for *Mad* in the mid-1990s, around the same time I was doing some freelance writing for *Cracked*. Because of that, *Mad* requested that I not use my real name in their mag. They said, 'Look, if you're still writing for *Cracked*, we can't have the same writer's names appearing in both magazines. It makes *Mad* look bad. Why would people want to buy *Mad*, when they can get the same stuff in *Cracked*?' I used the name Larry Sutter in *Mad*. I wrote two or three pieces for them. It was the thrill of a lifetime. Then, from the day I was hired on staff at *Cracked*, *Mad* never wanted to speak with me again. I was so naïve; I would submit stuff to *Mad* while I was editor of *Cracked*. I'd be like, 'I'll save the really good stuff for *Mad*!' Well, then if *Mad* rejected it, I'd say, 'Well, let's stick it in *Cracked*.' Yeah, there was a period that I used to submit stuff to *Mad* all the time. They, basically, had no use for me anymore. At this point, there's no work for me at *Mad* as long as the current editorial staff is there.

"The Kulpa era of *Cracked* was much maligned. It was a tumultuous time. In the beginning it started off with the best of intentions, then you could say it quickly fell apart once AMI canceled the magazine a couple of times, and then Kulpa tried to continue with little or no funding. It was kind of doomed. Once it left New York, it was kind of doomed from the start. We gave it a good try."

Brian Buniak gives his observations about the demise of the black and white humor magazine: "Even if you get one of those things online that has absolutely everything that *Mad* ever did, all collected together. It is as brilliant now as when it first came out but there is no way that you could put yourself back in that time period when it came out on an almost monthly basis. What more could you do with a movie. How they'd do it and they knew where it was going and after a while. I later would put *Mad* down for how they'd correct everything. This is our world and there has never been anything like that, except for about 5-10 other movies that did the very same thing. And then the next thing you'd do is say, 'I never saw that coming.' That was how *Mad* was all about. This really is different because blah, blah, blah. There would be something about it that would make you want to read the book.

"Another parallel about *Mad* that made some sense too is that with *Mad* now on television probably is the variety show with Red Skelton. Every week there would be similar type fare like there's the juggler, there's the singer and things like that. It was a very popular medium. If you look at it that way with *Mad*, it was like a variety show. It would have the same things that they would specifically do like a variety show and variety shows have disappeared. They are virtually impossible to find, except maybe *Saturday Night Live*, and that's not exactly the way they did that type of show. I think that there's part of that with that too in that variety shows take on things and then *Mad* comes along and finally comes along.

"You're right there, but others could have taken chances that *Mad* couldn't. There was something that they could break away from. *National Lampoon* is an example that they could go different ways on their parodies than *Mad*. For them to do that, it was I guess the best. I can tell you the exact day in which *National Lampoon* became irrelevant, that was the day that Richard Nixon resigned. The second he was gone, they still had 99% of what they worked towards was gone. It made that magazine a weapon formed against him. Once that was gone, it was the same type of humor again.

"One of the weirdest things I saw was during the Clinton administration. I wasn't buying *Mad* with any regularity for years, but there was something where I wanted to see the *Mad* parody of it. I picked it up and looked through it as they stated that politics and entertainment are intertwined. They were making a joke, but it was hard to tell where the parody ended and the reality began. With the recent administration of George W. Bush, Hollywood did most of it. That was where the supposed reputation that they had with this administration."

The thing that I found appalling and it doesn't mean that we need to poke humor at this, but shortly after 9/11, *Mad* put in an editorial stating that they weren't going to do humor about the 9/11 tragedy, and they could just not do it, but don't tell us that you're not going to do it. *Mad* has never been known for good taste. It was suddenly, 'We're not going to make fun of the President anymore. We're not going to make fun of 9/11 anymore,' so what's the point of *Mad*? My point is, *Mad* never put an editorial during the Vietnam War saying, 'We're not going to make fun of the Vietnam War.' They did, but they never did a serious editorial one way or another. That was the death knell of *Mad* to make a serious editorial in that way. It kind of shows a weakness of some sort. Like I said, they could have made fun of 9/11 but it seemed very odd to me that they didn't.

Buniak continues, "I can understand back then. Today, I would say to comment about 9/11 that I'm sure they could do it, but it is kind of odd to come out and say that we won't do that.

"Humor is changing as what's considered acceptable now that never was before. It's what is acceptable and it's not just in the mood of what was really out there. They feel that not only do that have to do it, but also to top what's been done. I'm not sure after this point what will follow that. I'm not going to bother with that.

"I probably technologically hear anything remotely like that unless they are an Amish Ludite. I would say the humor is going be on the Internet. I don't know if you can make money with it. I don't know how you can make money with it. Why pay for what you can get for free, so why pay for it unless it is collected together and sold in collections. If you see your work and like it or you can take out an old one. People love it in a collection. You have your own group of people who go in there and love your work. It's crazy; you don't have anyone standing over you making a comic book or something. I don't know how if you had that goal, but before that nobody knew how you could fit that in.

"I tell my students that to read through the papers and see if there is a way to do a strip and not do a strip like your dying, so to try to do that with so little papers left. The ones that are there and have been there forever. If you're competing with a graveyard and the graveyard has the advantage that would be the time to start looking.

"The problem with the Internet is that it is killing a lot of tactile work."

Kevin Sacco adds, "In the old days, DC Comics was two blocks from Marvel Comics. Everything was right there and you used to be able to go, make an appointment and show your portfolio. Sometimes you'd walk out with work under your arm. Today, I don't know if you could find anyone to show your work."

Lou Silverstone gives his thoughts as to why magazines like *Mad* are fading away: "Both have lost their talents. We're all getting old. They had a great staff. Where are you going to find another Mort Drucker or Jack Davis or Jaffee or any of those guys? They can't be replaced and they had a good writing staff, too."

Mike Ricigliano laments the end of *Cracked*: "I miss drawing for it and writing for it. I enjoy doing my sports cartoons for newspapers and enjoyed doing the greeting cards and my audience is a little bit more adult audience so I enjoy that too, but *Cracked* I always liked because I was free and had a huge palette and have three pages worth of stuff to do so it opened up a lot of stuff to do. I could do a lot more stuff with *Cracked* even with the restrictions of drawing to a younger audience it has built in. I could still have a freer mind, I could do crazier stuff in *Cracked* than I can do sometimes with the sports stuff I do in the newspaper. I did crazy stuff at the greeting card company too, and that was a very fun place to work. I miss that and I guess I miss being on the stands. I definitely have a place in my heart for *Cracked* magazine and the people who worked there."

As far as Ricigliano going to *Mad*, he replied, "One time I approached one of the editors about it and his take on it was that we've got guys like that and it wasn't a very pleasant exchange and they were struggling at the time too and that was what he was trying to tell me on the phone. Unless you can give me something that hasn't been done or something new, I probably can't use you. I understood what he was talking about. Nick Meglin was the guy and I was kind of turned off by the conversation, so I never pursued it.

"I don't know if I had I pursued it, if I'm a good enough artist for *Mad*. I wouldn't have made it at all in this field if I couldn't write. I'm an artist/writer and that's where I kind of fit in, both in the magazines and in the newspapers. If I didn't have my writing skills, I'd probably develop my skills and *Cracked* helped me develop my skills, too. When I got my job at American Greetings, the fact that I worked at *Cracked* for a year as an editor helped me get the job, so they figured I was a specialist in humor working for *Cracked*.

"I read them both, but I preferred *Mad* by far. My thinking was that *Mad* already had their staff of artists and I can make *Cracked* better. I could write funnier and draw funnier and think funnier, therefore this would be a good place to go, but sometimes it doesn't flow that way. The thinking at the top is what the thinking at the top is. I kind of had to see more like a *Cracked* guy, than a *Mad* guy, so to speak. My thinking was more for *Mad* magazine. That's how I grew up."

Bruce Bolinger misses *Cracked*: "I do because the staff was fun to work with and the assignments were always interesting, always different each month. I appreciated their leadership and they appreciated my effort. I always looked forward to my phone calls with Andy Simmons because Andy kept me laughing. Andy is a bright, clever humorist and he went on to be the Senior Humor Editor for *Reader's Digest*. I also miss the free copies they sent each month…

"I'm old enough to have come in at the beginning of both humor magazines...back in the early fifties. I was raised on that humor from as far back as I remember. To me both magazines were the same—FUNNY—even though *Cracked* was always considered a poor cousin to *Mad*. I suppose that's because it came to life secondly. When you look back over magazine history there have been a couple hundred humor magazines born and dead but *Cracked* lasted about 50 years. So, yes, I was always a fan and I had a pile of *Mad* and *Cracked* that was waist deep."

Frank Cummings adds his comments on missing *Cracked*, "I do. I was much younger then."

Noel Anderson also misses *Cracked*: "I really miss *Cracked*. There just aren't any humor mags like that any more. Yes, read it for many years. Mainly during grade school in the late '70s...y'know, when all of the jokes were about *Star Wars*, Mork from Ork, *Jaws* and Fonzie!"

Roger Brown says, "I do miss writing for *Cracked* and the cast of artists and writers I got to work with every month. It was a very funny magazine and had good clean fun you could show your friends and share a laugh. I am saddened by some of what is called humor today that is vulgar and crude. I would love to see the magazine back in print."

And Alan Kupperberg agrees, "Yes, I surely do. Any time you are in the same publication as the awesomely talented John P. Severin, you are in good company."

Rick Altergott misses *Cracked*: "I think it's sad that *Cracked* is gone and that *Mad* seems heading for extinction. With a cover price of six dollars, I can't imagine anyone buying it, regularly. Someone really screwed it up with *Mad*. They don't seem to be able to put out an issue that has any current features, anymore. Mort was faced with the necessity of using all inventory for an issue once; and he had a bit of fun with it in the masthead calling that issue, 'An Inventory of Laffs.'

"I wish a new magazine would come out that featured the TV and movie stuff. I think it would be popular. I'd love to work on something like that."

Dan Fiorella comments: "I do miss *Cracked*. The income was very helpful at that time... No, really, Andy gave me a bunch of *Cracked* merchandise once, a couple of t-shirts, Frisbees and such. I keep them stored away. I have all my magazines tucked away, some pages in my scrapbook. I probably need to put that stuff in fancy comic-book protectors.

"I really wasn't a fan of *Cracked* before I worked there. I didn't read *Mad* regularly, either. I was a child of TV and movies and wasn't much of a reader until later in my teens. Then went right into *National Lampoon*."

Bill Sproul reminisced about what's left in his *Cracked* collection, "I don't have any old merchandise. If you look at the ad for *Cracked* Reporter T-Shirts,'79, '80 or '81, the kid in the reporter that was me at about 16-years-old. That damn picture was in every mag for about two years. It was my own fault for not rewriting the ad.

"We worked with some guy on a radio show once. It was pretty funny and well written but I don't think it was ever broadcast regularly. We did license our material to a German outfit who published *Kaputt*, the German *Cracked*. We also did a Portuguese version that sold in South America, but I can't recall the name of it. I have 10 copies of almost every magazine and there may be more. I also have a few John Severin original covers; both the *Star Wars* bar scene and the desert scene that were also double-sized posters. I have the 'I Like Mike' Michael Jackson cover art. And a few old favorites my dad had framed for me."

And Dave Berns says, "Yes, very much so. I miss having that outlet, and working with so many great artists. It was a lot of fun and very exciting, if frustrating. Unfortunately, it was not run as a business, despite its GREAT potential to be a linchpin of a successful one.

"The work Barry and I later did on *Gag!* magazine was just as much fun, it just didn't have that built in cache of an established name, so it was considerably harder to promote. Maybe another humor magazine is in my future, who knows? With the state of the world being as crappy as it is, given the economy, police state and war, I know I could use a good laugh now more than ever, as a creator or a reader!"

Steve Strangio laments the death of *Cracked*: "Hell yeah. Being a contributing writer for *Cracked* made me damn proud. One of the things that I always corrected people on was the "You guys are just a rip-off of *Mad* comments. Here's how I look at it. There are a lot of genres and/or styles of entertainment out there. You have talk shows on all of the networks basically doing the same format, but bringing their own style to it. You also have that with radio stations and their morning shows, newspapers with their differing editorial policies and yes … magazines. How many different types of magazines are there out there? Each one has its own style. You have gossip mags, sports mags, car mags, and the list goes on.

"*Cracked* was a humor mag. One of many. *Mad* was first and that's a given. *Cracked* was then created and developed its own style over time. I'm still damn proud that I was a part of it. I still get a kick out of seeing someone holding a *Cracked* magazine in a television show, movie, or even a cartoon."

Andy Lamberti misses *Cracked*: "Do I miss *Cracked*? Of course. It was part of my life from the time I was 12 until the 1990s. At that time, I had to quit writing altogether to take care of my wife. She had cancer and died in 2007. Now I'm retired and every so often find solace by flipping through those old *Cracked*'s in my collection. Ok, I'm 62, but sometimes you're still a kid of 12, right?

"My favorite articles for *Cracked*? *The Cracked List*: 'Signs Your Folks Hate Your Guts' in the October 1997 issue. Batman is on the cover. The piece is on the last page of the issue. The artist, Mike Ricigliano, was kind enough to give me the large original artwork which I have hanging in my office.

"My second favorite article is in the issue #352 (*Survivor* cover). Its called '*Cracked* Gross-Outs' on page 30."

Gary Fields misses *Cracked*, too: "I have very good memories of working for *Cracked*. It was early in my career, Michael, Lou and Andy were all great guys to work for and have lunch with. I tried to make it a social thing as well as a business thing. I'd always go in and drop work off, have lunch and try and leave with my next job. I really enjoyed all the work for Michael, Andy and Lou. Later on when things were going downhill, some of the stuff I was doing was not so great.

"I definitely miss *Cracked*! Especially after writing about my time there for this book. It's a shame that there aren't more humor magazines, besides *Mad*. I think I read more *Mad* magazines as a kid. Maybe the *Cracked* issues were harder to get? I don't know."

And, Warren Sattler comments, "Well you know Kurtzman created *Mad* and I feel that *Cracked* did a better job than *Panic*, which was the second one from EC, as a take-off of *Mad*, but I think *Cracked* was a good competition."

B.K. Taylor offers his insights: "It's a shame that so few humor magazines still exist today. *Mad* is now only quarterly...then there is *The Onion*, and a few college humor magazines, like the *Harvard Lampoon* and *Stanford Chaparral*. Actually I just recently did a cover for Cornell University's anniversary anthology of the *Cornell Lunatic*. I love college humor...the ideas are fresh and the editors aren't afraid to explore and take risks."

Kit Lively offers these observations: "Yeah, I really do miss *Cracked*. I was a fan long before I was a contributor, so as someone who simply enjoyed the magazine, it would be nice to still have it around. Plus, the assurance of a regular, paying gig is always a plus.

"*Cracked* was as good as the best places that I've worked for; in fact, I would count them as one of the best places. There doesn't seem to be a lot of grey area when it comes to working for magazines (and, in some instances, book publishers). Either you find yourself involved with great, approachable people (like *Cracked*, *Mad* and *Hustler*), or you're dealing with people who print your work without telling or paying you. During my initial run of 1997-2000, *Cracked* was one of my favorite places to work. They had a genuine appreciation for their contributors. Fortunately, I've found similar environments at *Mad*, *National Lampoon* and *Hustler*.

"I've loved humor and satire from about the age of seven, when I saw my first copies of *Cracked*, *Mad* and *Crazy*. From then on, I had a passion for any and all humor magazines, as well as humor in any avenue or medium, from records to television to movies. Published humor was always my favorite, and even though a lot of the humor magazines that were so funny to me when I was a kid haven't aged too well, a surprising number of them have. I can still pull out an issue of *Cracked*, *Mad*, *Crazy* or *National Lampoon* from many years ago and find quite a few laugh out loud bits. I can only hope my own stuff will age as well (although it probably already hasn't)."

Asked whether he misses *Cracked*, Peter Bagge said, "No, though its current online version occasionally has some very funny stuff on it. As a kid I just thought of *Cracked* as a lesser *Mad*, and as I got older and got into underground comics I had no use for *Mad* or *Cracked*. I thought some of the work in *Cracked* was fine though, while I was working for them. I especially liked a lot of the artists: Severin, Clowes, Martin, Fingerman etc. I also liked how all the covers during Mort's tenure routinely showed a bunch of celebrities beating the crap out of each other!"

Bagge comments as to whether *Cracked* or *Mad* was his first choice for humor magazines: "Are you kidding? Was *Cracked* anyone's first choice? For me it's a very similar experience: they contacted me first, and on occasion they ask me to do something for them and I do it. All very clean and simple, with no arguments of heavy-handedness on either end. The only difference is that *Mad* has only asked me to draw, and never write for them. Go figure!"

Ray Billingsley had this to say: ""I do miss *Crazy* and *Cracked*, as well as a number of other great magazines. These young artists today don't know of the truly creative-era they missed. I was a fan of *Cracked*. I was a fan of every humor publication there was at the time. Everything was so visual, so bright, and so creative. They pushed boundaries of society. No one does that anymore. They don't question the status quo. It's way too tame these days."

Tom Richmond offers this assessment, "I don't miss it, but I do not regret my time there, either. I wouldn't classify myself as a 'fan,' but I did read the occasional issue and liked much of the content and art. I certainly knew about the magazine and some of the artists working in it."

Pete Fitzgerald offers his comments on *Cracked*: "I miss the pre-Kulpa/American Media era. Especially my brief time with Mike Delle-Femine and Cliff Mott running things, which were a lot of fun. They seemed to be going for a general satire/humor approach, safe enough for the majority-kid readership, but not aimed 100% at that audience. Plus, they threw some parties that got some cartooning hermits like myself out and among others of my deranged kind.

"The Silverstone / Simmons / Mott years were pretty damn good, too. Content-wise, it was somewhat more kid-oriented, so some of the material got repetitive, lots of school bus chaos gags and lunch-lady gags—probably sales/subscriptions/demographics indicated that was the way things should go, at that point. But it was still fun to draw, and they were good people to work for.

"I was more of a *Mad* fan, though as a kid I'd sometimes get an issue of *Cracked* in my Christmas stocking, or when I was sick in bed. I liked it well enough. Lots of great John Severin work, plus Howard Nostrand and Warren Sattler—who I later heard lived down the road from me in the same town,

Brookfield, CT, but I never got to meet him. The film geek in me loved the joke-captioned photos from old movies… there was always at least two stills from *Frankenstein Conquers the World* when they did that, which I think was following some unwritten law of those days.

"Though not really cartoon-related, the number one magazine for me growing up was actually *Famous Monsters of Filmland*, though I guess that dove-tails with all the monster-related issues of *Cracked* over the years. Those were the *Cracked* issues I'd most often get."

George Gladir offers this summation about his years at *Cracked*: "The big joy in writing for *Cracked* were the many gifted cartoonists that worked there at the time…there was the legendary John Severin, whom I now regard not only as one of our nation's best cartoonists, but also the most versatile cartoonist ever! I was most fortunate to have him draw up some 1000 of the 2,000 pages I wrote for *Cracked* over a 30-year stretch. There was also Don Orehek, a *Playboy* cartoonist and frequent winner of the National Cartoonists Society award for best gag cartoonist of the year. Others that come to mind are Warren Sattler, Sururi Gumen, and Mike Ricigliano. The list is almost endless. It's no wonder that *Cracked* managed to be *Mad*'s only serious competitor over the years.

"It's hard to compare Archie with *Cracked*. They were two entirely different environments. At *Cracked* I was able to tackle subjects that I might not have been able to do. During the Vietnam War in the early '70s, I was able to write a satirical comic story about a hawkish super hero who felt frustrated because he couldn't bring the war to a successful conclusion.

"Yes, I do miss *Cracked*, but as a free lancer you learn not to dwell on the past. You learn to keep busy with what is at hand. How could I not help be a fan with all of the talented artists working there at the outset."

Marten Jallad salutes *Cracked* and also laments its end: "In no particular order, I really appreciated Severin's covers. He really did create many memorable scenes involving Sylvester P. Smythe. I think the technical aspect of his craft shined through consistently. Don Orehek would have to be right up there for me as I enjoyed his somewhat loose fluid style and his *Shut-Ups* were great. Acquiring Don Martin from *Mad* was most probably *Cracked*'s greatest moment. I think that this move greatly renewed his enthusiasm and energy for his art and writing. It was also great to see him do 10 regular covers and two specials (more than the four single issues and four specials that he did in his 30 plus years with *Mad*). Frank Cummings is also a favorite whose material I was very sad to see disappear by the time I was involved. I believe that he ended up drawing for Richard Simmons Corp. Art Bouthillier's *Naked Guy* was also excellent. It was nice that Tom Richmond got his feet wet at *Cracked*, too. Bruce Bolinger's absurd characters made him a natural to ink Don Martin's material during his time at *Cracked*. As you can tell I feel that there were many terrific talents at *Cracked* throughout its life. Those that I mentioned just happened to be my favorites.

"I am proudest of the fact that through my short tenure at *Cracked*, I was able to bring on new talent that had worked with me at *Thwak*. It is also great that at least three artist / writer contributors that I have worked with went on to do work for *Mad*. I am also proud of the fact that the amazing Kelley Freas actually painted the cover to our final issue, the November 2004 Presidential race issue #365. Unfortunately, it was to be the last magazine cover he did as he passed away a couple of months later. Lastly, I do feel that under our tenure Scott and I were on the path to maintaining a consistent contributor base, especially among many from the *Thwak* ranks.

"I am least proud of lack of consistency of the issues because of the haphazard way that they were put together with typos and old irrelevant filler material.

"I miss *Cracked* as a humor magazine purist absolutely! With no offense to the last incarnation led by Monty Sarhan, I wish that version had never come out, as it bore no resemblance to the magazine's then 47-year-old history. There has been no person that I have spoken to who has understood why a title would be purchased presumably for its name as a logo and recognition only to be changed into something completely different. Prior to actually seeing any web or printed content I did initially talk with Monty about joining their ranks as an editor but was informed that their new base was now back in New York and that my prior experience was too limited in the old style humor magazine. But I digress. Yes, I do miss the old *Cracked*, but given the fact that every other humor magazine has fallen by the wayside and with the most current announcement by *Mad* that they are going quarterly I sadly feel that the masses are saying that they really do not need a monthly humor magazine on the newsstands. My hopes are that both *Cracked* and *Mad* continue to put out trade paperbacks. Naturally this would be somewhat of a first for *Cracked* other than a few pocket books and only put out one trade paperback under Kulpa titled *The Cracked Guide to the Movies*.

"I had read *Cracked* since the '70s and enjoyed it but never thought that it came anywhere near *Mad*. I stopped buying *Mad* in early '81 but would occasionally glance at it when I passed it on the newsstand to read the Don Martin cartoons. When Don went to *Cracked* that certainly renewed my interest in *Cracked* somewhat. It wasn't really until the mid- to late '90s that I started buying *Cracked* and even took out a three-year subscription. I strongly feel / felt that *Cracked* was at its best under Lou Silverstone's and Andy Simmons' editorship and one of my immediate goals upon becoming an editor was to recapture that level of execution. Incidentally, I was collecting *Mad* again since the mid-'90s but felt that *Cracked* was the superior magazine at that point."

Carson Demmans comments, "Does *Cracked* have a legacy? I'd say so. It was the best of the *Mad* imitators. Is that a major accomplishment? I'd say so, considering how many competitors it had for this distinction. *Mad* tried its own imitation, *Panic*, and it was quickly cancelled. Marvel tried *Crazy*, two different books called *Spoof* and *What Th'*? None of them worked. *Sick* survived for quite a few years, through multiple publishers, but I suspect because it had production values that were so low it was impossible for it not to make money. The ink would literally come off in your hands and the paper would get brittle and break on the way home form the store after buying the latest issue. DC had *Plop!*, which had *Mad* artists like Aragonés and Wood and still failed. Archie, of all publishers, had *Madhouse*, which went through multiple format changes, but still managed to publish some very funny stuff and some great art. In their digests, they'd also sneak in stuff like *Super Duck* and stories from *Tales Calculated to Drive you Bats*. Kurtzman had a few magazines, which tried to recreate *Mad* but never succeeded in doing it. There was also *Nuts*, which was really weird and only lasted a couple of issues in the '90s. DC tried to do the Big Books series, and a sister newsstand magazine version of *Mad* type material, but neither caught on. I haven't done the math, but you could probably add up the issue runs of the other *Mad* imitators and they wouldn't equal the runs of *Cracked* and its spin-offs.

"It also taught me that I could write humor. I have been published about 1000 times since that first sale to *Cracked*, mainly as a gag writer for comic strips. I am not famous or the best at what I do, but I do it, and I never would have even gotten this far without *Cracked*."

Mike Arnold laments missing *Cracked* on the stands: "I do. The humor genre hasn't been the same without it. *Cracked* magazine got a lot of grief for being a poor-man's *Mad*, but there was a lot of funny stuff in it over the years. Remember *Shut-Ups*? 'Mommy, where's my canary? SHUT-UP and eat your chicken!' And those little fortune cookie sayings in the margins like '*Cracked* is thinking a karate chop is a new cut of meat.' Classic! So, for a fan of that type of humor magazine *Mad* just wasn't enough. When I was a kid, *Mad* only put out eight issues a year so I needed to supplement my humor addiction with *Cracked*. I guess you could say I was a '*Cracked* Addict' (groan). For me there could never be enough humor magazines. I read them all, *Cracked*, *Crazy*, *Trash*, *Plop!*, *National Lampoon*...Gimme more! I'm really bummed that *Mad* is the only one left, but at least I still have all my old issues of *Cracked* to read. I wish the new ownership would put out some *Cracked* compilations either in trade paperback form or put the entire catalog on a DVD the way *Mad* and *National Lampoon* did. *Cracked* was really funny in the late '90s but not many people were reading it then. That 'Absolut' ad parody was brilliant (if not gross).

"Not many people realize that there were a lot of *Mad* artists that worked for *Cracked* starting with the great John Severin. Others include Jack Davis, Don Martin, Angelo Torres, Bill Wray, Tom Richmond, Al Jaffee, Will Elder, Duck Edwing, Peter Bagge even John Ficarra and Lou Silverstone have worked for *Cracked*. *Spider-Man* artist Steve Ditko, *Daredevil* and *Tomb of Dracula* artist Gene Colan, fantastic "realistic" science-fiction/horror artist Gray Morrow, *Flash Gordon* and *Star Wars* artist Al Williamson, *Frontline Combat* artist Russ Heath, the creator of the original *Human Torch* Carl Burgos, *Sgt. Fury* and original *Ghost Rider* artist Dick Ayers, the creator of the *Sub-Mariner*, Bill Everett and Jack 'King' Kirby did work for *Cracked*. That's quite an impressive array of contributors which why I think it's such a shame that they don't put out some compilations or a DVD of the material. There's a treasure trove of talent hidden that should be mined."

Mike Kazaleh misses *Cracked*, too: "I miss *Cracked*. I miss the whole idea of a humor magazine. It's a concept that seems to be dying at the moment. Where's all the comedy gone? A lot of really great cartoonists worked for *Cracked* over the years. I particularly loved John Severin's work."

Jay Lynch offers his summation of *Cracked*: "It's just one big pulsating ever-growing organism not unlike *The Blob*. It all comes from Kurtzman. Over the decades fresh bodies are consumed by this creature, and they make satire in the mode established by Kurtzman in 1952. The belly of this beast has ingested the greatest satirical minds of our time: Grabianski, Laikin, Gladir, Clowes, Severin, Davis, even Elder worked on *Cracked* stuff at one time."

Severin comments on John's years with *Cracked*: "It was a good, good relationship and they treated him well. *Cracked* treated us well. Bob treated us well. Michael Delle-Femine did, too."

To conclude the story of *Cracked*, Mike Arnold found some "Fun Facts": "I was perusing the *Cracked* message board I started a few years ago and found some funny facts:

> Did you know that Sylvester appeared on the cover of the first 10 issues of *Cracked* but we didn't see his face until issue #11 in October 1959?
>
> Did you know that with issue #30 in July 1963 *Cracked* first became a "Mazagine"?
>
> Did you know that "The Fonz" has been on the cover of no less than ten different covers making him the most popular *Cracked* cover character in the history of *Cracked*?
>
> Did you also know that "The Fonze" was misspelled three times on the cover of issue #134? Did you know that in March 1958 as *Cracked* #1 was hitting the newsstands:
>
> Andy Gibb, Sharon Stone, Holly Hunter and Gary Oldman were born.
>
> American League batters were required to start wearing batting helmets.
>
> Perry Como's *Magic Moments* topped the charts.
>
> The United States launched the Vanguard 1 satellite.
>
> Nikita Khrushchev became Premier of the Soviet Union?

An Alfred E. Neuman cover and article appearance gallery from *Cracked*:

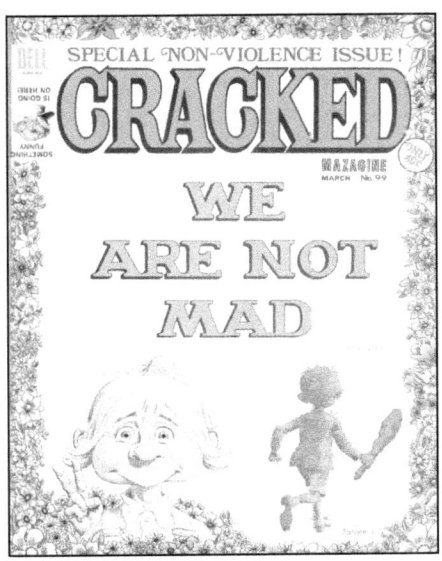

Cracked #99, March 1972,
art by John Severin.

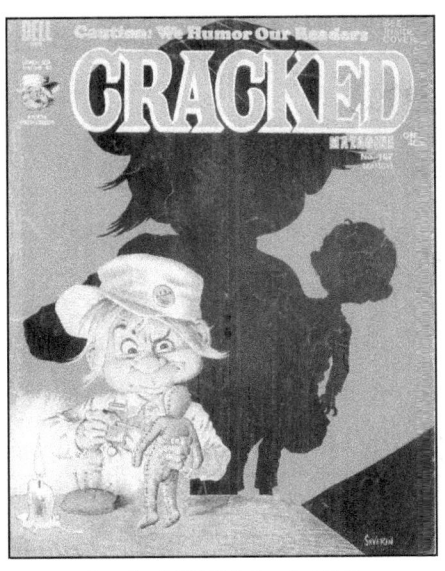

Cracked #107, March 1973,
art by John Severin.

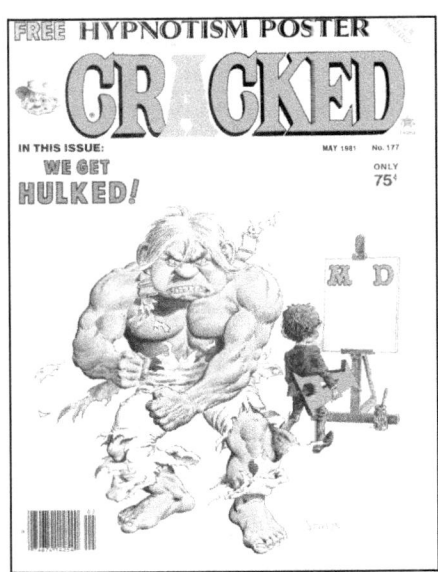

Cracked #177, May 1981,
art by John Severin.

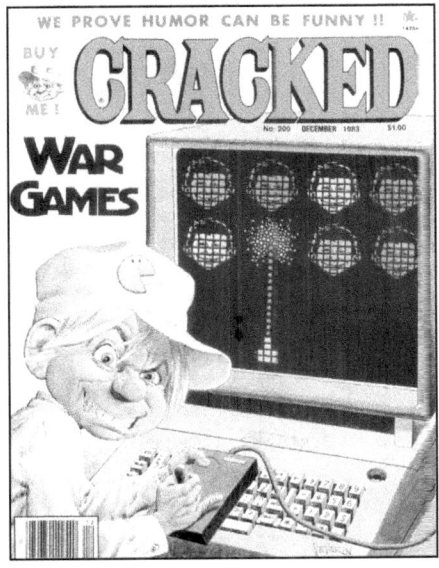

Cracked #200, December 1983,
art by John Severin.

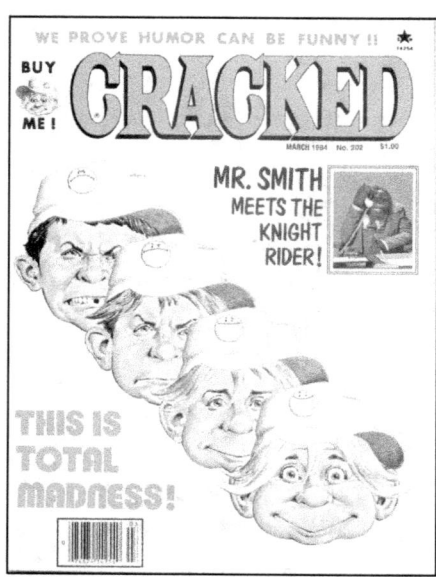

Cracked #202, March 1984,
art by John Severin.

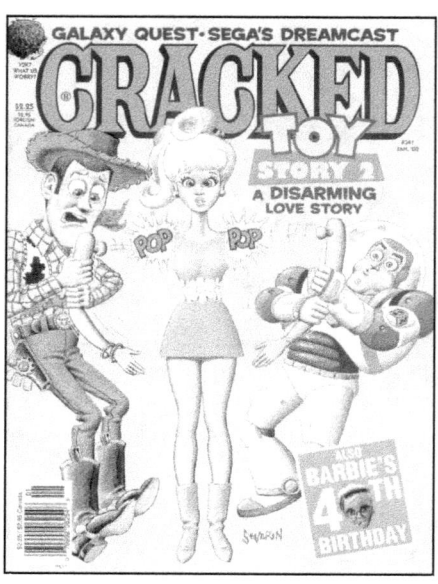

Cracked #341, January 2000,
art by John Severin.

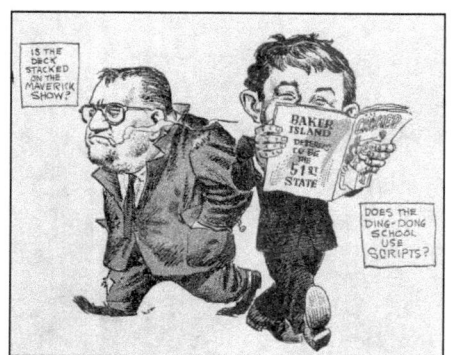

Cracked #13, March 1960,
art by John Severin.

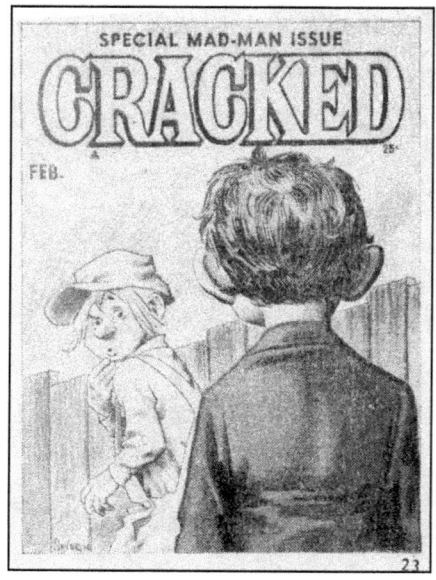

Cracked #21, September 1961,
art by John Severin.

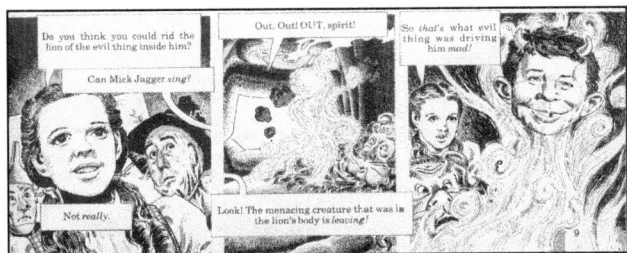

Cracked #131, March 1976, art by John Severin.

Cracked #141, May 1977, art by Bill Ward.

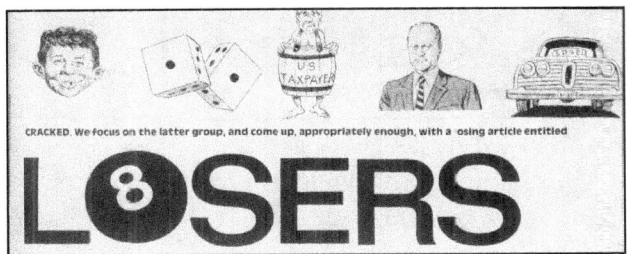

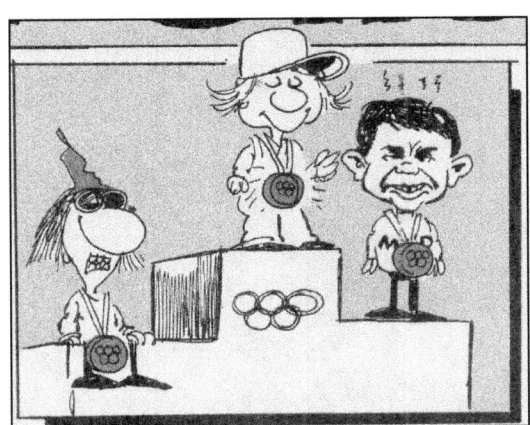

Cracked #238, September 1988, art by Mike Ricigliano.

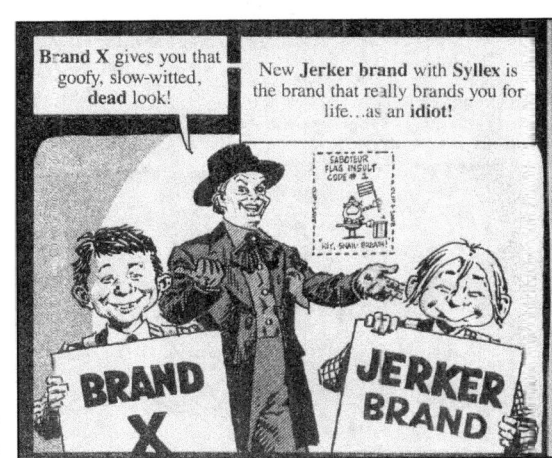

Cracked #249, November 1989, art by John Severin.

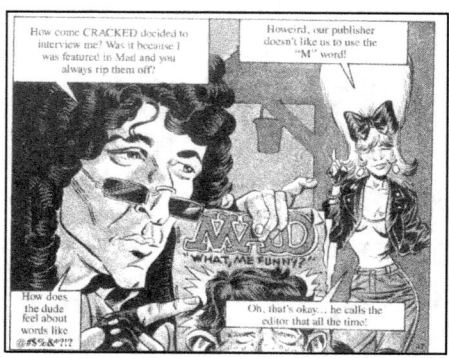

Cracked #273, August 1990,
art by Rob Orzechowski

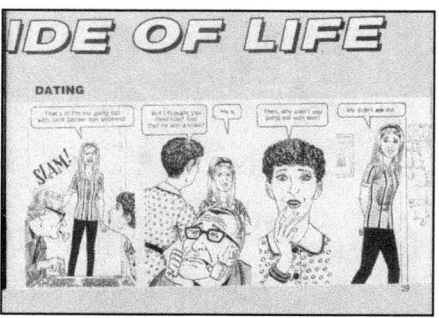

Severin does Dave Berg in "Another
Side of Life" from *Cracked* #202,
March 1984.

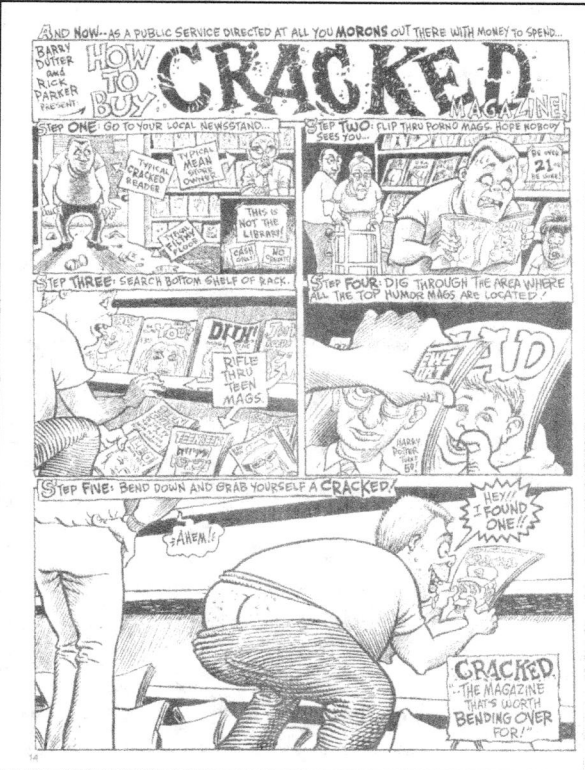

Rick Parker slipped in
yet another Alfred E.
Neuman appearance in
Cracked #349,
November 2000.

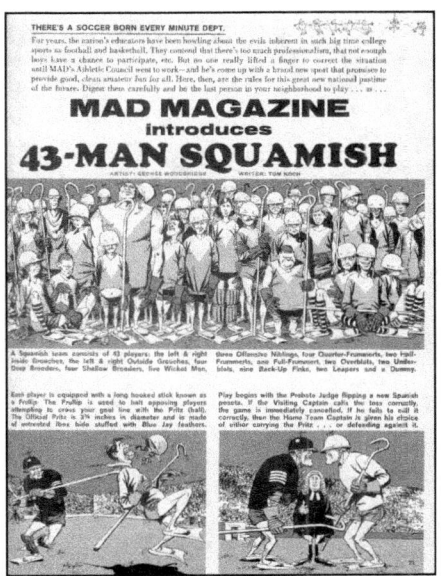

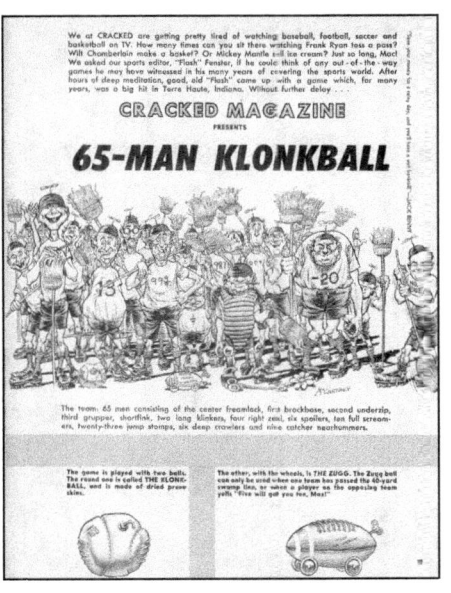

Mad's original "43-Man Squamish" became...

Cracked's "65-Man Klonkball."

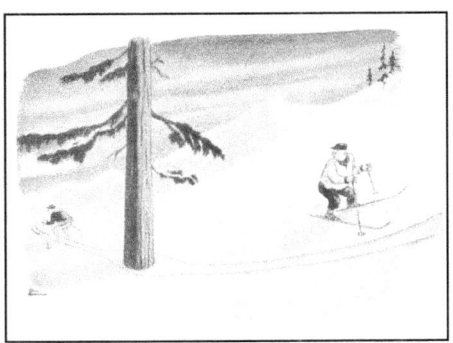

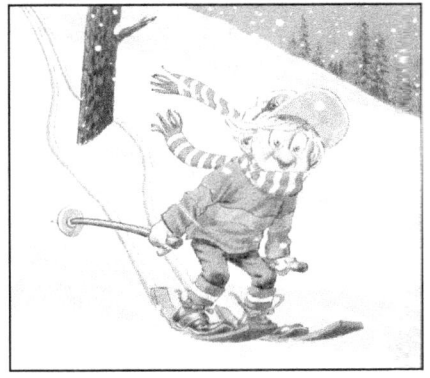

The infamous Charles Addams skiing cartoon from *The New Yorker* became...

The punchline from the cover of *Cracked* #67, March 1968, art by John Severin.

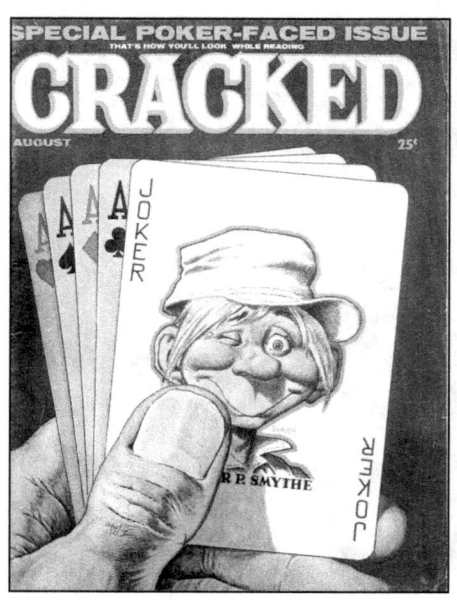

Here's a case where *Mad* rips off *Cracked*.
Cracked #15, August 1960…

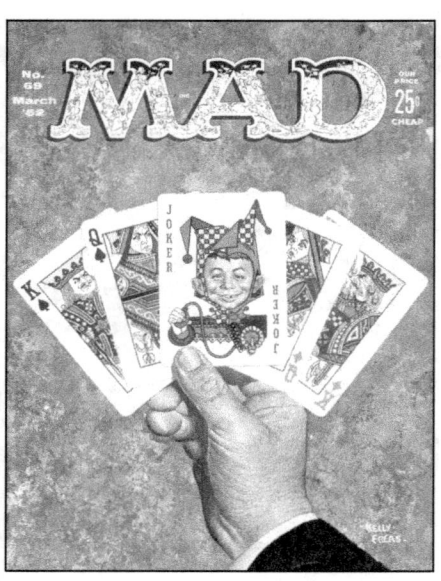

…and *Mad* #69, March 1962, art by
Frank Kelly Freas.

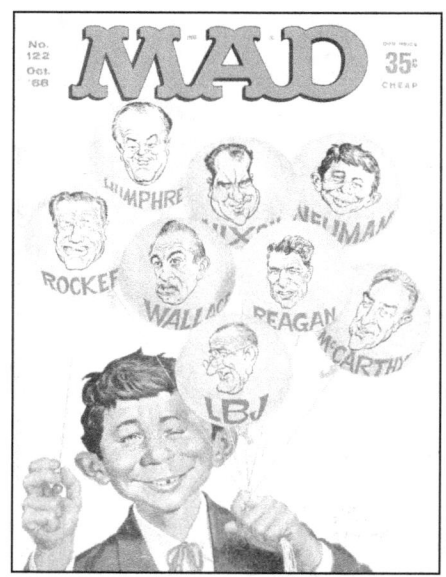

Mad #122, October 1968, art by
Norman Mingo, became…

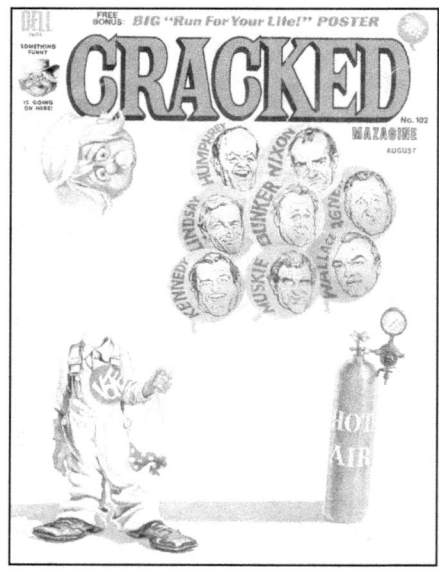

Cracked #102, August 1972, art by
John Severin.

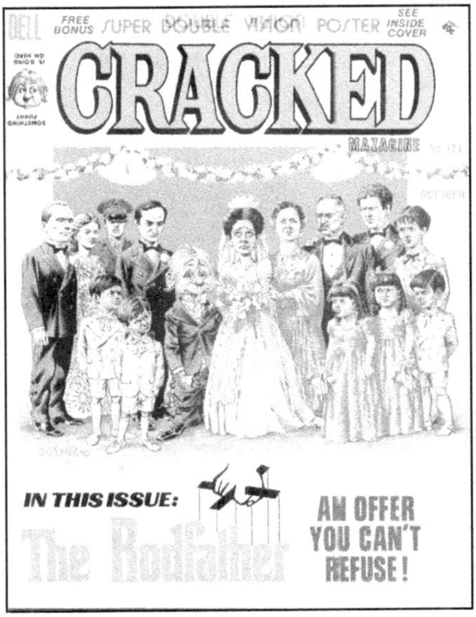
FREE BONUS SUPER DOUBLE VISION POSTER SEE INSIDE COVER
CRACKED
MAGAZINE
IN THIS ISSUE:
The Rodfather
AN OFFER YOU CAN'T REFUSE!

Cracked #104, October 1972, art by John Severin, became…

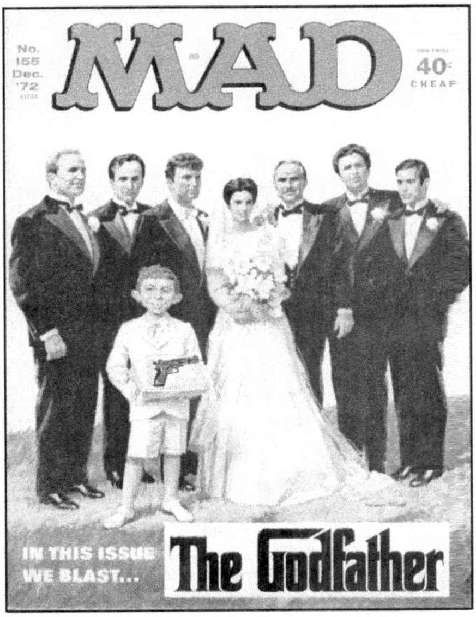
No. 155 Dec. '72
MAD
40¢ CHEAP
IN THIS ISSUE WE BLAST...
The Godfather

Mad #155, December 1972, art by Norman Mingo.

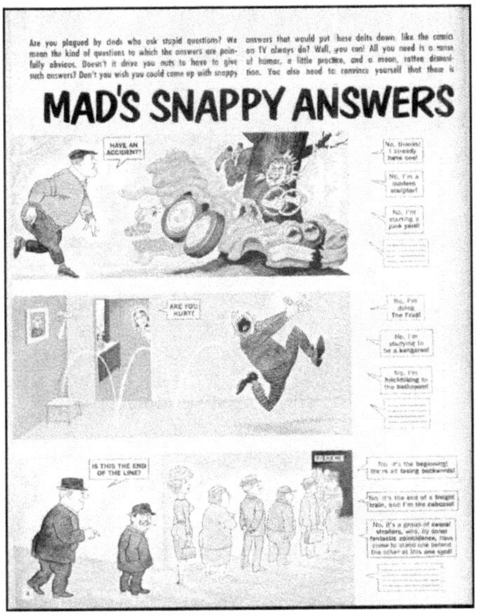
Are you plagued by clods who ask stupid questions? We mean the kind of questions to which the answers are painfully obvious. Doesn't it drive you nuts to have to give such answers? Don't you wish you could come up with snappy answers that would put these dolts down, like the comics on TV always do? Well, you can! All you need is a sense of humor, a little practice, and a mean, rotten disposition. You also need to convince yourself that there is
MAD'S SNAPPY ANSWERS
HAVE AN ACCIDENT?
No, thanks! I already have one!
ARE YOU HURT?
IS THIS THE END OF THE LINE?

Al Jaffee's "Snappy Answers to Stupid Questions" became…

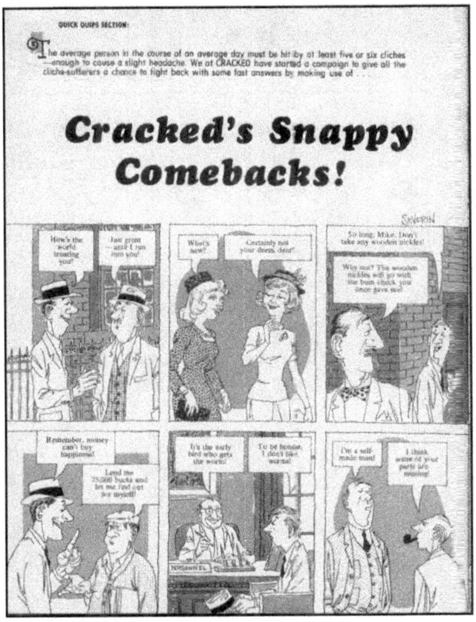
QUICK QUIPS SECTION:
The average person in the course of an average day must be hit by at least five or six cliches—enough to cause a slight headache. We at CRACKED have started a campaign to give all the cliche-sufferers a chance to fight back with some fast answers by making use of . . .
Cracked's Snappy Comebacks!
SEVERIN
How's the world treating you?
Just great—until I ran into you!
What's new?
Certainly not your dress, dear!
So long, Mike. Don't take any wooden nickles!

Cracked's "Snappy Comebacks."

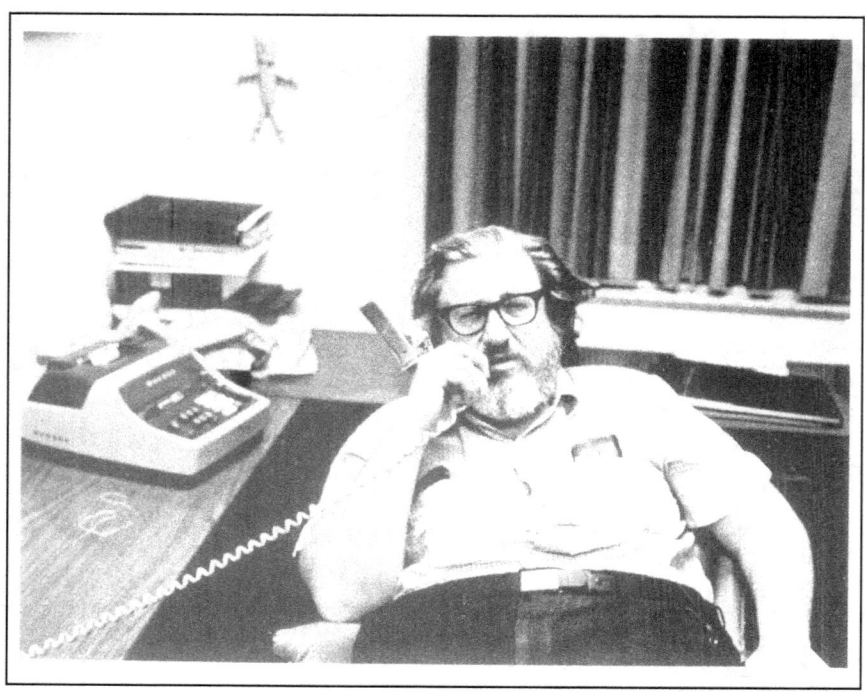

William M. Gaines with voodoo doll. Image courtesy of Frank Jacobs from his book *The Mad World of William M. Gaines*, 1972.

HOW DiD YOU GET STARTED
IN THE BUSiNESS?

Noel Anderson: I got into cartooning at a young age. As an adolescent in the '70s, I devoured every issue of humor magazines like *Mad*, *Cracked* and *Crazy* that I could get my hands on. I dreamed that one day I would see my work alongside that of John Severin and Bill Ward. I even convinced some of my school buddies to contribute their time and talents to a crudely drawn and stapled together humor magazine of our own called *Garbage*. As I grew older and my tastes matured, I discovered what was going on that 'top shelf' of my local newsstand. Adult comic publications by the likes of Robert Crumb and Gilbert Shelton soon influenced my artwork a great deal…but those comics were always something I had to hide from my mother. Sigh!

Mike Arnold: Well, like most adult cartoonists I started out drawing when I was about five or six copying my favorite characters out of the Sunday funnies and trying to recreate the coolest comic book covers from my collection. I don't know if I was all that good at it but because I liked doing it, I did it all the time and eventually I got better at it. I was a huge *Cracked* fan back in the mid-to-late '70s and John Severin was my hero. I just loved everything he did in *Cracked* and tried to emulate a lot of the expressions and body language he gave his characters into my drawings. I actually thought he owned the magazine because he did SO much work every month. It seemed like he did more than half the art in every issue (which was OK with me!) Then at some point in high school after one of those dreadful 'Career / College Days' where lots of colleges set up for recruitment in the gym and you go around gathering pamphlets and they help you decide which college to go to, I realized I did not want to go through another four years of academics and thought "I like drawing, how about Art School?"

It's funny because as much as I loved the funnies, comic books and *Cracked* and thought that's what I wanted to do when I got out of school, I started doing more cartoon illustration type work and then got into interactive

CD-Rom animation when I worked at *Sesame Street* through the '90s and I never submitted any work to *Cracked* until I started freelancing again around 2002 or so. I can't remember the exact chain of events but I finally decided to send them samples around 2003 and they were receptive.

Dave Berns: I was always "that guy" growing up who liked to draw and was a little better than everyone else I knew at it. As a wee lad I had a character Fido, that I used to draw incessantly… he started out as a failed attempt to draw Snoopy. Somewhere along the line he started wearing a cowboy hat and giving two thumbs up like the Fonz when he'd say "Aaaayyyy," only I don't think Fido ever spoke.

I'd read some comics as a kid, and of course *Mad* and *Cracked*, but was not hooked until my teen years. A good friend of mine had a stack of comic books during a study hall, and reading them seemed a lot more fun than submitting to coercion and doing actual homework. It was. I contracted comicgeekitus from then on.

In short order, I realized that people, flesh and blood human beings, just like me, got paid to draw that which I'd become obsessed with. This revelation gave direction and purpose to my artistic propensities and I quickly became just as, if not more, obsessed with trying to draw them myself.

The following year, I bumped into a funny looking little freshman, Travis Kramer, at the local comic shop. We went to a small prep/boarding school in the Adirondacks that was absolutely overrun with hockey players, skiers, etc… winter sports jock central (at least a half dozen people I knew from then went on to the Olympics, couple of guys in the NHL). Neither of us were into any of that shit, me being an overgrown goony long-haired freak from South Florida who was raised by a working mom (meaning, no dad to teach or push athletics, didn't even ride a bike 'til I was probably 10) and Travis, at that point, could have played lead in *Revenge of the Nerds: The High School Years*. Anyway, he was in the same head space as me, farting around with the notion of making comics, not just reading them, and we hit if off big time. Trav had the good fortune of coming across a little photocopied amateur small press comic book called *Mr. Mid-Nite*, self-published by a dude named Bob Elinskas, and instantly brought it to my attention. Once we realized all we needed was a photocopier and a few badly drawn bad ideas, it wasn't long before we were fledgling small press publishers ourselves.

We both joined the SPS (Small Press Syndicate), a collective of other self publishing enthusiasts who traded comics and advice with each other, at the time headed up by a mini comic revolutionary (no joke, he was, in fact, a revolutionary… giving rousing speeches at socialist rallies and the like, when he wasn't creating GREAT comics like Reverend Ablack: Adventures of the Anti-Christ) Chris Erwin (who later changed his name to Chris Paris, not sure why... hope it wasn't to distance himself from his revolutionary persona... lol) who promoted the organization with a flyer with the best call to action ever: "MAKE YOUR OWN DAMN COMICS!." Make our own damn comics, we did... one of which was Travis' parody comic "Biology Facts From Hell," to which I also contributed ideas and artwork. Other than drawing brutalized effigies of teachers and fellow students, this was our first crack at any kind of parody, and for the most part, it was fucking awful... but thankfully we didn't realize this fact at the time, because man was it fun!

Eventually I graduated, and moved back home to Florida, where I enrolled at Florida Atlantic University. I was more obsessed than ever with drawing and comics, and would skip class to work on them in the library or my car even. I did horribly there, I did not care, I was making my own damn comics, and improving by leaps and bounds! At some point I realized, why pretend to fight it and waste money on a university I couldn't have cared less about. I applied to and was accepted into the Joe Kubert School in New Jersey, where I was taught by and peer to some of the best in cartooning and comics until graduating in 1997.

After graduating from the Kubert School, instead of sticking around the Tri-state area, where all of comics and publishing lives and breathes, braniac that I am, I made the move back home to Florida. I continued to work on my own damn comics, picked up random freelance work, and began working day jobs as a graphic artist for different printing companies. I did a little bit of work for my friend Ricky Carallero's comic book company, High Impact Studios, but bounced from there when I realized my mom and grandma weren't going to pin pornographic lesbian action comics on their fridges. My loss, completely, as Ricky's life has definitely been 100x the adventure of my own. C'est la vie.

Eventually, my graphic design work led me to a small modeling industry magazine (*Military Miniatures in Review*), where those skills developed to a level (self taught really) of Art Director, rather than lowly designer. I also began working as art assistant to the great comic strip artist Carlos Castellanos, creator of *Baldo*, where I colored his Sunday strips and ghosted most of his freelance cartooning (for big-time educational publishers like McGraw Hill, Oxford University Press, etc...) allowing him to focus on the strip itself, and the licensing deals he was pursuing. I was double-timing it with both gigs at once and basically burnt out as a result. I got real unhealthy, gained a lot of weight (a running theme in my life), and burned out. September 11th had happened, anthrax attacks happened, the world was upside down."

So, around this time, like most of the country, I was possessed with anger, confusion, etc... at the state of the world. America had been attacked by fanatics on the other side of the planet, and they were going to do it again if we didn't turn their homelands to sheets of glass (what an a-hole I was for buying any of that malarkey... I wish I had the Who's "Won't Get Fooled Again" playing on a loop instead of corporate television then). I had the idiot box tuned in non-stop to talking heads blathering on about killing people who wanted to kill us on the news channels. I wanted to take up the fight, but was too obese and chicken to enlist, so I drew out my frustrations in the form of a series of editorial cartoons, I titled "NewsJunkie" and started shopping them around to syndicates. I got a couple of encouraging rejection letters, but those don't pay the bills or taste very good (not even with salsa) and eventually, I had to figure out what the hell to do with myself. My family helped me out here, sending me away to, I shit you not, fat camp. While trimming down and getting my head straight there, I began scouring the internet trying to figure out my next step in life, when low-and-behold, I happened upon *Cracked*'s website and found the office address was in the next town over from my own. A big-time magazine I was a perfect fit for in my backyard. I was not going to take no for an answer.

I was a fan of *Cracked*, but not a fanatic. I'd bought a few copies of the mazagine as a kid, but was not a subscriber. I subscribed to *Mad* off and on for many years. No disrespect, *Cracked*, I still love you and appreciate all the opportunities you've given to cartoonists the world over, but Alfred is Alfred after all.

Ultimately, even if I don't like the publication, I'm a fan of ANY of them that hire illustrators and cartoonists; as such publications have been a dying breed for decades!

Ray Billingsley: My debut into cartooning was not a regular one. I was first inspired by my older brother Richard, who was a fine artist. We shared a room and he always left his supplies around. I picked up a pencil and began to draw, until at a tender age, I began to get notice. Lucky for me he wasn't a drug dealer! I was in my seventh grade art class, and we were to build a 13-foot aluminum-can Christmas tree as part of a recycling effort. I thought it was a silly idea. I was already in the habit of sketching everywhere I was and I had a pad in my pocket. There was slight media coverage and the cameras were around. I had slipped off to the side and was doodling. A woman approached me and wanted to see what I was drawing. I gave her the drawing and that was that. That very next week, she got in touch with me and my family. She was an editor of *KIDS* Magazine, a mag for what else? Kids! She asked me down to the office to do some drawings. To my surprise, she paid me $5.00 for a small drawing. I felt really happy because my dad did not believe in allowances, and my brother, sister and I had to work for any money we got. I discovered people would pay for artwork! Then, I was offered a job as a staff artist. I had to show up at their office every day after school to draw, answer mail, and do page layouts. From that day on, life for me changed forever. It didn't make me more popular with my classmates and my art teachers were kind of miffed about it. I continued with *KIDS* and retired at age 18 as an Associate editor. So, basically, I was discovered off the streets, and just kept working and working ever since. To this day, I've never had any sort of job other than cartooning!

I was always interested in magazines and had a favorite news store, where I checked out all the mags I could. Can you imagine the look on the owners face when I told him I was looking at *Playboy* for the cartoons? And I was, like 14? Well, I read all the magazines offered—*Mad*, the *National Lampoon*, underground magazines-which featured the likes of R. Crumb, the *Village Voice*, where I was introduced to Feiffer. I was lost in all the great top magazines with cartoons in them. Then I stumbled across *Crazy* magazine. In those days, you could actually visit these magazine offices, without the Secretary Grinch stopping you at the door. I went in with a portfolio and was given a sample script to show how I would draw for it. As luck would have it, I was hired! *Crazy* was where I cut my teeth as a writer. After drawing others scripts, I submitted scripts of my own and they were accepted! I then began to write and draw my own features.

My time at *Crazy*, to me, was a very serious matter. I wanted to be noticed and that meant I had to concentrate and give them the best I could do. It was tough because I was freelancing and still had homework and tests to study for. I grew up on a deadline.

There were no real horror stories that I can think of. All in all, it was a great learning experience for a teenager. They left me free to experiment with story plots.

Bruce Bolinger: My interest in art was there from the beginning and while in high school I took all the creative classes I could. I headed for Art Center College in California after graduation, a college offering 4 years of education directed to the arts. Two years there, interrupted by Uncle Sam drafting my warm body to participate in a fruitless ten-year war effort. Fortunately I only commanded a desk. Marriage came, then my wife and I returned to California so I could finish college. My first job was with a publisher in the DC area where we remained until I could get my freelance business going. We moved to Pennsylvania where I freelanced all types of artwork until I decided, at age 45, to turn my attention to cartooning, an artwork form that always fascinated me.

Walter Brogan: I started drawing at the age of three. I still got some of the drawings like King Kong and Popeye. I would draw them on the blank pages in the back of encyclopedias. I would use those blank pages. Any piece of paper I could get, you know, the backs of photographs. That's how I pretty much started. I stayed with it.

I got hooked on the Disney and Warner Bros. cartoons, especially the Chuck Jones cartoons. Ken Harris, Milt Kahl, Freddie Moore, Ward Kimball, guys like that I was really attracted to. Then, I started picking up *Mad* magazine when I was about age 12-13 years old. That's when I saw Mort Drucker, and that guy just blew me away completely. Wow! Look at this; Mort…Jack Davis. Then I started picking up *Creepy* magazine and *Eerie*, and I saw those beautiful covers by Frank Frazetta, and Angelo Torres, Reed Crandall, and Neal Adams. Between Neal Adams and Mort Drucker, they were my main two guys really. Along the way you see guys like Ronald Searle. He was a big influence, too. He was also a big influence on Mort. If you look at some of Ronald Searle's paintings and then look at some of Mort's early paintings, there is a strong resemblance there. Also, Albert Dorn.

Remember that famous, Famous Art course? That was Albert Dorn's big thing. Robert Foster, illustrators from the '30s, '40s and '50s. Along the way, you pick a little bit from this guy and a little bit from that guy, and then I went to school in New York, and then I went to the Art Students League. I started working a little bit with Neal Adams. I used to go up and see Neal a lot. I asked him to critique my work. I got probably a better education from Neal than both the schools I went to. The guy didn't bullshit. He'd come right out and tell you that you got to take more modeling classes. You've got to start drawing from a model more. You've got to really sit down and learn how to draw now. He'd point to the bones and say the bones are everything. He'd go over it and critique my work and he'd spend a lot of time with it.

I did some work with him later on, some storyboard work. I did finish his continuities. While still in school, I went to the School of Visual Arts when I was 17, I would go over to his studio. His studio at that time was on 45th Street. I would meet some of the older guys like Bernie Wrightson, Mike Kaluta, and Walt Simonson. I don't know if you remember, but they were called the Crusty Bunkers? There were a bunch of other guys, too, but I got to meet those guys at his place. I would go up after school and Neal would sit down with me and he'd critique and go over my work. That was really nice of him to do that. He was one of the top guys in the business. He would spend time with me, showing me things with my artwork.

Crazy was my first published work. I think I was in my second year of college. I would go up to Marvel Comics. As a matter of fact, Marie Severin, who was working up there, gave me my first break. She called the editor who was named Paul Laikin, and that's how I got started working with *Crazy* magazine, thanks to Marie Severin.

I kind of fell into it. Actually I wanted to be an Art Director and do the comic book thing on the side. I took Harvey Kurtzman's class at SVA and he started me doing caricatures. He told me, "You've got a pretty good eye for doing this stuff. Keep doing that." I think there were four magazines out at that time, *Mad*, *Cracked*, *Crazy* and *Sick*. Originally, I wanted to be an Art Director.

What happened was Paul Laikin had left and Paul Laikin, he was a pretty good guy. The only problem was that he would tell me, "I want you to draw like Mort Drucker." And I said, "But I'm not Mort Drucker. I kind of got my own style. It might be similar to Mort's, but people will say I'm copying him. I don't think Mort would like that too much. He'd probably be pissed off at me." But Paul would say, "You've got to draw like Mort or else I can't give you work." So, what could I do, you know what I'm saying?

Kent Gamble, the problem with him is he's not as good of a draftsman than Mort. He's ok, but he's not in the same league as Mort, just for pure draftsmanship. I really didn't want to do that, but sometimes you go back and some stories I broke away from that, hopefully that Paul Laikin wouldn't see it and catch onto it. I went to California then. I was working as an assistant art director and I don't know what happened to *Crazy*. I think it folded or something.

Ok, '83. I was in California. I went to work at Walt Disney Studios in 1980. They had a training program. I had sent some sketches out and believe it or not the first person I met there was named Donald Duckwald. I thought it was some kind of a joke and I asked if that was really his name. He said, "That's my name." He was interviewing me. He went over my portfolio and I went all the way out there. He said, "I see some nice stuff here, but you got to work on some of your sketches more. You've got too much comic book stuff here. We need to see some action sketches." So I came back to New York. That's when I started going to the Art Students League. I sent some more sketches out and I met another guy named Ed Hanson, who was at Disney. They looked it over and I got a letter back from him and I was accepted.

We had to design our own little films, storyboards and animation. It was like a training school and that's where I met Eric Larson, one of Disney's nine old men. This guy was another fantastic draftsman who would show me certain things that I was doing wrong. I'd meet these people and I'd start learning more and more, the more people you'd meet. He was one hell of a nice guy too, Eric Larson. A really nice, great guy. And I met Ward Kimball, Frank Thomas, Ollie Johnston, and I stayed there and I didn't like California that much.

I just couldn't seem to get used to it. I was always thirsty and also during the Christmas holidays it was like 92 degrees. I wasn't used to that. I didn't get used to like waking up on the weekends and there'd be a smog alert, and walking out and there'd be nobody around and it would be like "What the hell is this?"

So then I came back and then I went to California again to work for Hanna-Barbera for a while, then I worked at Filmation for a little bit. At that point, I was kind of confused a little bit, not knowing what the hell I wanted to do. I kept saying, "What the hell did I leave advertising for? I was making a lot more money than I was making in California." That's when I came back to New York around 1982 or 1983 and then I started working doing storyboard work.

Roger Brown: While I was in high school I was always getting in trouble with my teachers because I would make something humorous out of an assignment when it was supposed to be serious. A friend told me the local radio station was looking for someone to write jokes for the morning DJ's show. So, I made up a couple of pages of one-liners he could use and dropped them off. The next week he called me wanting me to supply him with jokes daily. This is where I learned two things. One, you need to be able to write a lot of material for a daily show. The second, they don't want to pay a lot for all that work.

So, I started looking for other avenues to sell my work. That led me to gag-writing for nationally syndicated cartoonists who did magazine cartoons and comic strips.

Terry Colon: Not much of an interesting bio for me. A typically Midwestern American story that would never get on *Jerry Springer*. Anyway, I like to keep my private life private; otherwise it wouldn't be my private life any more.

I've liked cartoons and comic books since I was a lad. Submitted cartoons to various magazines and syndicates on and off over the years to little success. None being very little.

Frank Cummings: I've always loved cartooning ever since I was a child. Grew up drawing comic strips/cartoons and never considered anything else as a career possibility. Got into it because I never learned how to do anything else! It was cartoons or begging!

Carson Demmans: I started out as a reader, not a writer. *Mad* was everywhere in the 70s and 80s, even in my high school's library. I was not a big fan though, because Alfred E. Neuman always scared the hell out of me. Sylvester P. Smythe had a more appealing character design and was generally less creepy. There was also not as much as a difference between the magazines as people said. True, *Mad* had Don Martin in its prime, but *Cracked* had Severin, who could draw everything from movie satires to devil worshipping deer in an NRA parody; Ward, who somehow got away with drawing the same characters he regularly drew for *Sex to Sexty* in a children's magazine, and my personal favorite, Sattler, the chameleon who could adapt his style to any occasion. Eventually, *Cracked* had Martin too, for a while anyway. *Cracked* had lots of great talent over the years: Henry Boltinoff, Howard Nostrand, and I think on a couple of occasions, Ditko.

I started writing comics in public school. At least, I started getting rejected by comic publishers. DC Comics had *Dial H for Hero* and a talent search program. I was rejected. I sent a pro wrestling comic proposal to a Marvel editor who was also a noted pro wrestling fan. It was rejected, although at least with a personal rejection letter. Others followed. Lots of others followed, all rejected. In university, I discovered books with submission guidelines for magazines, including *Mad*. I was rejected, all with the same photocopied rejection letter. After I graduated university, I stopped submitting my writing for about three years. Then I started again. I now had a common law spouse with a word processor and lots of spare time due to getting fired from my day job. I wrote a brilliant (I thought) script, which parodied two popular properties of the day, *Darkwing Duck* and *The Punisher*. *Mad* rejected it so quickly I got it before I mailed the script to them. I then took a chance on *Cracked*.

Barry Dutter: When I was a little kid, I used to read *Cracked* magazine and draw my own *Cracked* magazines for fun. I was maybe 8, 9, 10 years old. I guess I was kind of born to work for *Cracked*. When we were kids, my older brother used to read *Mad* and I would read *Cracked*, just because I had to read something different. I later wound up reading *Mad* and enjoying that, too. In my early twenties, I got a job with Marvel Comics. I did writing and editing for them. I've written my own cartoon / humor books and *Mad*, *Cracked* and the various humor magazines. I probably started working for *Cracked* in 1996, and my book (*The Shy Guy's to Dating*) was published by St. Martin's Press in 1998.

Gary Fields: Like most cartoonists, I always drew as a kid. There was never any question about not being a cartoonist. I watched too many cartoons on Saturday morning, read *Mad* magazine and comic books. Really loved the old Hanna-Barbera cartoons. In high school I took a Saturday morning sketch class at the Joe Kubert School in Dover, NJ. After graduating from high school, I applied and was accepted Joe's school where I took two years of the cartooning program and two years of the new animation program. It's only a three-year school, but I wanted to get that extra year of animation and make it official.

Bob Fingerman: I'm born and bred in New York, raised in Rego Park, Queens, the same place Art Spiegelman's from, so I'm the other Rego Park comics person. I grew up in the city, always drew. Destiny's too big a word, but I think I was hardwired to do what I do. It was more a matter of compulsion than choice. I went to the High School of Art and Design, which is a specialty high school. Actually, that was quite good, though I did not take their cartooning course. I took illustration because I thought that would be more practical. After that, I went to the School of Visual Arts (SVA) for a few years and then dropped out, because basically I started getting work in the middle of my second year. I dropped out when I was getting paid. Why pay, when you are getting paid. I may have been a little cockier than I should have been. If you're 19 and you're not cocky, then there's something wrong with you. At least, you're supposed to be. I had some very good instructors there. Harvey Kurtzman was one of my instructors and Will Eisner was one of my instructors. I had good teachers. The first year there was a total write-off. The second year was quite good and at that point, I had had enough. It may have changed, but at that time, it was the only accredited art school that had cartooning and comics courses. At that point, I did decide to major in that. Other schools like Parsons and Pratt, they still hadn't condescended to have courses like that in their curriculum. They were still focusing on classic art. The reason I had left SVA, I had gotten a book contract to do a series of parodies popular at that time European comic. It was something I did on a lark. The artist did not want to do it, so the publishers thought a parody would be the way to continue it. I ended up getting this book deal to do 48 pages of short, self-contained parodies. I did about half the contract and then that thing never really came to fruition, but it gave me the confidence to leave SVA, so I was working, but I wasn't working on any sort of regular gig.

Dan Fiorella: Born and bred in Staten Island, I'd grown up watching old comedy movies like Abbott & Costello and Laurel & Hardy and always wanted to do that. I attended NYU, where I got to join the fledgling *Plague* humor magazine and started writing more prose pieces and some cartooning. Good times. Oddly, after college, one of the first things I sold was a cartoon gag to *Mad* that was drawn by Don Martin. They had run an ad in the *NY Times* looking for material! It was also the last thing I got into *Mad*. I've been freelancing since then, doing screenplays, radio scripts, industrials, Op-Ed pieces, animation, and PC games.

Pete Fitzgerald: I was born in Lowell, Massachusetts in 1968, and lived in the nearby town of Westford, MA, until 1975. My dad was an electrical engineer; my mom was a housewife, though later she ran a successful needlecraft shop. I'm the youngest of three children.

Our family moved down to Lynchburg, VA, where we lived until another move to Brookfield, CT, in 1982. I attended public schools, except for a two-year stint as a day student at a private school in Lynchburg, from 1980-82. During all this time, I had an insatiable appetite for classic cartoons (Warner

Brothers, Tex Avery, Fleischer Studios' Popeye, Bullwinkle, Speed Racer), dinosaurs, movies (especially monster movies) and TV, and to a lesser extent, comic books. *Mad* was a big influence, starting with copies my older brother brought home in the mid-1970s. I especially liked the Super Specials, with reprinted material from the 1950s, with Kurtzman/Elder, Wally Wood, Basil Wolverton, etc. Also, Don Martin was a god to me; I bought all the Don Martin paperbacks I could find, and would try to copy his drawings of Fester Bestertester and Karbunkle.

I always drew, but didn't consider cartooning as a vocation until high school. In middle school, I'd draw teachers as weird cartoon characters, who then took on a life of their own. While in high school, I created some cartoon characters, which made their way into some comic book / strip-style class assignments. Also around this time, I was becoming interested in animation directors like Bob Clampett, Chuck Jones and Tex Avery, via the book *Of Mice and Magic*; discovering the East Coast Comics reprints of *Tales from the Crypt* and *Vault of Horror*, Kitchen Sink's *Spirit* reprints and independent comics like Jim Valentino's *Normalman* at the local comic book store; and the great newspaper strips via *The Smithsonian Book of Newspaper Comics* (the *Comic Book Comics* volume as well, where I got my first look at Jack Cole's *Plastic Man*).

A high school friend was taking a Saturday cartooning class at a local art store, and convinced me to also sign up. The class was run by two comic book fans, then in their 20s, Rich Maurizio and Neil Hansen, who could both draw a little and had worked on the fringes of the comic book business. We'd talk animation and comics as much as we'd engage in drawing assignments. The class eventually morphed into a social group, and Rich eventually formed the short-lived company, Spotlight Comics, which eventually published *Underdog*, featuring my first semi-professional work, penciling and inking "The Eradicator" in issue #1 (I also drew the cover for issue #2, and penciled and partially inked "Prisoner of Love" in that issue).

The other big thing around that time was The Museum of Cartoon Art in Port Chester, NY. Besides all the great artwork on display, they would have famous cartoonists give lectures the first Sunday of every month, so I visited often, seeing Mort Walker, Milton Caniff, Jack Davis, Shamus Culhane and John Byrne, among others. One Sunday, the guests were Steve Bissette and Rick Veitch, both of whom were working on *Swamp Thing* at the time. They talked about The Joe Kubert School of Cartoon and Graphic Art, where they got much of their training, and recommended it to all aspiring young cartoonists.

That's all I needed to hear. After doing the appropriated research, I was interviewed, accepted and headed there after graduating high school. Three years at Kubert, learning all the right stuff and unlearning all the wrong stuff from Adam Kubert, Jose Delbo, Irwin Hasen, Hy Eisman, Mike Chen, Joe himself—oh, and here's a weird coincidence: the first comic book I ever owned was a reprint of Joe Kubert's *Tor*, given away as a shoe-store premium when I was probably about five! During the summer, away from school, I'd work on *Underdog* stuff for Spotlight.

Kent Gamble: Ever since I was small child I loved the Sunday funnies, I loved comic books, I loved to color and draw. It seems to be what I have always done. I was 10 years old and I discovered *Mad*, and that's where it all went down. I remember the issue. It was the one where Frankenstein is assembling a model of Alfred E. Neuman. I believe that the satire inside was of the TV show *The Fugitive*. I was just mesmerized by how this guy could draw David Janssen and it really looked like him but it was also distorted and exaggerated. I was just fascinated by that and to this day I'm still fascinated by that. That's got me started and through a series of events, *Mad* was the capper.

Caricatures were fun. I remember when I was a kid, we bought that *Mad* magazine and I went and I feverishly tried to draw that David Janssen. I showed it to my parents and they'd go, "Ah, we don't know who that is." So I remember I was crushed and then I worked on it and worked on it and finally they recognized him and I was elated at that point, so I guess caricatures were part of it. It was mostly just cartoons.

I had one instructor. When I was six years old my mom said, "We're going to go to this lady's house and she's going to give you art lessons." I said, "Oh, boy!" So, I had one lesson I remember we drew this dog and got some pastels and put in some grass and then the next week I asked, "Are we going to go?" And my mom said no as the lady had passed away. She was an elderly lady and she had passed away and that was my one lesson.

I think it was a conscious/unconscious notion at all times to draw like Drucker because I figured to me this guy was the best so if I could emulate him, I'd be set. The problem is, or the catch is, he's really talented. So you'd look at it and say, "I can see what he's going for here," and then you try to do it yourself and then it's really tough. It was probably more or less conscious.

I went to New York in 1976. I went to Texas Tech University, which was here in Lubbock and I was a senior advertising student with an art minor. They announced in one of the classes that there was going to be a trip to New York City, and top-flight students could do internships at advertising agencies. Well, I when I heard that I thought, "I don't want to work for an ad agency. I want to take my portfolio and go up and down Madison Avenue." So I went to the teacher who was sponsoring the thing—I'll never forget his name, it was Bernie Rosenblatt—and Bernie was from New York and he was a real live New Yorker. I wasn't a top-flight student by the way. I said, "Bernie, you've got to get me on that airplane so that I can go show off my cartoon portfolio." Everybody on the campus knew that I drew cartoons because I was a cartoonist for the college newspaper. Everybody saw my stuff so I said,

"Bernie, you've got to get me on that plane!" and bless his heart, he did. I didn't have to work. I just took my portfolio and went up and down the street. One day, of course, I went down to Marvel and I talked to Marie Severin. I showed her my portfolio and she said, "I like this and I like this." I remember and I put on a suit and she specifically commented and said, "You don't know how refreshing it is to see a young man dressed up for a job interview." Everybody there was wearing blue jeans and T-Shirts and I looked out of place. By the time it was all over, she said, "Well, I hate to tell you this, but you're probably going to have to work for *Crazy*! I'm going to tell Paul Laikin to give you a call and blah, blah, blah…" Well, a few weeks later I got a script in the mail from Paul. It was just a one-page thing with singers on it like Elton John, Frank Sinatra, a few singers. Anyway, I did that one page, he liked it, and a few weeks later I got a TV satire of *Barney Miller*. That was my first one. The very first one was that one or two-pager with the singers, but my first real satire was the *Barney Miller*. Paul said to make it look as much like Drucker as you can because he, then, and still is, the prototype for that type of work.

Paul was just amazing. Every script for the first few years was from Paul and he got a piece of typing paper, blocked out the panels. He put in the balloons. He wrote literally the script in the balloons as to who was saying what. He pretty much laid it out as far as the art and stuff. It was all written and laid out. I mean, the guy just did everything. He was amazing and he was one of these "this could be the start of something big!" You know, he was very positive and very motivating. I liked him. He was a really nice guy.

In 1980, it just seemed like they wanted to take *Crazy* in a different direction. When Larry Hama came on board, that was when Obnoxio the Clown came in, so it was kind of a more pointed, edgy type of humor. Paul's was funnier. They wanted it to be more of the sharp, pointed humor.

George Gladir: Growing up I wanted to be a cartoonist ever since the age of thirteen when I won a cartoon contest in *Tip Top Comics* by doing a one panel cartoon that solved a predicament that a cartoon character found himself in. Some years later, after graduating from the Cartoonists and Illustrators School I started doing gag cartoons for various magazines on a freelance basis. In 1959, an opening came up at Archie Comics for a writer. My experience in the humor field paid often enabled me to become a full-time writer for Archie. I discovered I found writing preferable to drawing.

In addition to writing one page gags and short stories at Archie I did a lot of writing for *Archie's Madhouse*, a publication similar to *Cracked* and *Mad*, only aimed at a somewhat younger audience. I used this experience to make the transition to *Cracked* when an opening came up. I continued writing for both publications simultaneously for many years thereafter.

Scott Gosar: I fancied myself a bit of a cartoonist throughout my childhood and most of my teen years. Although I didn't pursue cartooning as a vocation, I loved to draw in the styles of my favorite *Mad* artists, Mort Drucker and Jack Davis. When I was a junior in high school, I was placed in an "academically talented" program for kids who were basically board and unchallenged by the prescribed general educational curriculum and ended up taking an art class at our local university. I'll never forget the day that the nude female model showed up for class. The whole time, sketching out her form, I was thinking about how lucky I was to be able to take that class, and about all the other kids my age, sitting in their high school art classes, having to draw fruit or flowers or whatever else they make you draw in high school art classes. My first ever-published cartoons appeared in that university's student newspaper when I was still 16.

I have always been a news junkie and have read newspapers voraciously throughout my life. My earliest memory of a newspaper headline was when Nixon resigned the Presidency in August, 1974. I was 8 years old at the time, and can vividly remember how that giant, bold headline grabbed my attention and kept me interested in newspapers and print media in general.

It was around this time that my mother came home from the library with this strange new magazine called *Mad*. It was on a "free magazine" table and she just picked it up and brought it home, thinking that I would like it. Boy, did I ever. The issue was *Special* #8 from 1972, with the "*TV Guise* Fall Preview" insert inside. From that day forward, I had completely immersed myself in *Mad* and made it my #1 goal in life to acquire every back issue that I possibly could. Here I was, 9 and 10 years old, walking two miles each way, to the dank, funky, hippy-run Unique Book Stall where they sold back issues of *Mad* for 50c to $1.00 apiece. My childhood was a constant state of *Mad*-driven euphoria and I was very selfish when it came to my precious *Mad*s and my younger brother. It was during this period that I had also discovered *Cracked*, and it seemed, at the time, a perfect deterrent to keep my brother out of my *Mad* collection. It didn't work quite as well as I had hoped, but, by the end of the 1970s, we had amassed a pretty decent collection of *Cracked* magazines as well as *Mad*. The first issue of *Cracked* I can remember buying for my younger brother was #128, the one with Al Capone on the cover, from 1975.

Greg Grabianski: I've been drawing since I was a kid—my dad was a pretty well known cartoonist in Poland and so I naturally followed what he did. By the time I was a teenager, I got impatient with the drawing part of cartooning and started enjoying the writing of the gags more than the drawing. I started sending around panel cartoons to magazines when I was 15 or 16 and received tons of rejections! I also got rejections from *Cracked* and *Mad*. By the time I got to college at the University Of Illinois, I said "fuck 'em" and started printing and selling my own magazine (*Frenzied Scrawlings*) for $2 a pop—and at the same time I was writing a humor column in the school paper.

While I was still in college, I got an internship at *Mad* magazine (this was like '94, I think). Luckily, this was while they were still in the classic old offices on Madison Avenue, and I got to know a lot of the classic writers and artists. And the editors (Ficarra and Meglin—which was a huge let down!!) Refusing to do shit-work (like clipping magazine photos), I was soon rewriting articles by old humor warhorses like Frank Jacobs, Dave Berg, etc. Despite all the rewritten articles I helped revive, when the internship was over, *Mad* didn't want to hire me. So I contacted *Cracked*. I sent them samples and they quickly hired me as an associate editor / staff writer. This was like 1995.

Murad Gumen: I grew up watching my father, Sururi Gumen, labor over the drawing board, mainly while he was doing the ghost artwork for the comic strip, *Kerry Drake* (as he did for the major part of over thirty years). He was kind enough to pass on some of his drawing genes my way, and along with the general appreciation for cartooning and art that naturally developed; I got the bug to see what I could do as a cartoonist and illustrator. (I was especially a big fan of *Mad*, and to a lesser degree, *Cracked*. *Mad* served as a heavy influence for my humorous mindset.)

Mad and the distant-second *Cracked* served as the big leagues in the humor magazine arena, and when my father broke through, I decided to try my luck with the remaining one that was comparatively slumming, *Sick*. (If you want to succeed, aim for the bottom; everyone knows that.) The one in charge at the time, Paul Laikin, wrote back, saying he was impressed, but *Sick* was sick enough to (I believe) curtail publication at the time. "Sorry for the both of us" is how Mr. Laikin finished his rejection note, which nicely eased the pain of being told to scram.

Mr. Laikin remembered me when he moved over to *Crazy*. My family was scheduled for our annual vacation in Montauk, Long Island, and in order to meet the deadline, I had to work on my own two-page starter over the small kitchen table of the cabin we stayed in. I was thrilled, as I was still a teen-ager, and this was my big break. I think my next assignment was the satire for the television show, *Baretta*, and I was pleased to graduate to what I regarded as the prestige pieces for these magazines.

Larry Hama: I started out in undergrounds doing a strip for *Gothic Blimp Works* which was the Sunday Funnies of the *East Village Other*. Also did stuff for *OZ* magazine in London during this period (late '60s). In the early '70s I teamed up with Ralph Reese (I penciled, he inked) to do comics and illos for *National Lampoon*, *Esquire*, *Crazy* and CTW. I also did assistant work for Wally Wood at that time, and then got a freelancer desk at Neal Adams' Continuity Associates.

I think I got the *Crazy* job because I got imploded out of my editor slot at DC and Marvel was looking to spiff up their humor book. (That didn't mean they were going to raise the budget much). It wasn't long, maybe two to two and half years? It was great. Got to pick up the phone and say, *Crazy!* It was just me and Jim Owsley (now known as Christopher Priest) and one production guy, Jose Albelo. We did everything. Jim stayed at night and set the type. I designed the covers, and cooked up the feature concepts. Our page rate was so low; the only way we could afford to pay our freelancers decently was to produce like 20% of the editorial content in house for free.

Charles E. Hall: I was born June 5 in York, Maine. My father was a college professor, and my mother taught art, though there is more to it than that. I currently live in New York City.

I grew up around art and books, and there was always paper and crayons in the house, and drawing was always one of my favorite activities, if not my favorite. Even my earliest works would generally tell a story of some sort, and my mother has saved a number of newsprint murals, done in crayon, depicting violent conflict featuring Roman legionaries, Vikings, Civil War soldiers, and so on.

In school I would often draw when I wasn't supposed to, in math class particularly, math paper being unlined and well-suited to pencil, and me finding math stupefying. I would become very involved with certain time periods, usually relating to military history, learn about and draw very specific ships, or airplanes, or tanks, or uniforms, or what-have-you. In high school, I discovered science fiction, and drew lots of space ships, as well as the military stuff. When I drew, I would formulate detailed fantasies centered on my pictures, but seldom write them down, or finish anything I did write.

I did caricatures of classmates and teachers, and comic strips featuring characters I would make up. These I would pass around in class, or tape up in the halls. In my sophomore year I drew cartoons for the chapter headings in the school yearbook. Now that I think of it, I did a few comedy presentations at school assemblies; one featuring cartoons done on poster board. It's something to remember that high schools once had smoking areas. One of my posters presented an American Indian smoking a peace pipe. My monologue noted that the practice of passing the pipe had come down to our own times, and could be seen in our own smoking area.

My grades were erratic, averaging to poor. Art school was the common suggestion for me by people concerned with my interests, but I maintained that one either was or wasn't an artist, and that school had nothing to do with it. I ended up being thrown out of a community college and entered on to a series of jobs in restaurants: dishwasher, busboy, waiter, prep cook.

Around this time I started playing guitar. Rock and Roll had always seemed to me like the best and most important thing in the world, but I wasn't naturally good at music, as I was with art.

Punk rock made that seem a lot less important. I started making up songs, and hanging out in the Portland, Maine punk scene. It was there that I met Doug Delle-Femine, and was surprised but not particularly impressed to find out that his older brother Michael, a.k.a. Mort Todd, was the editor of *Cracked* magazine. I can't remember if I'd ever picked up a copy of *Cracked*, but I was certainly aware of it. Doug and I formed what was both of our first band, Shark Attack. We both played guitar, there was no bass player, just us, a singer and a drummer. We made fuzzy, reverb-laden racket, and were a big hit at the local punk club, the legendary Geno's, from the start. Shark Attack changed singers, and became The Moguls.

I still drew, but you can't draw and play guitar (or wash dishes), at the same time, so I ended up drawing a lot less. I did do lots of posters. I couldn't stand to let other people make posters for my band. We were really just getting drunk, playing the same club again and again, and driving around in cheap cars, but it seemed very glamorous and fantastic. And maybe it was, anyhow, I wasn't the only one who was fooled.

Russ Heath: I became friends of Harvey Kurtzman's as a luncheon buddy, and years later I realized that every time I called him for lunch, I'd end up with a job to do. If I had realized that sooner, I might have got in on some of those vacation trips that Gaines used to do. They went all around the world to France, Germany, all over the place. But I was like the first guy on the outside the inner ring, so I missed out on that. I more or less followed Harvey's career from when he was doing *Hey, Look!* That's where I met him. And then *Mad* magazine had lunches and so on and he left there, I don't know what the next thing was. It might have been *Humbug*. And I worked on that. Then he started *Help!*, a Warren magazine. I worked on that. I still got some of the pictures and I was in some of the fumettis, and it's fun to look at me when I was young and handsome. And then he called me on *Little Annie Fanny*. I got in on that then I think the second or fourth week, I wasn't sure if I completed the first or working on the second. Anyway, I joined into that and did that and of course, I was doing comics on the side always, either for Stan Lee and then I guess it was 1950 when I first started doing stuff for DC, war stories and so on.

I worked on *Trump*. I did an imitation of Petty. George Petty used to do all the girls in *Esquire* before Vargas did, and because of the "Y" on the "Petty" signature, I made a slash on the end of my name like the "Heathy" girl. They didn't like my transparent glass-like suit I had on her, so they got Willie Elder to make it opaque, which always wrangled me. You're not supposed to go to other artists and fix something. I like to go home with the girl you brought if you know what I mean.

Todd Jackson: I got into writing like a lot of nerdy teens did... by being a bookish kid who read everything from comic books to novels. I only really got interested in humor after I worked on my college humor magazine at Emory. With desktop publishing revolution in full swing, it was a great time to explore how to funny on the printed page, because you could do a lot of things that would have just been impossible... your parodies could really mimic your targets exactly.

It's hard to say. Comedy nerds were really rare then I think. I loved the late night programs—*Letterman, SNL.* And funny movies. Saw some *Python.* But it wasn't something that had a sway over what my future was going to be until I discovered my college humor magazine and realized there were people like me out there. I was always a bit of a comedy snob though—I was really bothered when one kid in high school got all this adulation for being funny because he did a top ten list over the intercom—a Letterman bit!

Marten Jallad: I started drawing at age 10 after discovering *Mad* magazine while living in Kuwait of all places. At first in the style of my all time favorite Don Martin and then others. My interest in humor had started a number of years earlier with the *Asterix the Gaul* series by wonderful Goscinny and Uderzo. I was also introduced to *Cracked, Crazy, Sick, CarToons* and *Plop!* in the '70s and although I picked up a few here and there, *Mad* was always the ultimate funny magazine for me. In the mid-'90s, I started collecting *Mad* again and that stimulated me to start contributing to some fanzines (including *The Journal of Madness*) and other publications while also submitting ideas to *Mad.* Around 2000 a friend suggested putting together a comic book of local Atlanta artists and while hanging out in my office (the *Mad* pad) we came up with the name *Thwak* (a Don Martin sound effect). After the first comic book, I decided to change the format and self publish as a magazine which was more akin to my own likes. *Thwak* was distributed across the country as well as in Diamond and was a thrill to work on. The format was that of a humor magazine / homage / fanzine all rolled into one as I included articles/interviews with the likes of Carmine Infantino, Kelley Freas and Bruce Bolinger. (A *Thwak* 128-page trade paperback is currently in the works.) At *Thwak*, I was both editor and publisher and was able to bring on board many artists and writers from across the country and the world. This included a number of *Cracked, National Lampoon, Hustler Humor* and various other humor magazine alumni.

Mike Kazaleh: I had a lot of work published by Fantagraphics. They were very easy going as far as letting me do my own thing went. I did freelance work writing and penciling for Disney Publications. They were extremely uptight about everything. Most of the stuff I'd done for them never escaped the studio. I did work for Mirage Studios on the Archie line of *Ninja Turtle* books. It was kind of fun and I liked working with Editor Dean Clarrion, but the deadlines were always brutal. Working for Marvel also meant crushing deadlines. It seemed like everything was always being done at the last possible moment. On the *Ren and Stimpy* books we had the added horror of dealing with the people at Nickelodeon's consumer products division. I worked for Acclaim after that. A lot of the stuff I did there never got off the ground either. They weren't in the comic book business very long. DC was very good. They had more relaxed schedules, and gave me a little room to interpret the characters. I'd spent ten years with them. I also work for Bongo Comics and they are really swell people. The hard part is sticking to the Simpsons' style of drawing.

Milton Knight: Born in 1962 in Mineola, NY. I started drawing, painting and creating my own attempts at comic books and animation at age two. Always enthused about drawing and creating characters, so much that it became a life force. I've never formed a barrier between fine art and cartooning. The art of expression was always the most important one to me, and growing up, I treasured Chinese watercolors, Breugel, Charlie Brown and Terrytoons equally. My very young childhood was during the era of "pop art," when fine artists were freely inspired by comics and other popular culture; I remember being captivated by these works during trips to museums and galleries in New York.

Graduated from BOCES Cultural Arts Center (Syosset, NY), then took a few college classes in art while beginning a freelance art and writing career. Left home at eighteen, eking out what some would call a semi-living at my crafts while enjoying a lovely semi-homeless existence on Manhattan's waterfront. Finally landed in a Brooklyn brownstone where I spent seven water buggy years.

Did everything I could, I wasn't particular. Wrote and drew comic books and comic strips for magazines and small newspapers, illustrated, designed record covers, posters, candy and T-Shirts, and exhibited paintings when I could. Spent the 1980s on the outskirts of the "radical art scene" of the East Village. A challenging time, if not always a happy one.

Labor on Ninja Turtles comics allowed me to get up a grubstake to come to the West Coast in 1991, lured by prospects of a more healthful existence. Lived through a riot and a few earthquakes while working in animation as a designer, animator, and breaking in as a director thanks to my good friend Felix the Cat.

Dick Kulpa: For twenty years I'd aspired to work inside the comics field, an industry which wowed me in the 1960s, but which followed a road of irrelevancy that I, as a reader, held little interest in. Subsequently, my main efforts during that period focused on political satire and advertising, with measurable success—particularly when "comics" were utilized. These projects were "regional" in scope, and kept me within close proximity—i.e. "reach"—of my audience. Here I would learn that, while comics in general continued their decline from mainstream consciousness, the art form remained highly viable with "mainstream" people, who not only enjoyed my work, but got a great kick out of seeing me appear in superhero tights as I promoted various causes.

And the only two self-published comic books I produced both generated headlines across the country.

In 1988, I joined *Weekly World News*—then a highly disciplined, million-plus circulation tabloid—as a well-paid senior editor. Within five years—and with prominent newspaper expert Iain "Ice-pick" Calder as one of my "forceful" mentors, I became one of its guiding forces, serving as art director and, eventually, editor-in-chief.

As Calder's disciplined, no-nonsense and reader-friendly editorial approach was beaten into me, my occasional look at the 1990s comics offerings caused me to predict that these books would never go beyond the "25-cent" boxes at conventions. That, and I truly believed every comic pro should work at least one month under this guy.

Four years after my *WWN* arrival, "Bat Boy" was born, courtesy of yours truly. Other "Kulpa"-originated features, i.e. "The Great Chinese Jump," "Space Train Orbiting Earth" and "Iraqi Submarine in Lake Michigan"—among others—would help etch *WWN* into the national consciousness. (The space train story generated a complaint from the Russian Embassy, and a Russian "knockoff *WWN*" featured a Kulpa cartoon showing a preacher "mooning" his congregation.) I had done "my part" into transforming Lantana, Florida into a new "Ground Zero."

I designed hundreds of *WWN* "Page 1s" in my 15 years there. In fact, one *WWN* front-page story featured "an actual photo" of Elvis Presley outside a movie theater in St. Louis. It was an "actual photo," however, that was me—with Elvis' face. In short, millions of people saw my work every week, far above and beyond the exposure average comics pros would ever enjoy. And my work translated into millions of single copy sales—over 200,000,000 copies! "Page 1s" generated impulse sales for this circulation-driven tab – and I was the "number one Page 1 guy." Trouble was, nobody outside the building knew it.

Alan Kupperberg: Born in Brooklyn, New York in May 1953, I feel as though I were born an artist. My father was a fine, award winning amateur photographer. My grandmother was a gifted artist and earned her living as a hand painter. She was married to a cinema-photographer. I suppose it was my love for Popeye the Sailor that brought forth my bent for writing and drawing. I could never get enough Popeye, so I began to write and draw his further adventures on my own.

A Fan? I was a fan of *Mad*. I've known Sergio Aragonés for 43 years. I knew their office on MADison Avenue like the back of my hand. John Putnam was a strange old crank. Lenny Brenner is a strange "young" crank. I knew Bill Gaines. I worked for Wally Wood and with Joe Orlando. I knew Prohias. Hell, EC and *Mad* alumnus Berni Krigstein was a TEACHER of mine at the High School of Art and Design.

I followed *Cracked* and *Sick* for a few years in the late 1960s, I guess. *Sick* was always third rate in my day. *Cracked* was only better by dint of having John Severin on their roster. Do you know that Marvel Comics paid Severin MORE to INK Dick Ayers pencils on *Sgt. Fury and his Howling Commandos* than they paid Dick for the pencils? I never had the heart to tell Dick.

Aron Laikin: I was born into the world of cartooning with *Mad*, *Cracked*, *Crazy*, *Sick*, *Wacko*, Marvel Comics, the whole gamut. My father, Paul Laikin, was a pioneer with the early magazines starting with *Mad* and then worked his way through all the other satire magazines. I grew up with the "gang of idiots" and they sort of were like Godfathers to me. I took an early interest in cartooning, the visual side vs. the literal side that my father was heading down. I would get lessons from the greats like Mort Drucker and Jack Davis. All those guys from *Mad* magazines. I used to go to all the parties and hang out in the offices. I remember sitting on Stan Lee's desk while my father was in a meeting. He would just plop down a whole bunch of comic books for me, which was almost like babysitting for me. I hung out at the bullpen at Marvel and watched everybody draw, and I thought, "That looks pretty easy. I think I can do that." That's how it began. It began just being in my blood and I took an early interest and started working. Probably by 8 or 9 years old, I was starting to work. I did some early work for *Crazy*. I did the masthead. Some spot illustration work and then when I got more comfortable I started doing some full-page back cover stuff. I would just kind of help out where I was needed. My father was not only a writer, but also the editor and was the art director. He helped me out and assigned all the jobs too to the artists and writers. If he needed something at the last minute, he had an in-house artist right there and I would accommodate him.

I did have the interest enough, but my father really pushed me and helped develop it more. It wasn't like child slavery or anything like that. It was more like he saw me take an interest in the art and then he did everything he could to make everything available for me, either with the artist's themselves or the actual artwork. The artist's at that time didn't care about the originals.

They would just send it to the magazines and then forget about it. It would just pile up and I wound up having access to all of that. I would copy it and see how they inked and penciled and used Zip-a-tone. I got a real early start and even in school I didn't compare myself to my peers. I always compared myself to the top people, not meaning that I was one of them at the time, but I would try to emulate the top people rather than my peers. I was so young and I didn't feel like my peers were at my level since I had such an early start.

Paul Laikin: At the age of 16, I discovered humor. I was a musician and I got some laughs on the stage and from there on, I began thinking about comedy. Someone in the neighborhood, his name was Julius Cohen, was a comedy writer, and it never occurred to me to be a comedy writer. From there I started collecting comedy material. I was just obsessed at 17 or 18 with comedy. I wanted to be a comedian on the stage and I saw that I wasn't good at it. Paul Lamont—that was my comedian name. When I started out, that was the name I used as a comic.

I went into the army right after that for a year and a half, and I came back. I went up to Milton Berle in his office. I wrote something and he was impressed and he sent me to the William Morris Agency. I'm just giving you the highlights. I went to *The Kate Smith Show*. It was a big show with Harry Savoy, the comedian. I went backstage and saw him. I went sort of pursuing this to be a comedian. It didn't occur to me to be a writer. I wasn't aware of how I was going to fit in. I had a background in there, so I became a writer because I saw that I couldn't go onstage and dressing up all the time.

While I was a musician, I went up to the Catskill Mountains with a band that I wasn't the leader. I was good enough to be a sideman. I participated in things onstage. I wasn't that outgoing. You might say I was a quiet tumler. I did material and they said, "What? Repeat!" They couldn't hear it. My parents were in the resort hotel business at that time. That was my sort of background at that time—resort hotels—as a musician and trumpet player. For comedy, Milton Berle was an idol of mine.

I wrote something for Berle but I just got my foot in the door. I was just 16 or 17. I just wanted to be around them. I didn't know how to proceed or how to break in, but all that ended when I went into the army at 18, based in Germany. Right after the war ended, they were still drafting people. I came out at 19 or 20 and I went to Manhattan and started submitting stuff to Earl Wilson's column. He had a column like Walter Winchell's. I was staggering in there with no foothold at all. My father was in the resort hotel business and I went in and he died in 1948. My mother and brother were there and I left Manhattan where I was floundering around so I went into the hotel business to take my father's place. This lasted for about four or five years. I still sort of dabbled in comedy, but nothing serious. I didn't figure out how I could contribute. We sold the hotel after five years and packed up and went to Brooklyn—my mother, my brother and myself—and I took a job as a shipping clerk and a waiter. I had experience as a waiter in the hotel. One day I was working at the Concord Hotel. One of the guests was reading a *Mad* magazine. As soon as I saw that magazine, I said, "This is it!" Humor, because there was nothing like it around. Humor was mother-in-law jokes. That was the humor of the day and that's what the comedians did. Soon, I was working in the office and I looked in the Sunday *Times* help wanted there and lo and behold there was an ad that said, "*Mad* magazine looking for writers." I don't remember the timeframe here, but I'm just telling you the highlights. A couple years may have transpired between the Concord and this, but not that much time. I went up and I guess I sold them, because I think I was in my late 20s.

I had a great background before I came to *Mad*. I started at the top, I used to say, I'm working my way down. I started with Milton Berle and *The Kate Smith Show* and wrote for the top comics, and now I'm working for Al Feldstein. I remember that this was a step down. Al Feldstein was a sweet guy. The only thing I didn't like about him is that he held my stuff and put it in the bottom drawer.

Andy Lamberti: When I was a kid of 12 (average age for a *Cracked* reader). I'd read the magazine and wondered what it would be like to do this for a living. Although the payment was poor (as are the magazines), I at least fulfilled a childhood dream. You can't put a price tag on that!

My life's work was as a comedy writer for comedians, disc jockeys and business speakers. I did it for 30+ years before the magazines dried up in the 1990s. I wrote humor pieces for every conceivable magazine market (from *Catholic Digest* to men's magazines).

I've been a fan/collector all of my life. In my opinion, *Sick* in the early '60s was tremendous. It went its own way, Lenny Bruce-style before trying to compete with the kids' market segment of *Mad* and *Cracked*. Did you ever hear of a magazine called *Help!*? It was the brainchild of Harvey Kurtzman and ran for 26 issues from 1960 to 1965. It's taken me 25 years to get the complete set for my collection. There's really nothing out there anymore, except for *Hustler Humor*.

Kit Lively: I began writing and drawing my own humor magazines, then selling them to unsuspecting friends and classmates, around the age of nine, a habit that continued through high school and into college. During my not-quite Ivy League years, I formed my college's first humor magazine, which only lasted one issue due to the fact that many found it to be gross and offensive (none of my assigned supervisors bothered to check the material before publication, dismissing me with a wave of their hand and assurances that they were "sure that it's fine"). After that, I was no longer allowed access to the school's printing facilities. I decided to keep publishing the magazine (*The Chopping Block*) myself, and it went on to gather critical acclaim from Joe Bob Briggs and others in the comedy community. It also had a nice write-up in the Penguin Press book *The World of Zines*. Through *The Chopping Block*, I was able to get my cartoons and humor writing into other small-press publications and eventually into newsstand humor magazines (like *Rubber Chicken, Hustler Humor, Mean, The Joe Bob Report*) and nudie mags (*Hustler, Swank*, etc.).

Jay Lynch: When we were kids we were doing fanzines around the year 1960. These were little mags with circulations of under a hundred copies that were printed on ditto machines and mimeograph machines. Titles like *Smudge, Wild, Jack High, Squire, Foo* and so on. These little mags contained news of the pro satire mag business, interviews with Al Feldstein, Will Elder, all those guys. They also contained the early cartooning efforts of Robert Crumb, Art Spiegelman, Skip Wiliamson, and me. Don Martin did a cover for one issue of *Smudge*. Don (Duck) Edwing did some stuff for *Smudge*. We all diligently studied the work of Kurtzman and wrote back and forth to each other about the intricacies of cartooning and satire. The kids who did these fanzines were around the ages of 14 thru 16.

Cliff Mott: I started drawing in front of the family TV (a tradition which continues) while watching the classic 60s *Batman* show. Learning to read led to an obsession with comics in any form and category. Any four-color process newsprint would do, even black and white for that matter. I wasn't very discerning at that point.

I eventually graduated to *Mad* and later *National Lampoon*. I was especially drawn to the 50s reprints that were included in *Mad* special editions in the 70s. While on the hunt for *Mad* paperbacks, I discovered the existence of underground comix, which opened up things considerably.

Don Orehek: I started drawing when I very young. I think even before I started grade school. My father used to draw Austrian soldiers when I was a little kid. My old man was an Austrian soldier many many years ago. All the Orehek kids were interested in art in school. The nuns used to teach art, painting, and things like that with all my older brothers and sisters, but I was always interested in drawing funny things. That's how I started was when I went to grade school. I used to draw almost anything and the nuns used to try to make me right-handed. They had no control over that left hand of mine. Finally, they stopped beating my wrist and my knuckles, and they had me doing Christmas cards, on the blackboard, Easter bunnies and all that kind of crap. Then, after grade school I went to the School of Industrial Arts and they taught cartooning there and photography and every other thing. All the cartoonists that went there were like Al Scaduto, Rube Goldberg, Sy Barry— all these guys went there. They learned more about cartooning there and they did it the rest of their lives. Then of course when I went into the Navy, the captain of the ship always wanted to see the boots when they came aboard. He asked me what I liked to do and I said that I liked to draw cartoons. We don't need a cartoonist aboard this ship. When you are over the side painting, you can do your cartoons over the side of the ship. Of course he said to beat it, really. I got a laugh out of that, and then I after two years on the ship, I got a job at the naval paper that was coming out once a week in that area where the ships were moored. I started doing a comic strip about a sailor who was toothless and beat up and must have been in the navy about 40 years. I did that for two years and then after I got out of the navy, I went to the Visual Arts. At that time it was called Cartoonists and Illustrators and I showed my cartoons from the navy to Burne Hogarth and he looked at it, and he put me in the cartoon class for magazine cartoons and illustration and that was the best move, because I wasn't sure I wanted to do the *Superman* type people, but he put me in his cartoon class. I continued with that and when I got out of school—well, when I was in school I was selling cartoons—so most of the cartoonists that were in that class like Jerry Marcus and Charles Rodrigues, he was a little guy, a Portuguese from Massachusetts. I always thought he was Spanish, but he had the Portuguese spelling with an "s" instead of a "z." Then, when I got out of school, Sam Beerman, who was doing a lot of joke books like *Army Laughs* and *Broadway Laughs* and *Dogs and Gals*, hired me to work for him. So I worked for him for about 3 years, I think. Then there was Peter Wyma and Orlando Busino who had a cartoon workshop in Manhattan in the Lincoln Building which later became Lincoln Center and I started doing I think in '56, I started to freelance, and I was working and going in everyday to that place. We got little jobs, which didn't pay much, but it helped. Finally, when Lincoln Center kicked us out of that place, I started working at home, and I've been freelancing ever since. Then of course, I used to sell girlies and general stuff to the magazines and then when I got married, my wife religiously sent my stuff to *Playboy* and started hitting *Playboy* like anything, doing *Playboy* stuff.

You know, when I was school—this was like 1949 or 1950 in Cartoonists and Illustrators—there was one cartoonist there who was selling cartoons, a guy by the name of Ray Forest, and I did this cartoon of a king sitting on the throne watching TV and on the TV screen is the court jester. He said, "That's a *New Yorker* cartoon. Send it to *New Yorker*. And I did, and I got a rejection and about a year later, the same cartoon appears in *New Yorker* by Krause.

I always heard that *New Yorker* used to steal gags and from unknown guys, especially. For 20 years I used to leave stuff there and never got anything. The only time I was in *The New Yorker* was when I started doing ads for a carpet outfit called Bigelow. They were paying $200 a piece for those things. The only time I was in *New Yorker* was in advertising.

Steph Ramsay: I started cartooning and drawing caricatures while still in high school. It was a way to make my friends laugh and keep the teachers from noticing that I didn't know one end of a Pythagorean theorem from the other.

Tom Richmond: I started drawing caricatures in a theme park during summers between college school semesters, and developed a fascination with the art form. Following college I managed a caricature operation at a Six Flags park for a concession company and started my own operation while I pursued freelance illustration work. I did some comic book work, which segued into magazine and advertising illustration, much of which had something to do with caricature…, which had become something of a forté for me.

Mike Ricigliano: I was a student at Buffalo State College and I was a fan of *Mad*. I was there to be an art teacher, but I got into the newspaper there called, *The Record* and I started to do a bunch of off the wall cartoons for the paper. One was called "The Beast that Ate Buffalo," about a tuna casserole that would go around and meet various administrators and teachers in school. It was kind of an editorial cartoon / horror type of thing. After I got out, I thought I could try my hand in that field. My first work was at *Crazy* at Marvel Comics. It was a wrestling cartoon that I wrote and drew and press-typed the headlines. I brought it in and they ran it as is and from there I got the bug and I wanted to get into the field and learn more about the field.

I had my loyalties to *Mad* and *Cracked* and *Crazy* was just a shot in the dark for me. I had the address, I walked into the city, I did the articles before I even went into the city, which is insane. I wish I had the article because you'd laugh at everything that I press-typed in that article. If you have that issue, look at it, it is all press-typed. They may have added type afterwards, but all the headlines that are on it and all of the type that I presented to them was press type.

I always signed my stuff "Ricig" in college, so if there is some stuff. I've always signed it even in college, "Ricig" with a little hat. I used to wear a little hat like that in college. I still wear hats. I have a huge collection of hats.

Kevin Sacco: I was poring over everything. I was very into the *Eerie* and *Creepy* stuff. That was beautiful stuff. I used to look at all the other humor magazines because I was fascinated by the artists. What started me off was *Mad* magazine. I'd look in the magazine and I was like "Wow! I want to do what Jack Davis does or I want to do what Harvey Kurtzman does." So, of course, you look at every other magazine.

The way I knew Marie Severin is that I had gone up to Marvel Comics and at the time she was in charge of hiring new talent. She was fabulous. She was such a sweetheart. She would help you in any way. She might not give you a job, but she would give you pointers. Later on, I found out, she introduced Kurtzman to his wife Adele, when Adele was working as a colorist at Marvel. It was sort of like a family affair with the Severins as artists. She was a pretty good artist, too. Everyone except for Davis, he was the kid from the South.

I sent Paul Laikin some samples of illustrations that I was doing when he was editing *Crazy*. He just responded by sending me a brief for me to do. So, I just started basically working on something then and there and doing something once a month, which was great, and a lot of fun. The only problem at that time was it was still "work for hire." Once you signed the back of the check, they owned all of the artwork. There were a lot of acrimonies about that one. You almost were crossing a picket line working for *Crazy* with that one. So that's how I got started working for *Crazy*.

Warren Sattler: My older brother was a natural born artist and when I was around five, my mother would keep a box of all his drawings. He was seven years older than me. He's since passed on. She kept a box of his drawings and when people would come to visit us, my mother would show these pictures and people would say, "Ooh, ah, look how wonderful that is." So, I kind of wanted that for myself so I started drawing, but to get into why I wanted to be a cartoonist, I fell in love—one Sunday I was looking at the Sunday pages and fell in love with Milton Caniff's *Terry and the Pirates*. I have that exact Sunday page on my wall. It was in March of '45 or '46, and when I saw that I went right to my mother, she was ironing and at the time I said, "Ma, I'm going to be a cartoonist like this man here," and that's what I wanted to do. Unfortunately, I wanted to do an adventure strip, but by the time I got into the business, humor had taken over and television had taken off all the adventure strips. I did get a chance to do some serious drawing when I started working for comic books. That's basically what happened.

I went to this trade school and there was this German teacher who was brought over to this country. Meredith at that time was the silver city of the world. It was all silverware and he was brought here to teach them and after a while he started to teach a course in the print school and that's where I got my basic training and when I tell other people how tough it was and how exacting he was as a teacher, they said that was better than a college education. I was always proud of that. His name was Ernst Lohrman. He taught art to me.

When I was a teenager I loved Jack Davis work as well. He and Harvey Kurtzman I learned how to draw hands and feet from. I loved their styles. I worked with Harvey Kurtzman too, which was a great honor on the early *Annie Fannys*. I was kind of a "way back" artist there. Kurtzman would think up the ideas, and he'd sketch out a rough sketch and give it to Will Elder. Will Elder would pencil in some stuff, and I would do all the background characters and tighten up the details so he could paint it later on.

I only did one or two pages one or two times with them. Trouble was, Kurtzman wanted me to work with him in New York. I live in Central Connecticut and I'd have to drive in to New York to Mount Vernon where Harvey lived, and then I'd have to go over to New Jersey—I forget the town—where Will Elder lived, and then drive all the way back to Connecticut and it was a monster trip whenever I had to do that. So, after two times I said I can't keep this up, and after that I just got the chance to draw *The Jackson Twins*, which was a syndicated comic strip, and all I had to do was stay home, and go down to work which was like an hour away from where I lived, and that was every two weeks I would have to deliver strips down through there. So I said, "I can't do this." So, I missed the opportunity of constant work with Harvey Kurtzman. That's why I'm probably not mentioned. That's the story of my life.

The one I did was about *La Dolce Vita* and was a Christmas issue. Like I said, I did the tightening up and some of the details. I think it was 1962. Well you can't miss it. It was all about Christmastime and buying Christmas presents. Yeah, that's the one I worked on. The last page I think you see her legs in a Christmas card. Something like that. Yeah I worked on that. All those Christmas cards are mine. Then the next one I don't recall what that one was because I was getting ready to leave anyway. I did all the people in the background. There's one where a bunch of people are given lights. I had the Statue of Liberty putting that out, but Harvey took that out.

I basically worked for Charlton for a number of years. I did a few jobs for Marvel and also for DC, but I did mostly for Charlton.

John Severin: He went to high school with these guys, Harvey Kurtzman, Will Elder, Al Jaffee, Al Feldstein and Joe Simon.

The way John got into comic books. It was supposed to be a party and him and Harvey and Bill and Harvey got John to work at EC. Before that, John had gone to American and there he worked with Jack Kirby. Then after Jack went over to Marvel and John went over to EC. A lot of years later, John did a lot of work on the *Hulk* for Marvel. So Harvey had gotten work at EC and they put out *Two-Fisted Tales* and worked on *Frontline Combat*.

So, John worked there with Harvey. When Harvey had Bill try a new one, with *Mad* and so naturally Harvey called John. But then Harvey always said something about deadlines, so John took over *Two-Fisted Tales* and then after that, they used John more and more because John loved it. At the time, Bill was having troubles with Harvey Kurtzman because Bill wanted to put him down. John worked for all the different companies. They could go back to Harvey. Harvey then went to *Trump* and he also did *Help!* and *Humbug*. John did not go, because about that time, he was always full with other work. He was with *Cracked* from then on.

He never went with Kurtzman on any other job. Severin went with Kurtzman early on at EC, but then Kurtzman did *Trump* and *Humbug* and they used all the other guys, but they didn't use Severin. He didn't go with *Humbug* or anything else.

Lou Silverstone: I grew up reading *Li'l Abner* and that was the big thing. I wanted to be a writer and an artist both like Al Capp. In college I worked on a humor magazine. As a kid I used to write my own comics and draw my own comics but they weren't very good. They were fun. When I got out of the Army I went to college in Illinois. There I started turning stuff out. The very first story I sent out was called "Boredom's going to be easy." The 25 bucks didn't last very long. It was for one of those men's magazines. Eventually I sent stuff to *Mad*, and they said it was very funny but wasn't quite mad enough but he invited me in. He had a conference and they gave me a shot and I was there for over 25 years. I started around 1960 or a little bit before that.

I sold a lot of one-panel cartoons and then they started buying more ideas than my drawings. Even in high school, I was by far the best artist in school. Then you see a Mort Drucker or someone like that and you think, "What the hell was I thinking?"

Steve Strangio: I wrote for a humor publication at Hofstra University called *Nonsense*. It was a great time and I hung out with a damn crazy and fun group of writers. I wanted to do more of that once I graduated, so I looked for magazines out there in the real world that needed writers. I'm a writer / producer and sometimes actor that really enjoys the entire creative process. Sometimes you do it alone and sometimes you learn from the other people you invite into the production. I'm happiest when I'm creating.

I got into writing because I felt a need to comment on the things I saw around me. Writing is also a great way to "get what's inside into the outside," and then take another look at it. I absolutely believe that people are writers because they have to be. It's who they are.

I've written and produced 10 short films, 15 one-act plays, hosted my own television show, appeared on national television, written an adventure ebook called *SAM Demon Hunter*, invented a few board games and even created my own team sport.

Basically, this is what I do for a living ...

- Screenwriter
- Filmmaker
- Television Writer/Producer/Creator
- Playwright
- Actor
- Voice Acting
- On-Air Host
- Author
- Comic Book Writer
- Game and Sports Creator

I'm planning on getting a business card that just reads, "I do lots o' stuff."

Seeing my first humor article published in *Cracked* was one of the highlights of my career so far. I collected a lot of humor magazines growing up and *Cracked* always stood out for me. Going from fan to regular contributor was one of the benchmarks in my career.

My goal was to do my best and make my writing stand out while contributing to the growth and the style of humor in this publication.

Having the chance to see my writing visualized by some of the industry's best artists really made me proud.

Tony Tallarico: I went to high school and specialized in art. It was called the School of Industrial Arts. After graduating I went on to art school. It was a cartoonists and illustrators school at the time, The School of Visual Arts now, and I went to Brooklyn Museum of Arts School. I always liked comics and I eventually started doing a few. It was very difficult in those years to do pulps which is what I really wanted to do. The pulps were gone. Comic books were the new pulps. I didn't mind and I enjoyed it. I worked for a lot of different places: I started off at Charlton, Hillman, Dell, just about everyone. It went on and on. Just about everybody. In '66, I did a book called *The Great Society Comic Book*, and it and became a bestseller.

It was a regular book publisher that took it on and it was sold in bookstores. It was a book that sold for a dollar, which would be the equivalent of about $6 or $7 now. It did very well. It sold several hundred thousand copies. It went back to press a couple of times. It did real well and right after that, as that was going on, I came up with an idea with a writer named DJ Armesen whom I collaborated with on *The Great Society* in the beginning, we did a book called *Lobo*, and *Lobo* was the first black hero comic book.

It was for Dell. We thought we had something really good, but it turns out after the second issue, they put a quick stop on it. The distributors were receiving packages of comics including *Lobo*, and because *Lobo* was in there, they would sending them right back. So that took care of that. It's funny, in that 40 years later, I got a call about 8-9 months ago from a motion picture studio in California that they're interested in doing a movie of it, so we'll just have to wait and see. I created the character.

I also did superhero versions of *Dracula* and *Frankenstein* for Dell. That was stupid. They were dumb! That was their idea. DJ Armasen was the editor at the time there. Lennie Coe had been caught with his hands in the till, and they bounced him. Helen Myers, she was the President of Dell at the time—she was the first female president of a publishing company—so Armasen presented the idea of the comic to her and she liked it. We did, I don't know, three or four issues of each. It was really quite stupid. There's no other way of saying it. For some strange reason, everybody asks about that. It must have touched something. In the '60s, you had to do that, although Dell was very good. I was getting a book a month out of them.

Then, I worked on some of the *Harvey Thrillers* for Joe Simon. He was a very nice guy. When he got ahold of it as a freelance editor, I don't think it lasted a year. I think comics were dying anyway. It was like that comics had it. The market wasn't there and shops were not real happy and they could put some other type of magazine in place of a comic book and charge a buck for it, so then comic books went into the 15c, maybe 20c category, which it just wasn't there for the dealer.

To generate interest in the candy storeowner in making a few dollars on it. If one comic book were stolen, there would be the entire week's money that they could make. It was really penny-ante stuff. Of course, *Playboy* they were the ones that really jacked up the price of magazines. I mean like a buck and a half, two dollars. Who ever thought of that? That was ridiculous.

After '66 with *The Great Society* and *Lobo*, I really started trying to do children's books. It was no easy thing, because at that point, if you did comic books, you were out. But I was doing coloring books and other books. Whatever I could do in the book field. I'm negotiating with the publisher to get the rights back.

B.K. Taylor: Well, I was very lucky; my father was a commercial artist. He did magazine illustration and ads for the auto companies and clients like Motown records. It was the perfect environment for me to become interested in illustration. I would go upstairs to his studio and watch him draw, or attempt to imitate what he was doing. The problem was, it was difficult for me to keep it serious -- my heart was in humorous illustration.

My dad had a great sense of humor (in fact he was the inspiration for Norm Appleton and the *National Lampoon* strip, *The Appletons*). But he didn't want me to be a cartoonist, as he didn't feel there was enough opportunity in cartooning. My teachers at school felt the same way. But I loved the challenge of making people laugh and creating the absurd, because it makes me laugh. It's fascinating to think that I may have made someone laugh on the other side of the country that I've never met, seen or heard from. I knew I wasn't ready for *Mad* magazine, since at that time they had (more or less) a closed stable of artists. I was still in art school when I first began sending my work around. I was fortunate to do a series of bubblegum cards for the Don Russ Company.

Mort Todd: I was a hardcore comic (and all media) geek since age seven and started writing and drawing my own comics soon after. I soaked up every comic I got my claws on and started recognizing artists' styles. I was boy editor of the summer camp newspaper and took the mimeograph machine home during the off-season to print my own comics, As a kid, of course you read *Cracked* when *Mad* wasn't around. Whenever anyone tells me, "Oh yeah, I always liked *Cracked* better than *Mad*," I just don't believe it! There was certainly excellent stuff in there with Severin and I really liked the Bill Ward stuff.

At thirteen, I brought my art samples to DC Comics and the art director then, the infamous Vinnie Colletta, told me I would never work in comics. Within ten years I was running my own mag hobnobbing with the industry greats. Vinnie was friends with the *Cracked* publisher and even came around sniffing for work but it sure wasn't gonna happen. At age seventeen, I moved from Maine to New York City and started doing comics, record covers, band logos and advertising. Soon we were publishing *Psycho Comics* and I was dabbling in film and animation. I was getting work from DC, Marvel and independents like Fantagraphics and Kitchen Sink so I dropped out of Parson's for art and went to SVA for film. Then Kevin McMahon and I sold a TV pilot called *The Ultimates* to a German company. It was about a band of teen superhero rock stars and starred a young Dan Clowes, who was then the spitting image of Speed Racer. I recently unearthed the original video and may use it to blackmail Clowes. Not long after I heard about *Cracked* from Pat at Marvel and the rest is comics history!

WHERE ARE THEY NOW?

Noel Anderson: I still do comics for *Hustler Humor* magazine, primarily doing Movie and TV satires, and have been working on several humor books with fellow *Cracked* alumni, Kit Lively. I do my best to carry over that *Cracked*-vibe in the parodies I create for them so it's kind of the same. Kind of the same except for the…um, ahem vaginas and what not!

Mike Arnold: I recently finished laying out and helping Marten redesign many of the pages for a 128-page *Thwak* trade paperback compilation. I love cartoon humor magazines and would love to do another and another and another. It's a labor of love and even though it's tough to find the time to work on pet projects it's always worth it in the end when you get to see it published and become a reality. You can look back and know that instead of just complaining that there are no more humor magazines being published, you made an effort to contribute to the genre.

  Other than that I'm doing same thing I was doing before *Cracked* had its unfortunate demise. I did a couple of things for *Mad* but mostly I do freelance cartoon illustration for books, magazines, greeting cards, kid's restaurant menus, character design, cartoon logos etc. Anything that needs my style of cartoon art. And reading my old issues of *Cracked*—America's Humorest Funny Mazagine!"

Peter Bagge: Graphic Novels. Yawn. Plus occasional comic strips for *Reason* and *Discover* magazines, and illustrations here and there.

Dave Berns: Sitting around in my pj pants writing answers to these interview questions… contemplating whether or not to delete half of this interview before sending it in… If you're reading this and legally represent any of the aforementioned bums and feel they've been maligned, I was only kidding, it's what I do! Cross my heart, hope to die and such.

Seriously, though I'm freelancing on illustration and design for the most part for whoever is paying me next (Marketing, package design, t-shirt illustration, caricature work, product design, conceptual illustration, logo design, publication design, etc... entertaining all offers when things are slow and only the fun ones when they're busy... again, I take requests!), working on some other ideas and collaborations that are proprietary in nature that I've yet to launch, and also dabbling in the local art scene a little lately. I invite you to check out daveberns.com for the latest and more specific updates.

Ray Billingsley: Currently doing *Curtis*. It is my second syndicated strip, the first being *Lookin' Fine*, which debuted when I was 21.

Bruce Bolinger: Presently I am "retired" but still create artwork for a couple websites and a T-Shirt distributor, Just4yucks.com. I do cartoon work that interests me and still turn down a lot of inquiries. At this very moment I just finished recreating artwork for Norma Martin, commissioned to bring back artwork Don drew for a couple vinyl LP record covers from 1950. I'm also involved in a couple other projects Norma is organizing. Since we live in the country my time is spent chopping wood, cleaning litter boxes, skinning things, keeping empties out of the driveway as well as creating artworks that don't provide an adequate income yet. In fact, my advice to aspiring cartoonists would be; learn a decent trade. We don't need the competition and there is definitely not enough money to go around. And good luck.

Roger Brown: Occasionally, I write for some of the independent comics and do some gag writing, but I mostly work on my inventions. I have several products licensed and on the market. I am finishing a book on how to get your products to market without going into debt. It is called Guerilla Inventing.

Brian Buniak: *Thunderbunny*: that really made the rounds. It first appeared at Charlton after being self-published, then it was at Red Circle Comics, one of the Archie imprints, then it was WaRP Graphics. Then WaRP turned into Apple Comics. We were all over the place. I loved *Thunderbunny*, but the amount of work that it took to draw and write, it needed much better sales to continue it. Really, I tried to make it pay off. The sales of the book were really low compared to what we were putting into it writing and art wise. I couldn't sustain it.

Right about the end of my run on *Thunderbunny*. I was looking around for other things and I was doing some caricature work and I went over there and they thought the things I was doing was good and they got hot when I left and I went home and I got a call and it was work in advertising and they paid more right there. We got all of our caricaturists anyway. He doesn't want to work it that way. Jack Davis doesn't want to. Mort Drucker doesn't want to. If they all say no, then we'll offer it to you. They always want to do more work not less, but show me what you got. "Do you really like it?" and they said yeah. I was working on the final issue of *Thunderbunny* and I got a phone call and they wanted me to work in two weeks and I said, "I'm working on this. Can I work on it a little longer?" and they said, "No. We want you to drop whatever it is and do this." I've never done that before. I've never really deliberately screwed someone. So I said, "I will be able to do that afterwards." I know what you're saying right now, "I'm Brian Buniak and he's turning up and down in order to not do this new thing. We want you to work full time and you'll never let us down." No, actually what I'm saying is that you're a jerk and I'm turning up and down to do this, and he hung up on me. I thought he was kidding. I thought he was being flippant. It was like touching the back of the Queen. Michelle Obama can get away with it, but I guess I can't. Once I did that I never worked there again. I tried and when Bill Gaines died I thought that would open things up and it got worse. When they were sort of taken over by Joe Orlando, I went in again, and they were all excited about my work until they go into another room and they come out and it looked like they looked at all the notes they had on me and they said, "No." I don't know if it said that I worked at *Cracked* or what and they come out and said, "W-w-w-we'll call you." I never got anything, not even after they went into hard times now. I'm happy now, but how many magazines have lasted so long that were so "hot" that have lasted so long. *Conan* comes to mind, you could barely buy the first couple of issues and then Marvel was starting to take a hit. I mean they had four or five different titles and then *Conan* comes along as this bloody barbarian. For a while it was great. Now, the fact that he can and that he's still alive. I looked at *Mad* and do you have time for one more analogy? Good. How I looked at *Mad* was when it first came out in the early 50s, but even in its early days as a magazine, *Mad* was an outcast. It was running around like Bugs Bunny, and they blasted everything. You couldn't do a normal thing with it. *Mad* was an outlaw, but it was a cool outlaw like Dirty Harry. It was wild. It was great. Such detail. It was great to look back on that stuff. After it moved into the 70s, it was still the law, but more like Andy Taylor. Kind of predictable, kind of "Come on, Barney." You still would chuckle, but you knew where it was going. The *Lampoon* was more worthwhile at that point. As time went on, it just became a bad old security guard. I don't know how well it holds up today. I don't know where it is. That's sort of how *Mad* evolved and I'm not sure I'd want to go through that.

The Joe Kubert School had seen my work and they had called me a number of times to see if I would do a caricatures class. I was excited to do it but I didn't know if I could actually teach something like that. I started it and tried it for a while as a temporary thing and I went in there and I really liked it. I liked explaining things to students. I liked showing things with humor. It isn't easy and it's much tougher to do it right. I drew some guy holding up a limp girl and looking up in the air and this is probably the most used cover idea of all. If you don't make people laugh, it just doesn't work no matter how well thought out it is or whatever. That element where you have to take things to explain them. Looking at what they did, it was about 80% there, but they couldn't figure what was wrong. They hoped that once they learned that timing, you could use that.

There's always something out there for it if you are a humor or caricature artist. You can do it on the spot if you are at a party or something like that. You have to be available for parties and other gigs where you have to draw for a couple of hours. Do a party to pay your rent or something, then take the rest of the time to do what you want. I'm not so funny to go on to do those as I've seen others do. I'm not so good at it. That work is up there with twisting and turning with kids. You cannot really do that with an age group like that. So if you really have a limited timetable.

It's 3 years and it's pretty intensive if you want to go there. It's about a 3½-year course if you put it all together. You have to put a lot of work into it. It does get easier as it goes on. I think a lot go there just essentially because they were drawing all the way through high school, so there looking and they go "Oh, wow! I'll be among my peers." It's not a school to just hang around and draw the things you like. You have a professional to tell you to avoid drawing what you like. If you like what you're doing, it won't earn you a nickel. You have to do it this way if you ever want to prosper as a cartoonist and you have to do it right. You have to do a lot of things that aren't important than drawing pictures and drawing cartoons. People out there love football and watch it every weekend. They can tell you every stat of every player, but you stick them on a field and they wouldn't know what to do. Similarly there are people who know and love comics, but they could never do this and leave after a year.

As far as humor is concerned it would be timing. A lot of time, guys and gals, the timing of a piece will sometimes save it or make it more readable than just throwing gags in some beautiful drawings. It has to really flow and I try to emphasize that. That's the kind of timing that works for a TV show or a fine film. It doesn't work in comedy without the rhythm for the gags. If you like to draw a certain way and a certain thing, then readers will detect a certain pattern from you, so you become not funny anymore. You got to work on each gag on a whole new level to keep it fresh forever and keep the rhythm and simplicity, or you'll dry up real quick. That's the most important thing. There are people that aren't that good of drawers but people love their work. Outside of *Cracked*, the ones that I would look at are like the strip out there now called, *Pearls Before Swine*. If you just look at it, you might say, "I hate this strip," because it is so limited in its drawing. I would say it is even poorly drawn. But it takes on a new level with the dialogue and it is really some of the best stuff that's out there. Limited drawings sometimes add to the humor of it. The very crudeness makes it that much funnier, sort of like a *Rocky and Bullwinkle*. If that were animated like a Disney's *Pinocchio*, it wouldn't be as funny as it is.

If the idea or concept isn't there, the movement won't matter. I love animation and movement, but a bad idea can put you to sleep. They can ruin it with animation that if you ever have any trouble nodding off, then...

Terry Colon: Lately I've been doing humor bits for *Reader's Digest*. The editor I work with there is Andy Simmons, whom I worked with at *Cracked*. I also write satire bits for *The People's Cube*. But I don't illustrate them.

Other than that, free-lance illustration. That's where I make my living. But that's sort-of another field. Though I use the same cartoonist-like sensibility for spot illustration. I like my art to border on a gag cartoon, if not actually being one.

Frank Cummings: I'm currently John Marshall's assistant on the comic strip *Blondie*. I do the Monday-Friday strips.

Barry Dutter: I had so much fun on *Cracked* despite a lot of the bad stuff that happened; there was stuff that I was proud of. I had a really good time with it. I actually started publishing my own humor magazine called *Gag!* I did two issues and they were like two years apart. I lost a ton of money on it, but had a great time. It was kind of my last hurrah with humor magazines. It was a lot of fun. I probably did it about 10 years too late. In the early '90s, I probably could have gotten some decent sales. If Warner Communications can't sell a humor magazine, what hope does a little guy working out of his apartment have? I'm here in LA now and like everyone else in LA, I'm working on a screenplay. I'm actually working on a graphic novel about my crazy adventures in Internet dating. All true stories. I'm mourning the end of humor magazines. If there was a way to produce a humor magazine and have it make a profit, I'd be more than happy to do it. These days, humor has moved to the Internet. We live in a culture that doesn't pay for anything anymore.

Gary Fields: In 1999, I started working at DC on their line of Hanna-Barbera comics. Marty Pasko was always telling me to go down to see the guys at *Mad*. They were one floor down. At that point, I felt loyal to *Cracked* and knew I probably couldn't work for both. Years later, after *Cracked* was dead I went to see Sam Viviano at *Mad*. He thought my stuff was "too cartoony" for *Mad*, but liked what I could do with ghosting other cartoonist's styles. Like when they would spoof comic strips and you'd have to do a *Peanuts*, *Beetle*

Bailey, Dick Tracy, etc. strip. Then he explained the hierarchy of things. He had his "A list" (Drucker, Sergio, etc.), he had his "B list," and if I was lucky I might be able to be on his "C list." I didn't mind being a "C lister" but I guess I didn't feel like jumping through any hoops at that time. So that was that.

As far as current freelance work goes, I've been a regular gag cartoonist for *Nickelodeon* magazine, which I love doing. Chris Duffy and Dave Roman are the best editors around. I continued to work for DC with their Cartoon Network comics and only stopped because the book I was working on got cancelled. I've worked for a lot of places, including Marvel. I always liked working for DC and Marvel, but was kind of out of the loop because I was doing the funny stuff. Maybe it was to my advantage. Who knows? *Cracked* was more like a bunch of friends who worked together, where Marvel and DC were more like the big companies they are.

I'm a full time artist working for The Children's Place doing graphics for our boy's graphic T-Shirts, clothes, and other fun stuff. I'm also still freelancing for *Nickelodeon* magazine, *National Geographic Kids*, *WWE Kids* magazine and trying to do a little more of my own comics and stuff just for myself.

Bob Fingerman: I think I became a pretty regular freelancer after that. I worked at the *Village Voice* after that and you know, various other magazines, too. It kept me out of *Cracked*, and I also started working for pornography, so it's a slippery slope. As I say, my early career isn't exactly one I can really crow about, but at least it paid my bills, which is better than what some people can say about drawing comics. I write and draw comics and I published a novel a couple of years ago. I'm definitely doing the kind of work I actually want to be doing—creator-owned, creator-driven stuff. I mainly do both graphic novels and prose novels.

Dan Fiorella: Presently I'm serving 9-5 in a brokerage house in lower Manhattan. I've been working my day job since school; gotta pay the bills and I have a family to support. But I'm still hacking away; I had a screenplay optioned by Warner Bros. (never produced). I worked on *The Adventures of the Galaxy Rangers* years ago (now on DVD!). I've written for Garrison Keillor's *Prairie Home Companion* (I like to think I have range). I contribute to All-Star Radio and American Comedy Network, a pair of radio syndicators who produce comedy sketches and to the Newsbusters website for their *Newsbusted* comedy news videos. (again, range.) My short story, a Sherlock Holmes parody *The Adventure of the Angry Author* was published in an anthology in France while a PC game I wrote is just coming out; *The Lost Adventures of Sherlock Holmes, Vol. 2* from Legacy Interactive. And still churning out screenplays. And there's my tale.

Pete Fitzgerald: Not so much cartooning these days, I'm afraid. Instead, I m working in the family business, which is the manufacture of rug-hooking frames, so I'm doing a lot of woodworking: sawing, sanding, routing, gluing, etc. The products are quite successful, so I'm making decent money, despite these rough economic times. I still do a bit of cartooning work now and again; I'll always have a hand in—I'm always up for doing some—even though it's not my livelihood at the present time. I'm still in CT, though no longer a Brookfield resident.

Subsequently, I did a little work for Mike, post-*Cracked*. A back cover for his *Pepito* comic, featuring a misassembled Terminator, and a two-page spread for the *Woodstock '94* commemorative comic, when he was working for Marvel Special Projects. Among the stuff I did soon after I left *Cracked* were some spot illos for Andy Simmons' newspaper-for-kids project, *Youthline USA*.

Kent Gamble: I'm 55 now. I'm doing my stuff from home. The script would come in the mail. I'd wrap it up, send it off to New York, and wait for the next script. That was it. I talked to Paul all the time and then for a stretch I illustrated a bunch of stuff where Murad Gumen was the writer and I was the writer. So, eventually I started to talk to Murad on the phone and we became buddies. At the time I took a trip up to New York years ago, I met with him and he showed me around town a little bit. We had fun. He was really the only guy, but I did meet Larry Hama one time. It was another trip and I went up to the offices but I had no idea what he looked like and he has this deep voice. When I saw him I guess he's Oriental a bit, and he had hair down to the middle of his back, and just straight black, jet-black hair.

He had this super-duper long hair when I saw him. I'm sure my mouth probably just fell open when I met him. I had no clue. That was not how I pictured him at all. And then Larry told me that at one point he was an actor, because he told me he was in an episode of *M*A*S*H*. I said, "Ah, come on," and he said, "I was in an episode of *M*A*S*H*. It was an episode where Burns is kidnapped by soldiers who he thinks are South Korean, but really turn out to be North Korean. Anyway, I saw that episode one time and I said, "My God, it is, it's Larry Hama!" So he was actually in an episode of *M*A*S*H*. He wasn't funnin' me, it was real.

I was in *Wacko* and *Parody*, I think it was. They were short-lived as well. One of the bigger names in *Parody* was Vance Rodewalt. I liked his stuff. He's good.

For years I have had a rep in New York, American Artists, which is Mike Mendelson. They've repped me for years and I've gotten some fairly good jobs from them. I have a rep and it sounds really big time, but I get a couple of jobs a year.

Yeah, and books. I've done a couple of books. Lynn Berman, he's the NBC sports anchor in New York on whatever the local channel is in New York. He's always on *The Today Show* a lot and he'll have films of sports blooper reels and then says, "And nobody got hurt." Well, he's written two kids books, which I illustrated called *And Nobody Got Hurt* and *And Nobody Got Hurt II*! I illustrated both of them. I still get a lot of work through them, and that's fun. I get a lot of sports stuff. Texas Tech is here and I do stuff for them. I do a lot of stuff like program rosters and art during football season for the football team.

If I get a job through Mendelson, great. Otherwise, you get calls. I've drawn a lot of stuff, locally for T-Shirts and billboards and stuff, so I'm kind of a local celebrity of sorts. I do a lot of stuff for Tech sports and I don't always get paid. I'm an alumnus and I do things for kicks and fun.

Somewhere I saw an issue of *The Journal of Madness* and I said, "Well, gee, this is neat. They're talking about *Mad* and they've got articles about them. I made some phone calls. I guess the phone number was inside. I called John and I wasn't sure if he had heard of me. I'm sure he had through *Crazy* or something. I asked him if I could mess around with a cover or something, so I did and he liked it and there we were.

I work for a title insurance company and have for almost 30 years. We close real estate transaction and close the titles. It pays the bills. I'm sure a lot of these guys had day jobs. A lot of my work was done either at night or on weekends. When I was young and I could stay up and still be ok at work the next. Well man, forget that now. It's hell to get old. We all did things late and at all hours. Looking back I always think, "My God, how did I do that?"

George Gladir: I am now in my fiftieth year at Archie, and enjoy what I am doing. I am also working on *Cindy and Obasan*, a comic book created by myself and comic book icon Stan Goldberg. We believe the book has movie potential. It's based on the knowledge I acquired on Japanese pop culture while writing manga for a Japanese publisher (Kodansha) back in the nineties.

I work closely with several comic book stores...Hi De Ho Comics and Golden Apple in California, as well as with Night Flight Comics in Utah. Would you believe the latter has its main store within a library?! ...the library is the famed Salt Lake City Library which was recently voted the #1 library in America by the National Library Association.

Charles E. Hall: I decided, against all sensible odds, to form another band here in the city. I still really liked playing, I was meeting a much larger and worldlier bunch of musicians than were to be found in Portland, and I was making up new songs all the time. I moved into a run-down, a seriously run-down, storefront on 5th Street between Avenues A and B. I was working at a record store when Mort was hired to be editor at Marvel Music, Marvel Comics' new Music division. Mort's first assignment was sort of "busy work" while deals were being made with prospective artists: a graphic novelization of the C.S. Lewis theological classic *The Screwtape Letters*, done in conjunction with Nelson Publishing. Mort looked at scripts from a couple other writers, then called me. The timing couldn't have been better, as shortly thereafter I was fired from the record store. I did very tight, specific layouts for the book, which I essentially abridged. Pat Redding did the inks.

My next assignment was an authorized and vetted three-part, 150-page, graphic biography of reggae legend Bob Marley. I then did a story for AC/ DC where the band goes to Hell to play a show with both Brian Johnson and Bon Scott.

My work experience wasn't that much different than it had been before, I worked freelance from home, and had little interaction with the Marvel personnel, except socially with some of the leather-jacket crew from the Bullpen. My storefront wasn't as comfy as my porch up in Maine, and in the winter I would sometimes run hot water over my hands to keep them limber when I was working.

I will say that it seems to me the people running the show at Marvel were as idiotic as the publisher at *Cracked* had been. They bagged Marvel Music after only a couple of years, but never tried to market their product properly. They saw music comic sales in terms of the percentage of comic fans who might be interested in say, Billy Ray Cyrus or Onyx, instead of as the percentage of music fans that might be interested in a comic about their favorite performer.

Marvel never put out he third installment of the Marley book, even though it was completed and ready to go. They also backed out of their deal with AC/DC, so that comic, one of my best, if I may say so myself, was never finished. The comic art featured inside the album *Ballbreaker* is it's only vestige.

I wasn't directly involved with it, but Marvel also rolled up an authorized Elvis Presley bio comic! It had actually been offered at a meeting—I wasn't there—that no one would be interested in either a Bob Marley or an Elvis comic! Nice work! Regardless of the quality of the product, putting those guys' images on any flat surface is a license to print money! And these books were done with the consent and involvement of the estates, with very high production values, at least under the circumstances. Marvel had no idea what they were commissioning and didn't want to pay for, or put the time in to, what was being created- a potential perennial.

It never fails to amaze me how people who, though not being creators themselves, make their living through the creative process, will so often seem to have no understanding of that process. At Marvel you got the impression that the people upstairs viewed The Hulk, Spider-Man, and so on as found property, like a vein of ore that needs to be dug out until there's nothing left, with no appreciation of the weird intellect that could come up with these sorts of pathetic, compelling, bizarre characters.

I am currently working as a carpenter. I've done a lot of good work on sheetrock and plywood, but it won't fit in my portfolio. Since my departure from Marvel, many years ago now, I've been researching and developing a broad and exotic piece of historical fiction—to be a graphic novel—set mostly in Africa and Europe during the tumultuous first decades of the 20th century. If I live long enough, I may finish it.

I continue to see Mort regularly, and count him among my closest friends. He was best man at my wedding, and I recently wrote and recorded a theme song—"Beware: Sadistik!"—for his character Sadistik, a skeleton-clad super-criminal with a propensity for assaulting scantily-clad women. But you can ask Mort about that!

Larry Hama: Writing comics, developing animation, script doctoring, storyboards.

Todd Jackson: I've mainly moved into Web Design and Development now—creating web sites for a variety of folks, some of them funny. You can see some of my work at toddjacksonworks.com. Comedy works on leaps of logic and web programming languages have a logic too. I think it uses an oddly similar part of my brain…

That career was an outgrowth of my creating Dead-Frog (dead-frog. com) a few years ago, a comedy blog that covers all things funny—stand-up, sketch, sitcoms, and, rarely (sadly), humor magazines. It's a lot more talking about funny things than being funny, but comedy is an art form that rarely gets the coverage it deserves. It started off as a small attempt to change that and it's just grown in ways I never expected. Very fulfilling in ways that I never expected.

Marten Jallad: Initially, I intended to continue *Thwak* even after I started working at *Cracked* but I really didn't have the time to try and do both, so much material was either used in *Cracked* #362 (incidentally a version of the center page pull out "Buy American or It's 'Bye America" from this issue initially ran in *Thwak* #2) or stashed away for later use. After *Cracked* was sold in early 2005, I was ready to try something with a new approach and published another humor magazine titled *Jokester* with Mike Arnold who had briefly contributed to *Cracked*'s last couple of issues. The magazine took a unique approach in that the front and back were like a playing card and the interior was separated by four categories: gag cartoons, one page multi panel, comic strips and text heavier pieces, each category being defined by a suit. It was a great looking book indeed. I then compiled and edited a comic with the Atlanta division of the National Cartoonists Society called *Southern Fried Comics* that came out in '06. Since then I have been working on *The Thwak Bonfire of Insanity Collection* trade paperback. It compiles some older material with new layout treatments as well as more than 50% brand new material and four interviews with the likes of Carmine Infantino on *Plop!*, Bruce Bolinger on inking for Don Martin at *Cracked*, Jay Lynch on his interesting career and Kelly Freas on *Mad*.

Mike Kazaleh: Working for Bongo Comics.

Milton Knight: Making a living with editorial illos, private commissions, painting and art classes. I'm also working on a stream of independent projects, which include those of a literary nature, and a ten-minute animated film, done solo and now in the ink and paint stage.

Alan Kupperberg: I live in Bohemian Splendor in New York's Greenwich Village with my lovely Debra and cats Bennett and Romana. I'm doing a 40-page commissioned comic right now and I've been preparing about fifty new pages to beef up a collection of my *Evil Clown* stories that ran in the *National Lampoon*. The whole collection will be in stunning color for the first time, thanks to the brilliant Tom Ziuko. I do a lot of commission work and advertising.

Aron Laikin: I'm 47 now. I'd been freelancing for most of my life. I did work for Disney and Warner Bros.' licensing departments. I worked at Marvel Comics for doing some other satirical work and then I did a lot of advertising work for the big ad agencies, BBD&O, all the big ones. I did storyboards and I had an education in animation, and I got involved in creating characters for different TV series and being brought up with my father, he was also a writer for Merv Griffin for 16 years. I was brought up in the entertainment industry, the television side. I would hang out on sets, so I got an early education on that side of the business, too. I was doing movie posters, marketing materials, flyers, mostly around the entertainment industry and then as I got more involved in animation, I started to represent a lot of the old Disney artists, their collections. I then formed Cartoon World, which was an animation art gallery and museum. So I opened up a chain of galleries and I did that for maybe 15 years, while I was doing other artwork, and then I sold off that business. I also started a documentary with the National Cartoonists Society and Jerry Robinson from *Batman* called *Cartoon America: A Centennial Celebration*. I went around the world interviewing probably over 375 of the top cartoonists in the business on video. We put a pilot that's still being developed with quite an archive with all the old *Mad* guys like Gaines, Feldstein, Mort, Jack, Nick Meglin, the whole gang. Now I have a business which sort of since I've been involved in so many different areas of various industries and publications in entertainment, it's sort of the perfect marriage to put together a company called The Creativity Zone, which is a multimedia design studio. We do all types of advertising, website design, all sorts of marketing packages. One of our specialties obviously is cartooning and that background we have a number of artists that work here. We do mascots, character design and licensing. It all formalizes all of these different aspects into one multimedia factory. We don't get too involved with the actual placement, although we consult and advise in that. We specialize more in the creative. We make sure we have a consistency along the line in all of their business endeavors. Starting with the logo, we really define building their identity in the culture of the business with a consistent message. We do all types of online animation, like flash and 3-D. That's what I'm doing at the present time.

Paul Laikin: Phil Hirsch was an editor at Pyramid Publishing. They did books, paperbacks, publishing from Madison Avenue, Pyramid. You may have seen their byline of Pyramid Publications. Anyhow, their big thing was paperbacks. Somehow, they got ahold of Joe Simon who was doing *Sick*, and Simon was too busy and couldn't handle it, and he called me, and I did *Sick*. That was a great experience. I liked doing *Sick* because *Sick* had a point of view. They weren't afraid to do text and political material, so I did *Sick* for quite some time.

Sick was in a good place. Phil Hirsch, does that name ring a bell? He was the editor who brought me in. It was one 5th Avenue or Madison Avenue, too, where I did *Sick*. Joe Simon did it from his home. They couldn't handle it all the time, so he gave it to me and Phil Hirsch called me in. I remember Madison Avenue, where *Sick* was.

What actually was funny, when I was working with Phil Hirsch on *Sick*. Phil Hirsch was the kind of guy that he wanted to see the material beforehand and he actually looked at it and said, "This is good. This is good." So, I figured a way to beat this guy. I brought all the material that came in. I gave it to him. He picked out the things that he liked, and I used those things. He was in fact the editor of the book, unknowingly. What am I going to do, fight with him? It didn't matter. He took all the good pieces and that's what I assigned to artists. That was how I worked. It didn't get better after that.

Then I went to *Crazy*. Sol Brodsky, at Marvel was there as their production manager. I don't know it happened, but it seemed to me that the segues were perfect. I never had to make a decision to go to Marvel. The only decision I ever made was leaving *Mad* to go to *Cracked*. If I could have my freedom, I was a top dog for the rest of my career. Here I would just have to be at the bottom at just another writer working for Al Feldstein.

Marv Wolfman was doing it and then he got busy with 30 magazines. Everyone came it at 9. It was a 9 to 5 job. They got busy and they needed an editor for *Crazy*, and I think Sol Brodsky was the one who told Stan Lee about me, and Stan Lee brought me in.

The transitions were kind of natural. I don't remember being kicked cut of *Crazy* or quitting, but I remember leaving. It was a natural progression. Somebody called me and gave me *Wacko*.

If some guy does not return my call, I wouldn't use 'em again, no matter how good he was. Tony Tallarico was always there, he always delivered.

Andy Lamberti: I tried *Mad* a few times, but it seemed to be a closed shop. At one instance, I was almost published in *Mad*, but was told in no uncertain terms how writing for *Cracked* was not appreciated.

Other than *Cracked*, I worked for comedy joke services, supplying one line gags for the entertainment field. The number of writers / artists is limited in this business and everyone is a fan. Kit Lively, whose illustrations were in *Cracked* in the 1990s, was a fan of my articles, as was Marten Jallad, a later *Cracked* editor.

I also wrote for *Thwak* in the past decade. It was edited by Marten Jallad who had a brief stint as editor for *Cracked* at American Media.

I don't write anymore since it became a job trying to make ends meet. For 43 years, I've been an avid road bicyclist. That's what I'm doing now in retirement, riding 15,000 miles a year.

Kit Lively: I continue to send in writing and cartoons to *Mad*, but it's a difficult magazine to sell to on a regular basis (well, for me, anyway). I still do cartoon work for the *Hustler* magazines from time to time, and I'm shopping around a collection of single-panel cartoons to various publishers. I was approached a while ago to join the writing staff of an animated comedy show that was being shown to MTV and Cartoon Network. Also, some friends and I have written a screenplay, and that's currently being handled by the agent of one of the aforementioned friends. Former *Cracked* editor Marten Jallad recently published a trade paperback collection of his previous humor magazine *Thwak*, which includes previously unpublished stuff like the rejected *Cracked* piece, "Pick-Up Lines to Use on Chicks at a Rock Concert." Of course, I continue to tour the amateur yodeling circuit, just for the thrill and the adrenaline. And the dames.

Cliff Mott: Presently, I'm finishing up illustrations for the *Heavy Metal Book of Lists* from Backbeat Books, follow-up to the wildly successful *Punk Rock Book of Lists*. Coincidentally, Mort and I recently worked on some animated cartoons for Playboy.com and we are eager to confab with Hef in the Grotto, with plans to save another magazine title from certain doom!

Don Orehek: *Playboy*: I heard that they're going to 11 issues a year. I just heard that. I usually sell something every time I send them something, and this time I didn't get an ok from them. Amanda mentioned that Hef likes my style and would like for me to continue, so that's good news. I never had any problem with them. I met him at the mansion back in '83, I think it was. He invited all the cartoonists and their wives and people to the mansion, when the Reuben awards were held there. I met him for the first time and got a picture taken. I got a picture taken with both of us and he sent it and bought six cartoons along with it. I send a batch of stuff. The last time I had a feeling that they weren't that great and they didn't buy anything, which I don't blame them. I looked at them and thought they wouldn't fall for that crap. He always buys and I always did very well with them. Whenever I mail a batch, I think it's good and I just mailed one recently. I feel that there are at least three or four ok's in there. I hope. It takes a while, you know, maybe four months, but as soon as I get my stuff back, I do the finishes and do it right away and then ship the stuff back to them, and then I always have another batch ready right away. I do roughs that you could print. With him, he wants you to do a finish. I use good paper. With *Cosmo*, they always bought your rough. A rough drawing always looks better to me. Then I have to do a finish from that rough, I trace is on a tracing board. It loses that simplicity, though. I try to make it look as close to that as possible.

Steph Ramsay: I am working to get my design Studio, Yellow Dog Studios, up and running in VA.

Tom Richmond: Doing freelance illustration for magazines, advertising and products. I still work regularly for *Mad*, and am currently illustrating a book.

Mike Ricigliano: No, I moved back to New York. I'm from New York, born in Brooklyn. I went back to live with my family for a year, and then I moved to Cleveland. That's where American Greetings was located. So, I lived in Cleveland for a year. American Greetings was an interesting place to work as a cartoonist because Don Martin had also worked there at one point in his career. He did greeting cards for a very short time. There were concept roughs by Don hanging around in this room that we all started in. It was for a very short time and they were concept roughs hanging around in this room that we all started in doing writing and art for greeting cards. You had to start in there with basic concepts and there was this R. Crumb things in there and there were some Don Martin things in there. At one point, they both worked for American Greetings, as did Steve O'Donnell, who works for David Letterman. They had a pretty good group of alumni that worked for that place. Anyway, I was there for a year and I got a job as a newspaper guy in Buffalo and that paper folded and I moved to Baltimore, then that paper folded and I moved to another one in Baltimore. I found my niche in newspapers anyway. I am an editorial cartoonist but I'm more of a sports fan than a political fan. Luckily, I found a place to be to do my stuff.

Kevin Sacco: I'm doing storyboards for advertising. Walter Brogan was at Benton & Bowles and he was doing storyboards and we met that way. I already knew about him. He was kind of well known, and over the years, we kind of kept in touch. We're just good friends. We worked together for Greenline Studios. We do it for different studios. Mainly for TV commercials. Every TV commercial you see is at first storyboarded. The studios they get the work from agencies all over the place. Now you just e-mail art around. Now everyone is now freelance and they do it on the computer.

Warren Sattler: I'm 74. I was in *National Lampoon* for a long time, probably around 15 times. My style has changed so many times. That's why I was working so much for *Lampoon*, because they wanted all different styles, and I was capable of doing that for them. There was one year that I did more drawings than the other cartoonists in that book.

I did a few comic book parodies. Other than that it was just articles — something that they needed an illustration for. My other work about why you didn't hear of me and where I was, I wanted to be in the comic strip field in the newspaper. I was a ghost artist on many comic strips. I ghosted on many strips and you don't see my name. I worked on *Barnaby*, *The Jackson Twins*, *Beauford*, *Comics for Kids*, *Bringing Up Father*...

Jerry De Fuccio and I were only friends over the telephone and I did quite a bit of work with him. He'd get little jobs I guess to keep him going because he was retired also. I did quite a bit and then he finally died of cancer. He was a good friend with Alex Toth, another great cartoonist. He would send me Toth postcards. I guess they were childhood friends. I got a stack of postcards from Alex Toth and I'd always write Toth, myself. I'd talk to other cartoonists and they'd call him up but I was kind of shy and all that. I never mixed around. I know a bunch of cartoonists. We used to go to dinner before my eyesight went, every Thursday. One of the times in Danbury, Connecticut. We'd have lunch and it would go on for hours, just gabbing away. There was Jerry Marcus, Bob Weber, Orlando Busino, I can't remember the rest. A lot of fellows. This was a funny story. My son was down at the Danbury Mall one day and he was walking through the book section and he saw two guys and they were talking about some subject, I don't know what it was, and my son walks over to them and says, "Are you guys cartoonists?" And they said, "Yeah, how did you know?" And he said, "You sound exactly like my father." I did it for about 10 years before my eyesight went and I could no longer drive that far and I had to give it up, but it was a joy. We had very similar interests of movies and books and politics. All similar.

John Severin: Once John got older, he didn't want to take on so much work, and after *Cracked* wound down, John went on to other comics. When you have one company like Marvel or Dark Horse, they'll call and everyone knows John. They'll call and John will say, "Ok, when's the deadline?" and all that.

Actually, once John was started and fortunately, he didn't have to do anything after he started. John did his books a lot. In fact, he did more than anyone else. Like I said, he really is not so fast. I think it was good for Dark Horse and for John and so they came up with this idea to do a list of things, and so they waited for him and like I say, they waited for him to finish. People who understand John, and people who want a commission will have to wait. I have a stack of things now. The man who called from Belgium and I said he tried to get a copy from him from France of American artists and they did a whole book of John's and I have tried to get a copy and the guy from Belgium got me a second hand copy and then he sent me some Belgium and we were trying to get a little sketch, but it takes John a long time.

It's amazing that John is still doing this. His line is so good and he can draw all night long.

Lou Silverstone: I'm responsible for Michael Jackson. Disney's Michael Eisner had seen the Jackson 5 in concert in Las Vegas and felt that that would make a good show for kids. He was the head of ABC at the time. Jack Davis was going through the caricatures and going through the stories and told me they needed a writer up there and they hired about three or four of the *Mad* guys and I got the job and did about four specials for ABC. A bunch of junky stuff. Today writers have so much freedom with the animation. They can say anything they want, practically. The ones we're doing had all these groups and I was doing a special for King Features that featured everyone of their characters like Popeye and I kept getting notes saying, "You can't have Popeye punching this guy. You can't have Popeye doing this. It took all the fun out of it." Now it doesn't matter what you say.

I finally got to work with Al Capp who was my boyhood idol and I did a piece called, "The Mad Liberals," and at the time Capp made fun of liberals. They wanted some anti-Joan Baez jokes. We broke up because this was during Watergate and I thought it would be so great to parody that, but he wouldn't touch it because it made fun of Nixon in it.

Bill Sproul: After the we sold the magazine I did all sorts of things: mall shopping guides, local advertising, opened a bar, owned two surf shops, I was always trying some new idea out (my hang-out threatened to wallpaper the bathrooms with my cards at one point) I ended up working for Home Depot as a manager, divisional operations trainer, HR specialist. I left when it stopped being a fun company to work for, after the founders were driven out. It treated me fairly well especially during the stock splitting days of late 80s to mid-90s. Incentive stock options were golden. I am now 54.

My younger sister gave me a kidney sixteen years ago. I've had my medical issues, but I'm still doing well and feeling great. I camp-out at few music festivals every year. As cooking and music are my passions. I have an 11-year-old daughter who is my biggest joy. My mother lives a couple of blocks from me and we see each other almost every day. I live with my girlfriend (not my daughter's mother). I dabble as a booking agent for local bands and clubs. Life is good, but I always knew it would be, because as you know, "When You're *Cracked*, You're Happy!"

Steve Strangio: I work as a writer/producer for television, stage and film. The two projects at the forefront right now are my first feature-length film called *Journey to the Strip Mall* and my full-length play *Happy Saturdays*. Both are really important to me since I've worked on them for more than a few years now.

The remainder of my time is spent on my other projects that include graphic novels, television pilots, voice over work, acting work, a new board game I invented, and even a new sport that I created.

I have 15 years of *Cracked* articles and I think it'd be great to see them reprinted in a book someday. Hell, I did Stand-Up Comedy professionally for 10 years. I'd kick some serious ass on a book tour.

Aside from all of that, I make time for my amazing and beautiful girlfriend Helena and we seek out damn fun things to do.

The career goal from this point on is to rotate projects and continue to work with talented people. I just go where the inspiration takes me and the journey has been exciting so far. People can check out my work at www.HappySaturdays.com.

B.K. Taylor: I really wasn't ready for *Mad* magazine. Eventually, years later, I did some work for them, but at that time I was doing work in television and Disney Animation in Burbank and, sadly, couldn't commit.

The *Lampoon* was total freedom in that I was writing and illustrating everything myself. I could just let my imagination run wild, with very little editing. (That is, except for my wife, Kathy, who did final edit on all my strips.)

Bananas was great for experimentation in color and exploring different media. The editor was incredibly easy to work with and very encouraging. Over the years, we became great friends. He called himself "Jovial Bob" back then, but later would change his name and become R.L. Stine (of the hugely popular *Goosebumps* book series fame). We remain the best of friends to this day.

I'm putting together an anthology of my *National Lampoon* cartoon strips, with additional new material. I'm also working with another writer who I worked with on the show *Home Improvement*. We're putting together pitches for a couple of animated television projects. It's been in the works for some time. I designed the characters and settings. I'm also doing production design on a film being shot in Michigan—believe it or not, a sci-fi horror film. Quite some time ago I worked on a low budget sci-fi film called *Moon Trap*, starring Bruce Campbell and Walter Koenig. I only mention this because most people are surprised when they hear that I'm working in that genre.

I am also working in tandem with another writer on a comedy film premise. I'd love to get back to doing more work in print, but I'm not sure where the market is now? I have to depend on my art agent for that.

I do have an idea for a comedic fantasy comic book. I think it would be fun to have the freedom to be able to tell a story and illustrate the entire book. In the meantime I'll develop the *Lampoon* book.

Mort Todd: Post-*Cracked*, I started my own comics company, AAA and put out a few titles, like the Bill Ward anthology, *W.O.W.*, shooting from his vintage original pin ups. We did a bi-lingual comic, *Pepito*, with work by Vic Martin, George Gladir, Cliff, Pat Redding and Pete Fitzgerald, I had planned a 5 issue *Mr. A* color series with Ditko, but lousy pre-orders from the direct market made it unfeasible. But we did put out a pile of Mr. A T-shirts and stickers that have become rare and collectible.

I soon took a gig with Marvel where I launched the Marvel Music line. We did licensed titles with bands and I got to work closely with superstars like KISS, AC/DC, Rob Zombie and the Bob Marley and Elvis estates along with creators like Neil Gaiman, Gene Colan, Kyle Baker and Severin. I also released a slew of Atlas/Marvel horror reprints representing the 1950s to the '70s. It included weird pre-Code never before reprinted, with rare things by Kubert, Wolverton, Kreigstein and Wally Wood. I also got new covers for them by Steve Ditko and work from Stan Lee and Jack Kirby's last piece for Marvel. I did the tabloid *Comic Book* with John Kricfalusi through his Spumco studio there, too.

At the turn of the century I started another company, Comicfix, and produce comics and other properties to develop for film and animation. Animation clients have included MTV, CBS, Disney and *Sesame Street*. I've directed a bunch of music videos, including one I just did for Peter Bagge's band. For a few years I did newspaper comic strips like *Speed Racer* and a biography strip with John Severin.

I acquired the rights to a dark Italian photo comic called *Sadistik* that I have been translating and publishing in English. I produced a documentary about the character called *The Diabolikal Super-Kriminal,* which has done well in Europe and I'm currently developing an animated series with Iggy Pop as the voice of Sadistik.

Hopefully, the end of the story will be that I get another opportunity to handle *Cracked*. In fact, some blog said that I was gonna. There's still an army of fans that grew up with me at *Cracked* but now they're getting a little gray!

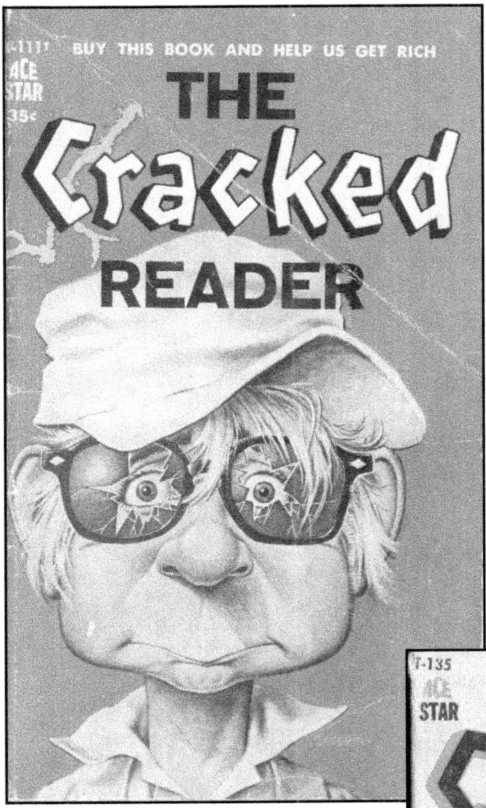
BUY THIS BOOK AND HELP US GET RICH
ACE STAR
35¢
THE
Cracked
READER

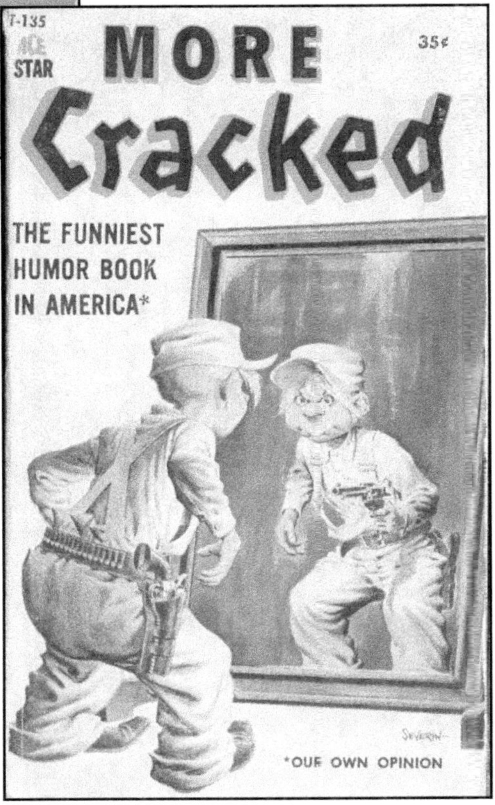
T-135
ACE STAR
MORE
35¢
Cracked
THE FUNNIEST HUMOR BOOK IN AMERICA*
*OUR OWN OPINION

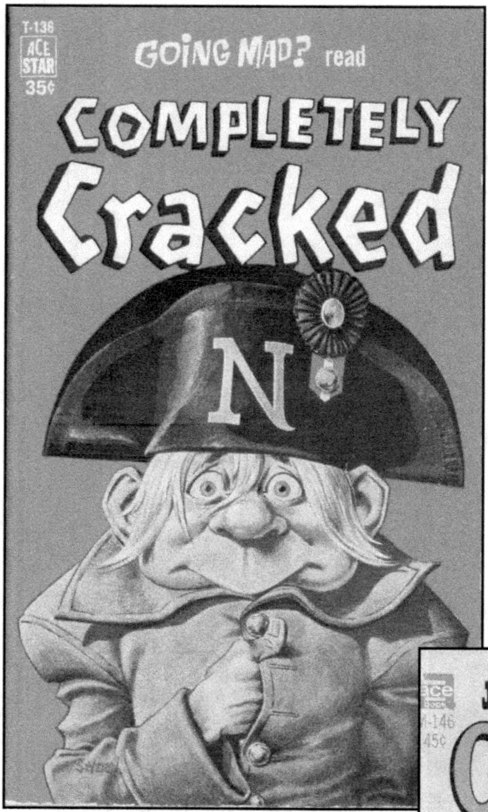
T-136
ACE STAR
35¢
GOING MAD? read
COMPLETELY
Cracked
N

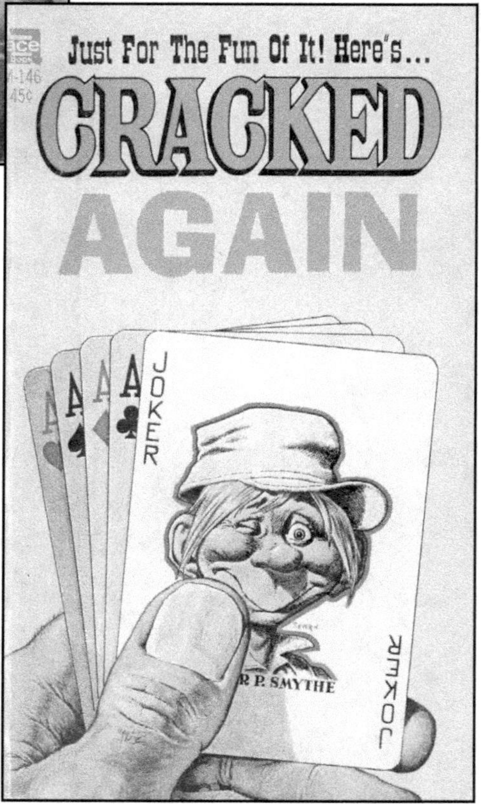
Just For The Fun Of It! Here's...
M-146
45¢
CRACKED
AGAIN
JOKER
R P. SMYTHE

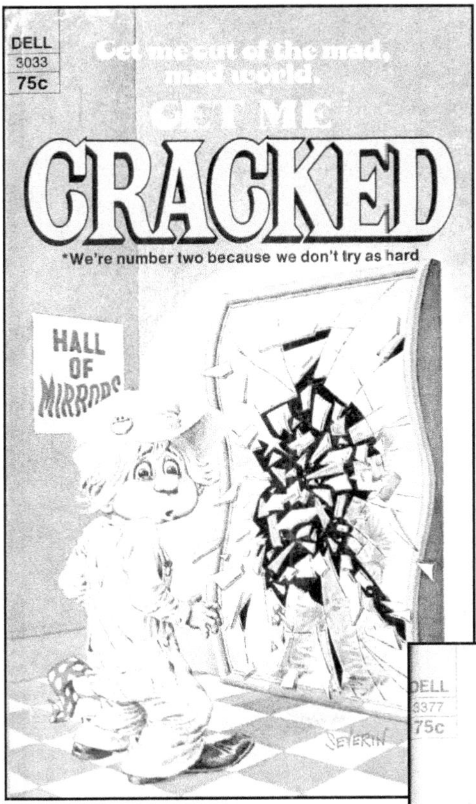
DELL
3033
75c
Get me out of the mad, mad world.
GET ME
CRACKED
*We're number two because we don't try as hard
HALL
OF
SEVERIN

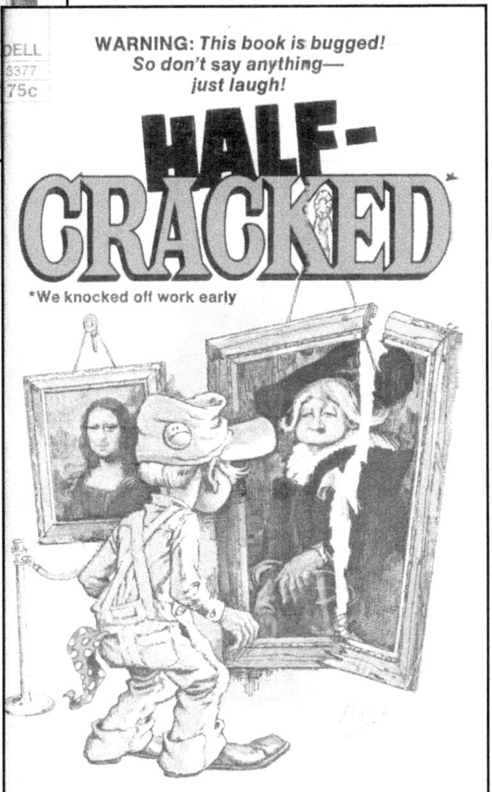
3377
75c
WARNING: *This book is bugged! So don't say anything— just laugh!*
HALF-
CRACKED
*We knocked off work early

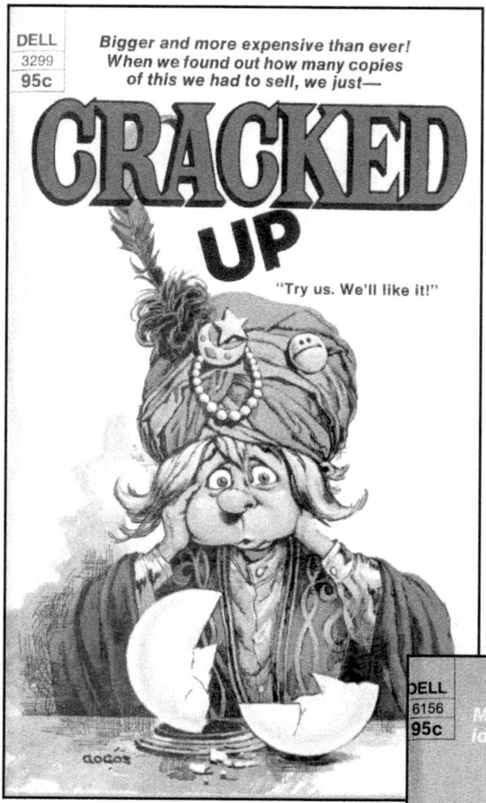
DELL
3299
95c
Bigger and more expensive than ever! When we found out how many copies of this we had to sell, we just—
CRACKED
UP
"Try us. We'll like it!"
GOGOS

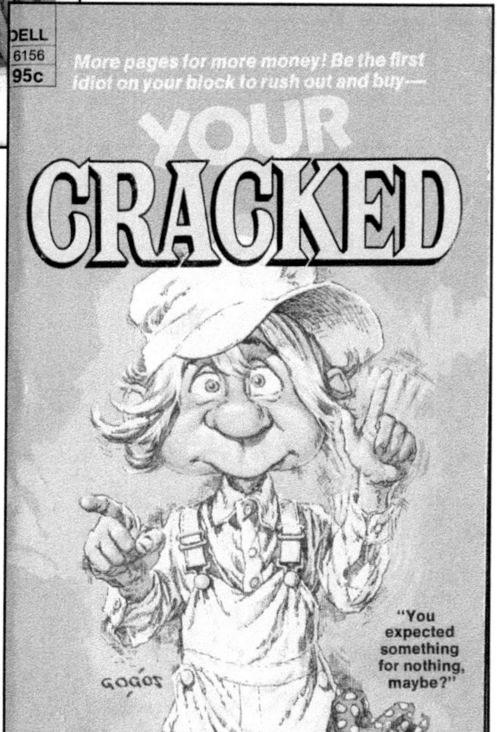
DELL
6156
95c
More pages for more money! Be the first idiot on your block to rush out and buy—
YOUR
CRACKED
"You expected something for nothing, maybe?"
GOGOS

DELL
5003
95c
Get set for a riotous
ride you'll never forget—
no matter how much you want to!
CRACKED
in the Saddle*
*As soon as we get
your money, we're
off and running!

DELL
5004
95c
We know why idiots
all over the globe will buy this book!
IT'S A
CRACKED
WORLD*
*If you don't
like it, you
know where
you can go.

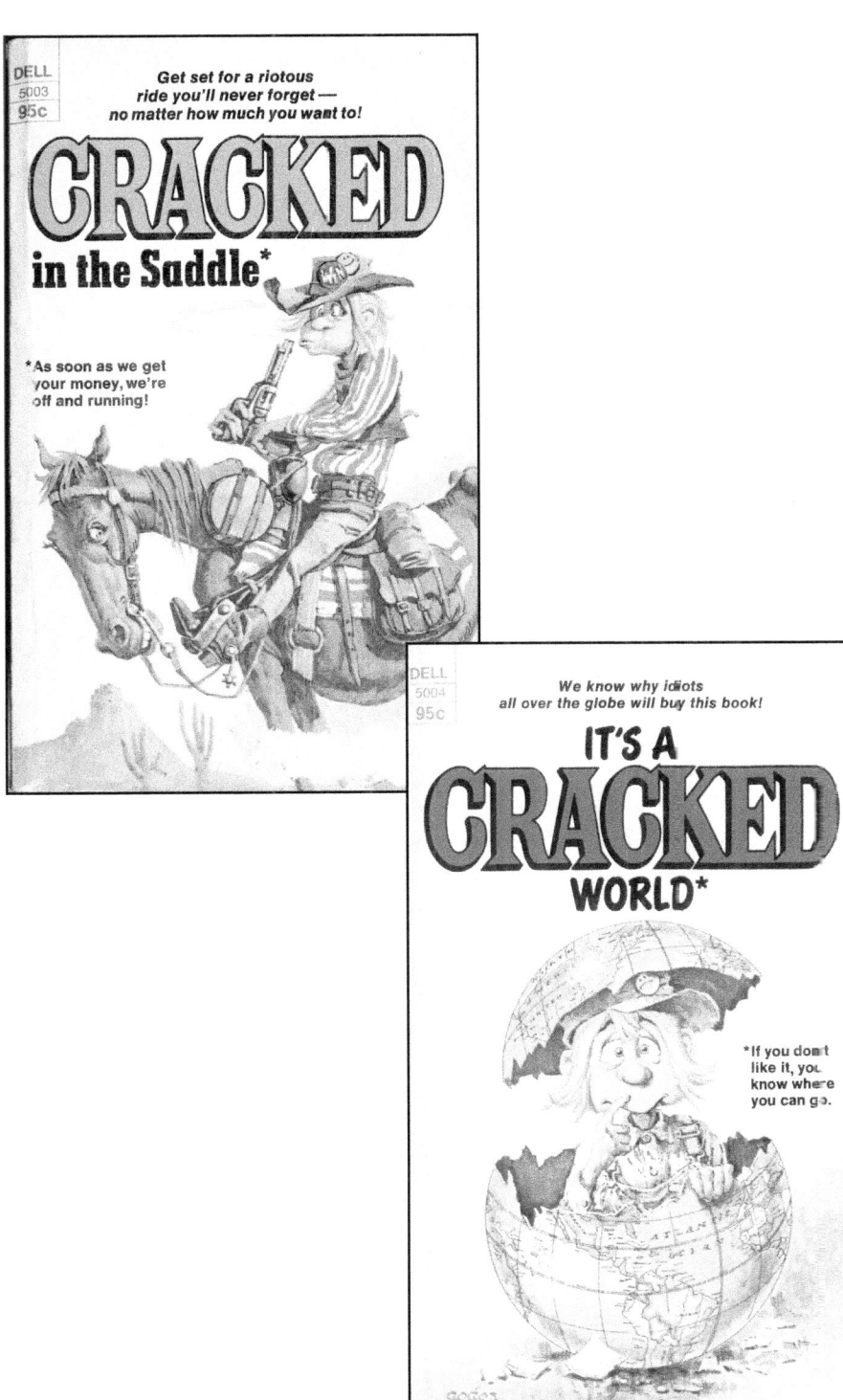

THE CRACKED MAGAZINE INDEX PART II

(Please note that reprints commonly were featured in regular issues of the magazine. Every attempt has been made to identify when an article has been reprinted and what issue was the original source. Also, art and writing credits are identified when known with the art credit first, followed by the writing credit. Finally, it has been confirmed through a number of sources that *Pow!* #3 and *Super Cracked* #27 do not exist. *Pow!*, *Zany*, *For Monsters Only* and *Don Martin's Droll Book* are included in this index due to the majority of the material either being reprinted in or reprinted from *Cracked*. The reprint information will only list the magazine title if it is anything other than *Cracked*.)

(Continued from Part I)

Cracked Collectors' Edition #49 (*Those Cracked Monsters*), September 1982 (52 pages) (90c)

Cover – Monster Fight – John Severin (reprint from *For Monsters Only* #2)

Page 2 – The Cracked Bookstore ad – John Severin

Page 3 – Contents

Page 4 – Planets of the Creatures - John Severin (reprint from #72)

Page 10 – Fun with Frankenstein's Monster (new)

Page 12 – A Tourist's Guide to Transylvania – Vic Martin (reprint from #60)

Page 16 – The Ghost and Mrs. Mire – John Severin (reprint from #83)

Page 22 – Stationery from Transylvania (reprint from *For Monsters Only* #1)

Page 24 – The Cracked TV Show/Movie Monster Quiz (new)

Page 26 – Transylvanian Cut-Out-Signs (reprint from *For Monsters Only* #2)

Page 28 – The Cracked Monster Lens (My goodness) (new)

Page 36 – Rosemary's Baby Devlin – Lugoze (reprint from #76)

Page 40 – Sylvester, the Blaw Son of Glock – Charles Rodrigues (reprint from #54)

Page 42 – The Cracked Fiendish Phrase Game (new)

Page 49 – Of the Apes – Ned Kelly (John Severin) / Don Edwing (reprint from #29)

Page 50 – The Terror Trip – BOJ (reprint from #55)

Page 51 – A Great, New Neighbor! (reprint from *For Monsters Only* #3)

Back Cover – Transylvania Travel Stickers (reprint from *For Monsters Only* #1)

Cracked Collectors' Edition #50 (*We Play with Video Games*), November 1982 (52 pages) (90c) (Another issue with predominantly new material.)

Cover – Pac-Man and Space Invaders

Page 2 – The Cracked Bookstore ad – John Severin

Page 3 – Contents

Page 4 – Lettuce to Crack Man / Subscription ad – Bob Taylor

Page 6 – A Cracked Review of Popular Video Games

Page 9 – Caption the Video Photo Contest

Page 10 – Video Games Go to School – Warren Sattler

Page 13 – The Ballad of Bob Hahn and the Video Game – Don Orehek

Page 17 – Future Ultra Realistic Electronic Games – Val Mayerik (reprint from #174)

Page 20 – Two Pictures Are Worth a Thousand Blips – Ron Zalme

Page 22 – Human-Like Video Games of the Future Will – John Langton

Page 24 – In the Electronic Game Room – Sururi Gumen (reprint from #181)

Page 25 – A Cracked Video Poster (Wanted)

Page 29 – Video Shut-Ups (Hyperspace!) – Mike Ricigliano

Page 30 – Arcade Machines for Adults – Arnoldo Franchioni

Page 33 – The Cracked Video Game Lens

Page 42 – A Cracked Look at an Amusement Area – Don Orehek (reprint from #142)

Page 44 – Video Games We'll Soon Be Seeing – Howard Nostrand (reprint from #141)

Page 47 – An Interview with the Video Game King – Bill Ward

Page 50 – The Cracked Video Iron-On

Cracked Collectors' Edition #51 (*Monsters*), December 1982 (52 pages) (90c)

Cover – Mr. Sardonicus and Company – John Severin (reprint from *Monster Howls* #1)

Page 2 – The Cracked Bookstore ad – John Severin

Page 3 – Contents

Page 4 – Monster Crack-Ups (new)

Page 6 – King Kung – John Severin (reprint from #140)

Page 13 – Transylvania's Airline Hostess of the Year! (reprint from *For Monsters Only* #5)

Page 14 – Quick Quiz (Lawrence Zelk) (reprint from *For Monsters Only* #9)

Page 16 – More Celebrity Nightmares – John Severin (reprint from #167)

Page 19 – Macabre Mirth (reprint from *For Monsters Only* #1)

Page 20 – The Colossus of New York (reprint from *For Monsters Only* #6)

Page 22 – More Combined Movies "Dracula" and "Snow White and the Seven Dwarfs" – John Severin (reprint from #132)

Page 23 – Bat Contest (new)

Page 24 – The Night Crawlers - Vic Martin (reprint from *For Monsters Only* #5)

Page 25 – Mayhem Mirth (reprint from *For Monsters Only* #5)

Page 30 – You Know You're the Biggest Thing Around if – Howard Nostrand (reprint from #142)

Page 33 – Our New "Merry Mailman" (reprint from *For Monsters Only* #5)

Page 34 – The Fiendish Delights! (reprint from *For Monsters Only* #8)

Page 40 – When Businesses Start Going After the Vampire Market – Warren Sattler (reprint from #166)

Page 44 – The Alligator People (reprint from *For Monsters Only* #3)

Page 46 – A Fiend from Up the Street (reprint from *For Monsters Only* #2)

Page 47 – Transylvania Go Go Football – Vic Martin (reprint from *For Monsters Only* #4)

Page 50 – Monster Shut-Ups (great blocks) – Mike Ricigliano (new)

Page 51 – ("Ugliest Student") *I Was a Teenage Werewolf* photo (reprint from *For Monsters Only* #3)

Back Cover – Monster Diploma (reprint from *For Monsters Only* #2)

Cracked Collectors' Edition #52 (Monsters), February 1983 (52 pages) (90c)

Cover – Earth Egg Hatching Monster – Nireves (John Severin) (reprint from *Giant Cracked* #8 with skull replacing egg-shaped Earth.)

Page 2 – The Cracked Bookstore ad – John Severin

Page 3 – Contents

Page 4 – Count Conrad's Corner (new)

Page 6 – The Cracked Monsters Lens (thrilled about dancing) (new)

Page 11 – The Desert Island Guest – John Severin (reprint from *For Monsters Only* #3)

Page 12 – Mighty Monster Laughs!! (reprint from #45)

Page 14 – The Wacky Weirdos (reprint from *For Monsters Only* #6)

Page 16 – Monster Phrases – Vic Martin (reprint from *For Monsters Only* #5)

Page 18 – Big Things are Happening! (reprint from *For Monsters Only* #7)

Page 19 – Shoot to Kill – John Severin (reprint from #33)

Page 20 – Horror Hee-Haw (reprint from *For Monsters Only* #10)

Page 22 – Monster Paper Doll Page – Warren Sattler (new)

Page 24 – The Biggies Break it Up! (reprint from *For Monsters Only* #10)

Page 26 – Son of Monster Mirth!!! (reprint from *For Monsters Only* #3)

Page 27 – The Painter's Fantasy – Oskar Blotta (reprint from #85)

Page 28 – Let's Meet the Ladies (reprint from *For Monsters Only* #9)

Page 30 – Mad Mirth Makers! (reprint from *For Monsters Only* #10)

Page 32 – McCartney's Mighty Monsters – Bill McCartney (Bill Ward) (reprint from *For Monsters Only* #5)

Page 33 – Girls and Ghouls (reprint from *For Monsters Only* #3)

Page 34 – Monsterous Merriment (reprint from #98)

Page 36 – Transylvanian TV – Bill McCartney (Bill Ward) (reprint from #36)

Page 40 – The Chiller-Dillers Swing Again! (reprint from *For Monsters Only* #6)

Page 41 – Orders – John Severin (reprint from #38)

Page 42 – Howl Makers (reprint from *For Monsters Only* #10)

Page 44 – Cracked Visits the Munsters (reprint from #52)

Page 45 – Cracked's Monster Puzzle Book – John Severin (new)

Page 51 – The Most Horrible Monster of All – Walt Lardner (reprint from #93)

Back Cover – Transylvania Life ad – John Severin (reprint from #35)

Cracked Collectors' Edition #53 (*Monsters*), May 1983 (52 pages) ($1.00)

Cover – Karloff as *The Mummy* photo with border by John Severin (new)

Page 2 – "Stop Eating Sweets" photo (new)

Page 3 – Contents

Page 4 – Monster Crack-Ups (new)

Page 6 – The Movie Monsters Strike – John Severin (reprint from #32)

Page 12 – The Cracked Monsters Lens (Will you call Junior) (new)

Page 16 – More Combined Movies "My Fair Lady" & "King Kong" – John Severin (reprint from #133)

Page 17 – Escape from the Boredom of the Apes – John Severin (reprint from #97)

Page 22 – Orehek's Horror Humor! – Don Orehek (new)

Page 26 – Fun Time Monsters – Vic Martin (reprint from *For Monsters Only* #3)

Page 27 – When Willard-Type Movies Take Over Hollywood – Nireves (John Severin) (reprint from #100)

Page 30 – Monster Cliches Match Game

Page 34 – It Happened at the Cemetery – Caracu (reprint from #69)

Page 36 – Another Combined Movie "Godzilla" vs. "The Towering Inferno" – Sururi Gumen (reprint from #137)

Page 37 – Cracked Monster Trading Cards – John Severin (new)

Page 41 – King Author and the Knights of the Reserved Table – John Severin (reprint from #171)

Page 48 – Monsters in the News – John Severin (reprint from #59)

Page 50 – Cracked's Monster Movie Scenes (new)

Page 51 – (Nonchalant) *King Kong* photo (reprint from *For Monsters Only* #2)

Back Cover – The Lonely Convict and the Pet – Oskar Blotta (reprint from #141)

Cracked Collectors' Edition #54 (*M*A*S*H Fun Book*), September 1983 (52 pages) ($1.00)

Cover – We Salute M*A*S*H – John Severin (reprint from #175)

Page 2 – The Cracked Bookstore ad – John Severin

Page 3 – Contents

Page 4 – M*U*S*H (Mail call!) – John Severin (reprint from #159)

Page 11 – M*U*S*H Again (probably wondering why I called you) – John Severin (originally called "M*U*S*H") (reprint from #168)

Page 17 – M*A*S*H*E*D – John Severin (reprint from #182)

Page 23 – The Cracked M*A*S*H Flip the Faces Game – John Severin (revised reprint from *Giant Cracked* #3)

Page 41 – M*U*S*H Some More (Dear Dad) – John Severin (originally called "M*U*S*H") (reprint from #115)

Page 46 – And Even More M*U*S*H (Colonel Potted) – John Severin (originally called "M*U*S*H") (reprint from #175)

Page 51 – Gary Burghoff photo (new)

Back Cover – Alan Alda, Loretta Swit, Wayne Rogers photo (new)

Cracked Collectors' Edition #55 (Sharks!), November 1983 (52 pages) ($1.00)

Cover – Jawz – John Severin (reprint from #129)

Page 2 – Avoid Shark Attacks (reprint from #129)

Page 3 – Contents

Page 4 – Lettuce to Sharks (new) / Official Cracked Fan Club ad – John Severin

Page 6 – Jawz – John Severin (reprint from #129)

Page 12 – A Cracked Look at Sharks – Don Orehek (reprint from *Cracked Collectors' Edition* #26)

Page 16 – The World's Best Shark Jokes (reprint from *Cracked Collectors' Edition* #26)

Page 22 – How to Ward Off Sharks – John Severin (reprint from *Cracked Collectors' Edition* #26)

Page 25 – One Day On the Atlantic Ocean – Howard Nostrand (reprint from *Cracked Collectors' Edition* #26)

Page 26 – Cracked's Shark Identification Chart – Bill Ward (reprint from *Cracked Collectors' Edition* #26)

Page 28 – A Visit to the Beach – LePoer (John Severin) (reprint from #38)

Page 30 – Sharks....Another View (reprint from *Cracked Collectors' Edition* #26)

Page 36 – The History of Sharks – Bill Ward (reprint from *Cracked Collectors' Edition* #26)

Page 41 – What to do in Case of Shark Attack – Warren Sattler (reprint from *Cracked Collectors' Edition* #26)

Page 43 – Jaws Too! – John Severin (reprint from #154)

Page 50 – Shark Shut-Ups (shark disguise) – Don Orehek (reprint from *Cracked Collectors' Edition* #26)

Page 51 – Smile! You're On Candid Shark! Iron-On (reprint from #154)

Back Cover – Great Moments in History 1,000,342 B.C. – Howard Nostrand (reprint from #142)

Cracked Collectors' Edition #56 (*We Have Fun with Video Games*), December 1983 (52 pages) ($1.00) (Another issue with predominantly new material.)

Cover – Pac-Man and Space Invaders Again

Page 2 – The Cracked Bookstore ad – John Severin

Page 3 – Contents

Page 4 – Lettuce to Crack Man

Page 6 – The Cracked World of Video Games – Samuel B. Whitehead (reprint from #184)

Page 10 – Arcade Heaven

Page 12 – The Cracked Video Lens

Page 15 – Video Tech College for Video Game Players – Mike Ricigliano

Page 20 – TV Contraptions We'll Soon Be Seeing – Val Mayerik (reprint from #157)

Page 23 – The Joystick Report – Warren Sattler
Page 25 – A Cracked Video Poster (Wanted) (reprint from *Cracked Collectors' Edition* #50)
Page 29 – Great Moments in Video History
Page 33 – Video Game Quiz Book
Page 37 – Illustrated Video Game News
Page 40 – You Know You're Really a Video Game Freak if – Walt Lardner
Page 42 – New Forms of Home Entertainment – Warren Sattler (reprint from #143)
Page 44 – Video Game Calculator Readouts
Page 45 – Cracked Interviews the Video King – Bill Ward (reprint from #181)
Page 50 – Lunch Time – Oskar Blotta (reprint from #89)
Page 51 – Video Put-Downs
Back Cover – Great Moments in History 1656 – Charles Rodrigues (reprint from #132)

Cracked Collectors' Edition #57 (*Monsters*), February 1984 (52 pages) ($1.00)

Cover – Monster Picnic – O.O. Severin (John Severin) (reprint from #54)
Page 2 – The One That Got Away! (reprint from *For Monsters Only* #5)
Page 3 – Contents
Page 4 – Frankenstein the Untold Story (reprint from *Cracked Collectors' Edition* #43)
Page 12 – Monster Mother Goose – Bill McCartney (Bill Ward) (reprint from *For Monsters Only* #1)
Page 14 – Transylvanian Calculator Readouts – John Severin (new)
Page 15 – Cracked Puts the Bite on Dracula – Howard Nostrand (reprint from #155)
Page 19 – The Birthday Gift! – John Langton (reprint from #67)
Page 20 – Quick Quiz (watered the front lawn) (reprint from *For Monsters Only* #3)
Page 22 – What Goes on in a Monster's Mind – Don Orehek (reprint from #138)
Page 25 – More Monster Mirth (reprint from *For Monsters Only* #2)
Page 26 – Monster Party! – John Severin (reprint from #31)
Page 28 – Transylvanian Rock 'n' Roll Monsters – Vic Martin (reprint from *For Monsters Only* #5)
Page 30 – The Stone Age – Oscar Blotta (reprint from *For Monsters Only* #5)
Page 32 – A Transylvanian Family Album (reprint from *For Monsters Only* #1)

Page 35 – Make Mine Well Done! – John Langton (reprint from #62)

Page 36 – The Nightmares of Monsters – Bill McCartney (Bill Ward) (reprint from *For Monsters Only* #5)

Page 38 – Chiller Dillers – John Severin, Joe Kiernan, Benson, Pete Wyma, Art Pottier, Lennie Herman, Norm Sutt, Bob (reprint from *For Monsters Only* #1)

Page 40 – Cracked Examines All the Possibilities of Flying Saucers – Bill McCartney (Bill Ward) (reprint from #68)

Page 44 – Fun, Games and Monsters – Vic Martin (reprint from *For Monsters Only* #4)

Page 45 – Masters of Evil (reprint from #174)

Page 48 – Modern Day Monsters – Joe Maneely (reprint from #5)

Page 50 – Ugghh!!-Break - Bob Zahn (reprint from *For Monsters Only* #3)

Page 90 – Fangmann's ad – John Severin (reprint from #36)

Back Cover – The Man and the Mousey – Oskar Blotta (reprint from #124)

Cracked Collectors' Edition #58 (*Shut-Ups*), May 1984 (52 pages) ($1.00)

Cover – Star Trek – John Severin, Don Orehek (partial reprint from #127)

Page 2 – The Cracked Bookstore ad – John Severin

Page 3 – Contents

Page 4 – Shut-Ups (your eyes) – Don Orehek (reprint from #165)

Page 5 – Shut-Ups (play like you never played) – Don Orehek (reprint from #166)

Page 6 – Shut-Ups (winning tickets) – S. Gross Jr. (Charles Rodrigues) (reprint from #103)

Page 7 – Shut-Ups (Have a good time!) – Mike Ricigliano (reprint from #138)

Page 8 – Shut-Ups (married 25 years) – Don Orehek (reprint from #167)

Page 9 – Shut-Ups (Main Street) – Bill Ward (reprint from *Cracked Collectors' Edition* #27)

Page 10 – Shut-Ups (ain't got no horses) – Charles Rodrigues (reprint from #121)

Page 11 – Shut-Ups (uncomfortable) – Charles Rodrigues (reprint from #130)

Page 12 – Shut-Ups (best nap) – Don Orehek (reprint from #148)

Page 13 – Shut-Ups (my greatest work of art) – Don Orehek (reprint from #174)

Page 14 – Shut-Ups (snooping around) – Sam Gross Jr. (Charles Rodrigues) (reprint from #100)

Page 15 – Shut-Ups (No cavities) – Sam Gross Jr. (Charles Rodrigues) (reprint from #99)

Page 16 – Shut-Ups (any other questions) – Don Orehek (reprint from #160)
Page 17 – Shut-Ups (I object) – Don Orehek (reprint from #155)
Page 18 – Shut-Ups (put his footprints) – Mike Ricigliano (reprint from #142)
Page 19 – Shut-Ups (Can I sit) – Glenn Mukheryee (Charles Rodrigues) (reprint from #94)
Page 20 – Shut-Ups (Squeaky's breaking out) – Don Orehek (reprint from #156)
Page 21 – Shut-Ups (big game) – Don Orehek (reprint from #157)
Page 22 – Shut-Ups (provide a blindfold) – Charles Rodrigues (reprint from #128)
Page 23 – Shut-Ups (good year) – Charles Rodrigues (reprint from #126)
Page 24 – Shut-Ups (drive-in movie) – Charles Rodrigues, Vic Martin (reprint from #93)
Page 25 – Shut-Ups (It's a mirage) – Charles Rodrigues (reprint from #131)
Page 26 – Shut-Ups (difficult time) – Charles Rodrigues (reprint from #115)
Page 27 – Shut-Ups (KUH-RRRAK!) – Charles Rodrigues (reprint from #125)
Page 28 – Shut-Ups (make up my mind) – Don Orehek (reprint from #147)
Page 29 – Shut-Ups (losing your hair) – Don Orehek (reprint from #153)
Page 30 – Shut-Ups (the score's tied) – Mike Ricigliano (reprint from #135)
Page 31 – Shut-Ups (grown man playing with a doll) – Charles Rodrigues (reprint from #120)
Page 32 – Shut-Ups (curtain about to go up) – Charles Rodrigues (reprint from #116)
Page 33 – Shut-Ups (electronic calculator) – Charles Rodrigues (reprint from #117)
Page 34 – Shut-Ups (pastrami on rye) – Don Orehek (reprint from #164)
Page 35 – Shut-Ups (hospital gowns) – Don Orehek (reprint from *Cracked Collectors' Edition* #27)
Page 36 – Shut-Ups (practice your violin) – Charles Rodrigues (reprint from #113)
Page 37 – Shut-Ups (good clean fight) – Mike Ricigliano (reprint from #134)
Page 38 – Shut-Ups (our little diet) – Don Orehek (reprint from #161)

Page 39 – Shut-Ups (Here's his picture) – Charles Rodrigues (reprint from #118)

Page 40 – Shut-Ups (Hollywood contract) – Don Orehek (reprint from #150)

Page 41 – Shut-Ups (best tattoo jobs) – Don Orehek (reprint from #159)

Page 42 – Shut-Ups (not going to forgive) – Don Orehek (reprint from #154)

Page 43 – Shut-Ups (drive away your customers) – Don Orehek (reprint from #162)

Page 44 – Shut-Ups (I LOVE a parade) – Don Orehek (reprint from #163)

Page 45 – Shut-Ups (let's go out dancing) – Mike Ricigliano (reprint from #136)

Page 46 – Shut-Ups (home cooked meal) – Don Orehek (reprint from *Cracked Collectors' Edition* #27)

Page 47 – Shut-Ups (Looks like a Picasso) – Don Orehek (reprint from *Cracked Collectors' Edition* #27)

Page 48 – Shut-Ups (bad luck to see bride) – Sam Gross Jr. (Charles Rodrigues) (reprint from #110)

Page 49 – Shut-Ups (innocent) – S. Gross (Charles Rodrigues) (reprint from #104)

Page 50 – Shut-Ups (take it from the top) – Don Orehek (reprint from #149)

Page 51– Shut-Ups (stopping the fight) – Charles Rodrigues (reprint from #132)

Back Cover – Shut-Ups (I remember) – Charles Rodrigues (reprint from #108)

Cracked Collectors' Edition #59 (*Monsters*), July 1984 (52 pages) ($1.00)

Cover – Rubber Monster photo (new)

Page 2 – ("Go to the barber") *I Was a Teenage Werewolf* photo (new)

Page 3 – Contents

Page 4 – School For Monsters – Nireves (John Severin) (reprint from #26)

Page 9 – Transylvania's Handyman (reprint from *For Monsters Only* #3)

Page 10 – Vampires of the World – Bernard Baily (reprint from #108)

Page 14 – Quick Quiz (typical father) (reprint from *For Monsters Only* #8)

Page 16 – Martin's Screams – Vic Martin (reprint from *For Monsters Only* #2)

Page 17 – King Kong's Boyhood – Bill Ward (reprint from #141)

Page 21 – Dungeon of Horror Game – Don Orehek, John Severin (new)

Page 33 – A Friend from Next Door (reprint from *For Monsters Only* #1)

Page 34 – Cracked Takes a Look at the Transylvanian Teen Scene – John Severin (reprint from #40)

Page 39 – Merry Old England Life ad (reprint from #47)

Page 40 – Transylvania's New Basketball Coach! (reprint from *For Monsters Only* #4)

Page 41 – Great Scenes from Great Horror Movies – John Severin (reprint from #42)

Page 43 – Here Comes the Bride and Gloom! (reprint from *For Monsters Only* #3)

Page 44 – Frankenstein and Rock 'n Roll! – Joe Maneely (reprint from #2)

Page 47 – The Search for Bigfoot – John Severin (reprint from #141)

Page 48 – The Monsters Laugh it Up! (reprint from #56)

Page 50 – The Evil Experiment! – John Langton (reprint from #75)

Page 51 – Transylvania's Number One Hot Shot (reprint from *For Monsters Only* #8)

Back Cover – The Screamers (reprint from *For Monsters Only* #5)

Cracked Collectors' Edition #60 (*Michael Jackson*), November 1984 (52 pages) ($1.25) (Another issue with predominantly new material.)

Cover – Michael Jackson Reads *Cracked* #207 – John Severin

Page 2 – Michael Jackson balloons photo

Page 3 – Contents

Page 4 – Michael Jackson Letters

Page 6 – A Day in the Life of Michael Jackson – Vance Rodewalt

Page 11 – Celebrity Odes to Michael

Page 14 – Rock and Roll Your Eyeballs Out – John Severin (reprint from #163)

Page 21 – Rock Calculator Readouts

Page 23 – One Afternoon in a Local Stereo Store – Sururi Gumen (reprint from #138)

Page 24 – Goldie Oldie Rock Yocks (reprint from #91)

Page 26 – Rock 'n' Roll Heaven – John Severin

Page 28 – Mike at Work

Page 30 – Michael Jackson's Scrapbook – Don Orehek

Page 35 – The Michael Jackson Book of Games and Puzzles – Don Orehek

Page 39 – National Gossip Rock Inquirer

Page 40 – Cracked Flip the Faces Book – John Severin (revised reprint from *Giant Cracked* #3)

Page 51 – Michael Jackson with E.T. photo

Back Cover – Michael Jackson with llama photo ("chew up those Lionel Richie albums")

Cracked Collectors' Edition #61 (*Monsters and Other Bad Guys*), February 1985 (52 pages) ($1.25)

  Cover – Alien – Don't Look it's too Scary! – John Severin, Vic Martin (partial reprint from #164 and others)

  Page 2 – The Man & the Fly – Oskar Blotta (reprint from #95)

  Page 3 – Contents

  Page 4 – The Cracked Monsters Lens (nuclear power) (new)

  Page 6 – The Rodfather – O.O. Severino (John Severin) (reprint from #104)

  Page 12 – Horrible Humor (reprint from #97)

  Page 15 – Big-John is Coming – LePoer (John Severin) (reprint from #31)

  Page 19 – The Howls Are Here! (reprint from *For Monsters Only* #9)

  Page 20 – The Pirate Treasure Chest (reprint from #64)

  Page 22 – Hiss the Villains (reprint from #94)

  Page 26 – Monster Party – John Severin (reprint from #43)

  Page 28 – Guns and Gags for Hire! (reprint from #62)

  Page 30 – The Cracked Camera (reprint from #102)

  Page 33 – The Train Robber – Bill McCartney (Bill Ward) (reprint from #34)

  Page 34 – The Cosa Nostra First Reader – Bill McCartney (Bill Ward) (reprint from #35)

  Page 39 – Monster Madness! (reprint from *For Monsters Only* #8)

  Page 40 – The Big Big Guys! (reprint from #102)

  Page 42 – Fiendish for Fun! (reprint from *For Monsters Only* #10)

  Page 44 – Wild Wheels (reprint from #104)

  Page 46 – Going Great Guns (reprint from #80)

  Page 48 – Heavy on the Horror, Please (reprint from #95)

  Page 50 – Cracked Space Shut-Ups! (most beautiful girl) – Bill McCartney (Bill Ward) (reprint from #8)

  Page 51 – The Way They Should Have Filmed it – John Severin (reprint from #29)

  Back Cover – The Man and the Beast – Oskar Blotta (reprint from #80)

Cracked Collectors' Edition #62 (*Cracked Looks at Celebrities*), September 1985 (52 pages) ($1.25)

  Cover – Michael Jackson Meets Mr. T! – John Severin, Aron Laikin (reprint from #206)

  Page 2 and 51 – Formal Portrait of Sylvester P. Smythe – Cracked Poster – John Severin (reprint from #147)

  Page 3 – Contents

  Page 4 – A Day in the Life of Michael Jackson – Vance Rodewalt (reprint from *Cracked Collectors' Edition* #60)

Page 9 – The True Story of The Lone Ranger – Brian Buniak (reprint from #198)

Page 12 – If Arnold Were Treated and Behaved Like a Real-Life Kid – John Severin (reprint from #171)

Page 16 – Future All-Star TV Specials – Samuel B. Whitehead (reprint from #191)

Page 20 – Cracked's Inquiring Photographer Visits the Stars (reprint from #152)

Page 25 – More Celebrity Garbage – John Severin (reprint from #187)

Page 28 – If Other Actors Played the Parts Made Famous by Somebody Else – John Severin (reprint from #151)

Page 32 – When Hollywood Totally Takes Over Washington – Samuel B. Whitehead (reprint from #180)

Page 35 – The Cracked Handbook of Acting – Warren Sattler (reprint from #159)

Page 39 – The Making of Thriller (reprint from #207)

Page 45 – Cracked Interviews the Comedy King – Bill Ward (reprint from #180)

Page 50 – Every Joke Ever Made – John Langton (reprint from #191)

Back Cover – Great Moments in Entertainment 1,432,600 B.C. – Warren Sattler (reprint from #193)

Cracked Collectors' Edition #63 (*Summer Camp Issue*), November 1985 (52 pages) ($1.25)

Cover – Life Guard – John Severin (reprint from #88)

Page 2 and 51 – Public Park Rules – Cracked Poster #188 (reprint from #188)

Page 3 – Contents

Page 4 – A Cracked Look at Summer Camps – Howard Nostrand (reprint from #145)

Page 8 – Snide Guide to Camping – John Severin (reprint from #61)

Page 11 – The Cracked Book of Summer Games and Puzzles That Anyone Can Do – Warren Sattler (reprint from *Cracked Collectors' Edition* #44)

Page 17 – Go Fly a Kite – John Severin (reprint from #74)

Page 18 – The Cracked World of Summer – Don Orehek (reprint from #155)

Page 20 – Prof. Whiffle-Bird Discovers a New Species – Tony Tallarico (reprint from #64)

Page 24 – Summer is – John Langton (reprint from #128)

Page 26 – Cracked Looks at Camping – Don Orehek (reprint from #119)

Page 28 – Cracked's Guide to Backpacking – John Severin (reprint from #108)

Page 33 – The Scuba Diver – Howard Nostrand (reprint from #159)

Page 34 – Creating Your Own Summer Jobs – Don Orehek (reprint from #197)

Page 36 – A Dozen Things Never to Do at the Beach – John Langton (reprint from #173)

Page 38 – The Cracked Guide to Canoeing – Warren Sattler (reprint from #146)

Page 42 – You Know It's Really Summer When – Don Orehek (reprint from *Cracked Collectors' Edition* #44)

Page 45 – Cracked Interviews the Camp King – John Langton (reprint from #111)

Page 50 – Shark Shut-Ups (shark disguise) – Don Orehek (reprint from *Cracked Collectors' Edition* #26)

Back Cover – Gorkel House – Tony Tallarico (reprint from #64)

Cracked Collectors' Edition #64 (*TV Spectacular*), December 1985 (52 pages) ($1.25)

Cover – Sylvester's Explosive Remote Control – John Severin (new)

Page 2 and 51 – We're Experiencing Technical Difficulties – Cracked Poster #159 (reprint from #159)

Page 3 – Contents

Page 4 – The A-a-aayy Team Takes a Ride on the Lovely Boat – John Severin (reprint from #197)

Page 11 – Magnumb Public Idiot – John Severin (reprint from #191)

Page 19 – Knight Rider Meets The Dukes of Hazzardous – John Severin (reprint from #196)

Page 26 – You Know You're an MTV Freak When – Bill Powers (John Severin) (reprint from #210)

Page 28 – The Falling Guy (Oh, Homer) – John Severin (reprint from #188)

Page 35 – If T.V. Warnings Appeared in Everyday Life – Don Orehek (reprint from #191)

Page 38 – The Silly Cosbey Show – John Severin (reprint from #212)

Page 41 – TV Contraptions We'll Soon Be Seeing – Val Mayerik (reprint from #157)

Page 44 – Simian & Simian – John Severin (reprint from #197)

Page 50 – Are You P.M. Magazine Material? – John Langton (reprint from #192)

Back Cover – Great Moments in Comedy 1391 – Mike Ricigliano (reprint from #194)

Cracked Collectors' Edition #65 (Best Movie Satires of the 80's), **February 1986 (52 pages) ($1.25)**

> Cover – Cracked Carnival of Fun – John Severin (partial reprints from *King-Sized Cracked* #2 and #155, 169, 181, 195, 208)
> Page 2 and 51 – King Kong – Cracked Poster #140 – John Severin (reprint from #140)
> Page 3 – Contents
> Page 4 – Traitors of the Lost Ark – John Severin (reprint from #183)
> Page 12 – Jawz – John Severin (reprint from #129)
> Page 18 – Star Drek the Moving Picture – John Severin (reprint from #169)
> Page 26 – Suped-Upman The Satire – Nireves (John Severin) (reprint from #160)
> Page 33 – E.T.'s Report My Experiences on Earth – Don Orehek (reprint from #192)
> Page 37 – Close Encounters of the Worst Kind – Michael Severin (John Severin) (reprint from #150)
> Page 44 – Indianapolis Bones and the Temple of Gloom – John Severin (reprint from #208)
> Back Cover – Landing On Mars – Howard Nostrand / Murad Gumen (reprint from #156)

Cracked Collectors' Edition #66 (Crime's War on Law!), **May 1986 (52 pages) ($1.25)**

> Cover – Capone – John Severin (reprint from #128)
> Page 2 and 51 – Support Non Violence or We'll Kill Ya!! – Cracked Poster – John Severin (reprint from #99)
> Page 3 – Contents
> Page 4 – Bullet Proof Car – John Severin (reprint from #35)
> Page 5 – The War on Law – John Severin (reprint from #57)
> Page 9 – Hudd & Dini (painted wall) – Vic Martin (reprint from #76)
> Page 11 – Criminal She-Nanigans – John Severin (reprint from #138)
> Page 15 – Which One is a Banker? Ad – John Severin (reprint from #23)
> Page 16 – Awards from the Syndicate – Bill Elder (reprint from #12)
> Page 19 – What are the Old TV & Movie Detectives Doing Today? – John Severin (reprint from #121)
> Page 24 – How Times Have Changed (reprint from #2)
> Page 26 – Guns and Gags for Hire! (reprint from #62)
> Page 28 – Notes – Don Orehek (reprint from #35)
> Page 30 – Capony – John Severin (reprint from #128)
> Page 36 – Come and Get Me, Copper! (reprint from #64)
> Page 37 – Julius "Little" Caesar – John Severin (reprint from #6) (originally called "Julius Caesar in Modern Dress")

Page 40 – Music Hath Charm – Bill McCartney (Bill Ward) (reprint from #42)
Page 41 – The Great Chicago Heist – John Severin (reprint from #176)
Page 49 – Subscription ad – John Severin
Page 50 – Hudd & Dini (Vacancy) – Vic Martin (reprint from #79)
Back Cover – Wanted Poster (reprint from #19) (originally called "Reward Poster")

Cracked Collectors' Edition #67 (*The Many Faces of Sylvester P. Smythe*), September 1986 (52 pages) ($1.25)

Cover and Back Cover – Many Faces of Sylvester P. Smythe – John Severin (reprints from #14, 15, 24, 50, 67, 81, 84, 87, 98, 140, 177, 188, *Cracked Collectors' Edition* #41)
Page 2 and 51 – Formal Portrait of Sylvester P. Smythe – Cracked Poster – John Severin (reprint from #147)
Page 3 – Contents
Page 4 – Sylvester for President – John Severin (reprint from #36)
Page 11 – The Losingest Family in History! – John Severin (reprint from #77)
Page 14 – Sylvester P. Smythe As Seen by Different Artists (reprint from #14)
Page 16 – Home Sweet Home – John Severin (reprint from #24)
Page 18 and 35 – Great War Heroes – Jack Davis (reprint from #15)
Page 19 – Giant Jig-Saw Puzzle – Jack Davis, John Severin, Bill Everett, Al Jaffee, (new, with reprints from #1, 2, 5, 11, 12, 14)
Page 29 – Sliding Down the Family Tree – John Severin (reprint from #128)
Page 31 – The Completely Rebuilt Person – Vic Martin (reprint from #76)
Page 36 – Sylvester Meets the Mets – John Severin (reprint from #64)
Page 40 – The Smythes – Losers Throughout History! – John Severin (reprint from #75)
Page 42 – The World's First Psychedelic Janitor – John Severin (reprint from #71)
Page 45 – Learning to Fly – John Severin (reprint from #80)

Cracked Collectors' Edition #68 (*Year's Best*), November 1986 (52 pages) ($1.25)

Cover – Slippery Ink – John Severin (reprint from #71)
Page 2 and 51 – Sylvester P, Smythe is Rambozo! – Cracked Movie Poster – Bob Fingerman (reprint from #219)
Page 3 – Contents

Page 4 – Laughing Matter – Hark Abner / Tom Bacas (reprint from #218)

Page 5 – Box Office Future – John Severin / Joe Catalano, Mort Todd (reprint from #218)

Page 11 – Robot Wars (heh heh bbbzzz) – Steve Ditko / Mort Todd (reprint from #218)

Page 12 – Cracked Visits a Midnight Monster Picnic – Al Scaduto (reprint from #217)

Page 14 – Cracked Max III Beyond Blunderdome! – Bob Fingerman (reprint from #217)

Page 18 – The Uggly Family "Melbin Goes to School" – Stosh Gillespie (Dan Clowes) / Eel O'Brian (Mort Todd) (reprint from *Extra Special Cracked* #9)

Page 28 – G.I. Joke "A Real American Nut!" – Bob Fingerman (reprint from #218)

Page 29 – A Fish Story – Milton Knight (reprint from #219)

Page 30 – Aren't You Nervous When – Dan Clowes / Michael Weitz (reprint from #216)

Page 32 – Cracked Look at Super-Zeros! – Mort Todd / Tom Bacas (reprint from #218)

Page 35 – Miami Nice – John Reiner (reprint from #216)

Page 40 – Mr. Rockey's Neighb'hood! – John Reiner / Mark Lewis (reprint from #219)

Page 42 – Arnold Fluffernutter Commandope – Bob Fingerman / Mort Todd (reprint from #219)

Page 47 – A Cracked Look at 007! – O.O. Severin (John Severin) / Mort Todd (reprint from #216)

Page 50 – Wrasslin' Shut-Ups (wear that mask) – Mort Todd (reprint from #215)

Back Cover – *Cracked Digest* #1 ad

Cracked Collectors' Edition #69 (Nanny Dickering's Best Interviews), December 1986 (52 pages) ($1.25)

Cover – Nanny Dickering – John Severin

Page 2 – Contents

Page 3 – Cracked Interviews the Rock Video King! – Mort Todd (new) (Fumetti-style photo comic of Nanny Dickering featuring Bebe Buell, Liv Tyler (Rundgren), Mort Todd and Charles E. Hall.)

Page 9 – Cracked Interviews the Skateboard King – Bill Ward (reprint from #152)

Page 14 – Cracked Interviews the Art King – John Severin (reprint from #137)

Page 19 – Cracked Interviews the Traveling Carnival King – Bill Ward (reprint from #140)

Page 24 – Cracked Interviews the Stunt King – Sururi Gumen (reprint from #128)

Page 26 – Nanny Dickering's Pin-Up Page – Bill Ward (new)

Page 31 – Cracked Interviews the Monster King – Bill Ward (reprint from #143)

Page 36 – Cracked Interviews the Newspaper King – Powers (John Severin) (reprint from #124)

Page 41 – Cracked Interviews the Insurance King – Bill Ward (reprint from #146)

Page 46 – Cracked Interviews the Outdoor King – Bill Ward (reprint from #138)

Page 51 – The Many Looks of Nanny Dickering – Bill Ward, John Severin, John Langton, Bob Taylor, Sururi Gumen, Stan Goldberg (new)

Back Cover – Rock Video King ad (new)

Cracked Collectors' Edition #70 (Cracked #1), April 1987 (52 pages) ($1.25) (Despite the title, only about 2/3 of issue #1 is actually reprinted.)

Cover and Back Cover – Cracked World – Bill Everett, John Severin (reprint from #1 and #147)

Page 2 – Subscription ad – John Severin (reprint from #1)

Page 3 – Contents (reprint from #1)

Page 4 – Letters From the Editor (reprint from #1)

Page 5 – Gunsmokes – Russ Heath (reprint from #1)

Page 8 – How to Build a Hot Hot Rod (reprint from #1)

Page 10 – The $64,000,000 Cracked-Pot Question – John Severin (reprint from #1)

Page 12 – Little Mercurochrome and Denny the Menaces (reprint from #1)

Page 13 – Max Wallis Interviews Jayne Womansfield – Russ Heath (reprint from #1)

Page 16 – Chef of the Month – John Severin (reprint from #1)

Page 18 – Science Fiction – Don Orehek (partial reprint from #1)

Page 19 – How I'll Beat the Champ – John Severin (reprint from #1)

Page 22 – Cracked Brings You Greetings – Bill Everett (reprint from #1)

Page 24 – Your Christmas Shopping Guide – John Severin (reprint from #1)

Page 25 – Shakespeare (reprint from #1)

Page 28 – He's Really a Lone Ranger Now! – Bill Ward (reprint from #1)

Page 29 – The Breaking Point (reprint from #2)

Page 30 – Wacky Inventions – Joe Sinnott (reprint from *Zany* #2)

Page 32 – Bridge on the River Kweer – John Severin (reprint from #2)

Page 35 – Cracked Shut-Ups (send me in) – Bill McCartney (Bill Ward) (reprint from #3)

Page 36 – American Grandstand – John Severin (reprint from #2)

Page 2 – Shut-Ups (Europe) – Bill McCartney (Bill Ward) (reprint from #2)

Page 3 – Contents

Page 4 – Cracked Calendar – John Severin (revised reprint from #19)

Cracked Collectors' Edition #71 (Summer Fun!), **July 1987 (52 pages) ($1.35)**

Cover – Jawz – John Severin (reprint from #129)

Page 2 – Things Are Tough All Over! – Bill McCartney (Bill Ward) (reprint from #7)

Page 3 – Contents

Page 4 – Throughout History with Home Movies – Ned Kelly (John Severin) (reprint from #38)

Page 10 – Camp Kicey Doo-Bee – Bill McCartney (Bill Ward) (reprint from #55)

Page 12 – A Visit to the Beach – LePoer (John Severin) (reprint from #38)

Page 14 – It All Depends on the Point of View (snake) – Bill McCartney (Bill Ward) (reprint from #10)

Page 16 – Beatlezania – John Severin (reprint from #42)

Page 21 – The Martian Report on Earth – Bill McCartney (Bill Ward) (reprint from #51)

Page 25 – Rock, Rattle & Moan! – Bob Fingerman (reprint from #221)

Page 31 – California Here I Went! – Bill McCartney (Bill Ward) (reprint from #57)

Page 34 – Ignited Air Lines ad – John Severin (reprint from #13)

Page 36 – If Picture Postcards Told the Truth! – John Severin (reprint from #59)

Page 38 – A Sunday at Coney Island – Bill McCartney (Bill Ward) (reprint from #40)

Page 40 – Banks Unlimited or (Money Does Grow on Trees) – McCarty (John Severin) (reprint from #51)

Page 43 – Bank of America Travelers Checks ad – John Severin (reprint from #28)

Page 44 – The Cracked Campaign Against Foreign Travel – Bill McCartney (Bill Ward) (reprint from #53)

Page 48 – Wild Record Albums – Bill McCartney (Bill Ward) (reprint from #13)

Page 50 – Popular Songs Shut-Ups (smile umbrella) – Bill McCartney (Bill Ward) (reprint from #22)

Page 51 – Cracked Takes You Back to When it all Started (blood pressure) – Jack Davis (reprint from #15)

Back Cover – A Way-Out Summer Extravaganza – Bob Fingerman (new)

Cracked Collectors' Edition #72 (*Year's Best!*), September 1987 (52 pages) ($1.35)

> Cover – "See Thru" Mirror Sandwich Board – John Severin (reprint from #76)
>
> Page 2 – Count Dracula …2086 A.D. – John Severin / George Gladir (reprint from #224)
>
> Page 3 – Contents
>
> Page 4 – The Cracked List of Stupid Things That Only Kids Like! – Bill Wray / Peter Bagge (reprint from #221)
>
> Page 6 – The Cosby Show – John Severin (reprint from #224)
>
> Page 11 – Garbage Dump Pop Stars (Paul Shaver) (reprint from #224)
>
> Page 14 – G.I. Joke in Peace, Love & Harmony – Shawn Kerri (reprint from #225)
>
> Page 19 – The Uggly Family (Whatcha got there) – Stosh Gillespie (Dan Clowes) / Eel O'Brian (Mort Todd) (reprint from #224)
>
> Page 22 – Ron Rover – Rick Altergott / Dan Knotts (reprint from #225)
>
> Page 25 – Rockey IV – Bob Fingerman / Mort Todd (reprint from #220)
>
> Page 30 – Gorbachev in America! – John Severin / Moe McMahon (Marian McMahon) (reprint from #221)
>
> Page 33 – Squeeeal of Fortune!! – John Reiner / Joe Catalano (reprint from #222)
>
> Page 37 – Movie Mystery Credits – Thyme Foxpound (John Severin) / E. Nelson Bridwell (reprint from #223)
>
> Page 39 – Canine the Barbarian (The Coming of Canine) – Gary Fields (partial reprint from *Super Cracked* #32)
>
> Page 43 – Real Competition! – Shawn Kerri (reprint from #223)
>
> Page 45 – Hudd & Dini (CLICK!) – Vic Martin (reprint from #221)
>
> Page 46 – Cracked Interviews the Vice Kings – Rob Orzechowski / Joe Catalano (reprint from #223)
>
> Page 50 – Shut-Ups (holding up the works) – Don Orehek (reprint from #221)
>
> Page 51 – Robot Wars (giant destroy-bots on their way here) – Steve Ditko / Mort Todd (reprint from #223)
>
> Back Cover – Dee Sylvester and Sylvester P. Reagan (reprints from #221 and 222)

Cracked Collectors' Edition #73 (*Monster Party*), January 1988 (100 pages) ($2.75)

> Cover – Sylvester's Nightmares – Bob Fingerman (new)
>
> Page 2 and 51 – The Greatest Monster Battle of all Time! – John Severin (reprint from *For Monsters Only* #2)
>
> Page 3 – Contents (green color added)

Page 4 and 91 – Frankenstein's Monster Party – Dick Briefer (new to *Cracked*) (green color added)

Page 11 – The Alien – Brian Buniak (reprint from #201)

Page 12 – King Kung – John Severin (reprint from #140)

Page 19 – When it all Ended (The Science Fiction Movie) – John Severin (reprint from #24)

Page 20 – The Old Lady and the Laundromat – Bill McCartney (Bill Ward) (reprint from #28)

Page 22 – Satan's Campaign to Promote Hell – Makbush (Sururi Gumen) (reprint from #134)

Page 26 – If Hit Movies Were Combined – John Severin (reprint from #131)

Page 30 – The Little World of Don Swanson (chinning hanger) – Don Swanson (reprint from #20)

Page 31 – Grumblins – John Severin (reprint from #209)

Page 38 – The Cracked Monsters Lens (Will you call Junior?) (reprint from *Cracked Collectors' Edition* #53)

Page 42 – A Tourist's Guide to Transylvania – Vic Martin (reprint from #60)

Page 47 – More Combined Movies "My Fair Lady" & "King Kong" – John Severin (reprint from #133)

Page 48 – How to Ward Off Sharks – John Severin (reprint from *Cracked Collectors' Edition* #26)

Page 51 – Orehek's Horror Humor! – Don Orehek (reprint from *Cracked Collectors' Edition* #53)

Page 55 – Hudd & Dini (CLICK!) – Vic Martin (reprint from #221)

Page 56 – Monster Paper Doll Page – Warren Sattler (reprint from *Cracked Collectors' Edition* #52)

Page 58 – Throughout History with the Real Gremlins – John Severin (reprint from #209)

Page 60 – Cracked Monster Phrases – Vic Martin (reprint from *For Monsters Only* #5) (originally called "Monster Phrases")

Page 62 – Black Movie Monsters – LePoer (John Severin) (reprint from #111)

Page 66 – What Goes on in a Monster's Mind – Don Orehek (reprint from #138)

Page 68 – Cracked Presents Future Insect Monster Movies – Sururi Gumen (reprint from #125)

Page 72 – Masters of Evil (reprint from #174)

Page 74 – You Know You're a Real Monster if – Brian Buniak (reprint from #199)

Page 76 – Earthshake – Ty Dahlwave (John Severin) (reprint from #125)

Page 82 – 3-D Horror Shows – Sururi Gumen (reprint from #194)

Page 85 – Another Combined Movie "Godzilla" vs. "The Towering Inferno" – Sururi Gumen (reprint from #137)

Page 86 – Cracked Interviews Stephen Kink the Horror King! – Stan Goldberg, Mike Esposito / Joe Catalano (reprint from #221)

Page 94 – Absolutely, Positively the Very Last of Those Cracked Monsters (reprint from #168) (green color added)

Page 97 – More Combined Movies "Dracula" and "Snow White and the Seven Dwarfs" – John Severin (reprint from #132) (green color added)

Page 98 – Shut-Ups (Mad Doctors' Monsters!) – Charles Rodrigues (reprint from #184) (green color added)

Back Cover – The Uggly Family Poster – Stosh Gillespie (Dan Clowes) / Eel O'Brian (Mort Todd) (reprint from #226)

Cracked Collectors' Edition #74 (*30 Years of Cracked*), April 1988 (100 pages) ($2.75)

Cover – 30 Years of Cracked – Bill Wray (new)

Page 2 and 99 – Cracked Cover Gallery (new and reprints from #1, 2, 6, 12)

Page 3 – Contents

Page 4 – 30 Years of Cracked / Cracked on TV! (new)

Page 6 – Gunsmokes – Russ Heath (reprint from #1)

Page 9 – Shut-Ups (Europe) – Bill McCartney (Bill Ward) (reprint from #2)

Page 10 – American Grandstand – John Severin (reprint from #2)

Page 12 – Psychological Predictions – Bill Elder (reprint from #6)

Page 14 – So You Think It's Easy to Buy Cracked? – John Severin (reprint from #6)

Page 17 – Cracked Brings You Greetings – Bill Everett (reprint from #1)

Page 18 – The Last of the Hollywood "B" Movies – Gray Morrow (reprint from #8)

Page 21 – A Beatnik Goes to a Party – Jack Davis (reprint from #12)

Page 23 – Those False Rumors About Cracked Magazine – John Severin / George Gladir (reprint from #25)

Page 27 – Big-John is Coming – LePoer (John Severin) (reprint from #31)

Page 31 – Shut-Ups (20 cents) – Rodrigliani (Charles Rodrigues) (reprint from #46)

Page 32 – The Flipsides! – O.O. Severin (John Severin) / George Gladir (reprint from #52)

Page 36 – The Cracked Office as it Would be Portrayed on TV – John Severin (reprint from *Giant Cracked* #45)

Page 38 – Sagebrush (don't lag behind) – John Severin (reprint from *King-Sized Cracked* #5)

Page 40 – Commercializing the Moon – John Severin (reprint from #81)

Page 44 – Hudd & Dini (garbage cans) – Vic Martin (reprint from #82)

Page 45 – Hawk – John Severin (reprint from #105)

Page 49 – The First Dollar – Bernard Baily (reprint from #107)

Page 50 – A Cracked History of the Movies – Vic Martin (reprint from #109)

Page 54 – Ye Hang Ups (Skrunch) – Nireves (John Severin) (reprint from #114) / Ye Hang Ups #3 (He hates to drink alone) – John Severin (reprint from #115)

Page 55 – If We Didn't Have Hair – John Severin (reprint from #115)

Page 58 – Cracked Interviews the Advertising King – Bill Ward (reprint from #117)

Page 63 – Late One Evening – Howard Nostrand (reprint from #142)

Page 64 – Cracked Looks at the T-Shirt Craze – Howard Nostrand (reprint from #143)

Page 66 – Shut-Ups (I think I can K.O.) – Don Orehek (reprint from #145)

Page 67 – Star-Warz – O.O. Severin (John Severin) / Joe Catalano (reprint from #146)

Page 74 – The Cracked Lens (reprint from #154)

Page 76 – The Talking Blob – John Severin / Joe Catalano (reprint from #149)

Page 82 – Magazines That Tried to Copy Cracked, But Failed – M.E. Tate (John Severin) (reprint from #212)

Page 86 – Laughing Matter – Hark Abner / Tom Bacas (reprint from #218)

Page 87 – G.I. Joke "A Real American Nut!" – Bob Fingerman (reprint from #218)

Page 91 – Robot Wars (heh heh bbbzzz) – Steve Ditko / Mort Todd (reprint from #218)

Page 92 – The Uggly Family "Melbin Goes to School" – Stosh Gillespie (Dan Clowes) / Eel O'Brian (Mort Todd) (reprint from *Extra Special Cracked* #9)

Back Cover – The Cracked Cover Art of John Severin (reprints from #8, 13, 22, 27, 28, 31, 40, 45, 53, 65, 69) (Same images that were used for the stickers in #146.) (reprint from *Giant Cracked* #46)

Cracked Collectors' Edition #75 (*Year's Best!*), July 1988 (100 pages) ($2.75)

Cover – Sylly Awards – John Severin (new)

Page 2 – Evolution of Smythe – Bill Wray (reprint from #226)

Page 3 – Contents

Page 4 – Behind the Cracked Classics (new)

Page 6 – Goonlighting – Bob Fingerman / Stu Schwartzberg (reprint from #226)

Page 11 – Hudd & Dini (street rock king) – Vic Martin (reprint from #226)

Page 12 – Blundercats – Steve Ditko / Mike Carlin (reprint from #226)

Page 17 – Shut-Ups (pumpkin pie) – Don Orehek (reprint from #226)

Page 18 – Communist Broadcasting System's New TV Lineup! – Ivan Severinovitch (John Severin) (reprint from #227)

Page 23 – Russian One-Shots (Miss Moscow) – Mike Ricigliano (reprint from #227)

Page 25 – Life in Amerika Magazine – O.O. Severin (John Severin) (reprint from #227)

Page 28 – You Know You're a Rad Biker When – Brad Joyce / George Gladir (reprint from #228)

Page 30 – Hurry-Ups (Neutral Zone) – Rick Altergott (reprint from #228)

Page 31 – Eeeeekualizer – O.O. Severin (John Severin) / Joe Catalano (reprint from #228)

Page 35 – Cracked Lens? (That's weird) – Randy Epley (reprint from #228)

Page 36 – Gross is Great – Stosh Gillespie (Dan Clowes) / Eel O'Brian (Mort Todd) (reprint from #228)

Page 38 – R.A.L.F. Real Alien Life Form – Walter Brogan / Joe Catalano (reprint from #228)

Page 41 – Cracked Guide to Guitars! – John Severin / Charles E. Hall (reprint from #228)

Page 45 – Monster One-Shots (Alien dental floss) – Mike Ricigliano / Roger Brown (reprint from #229)

Page 46 – Fright Court – Bob Fingerman / Joe Catalano (reprint from #229)

Page 50 – Uggly Family in "Meet the Trashformers" – Stosh Gillespie (Dan Clowes) / Eel O'Brian (Mort Todd) (reprint from #229)

Page 54 – Cracked Super Party! – John Severin / Jerry De Fuccio (reprint from #229)

Page 56 – Fadballs – Rick Parker / Pete Ciccone (reprint from #229)

Page 57 – Fangorier Magazine – Gray Morrow / George Gladir (reprint from #229)

Page 60 – Monsters Get Teed Off! – Rob Orzechowski /George Gladir (reprint from #229)

Page 62 – G.I. Joke Super-Macho Coloring Book – Shawn Kerri (reprint from #229)

Page 65 – The Minute After the Meineke Commercial! – Don Orehek / Jerry De Fuccio (reprint from #230)

Page 66 – Murder, She Wrot – Marie Severin / Stu Schwartzberg (reprint from #230)

Page 70 – What's On Their Minds? (Rambo) – Bill Wray / Peter Bagge (reprint from #230)

Page 71 – The Donkees – John Severin / Charles E. Hall, Mort Todd (reprint from #230)

Page 76 – Hollyweird Squares! – Rob Orzechowski / Moe McMahon (Marian McMahon), Mort Todd (reprint from #231)

Page 80 – Canine the Barkbarian (hasty exit) – Gary Fields (reprint from #231)

Page 82 – Robot Horror Story (what's that?) – Steve Ditko (reprint from #231)

Page 83 – Cracked Lens (cup of coffee) – Randy Epley (reprint from #231)

Page 86 – Cracked Interviews Bill Cozby! – Rob Orzechowski / Joe Catalano (reprint from #232)

Page 90 – Cracked Birds! – Alba Ballard / Kevin McMahon (reprint from #232)

Page 92 – New Jobs for Vanna! – John Severin / Joe Catalano (reprint from #232)

Page 94 – Cracked Interviews Michael J. Foxy – Rob Orzechowski / Joe Catalano (reprint from #232)

Page 98 – Shut-Ups (garbage disposal) – Don Orehek (reprint from #232)

Page 99 – Hudd & Dini (wrestling) – Vic Martin (reprint from #228)

Back Cover – Shut-Ups (get my hands on) – Don Orehek / Mort Todd (reprint from #228)

Cracked Collectors' Edition #76 (*3 Cracked Magazines in 1*), September 1988 (100 pages) ($2.75)

Cover – Michael Jackson Reads Cracked #207 – John Severin (reprint from *Cracked Collectors' Edition* #60)

Page 2 – The Sports Fan – Bill McCartney (Bill Ward) (reprint from #54)

Page 3 – Contents

Page 4 – Rock and Roll Your Eyeballs Out – John Severin (reprint from #163)

Page 11 – The Olympics go Commercial – Warren Sattler (reprint from #207) (originally called "The '84 Olympics go Commercial")

Page 14 – The Cult of Culture Snobbery – Bill McCartney (Bill Ward) (reprint from #46)

Page 17 – If Michael Jackson had Starred in – John Severin (reprint from #207)

Page 23 – The Cracked Guide to Swimming – Don Orehek (reprint from #207)

Page 27 – Shut-Ups (the score's tied) – Mike Ricigliano (reprint from #135)

Page 28 – Hypnotism – Richard Doxsee (reprint from #6)

Page 31 – Rock Calculator Readouts (reprint from *Cracked Collectors' Edition* #60)

Page 33 – The Making of Thriller (reprint from #207)

Page 39 – Cracked Hold-Ups! (horoscope) – Sururi Gumen (reprint from #203)

Page 41 – Sports Smiles – John Severin (reprint from #56)

Page 43 – The Cracked Game of Saboteurs and Investigators – Mike Ricigliano, John Severin, Don Orehek, Bill Ward, Catherine Severin, Warren Sattler, Sururi Gumen (reprint from *Super Cracked* #17) (red color added)

Page 59 – Sticks and Stitches – John Severin (reprint from #42)

Page 63 – Goldie Oldie Rock Yocks (reprint from #91)

Page 65 – Shut-Ups (haven't had this much fun) – Don Orehek (reprint from #210)

Page 66 – Real Cracked Books – Vic Martin (reprint from #18)

Page 68 – When Doctors Advertise! – Jack Davis, John Severin (reprint from #24)

Page 72 – You Know You're an MTV Freak When – Bill Powers (John Severin) (reprint from #210)

Page 74 – A Cracked Salute to the Olympics – Bill Ward (reprint from #135)

Page 79 – The Big Budget Epic vs. The Low Budget Quickie – John Severin (reprint from #135)

Page 83 – One Afternoon in a Local Stereo Store – Sururi Gumen (reprint from #138)

Page 84 – Absolutely, Unquestionably, Positively, Undeniably, the Very, Very, Last of The Cracked Lens (and we really, really mean it this time, for sure!) Part XXVI (reprint from #207)

Page 88 – Michael Jackson's Scrapbook – Don Orehek (reprint from *Cracked Collectors' Edition* #60)

Page 93 – Cracked Interviews the Olympic Training King – Bill Ward (reprint from #136)

Page 98 – Shut-Ups (stuck on this job) – Don Orehek (reprint from #207)

Page 99 – Sagebrush (Abundant Bull) – John Severin (reprint from #192)

Back Cover – Great Moments in Gardening 1708 – Howard Nostrand (reprint from #140)

***Cracked Collectors' Edition #77 (Rad)*, January 1989 (100 pages) ($2.75)**

Cover – Four-Eyed Sylvester – John Severin (reprint from #24)

Page 2 – The Machine Gun Nest – Ned Kelly (John Severin) / Don
   Edwing (reprint from #30)

Page 3 – Contents

Page 4 – The Searcher – Jack Davis (reprint from #14)

Page 5 – Smothered Brothers Show! – Rob Orzechowski / Peter Bagge
   (new)

Page 9 – Learn While You Snore! – Al Jaffee (reprint from #6)

Page 11 – The World's First Psychedelic Janitor – John Severin (reprint
   from #71)

Page 14 – Cracked Previews the New Groups – Vic Martin (reprint
   from #72)

Page 18 – Snow Flake and the Seven Dwarfs – John Severin (reprint
   from #70)

Page 23 – The Quick Quippers! (reprint from #69)

Page 24 – Shut-Ups (only girl) – Carlos Gerdel (Charles Rodrigues)
   (reprint from #86)

Page 25 – Fine Art Captions – Jack Davis (reprint from #17)

Page 28 – Build This Beautiful Yacht – Bill Everett (reprint from #2)

Page 30 – Around the World in Hats (reprint from #43)

Page 32 – The Man with the Sign – Caracu (reprint from #68)

Page 33 – Sub Suburbia – Bill McCartney (Bill Ward) (reprint from
   #46)

Page 36 – Take the 1968 Cracked Current Events Test – John Severin
   (reprint from #67) (originally called "Take the Cracked Current
   Events Test")

Page 38 – Company Names – Al Jaffee (reprint from #7)

Page 40 – Final Proof – John Severin / Don Edwing (reprint from #33)

Page 41 – Low Calorie Everything – Bill McCartney (Bill Ward)
   (reprint from #58)

Page 43 – Shut-Ups (five pounds of tea) – Charles Rodrigues (reprint
   from #66)

Page 44 – Everybody's Got Something to Be Thankful For – Angelo
   Torres (reprint from #7)

Page 46 – The Evolution of Beauty Contests – John Severin (reprint
   from #32)

Page 49 – Stories of the Month (My problem, Doctor) – Vic Martin
   (reprint from #19)

Page 50 – If Racketeers Took Over the Children's World – Jack Davis
   (reprint from #11)

Page 54 – Cannibal Chuckles – Charles Rodrigues (reprint from #39)

Page 55 – Surfing U.S.A. – Bill McCartney (Bill Ward) (reprint from #39)

Page 60 – The Garbage Can – Caracu (reprint from #66)

Page 61 – A Funny Thing Happened to Me on the Way to the Happening – O.O. Severin (John Severin) (reprint from #66)

Page 65 – Handshakes – John Severin (reprint from #11)

Page 67 – Saturday Night Dance – Joe Maneely (reprint from #4)

Page 70 – How I Rebuilt My Punk Lawn (reprint from #4)

Page 72 – Restaurants to Make You Feel at Home! (reprint from #8)

Page 74 – The Establishment Goes Hippy – O.O. Severin (John Severin) (reprint from #67)

Page 78 – Four for Fun (reprint from #41)

Page 79 – Why People Move to the Suburbs – Jack Davis (reprint from #14)

Page 83 – Male College Types to Be Wary Of – Bill McCartney (Bill Ward) (reprint from #6)

Page 85 – At the Barber Shop – Caracu (reprint from #67)

Page 86 – Architecture – Bill Elder (reprint from #12)

Page 88 – Charm Bracelets for Teens (reprint from #40)

Page 90 – Interior Decorating to Fit Your Job! – Bill McCartney (Bill Ward) (reprint from #23)

Page 92 – Black Thoughts – Caracu (reprint from #69)

Page 93 – Sylvester for President – John Severin (reprint from #36)

Page 98 – Shut-Ups (drive away your customers) – Don Orehek (reprint from #162)

Page 99 – Cracked Takes you Back to When it All Started! (The Telephone) – Angelo Torres (reprint from #10)

Back Cover – The Stone Age – Oskar Blotta (reprint from #125)

Cracked Collectors' Edition #78 (*Top 100 Laughs*), April 1989 (100 pages) ($2.75) (Each article condensed to a single page.)

Cover – Skiing – John Severin (reprint from #67)

Page 2 – The Beanstalk – Conky Nostrand (Howard Nostrand) (reprint from #167)

Page 3 – Contents – Ye Hang Ups (Skrunch) – Nireves (John Severin) (reprint from #114) (red color added)

Page 4 – Believe it or No! – Jack Davis (reprint from #11) (red color added)

Page 5 – Sagebrush (don't lag behind) – John Severin (reprint from *King-Sized Cracked* #5) (red color added)

Page 6 – Hurry-Ups (Sarge is pinned) – Bill McCartney (Bill Ward) (reprint from #36) (red color added)

Page 7 – Hudd & Dini (missing key) – Vic Martin (reprint from #77) (red color added)

Page 8 – The Little World of Don Swanson (chinning hanger) – Don Swanson (reprint from #20) (red color added)

Page 9 – Bunt's Catsup ad (reprint from #49) (red color added)

Page 10 – Brand X Cigarette Box Cut-Out (reprint from #12) (red color added)

Page 11 – Shakespearean Shut-Ups (Romeo) – John Severin (partial reprint from #17)

Page 12 – Cracked Looks at a Dog Show – Don Orehek (reprint from #105)

Page 13 – Cracked Sympathy Cards (reprint from #20)

Page 14 – Sagebrush (peace-pipe) – John Severin (reprint from #84)

Page 15 – Hudd & Dini (foot race) – Vic Martin (reprint from #104)

Page 16 – It Shouldn't Happen to a Dog – LePoer (John Severin) (reprint from #4)

Page 17 – Stories of the Month (I don't mean to be nosey) – Jerry Kirschen (reprint from #16)

Page 18 – A Swinging Good Time! (reprint from #71)

Page 19 – If Wedding Cakes Really Symbolized Marriages – Bill McCartney (Bill Ward) (reprint from #55)

Page 20 – The Suntan – Caracu (reprint from #70)

Page 21 – Shut-Ups (forbidden volcano) – Don Orehek (reprint from #209)

Page 22 – Sagebrush (wide open spaces) – John Severin (reprint from *Cracked Collectors' Edition* #9)

Page 23 – Guess Who…? – Bill McCartney (Bill Ward) (reprint from #76)

Page 24 – Go Fly a Kite – John Severin (reprint from #74)

Page 25 – Shut-Ups! (stick-in-the-mud) – Vito Montigliani (Charles Rodrigues) (reprint from #73)

Page 26 – Absolutely, Unquestionably, Positively, Undeniably, the Very, Very, Last of The Cracked Lens (and we really, really mean it this time, for sure!) Part XIX (reprint from #194)

Page 27 – Cracked's Snappy Comebacks! – John Severin (reprint from #75)

Page 28 – Cracked Looks at Television – Bill McCartney (Bill Ward) (reprint from #85) (originally called "Cracked Looks at Television Viewers")

Page 29 – Shut-Ups (I remember) – Charles Rodrigues (reprint from #108)

Page 30 – Sagebrush (KLOMK!) – John Severin (reprint from #104)

Page 31 – Orehek on Wry – Don Orehek (reprint from #108)

Page 32 – A Day at the Zoo – Charles Rodrigues (reprint from #108)

Page 33 – The Parakeet – John Severin (reprint from #77)
Page 34 – The Marx Brothers Ride Again! (reprint from #75)
Page 35 – Rodrigues' Side Show – Charles Rodrigues (reprint from #106)
Page 36 – Just What the Doctor Ordered (reprint from #78)
Page 37 – Shut-Ups (prison reforms) – Noah Sark (Charles Rodrigues) (reprint from #106)
Page 38 – Sagebrush (Hi! Hey!) – John Severin (reprint from #108) / Your (Ugh) Ancestors? (waterwheel) – Lo Linkert (reprint from #110)
Page 30 – Hudd & Dini (mousetrap) – Vic Martin (reprint from #83)
Page 40 – The Dungeon – Don Orehek (reprint from *Monster Howls* #1)
Page 41 – Stories of the Month (The Panhandler) – Jerry Kirschen (reprint from #18)
Page 42 – Cracked's Fractured Nursery Rhymes (reprint from #86)
Page 43 – Don't Believe a Word of it – John Severin (reprint from #82)
Page 44 – Shut-Ups (duck call) – Vic Martin (reprint from #52)
Page 45 – The Generation Gap! (reprint from #78)
Page 46 – Nasty Neighbors – Caracu (reprint from #82)
Page 47 – Blind Date Phone Calls – Bob Taylor (reprint from #84)
Page 48 – Shut-Ups (plastic surgery) – Charles Rodrigues (reprint from #109)
Page 49 – Look! Four Kooks! (reprint from #63)
Page 50 – Cracked Takes a Look at Skiing – Bill McCartney (Bill Ward) (reprint from #48)
Page 52 – Boys and Girls Together (reprint from #44)
Page 53 – Sagebrush (Howdy Shage) – John Severin (reprint from #113)
Page 54 – The Last of the 'Desert Island' Cartoons! – Irit Kajiij Jr. (Charles Rodrigues) (reprint from #109)
Page 55 – Adolt Education! (reprint from #83)
Page 56 – The World of Mr. Orehek – Don Orehek (reprint from #109)
Page 57 – The Explorer, the Dog & the Bone – Oskar Blotta (reprint from #84)
Page 58 – Hip Shut-Ups (I'm floatin') – John Severin (reprint from #11)
Page 59 – Cracked Looks at a Fender Bender – Don Orehek (reprint from #109)
Page 60 – Medicinal Mirth (reprint from #85)
Page 61 – Cracked Blasts Nasa – Don Orehek (reprint from #209)
Page 62 – Pow Pix Strike Again! (reprint from *Pow!* #2)
Page 63 – The Information Clerk – Caracu (reprint from #114)
Page 64 – Cracked Evolution Revolution – Mike Ricigliano (reprint from #194)

Page 65 – Cracked Looks at Stock Car Racing – Don Orehek (reprint from #114)

Page 66 – Shut-Ups (innocent) – S. Gross (Charles Rodrigues) (reprint from #104)

Page 67 – The Wide World of Laughs (reprint from #54)

Page 68 – Ye Hang Ups #9 (Hurry it up) – M.L. Severin (Margaret Severin) (reprint from #189)

Page 69 – Hudd & Dini (saint Bernard) – Vic Martin (reprint from #108)

Page 70 – Lights Camera Action! – John Severin (reprint from #60)

Page 71 – Your (Ugh) Ancestors? (snow tire sale) – Lo Linkert (reprint from #109) / Hudd & Dini (guard disguise) – Vic Martin (reprint from #109)

Page 72 – The Translator & the Duel – Mike Ricigliano (reprint from #189)

Page 73 – Cracked Looks at Archeology – Warren Sattler (reprint from #209)

Page 74 – Shut-Ups (magnifique) – S. Gross Jr. (Charles Rodrigues) (reprint from #105)

Page 75 – Ship Shape (reprint from #82)

Page 76 – Sagebrush (He sure hates rattlers) – John Severin (reprint from #80)

Page 77 – Board Her, Men! – Bill McCartney (Bill Ward) (reprint from #35)

Page 78 – The Smythes – Losers Throughout History! – John Severin (reprint from #75)

Page 79 – Absolutely, Unquestionably, Positively, Undeniably, the Very, Very, Last of The Cracked Lens (and we really, really mean it this time, for sure!) Part XXVIII (reprint from #209)

Page 80 – Fruity Tunes – Vic Martin (reprint from #88)

Page 81 – Shut-Ups (Ladies first) – Rodrigliani (Charles Rodrigues) (reprint from #77)

Page 82 – Saturday Night in India – Oskar Blotta (reprint from #86)

Page 83 – Shut-Ups (piece of my mind) – Don Orehek (reprint from #189)

Page 84 – Sagebrush (thinnin' hair) – John Severin (reprint from #115) / Ye Hang Ups #3 (He hates to drink alone) – John Severin (reprint from #115)

Page 85 – Goofed-Up Genes – Vic Martin (reprint from #86)

Page 86 – The Man and the Bird – Oskar Blotta (reprint from #87)

Page 87 – Sagebrush (water) – John Severin (reprint from #82)

Page 88 – Hudd & Dini (kite) – Vic Martin (reprint from #86)

Page 89 – Cracked's Romantic Greeting Cards That Express Everything – John Langton (reprint from #109)

Page 90 – Ye Hang Ups (rioting again) – John Severin (reprint from #217)

Page 91 – Cracked Looks at Hunting and Fishing – LePoer (John Severin) (reprint from #86) (red color added)

Page 92 – Shut-Ups (shoplifting) – Charles Rodrigues (reprint from #114) (red color added)

Page 94 – The Electric Shave – Oskar Blotta (reprint from #86) (red color added)

Page 95 – The Piggy Bank – Caracu (reprint from #87) (red color added)

Page 96 – Reel Gone! (reprint from #54) (red color added)

Page 97 – Ye Hang Ups (Autumn again) – O.O. Severin (John Severin) (reprint from #209) (red color added)

Page 98 – In Case of Emergency – Warren Sattler (reprint from #160) (red color added)

Page 99 – The Curious and the Modern Sculpture – Oskar Blotta (reprint from #127)

Back Cover – Great Moments in Sports 1972 – Howard Nostrand (reprint from #150)

Cracked Collectors' Edition #79 (Cracked Artists' Portfolio), **July 1989 (100 pages) ($2.75)**

Cover and Back Cover – Self Portraits – John Severin, Bill Ward, Don Orehek, Vic Martin (new)

Page 2 and 99 – Collage – John Severin, Bill Ward, Don Orehek, Vic Martin (new, featuring reprinted art images)

Page 3 – Contents for Severin

Page 4 – The Artist Selects his Model – John Severin (reprint from #41)

Page 5 – How Family Life Would be if the Sexes Changed Places – John Severin (reprint from #15)

Page 8 – Get Out the Vote! – John Severin (reprint from #51)

Page 9 – Romeo and Juliet – John Severin (reprint from #8)

Page 12 – Illustrated Little Willies – LePoer (John Severin) (reprint from #12)

Page 14 – At the Art Gallery – J. Lewis (John Severin) / Jay Lynch (reprint from #27)

Page 16 – Brigitte Bardot as Seen by Different Artists – John Severin (reprint from #12)

Page 19 – Curvy Sewer Cognac ad – John Severin (reprint from #28)

Page 20 – Am I Really in Love? – John Severin (reprint from #11)

Page 22 – A Cracked Gallery of New Artists – Oswaldo Laino, John Severin (reprint from #21)
Page 26 – Ye Hang Ups (giant Norwegian troll) (new)
Page 27 – Contents for Orehek
Page 28 – Science Fiction – Don Orehek (partial reprint from #1)
Page 29 – Orehek on Wry – Don Orehek (reprint from #108)
Page 32 – Cracked's Catchy First Lines For – Don Orehek (reprint from #111)
Page 34 – Guest Appearances by the World's Top Humor Artists – Don Orehek (reprint from #106)
Page 36 – The Growing Complexity of Pro Football – Don Orehek (reprint from #67)
Page 40 – Hurry-Ups (daddy fell out) – Don Orehek (reprint from #34)
Page 41 – Tales for Tots – Don Orehek (reprint from #66)
Page 44 – Notes – Don Orehek (reprint from #35)
Page 46 – Cracked Goes to Las Vegas – Don Orehek (reprint from #108)
Page 48 – Story of the Month (finish your oatmeal) – Don Orehek (reprint from #13)
Page 49 – Hurry-Ups (five dollar raise) – Don Orehek (reprint from #35)
Page 50 – Shut-Ups (mean he's out) – Don Orehek (new)
Page 51 – Contents for Ward
Page 52 – The Joker's Wild – Bill McCartney (Bill Ward) (reprint from #5)
Page 53 – The Big Wig Gig – Bill McCartney (Bill Ward) (reprint from #35)
Page 56 – The Public Links Golfer – Bill McCartney (Bill Ward) (reprint from #41)
Page 61 – Hurry-Ups (fly in soup) – Bill McCartney (Bill Ward) (reprint from #41)
Page 62 – A Cracked Guide to Footwear – Bill McCartney (Bill Ward) (reprint from #42)
Page 64 – Shut-Ups (Europe) – Bill McCartney (Bill Ward) (reprint from #2)
Page 65 – Music Hath Charm – Bill McCartney (Bill Ward) (reprint from #42)
Page 66 – Bridgette Barf-arf-arf-doe – Bill McCartney (Bill Ward) (reprint from #6)
Page 69 – Cracked Interviews the Skateboard King – Bill Ward (reprint from #152)
Page 74 – The Ward World of Sports (nothin' in the rule book) – Bill Ward (new)
Page 75 – Contents for Martin

Page 76 – HIP Alphabet Book – Vic Martin (reprint from #13)

Page 79 – Famous Scenes from Great "Dog Hero" Movies – Vic Martin (reprint from #47)

Page 81 – Hudd & Dini (painted wall) – Vic Martin (reprint from #76)

Page 82 – Churly – Vic Martin (reprint from #81)

Page 88 – Modern Tattoo Designs – Vic Martin (reprint from #65)

Page 91 – Famous Scenes from Great Lawyer-Type Movies! – Vic Martin (reprint from #53)

Page 93 – Ploys Against Noise – Vic Martin (reprint from #65)

Page 97 – Hudd & Dini (Vacancy) – Vic Martin (reprint from #79)

Page 98 – You Wanna Bet? – Vic Martin (new)

Cracked Collectors' Edition #80 (*Year's Best*), September 1989 (100 pages) ($3.25)

Cover – Comedy? Tragedy! – John Severin (new)

Page 2 – The Uggly Family (Why are we having dinner) – Stosh Gillespie (Dan Clowes) / Eel O'Brian (Mort Todd) (reprint from #234)

Page 3 – Contents

Page 4 – Progress of a Cracked Technophile! – John Severin / Peter Bagge (reprint from #233)

Page 6 – Winfrah Oprey! – Bill Wray / Peter Bagge (reprint from #233)

Page 10 – Bon Jovi vs. Bruce! – Frank Caruso (reprint from #233)

Page 12 – Form & Function (skateboards) – Bo Badman (Rurik Tyler) (reprint from #234)

Page 14 – Cracked Star Cars! – John Severin / Cliff Mott (reprint from #234)

Page 17 – Cyborgs Unlimited – John Severin / George Gladir (reprint from #234)

Page 20 – Hurry-Ups! (sit tight) – Rick Altergott (reprint from #235)

Page 21 – Cracked Interviews R.A.L.F. – Rob Orzechowski / Joe Catalano (reprint from #235)

Page 24 – Star Drek The Next Cancellation – Bo Badman (Rurik Tyler) (reprint from #235)

Page 28 – Cracked Mirrors – Vic Martin (reprint from #235)

Page 31 – My Two Duds! – Walter Brogan / Joe Catalano (reprint from #236)

Page 34 – Forgotten Funnies! – Gary Fields (reprint from #236)

Page 36 – Teen-Age Movie Monsters – Rob Orzechowski / George Gladir (reprint from #236)

Page 39 – Hudd & Dini (football) – Vic Martin (reprint from #236)

Page 40 – The Sabotage Handbook – Mike Ricigliano (reprint from #237)

Page 43 – The Uggly Family Go to the Olympics! – Stosh Gillespie (Dan Clowes) / Eel O'Brian (Mort Todd) (reprint from #237)
Page 46 – Cracked Interviews Rambozo! – Rob Orzechowski / Joe Catalano (reprint from #238)
Page 49 – G.I. Joke Gets Totally Thrashed! – Shawn Kerri (reprint from #238)
Page 54 – Cracked 30th Anniversary Party! – John Severin / Joe Catalano (reprint from #238)
Page 56 – What Rock Stars Were Like as Children – Rob Orzechowski / Joe Catalano (reprint from #238)
Page 58 – The Cracked List of What's Hot and What's Not – Gary Fields (reprint from #238)
Page 60 – Vernon Swallowing's Friend – Jeremy Banx (reprint from #238)
Page 61 – Spittlejuice – John Severin / Mort Todd (reprint from #239)
Page 65 – Martyred with Children – Rob Orzechowski / Murad Gumen (reprint from #239)
Page 68 – Blunder Years – Walter Brogan / Joe Catalano (reprint from #239)
Page 71 – Cracked Interviews Mike Dyson the Boxing King! – Rob Orzechowski (reprint from #239)
Page 74 – Shut-Ups (well-preserved mummy) – Don Orehek (reprint from #239)
Page 75 – If – John Severin / John Arcudi (reprint from #240)
Page 76 – Freddy's Celebrity Nightmares! – John Severin / Tony Frank (Lou Silverstone) (reprint from #240)
Page 78 – Garbage Dump Pop Stars (Linda Roundsnout) (reprint from #240)
Page 81 – Wow! (sensational) – Pat Boyette (reprint from #240)
Page 82 – If Morton Downey, Jr. was President! – Frank Caruso / Tony Frank (Lou Silverstone) (reprint from #241)
Page 85 – Ye Hang Ups (The Wall!!) – John Severin (reprint from #241)
Page 86 – Quentin Plasma's Life-Form – Jeremy Banx (reprint from #240)
Page 87 – Pig – Rob Orzechowski / Tony Frank (Lou Silverstone) (reprint from #241)
Page 92 – Who Framed Roger Wabbit / Wawwy Bwogan (Walter Brogan) / Rich Kriegel (Lou Silverstone) (reprint from #241)
Page 98 – Rock and Roll Shut-Ups (3000 people) – Don Orehek / Charles E. Hall (reprint from #241)
Page 99 – Two Heads Are Better Than – John Severin (reprint from #236)
Back Cover – Sylvester as Freddy! – Bob Fingerman (reprint from *Cracked Monster Party* #1)

Cracked Collectors' Edition #81 (*Sick Salute to the 1980s*), January 1990 (100 pages) ($2.75)

 Cover – Various 1980s Covers (reprints from #169, 183, 192, 198, 206, 229)
 Page 2 – Atlas Takes Recess – Rurik Tyler (new)
 Page 3 – Contents
 Page 4 – The Dorks of Hazzardous With Chipps to go – John Severin (reprint from #172)
 Page 11 – If Arnold Were Treated and Behaved Like a Real-Life Kid – John Severin (reprint from #171)
 Page 16 – Real Incredible People – John Severin (reprint from #174)
 Page 22 – My Buddyguard – John Severin (reprint from #177)
 Page 29 – The JR Family Photo Album – John Severin (reprint from #181)
 Page 32 – The Incredible Shrunken Woman – John Severin (reprint from #180)
 Page 39 – Magnumb Public Idiot – John Severin (reprint from #191)
 Page 46 – Heart to Heart – John Severin (reprint from #192)
 Page 52 – The A-a-aayy Team Takes a Ride on the Lovely Boat – John Severin (reprint from #197)
 Page 59 – Tootsie Roll – John Severin (reprint from #196)
 Page 66 – If Michael Jackson had Starred in – John Severin (reprint from #207)
 Page 72 – You Know You're an MTV Freak When – Bill Powers (John Severin) (reprint from #210)
 Page 74 – If TV Shows Were Combined – John Severin (reprint from #205)
 Page 79 – The Silly Cosbey Show – John Severin (reprint from #212)
 Page 82 – Simple & Simple – John Severin (reprint from #212)
 Page 89 – Rockey: 2001 – John Severin / Eel O'Brian (Mort Todd) (reprint from #219)
 Page 93 – Box Office Future – John Severin / Joe Catalano, Mort Todd (reprint from #218)
 Page 99 – The Tonsillectomy – Mike Ricigliano / Roger Brown (new)
 Back Cover – Sylvester P. Reagan, Mikhail Gorbasmythe, Aerosmythe, Mike P. Smyson – Bill Wray (reprints from #222, 227, 239, 243)

Cracked Collectors' Edition #82 (*The Comedy of Jack Davis*), April 1990 (100 pages) ($2.75) (Every Jack Davis article from *Cracked* reprinted.)

 Cover – Trick Mirror – Jack Davis (reprint from #16)
 Page 2 – Sylvester Jig-Saw Puzzle – Jack Davis (reprint from #12)
 Page 3 – Contents
 Page 4-5, 27-29 – Wallpapering the World...From Guam to Gum: The Cracked Visions of Jack Davis – Bhob Stewart

Page 6 – All Weather Drive-In Movie – Jack Davis (reprint from #5)

Page 8 – When it all Started (take the nice gun) – Jack Davis (reprint from #11)

Page 9 – Story of the Month (I'm afraid) – Jack Davis (reprint from #11)

Page 10 – If Racketeers Took Over the Children's World – Jack Davis (reprint from #11)

Page 14 – Endings for Old TV Shows – Jack Davis (reprint from #11)

Page 17 – Believe it or No! – Jack Davis (reprint from #11)

Page 18 – Restaurants – Jack Davis (reprint from #11)

Page 20 – Man's Best Friend? – Jack Davis (reprint from #11)

Page 21 – Way Out West! – Jack Davis (reprint from #11)

Page 23 – Judo – Jack Davis (reprint from #11)

Page 26 – Subscription ad – Jack Davis (reprint from #11)

Page 30 – Realistic Children's Games – Jack Davis (reprint from #12)

Page 32 – Story of the Month (You look terrible!) – Jack Davis (reprint from #12)

Page 33 – Civil War Facts – Jack Davis (reprint from #12)

Page 36 – A Beatnik Goes to a Party – Jack Davis (reprint from #12)

Page 38 – Subscription ad – Jack Davis (reprint from #12)

Page 39 – Peter Goon – Jack Davis (reprint from #12)

Page 42 – Marriages Are Made in Heaven – Jack Davis (reprint from #12)

Page 44 – Editor's Note: Jack Davis at Cracked – Michael Delle-Femine (Mort Todd)

Page 46 – When it all Started (Ponce DeLeon) – Jack Davis (reprint from #15)

Page 47 – Bat Masteyson – Jack Davis (reprint from #13)

Page 51 – Freezing People – Jack Davis (reprint from #13)

Page 56 – Cartoons of the Year – Jack Davis (reprint from #13)

Page 58 – Subscription ad – Jack Davis (reprint from #13)

Page 59 – The Searcher – Jack Davis (reprint from #14)

Page 60 – Why People Move to the Suburbs – Jack Davis (reprint from #14)

Page 64 – Band-Aides for Weird Color Skin – Jack Davis (reprint from #14)

Page 65 – Sea Haunt – Jack Davis (reprint from #14)

Page 69 – Believe it or Nuts!! – Jack Davis (reprint from #13)

Page 70 – Sports Oddities (Hank Luckeezi) – Jack Davis (reprint from #15)

Page 71 – Cracked Takes You Back to When it all Started (blood pressure) – Jack Davis (reprint from #15)

Page 72 – Great War Heroes – Jack Davis (reprint from #15)

Page 74 – They Shoulda Listened – Jack Davis (reprint from #15)

Page 77 – Sports Oddities (Fullback Arnold) – Jack Davis (reprint from #15)

Page 78 – Illustrated Limericks – Jack Davis (reprint from #15)

Page 79 – Subscription ad – Jack Davis (reprint from #15)

Page 82 – Cracked Playing Cards – Jack Davis (reprint from #16)

Page 83 – Magazine Covers – Jack Davis (reprint from #16)

Page 87 – Rare Olde Shut-Upf – Jack Davis (reprint from #16)

Page 88 – *The Cracked Reader* ad – Jack Davis (reprint from #16)

Page 89 – Fine Art Captions – Jack Davis (reprint from #17)

Page 92 – Things We Shoulda Done – Jack Davis (reprint from #17)

Page 95 – When Doctors Advertise! – Jack Davis, John Severin (reprint from #24)

Page 99 – The Descent of Man – Jack Davis (reprint from #14)

Back Cover – Showcasing the Humor of Jack Davis – Jack Davis (new to *Cracked*)

Cracked Collectors' Edition #83 (*What's Hot and Not*), July 1990 (100 pages) ($3.50)

Cover – Hot and Not – Gary Fields, John Severin (new with reprint from *Cracked Collectors' Edition* #80)

Page 2 – Contents

Page 4 – Elvis What's Hot and What's Not – Gary Fields (reprint from #244)

Page 5 – Family Ties – Vance Rodewalt (reprint from #202)

Page 12 – You Know You're a Super Type – Warren Sattler (reprint from #211)

Page 14 – Noid's Raisin Hell! – Frank Caruso / Eel O'Brian (Mort Todd) (reprint from #242)

Page 15 – Past, Present and Future Changes in Sports – Don Orehek (reprint from #199)

Page 19 – Jeraldo Revoltin's Guide to Be an Expert at Trash TV – Rob Orzechowski / Joe Catalano (reprint from #245)

Page 22 – Hee-Man, Mister of the Universe – Walter Brogan (reprint from #213)

Page 24 – Aren't You Nervous When – Dan Clowes / Michael Weitz (reprint from #216)

Page 26 – Shut-Ups (here's my plan) – Bill Burke (reprint from #213)

Page 27 – Beverly Hills Slop – Kent Gamble (reprint from #215)

Page 32 – Double Scare! – Frank Caruso / Joe Catalano (reprint from #242)

Page 36 – Alaffin's Magic Lamp – Fran Matera (reprint from #204)

Page 37 – The Final Episode of Comic Strips – Tony Tallarico (reprint from #216)

Page 40 – Movie Monsters Based on Video Games – Walter Brogan (reprint from #214)

Page 43 – Batman What's Hot and What's Not – Gary Fields (reprint from #248)
Page 44 – Cracked Hot Stove League Baseball Cards! – John Severin / George Gladir (reprint from #243)
Page 47 – Harried…with Children – Rob Orzechowski / Rich Kriegel (Lou Silverstone) (reprint from #248)
Page 51 – Hudd & Dini (Batman) – Vic Martin (reprint from #248)
Page 53 – Miami Nice – John Reiner (reprint from #216)
Page 58 – Comic Strip Oddities! – John Severin / George Gladir (reprint from #245)
Page 60 – Shut-Ups (watered down drinks) – Don Orehek (reprint from #243)
Page 61 – Cracked Interviews Edward Kroch The Big Apple Mayor! – Bill Ward / Tony Frank (Lou Silverstone) (reprint from #242)
Page 66 – Elvis Paper Doll Pages – Rob Orzechowski / George Gladir (reprint from #244)
Page 68 – More Positive Thinking – Warren Sattler (partial reprint from #217) (originally called "Positive Thinking is")
Page 69 – Cracked Max III Beyond Blunderdome! – Bob Fingerman (reprint from #217)
Page 73 – Wrestlin' T 'n' T – Bill Burke (reprint from #215)
Page 78 – More Cracked List of What's Hot and What's Not – Gary Fields (reprint from #242)
Page 80 – The Cozby Kids Meet the A-Teem – John Reiner (reprint from #217)
Page 84 – Sylvester's Corner The Painting – Kevin Sacco (reprint from #218)
Page 85 – Rambozo: Worst Blood II – Kent Gamble (reprint from #217) (originally called "Rambo First Blood Part II")
Page 90 – The Greenhouse Effect – John Severin / George Gladir (reprint from #244)
Page 93 – One Evening in a Fancy Restaurant – Bob Taylor (reprint from #135)
Page 94 – Misleading Movie and TV Titles – Don Orehek (reprint from #199)
Page 96 – The Aliens are Here!! – Tom Short (reprint from #216)
Page 98 – Shut-Ups (wonderful to sleep) – Don Orehek (reprint from #242)
Page 99 – Cracked Coming Distractions / Black T-Shirt / Severin Cracked T-Shirt / Sylvester Doll / Cracked Hat / Subscription ad
Back Cover – Sylvester Mask – Aron Laikin (reprint from #217)

Cracked Collectors' Edition #84 (*Year's Best*), September 1990 (100 pages) ($3.50)

Cover – We Pick Our Year's Best – Don Martin (new, but based on cover drawing from *Don Martin Digs Deeper* paperback done while at *Mad*, also used on *Honk* #1.)

Page 2 and 99 – Formal Sylvester P. Smythe Portrait – John Severin (reprint from #251)

Page 3 – Contents

Page 4 – Bat$man – John Severin / Mort Todd (reprint from #249)

Page 12 – Elvis Bubble Gum Cards – Pat Redding / Joe Catalano (reprint from #244)

Page 14 – The F.B.I. Ten Most Wanted Saboteurs – Mike Ricigliano (reprint from #248)

Page 15 – Grossanne – Walter Brogan / Rich Kriegel (Lou Silverstone) (reprint from #244)

Page 19 – Cracked Arena Rock Show! – John Severin / Charles E. Hall (reprint from #249)

Page 23 – Shut-Ups (found a roach) – Don Orehek (reprint from #250)

Page 24 – 21 Dump Street – Rob Orzechowski / Joe Catalano (reprint from #242)

Page 28 – Beam Us Up, Scotty! – Mike Ricigliano / Roger Brown (reprint from #247)

Page 29 – Cracked Sunday Comics – Gary Fields / John Arcudi (reprint from #245)

Page 33 – Cracked Guide to Customized Skateboards – John Severin / George Gladir (reprint from #251)

Page 36 – A Crummy Affair – Frank Caruso / Joe Catalano (reprint from #247)

Page 39 – The Dead Fool – Peter McDonnell / Tony Frank (Lou Silverstone) (reprint from #242)

Page 43 – The Zillionaire Starring the Uggly Family – Stosh Gillespie (Dan Clowes) (reprint from #243)

Page 47 – Wiseass – Walter Brogan / Vic Bianco (Lou Silverstone) (reprint from #248)

Insert – Varoom! – Vic Martin (reprint from #248)

Insert – We Pick Our Year's Best Poster – Don Martin

Insert – How Would You Like to be Interviewed by Nanny Dickering? – Skene Catling (reprint from "Cracked Party Pack" #4)

Page 51 – Guillotine Gags! – Don Orehek / George Gladir (reprint from #247)

Page 55 – The Ward World of Sports (forgot your contacts) – Bill Ward (reprint from #247)

Page 56 – Cracked Survival Primer – LePoer (John Severin) / Vic Bianco (Lou Silverstone) (reprint from #246)

Page 60 – Cracked Ghostbuggers Gear – Rurik Tyler (reprint from #249)

Page 62 – Hudd & Dini and Ye Hang Ups – Vic Martin, John Severin (reprint from #250)

Page 63 – Ailing Nation – Walter Brogan / Vic Bianco (Lou Silverstone) (reprint from #244)

Page 67 – The Coming Environmental Crisis! – John Severin / George Gladir (reprint from #247)

Page 71 – Slumming in America – Walter Brogan / Tony Frank (Lou Silverstone) (reprint from #242)

Page 76 – Cracked Toon Videos – Gary Fields (reprint from #249)

Page 87 – Goon with the Wind: 1990 – Walter Brogan / Rich Kriegel (Lou Silverstone) (reprint from #246)

Page 83 – Travel Ads Before and After – John Severin / Charles E. Hall (reprint from #246)

Page 86 – Star Drek the Next Generation – Mike Ricigliano / Roger Brown (reprint from #247)

Page 87 – Honey, I Stunk the Kids! – Walter Brogan / Charles E. Hall (reprint from #251)

Page 92 – A Cracked Look at Batman – Mike Ricigliano / Roger Brown (reprint from #248)

Page 94 – Pla'Toons – Walt Disbroganey (Walter Brogan) / Matthew Sweney (reprint from #245)

Page 97 – Spy and Saboteur in The Peace Treaty – Mike Ricigliano (reprint from #251)

Page 98 – Shut-Ups (we saw Elvis) – Don Orehek (reprint from #244)

Back Cover – Subscription ad / Cracked Hat / Severin Cracked T-Shirt / Black Cracked T-Shirt / Sylvester Doll ad (reprint from #66)

Cracked Collectors' Edition #85 (*Sports 'R' Us*), January 1991 (100 pages) ($3.50)

Cover – Sports 'R' Us – John Severin (new)

Page 2 and 99 – Sports 'R' Us Poster – John Severin (new)

Page 3 – Contents – John Severin

Page 4 – Rockey – John Severin (reprint from #143)

Page 10 – The Cracked Guide to Soccer – Warren Sattler (reprint from #145)

Page 14 – Take Me Out to the Old Cracked Ball Game – Charles Rodrigues (reprint from #53)

Page 16 – Cracked Interviews the Sports King – John Severin (reprint from #130)

Page 21 – The Hottest Questions in Basketball – Bill McCartney (Bill Ward) (reprint from #59)

Page 24 – A Cracked Look at a Skateboard Park – Sururi Gumen (reprint from #145)

Page 26 – Cracked's New Type Baseball Cards that Tell it Like it is – Howard Nostrand (reprint from #138)

Page 29 – Shut-Ups (good clean fight) – Mike Ricigliano (reprint from #134)

Page 30 – Footboxhockbasetennbasketgolfpoly – John Severin (reprint from #97)

Page 34 – Jock State University Bulletin – Warren Sattler (reprint from #183)

Page 37 – Exercise Manual and Hot Dog Stunts for Super Heroes – Powers (John Severin) (reprint from #147)

Page 41 – The Growing Complexity of Pro Football – Don Orehek (reprint from #67)

Page 45 – Big Business of Little League – Tony Tallarico (reprint from #62)

Page 49 – How to Make Baseball More Interesting – Bill Ward (reprint from #137)

Page 53 – The Cracked Guide to Football – Howard Nostrand (reprint from #140)

Page 58 – You Know You're a Skateboard Freak When – Warren Sattler (reprint from #154)

Page 60 – Sylvester Meets the Mets – John Severin (reprint from #64)

Page 64 – A Cracked Look at a Wrestling Match – Bill Ward (reprint from #137)

Page 66 – Cracked Guide to Sky Diving – Sururi Gumen (reprint from #130)

Page 70 – Past, Present and Future Changes in Sports – John Severin (reprint from #24)

Page 73 – The Cracked Guide to Bowling – Bill Dubay (reprint from #141)

Page 78 – Females Participating in All Sports – John Severin (reprint from #81)

Page 83 – Cracked Guide to Surfing – John Severin (reprint from #136)

Page 88 – The Wider World of Sports – John Severin (reprint from #139)

Page 94 – The Bad News Bores – John Severin (reprint from #136)

Back Cover – Robojock (new)

Cracked Collectors' Edition #86 (*Spies, Saboteurs, Secret Agents and Other Subversives*), April 1991 (100 pages) ($3.50)

Cover – Spies, Saboteurs and Sylvester – John Severin, Mike Ricigliano (gatefold cover) (new)

Page 2, 3 and 99 – Spies, Saboteurs and Sylvester – John Severin, Mike Ricigliano (inside gatefold cover) (new)
Page 3 – Contents – Mike Ricigliano
Page 4 – The Spy Who Snubbed Me – O.O. Severin (John Severin) (reprint from #148)
Page 10 – The Sabotage Handbook – Mike Ricigliano (reprint from #237)
Page 13 – The A-a-ayy Team (Excuse me, waitress) – O.O. Severin (John Severin) (reprint from #203)
Page 20 – Russian One-Shots (Miss Moscow) – Mike Ricigliano (reprint from #227)
Page 22 – Mission: Implausible – O.O. Severin (John Severin) (reprint from #80)
Page 28 – Lifesize Saboteurs – Mike Ricigliano (reprint from #240)
Page 30 – Red Meat – Rick Altergott / Vic Bianco (Lou Silverstone) (reprint from #241)
Page 35 – The Sabotron! – Mike Ricigliano (reprint from #250)
Page 36 – .007 Devices that Bombed! – Rob Orzechowski / Eel O'Brian (Mort Todd) (reprint from #233)
Page 39 – Spy and Saboteur Paper Airplanes Pilots – Mike Ricigliano (reprint from #242)
Page 40 – A Red-White-and-Blueprint for Unspying an Amerikan Hotel Room! (reprint from #227)
Page 42 – Spies and Saboteurs Activity Pages! – Mike Ricigliano (reprint from #232)
Page 44 – Eeeeekualizer – O.O. Severin (John Severin) / Joe Catalano (reprint from #228)
Page 48 – Spy and Saboteur in The Peace Treaty – Mike Ricigliano (reprint from #251)
Page 50 – Ill-Legal Weapons – Walter Brogan / Vic Bianco (Lou Silverstone) (reprint from #251)
Page 54 – A Cracked Look at 007! – O.O. Severin (John Severin) / Mort Todd (reprint from #216)
Page 58 – Better Off Red! – Bo Badmananoff (Rurik Tyler) (reprint from #227)
Page 61 – The Soviet Shut-Ups (beautiful clear night) – Don Orehek (reprint from #227)
Page 62 – On the Beach the Day After with Dr. Strangelove or How I Learned to Live with and Love Roaches – Wally Kubrogan (Walter Brogan) / Rich Kriegel (Lou Silverstone) (reprint from #246)
Page 66 – Marathon Jam – John Severin (reprint from #141)
Page 72 – Moonwrecker – Sururi Gumen (reprint from #166)

Page 79 – Hudd & Dini (You are now leaving Russia) – Vic Martinov (Vic Martin) (reprint from #227)

Page 80 – The Transinformers vs the Defecticons! – Steve Ditko (reprint from #227)

Page 82 – Laff and Let Die – O.O. Severin (John Severin) (reprint from #116)

Page 88 – Cracked Survival Primer – LePoer (John Severin) / Vic Bianco (Lou Silverstone) (reprint from #246)

Page 92 – Russian Commie Strips! – Gary Fieldsky (Gary Fields) / Pyoter Cicconewicz (reprint from #227)

Page 94 – More Spies and Saboteurs Than You'll Ever Need! – Mike Ricigliano (new)

Page 98 – I Survived the Cracked Saboteurs (So Far) – Mike Ricigliano (new)

Back Cover – Great Moments in Espionage 1990 – Mike Ricigliano (new)

Cracked Collectors' Edition #87 (*Ecology Edition*), July 1991 (100 pages) ($3.50)

Cover – Cracked Trash – Rurik Tyler (new)

Page 2 – The Forest's Prime Evil! – John Severin (reprint from #84)

Page 3 – Contents – Mike Ricigliano

Page 4 – Traitors of the Lost Ark – John Severin (reprint from #183)

Page 12 – Indianapolis Bones and the Temple of Gloom – John Severin (reprint from #208)

Page 19 – Indiana Bones and the Loot Crusade – Walter Brogan / Tony Frank (Lou Silverstone) (reprint from #249)

Page 24 – Couch Potato Catalog – Vic Martin / George Gladir (reprint from #237)

Page 27 – Dull House – Walter Brogan / Vic Bianco (Lou Silverstone) (reprint from #240)

Page 31 – E.T.'s Report My Experiences on Earth – Don Orehek (reprint from #192)

Page 35 – Murder, She Wrot – Marie Severin / Stu Schwartzberg (reprint from #230)

Page 39 – History of Cracked – Don Orehek / Darren Auck, John Arcudi (reprint from #237)

Page 42 – Talking Vending Machines – Sururi Gumen (reprint from #188)

Page 44 – Robocops and Roborobbers – John Severin / John Arcudi (reprint from #237)

Page 47 – Who's Who in the Classroom – John Reiner (reprint from #215)

Page 49 – Future At-Home Merchandising Parties – Warren Sattler (reprint from #184)

Page 51 – The Ninja – Mike Ricigliano / Roger Brown (reprint from #240)

Page 52 – Freddy's Celebrity Nightmares! – John Severin / Tony Frank (Lou Silverstone) (reprint from #240)

Page 54 – Ye Hang Ups (The moon is full) – John Severin (reprint from #240)

Page 55 – Cracked Evolution Revolution – Mike Ricigliano (reprint from #194)

Page 58 – Farewell M*A*S*H*E*D a Cracked Remembrance – John Severin (reprint from #194)

Page 65 – The Cracked Video Revolution! – Vic Martin / George Gladir (reprint from #231)

Page 68 – The Very Rich and the Very Poor – Warren Sattler (reprint from #193)

Page 72 – Cracked Visits a Midnight Monster Picnic – Al Scaduto (reprint from #217)

Page 74 – The Good Old Daze of the Automobile – John Severin (reprint from #193)

Page 78 – Can You Pass the Teen-Age Drivers Test? – Warren Sattler (reprint from #200)

Page 81 – The Silly Cosbey Show – John Severin (reprint from #212)

Page 84 – Advertising on Postage Stamps – Arnoldo Franchioni (reprint from #217)

Page 86 – How Popular Are You? – Warren Sattler (reprint from #192)

Page 90 – The Making of Jawz #23 – John Severin (reprint from #198)

Page 96 – Movie Monsters Based on Video Games – Walter Brogan (reprint from #214)

Page 99 – Subscription ad – Rurik Tyler

Back Cover – We're Litterbugged by an Untidy Accumulation of Yeech! – John Severin (reprint from #87)

Cracked Collectors' Edition #88 (*Year's Best*), September 1991 (100 pages) ($2.95)

Cover – We Pick Out Our Year's Best! – John Severin (new)

Page 2 – Dorkitos ad – Walter Brogan (reprint from #252)

Page 3 – Contents – Mike Ricigliano

Page 4 – Toon-Age Mutant Ninjerk Turtles – John Severin / Tony Frank (Lou Silverstone) (reprint from #256)

Page 10 – Japanese Entertainment Take Overs – Severino San (John Severin) / Gladir San (George Gladir) (reprint from #253)

Page 13 – The Sabotron! – Mike Ricigliano (reprint from #250)

Page 14 – Cracked Dinosaur True or Fossil Quiz? – Rurik Tyler (reprint from #252)
Page 16 – One Day in Chinese Acupuncture Hospital – Don Orehek (reprint from #250)
Page 18 – Doggie Hoser M.D. – Walter Brogan / Tony Frank (Lou Silverstone) (reprint from #254)
Page 22 – Unknown Facts About the California Raisins – Rurik Tyler (reprint from #251)
Page 24 – Robocop-Out, Too! – Frank Borth (reprint from #259)
Page 30 – The Last Issues of Popular Comic Books – Pete Fitzgerald / George Gladir (reprint from #258)
Page 34 – More Freak Outs from Back in the Future! – John Severin / George Gladir (reprint from #253)
Page 38 – Yertle the Mutant Ninja Turtle! – Gary Fields (reprint from #256)
Page 42 – Totally Recalled – Walter Brogan (reprint from #258)
Page 47 – Teenage Mutated Ninjerk Turdles Unfit Role Models for Our Children! – Rurik Tyler (reprint from #255)
Page 48 – Rejected Cracked Covers – John Severin / George Gladir (reprint from #257)
Page 50 – Get the New Kids Off the Block – Pete Fitzgerald (reprint from #259)
Page 52 – Spy and Saboteur in The Library – Mike Ricigliano (reprint from #252)
Page 54 – The Simplesons – Gary Fields / Rich Kriegel (Lou Silverstone) (reprint from #257)
Page 57 – Freddy Krocker Food Company – Rurik Tyler (reprint from #251)
Page 60 – Sabotage in the 1990's – Mike Ricigliano (reprint from #254)
Page 62 – Dink Trazy – Walter Brogan (reprint from #258)
Page 68 – Spy and Saboteur go Dancin' – Mike Ricigliano (reprint from #259)
Page 69 – Video Games & Equipment of the Future IV! – Pete Fitzgerald / George Gladir (reprint from #256)
Page 73 – Shut-Ups (Dick, what's your pleasure) – Don Orehek (reprint from #258)
Page 74 – Ill-Legal Weapons – Walter Brogan / Vic Bianco (Lou Silverstone) (reprint from #251)
Page 80 – Cracked Trading Cards for Less Glamorous Professions – Pete Fitzgerald (reprint from #259)
Page 82 – Aiming Gun Ads at Specific Groups – John Severin / George Gladir (reprint from #252)

Page 85 – New Villains for Future Dick Tracy Movies – John Severin / George Gladir (reprint from #256)

Page 89 – Good News and Bad News for Teenage Mutated Ninjerk Turdles – Rurik Tyler (reprint from #255)

Page 92 – Random Funnies (having a sale) – Mike Ricigliano / Roger Brown (reprint from #255)

Page 93 – The Hunt for Rad Crackedober – Walter Brogan / Tony Frank (Lou Silverstone) (reprint from #256)

Page 98 – Subscription ad – Rurik Tyler

Page 99 – Tinoctin ad – John Severin (reprint from #258)

Back Cover – Cracked Mutant Turtle Soup Cut-Up! – Rurik Tyler (reprint from #255)

Cracked Collectors' Edition #89 (*TV Misguided Fall Preview*), January 1992 (100 pages) ($2.95)

Cover – TV Misguided Fall Preview – Gary Fields (new)

Page 2 – The Emergency – Mike Ricigliano / Roger Brown (reprint from #243)

Page 3 – Contents – Mike Ricigliano

Page 4 – Blunder Years – Walter Brogan / Joe Catalano (reprint from #239)

Page 8 – Saturday Morning TV Cartoon Shows We Want to See – Tony Tallarico (reprint from #214)

Page 11 – Wrestlin' T 'n' T – Bill Burke (reprint from #215)

Page 16 – Remote Controls We'll Soon Be Seeing! – Gray Morrow / George Gladir (reprint from #249)

Page 18 – Double Scare! – Frank Caruso / Joe Catalano (reprint from #242)

Page 22 – New Jobs for Vanna! – John Severin / Joe Catalano (reprint from #232)

Page 24 – Harried…with Children – Rob Orzechowski / Rich Kriegel (Lou Silverstone) (reprint from #248)

Page 28 – The Final Episodes of Soured Sitcoms! – Frank Caruso (reprint from #232)

Page 30 – Jeers II – Walter Brogan / Joe Catalano (reprint from #238)

Page 33 – Video Nut Magazine – Arnoldo Franchioni (reprint from #213)

Page 40 – Cracked Interviews The Simpersons – Gary Fielding (Gary Fields) / Lou Silverstoning (Lou Silverstone) (reprint from #258)

Page 44 – Star Drek: The Next De-Generation – Bo Badman (Rurik Tyler) (reprint from #232)

Page 47 – Future Uses of Video (reprint from #216)

Page 49 – TV Misguided Fall Preview – Gary Fields (new)

Page 50 – T.V. Misguided Big Preview – Rurik Tyler (new)

Page 54 – Yotota ad – Frank Borth (new)

Page 55 – A Cracked Look at TV Commercials You'll Never Get to See – Bill Burke (reprint from #213)

Page 58 – The Final Episodes of Fantasy Shows – Rick Altergott (reprint from #246)

Page 64 – If Television Censors Had Their Way – John Severin (reprint from #212)

Page 67 – Cracked Interviews Bill Cozby! – Rob Orzechowski / Joe Catalano (reprint from #232)

Page 71 – Cracked Interviews Michael J. Foxy – Rob Orzechowski / Joe Catalano (reprint from #232)

Page 74 – 21 Dump Street – Rob Orzechowski / Joe Catalano (reprint from #242)

Page 77 – It's a Wonderful Laff – Peter McDonnell / Tony Frank (Lou Silverstone) (reprint from #243)

Page 82 – Remotely Controlled – Frank Caruso / Joe Catalano (reprint from #243)

Page 85 – VCR Home Movie Accessories Catalog – Warren Sattler (reprint from #212)

Page 88 – Nightlife with Ked Toppel – Frank Caruso / Steve Skeates (reprint from #234)

Page 33 – The ABC's of Video – Warren Sattler (reprint from #206)

Page 93 – Toilet Zone – Bob Fingerman / Steve Skeates (reprint from #236)

Page 95 – Jeraldo Revoltin's Guide to Be an Expert at Trash TV – Rob Orzechowski / Joe Catalano (reprint from #245)

Page 98 – Subscription ad – Rurik Tyler

Page 2 – Suds MacFrenzie – John Severin / Jerry De Fuccio (reprint from #235)

Back Cover – TV Guise Pee-Wee Herman Cover – Rurik Tyler (reprint from #253)

Cracked Collectors' Edition #90 (*Sci-Fi Special*), April 1992 (100 pages) ($2.95)

Cover – Star Trek and Star Trek: The Next Generation – John Severin (new)

Page 2 and 99 – More Star Wars – Cracked Poster – Powers (John Severin) (reprint from #148)

Page 3 – Contents – Pete Fitzgerald

Page 4 – Star Drek the Moving Picture – John Severin (reprint from #169)

Page 12 – Odd Jobs for Star Wars Stars – Howard Nostrand (reprint from #154)

Page 14 – If the Characters of Star Wars Appeared in Other Movies and TV Shows – Powers (John Severin) (reprint from #149)
Page 18 – You Know You're a Robot – Brad Joyce / George Gladir (reprint from #226)
Page 20 – The Six Billion Dollar Man vs. Dark Badar – O.O. Severin (John Severin) (reprint from #149)
Page 26 – Hee-Man, Mister of the Universe – Walter Brogan (reprint from #213)
Page 28 – Digital Instruments of the Future – Warren Sattler (reprint from #144)
Page 31 – Beam Us Up, Scotty! – Mike Ricigliano / Roger Brown (reprint from #247)
Page 32 – The Aliens are Here!! – Tom Short (reprint from #216)
Page 34 – Rockey: 2001 – John Severin / Eel O'Brian (Mort Todd) (reprint from #219)
Page 38 – Talking Computer Devices of Tomorrow – Cuz (reprint from #215)
Page 40 – The Machine Mania Monopolizes the Movies – Warren Sattler (reprint from #148)
Page 43 – Star Drek the Next Generation – Mike Ricigliano / Roger Brown (reprint from #247)
Page 44 – Cy-Threepiu & Arty-Ditto A Souvenir Photo Album of Their Visit to Earth – Cosa Nostrand (Howard Nostrand) (reprint from #148)
Page 48 – Star Trek Funnies – Mike Ricigliano / Roger Brown (reprint from #252)
Page 50 and Insert – 12 Cracked Collector Cards! The Extra Terrestrial Wrestling Federation – Mike Ricigliano, Pete Fitzgerald / Steve Strangio (full color, glossy) (new)
Page 51 – Star Drek IV: The Voyage Back Home to the Future! – Bill Wray / Mort Todd (reprint from #228)
Page 56 – Alien TV! – John Severin / Gene Perone, Mort Todd (reprint from #217)
Page 61 – On the Beach the Day After with Dr. Strangelove or How I Learned to Live with and Love Roaches – Wally Kubrogan (Walter Brogan) / Rich Kriegel (Lou Silverstone) (reprint from #246)
Page 65 – Star People Weekly and Creatures and Things Magazine – John Severin (reprint from #148)
Page 70 – The Happy Dazes' Close Encounters of the Third Kind – John Severin (reprint from #153)
Page 76 – If UFO's Ever Do Land – Bill Ward (reprint from #155)

Page 79 – Close Encounters of the Worst Kind – Michael Severin (John Severin) (reprint from #150)

Page 86 – Past Predictions of the Future – Sururi Gumen (reprint from #121)

Page 90 – Subscription ad – Rurik Tyler

Page 91 – The Cracked Investigation of the UFO Phenomenon – Howard Nostrand (reprint from #155)

Page 94 – Star Drek V The Finite Frontier – Rick Altergott / Tony Frank (Lou Silverstone) (reprint from #252)

Back Cover – Syl Spaces Out! – John Severin (reprint from #159)

Cracked Collectors' Edition #91 (*Beauty and the Feast*), July 1992 (100 pages) ($2.95)

Cover – We Roast Beauty and the Feast – Walter Brogan (new)

Page 2 – The Man and the Beast – Oskar Blotta (reprint from #80)

Page 3 – Contents – Mike Ricigliano

Page 4 – Hollywood Version of Nursery Rhymes – John Reiner (reprint from #214)

Page 9 – Forgotten Funnies! – Gary Fields (reprint from #236)

Page 11 – Would Columbus Have Discovered America Etc.? – O.O. Severin (John Severin) (reprint from #64)

Page 16 – One-Shots (surfing torpedo) – Mike Ricigliano / Roger Brown (reprint from #237)

Page 18 – Supedupman's 50th Birthday! – John Severin / George Gladir (reprint from #235)

Page 22 – Cracked's Random Samplings – Howard Nostrand (reprint from #170)

Page 26 – Ye Hang Ups (mind closing the door) – C.E. Severin (Catherine Severin) (reprint from #170)

Page 27 – We K.O. Rocky – John Severin (reprint from #143) (full color)

Page 28 – Rockey – John Severin (reprint from #143)

Page 34 – Using Star Trek Logic and Technology to Solve Life's Everyday Problems – Don Orehek (reprint from #170)

Page 37 – Who'd Like to Kill Roger Wabbit – John Severin (reprint from #241) (full color)

Page 38 – Cracked Interviews Roger Wabbit – John Severin / Vic Bianco (Lou Silverstone) (reprint from #245)

Page 41 – Loser Magazine – John Severin (reprint from #172)

Page 47 – Cracked Look at Teacher Types – John Severin (reprint from #186)

Page 49 – Walt Dizzy's Beauty and the Feast – Walter Brogan / Lou Silverstone (full color)

Page 53 – Real Kids Don't Eat Spinach – Warren Sattler (reprint from #197)

Page 57 – Constitutional Crisis! – John Severin / George Gladir (reprint from #235)

Page 58 – The Cracked World of Vic Martin – Vic Martin (reprint from #222)

Page 61 – We Take a Shot at 'Toons – John Severin / Mort Todd (reprint from #245) (full color)

Page 62 – If Comic Strip Heroes Had Hang-Ups Like the Rest of Us – Lugoze (reprint from #96)

Page 66 – Exposing the Con in Contests – Howard Nostrand (reprint from #144)

Page 70 – Railroad Crossing – Mike Ricigliano / Roger Brown (reprint from #235)

Page 71 – Sagebrush (such a bad character) – John Severin (reprint from *Cracked Collectors' Edition* #9)

Page 72 – Sagebrush (gettin' fed-up) – John Severin (reprint from #235)

Page 73 – Run Away Humor – John Severin / Mort Todd (reprint from #252) (full color)

Page 78 – Cracked Star Cars! – John Severin / Cliff Mott (reprint from #234)

Page 77 – What Your Mother/Father Would Say – Don Orehek (reprint from #197)

Page 80 – Perry Mazin The Case of the Guilty Client – Bill Wray / Robert Loren Fleming (reprint from #235)

Page 83 – Acme Manual for Nabbing Road Runners! – Walter Brogan / George Gladir (reprint from #245)

Page 86 – How is it That? – Warren Sattler (reprint from #199)

Page 89 – Crackadile Dandee, Too! – Gray Morrow / Tony Frank (Lou Silverstone) (reprint from #241)

Page 94 – When Comic Strips Go Madison Avenue – Lugoze (reprint from #80)

Page 98 – Shut-Ups (cook a pizza) – Don Orehek (reprint from #233)

Page 99 – Subscription ad – Mike Ricigliano

Back Cover – Smythe Character (Mammal Killers ad) – Bill Wray (reprint from #251)

Cracked Collectors' Edition #92 (*Year's Best*), **September 1992 (100 pages) ($2.95)**

Cover – We Pick Our Year's Best – Rurik Tyler (new)

Page 2 and 99 – The Twin Geaks Game – Mike Ricigliano (reprint from #261)

Page 3 – Contents – Mike Ricigliano

Page 4 – Familiar Patter – Walter Brogan / Lou Silverstone (reprint from #265)

Page 10 – Spies and Saboteurs Hit Baseball – Mike Ricigliano (reprint from #265)
Page 12 – Werewolves Were Affected by Other Types of Moons – Rurik Tyler (reprint from #264)
Page 14 – It Wasn't So Long Ago When – John Severin / Bill Ignizio (reprint from #268)
Page 16 – Fairy Tale Characters Where Are They Now? – Rurik Tyler / Steve Strangio (reprint from #266)
Page 19 – Totally Turtle! – Mike Ricigliano (reprint from #263)
Page 22 – Goodfelons – Walter Brogan / Vic Bianco (Lou Silverstone) (reprint from #261)
Page 28 – Cracked Horses Around – Arnoldo Franchioni (reprint from #268)
Page 30 – Cracked's Comparative Guide to Learning Institutions – Pete Fitzgerald / Steve Strangio (reprint from #268)
Page 34 – Mother Goose Goes to Court – Gary Fields / Ronnie Nathan (reprint from #261)
Page 37 – Orehek at Large Goes to a Rock Concert – Don Orehek (reprint from #266)
Page 40 – Transylvania's Funniest Home Videos – John Severin / Jack Harris (reprint from #261)
Page 45 – National Pooch Press & Tabby Tattler – Vic Martin / George Gladir (reprint from #265)
Page 49 – Cracked Looks Back at '92 (So Far) (new)
Page 52 – Subscription ad – Rurik Tyler
Page 53 – Cracked's New Magazines for the New America – Pete Fitzgerald / Howie Mitchell (reprint from #261)
Page 55 – How the Glitch Sold a Crisis! – Gary Fields / Ronnie Nathan (reprint from #264)
Page 58 – Robbing Hood Prance of Thieves – Walter Brogan / Lou Silverstone (reprint from #267)
Page 65 – U.S. Arsenal Munitions Catalog 1996 – Frank Borth (reprint from #265)
Page 66 – Superman's Bachelor Party! – Mike Ricigliano / Jerry De Fuccio (reprint from #266)
Page 68 – Cracked's Joy of Working – Pete Fitzgerald / Steve Strangio (reprint from #267)
Page 71 – Slamming the Doors – Rurik Tyler / Ronnie Nathan (reprint from #265)
Page 74 – R-Rated Ads for Family Films – Gary Fields / Evelyn Gabai (reprint from #267)
Page 76 – Cracked's College President of the Year – Walter Brogan / Lou Silverstone (reprint from #266)

Page 80 – One Afternoon in Jersey City – Don Orehek (reprint from #266) Page 81 – Cracked Helpful Hints for Shooting Snappier Snapshots – Vic Martin (reprint from #262)

Page 85 – Roadside Historical Markers – Frank Borth / Howie Mitchell (reprint from #261)

Page 88 – Another Collection of Cracked Baseball Cards – Pete Fitzgerald / Fred Sahner (reprint from #266)

Page 91 – Smurphy Brown – John Severin / Vic Bianco (Lou Silverstone) (reprint from #260)

Page 96 – Edward Scissorshandy – Frank Borth (new)

Page 97 – Twin Geaks Game Suspect Cards – Mike Ricigliano (reprint from #261)

Back Cover – Anygizer ad – John Severin / Scott Thaler (reprint from #263)

Cracked Collectors' Edition #93 (*Cracked Goes to School*), January 1993 (100 pages) ($2.95)

Cover – W.M. Gaines Memorial High School – John Severin (new)

Page 2 – Subscription ad – Frank Borth

Page 3 – Contents – Mike Ricigliano

Page 4 – The Joy of Cheating – Bruce Bolinger / Daniel O'Keefe (new)

Page 6 – Red Meat – Rick Altergott / Vic Bianco (Lou Silverstone) (reprint from #241)

Page 11 – If Colleges Advertised – John Severin (reprint from #29)

Page 16 – G.I. Laugh-In! (reprint from #75)

Page 18 – Reducing the Violence in Movies – Lugoze (reprint from #75)

Page 22 – Letters

Page 23 – A Brochure from P.T.U. (Prime Time University) – Bill Ward (reprint from #148)

Page 26 – If Rambo Fought Other Wars! – John Severin / George Glacir (reprint from #238)

Page 29 – Sylvester P. Smythe Junior College Catalogue of Courses – John Langton (reprint from #75)

Page 34 – As the Trend Towards Violence Increases – Lugoze (reprint from #69)

Page 40 – Metropolis the Slave – Arnoldo Franchioni (reprint from #63)

Page 42 – Arnold Fluffernutter Commandope – Bob Fingerman / Mort Todd (reprint from #219)

Page 47 – The Cracked Museum of Historical Trivia – Tony Tallarico (reprint from #69)

Page 50 and Insert – Cracked's Spy and Sab Bookmarks – Mike Ricigliano (full color and glossy) (new)

Page 51 – Come and Get Me, Copper! (reprint from #64)

Page 52 – The College Entrance Rat Race – John Langton (reprint from #75)

Page 56 – The Pirate Treasure Chest (reprint from #64)

Page 58 – Awards for School Kids – Bill McCartney (Bill Ward) (reprint from #77)

Page 62 – 11 Sure-Fire, Far-Out, Cool, New, Neat Ways to be Popular in College! – Joe Mead (reprint from #72)

Page 64 – School for Baby Sitters – Vic Martin (reprint from #78)

Page 67 – If – John Severin / John Arcudi (see note on issue #214) (reprint from #240)

Page 68 – How to Interpret All Those Professional School Ads – Samuel B. Whitehead

(reprint from #177)

Page 71 – Premedator – William York Wray (Bill Wray) / Robert Loren Fleming (reprint from #233)

Page 76 – What if There Had Been Guidance Counselors Throughout History? – O.O. Severin (John Severin) (reprint from #53)

Page 79 – Cracked Interviews Rambozo! – Rob Orzechowski / Joe Catalano (reprint from #238)

Page 82 – How to Win a School Election – T. Severin (John Severin) (reprint from #174)

Page 86 – A Cracked Look at a High School – Bill Ward (reprint from #116)

Page 88 – Cracked Takes You Back to When it all Started (blood pressure) – Jack Davis (reprint from #15)

Page 89 – Gift Catalogue for Teen-Agers – Don Orehek (reprint from #196)

Page 93 – Throughout History with the Isolated Camera – John Severin (reprint from #48)

Page 97 – Cracked's Specialized Greeting Cards – Don Orehek (reprint from #143)

Page 99 – Cracked X-15 Survival Knife – Bob Fingerman (reprint from #221)

Back Cover – Arnie Sylvesternegger – Bill Wray (reprint from #236)

Cracked Collectors' Edition #94 (We Lampoon Aladdin!), **April 1993 (100 pages) ($2.95)**

Cover – Aladdin's Bananas – Walter Brogan (new)

Page 2 – The Man and the Mousey – Oskar Blotta (reprint from #124)

Page 3 – Contents – Mike Ricigliano

Page 4 – Aladumb's Letters

Page 5 – Snow Flake and the Seven Dwarfs – John Severin (reprint from #70)

Page 10 – Video Games of the Future – Warren Sattler (reprint from #186)

Page 12 – Who in the World Decided That – Arnoldo Franchioni (reprint from #194)

Page 15 – Kitchenland – Rurik Tyler (reprint from #211)

Page 18 – The Female Role in American History – Don Orehek (reprint from #131)

Page 22 – More Believe it or Nots (Will Steele) (reprint from #187)

Page 25 – Wonderland Revisited – Brad Joyce / George Gladir (reprint from #239)

Page 26 – Subscription ad – Rurik Tyler

Page 27 – E.T. Pizza Delivery – John Severin (reprint from #192) (full color)

Page 28 – E.Z. Meets Clodzilla – Rob Orzechowski (reprint from *Cracked Monster Party* #12)

Page 33 – Sylvester: Supermarket Stock Boy – Al Scaduto (reprint from #220)

Page 34 – The Final Episode of Comic Strips – Tony Tallarico (reprint from #216)

Page – We Salute Michael Jackson – John Severin (reprint from #207) (full color)

Page 38 – Michael Jackson's Scrapbook – Don Orehek (reprint from *Cracked Collectors' Edition* #60)

Page 43 – The Making of Thriller (reprint from #207)

Page 49 – Dizzy's Aladumb – Walter Brogan / Lance Contrucci (full color) (new)

Page 53 – Inside the Genie's Lamp – Rurik Tyler (new)

Page 56 – Alaffin's Magic Lamp – Fran Matera (reprint from #204)

Page 57 – Cracked Toon Videos – Gary Fields (reprint from #249)

Page 60 – The Wish – Brian Buniak (reprint from #207)

Page 61 – Cracked Says Goodbye – John Severin (reprint from #133) (full color)

Page 62 – What Athletes Do on the Off Season – Warren Sattler (reprint from #209)

Page 65 – "Memorable Moments From Presidential History" – Val Mayerik (reprint from #177)

Page 69 – Cracked Looks at Archeology – Warren Sattler (reprint from #209)

Page 73 – Rocky and Home Alone – John Severin (reprint from #262) (full color)

Page 74 – Homeboy Alone – John Severin (reprint from #262)

Page 81 – Home Alone Goes Public – Don Orehek (reprint from #263)

Page 82 – Even More Sequels to Home Alone – Mike Ricigliano (new)

Page 84 – Jobs You Never Dreamed Someone Does – John Severin (reprint from #181)

Page 86 – Socky V – Walter Brogan (new)

Page 91 – Shut-Ups (Checkmate!!) – Don Orehek (reprint from #203) (red color added)

Page 92 – Comic Strip Oddities! – John Severin / George Gladir (reprint from #245)

Page 94 – Cracked's More Practical Tranzformer-type Toys – Bill Burke (reprint from #213) (Not only did they reprint this article, they also reprinted the contest which had a deadline of 1985 to send in entries.)

Page 99 – Shut-Ups (Happy Birthday, Muckey!) – Don Orehek (reprint from #246)

Back Cover – Peter Pan Reads a Bedtime Story – Mike Ricigliano / Roger Brown (reprint from #247)

Cracked Collectors' Edition #95 (*Cops in Toontown!*), July 1993 (100 pages) ($2.95)

Cover – Cops in Toontown! – Walter Brogan, Tom Grimes (new) (Brogan is also the cover photo model.)

Page 2 – Shut-Ups (get my hands on) – Don Orehek / Mort Todd (reprint from #228)

Page 3 – Contents – Mike Ricigliano

Page 4 – "Chops" in Toontown – Walter Brogan / Eric Goldberg, Mark Howard (new)

Page 8 – "Cops and Robbers" Section (new)

Page 9 – Capony – John Severin (reprint from #128)

Page 15 – Crimedom's Mail Order Catalogue – Warren Sattler (reprint from #146)

Page 19 – Columbum – Walter Brogan / Tony Frank (Lou Silverstone) (reprint from #247)

Page 23 – Cracked's Guide to Burglary Prevention – Vic Martin (reprint from #136)

Page 26 – Murder, She Wrot – Marie Severin / Stu Schwartzberg (reprint from #230)

Page 30 – Cracked's 10 Most Unwanted List – Bill Wray (reprint from #230)

Page 32 – Sherlock Holmes vs Jack the Ripper – John Severin / Tony Frank (Lou Silverstone) (reprint from #247)
Page 36 – Kojerk – Walter Brogan / Tony Frank (Lou Silverstone) (reprint from #255)
Page 40 – Don't You Hate it at the Movies – Sururi Gumen (reprint from #204)
Page 42 – Bad Professionals! – Tom Bacas (reprint from #219)
Page 45– Sylvester's Photo Album – John Severin (reprint from #35)
Page 49 – It's Those Ghastly Toothpaste People! – Jeremy Banx (reprint from #245)
Page 50 and Insert – Cracked Toon Wanted Posters – Mike Ricigliano, Gary Fields / Daniel O'Keefe (full color, glossy) (new)
Page 51 – Pla'Toons – Walt Disbroganey (Walter Brogan) / Matthew Sweney (reprint from #245)
Page 54 – Comic Character Evolution! – Bo Badman (Rurik Tyler) (reprint from #245)
Page 56 – Blundercats – Steve Ditko / Mike Carlin (reprint from #226)
Page 61 – Superswine – Gary Fields (reprint from #250)
Page 62 – Freddie the Menace – Gary Fields (reprint from #245)
Page 64 – Stars' Wars – Pat Boyette (reprint from #245)
Page 66 – Toontown Movie Posters – Gary Fields (reprint from #265)
Page 68 – Fairy Tale Characters – Mike Ricigliano / Roger Brown (reprint from #247)
Page 71 – Ninjerk Magazine – Walter Brogan (reprint from #224)
Page 76 – Things You Should Have Done – Walt Lardner (reprint from #203)
Page 80 – Sylvester P. Smythe As Seen by Different Artists (reprint from #14)
Page 82 – The Cracked History of the Automobile – Warren Sattler (reprint from #167)
Page 86 – The More Things Change the More They Stay the Same – Warren Sattler (reprint from #204)
Page 90 – Famous Funny Animals – Gary Fields (reprint from #255)
Page 91 – The Cracked Lens (I can't stop it) (reprint from #219)
Page 94 – Cracked's New Sidewalk, Street and Playground Games – Warren Sattler (reprint from #173)
Page 98 – Shut-Ups (drive-in movie) – Charles Rodrigues, Vic Martin (reprint from #93)
Page 99 – The Stone Age – Oskar Blotta (reprint from #125)
Back Cover – I Want You to Buy This Magazine – James Montgomery Flaggione (John Severin) (reprint from #106)

Cracked Collectors' Edition #96 (*Year's Best*), September 1993 (100 pages) ($2.95)

Cover – You've Got the Wrong One Baby Uh Huh! – John Severin (new)

Page 2 – *Cracked Summer Special #3* ad

Page 3 – Contents – Mike Ricigliano

Page 4 – Barferly Hills-911 – John Severin / Lou Silverstone (reprint from #270)

Page 10 – Cracked Prison Greeting Cards – Bruce Bolinger / Patric Abedin (reprint from #277)

Page 12 – Spies and Saboteurs Hit the Winter Olympics Part I – Mike Ricigliano (reprint from #271)

Page 13 – The Crash Test Dummies Test Other Products – Tim Grimes / Eric Goldberg, Mark Howard (reprint from #276)

Page 16 – Cracked on Safari – Arnoldo Franchioni (reprint from #272)

Page 18 – New Muppets! – Pete Fitzgerald / Rob Weske (reprint from #272)

Page 21 – Snacks That Time Forgot – John Severin / Lenore Skenazy (reprint from #276)

Page 24 – Spies and Saboteurs Hit an Amusement Park – Mike Ricigliano (reprint from #274)

Page 26 – Viering Off (Billy the Squid) – Gary Fields / Jed Vier (reprint from #273)

Page 27 – Megasuperultramania Magazine – Rurik Tyler / Steve Strangio (reprint from #275)

Page 32 – Dan Quayle's Career Opportunities – Jim Bennett / Eric Goldberg, Mark Howard (reprint from #277)

Page 34 – Book Reports of the Rich and Famous – John Severin / Lenore Skenazy (reprint from #273)

Page 30 – Some Improvement – Walter Brogan / Tony Frank (Lou Silverstone) (reprint from #273)

Page 42 – Transylvanian Breakfast Cereals – Gary Fields (reprint from #270)

Page 44 – Spies and Saboteurs Hit the Winter Olympics Part II – Mike Ricigliano (reprint from #271)

Page 45 – The Fuzzy Image Catalogue – John Severin / Lance Contrucci (reprint from #274)

Page 48 – Subscription ad

Page 49 – Cracked's 2nd Annual Year in Review – 1993 So Far (new)

Page 53 – Soak-Mart – Mike Ricigliano (reprint from #276)

Page 56 – Nun's the Word! – Rurik Tyler / Andrew Osborne (reprint from #277)

Page 58 – Magazines for the Psychologically Disturbed – Pete Fitzgerald / Lenore Skenazy (reprint from #273)

Page 61 – When Government Regulations Apply to the Wild Kingdom! – Don Orehek / Dan Birtcher (reprint from #278)

Page 64 – Wayne's Hurled – John Severin / Lou Silverstone (reprint from #273)

Page 69 – More Interesting, Livelier Summer Olympics! – Mike Ricigliano (reprint from #275)

Page 72 – Our Real Keyboard For Rock Star Wannabes! – Bruce Bolinger / Dan Birtcher (reprint from #278)

Page 74 – Cracked Conspiracy Theories – Rob Orzechowski / Daniel O'Keefe (reprint from #276)

Page 76 – The Cracked Top Ten List Least Popular Ballpark Promotional Dates – Mike Ricigliano (reprint from #275)

Page 77 – Money-Ball: The New Baseball – John Severin / Andy Simmons (reprint from #275)

Page 81 – Cracked's Big City Gift Catalog – Frank Borth / Scott Franklin (reprint from #273)

Page 84 – Spies and Saboteurs Hit American Gladiators – Mike Ricigliano (reprint from #277)

Page 86 – How Cartoon Characters are Coping with the Recession – Gary Fields / Andy Simmons (reprint from #275)

Page 88 – Presents for Hard to Please Monsters – John Severin (reprint from #272)

Page 91 – Why/When – Don Orehek / Joseph O'Brien (reprint from #276)

Page 93 – Battyman Return? – Walter Brogan / Lou Silverstone (reprint from #276)

Page 99 – Bitterfinger ad – Gary Fields / Lou Silverstone (reprint from #272)

Back Cover – The Straw-Man Writes a Book – Jeff Wong / Lou Silverstone (reprint from #274)

***Cracked Collectors' Edition* #97 (*5 Decades of Decadent Humor*), January 1994 (68 pages) ($2.95) (This issue came polybagged with a separate virtual reprint of *Cracked* #1.)**

Cover – 35th Anniversary Issue – John Severin (new)

Page 2 – Special Swimsuit Issue – Don Martin (reprint from #280)

Page 3 – Contents – Mike Ricigliano

Page 4 – 1st Anniversary (pictures all six previous covers) – John Severin, Russ Heath, Bill Everett (reprint from #7)

Page 5 – Sylvester for President – John Severin (reprint from #36)

Page 10 – Perry Masonry – John Severin (reprint from #10)

Page 12 – Civil War Facts – Jack Davis (reprint from #12)

Page 15 – Cracked Shut-Ups (daddy run) – Al Jaffee (reprint from #5)
Page 16 – Sylvesters on the Moon – John Severin (reprint from #68)
Page 17 – Would Columbus Have Discovered America Etc.? – O.O. Severin (John Severin) (reprint from #64)
Page 22 – When Doctors Advertise! – Jack Davis, John Severin (reprint from #24)
Page 26 – Shakespearean Shut-Ups (Romeo) – John Severin (reprint from #17)
Page 28 – Sweeping Up – John Severin (reprint from #87)
Page 29 – The Brainy Bunch – John Severin (reprint from #89)
Page 34 – If Mork Appeared in Other TV Shows and Movies (Star Trek) – John Severin (reprint from #164)
Page 39 – Shut-Ups (How do you address a king) – Charles Rodrigues (reprint from #183)
Page 40 – Who'd Like to Kill Roger Wabbit – John Severin (reprint from #241)
Page 41 – Couch Potato Catalog – Vic Martin / George Gladir (reprint from #237)
Page 44 – Who Framed Roger Wabbit / Wawwy Bwogan (Walter Brogan) / Rich Kriegel (Lou Silverstone) (reprint from #241)
Page 50 – Rock and Roll Shut-Ups (3000 people) – Don Orehek / Charles E. Hall (reprint from #241)
Page 51 – Subscription ad – Rurik Tyler
Page 52 – Welcome to the 1990s! – John Severin / Mort Todd (reprint from #251)
Page 53 – Spies and Saboteurs Hit Baseball – Mike Ricigliano (reprint from #265)
Page 56 – What is a Bummer Summer Vacation? – Frank Borth (reprint from #265)
Page 58 – Don't Ya Hate – Gary Fields (reprint from #269)
Page 59 – Cracked's Comparative Guide to Learning Institutions – Pete Fitzgerald / Steve Strangio (reprint from #268)
Page 63 – Wrestling Hype for Boring Sports – Rurik Tyler / Bill Ignizio (reprint from #267)
Page 66 – Shut-Ups (There's a seat) – Don Orehek / Gayle-Adams Pierpont (reprint from #272)
Page 67 – Covers to #14, 25, 27, 33, 70, 71, 77, 82, 89 – Jack Davis, John Severin, Basil Gogos.
Back Cover – Covers to #97, 124, 150, 239, 248, 255, 258, 265, 267 – John Severin, Rurik Tyler, Walter Brogan

Bonus Reprint of *Cracked* #1, March 1958 (44 pages) (This reprint is virtually identical to the original except for the following changes noted below.)

Cover – Cracked World – Bill Everett (The "25c" has been replaced with a large "#1.")

Page 2 – Wincin Cigarette ad – Paul Reinman

Page 3 – Contents (Indicia is changed to reflect *Cracked Collectors' Edition* #97 and 1994 information.)

Page 4 – Editor's Press Interview – Russ Heath

Page 6 – Letters From the Editor

Page 7 – Gunsmokes – Russ Heath

Page 10 – How to Build a Hot Hot Rod

Page 12 – Brave Guy – Paul Reinman

Page 13 – Ad Slogans

Page 14 – The $64,000,000 Cracked-Pot Question – John Severin

Page 16 – Little Mercurichrome and Denny the Menaces

Page 17 – Max Wallis Interviews Jayne Womansfield – Russ Heath

Page 20 – Chef of the Month – John Severin

Page 22 – News Flash From Behind the Iron Curtain

Page 24 – Science Fiction – Don Orehek, Bob Campbell, J. Kiernan (Kiernan's joke has been removed from this reprint.)

Page 25 – How I'll Beat the Champ – John Severin

Page 28 – Cracked Brings You Greetings – Bill Everett

Page 30 – Your Christmas Shopping Guide – John Severin

Page 31 – Marjorie Morninglory

Page 33 – Shakespeare

Page 36 – Sixteen and a Half Tons of Friendship – Paul Reinman

Page 38 – Famous Proverbs

Page 40 – So You're Going to College?

Page 42 – Why Doesn't This Ever Happen? – Bill Ward (Title changed to "He's Really a Lone Ranger Now!)

Page 43 – Subscription Ad – John Severin (Address and price modified to 1994 location and rates with a small note about 1958 prices added.)

Back Cover – Voto ad – Paul Reinman

***Cracked Collectors' Edition* #98 (*Beethoven's #1*), April 1994 (100 pages) ($2.95)**

Cover – Three Dogs Enjoying a Good Pee – Walter Brogan, Jeff Wong (new)

Page 2 – Training the Dog – Samuel B. Whitehead (reprint from #163)

Page 3 – Contents – Mike Ricigliano

Page 4 – Beerbellythoven's 2rd – Bruce Bolinger / Andy Simmons (new)

Page 8 – Super Heavies – Pete Fitzgerald / Steve Strangio (reprint from #264)

Page 10 – Cracked Interviews Elvis the King – John Severin / Rich Kriegel (Lou Silverstone) (reprint from #244)

Page 13 – Rodrigues' Side Show – Charles Rodrigues (reprint from #106)

Page 16 – Untouchy Bulls! – John Severin / Mort Todd (reprint from #233)

Page 21 – Baseball Statisticiatic – John Severin (reprint from #10)

Page 24 – Tour of the Cracked Magazine Offices! – John Severin / Joe Catalano, Michael Delle-Femine (reprint from #226)

Page 26 – It's a Lot Worse in Buffalo – Warren Sattler (reprint from #149)

Page 29 – RoboCop Out – Mark Pacella / John Arcudi (reprint from #233)

Page 32 – What Preceded Famous Events – Bill McCartney (Bill Ward) (reprint from #106)

Page 34 – Aiming Gun Ads at Specific Groups – John Severin / George Gladir (reprint from #252)

Page 37 – The Cracked Guide to Bowling – Bill Dubay (reprint from #141)

Page 42 – Are you a Hypochondriac? – John Langton (reprint from #106)

Page 44 – At the Heavy Metal Concert – Mike Ricigliano (reprint from #252)

Page 45 – America's Least Wanted – Rob Orzechowski / Matt Sweney (reprint from #252)

Page 48 – The Put-Downers – Vic Martin (reprint from #106)

Page 50 – Beagle and Mutt-Head (new)

Insert – Have You Hugged Your Human Today? – Rurik Tyler (new) (full color, glossy)

Insert – Fetch Your Own Damn Ball! – Jeff Wong (new) (full color, glossy)

Insert – Out of Order – Walter Brogan (new) (full color, glossy)

Insert – Muttonna…The Puppy Tour – Bruce Bolinger (new) (full color, glossy)

Page 52 – Cracked Birds! – Alba Ballard / Kevin McMahon (reprint from #232)

Page 55 – Dogs Magazine – John Severin (reprint from #74)

Page 63 – Cat Gifts for Cats Who Have Everything – Mac Bush (Sururi Gumen) (reprint from #125)

Page 65 – The Dog House (reprint from #65)

Page 67 – The Spoiled Rotten Pet Catalogue – Sururi Gumen (reprint from #189)

Page 71 – The Inspection – Mike Ricigliano / Roger Brown (reprint from #252)

Page 72 – Man's Best Friend – Bernard Baily (reprint from #106)

Page 74 – Psychologically Dangerous Toys – Vic Martin (reprint from #106)

Page 77 – Ye Hang Ups #9 (Hurry it up) – M.L. Severin (Margaret Severin) (reprint from #189)

Page 78 – The Cracked World of Looking Good – Bill Ward (reprint from #189)

Page 82 – The Loser – John Severin (reprint from #131)

Page 84 – Jogging Throughout History – John Severin (reprint from #82)

Page 88 – Marx Brothers' Laff-In! (reprint from #73)

Page 91 – Cracked's New Learn-At-Home Schools – LePoer (John Severin) (reprint from #141)

Page 94 – Familiar Patter – Walter Brogan / Lou Silverstone (reprint from #265)

Page 99 – Subscription ad – Frank Borth

Back Cover – Sylvester the Bird! – Alba Ballard, Bill Wray (reprint from #232)

Cracked Collectors' Edition #99 (Mighty Ducks 2½), July 1994 (68 pages) ($2.95)

Cover – We Blast Might Ducks 2½ - Walter Brogan, Jeff Wong (new)

Page 2 – One Night at the Garden – Howard Nostrand (reprint from #165)

Page 3 – Contents – Mike Ricigliano

Page 4 – Mighty Dorks 2½ - Walter Brogan (new)

Page 10 – Literal Interpretations of Baseball Expressions – LePoer (John Severin) (reprint from #164)

Page 12 – Spies and Saboteurs Hit the Mats – Mike Ricigliano (reprint from #261)

Page 13 – Jock State University Bulletin – Warren Sattler (reprint from #183)

Page 16 – To the Victors – Mike Ricigliano (reprint from #262)

Page 17 – How to Make Baseball More Interesting – Bill Ward (reprint from #137)

Page 21 – The Cracked Guide to Ice Skating – John Severin (reprint from #168)

Page 25 – Shut-Ups (good clean fight) – Mike Ricigliano (reprint from #134)

Page 26 – Socky V – Walter Brogan (reprint from Cracked Collectors' Edition #94)

Page 33 and Insert – It's Celebrity Thumb Wrestling – Jeff Wong / Eric Goldberg, Mark Howard (full color, glossy) (new)

Page 36 – Absolutely, Unquestionably, Positively, Undeniably, the Very, Very, Last of The Cracked Lens (and we really, really mean it this time, for sure!) Part XX (reprint from #195)

Page 40 – Roadside Historical Markers – Frank Borth / Howie Mitchell (reprint from #261)

Page 43 – Cracked Hold-Ups! (population explosion) – Sururi Gumen (reprint from #208)

Page 45 – The History of Advertising – Howard Nostrand (reprint from #166)

Page 49 – Subscription ad – John Severin (reprint from *Cracked Collectors' Edition* #88)

Page 50 – The Hunt for Rad Crackedober – Walter Brogan / Tony Frank (Lou Silverstone) (reprint from #256)

Page 55 – Believe it or Nuts!! – Jack Davis (reprint from #13)

Page 56 – Cracked Rock 'n' Roll Museum! – John Severin / George Gladir (reprint from #250)

Page 58 – One-Shots! (mine blasting) – Mike Ricigliano / Roger Brown (reprint from #250)

Page 60 – Jawz – John Severin (reprint from #129)

Page 66 – Shut-Ups (found a roach) – Don Orehek (reprint from #250)

Page 67 – Cracked Presents the Real Mighty Ducks – Walter Brogan (reprint from #279)

Back Cover – Great Moments in Sports 1,217,003 B.C. – Conky Nostrand (Howard Nostrand) (reprint from #171)

Cracked Collectors' Edition #100 (*Year's Best*), September 1994 (100 pages) ($2.95)

Cover – We Pick Our Year's Best – Walter Brogan, John Severin (new)

Page 2 – *Cracked Summer Special* #4 ad

Page 3 – Contents – Mike Ricigliano

Page 4 – Jurassick Park – Walter Brogan / Lou Silverstone (reprint from #283)

Page 11 – Yo, Santa! – Arnoldo Franchioni (reprint from #279)

Page 12 – Dangerous Toys – Ron Barrett (reprint from #279)

Page 14 – Cracked's Summertime Word Problem – Pete Fitzgerald / Judd Stomp (reprint from #285)

Page 16 – The Monkey Quotient – Bruce Bolinger / Arnie Bernstein (reprint from #281)

Page 20 – Pez Dispensers That Didn't Quite Make it – John Severin / Eric Goldberg, Mark Howard (reprint from #285)

Page 22 – Banned Children's Books – Gary Fields / David Boone (reprint from #282)

Page 25 – Beverly Hills High School Yearbook – Jim Bennett (reprint from #284)
Page 30 – TV Gameshows Through History – Pete Fitzgerald / Rob Weske (reprint from #282)
Page 32 – Landmark Remodeling – Terry Colon (reprint from #283)
Page 36 – Martian – John Severin / Andrew Osborne (reprint from #283)
Page 41 – Shut-Ups (I hope dis noize) – Don Orehek / Eric Goldberg, Mark Howard (reprint from #286)
Page 42 – Spies and Saboteurs Hit the Shopping Mall – Mike Ricigliano (reprint from #279)
Page 44 – The Crusty Spoon Placemat – Bruce Bolinger / Lenore Skenazy (reprint from #279)
Page 46 – Proper Football Safety Techniques – Rurik Tyler / Andy Simmons (reprint from #279)
Page 49 – Cracked's Annual Year in Review (1994 So Far) – Don Orehek (new)
Page 53 – When Government Regulations Apply to the Wild Kingdom! – Don Orehek / Dan Birtcher (reprint from #278)
Page 56 – Newly-Discovered Greek Theater Masks! – John Severin / Dan Birtcher (reprint from #283)
Page 58 – The Mighty Dorks – Pete Fitzgerald (reprint from #279)
Page 59 – Victor's Secret Catalogue – Bruce Bolinger / Steve Strangio (reprint from #282)
Page 62 – Kenny the Cockroach's Toy Tenement Sale! – Frank Borth / Scott Franklin (reprint from #280)
Page 66 – Charlie Brown Specials for the 90's – Gary Fields / Craig Farrell (reprint from #283)
Page 68 – Subscription ad
Page 69 – Smelrose Place – John Severin / Vic Bianco (Lou Silverstone) (reprint from #278)
Page 74 – Sani-Strips – Ron Barrett (reprint from #284)
Page 76 – Celebrity Answering Machines – Jeff Wong / David Boone (reprint from #278)
Page 78 – When 90's Headlines Catch Up with Comic Strips – Gary Fields / Mike Mikula (reprint from #285)
Page 81 – Monster Football League – Mike Ricigliano (reprint from #278)
Page 85 – Cracked's Truly Atrocious Trading Cards – Rurik Tyler / Dan Birtcher (reprint from #282)
Page 88 – Barney: The Missing Episodes – Rob Orzechowski / Eric Goldberg, Mark Howard (reprint from #284)
Page 90 – Self Help Books for Pre-Schoolers – John Severin / Lenore Skenazy (reprint from #279)

Page 92 – Gunforgiven – Walter Brogan / Lou Silverstone (reprint from #278)

Page 98 – The Cracked List 14 Versions of "Last Action Hero" That Would've Been Better – Mike Ricigliano / Link Pershad (reprint from #285)

Page 99 – Looose Leevi's – Tom Grimes / Steve Strangio (reprint from #280)

Back Cover – Marky Mark Bears All – Jeff Wong (reprint from #282)

Cracked Collectors' Edition #101 (*Lion King*), January 1995 (100 pages) ($2.95)

Cover – We Shoot the Lion King! – Walter Brogan (new)

Page 2 and 99 – Toon In! – Gary Fields (reprint from #267)

Page 3 – Contents – Mike Ricigliano

Page 4 – Dink Trazy – Walter Brogan (reprint from #258)

Page 10 – R-Rated Ads for Family Films – Gary Fields / Evelyn Gabai (reprint from #267)

Page 12 – Fairy Tales for the 1990s! – Mike Ricigliano / Roger Brown (reprint from #259)

Page 15 – A Cracked Look at Future Specialized Camps – Frank Borth / Tony Frank (Lou Silverstone) (reprint from #264)

Page 18 – Cracked Takes a Look at the Big Cats of the Big Top – Warren Sattler (reprint from #158)

Page 20 – Spies & Saboteurs Hit the Toons – Mike Ricigliano (reprint from #267)

Page 24 – Cracked's Joy of Working – Pete Fitzgerald / Steve Strangio (reprint from #267)

Page 27 – Harried…with Children – Rob Orzechowski / Rich Kriegel (Lou Silverstone) (reprint from #248)

Page 31 – Wrestling Hype for Boring Sports – Rurik Tyler / Bill Ignizio (reprint from #267)

Page 34 – You Know You're Courting "Big" Trouble When – Don Orehek (reprint from #267)

Page 36 – In Case of Emergency – Warren Sattler (reprint from #160)

Page 38 – A Cracked Look at Phobias – Warren Sattler (reprint from #158)

Page 42 – A Cracked Look at a Backyard Barbecue – Don Orehek (reprint from #155)

Page 44 – Increasing Consumption in Order to Maintain Full Employment – LePoer (John Severin) (reprint from #134)

Page 48 – Shut-Ups (man cannot live on bread) – Don Orehek (reprint from #199)

Page 49 – The Making of the Lion King – Walter Brogan, Chris Bartlett / Lou Silverstone (full color) (new)

Page 53 – A Modern Parent vs. Traditional Parent – Warren Sattler (reprint from #155)

Page 56 – Subscription ad (full color)

Page 57 – Bull & Tad's Excrement Adventure – Rick Altergott (reprint from #253)

Page 62 – The Non-Celebrity Workout Video – Pete Fitzgerald / Paul Giles (reprint from #264)

Page 64 – The Melanie Joy is Missing – John Severin / Jerry De Fuccio (reprint from #264)

Page 68 – Absolutely, Unquestionably, Positively, Undeniably, the Very, Very, Last of The Cracked Lens (and we really, really mean it this time, for sure!) Part XXII (reprint from #199)

Page 72 – Vermin Fight Back – Warren Sattler (reprint from #155)

Page 74 – Roasting Mother Goose (Little Jack Horner) – Vic Martin (reprint from #267)

Page 75 – The Cracked Fix-It Yourself Manual – Bill Ward (reprint from #199)

Page 79 – Orehek at Large on a Field Day at the Zoo – Don Orehek (reprint from #264)

Page 82 – Animal One-Shots – Mike Ricigliano / Roger Brown (reprint from #258)

Page 84 – "The Villain" – Val Mayerik (reprint from #158)

Page 85 – Airline Fares – Warren Sattler (reprint from #160)

Page 88 – Script Your Own Steven Seagul Movie – John Severin / Tony Frank (Lou Silverstone) (reprint from #266)

Page 92 – Cracked Trading Cards for Less Glamorous Professions – Pete Fitzgerald (reprint from #259)

Page 94 – Twits – Walter Brogan (reprint from #245)

Page 98 – Shut-Ups (two cowpokes) – Don Orehek (reprint from #262)

Back Cover – Ye Hang Ups (feed her cats) – John Severin (reprint from #252)

Cracked Collectors' Edition #102 (*Canned Laughter*), April 1995 (100 pages) ($2.95)

Cover – Our Canned Laughter Issue! – Pete Fitzgerald (new)

Page 2 – Anygizer ad – John Severin / Scott Thaler (reprint from #263)

Page 3 – Contents – Mike Ricigliano (red color added)

Page 4 – Sicken of the Sea, Nastea – Pete Fitzgerald / Greg Grabianski (full color) (new)

Page 5 – Cracked Fake-Out Grocery Labels – Pete Fitzgerald / Greg Grabianski (new)

Page 6 – Subscription ad – Frank Borth (full color)

Page 7 – The Naked Bun 2½ The Smell of Beer – Walter Brogan (reprint from #269)

Page 14 – What Rock Stars Were Like as Children – Rob Orzechowski / Joe Catalano (reprint from #238)

Page 16 – Cracked's Guide to Good Eating – Pete Fitzgerald / Howie Mitchell (reprint from #263)

Page 18 – Cracked's New Type Baseball Cards that Tell it Like it is – Howard Nostrand (reprint from #138)

Page 21 – Ass Ventoro, Pest Detective & On Shaky Ground – Walter Brogan / Lou Silverstone (reprint from #291)

Page 26 – Hazards of: (saying the wrong thing) – Mike Ricigliano / Roger Brown (reprint from #255)

Page 28 – "Going Out" Simulation Kits for Stay at Home People – Sean LePeor (John Severin) (reprint from #139)

Page 32 – Golf Oil Company ad (reprint from #169)

Page 33 – Orehek at Large in a Tacky Department Store – Don Orehek (reprint from #262)

Page 36 – Believe it or Not Again (reprint from #183)

Page 38 – Hot Snots! – John Severin / Tony Frank (Lou Silverstone) (reprint from #269)

Page 43 – How is it That? – Warren Sattler (reprint from #199)

Page 46 – The Condemned Man – John Severin (reprint from #64)

Page 47 – Camelsmells Islamic Alphabet Soup – Pete Fitzgerald / Greg Grabianski (full color) (new)

Page 48 – Shut-Ups (slow down) – Don Orehek (reprint from #258) (full color)

Page 49 – Old El Gaso WhoDied? Refried Beans – Pete Fitzgerald / Greg Grabianski (full color) (new)

Page 50 – A Dignified Evening at the Strongarm Social & Unity Club – Mike Ricigliano / Jerry De Fuccio (reprint from #263) (full color)

Page 51 – Peter Pain Sadistic Peanut Butter – Pete Fitzgerald / Greg Grabianski (full color) (new)

Page 52 – Goin' Up the Country – Frank Caruso (reprint from #249) (full color)

Page 53 – Hurt's Womanwich Original Sloppy Jane Sauce – Pete Fitzgerald / Greg Grabianski (full color) (new)

Page 54 – Exclusive Simpsons Interview – John Severin (reprint from #258)

Page 55 – The Simplesons – Gary Fields / Rich Kriegel (Lou Silverstone) (reprint from #257)

Page 59 – The Sabotage Handbook – Mike Ricigliano (reprint from #237)

Page 62 – Your Dentist is Your Friend – Don Orehek (reprint from #158)

Page 64 – Cracked Work Songs for Today's Monotonous Jobs Songbook – Frank Borth / Howie Mitchell (reprint from #266)

Page 68 – It's a Wonderful Laff – Peter McDonnell / Tony Frank (Lou Silverstone) (reprint from #243)

Page 73 – A Cracked Eye View of the Gulf – Rurik Tyler (reprint from #263)

Page 75 – Absolutely, Unquestionably, Positively, Undeniably, the Very, Very, Last of The Cracked Lens (and we really, really mean it this time, for sure!) Part XVIII (reprint from #193)

Page 78 – Cracked Highways for Tourists – Mike Ricigliano / Howie Mitchell (reprint from #261)

Page 80 – On the Beach the Day After with Dr. Strangelove or How I Learned to Live with and Love Roaches – Wally Kubrogan (Walter Brogan) / Rich Kriegel (Lou Silverstone) (reprint from #246)

Page 84 – Bomb Shelters of the Rich & Famous! – Bo Badman (Rurik Tyler) (reprint from #246)

Page 86 – Shut-Ups (I think I can K.O.) – Don Orehek (reprint from #145)

Page 87 – TV Cable Guide Magazine (reprint from #212)

Page 91 – Grossanne – Walter Brogan / Rich Kriegel (Lou Silverstone) (reprint from #244)

Page 95 – Chef Boylardy Fat-Encrusted Heart Shaped Pasta – Pete Fitzgerald / Greg Grabianski (full color) (new)

Page 96 – Jungle Rot – Frank Borth / Scott Thaler (reprint from #262) (full color)

Page 97 – Dumb-Maid Raisins – Pete Fitzgerald / Greg Grabianski (full color) (new)

Page 98 – The Dud Bowl – John Severin / Jerry De Fuccio (reprint from #264) (full color)

Page 99 – Roasting Mother Goose (Jack and Jill) – Vic Martin / Bob Kain (reprint from #268)

Back Cover – Cracked Mutant Turtle Soup Cut-Up! – Rurik Tyler (reprint from #255)

***Cracked Collectors' Edition* #103 (*We Detour Voyager*), July 1995 (84 pages) ($2.95)**

Cover – To Boldly Go Where No Man Has Gone Before – Walter Brogan (gatefold) (new)

Page 2 and 83 – Star Trek Voyajerk Game – Mike Ricigliano (gatefold) (new)

Page 3 – Contents – Mike Ricigliano (pink color added)

Page 4 – Star Drek: Voyeur – Walter Brogan / Lou Silverstone (new)

Page 9 – Beam Us Up, Scotty! – Mike Ricigliano / Roger Brown (reprint from #247)

Page 10 – Star Wreck Deeply Spaced Out Nine – Walter Brogan / Lou Silverstone (reprint from *Cracked Spaced Out* #1)

Page 16 – Star Trek Funnies – Mike Ricigliano / Roger Brown (reprint from #252)

Page 18 – Star Wreck The Next Degeneration – John Severin / Lou Silverstone (reprint from #271)

Page 25 – Star Drek the Next Generation – Mike Ricigliano / Roger Brown (reprint from #247)

Page 26 – Star Drek V The Finite Frontier – Rick Altergott / Tony Frank (Lou Silverstone) (reprint from #252)

Page 31 – I.M.A. Gravs Earthling Zoo – Gene Colan (reprint from #255)

Page 35 – One Day in the Department Store – Mike Ricigliano (reprint from #188)

Page 36 – Unknown Facts About the California Raisins – Rurik Tyler (reprint from #251)

Page 38 – Footboxhockbasetennbasketgolfpoly – John Severin (reprint from #97)

Page 42 – Cracked's Little Known Trivia Facts (reprint from #211)

Page 45 – Lifestyles of the Rich and Famous Toons – Walter Brogan / Steve Strangio (reprint from #270)

Page 48 – A Cracked Look at a College Campus – Al Scaduto (reprint from #214)

Page 50 – Cracked Senator of the Year – Walter Brogan / Lou Silverstone (reprint from #271)

Page 54 – Talking Computer Devices of Tomorrow – Cuz (reprint from #215)

Page 56 – Cracked Survival Primer – LePoer (John Severin) / Vic Bianco (Lou Silverstone) (reprint from #246)

Page 60 – Progress of a Cracked Technophile! – John Severin / Peter Bagge (reprint from #233)

Page 62 – Shut-Ups (wrong man) – Don Orehek (reprint from #256)

Page 63 – Cracked Interviews the Skateboard King – Bill Ward (reprint from #152)

Page 68 – Baby One-Shots – Mike Ricigliano / Roger Brown (reprint from #254)

Page 70 – Don't Even Start!! – Al Scaduto (reprint from #221)

Page 73 – The Arsenico Gall Show – Gary Fields / Lou Silverstone (reprint from #260)

Page 76 – Shut-Ups (big struggle) – Don Orehek (reprint from #168)

Page 77 – Subscription ad – John Severin (reprint from #159) (full color)

Page 78 – Star Trek Voyajerk Game Instructions – Mike Ricigliano (blue and pink color added) (new)

Back Cover – Landing On Mars – Howard Nostrand / Murad Gumen (reprint from #156)

Cracked Collectors' Edition #104 (*Year's Best*), September 1995 (100 pages) ($2.95)

Cover – We Roll Out Our Year's Best – Tom Grimes, John Severin, Walter Brogan / Nathaniel Cardonsky (new)

Page 2 – You Drink Milk and It Shows ad – Ron Barrett (reprint from #291)

Page 3 – Contents – Tom Grimes

Page 4 – Cracked's 187th Annual Year in Review (so far) (new)

Page 8 – The Mighty-Moron Chowder Rangers – John Severin / Greg Grabianski (reprint from #290)

Page 14 – Cracked's Practical Joke Items for Emergency Workers – Gary Fields / Scott Franklin (reprint from #293)

Page 16 – What if Everyone Talked Like a Race Car Driver? – Bruce Bolinger / Eric Bohlen (reprint from #290)

Page 18 – Saturday Morning Commercial Shut-Ups (Rice Krispies) – Don Orehek / Eric Goldberg, Mark Howard (reprint from #291)

Page 19 – Cracked Tattoons – Mike Ricigliano (reprint from #289)

Page 22 – Sin-filled – Walter Brogan / Lou Silverstone (reprint from #290)

Page 28 – New Dance Steps for Urban Street Survival – Rurik Tyler / Barry Zeger (reprint from #292)

Page 30 – What if Comic Strips Featured Guest Stars? – Gary Fields / Ed Subitzky (reprint from #292)

Page 33 – Angels in the Sapfield – John Severin / Andy Simmons (reprint from #295)

Page 38 – New Rules of Thumb! – Pete Fitzgerald / Daniel Birtcher (reprint from #289)

Page 40 – Subscription ad – John Severin (reprint from *Cracked Collectors' Edition* #88)

Page 41 – Crush People's Heads – The Morty Lee Way – Tom Grimes / Eric Goldberg, Mark Howard (reprint from #290)

Page 45 – The Beaver Newspaper – Ron Barrett (reprint from #292)

Page 48 – Prehistoric Cocktail Party – Bruce Bolinger / Lenore Skenazy (reprint from #295)

Page 50 – Spies and Sabs Hit the NFL Game – Mike Ricigliano (reprint from #288)

Page 52 – The Loin King – Walter Brogan (reprint from #294)

Page 58 – Where's Oswaldo? – Rurik Tyler / David Boone (reprint from #294)

Page 60 – Bad Professionals – Randy Jones / Randy Epley (reprint from #295)

Page 62 – Saturday Morning Cartoon Shut-Ups (Don't shoot me!) – Don Orehek / Eric Goldberg, Mark Howard (reprint from #290)

Page 63 – The Simpson – Don Orehek / Greg Grabianski (reprint from #295)

Page 69 – Just Plane Stupid – Terry Colon (reprint from #290)

Page 72 – Desperate Cigarette Ad Campaigns! – Ron Devue (John Severin) – Scott Franklin, Rick Rodgers (reprint from #288)

Page 74 – Drawnout Crime Scenes – Arnoldo Franchioni (reprint from #287)

Page 76 – Peed – Walter Brogan / Lou Silverstone (reprint from #294)

Page 80 – Cracked Goodies – Gary Fields / Rob Weske (reprint from #288)

Page 81 – Cracked's Guide to Specialized Summer Camps! – John Severin / Rob Weske (reprint from #293)

Page 85 – Fashion Pages for Teachers (and Other School Types) – Chris Bartlett / Greg Grabianski (reprint from #294)

Page 88 – Numbtendo's Megaplex Mania – Pete Fitzgerald / Steve Strangio (reprint from #287)

Page 90 – Television Warnings – Jim Bennett / Eric Goldberg, Mark Howard (reprint from #287)

Page 93 – The Fresh Prance of Bel Air – Walter Brogan / Lance Contrucci (reprint from #288)

Page 98 – The Cracked List 10 Toy Ideas That Didn't Make it – Mike Ricigliano / Michael Kaufman (reprint from #295)

Page 99 – Da Diss Dat Made Chester a Gangster – Alan Kupperberg / Barry Zeger (reprint from #295)

Back Cover – A Really Grimm Fairy Tale The Pied Piper of Encino – Jeff Wong (reprint from #287)

Cracked Collectors' Edition #105 (*Cracked Goes to School*), January 1996 (84 pages) ($2.99)

Cover – The School Cafeteria – Jim Bennett (new)

Page 2 – A TV Commercial You'll Never See (Klog's Totally) – John Severin / Spark (reprint from #273)

Page 3 – Contents – Mike Ricigliano

Page 4 – Shnook – John Severin / Lou Silverstone (reprint from #272)

Page 11 – Trasher! Magazine – Brad Joyce / Bo Badman (Rurik Tyler) (reprint from #239)
Page 15 – The 7 Deadly Sins – Phillips Studios (reprint from #258)
Page 18 – The New Fast Food Restaurants – John Severin / Fred Sahner (reprint from #266)
Page 20 – The Final Episode of Comic Strips – Tony Tallarico (reprint from #216)
Page 23 – Doctor Ricig – Mike Ricigliano (reprint from #264)
Page 24 – Cracked's Kid-Vid Clearance – Gary Fields (reprint from #278)
Page 26 – Another Collection of Cracked Baseball Cards – Pete Fitzgerald / Fred Sahner (reprint from #266)
Page 29 – Some Things Never Change – John Severin / George Gladir (reprint from #263)
Page 32 – YuckTales – Gary Fields / John Arcudi (reprint from #236)
Cover – Lethal Weapon 3½ – John Severin (reprint from #275) (full color)
Page 35 – Ill-Legal Weapon 3½ - Walter Brogan / Lou Silverstone (reprint from #275)
Page 41-44 and 82 – Cracked's 3-D Image – Gary Fields, John Severin (full color) (new)
Page 45 – W.M. Gaines Memorial High School – John Severin (reprint from *Cracked Collectors' Edition* #93) (full color)
Page 46 – Cracked's Spy and Sab Bookmarks – Mike Ricigliano (full color) (reprint from *Cracked Collectors' Edition* #93)
Page 51 – Orehek at Large Back to School – Don Orehek / Suzy Orehek (reprint from #269)
Page 54 – Reasons Why We Love School – Bruce Bolinger / Missy Wheathins (new)
Page 58 – Self Help Books for Pre-Schoolers – John Severin / Lenore Skenazy (reprint from #279)
Page 60 – The Cracked Student Profile – Pete Fitzgerald / Steve Strangio (reprint from #276)
Page 62 – The Illiterati – Bruce Bolinger / Andy Simmons (reprint from #276)
Page 66 – Orehek at Large in a Grade School – Don Orehek (reprint from #263) Page 68 – Don't Ya Hate – Gary Fields (reprint from #269)
Page 70 – Cracked Classroom TV Scream – John Severin / George Gladir (reprint from #255)
Page 73 – Cracked's Plan to Help Our Schools – Don Orehek / George Gladir (reprint from #277)
Page 76 – Awards for School Kids – Bill McCartney (Bill Ward) (reprint from #77)

Page 80 – The Joy of Cheating – Bruce Bolinger / Daniel O'Keefe (reprint from *Cracked Collectors' Edition* #93)

Page 83 – Subscription ad – John Severin (reprint from #159)

Back Cover – Great Moments in Education 2021 – Jeff Wong (reprint from #276)

Cracked Collectors' Edition #106 (*Best of Cracked TV*), April 1996 (100 pages) ($2.99)

Cover – We Go Channel-Surfing – John Severin (new)

Page 2 – A TV Commercial You'll Never See (Milk) – Walter Brogan / Spark (reprint from #269)

Page 3 – Contents – Mike Ricigliano

Page 4 – Grossanne: the Second Helping – John Severin / Greg Grabianski (reprint from #291)

Page 9 – Shut-Ups (for your muffler) – Don Orehek / Lou Silverstone (reprint from #278)

Page 10 – The Cracked Vidiot Musick Awards – Pete Fitzgerald / Paul Castiglia (reprint from #271)

Page 14 – Familiar Patter – Walter Brogan / Lou Silverstone (reprint from #265)

Page 19 – The Replacement Shows – John Severin / Steve Strangio (reprint from #271)

Page 22 – Cracked Interviews The Simpsons – Gary Fielding (Gary Fields) / Lou Silverstoning (Lou Silverstone) (reprint from #258)

Page 25 – The Cracked List 47 Future Sequels to "Saved By the Bell – The College Years" – Mike Ricigliano (reprint from #291)

Page 26 – Kops – John Severin / Greg Grabianski (reprint from #289)

Page 31 – NCC-1701-D Today (A Message from the Captain's Desk) – Rurik Tyler / Steve Strangio (reprint from *Cracked Spaced Out* #1)

Page 34 – SeaPest DDT – Bruce Bolinger / Lou Silverstone (reprint from *Cracked Spaced Out* #3)

Page 39 – Spies and Saboteurs Hit TV – Mike Ricigliano (reprint from #273)

Page 42 – America's Crummiest Home Videos – Vic Martin / Charles E. Hall (reprint from #257)

Page 46 – Cracked's Personalized Remotes – Terry Colon (reprint from #279)

Page 49 – The Saturday Morning TV Show Awards – Walter Brogan / Andy Simmons (full color) (new)

Page 53 – Barney Has a Snack – Don Orehek / Rob Weske (reprint from #285)

Page 54 – Smurphy Brown – John Severin / Vic Bianco (Lou Silverstone) (reprint from #260)

Page 59 – Accessories for the TV Football Freak – Bill Ward (reprint from #114)

Page 63 – Some Improvement – Walter Brogan / Tony Frank (Lou Silverstone) (reprint from #273)

Page 69 – If T.V. Warnings Appeared in Everyday Life – Don Orehek (reprint from #191)

Page 72 – Shut-Ups (SLOOP-SUP) – Don Orehek (reprint from #260)

Page 73 – Beers – John Severin / Andy Simmons (reprint from #282)

Page 78 – Instant Talk Show – Jeff Wong / Lenore Skenazy (reprint from #277)

Page 80 – Blossomed – Walter Brogan / Steve Strangio (reprint from #284)

Page 85 – A Cracked Interview with a Minor-League Manager – Bruce Bolinger / Randy Epley (reprint from #284)

Page 88 – Aquatic Leap – John Severin / Eric Goldberg, Mark Howard (reprint from #280)

Page 92 – TV Gameshows Through History – Pete Fitzgerald / Rob Weske (reprint from #282)

Page 94 – America's Most Daunted – Rurik Tyler / Judd Stomp (reprint from #287)

Page 99 – Subscription ad – John Severin (reprint from #160)

Back Cover – Bitterfinger ad – Gary Fields / Lou Silverstone (reprint from #272)

Cracked Collectors' Edition #107 (*It's Our Gross Issue!*), July 1996 (84 pages) ($2.99)

Cover – Gross – John Severin (new)

Page 2 – The Lonely Convict and the Pet – Oskar Blotta (reprint from #141)

Page 3 – Contents – Mike Ricigliano

Page 4 – Wayne's Hurled – John Severin / Lou Silverstone (reprint from #273)

Page 9 – Pet Movie Remakes – Pete Fitzgerald / Lenore Skenazy (reprint from #275)

Page 12 – How Governments Work – Mike Ricigliano / Roger Brown (reprint from #257)

Page 14 – Celebrity Garbage – John Severin (reprint from #131)

Page 18 – Judo – Jack Davis (reprint from #11)

Page 21 – Cracked to the Future Part III – John Severin / Tony Frank (Lou Silverstone) (reprint from #258)

Page 27 – Random Funnies (having a sale) – Mike Ricigliano / Roger Brown (reprint from #255)

Page 28 – Flip Flop – Rurik Tyler / George Gladir (reprint from #251)

Page 30 – Daredevils, Stuntmen and Stand-Ins – Arnoldo Franchioni (reprint from #274)
Page 33 – National Pooch Press & Tabby Tattler – Vic Martin / George Gladir (reprint from #265)
Page 37 – The Hunt for Rad Crackedober – Walter Brogan / Tony Frank (Lou Silverstone) (reprint from #256)
Page 42 – Viering Off (Billy the Squid) – Gary Fields / Jed Vier (reprint from #273)
Insert – Gross Section – John Severin (reprint from #273) (full color, glossy)
Insert – Cracked's Gross Pig Test – Bruce Bolinger / Barry Zeger (full color, glossy) (new)
Page 43 – Cracked Interviews the Grossout King! – Rob Orzechowski / Joe Catalano (reprint from #229)
Page 47 – Rodrigues' Hospital-ity – Charles Rodrigues (reprint from #110)
Page 50 – Sparky's Dog House Placemat – Bruce Bolinger / Lenore Skenazy (reprint from #279)
Page 52 – The Cracked Top Ten List Least Popular Ballpark Promotional Dates – Mike Ricigliano (reprint from #275)
Page 53 – Zit Happens! Starring Macaulay Culkin – Rurik Tyler / Andy Simmons (reprint from #278)
Page 56 – Warning Labels for People – Pete Fitzgerald / Eric Goldberg, Mark Howard (reprint from #278)
Page 58 – The Fast Food Wars! – Gary Fields / Paul Castiglia (reprint from #273)
Page 61 – Rock and Roll Mutations! – Bob Fingerman / Hilary Zatz (reprint from #231)
Page 64 – That Snot Funny – Arnoldo Franchioni (new)
Page 66 – Jeraldo Revoltin's Guide to Be an Expert at Trash TV – Rob Orzechowski / Joe Catalano (reprint from #245)
Page 69 – End of Gross Section – Mike Ricigliano (new)
Page 70 – Book Reports of the Rich and Famous – John Severin / Lenore Skenazy (reprint from #273)
Page 72 – Cracked Mental Implant Fantasies – Pete Fitzgerald / George Gladir (reprint from #262)
Page 75 – It Happened on Main and First – Caracu (reprint from #103)
Page 76 – Rockey – John Severin (reprint from #143)
Page 82 – Shut-Ups (My debts) – Mike Ricigliano (reprint from #143)
Page 83 – Subscription ad – Jeff Wong (reprint from #305)
Back Cover – Great Moments in Science 1699 – Mike Ricigliano (reprint from #138)

Cracked Collectors' Edition #108 (*Year's Best*), **September 1996 (100 pages) ($2.99)**

Cover – Year's Best – John Severin (new with reprint from #296 and #301)

Page 2 – *Cracked Summer Special* #6 ad

Page 3 – Contents – Mike Ricigliano

Page 4 – Friendzy – Walter Brogan / Greg Grabianski (reprint from #304)

Page 10 – Cracked Bell's New Phone Services – Pete Fitzgerald / Eric Goldberg, Mark Howard (reprint from #303)

Page 12 – MFL Hall of Fame – Mike Ricigliano (reprint from #295)

Page 14 – How the Gingrinch Stole Congress! – Gary Fields / Lenore Skenazy (reprint from #298)

Page 18 – The Techno-Geek Geeks – Bruce Bolinger / Mike Mikula (reprint from #303)

Page 20 – Moron Kombat – John Severin / Andy Simmons (reprint from #303)

Page 27 – Cracked Valentine's Day Cards – Randy Jones / Randy Epley (reprint from #298)

Page 29 – Trojan Horse Designs that Didn't Quite Make it – Terry Colon (reprint from #296)

Page 33 – The Lost Batman Villains Files – Pete Fitzgerald / Rob Weske (reprint from #302)

Page 36 – Shut-Ups (Hey, Bro) – Don Orehek / Eric Goldberg, Mark Howard (reprint from #300)

Page 37 – Cracked's Militia Man of the Year – Bruce Bolinger / Lou Silverstone (reprint from #302)

Page 42 – The Cracked Guide to Professional Jargon – Randy Jones / Lenore Skenazy (reprint from #303)

Page 44 – Family Mob Values – Arnoldo Franchioni (reprint from #302)

Page 45 – The Lyons Township Imbecile – Tom Grimes / Greg Grabianski (reprint from #303)

Page 50 – Spies and Sabs Hit the Toy Store – Mike Ricigliano (reprint from #297)

Page 52 – Subscription ad – John Severin (reprint from *Cracked Collectors' Edition* #88)

Page 53 – Duh-mb and Duh-mber – Walter Brogan / Lou Silverstone (reprint from #299)

Page 59 – Doom and Doomer – Rurik Tyler / Todd Jackson, Andy Simmons (reprint from #300)

Page 64 – The Cracked List 10 Superheroes and Their Not-So-Super Day Jobs – Mike Ricigliano (reprint from #300)

Page 65 – Rules for Making Soccer Less Boring – John Severin / Rob Weske (reprint from #299)

Page 69 – Scientific Principles That Every Kid Knows – Pete Fitzgerald / Darren Johnson (reprint from #301)

Page 72 – Frozen – Walter Brogan / Greg Grabianski (reprint from #297)

Page 77 – Creative Casting Ideas for Future Hollywood Remakes and Sequels – Gunnar Johnson (reprint from #304)

Page 80 – The Beginner's Guide to Roller Hockey – Mike Ricigliano (reprint from #302)

Page 85 – Apollogy 13 – John Severin / Lou Silverstone (reprint from #302)

Page 91 – Catchy Jingles for Unpleasant Yet Necessary Products – Bruce Bolinger / Barry Zeger (reprint from #296)

Page 94 – Barf, Man. Forever! – Walter Brogan / Lou Silverstone (reprint from *Cracked Super* #10)

Page 98 – Tennis, Anyone? – J. Kelly (reprint from #304)

Page 99 – Breast Milk What a Surprise! – Officer Smythe, LAPD (reprint from #304)

Back Cover – John Madden Free Agency Football – Jeff Wong / Missy Wheathins (reprint from #300)

Cracked Collectors' Edition #109 (*Video Game Special*), January 1997 (100 pages) ($2.99)

Cover – We Level Nintendo 64! – John Severin (new)

Page 2 – The Special on Aisle 9 – Bruce Bolinger (reprint from #282)

Page 3 – Contents – Mike Ricigliano

Page 4 – Cracked Interviews Mario of Ninnytendo – Frank Cummings / Todd Jackson (new)

Page 8 – Jobs Video Games Will Prepare You For – Pete Fitzgerald / Paul Giles (reprint from #280)

Page 10 – Video Games We'll Soon Be Seeing – Howard Nostrand (reprint from #141)

Page 12 – A Cracked Numbtendo Video Game Shopping Mall Adventure – Pete Fitzgerald / Steve Strangio (reprint from #269)

Page 15 – SamePro Magazine – Rurik Tyler / Eric Goldberg, Mark Howard, Odd Todd (reprint from #301)

Page 22 – Virtual-Reality Games We Won't Be So Quick to Try – Pete Fitzgerald / Greg Grabianski (reprint from #291)

Page 24 – Lifestyles of the Rich and Violent – Rurik Tyler / Judd Stomp (reprint from #291)

Page 28 – The Family Gathering of Doom – Pete Fitzgerald / Steve Strangio (reprint from #274)

Page 31 – Another Cracked Look at a Video Arcade – Sururi Gumen (reprint from #208)

Page 34 – Meat-Fighter – John Severin (reprint from #297)

Page 39 – Cracked's Uses for Used Computers – Mike Ricigliano / Roger Brown (reprint from #258)
Page 41 – Video Games & Equipment of the Future IV! – Pete Fitzgerald / George Gladir (reprint from #256)
Page 45 – Super Mario Brothers: The Movie – Walter Brogan / Andy Simmons (reprint from *Cracked Summer Special* #3)
Page 50 – Spies and Sabs Hit the Video Arcade – Mike Ricigliano (reprint from #291)
Page 52 – Easy-to-Read EKG Readings For – John Severin / Rob Weske (reprint from #283)
Page 54 – Proper Football Safety Techniques – Rurik Tyler / Andy Simmons (reprint from #279)
Page 57 – Cracked's Joy of Sports – Pete Fitzgerald / Fred Sahner (reprint from #265)
Page 60 – You Know the Clear Products Trend Has Gone Too Far When – John Severin / Dan Birtcher (reprint from #286)
Page 62 – Totally Recalled – Walter Brogan (reprint from #258)
Page 67 – Ye Hang Ups (Oh No NO!) – John Severin (reprint from #267)
Page 68 – Einstein's Other Theories of Relativity – Frank Borth / Larry Macloud (reprint from #278)
Page 70 – Hello, Columbus! – Arnoldo Franchioni (reprint from #277)
Page 73 – The High Lama – Eric Cartier / Tom Bacas (reprint from #220)
Page 74 – Spies and Saboteurs Hit a Political Convention – Mike Ricigliano (reprint from #276)
Page 76 – Hackdraft – John Severin / Tony Frank (Lou Silverstone) (reprint from #267)
Page 82 – After-School Job Opportunities – Ron Barrett (reprint from #280)
Page 84 – Cracked's Saturday Morning TV Review – Walter Brogan / Judd Stomp (reprint from #287)
Page 86 – The Fuzzy Image Catalogue – John Severin / Lance Contrucci (reprint from #274)
Page 89 – Ye Hang Ups #77 (small serving) – John Severin (reprint from #219)
Page 90 – If There Was Truth in Advertising – Gary Fields / Gayle Adams-Pierpont (reprint from #281)
Page 92 – Ill-Legal Weapons – Walter Brogan / Vic Bianco (Lou Silverstone) (reprint from #251)
Page 98 – The Cracked List 14 Tipoffs That You're Dating Princess Di – Mike Ricigliano / Dan Birtcher (reprint from #283)
Page 99 – Subscription ad – Frank Borth
Back Cover – Immoral Kombat – Rurik Tyler / Steve Strangio (reprint from #288)

Cracked Collectors' Edition #110 (*101 Dalmatians / Mars Attacks*), **April 1997 (84 pages) ($2.99)**

Cover – We Stink Up 101 Dalmatians! – Frank Cummings, Rurik Tyler (new)

Page 2 – Muttonna…The Puppy Tour – Bruce Bolinger (reprint from *Cracked Collectors' Edition* #98)

Page 3 – Contents – Mike Ricigliano

Page 4 – Dizzy's 101 Dullmatians – Bruce Bolinger / Andy Simmons (new)

Page 10 – The Dog House (reprint from #65)

Page 12 – Cats Are People Too! – P.C. Vey (reprint from #280)

Page 13 – Dogs Magazine – John Severin (reprint from #74)

Page 21 – Man's Best Friend – Bernard Baily (reprint from #106)

Page 23 – Beerbellythoven's 2nd – Bruce Bolinger / Andy Simmons (reprint from *Cracked Collectors' Edition* #98)

Page 27 – Cracked's Creative Concepts for Jump-Starting the Economy – Mike Ricigliano (reprint from #285)

Page 30 – Pez Dispensers That Didn't Quite Make it – John Severin / Eric Goldberg, Mark Howard (reprint from #285)

Page 32 – Sports Strikes for '97! – Tom Short (reprint from #218) (originally called "Sports Strikes for '86!")

Page 35 – Script Your Own Steven Seagul Movie – John Severin / Tony Frank (Lou Silverstone) (reprint from #266)

Page 39 – Shakespearean Shut-Ups (To be, or not to be) – Don Orehek / Dan Birtcher (new)

Page 40 – Miniature Golf from Hell!! – Rob Barrett (reprint from #287)

Page 42 and Insert – Cracked Monster Attacks Cards! – Rurik Tyler, Mike Ricigliano / Steve Strangio (full color, card stock) (new)

Page 43 – The Cracked List 10 Most Unpopular Tropical Island Activities at Club Med – Mike Ricigliano / Greg Grabianski (reprint from #290)

Page 44 – A Few Odd Men – John Severin / Lou Silverstone (reprint from #281)

Page 50 – Slimeco Chemical and Food Industries Presents Genetically Enhanced Food for the 90's – Bruce Bolinger / Joseph O'Brien (reprint from #282)

Page 52 – Landmark Remodeling – Terry Colon (reprint from #283)

Page 56 – More Shakespearean Shut-Ups (Damn Spot!) – Don Orehek / Dan Birtcher (reprint from #288)

Page 57 – Disaster Movies You May Be Soon Seeing – John Severin (reprint from #128)

Page 60 – The Family Profile – Pete Fitzgerald / Steve Strangio (reprint from #284)

Page 62 – Tabloids Through History – Bruce Bolinger / David Levesçue (reprint from #288)

Page 64 – Screwge – Wally Dickens Brogan (Walter Brogan) / Vic Bianco (Lou Silverstone) (reprint from #243)

Page 68 – Great Views from Your Typical Airline Coach Seat – John Severin / Jim Bauer (reprint from #282)

Page 70 – Put Your Best Foot Back! – Mike Ricigliano (reprint from #228)

Page 71 – Cracked Guide to Guitars! – John Severin / Charles E. Hall (reprint from #228)

Page 75 – Arctic Antic – Henry Boltinoff (reprint from #243)

Page 76 – Barney: The Missing Episodes – Rob Orzechowski / Eric Goldberg, Mark Howard (reprint from #284)

Page 78 – Rookie of the Weird – Walter Brogan / Andy Simmons (reprint from #286)

Page 83 – Subscription ad – John Severin (reprint from #260)

Back Cover – Have You Hugged Your Human Today? – Rurik Tyler (reprint from *Cracked Collectors' Edition* #98)

***Cracked Collectors' Edition* #111 (*The Internet*), July 1997 (100 pages) ($2.99)**

Cover – We Salute the Internet – Pete Fitzgerald (new)

Page 2 – A TV Commercial You'll Never See! (UT&T) – John Severin / R. Rhine (reprint from #293)

Page 3 – Contents – Mike Ricigliano

Page 4 – Cracked Salutes the Internet (new)

Page 5 – Cracked's Guide to the Internet – Frank Cummings / Greg Grabianski (new)

Page 11 – An Owner and a Player Negotiating a Contract – Ron Zalme (reprint from #194) (originally called "An Owner and a Player Negotiating a Contract 1982")

Page 12 – If More Holidays Were Combined – Bruce Bolinger / Judd Stomp (reprint from #286)

Page 14 – Tomorrow's High-Tech Gadgets for Couch-Potato Sports Fans – John Severin / George Gladir (reprint from #284)

Page 17 – Cracked Evolution Revolution – Mike Ricigliano (reprint from #194)

Page 20 – NYPD Blue Moon – Walter Brogan / Lou Silverstone (reprint from #293)

Page 25 – Curses for Our Time – Ron Barrett (reprint from #290)

Page 28 – More Press Mistakes! (Lady Diana) – John Langton (reprint from #185)

Page 30 – The Cracked History of Aviation – Bill Ward (reprint from #185)

Page 34 – Cyber Love – Bruce Bolinger / Todd Jackson (new)

Page 35 – Doomed III Hell Up in High School – Pete Fitzgerald / Eric Goldberg, Mark Howard (reprint from #304)
Page 38 – The Cosby Show – John Severin (reprint from #224)
Page 43 – The Difference Between Upper Class & Middle Class – Warren Sattler (reprint from #186)
Page 46 – When 90's Headlines Catch Up with Comic Strips – Gary Fields / Mike Mikula (reprint from #285)
Page 49 – Barney Has a Snack – Don Orehek / Rob Weske (reprint from #285)
Page 50 – Spies and Saboteurs Hit School – Mike Ricigliano (reprint from #286)
Page 52 – Cracked's Sneaker Manufacturer of the Year – Walter Brogan / Lou Silverstone (reprint from #289)
Page 56 – Talking Vending Machines – Sururi Gumen (reprint from #188)
Page 58 – Rule the School! – Pete Fitzgerald / Steve Strangio (reprint from #277)
Page 60 – Spies and Saboteurs Hit Baseball – Mike Ricigliano (reprint from #265)
Page 63 – The Three Moosekateers – John Severin (reprint from #205)
Page 70 – Cracked's Video Cartoon Showcase – Jeff Keate (reprint from #194)
Page 72 – Future Crocodile Dundee Movies – Gray Morrow / George Gladir (reprint from #228)
Page 75 – Bragging Rights – Bruce Bolinger / Todd Jackson (new)
Page 76 – Signs That It's a Computer Age – Warren Sattler (reprint from #199)
Page 78 – Remote Controls We'll Soon Be Seeing! – Gray Morrow / George Gladir (reprint from #249)
Page 82 – A Cracked Look at Household Chores – Samuel B. Whitehead (reprint from #188)
Page 85 – Cracked's Joy of Sports – Pete Fitzgerald / Fred Sahner (reprint from #265)
Page 88 – Cracked Horses Around – Arnoldo Franchioni (reprint from #268)
Page 90 – It Wasn't So Long Ago When – John Severin / Bill Ignizio (reprint from #268)
Page 92 – Sin-filled – Walter Brogan / Lou Silverstone (reprint from #290)
Page 98 – The First Interactive Cracked Article – Gary Fields / Todd Jackson (new)
Page 99 – Subscription ad – Jeff Wong (reprint from #305)
Back Cover – NBA Scam – Rurik Tyler (new)

Cracked Collectors' Edition #112 (*Year's Best*), September 1997 (100 pages) ($2.99)

Page 66 – McPoop's Dilemma – J. Kelly (reprint from #311)

Page 67 – Killer Stinky Instruction Booklet – Rurik Tyler / Steve Strangio (reprint from #308)

Page 72 – Subscription ad – John Severin (reprint from #44)

Page 73 – Ass Venturda: When Nature Fails – Walter Brogan / Lou Silverstone (reprint from #305)

Page 80 – The Real Handbook of School Decorum – Frank Cummings / Greg Grabianski (reprint from #312)

Page 84 – Cracked's American Hand Signing – Bruce Bolinger (reprint from #312)

Page 85 – Comic Book vs. Comic Strip Crossover Battles! – Alan Kupperberg / Judd Stomp (reprint from #307)

Page 89 – Aphorisms from Round the World – Randy Jones / Lenore Skenazy (reprint from #305)

Page 92 – Oy, Whatta Story – John Severin / Andy Simmons (reprint from #306)

Page 98 – The Cracked List 11 Oscar Categories We Don't Hear About – Mike Ricigliano / Todd Jackson (reprint from #308)

Page 99 – Dole and Clinton Vie for the Youth Vote – Jeff Wong (reprint from #313)

Back Cover – Coffin Stickers – Frank Cummings (new)

Cracked Collectors' Edition #113 (*Football Special*), January 1998 (68 pages) ($2.99)

Cover – Football Special – Frank Cummings (new)

Page 2 – Great Moments in Sports 1972 – Howard Nostrand (reprint from #150)

Page 3 – Contents – Mike Ricigliano

Page 4 – A Cracked Peek at Monday Night Football – Bruce Bolinger / Rob Weske (reprint from #306)

Page 8 – The Bloody Ryan Smashmouth NFL Playbook – Mike Ricigliano (reprint from #304)

Page 12 – The Cracked Guide to Football – Howard Nostrand (reprint from #140)

Page 17 – Jock State University Bulletin – Warren Sattler (reprint from #183)

Page 20 – The Growing Complexity of Pro Football – Don Orehek (reprint from #67)

Page 24 – New NFL Rules – Bruce Bolinger (reprint from #297)

Page 26 – R.I.P. Pallbearer, All-Transylvanian – Walter Brogan / Lou Silverstone (reprint from *Cracked Monster Party* #23)

Page 30 – Shut-Ups (pull them offside) – Don Orehek (reprint from #261)

Page 31 – Monster Sports Card Collector's Guide – Mike Ricigliano (reprint from #286)

Page 34 – Why is This Man Laughing? – Frank Cummings (new)

Insert – Cracked Football Guidebook – Mike Ricigliano, Terry Colon, Al Shwump / Todd Jackson, Cliff Mott, Lou Silverstone, Andy Simmons (full color, glossy covers, half size, 16 pages) (new)

Page 35 – Your High School Reunion – Pete Fitzgerald / Patric Abedin (reprint from #286)

Page 38 – Memphis Bull! – John Severin (reprint from #261)

Page 44 – Cracked's Guide to Subspecies of Everyday Imbeciles and Idiots – Walter Brogan / Barry Zeger (reprint from #291)

Page 46 – You Know You're a Robot – Brad Joyce / George Gladir (reprint from #226)

Page 48 – Feed Whaley – Jeff Wong / Vic Bianco (Lou Silverstone) (reprint from #286)

Page 52 – Who in the World Decided That – Arnoldo Franchioni (reprint from #194)

Page 54 – Cracked's Practical Joke Items for Emergency Workers – Gary Fields / Scott Franklin (reprint from #293)

Page 56 – The Animal Rights Debate – Randy Jones / Lenore Skenazy (reprint from #292)

Page 58 – Ill Literacy – Arnoldo Franchioni (reprint from #286)

Page 59 – Farewell M*A*S*H*E*D a Cracked Remembrance – John Severin (reprint from #194)

Page 66 – Shut-Ups (pole-vaulting) – Don Orehek (reprint from #194)

Page 67 – Subscription ad – John Severin (reprint from *Cracked Collectors' Edition* #85)

Back Cover – The Salad Bowl – John Severin / Jerry De Fuccio (reprint from #264) (originally called "The Dud Bowl")

***Cracked Collectors' Edition* #114 (*NHL Crashes Olympics*), April 1998 (100 pages) ($2.99)**

Cover – NHL Crashes Olympics – Walter Brogan (new)

Page 2 – The Day the Paulsbury Doughboy's Oven Overheated! – John Severin / Scott Thaler (reprint from #266)

Page 3 – Contents – Mike Ricigliano

Page 4 – Team NHL Goes to the Olympics – Pete Fitzgerald / Link Pershad (new)

Page 5 – 1998 Winter Olympic Guide – Rurik Tyler / Greg Grabianski (new)

Page 10 – Things You Hate So Much – Mike Ricigliano / Roger Brown (reprint from #257)

Page 12 – Rejected Cracked Covers – John Severin / George Gladir (reprint from #257)

Page 14 – Mighty Dorks 2½ - Walter Brogan (reprint from *Cracked Collectors' Edition* #99)
Page 20 – Spies and Saboteurs Hit the Winter Olympics Part I – Mike Ricigliano (reprint from #271)
Page 21 – The Winter Exhibition at the Buffalo Museum of Art – John Severin / Mike Ricigliano (reprint from #298)
Page 24 – New Cracked Dances! – Al Scaduto (reprint from #222)
Page 26 – The Cracked List 13 Ways to Know You've Had Enough of Winter – Mike Ricigliano / Andy Simmons (reprint from #280)
Page 27 – Paint Gunner Magazine – Pete Fitzgerald / Matt Sweney (reprint from #255)
Page 31 – Canine the Barbarian (the most savage barbarian) – Gary Fields (reprint from #225)
Page 34 – The Forrest Gump Scrapbook – Randy Jones / Mike Mikula (reprint from #296)
Page 36 – Cobrat – Bill Wray / Mort Todd (reprint from #225)
Page 42 – Advertising Fantasy vs. Everyday Reality – Pete Fitzgerald / Barry Zeger (reprint from #293)
Page 44 – When an Owner Sez…He Really Means – Bruce Bolinger / Lou Silverstone (reprint from #291)
Page 46 – The Fightin' Cracked Lens! – Randy Epley (new)
Page 49 – The NHL Goes to the Olympics (in Nagano, Japan) – Mike Ricigliano (new)
Page 52 – Cracked Interviews Broke Shields the Glamour Queen! – Rob Orzechowski / Moe McMahon (Marian McMahon) (reprint from #226)
Page 56 – Celebrity Phobias! – Frank Caruso (reprint from #222)
Page 58 – Ye Hang Ups (Guards!) – John Severin (reprint from #251)
Page 59 – Cracked Multi-Mini-Plex – Walter Brogan / Linc Pershad (reprint from #252)
Page 62 – Taking it Literally – Mike Ricigliano / Roger Brown (reprint from #251)
Page 64 – The Cracked Guide to Ice Skating – John Severin (reprint from #168)
Page 68 – Real Life Nature Tapes – Pete Fitzgerald / Aimee Keillor (reprint from #298)
Page 70 – Before Heimlich! – Vic Martin (reprint from #222)
Page 71 – Goonlighting – Bob Fingerman / Stu Schwartzberg (reprint from #226)
Page 76 – Hollywood Sports Fantasy vs. Everyday Reality – Walter Brogan / Barry Zeger (reprint from #297)
Page 79 – TV Sets for Watching Specific TV Shows! – John Severin / Charles E. Hall (reprint from #254)

Page 83 – The Silly Cosbey Show – John Severin (reprint from #212)

Page 86 – Shut-Ups (little off the top) – Don Orehek (reprint from #217)

Page 87 – G.I. Joke in Peace, Love & Harmony – Shawn Kerri (reprint from #225)

Page 92 – Sylvester's Corner The Rubber Duck – Kevin Sacco (reprint from #222)

Page 93 – Untouchy Bulls! – John Severin / Mort Todd (reprint from #233)

Page 98 – Spies and Saboteurs Hit the Winter Olympics Part II – Mike Ricigliano (reprint from #271)

Page 99 – Subscription ad – Walter Brogan (reprint from #279)

Back Cover – Olympic Thumb Wrestling – Jeff Wong / Eric Goldberg, Mark Howard (partial reprint from *Cracked Collectors' Edition* #99)

Cracked Collectors' Edition #115 (*Tomb Raider*), July 1998 (84 pages) ($2.99)

Cover – Tomb Raider of the Lost Video Games – Rurik Tyler (new)

Page 2 – The Truth About Pac-Man (reprint from #196)

Page 3 – Contents – Mike Ricigliano

Page 4 – Cracked Gallery of Fun Products You Can't Live Without – Bruce Bolinger (reprint from #301)

Page 5 – Tomb Raider III – Frank Cummings / Todd Jackson (full color) (new)

Page 9 – Ye Hang Ups (starting to resent) – John Severin (reprint from #252)

Page 10 – Shoe Biz is Going Show Biz! – Bill Ward / George Gladir (reprint from #255)

Page 13 – Cracked Video Games – Pete Fitzgerald / Steve Strangio (reprint from *Cracked Summer Special* #3) (full color)

Page 17 – Cracked's Fantastic Facts – Walter Brogan / Bill Ignizio (reprint from #272)

Page 19 – Recipes from Celebrity Cookbooks – Tom Grimes / Ricky Sprague (reprint from #305)

Page 22 – Traitors of the Lost Ark – John Severin (reprint from #183)

Page 30 – Cracked on Safari – Arnoldo Franchioni (reprint from #272)

Page 32 – Rule the School! – Pete Fitzgerald / Steve Strangio (reprint from #277)

Page 34 – The "How to Insult" Manual – Powers (John Severin) (reprint from #148)

Page 38 – Battle of the Tattoo Artists – Mike Ricigliano (reprint from #258)

Page 39 – Cracked's Joy of Sports – Pete Fitzgerald / Fred Sahner (reprint from #265)

Page 42 – Spies and Sabs Hit the World Cup – Mike Ricigliano (reprint from #292)

Page 44 – Indianapolis Bones and the Temple of Gloom – John Severin (reprint from #208)

Page 51 – Spy and Saboteur at Echo Canyon – Mike Ricigliano (reprint from #256)

Page 52 – Awkward Moments for Limbs to Fall Off (Archie Bunker) – Gray Morrow / Ricky Sprague (reprint from #296)

Page 53 – Ill-Legal Weapon 3½ - Walter Brogan / Lou Silverstone (reprint from #275)

Page 58 – The Back Room of the Hall of Fame – Bruce Bolinger / Andy Simmons (reprint from #285)

Page 60 – Road Sign – Mike Ricigliano / Roger Brown (reprint from #253)

Page 61 – Kops – John Severin / Greg Grabianski (reprint from #289)

Page 66 – Bizarre Business Cards We Hope We Never See – Terry Colon (reprint from #289)

Page 68 – The Water Skier – Don Orehek / Rob Weske (reprint from #296)

Page 69 – The Spy and Saboteur Reunion Photo – Mike Ricigliano (reprint from #239) (full color)

Page 70 – Where's Weirdo Poster – Rurik Tyler (reprint from *Cracked Blockbuster* #6) (full color)

Page 72 – Subscription ad – Jeff Wong (reprint from #305)

Page 73 – Indiana Bones and the Loot Crusade – Walter Brogan / Tony Frank (Lou Silverstone) (reprint from #249)

Page 78 – The Cracked List 11 Baseball Mascots that Didn't Work Out – Mike Ricigliano (reprint from #292)

Back Cover – Fighter Beat Magazine – Walter Brogan (reprint from #297)

Cracked Collectors' Edition #116 (*Years Best*), July 1998 (84 pages) ($2.99)

Cover – We Chews Our Years Best – Walter Brogan, Jeff Wong, John Severin (new and reprint from #315, 316, 318, 319)

Page 2 – Cartoon Makeovers – Gary Fields / Mike Ricigliano (reprint from #315)

Page 3 – Contents – Mike Ricigliano

Page 4 – Meet Our Guest Editors – Walter Brogan (new)

Page 5 – The Ecchhh Files – Walter Brogan / Lou Silverstone (reprint from #318)

Page 11 – Rejected Kids Meals – John Severin / Rob Weske (reprint from #314)

Page 14 – Cracked Visits a Modern Hospital – Frank Cummings / Fred Sahner (reprint from #320)

Page 16 – The Stupid Idiot's Guide to Watching Football – Mike Ricigliano (reprint from #314)
Page 20 – Police Line-Ups Around the World (and Beyond) – Terry Colon (reprint from #314)
Page 22 – The Loot World Jurassick Park – John Severin / Lou Silverstone (reprint from #319)
Page 28 – Dog's Best Friend – Don Orehek / Kit Lively (reprint from #320)
Page 29 – Batgirl's Super Rules – Pete Fitzgerald / Todd Jackson (reprint from #321)
Page 32 – Unique Suicide Techniques – Oskar Blotta / Luciano Blotta (reprint from #315)
Page 34 – Leech Lake Camp – Ron Barrett (reprint from #320)
Page 38 – Self-Hurt Books – Randy Jones / Oliver Fultz (reprint from #319)
Page 40 – Beaver & Putz-Head Dupe America – Walter Brogan / Judd Stomp (reprint from #315)
Page 46 – Men in Black Manual – Frank Cummings / Andy Simmons (reprint from #322)
Page 50 – Spies and Sabs Hit the Star Wars Bar – Mike Ricigliano (reprint from #316)
Page 52 – Subscription ad – John Severin (reprint from *Cracked Collectors' Edition* #88)
Page 53 – Lawyer, Lawyer – Nireves (John Severin) (reprint from #317)
Page 58 – Cracked Clip (Vice Girls) – Cliff Mott / Barry Zeger (reprint from #321)
Page 60 – Diary of a Tamgotchi Owner – Bruce Bolinger / Mike Lotter (reprint from #321)
Page 64 – Somber Toddler's Book Club – Rurik Tyler / Lenore Skenazy, Oliver Fultz (reprint from #322)
Page 66 – McPoop's New Fall Sneezin' – J. Kelly (reprint from #314)
Page 67 – Field & Streaming Blood Magazine – John Severin / Greg Grabianski (reprint from #322)
Page 72 – The Upside and Downside of Future Inventions – Gary Fields / Dan Fiorella (reprint from #322)
Page 74 – When Gay-Themed TV Shows Get Completely Out of Hand – Harold Bluetooth (Gunnar Johnson) (reprint from #322)
Page 78 – Cloning: Cloning: How How I I Made Made Miss Miss Dolly Dolly – Ron Barrett (reprint from #319)
Page 81 – The Tiger Woods Phenomenon – Frank Cummings / Ricky Sprague (reprint from #321)
Page 86 – Other Mythological Creatures Left Out of Hercules – Pete Fitzgerald / Steve Strangio (reprint from #321)

Page 88 – The Wishing Well – Bruce Bolinger / Kit Lively (reprint from #319)

Page 89 – Roller Coaster Mania – Terry Colon (reprint from #318)

Page 92 – Goosedumps – John Severin / Greg Grabianski (reprint from #316)

Page 98 – The Cracked List 10 Daytime TV Talk Show Guests They'll Soon Be Resorting To – Mike Ricigliano / Dan Birtcher (reprint from #315)

Page 99 – The Tickle Me Elmo Rip-Offs – Frank Cummings (reprint from #317)

Back Cover – Space Jam – Tom Grimes, Gary Fields (reprint from #314)

Cracked Collectors' Edition #117 (Got Milk), January 1999 (84 pages) ($2.99)

Cover – Got Milk Posters – Frank Cummings (new)

Page 2 – Breast Milk What a Surprise! – Officer Smythe, LAPD (reprint from #304)

Page 3 – Contents – Mike Ricigliano

Page 4 – The Phewww-gitive – John Severin / Lou Silverstone (reprint from #287)

Page 10 – Give-Away Items That Would Really Make Money for Businesses – Pete Fitzgerald / Greg Grabianski, Aimee Keillor (reprint from #299)

Page 12 – The Second Time Around for Commercial Pitchmen – Walter Brogan / Eric Goldberg, Mark Howard (reprint from #303)

Page 15 – The Very Rich and the Very Poor – Warren Sattler (reprint from #193)

Page 19 – Cracked Gallery of Fun Products You Can't Live Without – Bruce Bolinger (reprint from #301)

Page 20 – Cracked "You Know You're _____ When" – Don Orehek (reprint from #186)

Page 22 – The Abyssmal – John Severin / Terry Gentile (reprint from #252)

Page 26 – The 1st Annual Cracked NFL All-Dough Team – Mike Ricigliano (reprint from #284)

Page 28 – What if Comic Strips Featured Guest Stars? – Gary Fields / Ed Subitzky (reprint from #292)

Page 31 – Cracked's Comparative Guide to Learning Institutions – Pete Fitzgerald / Steve Strangio (reprint from #268)

Page 35 – Tree's Company – John Severin (reprint from #201)

Page 42 – Absolut Idiot – John Severin (new with reprint from #127)

Insert – 4 Got Milk Posters (full color, glossy) (new)

Page 43 – More Cracked Fun Products You Can't Live Without – Bruce
Bolinger (reprint from #301)

Page 44 – Dumb and Dumber – Rurik Tyler / Randy Epley (reprint
from #298)

Page 46 – Classroom Turmoil Accessories – Todd James / Greg
Grabianski (reprint from #294)

Page 48 – Peed – Walter Brogan / Lou Silverstone (reprint from #294)

Page 52 – The Pondering Plumber – Sururi Gumen (reprint from
#193)

Page 53 – The 7 Deadly Sins – Phillips Studios (reprint from #258)

Page 56 – Where the Money We Spend on Things Really Goes! – Terry
Colon / Dan Birtcher (reprint from #300)

Page 58 – Yahoo Wild West Part II – Arnoldo Franchioni (reprint from
#293)

Page 60 – Designer Genes – Bob Fingerman / George Gladir (reprint
from #230)

Page 63 – Voila! – A. Blinken (John Severin) / Andy Simmons (reprint
from #289)

Page 67 – Least Popular Frozen Dinner Coupons – Chris Bartlett /
David Boone (reprint from #297)

Page 70 – Cracked's Cartoon Showcase Featuring Jeff Keate (Running
Weasel) – Jeff Keate (reprint from #191)

Page 72 – If America Really was Policeman to the World! – Gary Fields
/ Dan Birtcher (reprint from #296)

Page 74 – One-Shots! (mine blasting) – Mike Ricigliano / Roger Brown
(reprint from #250)

Page 76 – Cracked to the Future Part III – John Severin / Tony Frank
(Lou Silverstone) (reprint from #258)

Page 82 – Subscription ad – John Severin (reprint from #26)

Page 83 – Absolut Drunk – Tom Grimes (reprint from #308)

Back Cover – Milk May the Mustache Be With You (reprint from
Cracked Monster Party #36)

**Cracked Collectors' Edition #118 (*TeleTubbies*), April 1999 (84 pages)
($2.99)**

Cover – We Terrorize the TeleTubbies – John Severin (new)

Page 2 – You Drink Milk and It Shows ad – Ron Barrett (reprint from
#291)

Page 3 – Contents – Mike Ricigliano

Page 4 – Frozen – Walter Brogan / Greg Grabianski (reprint from #297)

Page 9 – Fairy Tales for the 1990s! – Mike Ricigliano / Roger Brown
(reprint from #259)

Page 12 – Cracked's Guide to Good Eating – Pete Fitzgerald / Howie Mitchell (reprint from #263)
Page 14 – The Lion King Returns to his Kingdom – Don Orehek / Rob Weske (reprint from #293)
Page 15 – Winter TV Replacement Shows – John Severin / Scott Franklin (reprint from #306)
Page 18 – Cracked Ponders Death – Frank Cummings / Coyote J. Calhoun (reprint from #305)
Page 20 – The F.B.I. Ten Most Wanted Saboteurs – Mike Ricigliano (reprint from #248)
Page 21 – The Cracked Family Travel Map – Bruce Bolinger / Greg Grabianski (reprint from #301) (originally called "The Cracked Family Travel Map 1995")
Page 25 – Cracked's Complete Guide to Piercing – Terry Colon (reprint from #304)
Page 28 – Dictionary of Disgusting Phrases – Randy Jones / Barry Zeger, Sue Zeger (reprint from #302)
Page 30 – Cuteness – John Severin / Lou Silverstone (reprint from #304)
Page 35 – Letterboxed Comics!!! – Gary Fields / Michael Gilbert (reprint from #300)
Page 38 – The Sabotron! – Mike Ricigliano (reprint from #250)
Page 39 – Orehek at Large on a Field Day at the Zoo – Don Orehek (reprint from #264)
Page 42 and Insert – TeleTubby Viewer and Filmstrips – Walter Brogan, Frank Cummings, Rurik Tyler (full color, glossy) (new)
Page 43 – The Finkstones – Walter Brogan / Lou Silverstone (reprint from #292)
Page 49 – Wrestling Hype for Boring Sports – Rurik Tyler / Bill Ignizio (reprint from #267)
Page 52 – Spies and Saboteurs Hit Ice Hockey – Mike Ricigliano (reprint from #272)
Page 54 – Remote Controls We'll Soon Be Seeing! – Gray Morrow / George Gladir (reprint from #249)
Page 58 – The Non-Celebrity Workout Video – Pete Fitzgerald / Paul Giles (reprint from #264)
Page 60 – Politically Incorrect Kids Games for the 90's – John Severin / Barry Zeger (reprint from #295)
Page 63 – Doggie Hoser M.D. – Walter Brogan / Tony Frank (Lou Silverstone) (reprint from #254)
Page 67 – Things are Gonna Get a Lot Worse Before They Get Better! – John Severin / George Gladir (reprint from #274)

Page 70 – Cracked's Uses for Used Computers – Mike Ricigliano /
Roger Brown (reprint from #258)
Page 72 – Cracked Guide to Behavior in Public Places – John Severin /
Fred Sahner (reprint from #270)
Page 74 – Prehistoric Cocktail Party – Bruce Bolinger / Lenore Skenazy
(reprint from #295)
Page 76 – Roasting Mother Goose (Little Tommy Tucker) – Vic Martin
/ Lyle Roberts Kain (reprint from #269)
Page 77 – Schlep by Schlep – John Severin / Greg Grabianski (reprint
from #305)
Page 82 – Shut-Ups (call a doctor) – Don Orehek (reprint from #291)
Page 83 – Subscription ad – John Severin (reprint from #125)
Back Cover – Cracked's Great Moments in Education Kermit the Frog
Goes Back to School – Jeff Wong / Rob Weske (reprint from #294)

**Cracked Collectors' Edition #119 (*Star Wars for Dummies*), July 1999 (68
pages) ($2.99)**
Cover – Star Wars for Dummies – Frank Cummings (new)
Page 2 – The Cracked "Spaced Out" List Other Upcoming "Star Trek"
Spinoffs – Mike Ricigliano (reprint from *Cracked Spaced Out #1*)
Page 3 – Contents – Mike Ricigliano
Page 4 – Star-Warz – O.O. Severin (John Severin) / Joe Catalano
(reprint from #146)
Page 11 – Star Warts Lost Footage Star Warz: An Old Joke – Walter
Brogan / Todd Jackson (reprint from *Cracked Monster Party #35*)
Page 12 – Shut-Ups (I can do no moore!) – Don Orehek / Eric
Goldberg, Mark Howard (reprint from #289)
Page 13 – Hollywoodworld Resort – Bruce Bolinger / Rob Weske
(reprint from #289)
Page 17 – Soak-Mart – Mike Ricigliano (reprint from #276)
Page 20 – New Rules of Thumb! – Pete Fitzgerald / Daniel Birtcher
(reprint from #289)
Page 22 – Parents! Can't Live With 'em, Can't Live Without 'em – P.C.
Vey (reprint from #284)
Page 23 – Money-Ball: The New Baseball – John Severin / Andy
Simmons (reprint from #275)
Page 27 – Cracked Animal Species That Didn't Quite Make it – Bruce
Bolinger / Donald Neiswinger (reprint from #280)
Page 30 – Cracked Horses Around – Arnoldo Franchioni (reprint from
#268)
Page 32 – Spies and Saboteurs Hit the Jungle! – Mike Ricigliano (reprint
from #293)

Page 34 – Star Wars Dummies Guide – Tom Grimes (reprint from *Cracked Monster Party* #36)

Insert – Star Wars for Dummies – Frank Cummings, Cliff Mott, Mike Ricigliano, Rurik Tyler / Jay Oakes (full color, glossy covers, half size, 16 pages) (new)

Page 35 – Shut-Ups (autobiography) – Don Orehek (reprint from #252)

Page 36 – The Empire Strikes Out – O.O. Severin (John Severin) (reprint from #173)

Page 43 – Star Warts Lost Footage The Empire Strikes Out – Walter Brogan / Todd Jackson (reprint from *Cracked Monster Party* #36)

Page 44 – Water Parks of the Damned! – Ron Barrett (reprint from #293)

Page 46 – If I Won the Lottery – Mike Ricigliano (reprint from #264)

Page 49 – Gangland Land America's First Urban Decay Theme Park – Don Orehek / Bill Frenzer (reprint from #281)

Page 52 – Nun's the Word! – Rurik Tyler / Andrew Osborne (reprint from #277)

Page 54 – NCC-1701-D Today (A Message from the Captain's Desk) – Rurik Tyler / Steve Strangio (reprint from *Cracked Spaced Out* #1)

Page 57 – Returns of the Jed Eye – John Severin (reprint from #199)

Page 65 – Star Warts Lost Footage Returns of the Jed Eye – Walter Brogan / Todd Jackson (reprint from *Cracked Monster Party* #36)

Page 66 – Doctor Ricig – Mike Ricigliano (reprint from #264)

Page 67 – Subscription ad – John Severin (reprint from #296)

Back Cover – At the Star Trek Convention – Jim Bennett / Rob Weske (reprint from *Cracked Spaced Out* #4)

Cracked Collectors' Edition #120 (*Year's Best*), September 1999 (100 pages) ($2.99)

Cover – We Serve Up Our Year's Best – John Severin, Walter Brogan, Jeff Wong (new with reprint from #324, 326, 327, 330, 331)

Page 2 – Mr. Beanie Babies – Gunnar Johnson / Sherry Johnson (reprint from #326)

Page 3 – Contents – Mike Ricigliano

Page 4 – Tipanic! – John Severin / Andy Simmons (reprint from #325)

Page 10 – That's News to Us! – Don Orehek / Mike Lotter (reprint from #331)

Page 11 – History's Least Successful Proto Humans – Terry Colon (reprint from #328)

Page 14 – A Cracked Look at the Pyramids – Bruce Bolinger / Rob Weske (reprint from #323)
Page 18 – King of the Ill – Frank Cummings / Todd Jackson (reprint from #326)
Page 23 – Sports World Tamagotchis – Pete Fitzgerald / Dan Birtcher (reprint from #324)
Page 26 – Canes and Walkers for Oldsters On the Go – Ron Barrett (reprint from #331)
Page 28 – Cracked Looks at the Sport Utility Vehicle Craze – John Severin / Greg Grabianski (reprint from #331)
Page 32 – Toys of the Third Reich – Rurik Tyler / R.J. Reiley, C.L. Walker (reprint from #329)
Page 35 – Seinfeld Retrospective – Walter Brogan / Lou Silverstone (reprint from #327)
Page 41 – Modern Immaturity Magazine – Gunnar Johnson (reprint from #328)
Page 46 – Breaking the Code: Your Uncle's Magic Tricks Exploded. Starring the Masked Uncle – John Severin / Dan Fiorella (reprint from #330)
Page 50 – Spies and Sabs Hit a Mall Food Court – Mike Ricigliano (reprint from #327)
Page 52 – Extreme Ideas for Everyday Activities – Todd James / Mike Morse (reprint from #330)
Page 53 – If the Simpsons Starred in a TV Drama – Don Orehek / Lou Silverstone, Andy Simmons, Todd Jackson (reprint from #326)
Page 56 – D'er – Walter Brogan / Steve Strangio, Eric Goldberg, Mark Howard (reprint from #323)
Page 62 – America's Weirdest Restaurants – Randy Jones / Mike Morse (reprint from #331)
Page 64 – Cracked's Spring Fashion Preview – Mike Ricigliano (reprint from #327)
Page 67 – Dawson's Geeks – Frank Cummings / Greg Grabianski (reprint from #329)
Page 72 – Cracked Clip Jamiroquack Video Insanity – Cliff Mott / Barry Zeger (reprint from #325)
Page 73 – If Beavis and Butt-Head Were in Classic Christmas Films – Gary Fields / Judd Stomp (reprint from #324)
Page 76 – The Waterbug – John Severin / Andy Simmons (reprint from #331)
Page 81 – Cracked Rules for Bad Manners – Bruce Bolinger / Stu Vivetchek, Ricky Sprague (reprint from #328)
Page 85 – Mouth Park – Gary Fields / Greg Grabianski (reprint from #326)

Page 90 – Cracked's 1998 Calendar Concepts That Didn't Quite Make it – Mike Ricigliano (reprint from #324)

Page 92 – Clodzilla – Walter Brogan / Lou Silverstone (reprint from #328)

Page 98 – Subscription ad – John Severin (reprint from *Cracked Collectors' Edition* #106)

Page 99 – National Rifle Association ad – Alan Kupperberg / R.J. Reiley (reprint from #330)

Back Cover – I Want You for White House Intern – Jeff Wong (reprint from #327)

Cracked Collectors' Edition #121 (*Celebrate 3000*), January 2000 (68 pages) ($2.99)

Cover – We Celebrate the Year 3000! – Frank Cummings (new)

Page 2 – Oh, No…Do We Have to Start All Over Again? – Charles Rodrigues (reprint from #110)

Page 3 – Contents – Mike Ricigliano

Page 4 – The Yechh's Files – Walter Brogan / Rob Weske (reprint from *Cracked Monster Party* #31)

Page 9 – Orehek's Alien Humor – Don Orehek (reprint from *Cracked Spaced Out* #3)

Page 10 – Fly Me to the Moon – Oskar Blotta (reprint from #79)

Page 12 – Alien TV! – John Severin / Gene Perone, Mort Todd (reprint from #217)

Page 17 – The Sci-Fi Yellow Pages – Bruce Bolinger / Rob Weske (reprint from *Cracked Spaced Out* #2)

Page 20 – Dr. Fizzix (origin) – Gary Fields / Eric Goldberg, Mark Howard (reprint from *Cracked Spaced Out* #4)

Page 22 – Star Wreck The Next Degeneration – John Severin / Lou Silverstone (reprint from #271)

Page 29 – NCC-1701-D Today (Lt. Jadzia Dax) – Rurik Tyler / Steve Strangio (reprint from *Cracked Spaced Out* #4)

Page 32 – The Spaced Out Solar System (and Other Stuff) Chart – Mike Ricigliano (reprint from *Cracked Spaced Out* #3)

Page 34 – Cracked 1000 Year Calendar – Mike Ricigliano (new)

Insert – Cracked 1000 Year Calendar Poster – Frank Cummings (full color, glossy, oversize) (new)

Insert – X-Files Poster – Jeff Wong (full color, glossy, oversize) (reprint from #318)

Page 35 – Dr. Fizzix #432 Let's Make Pigs Fly – Gary Fields / Eric Goldberg, Mark Howard (reprint from *Cracked Spaced Out* #4)

Page 36 – Life in the 21st Century – John Langton (reprint from #195)

Page 38 – SeaPest DDT – Bruce Bolinger / Lou Silverstone (reprint from *Cracked Spaced Out* #3)

Cracked Collectors' Edition #122 (*Harry Pottey*), April 2000 (84 pages) ($2.99) (As mentioned in *Cracked* #345, this cover beat *Mad* #391 to the stands by two months.)

Page 42 and Insert – Harry Pottey and the Sorcerer's Throne Book Cover – Mike Ricigliano, Rurik Tyler (full color, card stock) (new)

Insert – Harry Potter Star Seeker For the Gryffindor Quidditch Team Poster – Rurik Tyler (full color, card stock) (new)

Page 43 – The Little Dread Schoolhouse – Lee Chenell (reprint from #268)

Page 44 – New NFL Rules – Bruce Bolinger (reprint from #297)

Page 46 – 007's Latest Supercool Spy Gadgets – Pete Fitzgerald / Barry Zeger (reprint from #305)

Page 49 – The Toys Not in Toy Story Catalogue – Brian Buniak / Ricky Sprague (reprint from #308)

Page 52 – The Cracked Teacher Creature Chart – Mike Ricigliano (reprint from #305)

Page 54 – King Ralf – Walter Brogan / Lou Silverstone (reprint from #264)

Page 60 – The Cracked Guide to Professional Jargon – Randy Jones / Lenore Skenazy (reprint from #303)

Page 62 – The Lonely Guy – Don Orehek / Rob Weske (reprint from #312)

Page 63 – The Beginner's Guide to Roller Hockey – Mike Ricigliano (reprint from #302)

Page 68 – School Prayers Everybody Can Use – Bruce Bolinger / John Fahs (reprint from #308)

Page 70 – When History Gets the Disney Treatment – Don Orehek / Rob Weske (reprint from #303)

Page 73 – Ye Olde Transport Catalogue – Terry Colon (reprint from #299)

Page 76 – Groundhog Daze – Walter Brogan / Lou Silverstone (reprint from #282)

Page 82 – The Cracked List 12 Dysfunctional Toys for Dysfunctional Kids – Mike Ricigliano / William Raschendorfer (reprint from #306)

Page 83 – Subscription ad – John Severin, Rurik Tyler, Jeff Wong (reprint from #66, 335, 337)

Back Cover – Pippi Longfilters – Frank Cummings / John Fahs (reprint from #310)

Cracked Collectors' Edition #123 (*Year's Best*), **Spring 2000 (84 pages) ($2.99)**

Cover – Year's Best Comics Parodies! – John Severin (new with reprint of #333, 337, 338, 339)

Page 2 – Austin Powers – Gunnar Johnson (reprint from #337)

Page 3 – Contents – Mike Ricigliano (full color)

Page 4 – Snore Wars Epic-Dud 1 The Phantom Cuteness – John Severin / Lou Silverstone (reprint from #338) (full color)

Page 10 – Chia Pest Chia Back & Crack – Aimee Keillor, Rurik Tyler, Tom Grimes (reprint from #338) (full color)
Page 11 – A Peek Inside Austin Powers' Scrapbook – Gunnar Johnson (reprint from #337)
Page 14 – Total Request Lovin' the Ego Stroke-a – Cliff Mott / Barry Zeger (reprint from #338)
Page 16 – Cracked's Guide to Braces – John Severin / Dan Fiorella, Jackie Rose (reprint from #334)
Page 19 – Jujubee Jury Rate Heaving Private Ryan – Walter Brogan / Lou Silverstone (reprint from #332)
Page 26 – When the Jesse "The Body" Ventura Trend Takes Over Washington – Gunnar Johnson (reprint from #334)
Page 28 – The Furby Phenomenon – Pete Fitzgerald / Greg Grabianski (reprint from #334)
Page 31 – Cracked Pharmaceuticals (reprint from #338)
Page 33 – One Miserable Day in Bombay – Oskar Blotta (reprint from #335)
Page 34 – Everybody Loathes Raymundane – John Severin / Greg Grabianski (reprint from #336)
Page 39 – Suplex Marks the Spot – Don Orehek / Katey Dash (reprint from #334)
Page 40 – When All Magazines Publish Special Editions Just For Kids – Gunnar Johnson / Anthony Zampano (reprint from #332)
Page 42 – The Cracked Guide to Boy Groups – Frank Cummings / Greg Grabianski (reprint from #338)
Page 46 – The First Kiddie Casino – Bruce Bolinger / Mike Morse (reprint from #332)
Page 48 – Upside/Downside of Cyberspace – Todd James / Dan Fiorella (reprint from #333)
Page 50 – A Hair in the Nose – Oskar Blotta (reprint from #339)
Page 51 – CDs That Today's Aging Pop Stars Will Be Releasing When They Get Really Old – Gunnar Johnson (reprint from #335)
Page 54 – Hot Toy Timeline – Rurik Tyler / Dan Fiorella (reprint from #339)
Page 56 – When All Organizations Offer Their Own Visa Cards – Gunnar Johnson (reprint from #333)
Page 58 – Game Shows to Play With Your Grandparents – Todd James / Dan Lee (reprint from #336)
Page 60 – When the Famous Join the Everyday Workforce – Jeff Wong / John Samony (reprint from #333)
Page 62 – Supermodel Shut-Ups (I'm a perfect size!) – Don Orehek / Eric Goldberg, Mark Howard (reprint from #336)

Page 63 – American Lie – Walter Brogan / Andy Simmons (reprint from #339)

Page 67 – The Latest Tomb Raider Games – Frank Cummings / Lou Motson (reprint from #335)

Page 71 – Cut Out a Can of Whoop Ass – Cliff Mott / Todd Jackson (reprint from #334)

Page 72 – Changes to the Currency We'd Really Like to See – Rurik Tyler / Dan Birtcher (reprint from #334)

Page 74 – The Choke's On You – Ian Baker (reprint from #340)

Page 75 – Mistletoe – Gary Fields / Kit Lively (reprint from #332)

Page 76 – What to Expect When All Corporations Merge – Gunnar Johnson / Sherry Johnson (reprint from #335)

Page 78 – Cracked Swimsuit Edition Fun & Frolic in South Park, Colorado – Rurik Tyler, Tom Grimes / Greg Grabianski (reprint from #333) (full color)

Page 83 – Get Ready to Thumble! – Jeff Wong (reprint from #334)

Back Cover – Tae Boba Workout – Eric Snodgrass, Jonathan Skaines, Matt Martelli / Todd Jackson (reprint from #337)

Cracked Collectors' Edition #124 (*Our Funniest Comics Ever!*), Summer 2000 (84 pages) ($3.99) (Page numbering changes.)

Cover – Our Funniest Comics Ever! – John Severin, Mike Ricigliano, J. Kelly, Walter Brogan, Gary Fields (new with reprint from #330, 334)

Inside Front Cover – Cartoon Nutwork Presents The Flopstones – Don Orehek / Greg Grabianski (reprint from #339)

Page 1 – Contents (full color)

Page 2 – If the Simpsons Were Guests on the Jerry Springer Show – Gary Fields / Greg Grabianski (reprint from #330) (full color)

Page 6 – Lawn Styles of the Rich and Famous – Terry Colon (reprint from #300) (full color)

Page 7 – A TV Commercial You'll Never See (Milk) – Walter Brogan / Spark (reprint from #269) (full color)

Page 8 – Peter Pan Reads a Bedtime Story – Mike Ricigliano / Roger Brown (reprint from #247) (full color)

Page 9 – You're a Worthwhile Individual, Churlish Brawn! – Gary Fields / Ricky Sprague (reprint from #338)

Page 10 – Cracked Super Party! – John Severin / Jerry De Fuccio (reprint from #229)

Page 12 – Germinator 2: Judgment Daze – Walter Brogan / Tony Frank (Lou Silverstone) (reprint from #268)

Page 19 – Fairy Tale Characters – Mike Ricigliano / Roger Brown (reprint from #247)

Page 22 – Dictionary of Disgusting Phrases – Randy Jones / Barry Zeger, Sue Zeger (reprint from #302)
Page 24 – Radzilla – Mike Ricigliano / Roger Brown (reprint from #237)
Page 25 – Unlikely Celebrity Product Endorsements – Jim Bennett / Eric Goldberg, Mark Howard, Mike Mikula (reprint from #286)
Page 26 – Other Celebrity Name Brand Products – Sven Forkbeard (Gunnar Johnson) (reprint from #321)
Page 32 – The Next Don – Don Orehek / Mike Lotter (reprint from #340)
Page 33 – McPoop's New Fall Sneezin' – J. Kelly (reprint from #314)
Page 34 – You Think You Got it Bad? – Oskar Blotta / Luciano Blotta (reprint from #322)
Page 36 – Other Big-Time Hollywood Productions of Classic TV Shows – Gunnar Johnson (reprint from #329)
Page 40 – Spies and Sabs Hit a Softball Game – Mike Ricigliano (reprint from #335)
Page 42 – Gramps and the Flies – J. Kelly (reprint from #305)
Page 43 – The Boat Ride – Mike Ricigliano / Roger Brown (reprint from #231)
Page 44 – A Grizzly Escape! – Mike Ricigliano / Roger Brown (reprint from #231)
Page 45 – The Cracked List – 10 Bad Signs – Mike Ricigliano (reprint from #294)
Page 46 – The Wishing Well – Bruce Bolinger / Kit Lively (reprint from #319)
Page 47 – Jeoparty! – John Severin / Joe Catalano (reprint from #231)
Page 49 – Spaced Out Shut-Ups (no man has gone) – Don Orehek / Eric Goldberg, Mark Howard (reprint from *Cracked Spaced Out* #3)
Page 50 – McPoop's Dilemma – J. Kelly (reprint from #311)
Page 51 – Bowling Bummer – Gary Fields / Ricky Sprague (reprint from #343)
Page 52 – When Gay-Themed TV Shows Get Completely Out of Hand – Harold Bluetooth (Gunnar Johnson) (reprint from #322)
Page 56 – Bummers! – Dick Ayers / Moe McMahon (Marian McMahon) (reprint from #235)
Page 58 – Star Drek the Next Generation – Mike Ricigliano / Roger Brown (reprint from #247)
Page 59 – The First Proposal – Henry Boltinoff (reprint from #240)
Page 60 – Gangster or Gangsta Do You Know the Difference? – Randy Jones / Jay Oakes (reprint from #330)
Page 62 – Summer Jobs for Aliens – Arnoldo Franchioni (reprint from *Cracked Spaced Out* #3)

Page 64 – Monster One-Shots (Alien dental floss) – Mike Ricigliano / Roger Brown (reprint from #229)

Page 65 – The Monster – Sururi Gumen (reprint from #130)

Page 66 – Monster Pets – John Severin / Moe McMahon (Marian McMahon) (reprint from #229)

Page 67 – Cracked Guide to Customized Skateboards – John Severin / George Gladir (reprint from #251)

Page 68 – Hazards of: Being a Superhero – Mike Ricigliano / Roger Brown (reprint from #243)

Page 69 – The Grip – Mike Ricigliano / Roger Brown (reprint from #232)

Page 70 – Dog's Best Friend – Don Orehek / Kit Lively (reprint from #320)

Page 71 – A Stork's Tale – Gary Fields / Kit Lively (reprint from #320) (full color)

Page 72 – An Earrie Tale – Oskar Blotta / Luciano Blotta (reprint from #329) (full color)

Page 73 – Don Archie – Gary Fields / R.J. Reiley (reprint from #334) (full color)

Page 79 – Tummy Hillfigure ad (full color) (new)

Page 80 – The Cracked List 8 Ways to Make This a Special Fathers Day – Mike Ricigliano (reprint from #336) (full color)

Inside Back Cover – *Cracked* #346 ad

Back Cover – National Rifle Association ad – Alan Kupperberg / R.J. Reiley (reprint from #330)

Cracked Collectors' Edition #125 (*Newspaper Funnies*), Fall 2000 (84 pages) ($3.99)

Cover – We Spoof Your Favorite Newspaper Funnies – Basil Gogos, Gary Fields, Tony Tallarico (reprint from #71)

Inside Front Cover and Inside Back Cover – Toon In! – Gary Fields (reprint from #267)

Page 1 – Contents – Gary Fields / Barry Dutter (full color)

Page 2 – Cracked Sunday Comics – Gary Fields / John Arcudi (reprint from #245) (full color)

Page 5 – Great Moments in Police Technology 1931 – Mike Ricigliano (reprint from #257) (full color)

Page 6 – Da Diss Dat Made Chester a Gangster – Alan Kupperberg / Barry Zeger (reprint from #295) (full color)

Page 7 – The Thanksgiving Day Parade: The Morning After – Arnoldo Franchioni (reprint from #287) (full color)

Page 8 – The Emergency – Mike Ricigliano / Roger Brown (reprint from #243) (full color)

Page 9 – Superheroes Fly Over the Hill! – Brian Buniak / Dan Birtcher (reprint from #310)

Page 12 – If Classic Cartoonists had Painted the Mona Lisa! – John Severin (reprint from #25) (originally called, "If Different Cartoonists had Painted the Mona Lisa")

Page 14 – One Day in Metropolitis – Don Orehek (reprint from #136)

Page 15 – Batman to the Rescue – Mike Ricigliano / Roger Brown (reprint from #248)

Page 16 – How to Draw Superhero Comic Books – Alan Kupperberg / Greg Grabianski, Ricky Sprague (reprint from #315)

Page 20 – The Final Episode of Comic Strips – Tony Tallarico (reprint from #216)

Page 23 – Super Hurry-Ups! (Sure is romantic) – Rick Altergott (reprint from #243)

Page 24 – The Day That Nothing Seemed to Go Right for the Ape Man – Fal Hoster (John Severin) (reprint from #55)

Page 27 – Cracked Presents Superheroes of the Future – Willy Orwonte (John Severin) (reprint from #160)

Page 30 – Plastic Surgery of the Cartoon Stars – Mike Ricigliano / Jerry De Fuccio (reprint from #273)

Page 32 – Things a Hero's Mom Could Never Get Used To! – Kurt Schaffenberger (reprint from #243)

Page 34 – Freddie the Menace – Gary Fields (reprint from #245)

Page 36 – Superhero Long-Shots – Mike Ricigliano / Roger Brown (reprint from #257)

Page 39 – Saturday Morning Cartoon Shut-Ups (Don't shoot me!) – Don Orehek / Eric Goldberg, Mark Howard (reprint from #290)

Page 40 – Little Mercurochrome and Denny the Menaces (reprint from #1)

Page 41 – Cracked Shut-Ups (diamond ring) – Bill McCartney (Bill Ward) (reprint from #5) (In this reprint, they mention that this one originally appeared in *Cracked* #2, but it's not true.)

Page 42 – If Comic Strip Heroes Had Hang-Ups! – Lugoze (reprint from #96) (originally called, "If Comic Strip Heroes Had Hang-Ups Like the Rest of Us")

Page 46 – Hazards of: Being a Superhero – Mike Ricigliano / Roger Brown (reprint from #243)

Page 48 – Mr. Wilson's Revenge – Gary Fields / Eric Goldberg, Mark Howard (reprint from #284)

Page 50 – The Day Comic Strip Characters Got up on the Wrong Side of the Bed! – John Severin (reprint from #76) (originally called, "The Day Comic Strip Characters Got up on the Wrong Side of Bed")

Page 53 – Exclamation!!! – Don Perlin (reprint from #50)

Page 54 – Comic Strip Mergers! – Bill McCartney (Bill Ward) (reprint from #37) (originally called, "Merged Comic Strips")

Page 57 – Daddy-Long Legs-Man – Alan Kupperberg / Andy Simmons (reprint from #304)

Page 62 – Just How Fast is the Flash? – Rurik Tyler (reprint from #264)

Page 64 – Daily Times-News-Sun-Post-Globe – Bill McCartney (Bill Ward) (reprint from #45)

Page 66 – Bat On a Hot Tin Roof – Mike Ricigliano (reprint) (originally called something else, not from #248)

Page 67 – How the Movies Wrecked Supedupman – Rick Altergott / Mort Todd (reprint from #233)

Page 71 – Peanutz – Gary Fields / Martin Heeley (reprint from #348)

Page 73 – Cartoon Makeovers – Gary Fields / Mike Ricigliano (reprint from #315) (full color)

Page 74 – It Ain't Easy Being Ghost Rider – Gary Fields (reprint from *Cracked Super* #7) (full color)

Page 75 – Shut-Ups (Happy Birthday, Muckey!) – Don Orehek (reprint from #246) (full color)

Page 76 – Cracked.com ad (full color)

Page 77 – Tinoctin ad – John Severin (reprint from #258) (full color)

Page 78 – X-Funnies – Gary Fields / Barry Dutter (reprint from #346) (full color)

Back Cover – Stan Lee's Press-On Nails – John Severin / Gene Perone (reprint from #283)

Cracked Digest #1, October 1986 (148 pages) ($1.75) (New Spy vs. Saboteur Flip-Cartoon in corner of every page by Mike Ricigliano.)

Cover – Sylvester's Newsstand Toothache – John Severin (reprint from #82)

Page 2 – Sagebrush (thinnin' hair) – John Severin (reprint from #115)

Page 3 – Contents

Page 4 – Editor's Note

Page 6 – Rambozo: The Second First Blood (the Second Time!) – Kent Gamble (reprint from #217) (originally called "Rambo First Blood Part II")

Page 19 – Push Button War – Bill Everett (reprint from #9)

Page 25 – Cat Gifts for Cats Who Have Everything – Mac Bush (Sururi Gumen) (reprint from #125)

Page 30 – Hudd & Dini (mousetrap) – Vic Martin (reprint from #83)

Page 33 – Ultra-Realistic Barbra & Ben Doll Accessories – Bill McCartney (Bill Ward) (reprint from #52)

Page 38 – Cannibal Chuckles – Charles Rodrigues (reprint from #39)

Page 41 – School for T.V. Wrestlers – Sean Powers (John Severin) (reprint from #48)

Page 58 – Hurry-Ups (fly in soup) – Bill McCartney (Bill Ward) (reprint from #41)

Page 61 – Celebrities and Their Screen Idols – John Severin (reprint from #107)

Page 67 – Surfing U.S.A. – Bill McCartney (Bill Ward) (reprint from #39)

Page 84 – The Beach Balloon – John Severin (reprint from #27)

Page 88 – Take Me Out to the Old Cracked Ball Game – Charles Rodrigues (reprint from #53)

Page 91 – The Cracked Lens (reprint from #154)

Page 99 – Cracked Interviews the Magic King – Bill Ward (reprint from #131)

Page 114 – Silly Things We Do – John Severin (reprint from #101)

Page 122 – One Extremely Foggy Night in Minnesota – Howard Nostrand (reprint from #139)

Page 125 – The Towering Infernal – John Severin (reprint from #126)

Page 144 – Rare Olde Shut-Upf – Jack Davis (reprint from #16)

Page 147 – Sagebrush (BOM-BIDDY) – John Severin (reprint from *Cracked Collectors' Edition* #9)

Back Cover – Shut-Ups (I'll find you) – John Severin (reprint from #13)

Cracked Digest #2, January 1987 (148 pages) ($2.00)

Cover – Earth Egg Hatching Monster – Nireves (John Severin) (reprint from *Giant Cracked* #8 with skull replacing egg-shaped Earth)

Page 2 – Orders – John Severin (reprint from #38)

Page 3 – Contents

Page 4 – The Cracked Monsters Lens (Gatorade) (new)

Page 8 – Cracked Takes a Look at the Transylvanian Teen Scene – John Severin (reprint from #40)

Page 20 – Cracked's Scariest Laughs! – Vic Martin, Bill Ward, Don Orehek (reprints from various issues)

Page 27 – Frankenstein and Rock 'n Roll! – Joe Maneely (reprint from #2)

Page 31 – Hudd & Dini (skeleton) – Vic Martin (reprint from #95)

Page 34 – Cracked Look at Godzilla! – Bill Wray / Joe Catalano (reprint from #219)

Page 41 – Transylvania's Montgomery & Morgue – John Severin (reprint from *For Monsters Only* #2)

Page 51 – Bill Ward's Chiller Dillers – Bill Ward (reprint from *For Monsters Only* #3)

Page 52 – Gunspook – Don Orehek (reprint from *Zany* #2)

Page 60 – Basil Wolverton's Weird Trading Cards – Basil Wolverton (reprint from *Giant Cracked* #43) (originally called "Cracked Alien Trading Cards)

Page 65 – Allien and How to Watch it – John Severin (reprint from #164)

Page 84 – Cracked Monster Lens (so much for scuba diving) (new)

Page 88 – Hard-to-Digest Letters (new) Page 90 – Monster Mother Goose – Bill McCartney (Bill Ward) (reprint from *For Monsters Only* #1)

Page 95 – Frankenstein and the Mummies – (new to *Cracked*.)

Page 117 – The Uggly Family "My Real Weird Science Project" – Stosh Gillespie (Dan Clowes) / Eel O'Brian (Mort Todd) (reprint from *Giant Cracked* #43)

Page 131 – Polter-Psycho-Geist – John Reiner / Mortimer Post, Mort Todd (reprint from #221)

Page 136 – Transylvanian Rock 'n' Roll Monsters – Vic Martin (reprint from *For Monsters Only* #5)

Page 138 – Monster High School – J.D. King / Jane King (new)

Page 145 – Monster Shut-Ups (great blocks) – Mike Ricigliano (reprint from *Cracked Collectors' Edition* #51)

Page 147 – Gigantic Monster Mobile Bonus! – Vic Martin (reprint from *For Monsters Only* #6)

Cracked Digest #3, April 1987 (148 pages) ($2.00)

Cover – Sylvester's Explosive Remote Control – John Severin (reprint from *Cracked Collectors' Edition* #64)

Page 2 – Excedruin ad – John Severin (reprint from #86)

Page 3 – Contents

Page 4 – Alien TV! – John Severin / Gene Perone, Mort Todd (reprint from #217)

Page 19 – Personalized TV Sets – Bill McCartney (Bill Ward) (reprint from #41)

Page 25 – Lowering the Mental Level of TV Programs – John Severin (reprint from #70)

Page 33 – What's the Beef? – John Reiner / Joe Catalano (reprint from #220)

Page 37 – Mission: Implausible – O.O. Severin (John Severin) (reprint from #80)

Page 52 – The Moldin Girls – Marie Severin / Stu Schwartzberg (reprint from #222)

Page 66 – On-the-Spot Test Commercials – John Severin (reprint from #21)

Page 73 – The Transdeformers vs Boltron – Steve Ditko / Mort Todd, John Arcudi (reprint from #222)

Page 83 – Cracked Interviews Dick Clog the Blooper & Practical Joke King – John Severin / Mort Todd (reprint from #220)

Page 94 – Have Gun Won't Travel – Bill McCartney (Bill Ward) (reprint from #5)

Page 102 – Star Yecch! – John Severin (reprint from #127)

Page 115 – As the General, Young, and Restless Hospital Turns – Bill Ward (reprint from #137)

Page 125 – TV Cable Guide Magazine (reprint from #212)

Page 130 – He's Really a Lone Ranger Now! – Bill Ward (reprint from #1)

Page 132 – Rival TV Shows Cry U.N.C.L.E. – McCarthy (John Severin) (reprint from #46)

Page 138 – Sea Haunt – Jack Davis (reprint from #14)

Page 147 – Television Shut-Ups (cashier's check) – John Severin (reprint from #21)

Page 148 – Cracked Interviews Cracked ad (new, with reprint from #19)

Cracked Digest #4, July 1987 (148 pages) ($2.00)

Cover – The Cracked Book of Shut-Ups! – Don Orehek (new)

Page 2, 129-130 – Hip Shut-Ups (I'm floatin') – John Severin (reprint from #11)

Page 3 – Contents

Page 4-5, 12 – Shut-Ups (don't want to run) – John Severin (reprint from #42)

Page 6-7, 9 – Shut-Ups (first men on moon) – Charles Rodrigues (reprint from #79)

Page 8, 70-71 – Shut-Ups (C-A-T) – Charles Rodrigues (reprint from #57)

Page 9-11 – Shut-Ups (astronaut) – Charles Rodrigues (reprint from #80)

Page 13-15 – Shut-Ups (don't need haircut) – Vic Martin (reprint from #49)

Page 16-18 – Shut-Ups (No cavities) – Sam Gross Jr. (Charles Rodrigues) (reprint from #99)

Page 19-21 – Shut-Ups (jump) – Rodrigliani (Charles Rodrigues) (reprint from #55)

Page 22-24 – Shut-Ups (best tattoo jobs) – Don Orehek (reprint from #159)

Page 25-26, 30 – Shut-Ups (play like you never played) – Don Orehek (reprint from #166)

Page 27-29 – Shut-Ups (writing a book) – Don Orehek (reprint from #185)

Page 31, 44-45 – Shut-Ups (Monday morning paper) – Don Orehek (reprint from #212)

Page 32-34 – Shut-Ups (any other questions) – Don Orehek (reprint from #160)

Page 35-37 – Hurry-Ups (house on fire) – John Severin (reprint from #32)

Page 38-39 – Ye Hang Ups #4 (got a minute) – C.E. Severin (Catherine Severin) (reprint from #174)

Page 40-41 – Ye Hang Ups #8 (Uh! Oh!) – C.E. Severin (Catherine Severin) (reprint from #187)

Page 42-43 – Shut-Ups (Peanuts) – Ellsworth A. Sap (Charles Rodrigues) (reprint from #69)

Page 46, 68-69 – Shut-Ups! (Running Deer) – Charles Rodrigues (reprint from #62)

Page 47 – Shut-Ups (king's dinner) – Julius Siezure (Charles Rodrigues) (reprint from #96)

Page 48-49 – Fine Art Shut-Ups (lopsided hat) – John Severin (reprint from #19)

Page 50 – Ye Hang Ups #9 (Hurry it up) – M.L. Severin (Margaret Severin) (reprint from #189)

Page 51-52 – Ye Hang Ups #10 (He can't be serious) – C.E. Severin (Catherine Severin) (reprint from #190)

Page 53-55 – Russian Shut-Ups (Russia) – Bill McCartney (Bill Ward) (reprint from #12)

Page 56-59 – Cracked Shut-Ups (beastly hot) – Bill McCartney (Bill Ward) (reprint from #7)

Page 60-61 – Cracked Shut-Ups (daddy run) – Al Jaffee (reprint from #5)

Page 62-63 – Madison Avenue Shut-Ups (no cavities) – Vic Martin (reprint from #20)

Page 64-67 – Popular Songs Shut-Ups (smile umbrella) – Bill McCartney (Bill Ward) (reprint from #22)

Page 72, 74 – Ye Hang Ups (Autumn again) – O.O. Severin (John Severin) (reprint from #209)

Page 73 – Ye Hang Ups (which way to the john) – Nireves (John Severin) (reprint from #116)

Page 75-78 – Hold-Ups! (Comrade Mishkin) – Sururi Gumen, Don Orehek (reprint from #206)

Page 79-83 – Hurry-Ups (papa, papa) – John Severin (reprint from #33)

Page 84-86 – Hurry-Ups (daddy fell out) – Don Orehek (reprint from #34)

Page 87-89 – Hurry-Ups (five dollar raise) – Don Orehek (reprint from #35)

Page 90-92 – Ye Hang Ups #2 (castle) – C.E. Severin (Catherine Severin) (reprint from #173)

Page 93-96, 137-140 – Hold-Ups! (Nine Lives Louie) – Sururi Gumen (reprint from #207)

Page 97-99 – Shut-Ups (bottle of soda) – Vic Martin (reprint from #48)

Page 100-104 – Famous Proverb Shut-Ups (small packages) – John Severin (reprint from #15)

Page 105-106 – Famous Quotations Shut-Ups (Don't give up the ship) – Vic Martin (reprint from #23)

Page 107-110 – Cracked Shut-Ups (diamond ring) – Bill McCartney (Bill Ward) (reprint from #5)

Page 111-113 – Cracked Shut-Ups (Bwanna Jim) – Bill McCartney (Bill Ward) (reprint from #6)

Page 112-114 – Shut-Ups (missing a great show) – Don Orehek (reprint from #205)

Page 115-119 – Shut-Ups (pastrami on rye) – Don Orehek (reprint from #164)

Page 120-122 – Shut-Ups (martini) – Cosi Van Tutti (Charles Rodrigues) (reprint from #76)

Page 123-125 – Shut-Ups (unlimited talent) – Sam Gross Jr. (Charles Rodrigues) (reprint from #98)

Page 126-128 – Shut-Ups (baseball) – Bill McCartney (Bill Ward) (reprint from #43)

Page 131-133 – Hurry-Ups (Sarge is pinned) – Bill McCartney (Bill Ward) (reprint from #36)

Page 134-136 – Hurry-Ups (last cigarette) – Bill McCartney (Bill Ward) (reprint from #38)

Page 141 – Ye Hang Ups (hanging knight) – LePoer (John Severin) (originally called *Knights 'n' Daze* #36) (reprint from #128)

Page 142-144 – Shut-Ups (fly in my soup) – Dan Clowes (new)

Page 145, Back Cover – Hold this Cover up to the Light! – O.O. Severin (John Severin) (reprint from #55)

Cracked Digest #5, October 1987 (148 pages) ($2.00)

Cover – Sylvester's Skateboard – Bob Fingerman (new)

Page 2 – Believe it or No! – Jack Davis (reprint from #11)

Page 3 – When All of Television Goes 3-D – John Severin (reprint from #200)

Page 10 – On Capitol Hill – Howard Nostrand (reprint from #146)

Page 11 – The Cracked Guide to Martial Arts – Sean Severin (John Severin) (reprint from #150)

Page 20 – Cracked Interviews the Hobo King – Bill Ward (reprint from #148)

Page 35 – Hudd & Dini (octopus) – Vic Martin (reprint from #103)

Page 36 – Wild and Wacky Westerns! (reprint from #103)

Page 41 – Cracked Looks at the Neighborhood Movie House – Vic Martin (reprint from #103)

Page 44 – Escape from the Boredom of the Apes – John Severin (reprint from #97)

Page 58 – Success in Your Chosen Career – Bill McCartney (Bill Ward) (reprint from #96)

Page 67 – Jogging Throughout History – John Severin (reprint from #82)

Page 79 – Going Great Guns (reprint from #80)

Page 84 – Water Shortage (reprint from #38)

Page 96 – Daze & Knights (reprint from #82)

Page 100 – Goryson's Gorillas – John Severin (reprint from #71)

Page 114 – The Skyfighters of World War 1 – John Severin (reprint from #39)

Page 129 – Judo – Jack Davis (reprint from #11)

Page 138 – The Train Robber – Bill McCartney (Bill Ward) (reprint from #34)

Page 141 – Shut-Ups (best nap) – Don Orehek (reprint from #148)

Page 147 – Board Her, Men! – Bill McCartney (Bill Ward) (reprint from #35)

Back Cover – Great Moments in Hospitality 472 A.D. – Howard Nostrand (reprint from #158)

Cracked Monster Party #1, July 1988 (52 pages) ($1.49) (Many issues feature new material.)

Cover – Count Sylvestre – John Severin (new)

Page 2 and 51 – A Day in the Life of the Uggly Family Game – Stosh Gillespie (Dan Clowes) / Eel O'Brian (Mort Todd) (new)

Page 3 – Contents (green color added)

Page 4 – Monster Pets – John Severin / Moe McMahon (Marian McMahon) (reprint from #229) (green color added)

Page 5 – The Movie Monsters Strike – John Severin (reprint from #32)

Page 11 – The Horn – Bill McCartney (Bill Ward) (reprint from #32)

Page 13 – Frankenstein's Spring Fling! – Cliff Mott (new) (green color added)

Page 17 – Rodrigues' Hospital-ity – Charles Rodrigues (reprint from #110)

Page 20 – Alieens – Bill Wray / Joe Catalano, Mort Todd (reprint from #226)

Page 25 – Great Scenes from Great Horror Movies – John Severin (reprint from #42) (green color added)

Page 27 – Cracked Hold-Ups! (pressure on the cooler) – Sururi Gumen (reprint from #204) (green color added)

Page 29 – More Combined Movies "My Fair Lady" & "King Kong" – John Severin (reprint from #133)

Page 30 – The Nightmares of Monsters – Bill McCartney (Bill Ward) (reprint from *For Monsters Only* #5)

Page 32 – Heavy on the Horror, Please (reprint from #95)

Page 34 – You Know You're a Real Monster if – Brian Buniak (reprint from #199)

Page 36 – Another Combined Movie "Godzilla" vs. "The Towering Inferno" – Sururi Gumen (reprint from #137)

Page 37 – To the Top – Pete Wyma (reprint from *Monster Howls* #1) (green color added)

Page 38 – Cracked Nightmare Interview with Freddy! – Rob Orzechowski / Mort Todd (new) (green color added)

Page 41 – Monster Madness! (reprint from *For Monsters Only* #8)

Page 42 – The Big Big Guys! (reprint from #102)

Page 44 – A Tourist's Guide to Transylvania – Vic Martin (reprint from #60)

Page 49 – Monster Diploma (reprint from *For Monsters Only* #2) (green color added)

Page 50 – Shut-Ups (Have a good time!) – Mike Ricigliano (reprint from #138) (green color added)

Back Cover – Sylvester as Freddy! – Bob Fingerman

Cracked Monster Party #2, October 1988 (52 pages) ($1.49)

Cover – Monsters in Haunted House – John Severin (reprint from *For Monsters Only* #3)

Page 2 and 51 – King Kong – Cracked Poster #140 – John Severin (reprint from #140)

Page 3 – Contents

Page 4 – Cracked Visits the Munsters (reprint from #52)

Page 5 – Drecula – John Severin (reprint from #165)

Page 12 – You Know You're the Biggest Thing Around if – Howard Nostrand (reprint from #142)

Page 15 – Fun, Games and Monsters – Vic Martin (reprint from *For Monsters Only* #4)

Page 16 – Mixed Up Pocketbooks – Bill Elder (reprint from #12)

Page 18 – Hudd & Diri (witches) – Vic Martin (reprint from #102)

Page 19 – Quick Quiz (Peter Lawford) (reprint from *For Monsters Only* #1)

Page 21 – A Visit to Transylvania – Bill McCartney (Bill Ward) (reprint from #55)

Page 24 – It Happened at the Cemetery – Caracu (reprint from #69)

Page 26 – Dungeon Dan-Dan-Dandies! – John Severin (reprint from *For Monsters Only* #3)

Page 28 – King Kong's Boyhood – Bill Ward (reprint from #141)

Page 32 – Cracked Monster Phrases – Vic Martin (reprint from *For Monsters Only* #5)

Page 34 – Orehek's Horror Humor! – Don Orehek (reprint from *Cracked Collectors' Edition* #53)

Page 38 – Magazine Covers from Planet of the Apes – John Severin (reprint from #124)

Page 40 – Fiendish for Fun! (reprint from *For Monsters Only* #10)

Page 42 – Transylvania Go Go Football – Vic Martin (reprint from *For Monsters Only* #4)

Page 45 – Cracked Interviews the Monster King – Bill Ward (reprint from #143)

Page 50 – The Terror Trip – BOJ (reprint from #55)

Back Cover – Sicko Ties – Rick Parker (new)

Cracked Monster Party #3, January 1989 (52 pages) ($1.49)

Cover – More Star Wars – Powers (John Severin) (reprint from #148)

Page 2 and 51 – More Star Wars – Cracked Poster – Powers (John Severin) (reprint from #148)

Page 3 – Contents

Page 4 – EaTing – John Severin (reprint from *Giant Cracked Fun-Kit* #34)

Page 11 – Cracked Alien Trading Cards – Basil Wolverton (reprint from *Giant Cracked* #43)

Page 15 – Freezing People – Jack Davis (reprint from #13)

Page 20 – Cracked Space Lens (reprint from *Giant Cracked* #43)

Page 23 – Star People Weekly and Creatures and Things Magazine – John Severin (reprint from #148)

Page 28 – Interplanetary Magazines – Bill Everett (reprint from #8)

Page 30 – Allien and How to Watch it – John Severin (reprint from #164)

Page 37 – Hudd & Dini (rocket) – Vic Martin (reprint from #87)

Page 38 – Cracked Space Helmets – John Severin (reprint from #25)

Page 40 – Cloning: The Advantages and the Disadvantages – Howard Nostrand (reprint from #154)

Page 42 – It Happened on Main and First – Caracu (reprint from #103)

Page 43 – The American Space Base on Mars – John Severin (reprint from #32)

Page 45 – Cracked Interviews the Trekker King – Bill Ward (reprint from #169)

Page 50 – Alien Shut-Ups! (most beautiful girl) – Bill McCartney (Bill Ward) (reprint from #8)

Back Cover – Subscription ad – John Severin (reprint from #66)

***Cracked Monster Party* #4, April 1989 (52 pages) ($1.49)**

Cover – Elvira vs. Nanny – Skene Catling (new)

Page 2 – Great Moments in Sports 1967 – Warren Sattler (reprint from #175)

Page 3 – Contents (red color added)

Page 4, 16, 25-28, 37-40, 49-50 – 1989 Calendar (new) (red color added)

Page 5 – Monster One-Shots (Alien dental floss) – Mike Ricigliano / Roger Brown (reprint from #229)

Page 6 – You Can Write Like Stephen King! – Peter Dulligan / Doug Martin (new)

Page 8 – Transylvanian TV – John Severin (reprint from #229)

Page 13 – Cracked Monster Interview with Evilra – Bill Ward, Skene Catling / Joe Catalano (new) (red color added)

Page 17 – Painting the Town – John Severin / Roger Brown (reprint from #221)

Page 18 – Don Orehek's Horrible Humor – Don Orehek (reprint from #221)

Page 20 – Cracked Horror Lens – Randy Epley (reprint from #221)

Page 22 – Real Life Horror! – Milton Knight (reprint from #221)

Page 23 – Monstrous Practical Jokes! – John Severin / Hilary Zatz (reprint from #221)

Page 29 – Hudd & Dini (CLICK!) – Vic Martin (reprint from #221)

Page 30 – Horror Tales for the 80s – Shawn Kerri (reprint from #221)

Page 33 – Don Orehek's Horrible Humor II: A New Beginning! – Don Orehek (reprint from #229)

Page 35 – Cracked Monster Lens! (Was somebody already sitting) – Randy Epley (reprint from #229)

Page 41 – Monstrous Hurry-Ups! (sweetest cherries) – Rick Altergott / Charles Schneider (reprint from #229)

Page 42 – A Fiend for Life (reprint from *Cracked Collectors' Edition* #43)

Page 44 – Cracked Interviews the Grossout King! – Rob Orzechowski / Joe Catalano (reprint from #229)

Page 48 – Shut-Ups (holding up the works) – Don Orehek (reprint from #221)

Page 49 – The Man and the Beast – Oskar Blotta (reprint from #80)

Back Cover – Nanny's Pin Up Page – Skene Catling (reprint from #229)

***Cracked Monster Party* #5, July 1989 (52 pages) ($1.49)**

Cover – Horrifying Humor – Stosh Gillespie (Dan Clowes) / Eel O'Brian (Mort Todd) (new)

Page 2 and 51 – Monster Party Poster – John Severin (reprint from #43) (Now done as a poster with red color added.)

Page 3 – Contents (green color added)

Page 4 – The Phantom of the Gran' Ol' Opry – Rob Orzechowski (new) (green color added)

Page 5 – The Cracked Monsters Lens (thrilled about dancing) (reprint from *Cracked Collectors' Edition* #52)

Page 10 – Modern Day Monsters – Joe Maneely (reprint from #5)

Page 12 – The Desert Island Guest – John Severin (reprint from *For Monsters Only* #3)

Page 13 – Londumb After Midnight – Rob Orzechowski (new) (green color added)

Page 14 – Irving Claw's Cracked Monster Lens! (I've got to make this) (new) (green color added)

Page 18 – Monster Mother Goose – Bill McCartney (Bill Ward) (reprint from *For Monsters Only* #1)

Page 20 – More Horrors from Don Orehek – Don Orehek (new)

Page 22 – The Condemned Man – John Severin (reprint from #64)

Page 23 – The Stone Age – Oscar Blotta (reprint from *For Monsters Only* #5)

Page 25 – Count Sylvestula – Rob Orzechowski (new) (green color added)

Page 26 – Monster Party! – John Severin (reprint from #31) (green color added)

Page 28 – The Frankensmythe Monster – Rob Orzechowski (new) (green color added)

Page 29 – Frankenstein the Untold Story (reprint from *Cracked Collectors' Edition* #43)

Page 37 – Dr. Jerkyll & Mr. Deidnick – Rob Orzechowski (new) (green color added)

Page 38 – It's a Bad, Bad, Bad, Bad World! – Bo Badman (Rurik Tyler) (new) (green color added)

Page 40 – The Scummy – Rob Orzechowski (new) (green color added)

Page 41 – The Uggly Family Album – Stosh Gillespie (Dan Clowes) (new)

Page 49 – The Wuff Man – Rob Orzechowski (new) (green color added)

Page 50 – Shut-Ups (put his footprints) – Mike Ricigliano (reprint from #142) (green color added)

Back Cover – Sylobite the Smellraiser – Bill Wray

Cracked Monster Party #6, October 1989 (52 pages) ($1.49)

Cover – Freddy's Real Nightmare! – Rurik Tyler (new)

Page 2 – Nanny's Mystery Date – Skene Catling (new)

Page 3 – Contents – Mike Ricigliano (new)

Page 4 – The Original Frankensmythe (silent version) – Rob Orzechowski (new)

Page 5 – Monster Babie's Horror Tales – Bill Wray (reprint from #229)
Page 8 – Tale of the Full Moon – Henry Boltinoff (new)
Page 9 – Cracked Ugly Oracles #1 Psychic Psycho! – Bo Badman (Rurik Tyler) (reprint from #229)
Page 11 – Fetch! – John Severin (reprint from *For Monsters Only* #1)
Page 12 – Transylvanian Rock 'n' Roll Monsters – Vic Martin (reprint from *For Monsters Only* #5)
Page 14 – Nosylferatu – Rob Orzechowski (new)
Page 15 – When Businesses Start Going After the Vampire Market – Warren Sattler (reprint from #166)
Page 19 – The Shmegolem – Rob Orzechowski (new)
Page 20 – Monster Sandwich-Board Men – John Severin (reprint from #34)
Page 21 – The Ghost Finds a Friend – Milton Knight (new)
Page 22 – Monster Party Lines
Page 24 – The Hunchedback of Notre Dumb – Rob Orzechowski (new)
Page 25 – Fun Time Monsters – Vic Martin (reprint from *For Monsters Only* #3)
Page 26 – Fright Knights – Rurik Tyler (new)
Page 28 – Your Little Brother Really is a Monster When – Walter Brogan / Joe Catalano (reprint from #229)
Page 31 – The Man What Laffs – Rob Orzechowski (new)
Page 32 – Chiller Dillers – John Severin, Joe Kiernan, Benson, Pete Wyma, Art Pottier, Lennie Herman, Norm Sutt, Bob (reprint from *For Monsters Only* #1)
Page 34 – The Vampire Strikes – Henry Boltinoff (new)
Page 35 – The Eerie World of Don Orehek - Don Orehek (reprint from *Monster Howls* #1)
Page 37 – The Night Crawlers - Vic Martin (reprint from *For Monsters Only* #5)
Page 38 – Stationery from Transylvania (reprint from *For Monsters Only* #1)
Page 40 – Werewuff of Londum – Rob Orzechowski (new)
Page 41 – Cartoon Screams – Don Orehek (reprint from *For Monsters Only* #4)
Page 42 – The Effects of Horror Movies! (reprint from *Zany* #1)
Page 44 – Martin's Screams – Vic Martin (reprint from *For Monsters Only* #2)
Page 45 – Cracked Luv (based on The Hands of Sylac) – Rob Orzechowski (new)
Page 46 – Darn to Heck with Don Orehek! – Don Orehek (new)
Page 48 – Monster Sale – Henry Boltinoff (new)
Page 49 – The Bride of Frankensmythe – Rob Orzechowski (new)

Page 50 – Shut-Ups (needs salt) – Don Orehek (new)

Page 51 – Tales from the Creep! – Rob Orzechowski (new)

Back Cover – *Cracked Monster Party* #6 and *Monsters Attack!* #1 ad – Rurik Tyler, John Severin

Cracked Monster Party #7, November 1989 (52 pages) ($1.49)

Cover – Shreddy Freddy and Chasin' Jason – Rurik Tyler (new)

Page 2 and 51 – Monster Skate Poster – Phillips Studios (new)

Page 3 – Contents – Flash!! – John Severin (reprint from #?) (originally called ?)

Page 4 – The Curse of Frankensmythe – Rob Orzechowski (new)

Page 5 – The Monster's Advertising Agency – John Severin (reprint from #33)

Page 10 – Real Cracked Books – Vic Martin (reprint from #18)

Page 12 – Shreddy Kreuger – Rob Orzechowski (new)

Page 13 – The Honeymoaners – Win Mortimer / Rich Kriegel (Lou Silverstone) (new)

Page 17 – Schmole People – Rob Orzechowski (new)

Page 18 – Monster Greeting Cards – Don Orehek (reprint from #95)

Page 21 – It's the Great Punkin, Churlie Braun! – Gary Fields (new)

Page 23 – Jasyl – Rob Orzechowski (new)

Page 24 – Fiendish Florist Telephone Delivery ad – John Severin (reprint from #43)

Page 25 – McCartney's Mighty Monsters – Bill McCartney (Bill Ward) (reprint from *For Monsters Only* #5)

Page 26 – Reaper Madness – Rurik Tyler

Page 29 – Monster Shut-Ups (great blocks) – Mike Ricigliano (reprint from *Cracked Collectors' Edition* #51)

Page 30 – The Uggly Family "My Real Weird Science Project" – Stosh Gillespie (Dan Clowes) / Eel O'Brian (Mort Todd) (reprint from *Giant Cracked* #43)

Page 35 – Hudd & Dini (Cracked Annual Monster Party) – Vic Martin (reprint from #230)

Page 37 – Pre-Hystericals – Gary Fields (reprint from #240)

Page 39 – Creature from the Cracked Lagoon – Rob Orzechowski (new)

Page 40 – Hair-Raising Horror of Don Orehek – Don Orehek (new)

Page 43 – Monster Gags – Gary Fields (new)

Page 44 – Cracked Visits a Midnight Monster Picnic – Al Scaduto (reprint from #217)

Page 46 – Cracked Look at Godzilla! – Bill Wray / Joe Catalano (reprint from #219)

Page 49 – Syleatherface – Rob Orzechowski (new)

Page 50 – Monster Shut-Ups (sales climbing) – Rurik Tyler (new)
Back Cover – Sump Thing – Bill Wray (new)

Cracked Monster Party #8, January 1990 (52 pages) ($1.49)
Cover – Count Sylvestre – John Severin (reprint from *Cracked Monster Party* #1)
Page 2 and 51 – A Day in the Life of the Uggly Family Game – Stosh Gillespie (Dan Clowes) / Eel O'Brian (Mort Todd) (reprint from *Cracked Monster Party* #1)
Page 3 – Contents
Page 4 – A MonStar is Reborn – John Severin / George Gladir (reprint from *For Monsters Only* #1)
Page 10 – Vampires of the World – Bernard Baily (reprint from #108)
Page 14 – The Wacky Weirdos (reprint from *For Monsters Only* #6)
Page 16 – Cracked Nightmare Interview with Freddy! – Rob Orzechowski / Mort Todd (reprint from *Cracked Monster Party* #1)
Page 19 – Transylvania's Montgomery & Morgue – John Severin (reprint from *For Monsters Only* #2)
Page 24 – You Know You're a Real Monster if – Brian Buniak (reprint from #199)
Page 26 – More Horrors from Don Orehek – Don Orehek (reprint from *Cracked Monster Party* #5)
Page 28 – The Monster – Sururi Gumen (reprint from #130)
Page 29 – Frankenstein's Spring Fling! – Cliff Mott (reprint from *Cracked Monster Party* #1)
Page 33 – The Uggly Family Album – Stosh Gillespie (Dan Clowes) (reprint from *Cracked Monster Party* #5)
Page 41 – Orders – John Severin (reprint from #38)
Page 42 – It's a Bad, Bad, Bad, Bad World! – Bo Badman (Rurik Tyler) (reprint from *Cracked Monster Party* #5)
Page 44 – You Can Write Like Stephen King! – Peter Dulligan / Doug Martin (reprint from *Cracked Monster Party* #4)
Page 46 – Howl Makers (reprint from *For Monsters Only* #10)
Page 48 – Cracked Monster Interview with Evilra – Bill Ward, Skene Catling / Joe Catalano (reprint from *Cracked Monster Party* #4)
Back Cover – Count Sylvestre Poster – John Severin (reprint from *Cracked Monster Party* #1)

Cracked Monster Party #9, August 1990 (52 pages) ($1.75)
Cover – Syleatherface – Rob Orzechowski (new)
Page 2 and 51 – Syleatherface Poster – Rob Orzechowski (new)
Page 3 – Contents

Page 4 – Big Things are Happening! (reprint from *For Monsters Only* #7)

Page 5 – Spittlejuice – John Severin / Mort Todd (reprint from #239)

Page 9 – The Weirdo – Vic Martin (new)

Page 11 and 37 – It Can Happen to You – Basil Wolverton (new to *Cracked*.)

Page 12 – Orehek's Weird! – Don Orehek (new)

Page 15 – The Uggly Family in "Elvis, You're a Janitor?" – Stosh Gillespie (Dan Clowes) (reprint from #244)

Page 18 – Planets of the Creatures - John Severin (reprint from #72)

Page 24 – Summer Jobs for Movie Monsters – Kent Gamble (reprint from #216)

Page 26 – Form and Function Looks at the Roach! – Bo Badman (Rurik Tyler) (reprint from #246)

Page 28 – Freddie the Menace – Gary Fields (reprint from #245)

Page 30 – Monsters Get Off on Ecological Disasters! – Vic Martin / George Gladir (reprint from #246)

Page 33 – Handbook for Scaring People! – Bo Badman (Rurik Tyler) / George Gladir (reprint from #239)

Page 38 – Mighty Mad Monsters Strike Again (new) Page 40 – Sherlock Holmes vs Jack the Ripper – John Severin / Tony Frank (Lou Silverstone) (reprint from #247)

Page 45 – All-New Monster Party Activity Page – Rurik Tyler (new)

Page 47 – Cracked Interviews Frankenstein, the Movie Monster King – Bill Burke (reprint from #217)

Page 50 – Ghostbugger Shut-Ups (Class 5 apparitions) – Rurik Tyler (reprint from #249)

Back Cover – Cracked Monster Party Picnic Pin-Up – O.O. Severin (John Severin) (reprint from #54)

Cracked Monster Party #10, October 1990 (52 pages) ($1.75)

Cover – Sylvester, Pizza Delivery Boy – Rurik Tyler (new)

Page 2 and 51 – Monster Party Animal Poster – Mort Todd (new)

Page 3 – Contents

Page 4 – Tales From the Dork Side – Walter Brogan (new)

Page 8 – The Abominable Dr. Smythe – Rob Orzechowski (new)

Page 9 – The Zillionaire Starring the Uggly Family – Stosh Gillespie (Dan Clowes) (reprint from #243)

Page 13 – The Syl Fly – Rob Orzechowski (new)

Page 14 – Monsters in the News – John Severin (reprint from #59)

Page 16 – Jawz – John Severin (reprint from #129)

Page 22 – Cracked's Guide to Sharks – Don Orehek (reprint from #130)

Page 25 – The Syl-Creature – Rob Orzechowski (new)

Page 26 – Cracked Puts the Bite on Dracula – Howard Nostrand (reprint from #155)
Page 30 – Dork Shadows – Rob Orzechowski (new)
Page 31 – Cracked Takes a Look at the Transylvanian Teen Scene – John Severin (reprint from #40)
Page 36 – Don Orehek Back at the Board! – Don Orehek (new)
Page 38 – Mr. Smythdonicus – Rob Orzechowski (new)
Page 39 – The Painter's Fantasy – Oskar Blotta (reprint from #85)
Page 40 – Snore Johnson – Rob Orzechowski (new)
Page 41 – The Cremation of Sam McGee – John Severin (reprint from #19)
Page 45 – Monster Party Animal – Mort Todd (new)
Page 49 – Monster Laughs!!! (reprint from *For Monsters Only* #9)
Page 50 – Invasion of the Saucer-Smythe – Rob Orzechowski (new)
Back Cover – Shut-Ups (one big artichoke) – Don Orehek (new)

Cracked Monster Party #11, January 1991 (52 pages) ($1.75)
Cover – Monster Party Election – Rurik Tyler (new)
Page 2 – Simian "Gone Ape" Smythe – Rob Orzechowski, John Severin (new)
Page 3 – Contents – John Severin
Page 4 – Ghouls-R-Us – Rob Orzechowski (new)
Page 6 – Ye Hang Ups (getting off for good behavior) – John Severin (new)
Page 9 – Underneath the Planet of the Apes – John Severin (reprint from #90)
Page 13 – The Zombie Smythe – Rob Orzechowski (new)
Page 14 – Awesome and Bogus Robots of the Future – Mike Ricigliano / Roger Brown (new)
Page 16 – Rosemary's Baby Devlin – Lugoze (reprint from #76)
Page 19 – Shut-Ups (happiest day) – Don Orehek (new)
Page 20 – Horror Tales for the 80s – Shawn Kerri (reprint from #221)
Page 23 – Invisible Smythe – Rob Orzechowski (new)
Page 24 – Monster Party Animal in: Tis the Season to be Rowdy! – Cliff Mott, Mort Todd / John Arcudi (new)
Page 28 – Cracked Presents Future Insect Monster Movies – Sururi Gumen (reprint from #125)
Page 32 – Hudd & Dini (elephant) – Vic Martin (new)
Page 34 – Clodsylla – Rob Orzechowski (new) Page 35 – Ant-Ant! – Gary Fields (new)
Page 38 – The Creature from the Root Canal! – Don Orehek (new)

Page 40 – Masters of Evil (reprint from #174)

Page 43 – Cracked's Look at Superstitions – Warren Sattler (reprint from #178)

Page 46 – Amazing Collosyl Man – Rob Orzechowski (new)

Page 47 – Monster Vote Getters – John Severin / George Gladir (reprint from #241)

Page 50 – Vote for the Monster of Your Choice (new)

Page 51 – Of Grave Concern! (new)

Back Cover – Transylvanian Citizenship Certificate (new)

Cracked Monster Party #12, April 1991 (52 pages) ($1.75)

Cover – King Kong Sweeps Election! – Frank Borth (new)

Page 2 and 51 – Congratulations King Kong Poster – Rurik Tyler (new)

Page 3 – Contents – John Severin

Page 4 – The Transylvanian Glob (King Kong Write-In) – Rurik Tyler (new) (1st *Transylvanian Glob*)

Page 2 – Count Dracula …2086 A.D. – John Severin / George Gladir (reprint from #224)

Page 8 – Cesspool and Regurt Look at This Year's Horror Videos – Rurik Tyler (new)

Page 11 – Shut-Ups (money and credit cards) – Don Orehek (reprint from #170)

Page 12 – Sylvester: Creep of 1000 Faces (wolfman character) – Rob Orzechowski (new)

Page 13 – Cracked Interviews Stephen Kink the Horror King! – Stan Goldberg, Mike Esposito / Joe Catalano (reprint from #221)

Page 18 – There's a Small Motel – Mike Ricigliano (new)

Page 19 – How to Have a Fun Time on Earth – Don Orehek (reprint from #196)

Page 24 – Monster Combination Movies – Walter Brogan / Jim Wheelock (reprint from #221)

Page 26 – The Incredible Hunk – Sigbjorn (John Severin) (reprint from #177)

Page 31 – E.Z. Meets Clodzilla – Rob Orzechowski (new)

Page 36 – Monster Party Animal The Stinker – Cliff Mott (new)

Page 40 – Teen-Age Movie Monsters – Rob Orzechowski / George Gladir (reprint from #236)

Page 43 – Sylvester: Creep of 1000 Faces (witch character) – Rob Orzechowski (new)

Page 44 – King Kung – John Severin (reprint from #140)

Back Cover – Screaming Room Only! – O.O. Severin (John Severin) (reprint from #105)

Cracked Monster Party #13, August 1991 (52 pages) ($1.75)

Cover – Vote for the Thing of Your Choice! – Rurik Tyler (new)

Page 2 and 51 – Beeyootie Contest Poster – Rurik Tyler (new)

Page 3 – Contents – Rurik Tyler

Page 4 – Transylvanian Glob (Invisible Woman Goes Berserk!) – Rurik Tyler (new)

Page 8 – Grumblins – John Severin (reprint from #209)

Page 15 – The Transdeformers vs Boltron – Steve Ditko / Mort Todd, John Arcudi (reprint from #222)

Page 18 – A Visit to Grossland – Rob Orzechowski (new)

Page 20 – The Freakniks Meet the Wreckin' Crew (reprint from *Cracked Super* #2)

Page 27 – "Curse of the Wolfman" Sylvester – Rob Orzechowski (new)

Page 28 – Gross is Great – Stosh Gillespie (Dan Clowes) / Eel O'Brian (Mort Todd) (reprint from #228)

Page 30 – The Making of Thriller (reprint from #207)

Page 36 – A Reunion of Geraldo's Guests – Don Orehek (new)

Page 38 – Reptile Sylvester – Rob Orzechowski (new)

Page 39 – The Thing Most Likely to Succeed – Rurik Tyler (new)

Page 43 – Ghastly Ghoulies – Mike Ricigliano (Looking for Cheap Thrills) (new)

Page 46 – Ye Hang Ups (What makes you think) – John Severin (new)

Page 47 – Rock and Roll Mutations! – Bob Fingerman / Hilary Zatz (reprint from #231)

Page 50 – Subscription ad – Frank Borth

Back Cover – Shut-Ups (Dr. Jekyll) – Don Orehek (new)

Cracked Monster Party #14, October 1991 (52 pages) ($1.75)

Cover – Chucky's Back! – Rurik Tyler (new)

Page 2 and 51 – Monsters on Parade Poster – Arnoldo Franchioni (new)

Page 3 – Contents

Page 4 – Child's Plague 2¾ - Harry North (new)

Page 8 – Video Nightmares – Don Orehek (reprint from #205)

Page 12 – Mr. Moto Sylvester – Rob Orzechowski (new)

Page 13 – Throughout History with the Real Gremlins – John Severin (reprint from #209)

Page 15 – Female Movie Monsters – Rob Orzechowski / George Gladir (new)

Page 18 – Morbad News (reprint from #176)

Page 21 – The Monsters Laugh it Up! (reprint from #56)

Page 23 – Trouble's on the Way! – Harry North (new)

Page 26 – The Sabotaged Haunted House – Mike Ricigliano (new)

Page 28 – Polter-Psycho-Geist – John Reiner / Mortimer Post, Mort Todd (reprint from #221)

Page 33 – Big Head Sylvester – Rob Orzechowski (new)

Page 34 – What Goes on in a Monster's Mind – Don Orehek (reprint from #138)

Page 37 – The Most Horrible Monster of All – Walt Lardner (reprint from #93)

Page 38 – Don Orehek Off the Macabre – Don Orehek (new)

Page 41 – Crimedom's Mail Order Catalogue – Warren Sattler (reprint from #146)

Page 46 – Ye Hang Ups (one good turn) – John Severin (new)

Page 47 – Monster Diploma (reprint from *For Monsters Only* #2)

Page 48 – Subscription ad – Frank Borth

Page 49 – Cracked Hold-Ups! (ask alien for identification) – Don Orehek (new)

Back Cover – We'll Drive You Bats! – John Severin (reprint from #165)

Cracked Monster Party #15, January 1992 (52 pages) ($1.75)

Cover – Freddie's Dead…Not! – Rurik Tyler (new)

Page 2 – Cracked Monster Party! Pin-Up! – John Severin (reprint from #43)

Page 3 – Contents – Mike Ricigliano

Page 4 – Freddy's Dead The Final Rip-Off – Frank Borth / Steve Strangio (new)

Page 9 – Ghastly Ghoulies (Cleaning up one's act) – Mike Ricigliano / May Sakami (new)

Page 11 – Handbook for Scaring People! – Bo Badman (Rurik Tyler) / George Gladir (reprint from #239)

Page 15 – The Growing Cult of the Occult – Don Orehek (reprint from #96)

Page 18 – A Cracked Look at Monster Garbage – Rob Orzechowski (new)

Page 22 – Updated Torture Devices for Catching the Witches of Today – John Severin (reprint from #58) (The dates in the article were changed from 1567 and 1967 to 1591 and 1991.)

Page 25 – Monsters Get Off on Ecological Disasters! – Vic Martin / George Gladir (reprint from #246)

Page 28 – Real Cracked Books – Vic Martin (reprint from #18)

Page 30 – Make Mine Well Done! – John Langton (reprint from #62)

Page 31 – Cracked Hold-Ups! (stone carvings) – Don Orehek (new)

Page 33 – Freddy's Celebrity Nightmares! – John Severin / Tony Frank (Lou Silverstone) (reprint from #240)

Page 35 – Monster Party! Letters

Page 36 – Hiss the Villains (reprint from #94)

Page 40 – Movie Monster Museum – Rob Orzechowski / George Gladir

Page 43 – If Frankenstein's Monster Did Guest Appearances on T.V. – Howard Nostrand (reprint from #151)

Page 49 – Witches' Stew – Arnoldo Franchioni (new)

Back Cover – Fangmann's ad – John Severin (reprint from #36)

Cracked Monster Party #16, April 1992 (52 pages) ($1.75)

Cover – The Addams Family – John Severin (new)

Page 2 and 51 – Club Dred Poster – Rurik Tyler (new)

Page 3 – Contents – Mike Ricigliano

Page 4 – The Addarns Family – Walter Brogan / Lou Silverstone

Page 8 – Cryptic Commercials – Frank Caruso (reprint from #221)

Page 10 – Paranoia News Magazine – John Langton (reprint from #89)

Page 13 – Creature from the Cracked Lagoon! – Rurik Tyler (new)

Page 16 – How to Cure Superstitions (reprint from #19)

Page 18 – Old Movie Monster Films Updated for Today – Kent Gamble (reprint from #213)

Page 22 – I've Never Met a Monster I Didn't Like – Arnold Franchioni (new)

Page 24 – Don Orehek's Horrible Humor – Don Orehek (reprint from #221)

Page 26 – Spies and Saboteurs in an Egyptian Tomb – Mike Ricigliano (new)

Page 28 – Cracked Interviews Frankenstein, the Movie Monster King – Bill Burke (reprint from #217)

Page 32 – If Other Actors Played the Parts Made Famous by Somebody Else – John Severin (reprint from #151)

Page 36 – Monster Party! – John Severin (reprint from #31)

Page 38 – Madame Fatal's Advice to Monsters – Mike Ricigliano (new)

Page 39 – Real Scary Horror Videos – Rob Orzechowski / George Gladir (new)

Page 41 – Monsterous Merriment (reprint from #98)

Page 43 – Horror Tales for the 80s – Shawn Kerri (reprint from #22_)

Page 46 – The Adamns Family Photo Album – Gary Fields / George Gladir (new)

Page 50 – Subscription ad – Mike Ricigliano

Back Cover – Transylvania Life ad – John Severin (reprint from #35)

Cracked Monster Party #17, August 1992 (52 pages) ($1.75)

Cover – On the Set of Alien 3 – Rurik Tyler (new)

Page 2 – The Lonely Convict and the Pet – Oskar Blotta (reprint from #141)

Page 3 – Contents – Mike Ricigliano

Page 4 – Cracked Visits the Alien 3 Set – Walter Brogan / Scott Franklin, John Leary (new)

Page 9 – Godzilla Visits the Big Apple! – Arnoldo Franchioni (new)

Page 12 – Cracked's Detective Handbook – Bill Ward (reprint from #151)

Page 16 – Allien and How to Watch it – John Severin (reprint from #164)

Page 23 – Transylvania Go Go Football – Vic Martin (reprint from *For Monsters Only* #4)

Page 26 – Cracked Creates the Perfect Baseball Monster – Mike Ricigliano (new)

Page 28 – Monster Party! Letters

Page 29 – Subscription ad – Mike Ricigliano

Page 30 – Alien Shut-Ups! (most beautiful girl) – Bill McCartney (Bill Ward) (reprint from #8)

Page 31 – Cracked Hold-Ups! (that gimmick) – Don Orehek (new) Page 33 – Cracked Horror Lens – Randy Epley (reprint from #221)

Page 35 – Alieens – Bill Wray / Joe Catalano, Mort Todd (reprint from #226)

Page 40 – Witchcraft The & Now – Rob Orzechowski / George Gladir (new)

Page 43 – Monster Bummers – Don Orehek / Jed Vier (new)

Page 46 – Our Baby Alien Album – Rurik Tyler / Andy Simmons (new)

Page 51 – Ye Hang Ups (New Kids on the Block) – John Severin (reprint from #254)

Back Cover – Monster Party Time! Excellent! – Rurik Tyler (new)

Cracked Monster Party #18, October 1992 (52 pages) ($1.75)

Cover – Honey, We Blow Up Honey, I Blew Up the Kid! – Rurik Tyler (new)

Page 2 and 51 – Monster Go Round – Arnoldo Franchioni (new)

Page 3 – Contents – Mike Ricigliano

Page 4 – How to Raise Your 112 Foot Baby – Bruce Bolinger / Andy Simmons (new)

Page 8 – Cracked Look at Godzilla! – Bill Wray / Joe Catalano (reprint from #219)

Page 10 – King Kong's Boyhood – Bill Ward (reprint from #141)

Page 14 – Moonlighting Monsters – Don Orehek (new)

Page 16 – Ye Hang Ups #3 (screams) – C.E. Severin (Catherine Severin) (reprint from #172)

Page 17 – It's the Great Punkin, Churlie Braun! – Gary Fields (reprint from *Cracked Monster Party* #7)

Cracked Monster Party #19, January 1993 (52 pages) ($1.75)

Page 28 – The Honeymoaners – Win Mortimer / Rich Kriegel (Lou Silverstone) (reprint from *Cracked Monster Party* #7)

Page 32 – Cracked's Monster Dating Chart – Mike Ricigliano (new)

Page 34 – Monstrous Practical Jokes! – John Severin / Hilary Zatz (reprint from #221)

Page 36 – Shut-Ups (holding up the works) – Don Orehek (reprint from #221)

Page 37 – Real-Life Monsters from the Deepest Pits of School – Pete Fitzgerald / Daniel O'Keefe

Page 40 – When They Were Young – Don Orehek / George Gladir (new)

Page 42 – Circus of the Monsters – Arnoldo Franchioni (new)

Page 44 – Drecula – John Severin (reprint from #165)

Page 51 – Subscription ad – Mike Ricigliano

Back Cover – Sylobite the Smellraiser – Bill Wray (reprint from *Cracked Monster Party* #5)

Cracked Monster Party #20, April 1993 (52 pages) ($1.75)

Cover – Jason Goes to Hell! – John Severin (new)

Page 2 – Shut-Ups (one big artichoke) – Don Orehek (reprint from *Cracked Monster Party* #10)

Page 3 – Contents – Mike Ricigliano

Page 4 – Army of Dorkness Evil Dread III – Walter Brogan / Lou Silverstone (new)

Page 9 – What Kind of a Man Reads Cracked Monster Party? (new) (photos of Bruce Campbell, Michael Meyer, Doug Bradley, Tony Timpone, Walter Brogan and Lou Silverstone)

Page 10 – Fright Knights – Rurik Tyler (reprint from *Cracked Monster Party* #6)

Page 12 – Jason Goes to Hell – Bruce Bolinger / Daniel O'Keefe (new)

Page 16 – Cracked Horror Lens – Randy Epley (reprint from #221)

Page 18 – Monster Babie's Horror Tales – Bill Wray (reprint from #229)

Page 21 – 1st Annual Transylvanian Yard Sale – Rob Orzechowski / Gayle Adams-Pierpont (new)

Page 24 – Pre-Hystericals – Gary Fields (reprint from #240)

Page 26 – Form and Function Looks at the Roach! – Bo Badman (Rurik Tyler) (reprint from #246)

Page 28 – Jason's Body Count! – Kevin McMahon (reprint from *Monsters Attack!* #3)

Page 32 – Subscription ad

Page 33 – Your Little Brother Really is a Monster When – Walter Brogan / Joe Catalano (reprint from #229)

Page 36 – Monster Bummers – Don Orehek / Jed Vier (reprint from
  Cracked Monster Party #17)
Page 38 – Matlocch – Walter Brogan (new)
Page 43 – Ghouls-R-Us – Rob Orzechowski (reprint from *Cracked
  Monster Party* #11)
Page 51 – Great Moments in Sports 1967 – Warren Sattler (reprint from
  #175)
Back Cover – Sicko Ties – Rick Parker (reprint from *Cracked Monster
  Party* #2)

Cracked Monster Party #21, August 1993 (52 pages) ($1.75)
Cover – Barney Goes to Jurassic Park – Rurik Tyler (new)
Page 2 – *Cracked Super* #7 ad
Page 3 – Contents – Mike Ricigliano
Page 4 – Blarney and the Backyard Gang Go to Jurassic Park – Bruce
  Bolinger / Dan Birtcher (new)
Page 8 – Planets of the Creatures - John Severin (reprint from #72)
Page 10 – The Suicide – Caracu (reprint from #68)
Page 11 – Monster Medicine Cabinet – Rob Orzechowski / Gayle
  Adams-Pierpont (new)
Page 14 – Cracked Dinosaur True or Fossil Quiz? – Rurik Tyler (reprint
  from #252)
Page 16 – More Horrible Humor (reprint from #97) (originally called
  "Horrible Humor")
Page 18 – A Visit to the Museum of Unnatural History – Don Orehek /
  Rob Weske (new)
Page 19 – Shylock Homes and the Case of the Lifted Locket – Moe
  Riarty (John Severin) / Joe Catalano (reprint from #162)
Page 26 – A Prehysterical Look at Jurassic Park – Mike Ricigliano (new)
Page 28 – Cracked Takes You Back to the Year 1075 BC! – Bill
  McCartney (Bill Ward) (reprint from #74)
Page 30 – Black Movie Monsters – LePoer (John Severin) (reprint from
  #111)
Page 35 – T-Rex at Mann's Chinese Theater (new)
Page 37 – Subscription ad
Page 38 – Undiscovered Dinosaur Species – Gary Fields / Rob Weske
  (new)
Page 41 – Vampire Gags – Gary Fields (reprint from #252)
Page 44 – Ye Hang Ups (starting to resent) – John Severin (reprint from
  #252)
Page 45 – Take Me Out to the Ball Game! – Alan Kupperberg / Lou
  Silverstone (new)

Page 51 – Cracked presents the Aftermath of the Dinosaurs Attack Cards! – Bo Badman (Rurik Tyler) (reprint from #246)

Back Cover – The Barneysaurus – Jim Bennett (new)

Cracked Monster Party #22, Winter 1993 (52 pages) ($1.75)

Cover – Freddy Krueger Back to School Issue! – John Severin (new)

Page 2 – *Cracked Spaced Out* #2 ad

Page 3 – Contents – Mike Ricigliano

Page 4 – Freddy's Worst Nightmare – Walter Brogan / Rich Kriegel (Lou Silverstone) (new)

Page 8 – All-New Monster Party Activity Page – Rurik Tyler (reprint from *Cracked Monster Party* #10)

Page 10 – Cracked Nightmare Interview with Freddy! – Rob Orzechowski / Mort Todd (reprint from *Cracked Monster Party* #1)

Page 13 – Dreddy's Dead The Final Rip-Off – Frank Borth / Steve Strangio (new)

Page 18 – The Monster – Sururi Gumen (reprint from #130)

Page 19 – Hannibal Lecter's Places – Rob Orzechowski / Craig Farrell (new)

Page 22 – Stiffs – Walter Brogan / Andrew Osborne (new)

Page 26 – Monsterous Merriment (reprint from #98)

Page 28 – Modern Day Monsters – Joe Maneely (reprint from #5)

Page 30 – Subscription ad

Page 31 – Mr. Prince-of-Darkness (Christopher Lee photo) (new)

Page 32 – Transylvanian School Cafeteria – Don Orehek / Gayle Adams-Pierpont (new)

Page 34 – The Thing Most Likely to Succeed – Rurik Tyler (reprint from *Cracked Monster Party* #13)

Page 38 – Note to the Teacher – Don Orehek / Gayle Adams-Pierpont (new)

Page 40 – The Little Dread Schoolhouse – Lee Chenell (reprint from #268)

Page 41 – When Old Age Finally Hits Monsterdom – Vic Martin / George Gladir (reprint from #240)

Page 44 – Dungeon Dan-Dan-Dandies! – John Severin (reprint from *For Monsters Only* #3)

Page 46 – Monsterpiece Theater – Alan Kupperberg / Andy Simmons (new)

Page 51 – Sylvester as Freddy! – Bob Fingerman (reprint from *Cracked Monster Party* #1)

Back Cover – Cracked Monster Party Picnic Pin-Up – O.O. Severin (John Severin) (reprint from #54 and *Cracked Monster Party* #9)

Cracked Monster Party #23, Spring 1994 (52 pages) ($1.75)
Cover – Addams Family devalues – Jeff Wong (new)
Page 2 – *Cracked Spaced Out* #3 ad – John Severin (reprint from #129)
Page 3 – Contents – Mike Ricigliano
Page 4 – The Addamneds Family Devalued – Walter Brogan / Steve
    Strangio (new)
Page 9 – Don Orehek Back at the Board! – Don Orehek (reprint from
    Cracked Monster Party #10)
Page 11 – Transylvania's Montgomery & Morgue – John Severin
    (reprint from *For Monsters Only* #2)
Page 14 – Monsters and Mobsters – Arnoldo Franchioni (new)
Page 16 – R.I.P. Pallbearer, All-Transylvanian – Walter Brogan / Lou
    Silverstone (new)
Page 20 – Mixed Up Pocketbooks – Bill Elder (reprint from #12)
Page 22 – Monster Party Animal – Mort Todd (reprint from *Cracked
    Monster Party* #10)
Page 26 – Thing's Palm Reading – Gary Fields / Daniel O'Keefe (new)
Page 28 – Shut-Ups (Have a good time!) – Mike Ricigliano (reprint
    from #138)
Page 29 – The Monster's Advertising Agency – John Severin (reprint
    from #33)
Page 34 – Monster Day Dreams – Rob Orzechowski / George Gladir
    (new)
Page 36 – A Tourist's Guide to Transylvania – Vic Martin (reprint from
    #60)
Page 41 – The Screamers (reprint from *For Monsters Only* #5)
Page 44 – Subscription ad – John Severin
Page 45 – And the Defendant Answered – Bernard Baily (reprint from
    #110)
Page 46 – Monster Party Theater Blarney – Alan Kupperberg / Lance
    Contrucci (new)
Page 51 – The Man and the Beast – Oskar Blotta (reprint from #80)
Back Cover – Medusa Invents the Bad Hair Day – Jim Bennett (new)

Cracked Monster Party #24, Summer 1994 (52 pages) ($1.75)
Cover – Teen Creep – Jeff Wong (new)
Page 2 – Transylvanian Summertime – Vic Martin (reprint from #250)
Page 3 – Contents – Mike Ricigliano
Page 4 – Frightbore Before Christmas – Gary Fields / Lou Silverstone
    (new)
Page 10 – Ye Hang Ups (The moon is full) – John Severin (reprint from
    #240)

Page 12 – Cracked Monster Get Well Cards – Bruce Bolinger / Patric Adedin (new)

Page 15 – Transylvanian TV – John Severin (reprint from #229)

Page 19 – Cracked Look at Frankenstein – Cliff Mott / John Arcudi (reprint from #234)

Page 21 – Your Little Brother Really is a Monster When – Walter Brogan / Joe Catalano (reprint from #229)

Page 24 – Another Helping of Monster Goodies – Rob Orzechowski / Gayle Adams-Pierpont (new)

Page 26 – Subscription ad

Page 27 – Teen Creep Magazine – Jeff Wong (new)

Page 33 – Monster Babie's Horror Tales – Bill Wray (reprint from #229)

Page 36 – The Effects of Horror Movies! (reprint from *Zany* #1)

Page 38 – Tales From the Dork Side – Walter Brogan (reprint from *Cracked Monster Party* #10)

Page 42 – The Big Big Guys! (reprint from #102)

Page 44 – Painting the Town – John Severin / Roger Brown (reprint from #221)

Page 45 – Monster Party Theater Presents: Have an Ice Day! – Alan Kupperberg / Andy Simmons (new)

Page 50 – Monster Shut-Ups (sales climbing) – Rurik Tyler (reprint from *Cracked Monster Party* #7)

Page 51 – The Man and the Ink Spot – Oskar Blotta (reprint from #146)

Back Cover – Late One Night in a Cemetary (sic) – Don Orehek / Greg Grabianski (new)

***Cracked Monster Party* #25, Fall 1994 (52 pages) ($1.75)**

Cover – We Blow Up The Stand – John Severin (new)

Page 2 – Shut-Ups (Dr. Jekyll) – Don Orehek (reprint from *Cracked Monster Party* #13)

Page 3 – Contents – Mike Ricigliano

Page 4 – The Stunnded – Walter Brogan / Lou Silverstone (new)

Page 10 – More Horrible Horrors from the Spooky Pen of Don Orehek – Don Orehek (new)

Page 12 – Cesspool and Regurt Look at This Year's Horror Videos – Rurik Tyler (reprint from *Cracked Monster Party* #12)

Page 15 – Ghastly Ghoulies (Looking for Cheap Thrills) – Mike Ricigliano (reprint from *Cracked Monster Party* #13)

Page 18 – The Nightmares of Monsters – Bill McCartney (Bill Ward) (reprint from *For Monsters Only* #5)

Page 20 – Ye Hang Ups (basket of heads) – John Severin (new)

Page 21 – Cracked Interviews Stephen Kink the Horror King! – Stan Goldberg, Mike Esposito / Joe Catalano (reprint from #221)

Page 26 – First Annual Transylvanian Pet Show – Rob Orzechowski / Gayle Adams-Pierpont (new)

Page 28 – Subscription ad

Page 29 – Transylvanian Glob (Invisible Woman Goes Berserk!) – Rurik Tyler (reprint from *Cracked Monster Party* #13)

Page 32 – Fetch! – John Severin (reprint from *For Monsters Only* #1)

Page 33 – If Monsters Were Dealt With By Our Criminal Justice System! – Bruce Bolinger / Dan Birtcher (new)

Page 36 – Monster Party Animal The Stinker – Cliff Mott (reprint from *Cracked Monster Party* #12)

Page 40 – A Reunion of Geraldo's Guests – Don Orehek (reprint from *Cracked Monster Party* #13)

Page 42 – Masters of Evil (reprint from #174)

Page 45 – Monster Party Theater The Devil's Dinero – Alan Kupperberg / Lou Silverstone (new)

Page 50 – Shut-Ups (happiest day) – Don Orehek (reprint from *Cracked Monster Party* #11)

Page 51 – Sicko Ties – Rick Parker (reprint from *Cracked Monster Party* #2)

Back Cover – Samsonbites Coffins – Rurik Tyler / Randy Epley (new)

Cracked Monster Party #26, Winter 1994 (52 pages) ($1.75)

Cover – We Put On The Mask – Rurik Tyler (new)

Page 2 and 51 – King Kong – Cracked Poster #140 – John Severin (reprint from #140)

Page 3 – Contents – Mike Ricigliano

Page 4 – The Unmasked – Walter Brogan / Lou Silverstone (new)

Page 10 – Monsters in the News – John Severin (reprint from #59)

Page 12 – Monster Mother Goose – Bill McCartney (Bill Ward) (reprint from *For Monsters Only* #1)

Page 14 – Subscription ad

Page 15 – Monster Mini-Flips – Mike Ricigliano (new)

Page 17 – More Monster Mini-Flips – Mike Ricigliano (new)

Page 19 – E.Z. Meets Clodzilla – Rob Orzechowski (reprint from *Cracked Monster Party* #12)

Page 24 – It's a Bad, Bad, Bad, Bad World! – Bo Badman (Rurik Tyler) (reprint from *Cracked Monster Party* #5)

Page 26 – Cracked's Monster Sports – Arnoldo Franchioni (new)

Page 28 – School For Monsters – Nireves (John Severin) (reprint from #26)

Page 33 – Cracked Hold-Ups (prefer fast food) – Don Orehek / George Gladir (new)

Page 35 – Frankenstein the Untold Story (reprint from *Cracked Collectors' Edition* #43)

Page 43 – Cracked Monster Phrases – Vic Martin (reprint from *For Monsters Only* #5)

Page 45 – Monster Party Theater One Hell of a Chick – Alan Kupperberg / Greg Grabianski (new)

Page 50 – Shut-Ups (needs salt) – Don Orehek (reprint from *Cracked Monster Party* #6)

Back Cover – The Wolf Hunt – Jeff Wong / Missy Candytuft (new)

Cracked Monster Party #27, Spring 1995 (52 pages) ($1.75)

Cover – Interview With the Vampire – Jeff Wong (new)

Page 2 and 51 – Frankenstein '94 The Authorized Autopsy Poster – Rurik Tyler / Barry Zeger (new)

Page 3 – Contents – Mike Ricigliano

Page 4 – David Bloodletterman's Interview With a Vampire – Jeff Wong / Andy Simmons (new)

Page 10 – Witches Brew – Arnoldo Franchioni (new)

Page 12 – Cracked Takes a Look at the Transylvanian Teen Scene – John Severin (reprint from #40)

Page 17 – Sci-Fi Catalogue – Pete Fitzgerald / Rob Weske

Page 20 – Monster Sandwich-Board Men – John Severin (reprint from #34)

Page 22 – Freddy Krocker Food Company – Rurik Tyler (reprint from #251)

Page 25 – Dr. Fizzix #2452 – Let's Make a Tropical Volcano – Gary Fields / Eric Goldberg, Mark Howard (new)

Page 26 – Monster Party Cracked Collector Plates – Bruce Bolinger (new)

Page 28 – Subscription ad (reprint from #295)

Page 29 – The Schocky Horror Picture Show – Walter Brogan (new)

Page 34 – Orehek Gags! – Don Orehek (reprint from #251)

Page 36 – Heavy on the Horror, Please (reprint from #95)

Page 38 – Transylvania Go Go Football – Vic Martin (reprint from *For Monsters Only* #4)

Page 41 – Frankenstein's Spring Fling! – Cliff Mott (reprint from *Cracked Monster Party* #1)

Page 45 – Monster Party Theater Presents: "A Stiff Penalty" – Alan Kupperberg / Greg Grabianski (new)

Page 50 – One Moonlit Night – Arnoldo Franchioni (new)

Back Cover – Witches' Convention Parking – Arnoldo Franchioni (new)

Cracked Monster Party #28, Summer 1995 (52 pages) ($1.75)
Cover – Bleedvis and Bolt-Head – Walter Brogan (new)
Page 2 – Two Heads Are Better Than – John Severin (reprint from #236)
Page 3 – Contents – Mike Ricigliano
Page 4 – Bleedvis & Bolt-Head Check-Out MTV – Walter Brogan / Judd Stomp (new)
Page 9 – Ye Hang Ups (underarm deodorant) – John Severin (reprint from #255)
Page 10 – Awesome and Bogus Robots of the Future – Mike Ricigliano / Roger Brown (reprint from Cracked Monster Party #11)
Page 12 – Old Movie Monster Films Updated for Today – Kent Gamble (reprint from #213)
Page 16 – Werewolf of the 90s – Rob Orzechowski / Don DeBruin (new)
Page 18 – Transylvania's Funniest Home Videos – John Severin / Jack Harris (reprint from #261)
Page 23 – More Combined Movies "My Fair Lady" & "King Kong" – John Severin (reprint from #133)
Page 24 – Really Scary Creatures from Everyday Life! – Gary Fields / Bill Ignizio (reprint from #268)
Page 26 – Transylvanialand – Arnoldo Franchioni (new)
Page 28 – Ye Hang Ups (Sob! Moan!) – John Severin (reprint from #257)
Page 29 – Monster Party Theater Wes Craving's New Nightmare on Lexington Avenue – Alan Kupperberg / Lance Contrucci (new)
Page 34 – Werewolves Were Affected by Other Types of Moons – Rurik Tyler (reprint from #264)
Page 36 – Monster Shut-Ups (this smell) – Don Orehek / Barry Zeger (new)
Page 37 – Vic Martin's Monsters on Parade! – Vic Martin (reprint from #252)
Page 40 – Hiss the Villains (reprint from #94)
Page 44 – Cracked Ghostbuggers Gear – Rurik Tyler (reprint from #249)
Back Cover – TV Gore Magazine – Rurik Tyler (new)
Page 51 – Subscription ad – John Severin (reprint from Cracked Monster Party #1 and Cracked #297)

Cracked Monster Party #29, Fall 1995 (52 pages) ($1.75)
Cover – Casper the Snotty Ghost – Rurik Tyler (new)
Page 2 – Cracked Blockbuster #9 ad
Page 3 – Contents – Mike Ricigliano
Page 4 – Corpser – Don Orehek / Andy Simmons (new)

Page 10 – Transylvanian Breakfast Cereals – Gary Fields (reprint from #270)

Page 12 – The Effects of Horror Movies! (reprint from *Zany* #1)

Page 14 – Ye Hang Ups (The moss is out!) – John Severin (new)

Page 15 – Monster Junk Mail! – Rob Orzechowski / Rob Weske (new)

Page 18 – Orehek at Large Touring a Horror House – Don Orehek (reprint from #270)

Page 20 – Ghastly Ghoulies of the Gridiron – Mike Ricigliano (reprint from #270)

Page 23 – Martin's Screams – Vic Martin (reprint from *For Monsters Only* #2)

Page 24 – The Wacky Weirdos (reprint from *For Monsters Only* #6)

Page 26 – Hollyweird Transylvania – Arnoldo Franchioni (new)

Page 28 – Subscription ad – John Severin (reprint from *Cracked Monster Party* #1 and *Cracked* #297)

Page 29 – Ghostbuggers II – Walter Brogan / Vic Bianco (Lou Silverstone) (reprint from #250)

Page 34 – Monster Party Playground – Rob Orzechowski / Rob Weske (new)

Page 36 – Monsters Get Off on Ecological Disasters! – Vic Martin / George Gladir (reprint from #246)

Page 39 – The Cremation of Sam McGee – John Severin (reprint from #19)

Page 43 – Cracked Hold-Ups (make-up department) – Don Orehek / George Gladir (new)

Page 45 – The Launderliers – Walter Brogan / Lou Silverstone (new)

Page 50 – Monster Shut-Ups (great blocks) – Mike Ricigliano (reprint from *Cracked Collectors' Edition* #51)

Page 51 – Great Moments in Science 1934 – Charles Rodrigues (reprint from #118)

Back Cover – An Interview With the Vampire – Pete Fitzgerald / Patric Abedin (new)

Cracked Monster Party #30, Winter 1995-1996 (52 pages) ($1.75)

Cover – The Power Rangers Meet Ivan Uzi – Rurik Tyler (new)

Page 2 – *Cracked Super* #10 ad

Page 3 – Contents – Mike Ricigliano

Page 4 – Mighty Moronic Powder Rangers The Movie – Alan Kupperberg / Greg Grabianski (new)

Page 10 – Modern-Day Creatures We Could Do Without – Pete Fitzgerald / Spark (new)

Page 12 – Moonlighting Monsters – Don Orehek (reprint from *Cracked Monster Party* #18)

Page 14 – Monster Holidays – Rob Orzechowski / Patric Abedin (new)

Page 17 – Monster Kids – Gary Fields (reprint from #251)

Page 18 – Cracked's Killer Card Manufacturer of the Year – John Severin / Rich Kriegel (Lou Silverstone) (reprint from #275)

Page 22 – What a Riot! – Bruce Bolinger / Steve Strangio (reprint from #275)

Page 24 – What Goes on in a Monster's Mind – Don Orehek (reprint from #138)

Page 26 – Spies and Saboteurs in an Egyptian Tomb – Mike Ricigliano (reprint from *Cracked Monster Party* #16)

Page 28 – Subscription ad (reprint from #295)

Page 29 – The Addled Family – Walter Brogan / Vic Bianco (Lou Silverstone) (reprint from #271)

Page 35 – Monstrous Practical Jokes! – John Severin / Hilary Zatz (reprint from #221)

Page 38 – You Can Write Like Stephen King! – Peter Dulligan / Doug Martin (reprint from *Cracked Monster Party* #4)

Page 40 – Alienated 3 – John Severin / Tony Frank (Lou Silverstone) (reprint from #276)

Page 45 – Our Baby Alien Album – Rurik Tyler / Andy Simmons (reprint from *Cracked Monster Party* #17)

Page 50 – Monster One-Shots (Alien dental floss) – Mike Ricigliano / Roger Brown (reprint from #229)

Page 51 – Save the Aliens – Rurik Tyler (reprint from #276)

Back Cover – The Attack from Planet X – Rurik Tyler (new)

Cracked Monster Party #31, Spring 1996 (52 pages) ($1.75)

Cover – We Open the X Files – John Severin (new)

Page 2 and 51 – Gallery of Ghastly Ghoulies – Mike Ricigliano / May Sakami (reprint from #266)

Page 3 – Contents – Mike Ricigliano

Page 4 – The Yechh's Files – Walter Brogan / Rob Weske (new)

Page 9 – Goodies for Transylvanian Gourmets! – Rob Orzechowski / Gayle Adams-Pierpont (reprint from #279)

Page 12 – Cryptic Commercials – Frank Caruso (reprint from #221)

Page 14 – Monster Combination Movies – Walter Brogan / Jim Wheelock (reprint from #221)

Page 16 – Lunch Time – Oskar Blotta (reprint from #89)

Page 17 – Handbook for Scaring People! – Bo Badman (Rurik Tyler / George Gladir (reprint from #239)

Page 21 – Monster Olympic One-Shots – Mike Ricigliano / Roger Brown (reprint from #239)

Page 23 – Scooby Doo After the Case of the Real-Life Ghost – Gary Fields / Daniel O'Keefe (reprint from *Cracked Monster Party* #18)

Page 26 – Transylvania Road Signs – Arnoldo Franchioni (new)

Page 28 – Our First Annual Hell of a Time! – Jim Bennett / Andy Simmons (reprint from #279)

Page 30 – Cracked's Monster Dating Chart – Mike Ricigliano (reprint from *Cracked Monster Party* #19)

Page 32 – Subscription ad – John Severin (reprint from *Cracked Monster Party* #1)

Page 33 – Double Scare! – Frank Caruso / Joe Catalano (reprint from #242)

Page 37 – Monster Bummers – Don Orehek / Jed Vier (reprint from *Cracked Monster Party* #17)

Page 40 – Monster Bulletin Board – Rob Orzechowski / Rob Weske (new)

Page 42 – Monstrous Practical Jokes! – John Severin / Hilary Zatz (reprint from #221)

Page 44 – Monster Party! – John Severin (reprint from #31)

Page 46 – Vampire in Shnookland – Bruce Bolinger / Andy Simmons (new)

Back Cover – Leftover Halloween Treats – Gary Fields / Randy Epley (new)

Cracked Monster Party #32, Summer 1996 (52 pages) ($1.75)

Cover – We Dump on Goosebumps – Rurik Tyler (new)

Page 2 – Fangmann's ad – John Severin (reprint from #36)

Page 3 – Contents – Mike Ricigliano

Page 4 – Jerkules The Liesurely Journeys – Walter Brogan / Greg Grabianski (new)

Page 10 – Cracked Visits a Midnight Monster Picnic – Al Scaduto (reprint from #217)

Page 12 – Satan's Campaign to Promote Hell – Makbush (Sururi Gumen) (reprint from #134)

Page 16 – Throughout History with the Real Gremlins – John Severin (reprint from #209)

Page 18 – Real-Life Monsters from the Deepest Pits of School – Pete Fitzgerald / Daniel O'Keefe (reprint from *Cracked Monster Party* #19)

Page 21 – Spittlejuice – John Severin / Mort Todd (reprint from #239)

Page 25 – That Poisoned Pen of Don Orehek – Don Orehek (reprint from *Cracked Monster Party* #18)

Page 26 – Hell's Gift Shop – Rob Orzechowski / Lenore Skenazy (new)

Page 28 – The Transdeformers vs Boltron – Steve Ditko / Mort Todd, John Arcudi (reprint from #222)

Page 31 – Robot Report Magazine – John Severin (reprint from #194)

Page 35 – Count Dracula …2086 A.D. – John Severin / George Gladir (reprint from #224)

Page 36 – Summer Jobs for Movie Monsters – Kent Gamble (reprint from #216)

Page 38 – Transylvanian Rock 'n' Roll Monsters – Vic Martin (reprint from *For Monsters Only* #5)

Page 40 – Jaws Too! – John Severin (reprint from #154)

Page 47 – R.L. Slime Goosedumps – Rob Orzechowski (new)

Page 51 – Subscription ad – Frank Borth

Back Cover – Goosedumps Book Cover – Rurik Tyler / Cliff Mott (new)

Cracked Monster Party #33, Fall 1996 (52 pages) ($1.75)

Cover – We Grill on DragonHeart – Rurik Tyler (new)

Page 2 – *Cracked Blockbuster* #10 ad

Page 3 – Contents – Mike Ricigliano

Page 4 – Dragonfart – Bruce Bolinger / Andy Simmons (new)

Page 10 – Another Serving of Transylvanian Breakfast Cereals – Gary Fields / Randy Epley (reprint from #274)

Page 12 – You'll Know Your Nemesis Has Struck When – Rob Orzechowski / Rick Kriegal (new)

Page 15 – The Thing Most Likely to Succeed – Rurik Tyler (reprint from *Cracked Monster Party* #13)

Page 18 – Witches' Stew – Arnoldo Franchioni (reprint from *Cracked Monster Party* #15)

Page 20 – Dreddy's Dead The Final Rip-Off – Frank Borth / Steve Strangio (reprint from *Cracked Monster Party* #22)

Page 25 – Make Mine Well Done! – John Langton (reprint from #62)

Page 26 – Cracked Creates the Perfect Baseball Monster – Mike Ricigliano (reprint from *Cracked Monster Party* #17)

Page 28 – A Cracked Look at Useless Monster Junk Mail – Rob Orzechowski (reprint from *Cracked Monster Party* #17)

Page 30 – Trouble's on the Way! – Harry North (reprint from *Cracked Monster Party* #14)

Page 33 – Premedator – William York Wray (Bill Wray) / Robert Loren Fleming (reprint from #233)

Page 38 – 3-D Horror Shows – Sururi Gumen (reprint from #194)

Page 41 – Godzilla Visits the Big Apple! – Arnoldo Franchioni (reprint from *Cracked Monster Party* #17)

Page 44 – Eczema Wearisome Princess – Walter Brogan / Greg Grabianski (new)

Page 50 – Subscription ad – John Severin (reprint from #309)

Page 51 – Dead Fred's Discount Funeral Shack! – Rurik Tyler (reprint from #279)

Back Cover – Monster Olympics – Mike Ricigliano (new)

***Cracked Monster Party* #34, Winter 1996-1997 (52 pages) ($1.75)**

Cover – We Salute Alien Independence Day! – Rurik Tyler (new)

Page 2 and 51 – Club Dred Poster – Rurik Tyler (reprint from *Cracked Monster Party* #16)

Page 3 – Contents – Mike Ricigliano

Page 4 – A Cracked Interview With "The Alien" – Walter Brogan / Lou Silverstone (new)

Page 8 – Ghastly Ghoulies (Breaking Up an Old Partnership) – Mike Ricigliano / May Sakami (reprint from *Cracked Monster Party* #18)

Page 10 – Castle Dracula – Rurik Tyler / George Gladir (reprint from #280)

Page 12 – The 1996 Monster Elections – Rob Orzechowski / Dan Birtcher (new)

Page 16 – Alien TV! – John Severin / Gene Perone, Mort Todd (reprint from #217)

Page 21 – Monster Medicine Cabinet – Rob Orzechowski / Gayle Adams-Pierpont (reprint from *Cracked Monster Party* #21)

Page 24 – Movies From Hell – Jim Bennett / Andrew Osborne (reprint from #282)

Page 26 – The Sabotaged Haunted House – Mike Ricigliano (reprint from *Cracked Monster Party* #14)

Page 28 – Subscription ad

Page 29 – Bran Stuckey's Drecula – Rurik Tyler (new)

Page 34 – Your Little Brother Really is a Monster When – Walter Brogan / Joe Catalano (reprint from #229)

Page 37 – Cracked Ugly Oracles #1 Psychic Psycho! – Bo Badman (Rurik Tyler) (reprint from #229)

Page 39 – Hiss the Villains (reprint from #94)

Page 43 – Cracked Hold-Ups! (stone carvings) – Don Orehek (reprint from *Cracked Monster Party* #15)

Page 45 – The Crichtoners – Bruce Bolinger / Andy Simmons (new)

Page 50 – Ye Hang Ups #3 (screams) – C.E. Severin (Catherine Severin) (reprint from #172)

Back Cover – FBI Nine Most Wanted Aliens – Mike Ricigliano (new)

***Cracked Monster Party* #35, Spring 1997 (52 pages) ($1.75)**

Cover – We Slam Space Jam! – Walter Brogan (new)

Page 2 – Cracked presents the Aftermath of the Dinosaurs Attack Cards! – Bo Badman (Rurik Tyler) (reprint from #246)

Page 3 – Contents – Mike Ricigliano

Page 4 – Space Chump – Rurik Tyler / Ellen Lynch (new)

Page 9 – Movie Monster Museum – Rob Orzechowski / George Gladir (reprint from *Cracked Monster Party* #15)

Page 12 – Sab Trek We Deep-Six All the Generations – Mike Ricigliano (reprint from *Cracked Spaced Out* #1)

Page 14 – Updated Torture Devices for Catching the Witches of Today – John Severin (reprint from #58) (The dates in the article were changed from 1567 and 1967 to 1591 and 1997.)

Page 17 – The Adamns Family Photo Album – Gary Fields / George Gladir (reprint from *Cracked Monster Party* #16)

Page 21 – Creature from the Cracked Lagoon! – Rurik Tyler (reprint from *Cracked Monster Party* #16)

Page 24 – Real Scary Horror Videos – Rob Orzechowski / George Gladir (reprint from *Cracked Monster Party* #16)

Page 26 – Do the Monsta-Rena! – Mike Ricigliano

Page 28 – Stiffs – Walter Brogan / Andrew Osborne (reprint from *Cracked Monster Party* #22)

Page 32 – The Terror Trip – BOJ (reprint from #55)

Page 33 – Hannibal Lecter's Places – Rob Orzechowski / Craig Farrell (reprint from *Cracked Monster Party* #22)

Page 36 – Frightbore Before Christmas – Gary Fields / Lou Silverstone (reprint from *Cracked Monster Party* #24)

Page 42 – Rush Hour on Venus – Pete Fitzgerald / Lenore Skenazy (reprint from *Cracked Spaced Out* #1)

Page 44 – The Island of Dr. Moron – Bruce Bolinger / Lou Silverstone (new)

Page 49 – The Painter's Fantasy – Oskar Blotta (reprint from #85)

Page 50 – The Amazing New Ronco Borg! – Pete Fitzgerald / Todd Jackson (new) Page 51 – Subscription ad – John Severin (reprint from #125)

Back Cover – Gilligan's Island of Dr. Moreau – Randy Jones (new)

Cracked Monster Party #36, Summer 1997 (52 pages) ($1.75)

Cover – Star Wars The Final Cut – Tom Grimes (new)

Page 2 and 51 – More Star Wars – Cracked Poster – Powers (John Severin) (reprint from #148)

Page 3 – Contents – Mike Ricigliano

Page 4 – The Characters From the Star Wars Trilogy – Walter Brogan / Lou Silverstone (new)

Page 6 – Star-Warz – O.O. Severin (John Severin) / Joe Catalano (reprint from #146)

Page 13 – Star Warts Lost Footage Star Warz: An Old Joke – Walter Brogan / Todd Jackson (new)

Page 14 – Odd Jobs for Star Wars Stars – Howard Nostrand (reprint from #154)

Page 17 – Cy-Threepiu & Arty-Ditto A Souvenir Photo Album of Their Visit to Earth – Cosa Nostrand (Howard Nostrand) (reprint from #148)

Page 21 – Subscription ad – John Severin (reprint from #296)

Page 22 – Cracked Interviews Star Warts Creator George Lucre – John Severin (reprint from #200)

Page 26 – When Nerds Hit a Science Fiction Convention – Don Orehek / Eric Goldberg, Mark Howard (reprint from *Cracked Spaced Out* #2)

Page 28 – Mars Outtakes – Rurik Tyler (new)

Page 30 – The Empire Strikes Out – O.O. Severin (John Severin) (reprint from #173)

Page 37 – Star Warts Lost Footage The Empire Strikes Out – Walter Brogan / Todd Jackson (new)

Page 38 – Spaced Out Amusement Park – Arnoldo Franchioni (reprint from *Cracked Spaced Out* #2)

Page 40 – They Came From Real Life: Everyday Sci-Fi Comics! – Alan Kupperberg / Rob Weske (reprint from *Cracked Spaced Out* #2)

Page 42 – Returns of the Jed Eye – John Severin (reprint from #199)

Page 50 – Star Warts Lost Footage Returns of the Jed Eye – Walter Brogan / Todd Jackson (new)

Back Cover – Milk May the Mustache Be With You (new)

Cracked Monster Party #37, Fall 1997 (52 pages) ($1.75)

Cover – Men in Blecch! – Frank Cummings (new)

Page 2 – The Barneysaurus – Jim Bennett (reprint from *Cracked Monster Party* #21)

Page 3 – Contents – Mike Ricigliano

Page 4 – Men in Blecch – Frank Cummings / Lou Silverstone (new)

Page 10 – Home Shopping Club for Monsters – Rob Orzechowski / Barry Dutter (new)

Page 12 – Don Orehek's Horrible Humor – Don Orehek (reprint from #221)

Page 14 – Squeam – Walter Brogan / Andy Simmons (new)

Page 18 – Goodies for Transylvanian Gourmets! – Rob Orzechowski / Gayle Adams-Pierpont (reprint from #279)

Page 21 – Tales from the Creep – Bill Wray / Archie Falbo (John Arcudi) (reprint from #250)

Page 25 – Make Mine Well Done! – John Langton (reprint from #62)

Page 26 – Spies and Saboteurs Hit Jurassic Park – Mike Ricigliano (reprint from #283)

Page 28 – How Has Success Changed the Dinosaurs of "Jurassic Park"? – Jeff Wong / Missy Wheathins (reprint from #285)

Page 30 – Blarney and the Backyard Gang Go to Jurassic Park – Bruce Bolinger / Dan Birtcher (reprint from *Cracked Monster Party* #21)

Page 33 – Jurassic Park's Dinosaur Experiments Gone Bad! – Pete Fitzgerald / Mike Ricigliano (reprint from #283)

Page 36 – Undiscovered Dinosaur Species – Gary Fields / Rob Weske (reprint from *Cracked Monster Party* #21)

Page 39 – A Visit to Jurassic Park – Don Orehek / Rob Weske (reprint from #283)

Page 40 – A Prehysterical Look at Jurassic Park – Mike Ricigliano (reprint from *Cracked Monster Party* #21)

Page 42 – Jurassick Park – Walter Brogan / Lou Silverstone (reprint from #283)

Page 48 – Subscription ad – John Severin (reprint from #285)

Page 50 – A Visit to the Museum of Unnatural History – Don Orehek / Rob Weske (reprint from *Cracked Monster Party* #21)

Page 51 – The Auditions for "Jurassic Park" – Jeff Wong (reprint from #283)

Back Cover – The Lost World Jurassic Park Ad Poster – Rurik Tyler (new)

Cracked Monster Party #38, Winter 1997-1998 (52 pages) ($1.75)

Cover – We Squash Starship Troopers! – John Severin (new)

Page 2 – Save the Aliens – Rurik Tyler (reprint from #276)

Page 3 – Contents – Mike Ricigliano

Page 4 – Starship Troopers, 90210 – Walter Brogan / Andy Simmons (new)

Page 10 – Ghastly Ghoulies (Cleaning up one's act) – Mike Ricigliano / May Sakami (reprint from *Cracked Monster Party* #15)

Page 12 – Objects For Sale at a Hollywood Auction – John Severin (reprint from #90)

Page 15 – Allien and How to Watch it – John Severin (reprint from #164)

Page 22 – Shut-Ups (happiest day) – Don Orehek (reprint from *Cracked Monster Party* #11)

Page 23 – Our Baby Alien Album – Rurik Tyler / Andy Simmons (reprint from *Cracked Monster Party* #17)

Page 28 – Cracked Visits the Alien 3 Set – Walter Brogan / Scott Franklin, John Leary (reprint from *Cracked Monster Party* #17)

Page 33 – It's the Great Punkin, Churlie Braun! – Gary Fields (reprint from *Cracked Monster Party* #7)

Page 35 – Monsters Get Off on Ecological Disasters! – Vic Martin / George Gladir (reprint from #246)

Page 38 – Alieens – Bill Wray / Joe Catalano, Mort Todd (reprint from #226)

Page 43 – Alien Shut-Ups! (most beautiful girl) – Bill McCartney (Bill Ward) (reprint from #8)

Page 44 – Real Cracked Books – Vic Martin (reprint from #18)

Page 46 – The Alien Hollywood Megastar! – Mike Ricigliano (new)

Page 50 – Shut-Ups (holding up the works) – Don Orehek (reprint from #221)

Page 51 – Subscription ad – Rurik Tyler (reprint from *Cracked Monster Party* #17)

Back Cover – Releasing the Ghosts – Rurik Tyler (new)

Cracked Monster Party #39, Spring 1998 (52 pages) ($1.75)

Cover – We Take a Stab at Scream 2 – Frank Cummings (new)

Page 2 – A Sunday Afternoon in Jurassic Trailer Park – Rurik Tyler / Cliff Mott (reprint from #285)

Page 3 – Contents – Mike Ricigliano

Page 4 – Reamed, Too – Walter Brogan / Lou Silverstone (new)

Page 10 – Cracked's Star Warped – Arnoldo Franchioni (reprint from *Cracked Spaced Out* #1)

Page 12 – A Cracked Look at Monster Garbage – Rob Orzechowski (reprint from *Cracked Monster Party* #15)

Page 16 – Cracked Dinosaur True or Fossil Quiz? – Rurik Tyler (reprint from #252)

Page 18 – The Honeymoaners – Win Mortimer / Rich Kriegel (Lou Silverstone) (reprint from *Cracked Monster Party* #7)

Page 22 – Jason Goes to Hell – Bruce Bolinger / Daniel O'Keefe (reprint from *Cracked Monster Party* #20)

Page 26 – Addams Family Valentines – Jeff Wong / Scott Franklin (reprint from #289)

Page 28 – Cracked Nightmare Interview with Freddy! – Rob Orzechowski / Mort Todd (reprint from *Cracked Monster Party* #1)

Page 31 – Monster Football League – Mike Ricigliano (reprint from #278)

Page 35 – The Boulder and the Sword – Arnoldo Franchioni (reprint from #294)

Page 36 – The Monster Home Shopping Channel – Rob Orzechowski / Craig Farrell (reprint from #293)

Page 38 – Ghastly Ghoulies (Cleaning up one's act) – Mike Ricigliano / May Sakami (reprint from *Cracked Monster Party* #15)

Page 40 – Movie Monster Museum – Rob Orzechowski / George Gladir (reprint from *Cracked Monster Party* #15)

Page 43 – T-Rex at Mann's Chinese Theater (reprint from *Cracked Monster Party* #21)

Page 45 – I Know What You Wore Last Summer – Bruce Bolinger / Andy Simmons (new)

Page 50 – More Horrors from the Cracked Pen of Don Orehek – Don Orehek (reprint from #296)

Page 51 – Subscription ad – John Severin, Frank Cummings, Tom Grimes (reprint from *Cracked Monster Party* #1 and *Cracked* #283)

Back Cover – Goreton's Finger Sticks ad – Rurik Tyler (new)

Cracked Monster Party #40, Summer 1998 (52 pages) ($1.75)

Cover – We Abduct X-Files: The Movie – John Severin (new)

Page 2 – *Cracked Blockbuster* #12 ad

Page 3 – Contents – Mike Ricigliano

Page 4 – What if Mulder and Scully Starred in Other Movies? – Walter Brogan / Andy Simmons (new)

Page 9 – Monster Basketball Association MBA – Mike Ricigliano (reprint from #299)

Page 12 – Monster Party Cracked Collector Plates – Bruce Bolinger (reprint from *Cracked Monster Party* #27)

Page 14 – Another Helping of Monster Goodies – Rob Orzechowski / Gayle Adams-Pierpont (reprint from *Cracked Monster Party* #24)

Page 16 – Tales From the Dork Side – Walter Brogan (reprint from *Cracked Monster Party* #10)

Page 20 – Thing's Palm Reading – Gary Fields / Daniel O'Keefe (reprint from *Cracked Monster Party* #23)

Page 22 – One Moonlit Night – Arnoldo Franchioni (reprint from *Cracked Monster Party* #27)

Page 23 – Sci-Fi Gift Catalogue – Pete Fitzgerald / Rob Weske (new)

Page 26 – First Annual Transylvanian Pet Show – Rob Orzechowski / Gayle Adams-Pierpont (reprint from *Cracked Monster Party* #25)

Page 28 – Monsters and Mobsters – Arnoldo Franchioni (reprint from *Cracked Monster Party* #23)

Page 30 – Freddy's Worst Nightmare – Walter Brogan / Rich Kriegel (Lou Silverstone) (reprint from *Cracked Monster Party* #22)

Page 34 – Monsters in the News – John Severin (reprint from #59)

Page 36 – Dr. Fizzix #2452 – Let's Make a Tropical Volcano – Gary Fields / Eric Goldberg, Mark Howard (reprint from *Cracked Monster Party* #27)

Page 37 – Cesspool and Regurt Look at This Year's Horror Videos – Rurik Tyler (reprint from *Cracked Monster Party* #12)

Page 40 – Monster Party Theater One Hell of a Chick – Alan Kupperberg / Greg Grabianski (reprint from *Cracked Monster Party* #26)

Page 45 – Subscription ad – John Severin (reprint from #285)

Page 46 – How to Defend Your Town Against Godzilla – Bruce Bolinger / Andy Simmons (new)

Page 50 – Monster Shut-Ups (sales climbing) – Rurik Tyler (reprint from *Cracked Monster Party* #7)

Page 51 – "B"-Movies of Cartoon Characters! – John Severin / Rob Weske (reprint from #301)

Back Cover – A T.V. Commercial We'll Never See (Nicodork) – Frank Cummings (new)

Cracked Monster Party #41, Fall 1998 (52 pages) ($1.75)

Cover – We School Buffy the Vampire Slayer – Frank Cummings (new)

Page 2 – Spaced Out Miss Universe Pageant – Mike Ricigliano (reprint from *Cracked Spaced Out* #3)

Page 3 – Contents – Mike Ricigliano

Page 4 – Boffy the Vampy Slayer – Rurik Tyler / Todd Jackson (reprint from #322)

Page 9 – Monster Babie's Horror Tales – Bill Wray (reprint from #229)

Page 12 – Monster Mother Goose – Bill McCartney (Bill Ward) (reprint from *For Monsters Only* #1)

Page 14 – David Bloodletterman's Interview With a Vampire – Jeff Wong / Andy Simmons (reprint from *Cracked Monster Party* #27)

Page 20 – MFL Hall of Fame – Mike Ricigliano (reprint from #295)

Page 22 – Witchcraft Then & Now – Rob Orzechowski / George Gladir (new)

Page 25 – Cracked Science Fiction Convention Profiles – Bruce Bolinger / Steve Strangio (reprint from *Cracked Spaced Out* #4)

Page 28 – EaTing – John Severin (reprint from *Giant Cracked Fun-Kit* #34)

Page 35 – Shut-Ups (I feel pounds lighter) – Don Orehek / Gayle Adams-Pierpont (reprint from *Cracked Spaced Out* #1)

Page 36 – I've Never Met a Monster I Didn't Like – Arnold Franchioni (reprint from *Cracked Monster Party* #16)

Page 38 – How to Raise Your 112 Foot Baby – Bruce Bolinger / Andy Simmons (reprint from *Cracked Monster Party* #18)

Page 42 – Cloning: The Advantages and the Disadvantages – Howard Nostrand (reprint from #154)

Page 44 – Monster Pets – John Severin / Moe McMahon (Marian McMahon) (reprint from #229)

Page 45 – X-Files: The Rip-Off – Bruce Bolinger / Andy Simmons (new)

Page 50 – Shut-Ups (Have a good time!) – Mike Ricigliano (reprint from #138)

Page 51 – Subscription ad – John Severin (reprint from #125)
Back Cover – Puffy the Vampire Playa – Jeff Wong (new)

Cracked Monster Party #42, Winter 1998-1999 (52 pages) ($1.75)
Cover – Catch of the Day: I Still Know What You Did Last Summer – Frank Cummings (new)
Page 2 – The Man and the Ink Spot – Oskar Blotta (reprint from #146)
Page 3 – Contents – Mike Ricigliano
Page 4 – Horrorween – Walter Brogan / Lou Silverstone (new)
Page 11 – Cracked Real-Life Horror Movies – Rob Orzechowski / Gayle Adams-Pierpont (reprint from *Cracked Monster Party* #19)
Page 14 – Planets of the Creatures - John Severin (reprint from #72)
Page 16 – Note to the Teacher – Don Orehek / Gayle Adams-Pierpont (reprint from *Cracked Monster Party* #22)
Page 18 – Army of Dorkness Evil Dread III – Walter Brogan / Lou Silverstone (reprint from *Cracked Monster Party* #20)
Page 23 – If Monsters Were Dealt With By Our Criminal Justice System! – Bruce Bolinger / Dan Birtcher (reprint from *Cracked Monster Party* #25)
Page 26 – Transylvanian School Cafeteria – Don Orehek / Gayle Adams-Pierpont (reprint from *Cracked Monster Party* #22)
Page 28 – Drecula – John Severin (reprint from #165)
Page 35 – Ghouls-R-Us – Rob Orzechowski (reprint from *Cracked Monster Party* #11)
Page 38 – When They Were Young – Don Orehek / George Gladir (reprint from *Cracked Monster Party* #19)
Page 40 - Star Trek Technical Manual The Lost Pages – Terry Colon / Craig Farrell (reprint from *Cracked Spaced Out* #4)
Page 44 – Martin's Screams – Vic Martin (reprint from *For Monsters Only* #2)
Page 45 – I Still Know What I Did Last Summer…I Killed You! – Bruce Bolinger / Andy Simmons (new)
Page 50 – Shut-Ups (Have a good time!) – Mike Ricigliano (reprint from #138) (Geez! How lazy. This was just reprinted in the previous issue.)
Page 51 – Subscription ad – Rurik Tyler (reprint from *Cracked Monster Party* #17)
Back Cover – Bridal Died Magazine – Tom Grimes (new)

Cracked Monster Party #43, Spring 1999 (52 pages) ($1.75)
Cover – The Legend of Zelda Yuckarina of Time – Rurik Tyler (new)
Page 2 – An Interview With the Vampire – Pete Fitzgerald / Patric Abedin (reprint from *Cracked Monster Party* #29)
Page 3 – Contents – Mike Ricigliano

Page 4 – A Cracked Look at the X-Files – Bruce Bolinger / Rob Weske (reprint from #305)

Page 5 – The Dead Ends of Zelda – Frank Cummings / Todd Jackson (new)

Page 9 – Monstrous Practical Jokes! – John Severin / Hilary Zatz (reprint from #221)

Page 12 – Monster Day Dreams – Rob Orzechowski / George Gladir (reprint from *Cracked Monster Party* #23)

Page 14 – The Remarkable Similarities of Extraterrestrials and Earthlings – Pete Fitzgerald / George Gladir (new)

Page 17 – The Addamneds Family Devalued – Walter Brogan / Steve Strangio (reprint from *Cracked Monster Party* #23)

Page 22 – More Horrible Horrors from the Spooky Pen of Don Orehek – Don Orehek (reprint from *Cracked Monster Party* #25)

Page 24 – Really Scary Creatures from Everyday Life! – Gary Fields / Bill Ignizio (reprint from #268)

Page 26 – Transylvania Road Signs – Arnoldo Franchioni (reprint from *Cracked Monster Party* #31)

Page 28 – King Kung – John Severin (reprint from #140)

Page 35 – Freddy Krocker Food Company – Rurik Tyler (reprint from #251)

Page 38 – You Can Write Like Stephen King! – Peter Dulligan / Doug Martin (reprint from *Cracked Monster Party* #4)

Page 40 – Monster Bulletin Board – Rob Orzechowski / Rob Weske (reprint from *Cracked Monster Party* #31)

Page 42 – The Wacky Weirdos (reprint from *For Monsters Only* #6)

Page 44 – Mister and Myth – J. Kelly (reprint from #308)

Page 45 – Star Drek Imperfection – Bruce Bolinger / Andy Simmons (new)

Page 50 – Patient Complaints About Witch Doctors – Frank Cummings / Coyote J. Calhoun (reprint from #307)

Page 51 – Subscription ad – John Severin, Rurik Tyler, Tom Grimes (reprint from *Cracked Monster Party* #1 and #333)

Back Cover – The Jamie Lee Curtis Virus! – Alan Kupperberg (new)

Cracked Monster Party #44, Summer 1999 (52 pages) ($1.75)

Cover – We Cut Loose on Star Wars! – Rurik Tyler (new)

Page 2 – *Cracked Collectors' Edition* #120 and *Cracked Summer Special* #9 ad – John Severin (reprint from #86)

Page 3 – Contents – Mike Ricigliano

Page 4 – Dominatrix – Bruce Bolinger / Andy Simmons (new)

Page 9 – 1st Annual Transylvanian Yard Sale – Rob Orzechowski / Gayle Adams-Pierpont (reprint from *Cracked Monster Party* #20)

Page 12 – The Effects of Horror Movies! (reprint from *Zany* #1)

Page 14 – King Kong's Boyhood – Bill Ward (reprint from #141)

Page 18 – Monster Bummers – Don Orehek / Jed Vier (reprint from *Cracked Monster Party* #17)

Page 20 – Take Me Out to the Ball Game! – Alan Kupperberg / Lou Silverstone (reprint from *Cracked Monster Party* #21)

Page 26 – Hollyweird Transylvania – Arnoldo Franchioni (reprint from *Cracked Monster Party* #29)

Page 28 – Monster Holidays – Rob Orzechowski / Patric Abedin (new)

Page 31 – When Old Age Finally Hits Monsterdom – Vic Martin / George Gladir (reprint from #240)

Page 34 – The Stunned – Walter Brogan / Lou Silverstone (new)

Page 40 – Fright Knights – Rurik Tyler (reprint from *Cracked Monster Party* #6)

Page 12 – Cracked Monster Get Well Cards – Bruce Bolinger / Patric Adedin (reprint from *Cracked Monster Party* #24)

Page 45 – Tatooine Junior High School Yearbook – Frank Cummings / Greg Grabianski (new)

Page 50 – Subscription ad – Tom Grimes (reprint from *Cracked Monster Party* #36)

Page 51 – Tragic The Trial – Rurik Tyler (reprint from #303)

Back Cover – Medusa Invents the Bad Hair Day – Jim Bennett (reprint from *Cracked Monster Party* #23)

Cracked Monster Party #45, Winter 1999-2000 (52 pages) ($1.75)

Cover – We Burn the Blair Witch Project! – Rurik Tyler (new)

Page 2 – Samsonbites Coffins – Rurik Tyler / Randy Epley (reprint from *Cracked Monster Party* #25)

Page 3 – Contents – Mike Ricigliano

Page 4 – The Bladder Witch Project – Walter Brogan / Lou Silverstone

Page 10 – Witches' Stew – Arnoldo Franchioni (reprint from *Cracked Monster Party* #15)

Page 12 – The Thing Most Likely to Succeed – Rurik Tyler (reprint from *Cracked Monster Party* #13)

Page 15 – Transylvania's Montgomery & Morgue – John Severin (reprint from *For Monsters Only* #2)

Page 18 – Monster Party Theater Blarney – Alan Kupperberg / Lance Contrucci (reprint from *Cracked Monster Party* #23)

Page 23 – That Poisoned Pen of Don Orehek – Don Orehek (reprint from *Cracked Monster Party* #18)

Page 24 – Monster Party Playground – Rob Orzechowski / Rob Weske (reprint from *Cracked Monster Party* #29)

Page 26 – Meet the Rest of the Pinhead Family – Rurik Tyler (reprint from *Cracked Monster Party* #19)

Page 28 – Duhbrina the Teenage Witch – Walter Brogan / Lou Silverstone (reprint from #317)

Page 33 – Scooby Doo After the Case of the Real-Life Ghost – Gary Fields / Daniel O'Keefe (reprint from *Cracked Monster Party* #18)

Page 36 – Cracked Takes a Look at the Transylvanian Teen Scene – John Severin (reprint from #40)

Page 41 – Monster One-Shots (Alien dental floss) – Mike Ricigliano / Roger Brown (reprint from #229)

Page 42 – It's a Bad, Bad, Bad, Bad World! – Bo Badman (Rurik Tyler) (reprint from *Cracked Monster Party* #5)

Page 44 – Creepy Hollow – Frank Cummings / Andy Simmons (new)

Page 50 – Subscription ad – John Severin, Jeff Wong (reprint from *Cracked Monster Party* #1 and #337)

Page 51 – Witches' Convention Parking – Arnoldo Franchioni (reprint from *Cracked Monster Party* #27)

Back Cover – Leftover Halloween Treats – Gary Fields / Randy Epley (reprint from *Cracked Monster Party* #31)

Cracked Monster Party #46, Spring 2000 (52 pages) ($1.75)

Cover – Who Wants to Be a Vampire! – Jeff Wong (new)

Page 2 – *Cracked Super* #17 ad

Page 3 – Contents – Mike Ricigliano

Page 4 – The Making of Screamed 3 – Walter Brogan / Lou Silverstone (new)

Page 9 – Monster One-Shots (Alien dental floss) – Mike Ricigliano / Roger Brown (reprint from #229)

Page 10 – Real-Life Monsters from the Deepest Pits of School – Pete Fitzgerald / Daniel O'Keefe (reprint from *Cracked Monster Party* #19)

Page 13 – Satan's Campaign to Promote Hell – Makbush (Sururi Gumen) (reprint from #134)

Page 17 – Monster Medicine Cabinet – Rob Orzechowski / Gayle Adams-Pierpont (reprint from *Cracked Monster Party* #21)

Page 20 – Why It's a Bad Idea to Hire Zombie Workers – Todd James / Kit Lively (reprint from #322)

Page 21 – Boffy the Vampy Slayer – Rurik Tyler / Todd Jackson (reprint from #322)

Page 26 – Spies and Sabs Hit An Alien Attack – Mike Ricigliano (reprint from #321)

Page 28 – Creature from the Cracked Lagoon! – Rurik Tyler (reprint from *Cracked Monster Party* #16)

Page 31 – If Monsters Were Dealt With By Our Criminal Justice System! – Bruce Bolinger / Dan Birtcher (reprint from *Cracked Monster Party* #25)

Page 34 – Cracked's Monster Sports – Arnoldo Franchioni (reprint
  from *Cracked Monster Party* #26)
Page 36 – Aycaramba – John Severin / Lou Silverstone (reprint from #320)
Page 41 – Mother Goosebumps – Gary Fields / Dan Birtcher (reprint
  from #320)
Page 44 – Cracked's Monster Dating Chart – Mike Ricigliano (reprint
  from *Cracked Monster Party* #19)
Page 46 – Monsteroci-TV – Frank Cummings / Andy Simmons (new)
Page 50 – Buffy Does Frat Row – Bruce Bolinger / Todd Jackson (new)
Page 51 – Subscription ad – Rurik Tyler (reprint from #339)
Back Cover – Goosedumps Book Cover – Rurik Tyler / Cliff Mott
  (reprint from *Cracked Monster Party* #32)

**Cracked Party Pack #1, Summer 1987 (148 pages) ($2.00) (New Spy vs.
Saboteur Flip-Cartoon in corner of every page by Mike Ricigliano.) (This
issue only was digest-sized.)**
Cover – Party Pack – Walter Brogan (new)
Page 2 – Dry Paint Sign (reprint from *Biggest Greatest Cracked* #5)
Page 3 – Contents
Page 4 – Cracked Bubble Gum Cards – John Severin (reprint from #30)
Page 15 – Status Symbols for Dogs! – John Severin (reprint from #86)
Page 19 – Goofed-Up Genes – Vic Martin (reprint from #86)
Page 25 – Sagebrush (such a bad character) – John Severin (reprint
  from *Cracked Collectors' Edition* #9)
Page 28 – Why is it on T.V. You Never See – Bill Ward (reprint from #133)
Page 41 – Winners & Losers – Vic Martin (reprint from #133)
Page 47 – Cracked Frisbee Rating System – Bob Taylor (reprint from #133)
Page 56 – The Cracked Lens (reprint from #154)
Page 65 – Ancient Psychiatry – Bill Elder (reprint from #10)
Page 75 – Civil War Facts – Jack Davis (reprint from #12)
Page 84 – Cracked Interviews the Psychiatric King – Bill Ward (reprint
  from #162)
Page 98 – Iffy U.F.O. Info Magazine – Howard Nostrand (reprint from
  #156)
Page 108 – Beach Blanket Party – John Severin (reprint from #137)
Page 125 – Draw Your Own Conclusion – John Severin (reprint from #19)
Page 130 – Snide Guide to Camping – John Severin (reprint from #51)
Page 136 – Fruity Tunes – Vic Martin (reprint from #88)
Page 141 – Shut-Ups (drive away your customers) – Don Orehek
  (reprint from #162)
Page 144 – Shut-Ups (Squeaky's breaking out) – Don Orehek (reprint
  from #156)

Page 147 – Insult Cards (reprint from #45)

Back Cover – Sylvester-in-the-Box – Walter Brogan (new)

Cracked Party Pack #2, Summer 1988 (100 pages) ($3.25)

Cover – Celebrity Party Pack – Bill Wray (new)

Page 2 – Sylvester P. Alf – Bill Wray (reprint from #229)

Page 3 – Contents

Page 4 – Ronald Reagan's Photo Album – John Severin (reprint from #193)

Page 7 – Hurry-Ups (ship is sinking) – Bill McCartney (Bill Ward)
(reprint from #37)

Page 8 – A Visit to Ralf's Home Planet! – Walter Brogan / Joe Catalano
(reprint from #232)

Page 10 – The Marx Brothers Ride Again! (reprint from #75)

Page 11 – The Cosby Show – John Severin (reprint from #224)

Page 16 – Lifestyles of the Decadent and Opulent – Bob Fingermanski
(Bob Fingerman) (reprint from #227)

Page 18 – Cracked Interviews Max Headache – Rob Orzechowski / Ellis
O'Brien (reprint from #228)

Page 22 – Rasslin' Rowdies Magazine – John Severin / George Gladir
(reprint from #223)

Page 26 – I Don't Care Who You Are – John Severin (reprint from #96)

Page 28 – Valentino Vibrations (reprint from #94)

Page 30 – Messed up by Modern Times! – Bob Fingerman (reprint
from #222)

Page 36 – How Famous People Got Their Nicknames – LePoer (John
Severin) (reprint from #92)

Page 38 – Elvis Talks Salary (Like a Million!) – Vic Martin (reprint
from #87)

Page 41 – Cracked Interviews the Rock Video King! – Mort Todd
(reprint from *Cracked Collectors' Edition* #69)

Page 47 – Fine Art Shut-Ups (lopsided hat) – John Severin (reprint
from #19)

Page 48 – Mr. Rockey's Neighb'hood! – John Reiner / Mark Lewis
(reprint from #219)

Page 50 – Nanny Dickering's Pin-Up Page – Bill Ward (reprint from
Cracked Collectors' Edition #69)

Page 52 – Familiar Ties – John Severin / Joe Catalano (reprint from
#226)

Page 57 – How to Make an "X" Movie Out of a Classic Film – Bob
Taylor (reprint from #87)

Page 59 – Star Drek IV: The Voyage Back Home to the Future! – Bill
Wray / Mort Todd (reprint from #228)

Page 64 – Cracked Interviews Broke Shields the Glamour Queen! – Rob Orzechowski / Moe McMahon (Marian McMahon) (reprint from #226)

Page 68 – Late Nut with David Letterhead! (reprint from #232)

Page 72 – If Some Famous Married Couples had Divorce Hearings – John Severin (reprint from #17)

Page 76 – If Famous People Had Listened to Their Mothers – John Severin (reprint from #94)

Page 78 – Cracked Interviews the Doll Queen – Rob Orzechowski / Mortimer Post (reprint from #225)

Page 82 – Butch Cavity and the Sundrenched Kid – John Severin (reprint from #87)

Page 87 – Tricks Are For Kids! – Milton Knight (reprint from #220)

Page 88 – Future Crocodile Dundee Movies – Gray Morrow / George Gladir (reprint from #228)

Page 91– Sylvester's Photo Album – John Severin (reprint from #35)

Page 95 – Cracked Interviews Vainna White! – John Severin / Moe McMahon (Marian McMahon) (reprint from #231)

Page 98 – Shut-Ups (new Walkman) – Don Orehek (reprint from #224)

Page 99 – Sylvelvis Presley Smythe – Bill Wray (reprint from #230)

Back Cover – Goonlighting – Bill Wray (reprint from #231)

Cracked Party Pack #3, Summer 1989 (100 pages) ($2.75)

Cover – Poiyoit Pants – John Severin (reprint from *Super Cracked* #5)

Page 2 and 51 – Hudd & Dini Cracked Game! – Vic Martin (new)

Page 3 – Contents

Page 4 – The Cracked Puzzler of Puzzle Books – Jack Davis, Bob Taylor (reprint from *Biggest Greatest Cracked* #11)

Page 19 – The Breaking Point – Bill McCartney (Bill Ward) (reprint from #2)

Page 20 – Cracked's 8 Great Ways to Beat the Heat – Vic Martin (reprint from #54)

Page 22 – Insult Cards for All Occasions – Bill McCartney (Bill Ward) (reprint from #78)

Page 24, 25, 96, 97 – Cracked Stationery Kit – John Severin, Warren Sattler (reprint from *King-Sized Cracked* #15)

Page 26 – Hudd & Dini (inflatable man) – Vic Martin (reprint from #97)

Page 27 – Cracked's Shut-Ups Game – John Severin, Charles Rodrigues, Bill Ward (reprint from *Giant Cracked Fun-Kit* #29)

Page 42 – Dial 'A' for Africa – Bill McCartney (Bill Ward) (reprint from #42)

Page 43 – Cracked Insult Greeting Card Kit – Bill Ward, John Severin, John Langton, Bernard Baily (reprint from *Giant Cracked* #9) (originally called "Cracked Now Greeting Card Kit")

Page 59 – Cracked Comic Cube Kit – John Severin (reprint from *King-Sized Cracked* #14)

Page 62 – Dry Paint Sign (reprint from *Biggest Greatest Cracked* #5)

Page 64 – Heads I Win Tails You Lose Sign (new)

Page 66 – Danger! Beware of Stampeding Turtles – John Severin (reprint from #48)

Page 68 – The Breaking Point! – Vic Martin (reprint from #56)

Page 70 – Shut-Ups (Squeaky's breaking out) – Don Orehek (reprint from #156)

Page 72 – Hudd & Dini (books) – Vic Martin (reprint from #105)

Page 73 – Cracked Games and Puzzles That Almost Anyone Can Solve Vol. III – Don Orehek (reprint from *Biggest Greatest Cracked* #17)

Page 87 – Cracked Fishing Game Kit – Don Orehek (reprint from *Biggest Greatest Cracked* #16)

Page 93 – Insult Proclamation (partial reprint from *Giant Cracked* #7)

Page 95 – Subpoena and Parking Ticket (reprint from #27)

Page 98 – Shut-Ups (Can I Stop?) – Vic Martin (reprint from #44)

Back Cover – Insult Cards (reprint from #45)

Cracked Party Pack #4, Summer 1990 (100 pages) ($3.50) (Replaced by Cracked Summer Special in 1991.)

Cover – Nanny Dickering – Skene Catling (new)

Page 2 and 51 – How Would You Like to be Interviewed by Nanny Dickering? Poster – Skene Catling (new)

Page 3 – Contents

Page 4 – The Ward World of Sports (Burp Beer) – Bill Ward (reprint from #245)

Page 5 – Cracked Interviews the Skateboard King – Bill Ward (reprint from #152)

Page 10 – One Afternoon in a Local Stereo Store – Sururi Gumen (reprint from #138)

Page 11 – Martial Art Weapons and Techniques – Bill Ward (reprint from #118)

Page 14 – American Car-Daffy – Sururi Gumen (reprint from #121)

Page 20 – Cracked Interviews the Stunt King – Sururi Gumen (reprint from #128)

Page 25 – Pet Plaza – Bill Ward (reprint from #118)

Page 30 – Rock and Roll Your Eyeballs Out – John Severin (reprint from #163)

Page 37 – Cracked Interviews Edward Kroch The Big Apple Mayor! – Bill Ward / Tony Frank (Lou Silverstone) (reprint from #242)
Page 42 – Elvis Talks Salary (Like a Million!) – Vic Martin (reprint from #87)
Page 45 – Cracked Interviews the Monster King – Bill Ward (reprint from #143)
Page 50 – Nanny Dickering's Pin-Up Page – Bill Ward (reprint from *Cracked Collectors' Edition* #69)
Insert – Clynt Beastwood – Rob Orzechowski, John Severin (new)
Insert – Nanny Dickering's Cracked Summer Pin-Up – Skene Catling (new)
Insert – Cracked Interviews Rabid the Wonder Boy! – Skene Catling (reprint from #248)
Page 52 – W.O.W. World of Ward – Bill Ward (new)
Page 53 – Cracked Interviews Yoko Ohno – Bill Ward (reprint from #244)
Page 56 – Past Predictions of the Future – Sururi Gumen (reprint from #121)
Page 60 – The Hitler Nostalgia Craze – Bill Ward (reprint from #116)
Page 64 – Cracked Interviews the Jerker – Walter Brogan / Rich Kriegel (Lou Silverstone) (reprint from #250)
Page 68 – A Cracked Look at a High School – Bill Ward (reprint from #116)
Page 71 – Cracked Interviews Elvis the King – John Severin / Rich Kriegel (Lou Silverstone) (reprint from #244)
Page 74 – Nostalgic Amusement Parks – Bill Ward (reprint from #122)
Page 78 – Sagebrush (thinnin' hair) – John Severin (reprint from #115) / Ye Hang Ups #3 (He hates to drink alone) – John Severin (reprint from #115)
Page 79 – Cracked Interviews the Traveling Carnival King – Bill Ward (reprint from #140)
Page 84 – A Cracked Look at a Garage Sale – Ron DeLay (John Severin) (reprint from #125)
Page 86 – When the World Runs Out of Food – Sururi Gumen (reprint from #122)
Page 90 – A Cracked Look at a Bowling Alley – Don Orehek (reprint from #124)
Page 92 – The Cracked History of Television – Bill Ward (reprint from #124)
Page 96 – Cracked Interviews Roger Wabbit – John Severin / Vic Bianco (Lou Silverstone) (reprint from #245)
Back Cover – Subscription ad / Cracked Hat / Severin Cracked T-Shirt / Black Cracked T-Shirt / Sylvester Doll ad (reprint from #66)

Cracked Spaced Out #1, Summer 1993 (52 pages) ($1.75) (Many issues feature new material.)

Cover – We Wreck Star Trek – John Severin (new)

Page 2 – Spaced Out – Al Scaduto (reprint from #240)

Page 3 – Contents – Mike Ricigliano

Page 4 – Star Wreck Deeply Spaced Out Nine – Walter Brogan / Lou Silverstone (new)

Page 10 – Rush Hour on Venus – Pete Fitzgerald / Lenore Skenazy (new)

Page 12 – E.T.'s Report My Experiences on Earth – Don Orehek (reprint from #192)

Page 16 – Life in the 21st Century – John Langton (reprint from #195)

Page 18 – Cracked's Star Warped – Arnoldo Franchioni (new)

Page 20 – Star Wrek VI The Uninspired Conclusion – Walter Brogan / Tony Frank (Lou Silverstone) (reprint from #272)

Page 26 – Sab Trek We Deep-Six All the Generations – Mike Ricigliano (new)

Page 28 – Subscription ad

Page 29 – Iffy U.F.O. Info Magazine – Howard Nostrand (reprint from #156)

Page 34 – Job Trek – Jim Bennett / Craig Farrell (new)

Page 36 – Cracked Blasts Nasa – Don Orehek (reprint from #209)

Page 38 – Things That Have Bumps in the Night! – Mike Ricigliano (new)

Page 40 – Star Wreck The Next Degeneration – John Severin / Lou Silverstone (reprint from #271)

Page 47 – NCC-1701-D Today (A Message from the Captain's Desk) – Rurik Tyler / Steve Strangio (1st "NCC-1701-D Today") (new)

Page 50 – Shut-Ups (I feel pounds lighter) – Don Orehek / Gayle Adams-Pierpont (new)

Page 51 – Landing On Mars – Howard Nostrand / Murad Gumen (reprint from #156)

Back Cover – The Cracked "Spaced Out" List Other Upcoming "Star Trek" Spinoffs – Mike Ricigliano (new)

Cracked Spaced Out #2, Fall 1993 (52 pages) ($1.75)

Cover – Deep Space 90210 – Jim Bennett / Jeremy Bucovetsky (new)

Page 2 – *Cracked Blockbuster* #7 ad

Page 3 – Contents – Mike Ricigliano

Page 4 – Deep Space 9…0210 – Walter Brogan / Dan Birtcher (new)

Page 9 – Spaced Out Amusement Park – Arnoldo Franchioni (new)

Page 11 – Robot Report Magazine – John Severin (reprint from #194)

Page 15 – The Alien – Brian Buniak (reprint from #201)

Page 16 – They Came From Real Life: Everyday Sci-Fi Comics! – Alan Kupperberg / Rob Weske (new)

Page 18 – Cracked Examines All the Possibilities of Flying Saucers – Bill McCartney (Bill Ward) (reprint from #68)

Page 22 – Subscription ad

Page 23 – Nothing New Under, Around or Beyond the Sun! – Tom Short (reprint from #231)

Page 26 – When Nerds Hit a Science Fiction Convention – Don Orehek / Eric Goldberg, Mark Howard (new)

Page 28 – Star-Warz – O.O. Severin (John Severin) / Joe Catalano (reprint from #146)

Page 35 – The Sci-Fi Yellow Pages – Bruce Bolinger / Rob Weske (new)

Page 38 – Cracked's Superheroes Refresher Course – Mike Ricigliano / Jerry De Fuccio (new)

Page 40 – Alien TV! – John Severin / Gene Perone, Mort Todd (reprint from #217)

Page 45 – Didja Notice on Star Trek? – Gray Morrow / Douglas Martin (reprint from #238)

Page 47 – NCC-1701-D Today (Enterprise Carnival) – Rob Orzechowski / Steve Strangio (new)

Page 50 – Hurry-Ups (Neutral Zone) – Rick Altergott (reprint from #228)

Page 51 – It Happened on Main and First – Caracu (reprint from #103)

Back Cover – Become an Astronaut at NASA – Randy Epley (new)

Cracked Spaced Out #3, Spring 1994 (52 pages) ($1.75)

Cover – We Torpedo SeaQuest! – John Severin (new)

Page 2 – *Cracked Monster Party* #23 ad

Page 3 – Contents – Mike Ricigliano

Page 4 – SeaPest DDT – Bruce Bolinger / Lou Silverstone (new)

Page 9 – Orehek's Alien Humor – Don Orehek (new)

Page 11 – The Martian Report on Earth – Bill McCartney (Bill Ward) (reprint from #51)

Page 14 – Drink Coaster from Quark's Bar – Pete Fitzgerald (new)

Page 16 – Cracked's G.I. Space Set – Bill Kresse (reprint from #58)

Page 18 – Robocop Ramblings – John Severin (reprint from #259)

Page 22 – Subscription ad

Page 23 – Cracked Space Lens (reprint from *Giant Cracked* #43)

Page 26 – The Spaced Out Solar System (and Other Stuff) Chart – Mike Ricigliano (new)

Page 28 – A Look at a UFO – Don Orehek (reprint from #116)

Page 30 – ZZ Slop vs. the Space Pirates – Bob Fingerman (reprint from #223)

Page 36 – Summer Jobs for Aliens – Arnoldo Franchioni (new)

Page 38 – The Abyssmal – John Severin / Terry Gentile (reprint from #252)

Page 42 – Fly Me to the Moon – Oskar Blotta (reprint from #79)

Page 44 – A Closer Look at Star Trek Blueprints – Terry Colon / Craig Farrell (new)

Page 46 – Robot Wars (Whirrrrrrrr) – Steve Ditko / Mort Todd (reprint from #219)

Page 47 – NCC-1701-D Today (Transporter Mix-Up) – Rurik Tyler / Steve Strangio (new)

Page 50 – Spaced Out Shut-Ups (no man has gone) – Don Orehek / Eric Goldberg, Mark Howard (new)

Page 51 – Oh, No…Do We Have to Start All Over Again? – Charles Rodrigues (reprint from #110)

Back Cover – Spaced Out Miss Universe Pageant – Mike Ricigliano (new)

Cracked Spaced Out #4, Summer 1994 (52 pages) ($1.75)

Cover – Star Trek / NASA Argument – John Severin (new)

Page 2 and 51 – Official Location Map – Cracked Poster (reprint from #209)

Page 3 – Contents – Mike Ricigliano

Page 4 - Star Trek Technical Manual The Lost Pages – Terry Colon / Craig Farrell (new)

Page 8 – Dr. Fizzix (origin) – Gary Fields / Eric Goldberg, Mark Howard (1st *Dr. Fizzix*) (new)

Page 10 – Cracked Space Helmets – John Severin (reprint from #25)

Page 12 – The Empire Strikes Out – O.O. Severin (John Severin) (reprint from #173)

Page 19 – Cracked Space Lens (reprint from *Giant Cracked* #43)

Page 22 – Star Trek Fun Page! – Rob Orzechowski / Rob Weske (new)

Page 24 – Dr. Fizzix #432 Let's Make Pigs Fly – Gary Fields / Eric Goldberg, Mark Howard (new)

Page 25 – Cracked Science Fiction Convention Profiles – Bruce Bolinger / Steve Strangio (new)

Page 26 – Form & Function Q & A Looks at Robo Cop – Rurik Tyler (reprint from #258)

Page 28 – Commercializing the Moon – John Severin (reprint from #81)

Page 34 – Jiffy-Gloob – Mike Ricigliano (new)

Page 36 – Alien Shut-Ups! (most beautiful girl) – Bill McCartney (Bill Ward) (reprint from #8)

Page 37 – Cracked Interviews the Trekker King – Bill Ward (reprint from #169)

Page 42 – Married Couples In – Pete Fitzgerald / Eric Boihlen (new)

Page 44 – Odd Jobs for Star Wars Stars – Howard Nostrand (reprint from #154)

Page 46 – Subscription ad – John Severin (reprint from #159)

Page 47 – NCC-1701-D Today (Lt. Jadzia Dax) – Rurik Tyler / Steve Strangio (new)

Page 50 – Dr. Fizzix #692 Aeronutics 101 – Gary Fields / Eric Goldberg, Mark Howard (new)

Back Cover – At the Star Trek Convention – Jim Bennett / Rob Weske (new)

***Cracked Stocking Stuffer*, 1999 (68 pages) ($1.09) (This was a *Globe Mini-Mag* and measures approximately 2"x3" in size and is apparently very hard to find. It features a lot of new material.)**

Cover – Santa Stuffs Rudolph – Jorge Pacheco (new)

Page 2 – Santa Claus – John Severin (reprint from #41)

Page 3 – Contents

Page 4 – Ratolph the Red-Nosed Reindeer – Jorge Pacheco / Mike Lotter (new)

Page 25 – Frosted the Snowman – Jorge Pacheco / Mike Lotter (new)

Page 36 – Cracked's Christmas Quiz – Mike Ricigliano / Eric Bohlen (reprint from #288)

Page 44 – How the G-r-r-inch Lost Christmas in the Mail – Jorge Pacheco / Mike Lotter (new)

Page 64 – Christmas Gifts for the Dog on Your Shopping List – Jim Bennett / Eric Bohlen (reprint from #288)

Page 67 – Subscription ad – John Severin, Jeff Wong (reprint from #332, 337)

Back Cover – Santa Skateboarder – John Severin / Mort Todd (reprint from #243)

***Cracked Summer Special* #1, Summer 1991 (100 pages) ($3.50)**

Cover – Life Guard – John Severin (reprint from #88)

Page 2 and 51 – Public Park Rules – Cracked Poster #188 (reprint from #188)

Page 3 – Contents – Mike Ricigliano

Page 4 – National Limpoon's Groundhog Day Vacation – Walter Brogan / Lou Silverstone (new)

Page 9 – How Hot is it? – Don Orehek (reprint from #190)

Page 12 – Word Play (Room for One More) (reprint from #210)

Page 14 – The Cracked Guide to Windsurfing – Bill Ward (reprint from #190)

Page 18 – The Wheel of Fortune for Summer Jobs! – Bo Badman (Rurik Tyler) (reprint from #230)
Page 20 – Summer is – John Langton (reprint from #128)
Page 22 – How to Beat Those Video Game Players – Ron Zalme (reprint from #195)
Page 25 – The Cracked Guide to Hobbies – Warren Sattler (reprint from #200)
Page 29 – Growing Painful – Walter Brogan / Joe Catalano (reprint from #230)
Page 33 – The Cracked Step-by-Step Guide for Growing Your Own Garden – Warren Sattler (reprint from #190)
Page 37 – More Spy and Saboteur Mini-Flips – Mike Ricigliano (new)
Page 39 – Cracked Looks at Computers – Warren Sattler (reprint from #206)
Page 43 – The Cracked Guide to Kite Flying – Bill Ward (reprint from #199)
Page 47 – Shut-Ups (don't want to visit Grandma) – Don Orehek (reprint from #218)
Page 48 – A Dozen Things Never to Do at the Beach – John Langton (reprint from #173)
Page 49 and Insert – Cracked Personalized Mix-Your-Own-Glue Stickers – Arnoldo Franchioni (full color, glossy) (new)
Page 50 – Cracked Hold-Ups! (horoscope) – Sururi Gumen (reprint from #203)
Page 53 – The Cracked Money Diet – LePoer (John Severin) (reprint from #210)
Page 56 – Cat Gifts for Cats Who Have Everything – Mac Bush (Sururi Gumen) (reprint from #125)
Page 58 – You Know It's Really Summer When – Don Orehek (reprint from *Cracked Collectors' Edition* #44)
Page 60 – The Scuba Diver – Howard Nostrand (reprint from #159)
Page 61 – Another Cracked Look at a Video Arcade – Sururi Gumen (reprint from #208)
Page 64 – Go Fly a Kite – John Severin (reprint from #74)
Page 65 – The Cracked Book of Games and Puzzles That Anyone Can Solve – Warren Sattler (reprint from #159)
Page 71 – The Cracked Guide to Bicycle Motocross – Don Orehek (reprint from #201)
Page 75 – A Cracked Look at Summer Camps – Howard Nostrand (reprint from #145)
Page 79 – Cracked Interviews the Lemonade King – John Langton (reprint from #129)

Page 84 – The Cracked Guide to Boating – Sailor Sam (John Severin) (reprint from #129)

Page 88 – How to Make Baseball More Interesting – Bill Ward (reprint from #137)

Page 92 – Creating Your Own Summer Jobs – Don Orehek (reprint from #197)

Page 94 – The Honeymoaners – Win Mortimer / Rich Kriegel (Lou Silverstone) (reprint from *Cracked Monster Party* #7)

Page 98 – Subscription ad – Rurik Tyler

Back Cover – Sylvester Having a Beach Bawl! – John Severin (reprint from #95)

Cracked Don Martin Summer Special #2, Summer 1992 (100 pages) ($2.95) (This was the only time any of Don Martin's material was reprinted in *Cracked*, as Martin commanded a fairly high reprint royalty.)

Cover – Heimlich Maneuver – Don Martin (new)

Page 2 – Two Heads Are Better Than – John Severin (reprint from #236)

Page 3 – Contents – Mike Ricigliano

Page 4 – Ill-Legal Weapons – Walter Brogan / Vic Bianco (Lou Silverstone) (reprint from #251)

Page 10 – The '92 Olympics go Commercial – Warren Sattler (reprint from #207) (originally called "The '84 Olympics go Commercial")

Page 13 – Progress of a Cracked Technophile! – John Severin / Peter Bagge (reprint from #233)

Page 15 – Cracked Interviews Howeird Stern – Rob Orzechowski / Terry Gentile (reprint from #255)

Page 18 – A Good Date vs. A Bad Date – Frank Fitzgerald (reprint from #187)

Page 21 – Cracked Olympic Lens! – Randy Epley (reprint from #237)

Page 22 – Form & Function Looks at Little League Gear! – Bo Badman (Rurik Tyler) (reprint from #237)

Page 24 – Fringe Benefits Athletes Will Soon Be Demanding – Howard Nostrand (John Severin) (reprint from #146)

Page 27 – Video College – Warren Sattler (reprint from #187)

Page 31 – Olympic One-Shots (medals) – Mike Ricigliano / Roger Brown (reprint from #237)

Page 32 – Cracked's Guide to Backpacking – John Severin (reprint from #108)

Page 37 – Shut-Ups (li'l twit) – Don Orehek (reprint from #236)

Page 38 – The Cracked World of Relatives – Don Orehek (reprint from #187)

Page 41 – False Rumors About Cracked – John Severin / George Gladir (reprint from #237)

Page 44 – Great Moments in History (fishing) (reprint from #189)

Page 46 – Cracked Hot Stove League Baseball Cards! – John Severin / George Gladir (reprint from #243)

Page 49 – Cracked Olympic Lens II! – Randy Epley (reprint from #237)

Page 50 – Don Martin Rules! – Don Martin (new)

Insert – Don Martin's Jacques Cousteau in his Submarine – Don Martin (reprint from #264)

Insert – Don Martin's Olympics '92 – Don Martin (new)

Insert – Don Martin's Calling All Hands – Don Martin (reprint from #250)

Page 51 – Don Martin's One Fine Day on Duncan Avenue – Don Martin (reprint from #259)

Page 52 – Don Martin's One Electrifying Morning at the State Pen – Don Martin (reprint from #236)

Page 53 – Don Martin Presents the Sounds of Battyman! – Don Martin (reprint from #248)

Page 56 – Don Martin's One Fine Day in the Outback – Don Martin (reprint from #255)

Page 57 – Don Martin's Quasimodo at the Doctor's Office – Don Martin (reprint from #251)

Page 58 – Don Martin's Dork Tracy – Don Martin (reprint from #258)

Page 62 – Don Martin's One Fine Tuesday Afternoon…or Was it Wednesday? – Don Martin (reprint from #255)

Page 63 – Cracked Olympic Lens III! – Randy Epley (reprint from #237)

Page 64 – A Cracked Look at Cable TV – Don Orehek (reprint from #193)

Page 68 – When the Country Runs Out of Water – Bill Ward (reprint from #146)

Page 72 – A Cracked Alphabet Book for Home Owners – John Severin (reprint from #41)

Page 76 – Mod Fairy Tales (Humpty Dumpty) – C.E. Severin (Catherine Severin) (reprint from #193)

Page 77 – Pologloid No-Step ad (reprint from #161)

Page 78 – Cracked Looks at a Summer Camp – Don Orehek (reprint from #128)

Page 81 – The Cracked Guide to Gymnastics – John Langton (reprint from #167)

Page 85 – What You're Really Thinking – Warren Sattler (reprint from #172)

Page 87 – Ye Hang Ups (fat little guy) – John Severin (reprint from #237)

Page 89 – The Cracked Soccer Question and Answer Booklet – Don Orehek (reprint from #191)

Page 93 – Ghostbuggers II – Walter Brogan / Vic Bianco (Lou Silverstone) (reprint from #250)

Page 98 – Shut-Ups (pole-vaulting) – Don Orehek (reprint from #194)
Page 99 – Subscription ad – Mike Ricigliano
Back Cover – Chicken Soap label – John Severin (reprint from #108)

***Cracked Summer Special #3*, Summer 1993 (100 pages) ($2.95)**
Cover – We Flush Super Mario Bros: The Movie – John Severin (new)
Page 2 – *Cracked Collectors' Edition* #96 ad
Page 3 – Contents – Mike Ricigliano
Page 4 – Super Mario Brothers: The Movie – Walter Brogan / Andy Simmons (new)
Page 9 – Ripper's Believe it or Bail! (No Skateboarding) – Phillips Studios (reprint from #249)
Page 10 – Dear John Letters of History – John Severin (reprint from #27)
Page 12 – Grossanne – Walter Brogan / Rich Kriegel (Lou Silverstone) (reprint from #244)
Page 16 – Specialty Signs for Specialty Stores – Bill Ward (reprint from #143)
Page 18 – Freddie the Menace – Gary Fields (reprint from #245)
Page 20 – Cracked Map – John Langton (reprint from #63)
Page 22 – The Cracked History of Art – John Langton (reprint from #117)
Page 26 – You Know You're a Couch Potato When – Bud Jones / Gary Fields (reprint from #236)
Page 28 – Twits – Walter Brogan (reprint from #245)
Page 32 – Small is Beautiful – John Langton (reprint from #143)
Page 35 – When All TV Reflects the Simpson Influence – John Severin / George Gladir (reprint from #260)
Page 38 – Arachnomania – Mike Ricigliano (reprint from #260)
Page 40 – Double Scare! – Frank Caruso / Joe Catalano (reprint from #242)
Page 44 – Shut-Ups (two cowpokes) – Don Orehek (reprint from #262)
Page 45 – Cowtown U.S.A. (reprint from #150)
Page 50 – Vidiotic Games Section – John Severin (reprint from #200)
Insert – Cracked Video Games – Pete Fitzgerald / Steve Strangio (full color, glossy) (new)
Page 51 – Another Cracked Look at a Video Arcade – Sururi Gumen (reprint from #208)
Page 54 – Video Games We'll Soon Be Seeing – Howard Nostrand (reprint from #141)
Page 57 – Video Games & Equipment of the Future IV! – Pete Fitzgerald / George Gladir (reprint from #256)
Page 61 – A Cracked Numbtendo Video Game Shopping Mall Adventure – Pete Fitzgerald / Steve Strangio (reprint from #269)
Page 64 – Accessories That Duplicate the Thrills of Arcade Playing Right in the Home – Don Orehek (reprint from #200)

Cracked Summer Special #4, Summer 1994 (100 pages) ($2.95) (Major errors in this issue as certain pages were reprinted that shouldn't have been. They actually were supposed to be for *Cracked Collectors' Edition* #100. The table of contents reflects what should have been in the issue from pages 62-69. Also page 91 is reprinted twice.)

Page 22 – The Vanilla Ice Cream Story The Man, his Music, the Legend – John Severin / Vic Bianco (Lou Silverstone) (reprint from #264)
Page 26 – Our Lady of Garbage – Rurik Tyler / Ronnie Nathan (reprint from #266)
Page 28 – The Elvis Parsley Story – Bill Wray, John Severin / Tony Frank (Lou Silverstone) (reprint from #244)
Page 32 – At the Heavy Metal Concert – Mike Ricigliano (reprint from #252)
Page 33 – Woodstock – Don Orehek / Vic Bianco (Lou Silverstone) (reprint from #249)
Page 37 – An Owner and a Player Negotiating a Contract 1982 – Ron Zalme (reprint from #194)
Page 38 – The Last of The Cracked Lens (reprint from #164)
Page 44 – The Cracked Guide to Plant Care – John Severin (reprint from #130)
Page 47 – If I Won the Lottery – Mike Ricigliano (reprint from #264)
Page 50 and Insert – Unbelievably Sneaky Fake-Out Covers!!! – Mike Ricigliano, Rurik Tyler (full color, glossy) (new)
Page 51 – Subscription ad
Page 52 – The Dorks of Hazzardous With Chipps to go – John Severin (reprint from #172)
Page 59 – Kids, You Know You Really Have to Worry When – Don Orehek (reprint from #188)
Page 62 – Kenny the Cockroach's Toy Tenement Sale! – Frank Borth / Scott Franklin (reprint from #280) (mistaken reprint)
Page 66 – Charlie Brown Specials for the 90's – Gary Fields / Craig Farrell (reprint from #283) (mistaken reprint)
Page 68 – Subscription ad (mistaken reprint)
Page 69 – Smelrose Place – John Severin / Vic Bianco (Lou Silverstone) (partial reprint from #278) (mistaken reprint)
Page 70 – Things We've Often Wondered About – Bill Ward (partial reprint from #192)
Page 72 – The Great Chicago Heist – John Severin (reprint from #176)
Page 80 – Smooth Character Camels You'll Never See – Ron Wagner (reprint from #259)
Page 82 – Cracked Fantasies – Sururi Gumen (reprint from #172)
Page 85 – The Cracked Annoyance Barometer – Bill Ward (reprint from #185)
Page 88 – Everybody's Got Something to Be Thankful For – Angelo Torres (reprint from #7)
Page 90 – Spy and Saboteur in The Library – Mike Ricigliano (reprint from #252)

Page 91 – Homeboy Alone – John Severin (reprint from #262) (The first
   page of this story is reprinted twice.)

Page 98 – Shut-Ups (happiest day) – Don Orehek (reprint from *Cracked
   Monster Party* #11)

Page 99 – Memorhex ad – Rurik Tyler (new)

Back Cover – Great Moments in History 1656 – Charles Rodrigues
   (reprint from #132)

Cracked Summer Special #5, Summer 1995 (84 pages) ($2.95)

Cover – We Strip Poker Hontas – Walter Brogan (new)

Page 2 – *Cracked Blockbuster* #9 ad

Page 3 – Contents – Mike Ricigliano

Page 4 – Cracked's Sensational Full Color Fake-Out Video Covers! –
   Mike Ricigliano (new)

Page 5 – Beauty and the Feast – Water Brogan (full color) (new)

Page 6 – Walt Dizzy's Beauty and the Feast – Walter Brogan / Lou
   Silverstone (full color) (reprint from *Cracked Collectors' Edition* #91)

Page 9 – Mister Bignose – Jeremy Banx (butterflies) (reprint from #245)

Page 10 – Snot Wipe and the Seven Dwarfs – Water Brogan (full color)
   (new)

Page 11 – Magazines for the Psychologically Disturbed – Pete Fitzgerald
   / Lenore Skenazy (reprint from #273)

Page 14 – Cracked Looks at Baseball Trading Cards – John Severin /
   George Gladir (reprint from #250)

Page 18 – Form and Function Looks at the Roach! – Bo Badman (Rurik
   Tyler) (reprint from #246)

Page 20 – Honey, I Stunk the Kids! – Walter Brogan / Charles E. Hall
   (reprint from #251)

Page 26 – Cartoondom Confidential – Gary Fields (reprint from #267)

Page 28 – Proper Etiquette for Everyday Living – Mike Ricigliano /
   Roger Brown (reprint from #256)

Page 30 – How the Future has Changed – Gray Morrow / Charles E.
   Hall (reprint from #253)

Page 34 – Plastic Surgery of the Cartoon Stars – Mike Ricigliano / Jerry
   De Fuccio (reprint from #273)

Page 36 – How the West Was Lost – Gary Fields / Randy Epley (reprint
   from #240)

Page 38 – Everyday Neuroses – Rurik Tyler / Steve Strangio (reprint
   from #270)

Page 41 – Pocahoney – Walter Brogan / Andy Simmons (new)

Page 47 – Famous Scenes form Great World War I Aviation Movies!
   (reprint from #64)

Page 48 – Snacks That Time Forgot – John Severin / Lenore Skenazy (reprint from #276)

Page 51 – Mother Goose Goes to Court – Gary Fields / Ronnie Nathan (reprint from #261)

Page 54 – Robbing Hood Prance of Thieves – Walter Brogan / Lou Silverstone (reprint from #267)

Page 61 – More Cigarette Ads Aimed at Specific Groups! – John Severin / George Gladir (reprint from #255)

Page 64 – One-Shots (Biff Masters) – Mike Ricigliano / Roger Brown (reprint from #242)

Page 66 – Shut-Ups (soaring over the city) – Don Orehek (reprint from #237)

Page 67 – Toon Town Babylon – Bill Wray / Eel O'Brian (Mort Todd) (reprint from #245)

Page 71 – Cracked Interviews Howeird Stern – Rob Orzechowski / Terry Gentile (reprint from #255)

Page 74 – It's Those Ghastly Toothpaste People! – Jeremy Banx (reprint from #245)

Page 75 – The Return of Jafart – Water Brogan (full color) (new)

Page 76 – Dizzy's Aladumb – Walter Brogan / Lance Contrucci (full color) (reprint from *Cracked Collectors' Edition* #94)

Page 80 – Subscription ad – John Severin (reprint from #159) (full color)

Page 81 – Ye Hang Ups #10 (He can't be serious) – C.E. Severin (Catherine Severin) (reprint from #190)

Page 82 – The Lion Klutz – Water Brogan (full color) (new)

Page 83 – Shut-Ups (Happy Birthday, Muckey!) – Don Orehek (reprint from #246)

Back Cover – Nosepicchio – Water Brogan (full color) (new)

Cracked Summer Special #6, Summer 1996 (84 pages) ($2.99)

Cover – The Hunchback of Notre Lame – Walter Brogan (new)

Page 2 – *Cracked Collectors' Edition* #108 ad

Page 3 – Contents – Mike Ricigliano

Page 4 – Days of Plunder – Walter Brogan (reprint from #259)

Page 10 – The Last Issues of Popular Comic Books – Pete Fitzgerald / George Gladir (reprint from #258)

Page 12 – Court Room Capers – Don Orehek (reprint from #252)

Page 14 – It Came to Pass – Jeremy Banx (reprint from #242)

Page 15 – The Nielsen Ratings for Everyday Life! – Gary Fields / Dan Birtcher (reprint from #288)

Page 18 – Smooth Character Camels You'll Never See – Ron Wagner (reprint from #259)

Page 20 – Bill & Ted's Big Budget Journey – John Severin / Vic Bianco (Lou Silverstone) (reprint from #268)
Page 25 – Shut-Ups (autobiography) – Don Orehek (reprint from #252)
Page 26 – Cracked Mini-Movie Multiplex – Rurik Tyler, Frank Borth / Steve Strangio, Tony Frank (Lou Silverstone) (reprint from #263)
Page 30 – Viering Off (Sleeping Beauty) – Gary Fields / Jed Vier (reprint from #271)
Page 32 – Next Years' "Real Life" Shows – John Severin / Steve Glaser (reprint from #273)
Page 34 – Roasting Mother Goose (Little Tommy Tucker) – Vic Martin / Lyle Roberts Kain (reprint from #269)
Page 35 – The Hunchback of Notre Lame – Walter Brogan / Andy Simmons (full color) (new)
Page 39 – Cracked Hold-Ups! (now belong) – Don Orehek (reprint from #273)
Page 41 – Cracked Dinosaur Chart – Mike Ricigliano (reprint from *Cracked Blockbuster* #7) (full color)
Page 45 – Shut-Ups (watered down drinks) – Don Orehek (reprint from #243)
Page 46 – Subscription ad – John Severin (reprint from #260) (full color)
Page 47 – Highlights From the 1996 Summer Olympics in Atlanta (red color added) (new)
Page 48 – Cracked's Summer Olympic Pins – Mike Ricigliano (full color) (new)
Page 50 – A Cracked Salute to the Olympics – Bill Ward (reprint from #135)
Page 55 – Olympic One-Shots (medals) – Mike Ricigliano / Roger Brown (reprint from #237)
Page 56 – Cracked Form & Function Looks at the Summer Olympics! – Bo Badman (Rurik Tyler) (reprint from #238)
Page 58 – More Interesting, Livelier Summer Olympics! – Mike Ricigliano (reprint from #275)
Page 61 – Cracked Olympic Lens! – Randy Epley (reprint from #237)
Page 62 – Olympic Events Based on Everyday Stuff? – Walter Brogan (reprint from #276)
Page 64 – One-Shots Looks at the Olympics – Mike Ricigliano / Roger Brown (reprint from #238)
Page 66 – Cracked Olympic Lens II! – Randy Epley (reprint from #237)
Page 67 – Cracked Interviews the Olympic Training King – Bill Ward (reprint from #136)
Page 72 – The Olympics go Commercial – Warren Sattler (reprint from #207)

Page 75 – Spies and Saboteurs Hit the Olympics – Mike Ricigliano (reprint from #275)

Page 76 – Cracked Olympic Lens III! – Randy Epley (reprint from #237)

Page 77 – The Uggly Family Go to the Olympics! – Stosh Gillespie (Dan Clowes) / Eel O'Brian (Mort Todd) (reprint from #237)

Page 80 – So Here's a Cracked Look at Shoes on the Cutting Edge! – John Severin / Jeffery Wilson (new)

Page 82 – Olympic One-Shots (Alfred E. Neuman appearance) – Mike Ricigliano / Roger Brown (reprint from #239)

Page 83 – Peter Pan Reads a Bedtime Story – Mike Ricigliano / Roger Brown (reprint from #247)

Back Cover – Great Moments in Sports 1947 – Howard Nostrand (reprint from #160)

Cracked Summer Special #7, Summer 1997 (84 pages) ($2.99)

Cover – Hercules Versus Hercules – Walter Brogan (new)

Page 2 – Commemorative Plate Rejects – Rurik Tyler / Andy Lamberti (reprint from #290)

Page 3 – Contents – Mike Ricigliano

Page 4 – Hercules photo (new)

Page 5 – The 12 Labors of Disney's Jercules – Walter Brogan / Judd Stomp (full color) (new)

Page 9 – Once and For All – Mike Ricigliano (reprint from #263)

Page 10 – Cracked Prison Greeting Cards – Bruce Bolinger / Patric Abedin (reprint from #277)

Page 12 – Cracked Toon Wanted Posters – Mike Ricigliano, Gary Fields / Daniel O'Keefe (reprint from *Cracked Collectors' Edition* #95) (full color)

Page 17 – Cracked's Big City Gift Catalog – Frank Borth / Scott Franklin (reprint from #273)

Page 20 – Some Rhymes of the Times – Rurik Tyler / Lenore Skenazy (reprint from #274)

Page 22 – Martian – John Severin / Andrew Osborne (reprint from #283)

Page 27 – Unlikely Celebrity Product Endorsements – Jim Bennett / Eric Goldberg, Mark Howard, Mike Mikula (reprint from #286)

Page 30 – Numbtendo's Megaplex Mania – Pete Fitzgerald / Steve Strangio (reprint from #287)

Page 32 – Cracked Rock 'n' Roll Museum! – John Severin / George Gladir (reprint from #250)

Page 34 – Guillotine Gags! – Don Orehek / George Gladir (reprint from #247)

Page 38 – The Grip – Mike Ricigliano / Roger Brown (reprint from #232)

Page 39 – Rob Weske's Interpreting Cave Drawings – Bruce Bolinger / Rob Weske (reprint from #292)

Page 42 – Spies and Saboteurs Hit Summer Camp – Mike Ricigliano (reprint from #284)

Page 45 – Who Framed Roger Wabbit / Wawwy Bwogan (Walter Brogan) / Rich Kriegel (Lou Silverstone) (reprint from #241)

Page 50 – The Wheel of Fortune for Summer Jobs! – Bo Badman (Rurik Tyler) (reprint from #230)

Page 52 – The Final Episodes of Soured Sitcoms! – Frank Caruso (reprint from #232)

Page 54 – Cracked Interviews the Fast Food King – Bill Ward / Charles E. Hall (reprint from #252)

Page 58 – Beyond Beauty and the Beast – Mike Ricigliano (reprint from #272)

Page 60 – Jerkules The Liesurely Journeys – Walter Brogan / Greg Grabianski (reprint from *Cracked Monster Party* #32)

Page 66 – Daredevils, Stuntmen and Stand-Ins – Arnoldo Franchioni (reprint from #274)

Page 69 – Hercules photo (full color) (new)

Page 70 – Hercules Spin-Off Products – Don Orehek / Dan Birtcher (new)

Page 72 – Subscription ad – John Severin (reprint from #160) (full color)

Page 73 – Roasting Mother Goose (Little Boy Blue) – Vic Martin (reprint from #276)

Page 74 – How Clinton's Programs Have Affected Mother Goose – Gary Fields / Dan Birtcher (reprint from #291)

Page 77 – The Making of the Lion King – Walter Brogan, Chris Bartlett / Lou Silverstone (reprint from *Cracked Collectors' Edition* #101) (full color)

Page 81 – How the Other Half Lives – Mike Ricigliano (reprint from #263)

Page 82 – Dear Hercules – Dan Birtcher (new)

Page 83 – Jim Bum ad – John Severin / Cliff Mott (reprint from #278)

Back Cover – Looose Leevi's – Tom Grimes / Steve Strangio (reprint from #280)

Cracked Summer Special #8, Summer 1998 (100 pages) ($2.99)

Cover – Small Soldiers Search and De-Toy! – O.O. Severin (John Severin) (new)

Page 2 – The Cracked "Lose Weight Permanently" Diet Pyramid – Gary Fields / Brian Glass (reprint from #296)

Page 3 – Contents – Mike Ricigliano

Page 4 – Maul Soldiers – Walter Brogan / Lou Silverstone (new)

Page 10 – Cracked's Summertime Word Problem – Pete Fitzgerald / Judd Stomp (reprint from #285)

Page 12 – The Cracked World of Staying in Shape – Bill Dubay (reprint from #178)

Page 15 – $trikes Illustrated Magazine – Ron Zalme (reprint from #193)

Page 19 – Acnnie – John Severin (reprint from #191)

Page 27 – What's Really in Those Cigarettes? – Bruce Bolinger / Lenore Skenazy (reprint from #293)

Page 30 – Cracked Rates the New Thrill-Ride Roller Coasters – Mike Ricigliano (reprint from #291)

Page 32 – Cracked's New Sidewalk, Street and Playground Games – Warren Sattler (reprint from #173)

Page 36 – The Hunter – Don Orehek / Rob Weske (reprint from #292)

Page 37 – Cracked Interviews the Useless Products King – Bill Ward (reprint from #191)

Page 42 – A.C.R.O.N.Y.M.S. – Ron Zalme (reprint from #191)

Page 44 – A Dozen Things Never to Do at the Beach – John Langton (reprint from #173)

Page 46 – The Cracked World of Vacations – Don Orehek (reprint from #173)

Page 50 – Spies and Saboteurs Hit the Rodeo – Mike Ricigliano (reprint from #294)

Page 52 – Every Cloud has a Silver Lining – John Severin (reprint from #175)

Page 55 – Arnie Goes to the Movies – Bruce Bolinger / Andy Simmons (reprint from *Cracked Blockbuster* #7)

Page 60 – Other "No Frills" Items and Services – Don Orehek (reprint from #178)

Page 62 – Ye Hang Ups #2 (castle) – C.E. Severin (Catherine Severin) (reprint from #173)

Page 63 – The Very Rich and the Very Poor – Warren Sattler (reprint from #193)

Page 67 – Profile of a Coward – Bill Ward (reprint from #175)

Page 70 – How You Picture a Business Operates and How it Really Does – Samuel B. Whitehead (reprint from #178)

Page 72 – The Big Bird and the Little Old Lady – Arnoldo Franchioni (reprint from #289)

Page 73 – The Good Old Daze of the Automobile – John Severin (reprint from #193)

Page 77 – If Newspapers Emphasized Good News – Samuel B. Whitehead (reprint from #178)

Page 80 – A Cracked Look at Cable TV – Don Orehek (reprint from #193)

Page 84 – Random Funnies (upset) – Mike Ricigliano / Roger Brown (reprint from #251)

Page 86 – Celebrity Garbage – John Severin (reprint from #131)

Page 90 – The Animal Kingdom Gets Tattooed – Bruce Bolinger / Lenore Skenazy (reprint from #290)

Page 93 – Bull & Tad's Excrement Adventure – Rick Altergott (reprint from #253)

Page 98 – Royal Canadian Shut-Ups (La Forge) – Don Orehek / Eric Goldberg, Mark Howard (reprint from #287)

Page 99 – Subscription ad – John Severin (reprint from *Cracked Collectors' Edition* #85)

Back Cover – Great Moments in History 1314 – Mike Ricigliano (reprint from #250)

Cracked Summer Special #9, Summer 1999 (84 pages) ($2.99)

Cover – Austin Powers The Spy Who Shagged Us! – John Severin (new)

Page 2 – *Cracked Collectors' Edition* #120 ad

Page 3 – Contents – Mike Ricigliano (full color)

Page 4 – Swinging Sixties Section! – Walter Brogan (full color) (new)

Page 5 – Austin Poopers: The Spy Who Gagged Me – Frank Cummings / Andy Simmons (full color) (new)

Page 10 – Goin' Up the Country – Frank Caruso (reprint from #249) (full color)

Page 11 – A Funny Thing Happened to Me on the Way to the Happening – O.O. Severin (John Severin) (reprint from #66)

Page 15 – Now They're Hi-Jacking Everything! – Vic Martin (reprint from #78)

Page 18 – Black Thoughts – Caracu (reprint from #69)

Page 19 – The Hippies' Coloring Book – Lugoze (reprint from #79)

Page 22 – The Stones Keep Rollin! – John Severin (reprint from #57)

Page 26 – Cracked Looks at an Outdoor Art Exhibit! – Walter Gastaldo (reprint from #67)

Page 28 – The Establishment Goes Hippy – O.O. Severin (John Severin) (reprint from #67)

Page 32 – Life's Dropouts are Getting Younger and Younger – Bill McCartney (Bill Ward) (reprint from #66)

Page 36 – More Beatlezania – John Severin (reprint from #50)

Page 41 – The World's First Psychedelic Janitor – John Severin (reprint from #71)

Page 44 – Square Buttons for Squares (reprint from #70)
Page 46 – The Woodstock Tales – Don Orehek (new)
Page 49 – Swinging Sixties Section! – Walter Brogan (new)
Page 50 – The A-a-ayy Team (Excuse me officer) – John Severin (reprint from #201)
Page 57 – What Really Happens When – Bruce Bolinger / Ed Subitzky (reprint from #309)
Page 60 – Banned Children's Books – Gary Fields / David Boone (reprint from #282)
Page 62 – Goon with the Wind: 1990 – Walter Brogan / Rich Kriegel (Lou Silverstone) (reprint from #246)
Page 66 – Job Changes Caused by Downsizing – Don Orehek / Fred Sahner (reprint from #311)
Page 68 – The Hunt for Rad Crackedober – Walter Brogan / Tony Frank (Lou Silverstone) (reprint from #256)
Page 73 – Summer Shut-Ups (Woooo…woooo!!) – Don Orehek / Eric Goldberg, Mark Howard (reprint from #312)
Page 74 – Cracked Fake-Out Grocery Labels – Pete Fitzgerald / Greg Grabianski (reprint from *Cracked Collectors' Edition* #102)
Page 75 – Sicken of the Sea, Nastea – Pete Fitzgerald / Greg Grabianski (reprint from *Cracked Collectors' Edition* #102) (full color)
Page 76 – Camelsmells Islamic Alphabet Soup – Pete Fitzgerald / Greg Grabianski (reprint from *Cracked Collectors' Edition* #102) (full color)
Page 77 – Old El Gaso WhoDied? Refried Beans – Pete Fitzgerald / Greg Grabianski (reprint from *Cracked Collectors' Edition* #102) (full color)
Page 78 – Peter Pain Sadistic Peanut Butter – Pete Fitzgerald / Greg Grabianski (reprint from *Cracked Collectors' Edition* #102) (full color)
Page 79 – Hurt's Womanwich Original Sloppy Jane Sauce – Pete Fitzgerald / Greg Grabianski (reprint from *Cracked Collectors' Edition* #102) (full color)
Page 80 – Chef Boylardy Fat-Encrusted Heart Shaped Pasta – Pete Fitzgerald / Greg Grabianski (reprint from *Cracked Collectors' Edition* #102) (full color)
Page 81 – Dumb-Maid Raisins – Pete Fitzgerald / Greg Grabianski (reprint from *Cracked Collectors' Edition* #102) (full color)
Page 82 – Subscription ad – Jeff Wong (reprint from #305) (full color)
Page 83 – A Dignified Evening at the Strongarm Social & Unity Club – Mike Ricigliano / Jerry De Fuccio (reprint from #263)
Back Cover - Page 96 – Jungle Rot – Frank Borth / Scott Thaler (reprint from #262)

Cracked Super #5, Winter 1991-1992 (100 pages) ($3.50) (Formerly *Super Cracked*)

Cover – Sylvester, Comic Collector – Rurik Tyler (new)

Page 2 – Super-Sylvester – O.O. Severin (John Severin) (reprint from #53)

Page 3 – Contents – Mike Ricigliano

Page 4 – U.S.A. Superforce – John Severin / E. Nelson Bridwell (reprint from #225)

Page 9 – Stars' Wars – Pat Boyette (reprint from #245)

Page 11 – 1982 Catalog for Costumed Heroes – John Severin (reprint from #190)

Page 14 – Super Hero Ads – Bruce Day (reprint from #152)

Page 16 – If Comic Strip Characters Had Summer Replacements – Lugoze (reprint from #78)

Page 20 – Cracked Looks at the World of Superdom – Don Orehek (reprint from #139)

Page 24 – The Funnies in the Flicks! (reprint from #72)

Page 27 – Super Ms Magazine – Warren Sattler (reprint from #161)

Page 32 – Are Comics Ruining Our Children? – Bill Elder (reprint from #11)

Page 34 – If the Comics Were Drawn by Famous Movie Directors – Bill McCartney (Bill Ward) (reprint from #51)

Page 38 – You Know You're a Super Type – Warren Sattler (reprint from #211)

Page 40 – Cracked Look at Super-Zeros! – Mort Todd / Tom Bacas (reprint from #218)

Page 43 – Cracked Interviews the Saturday Morning Cartoon King – Bill Ward (reprint from #159)

Page 48 – Cracked Sunday Comics – Gary Fields / John Arcudi (reprint from #245)

Insert and 51 – X-Mental Patients Comic Book –Rurik Tyler (full color, glossy) (new)

Page 58 – Skata Curb (Skateboard Keyboard) – Phillips Studios (reprint from #247)

Page 59 – Cracked Presents Superheroes of the Future – Willy Orwonte (John Severin) (reprint from #160)

Page 62 – If Comic Strip Characters Had to Face Simple But Realistic Problems! – John Severin (reprint from #69)

Page 65 – Super People Magazine – Sururi Gumen (reprint from #163)

Page 70 – Super Types in Ordinary Life – Warren Sattler (reprint from #183)

Page 74 – Poopeye – Nireves (John Severin) (reprint from #179)

Page 81 – Toon Town Babylon – Bill Wray / Eel O'Brian (Mort Todd) (reprint from #245)

Page 85 – Tardzan the Apish Man – John Clayton (John Severin) / Joe Catalano, Mort Todd (reprint from #226)

Page 90 – When the Woman's Lib Movement Spreads to the Comics! – John Severin (reprint from #92)

Page 94 – When Comic Strips Go Madison Avenue – Lugoze (reprint from #80)

Page 98 – Help! Wanted – Garry Owen (John Severin) (reprint from #38)

Page 99 – Godzilla and Pow-Man – John Severin (reprint from Pow! #2)

Back Cover – A Man Can Fly? – John Severin (reprint from #160)

Cracked Super #6, Winter 1992 (100 pages) ($2.95)

Cover – Not to Worry, Batman – Rurik Tyler (new)

Page 2 – Cracked Interviews Rabid the Wonder Boy! – Skene Catling (reprint from #248)

Page 3 – Contents – Mike Ricigliano

Page 4 – X-Mess the Movie – Bill Wray, Tony Salmons / Robert Loren Fleming (reprint from #243)

Page 7 – Martial Art Weapons and Techniques – Bill Ward (reprint from #118)

Page 10 – 1-900-Cracked – Rurik Tyler (reprint from #249)

Page 12 – Super Hero Hall of Fame – O.O. Severin (John Severin) (reprint from #60)

Page 16 – The Government Gambol in Gambling – O.O. Severin (John Severin) (reprint from #68)

Page 20 – If Picture Postcards Told the Truth! – John Severin (reprint from #59)

Page 22 – Photos That Have Been Cropped – John Severin (reprint from #25)

Page 26 – Take Me Out to the Old Cracked Ball Game – Charles Rodrigues (reprint from #53)

Page 28 – Sly Stallone's Greatest Xmas Hits! (reprint from #243)

Page 29 – Cracked Goes Batty – Rurik Tyler / Mort Todd (reprint from #248)

Page 30 – Batzman Meets the Green Horned Bee! – M & O.O. Severin (Marie Severin, John Severin) (reprint from #74)

Page 36 – A Cracked Look at Batman – Mike Ricigliano / Roger Brown (reprint from #248)

Page 38 – What if Bruise Payne Didn't Become Battyman?! – Ron Wagner / George Gladir (reprint from #248)

Page 42 – The Day Bazman Almost Went Bats – John Severin (reprint from #73)

Page 44 – Battyman – Rick Altergott / Charles E. Hall (reprint from #234)

Page 48 – Shut-Ups (crummy issue of *Cracked*) – Don Orehek (reprint from #248)

Page 49 and Insert – Bat-Mobile – Rurik Tyler (full color, glossy) (new)

Page 51 – Batty-Weapons that Didn't Quite Make it to the Utility Belt! – John Severin / George Gladir (reprint from #248)

Page 54 – Cracked Interview with Rabid the Wonder Boy! – John Severin / Rich Kriegel (Lou Silverstone) (reprint from #248)

Page 58 – Batman to the Rescue – Mike Ricigliano / Roger Brown (reprint from #248)

Page 59 – The Cracked Lens Presents the Bat-Photo Scrapbook! (reprint from #248)

Page 61 – Battyman (Where's Dr. Freeze) – Rick Altergott (reprint from #257)

Page 66 – Geez...What Cushy Job Being Badtman – Pat Boyette (reprint from #248)

Page 68 – Batman What's Hot and What's Not – Gary Fields (reprint from #248)

Page 69 – Them Battyman Sequels We're Sure to See! – John Severin / George Gladir (reprint from #248)

Page 72 – Bat$man – John Severin / Mort Todd (reprint from #249)

Page 80 – Don't Even Start!! – Al Scaduto (reprint from #221)

Page 83 – From Bad to Worse – Mike Ricigliano / Roger Brown (reprint from #243)

Page 85 – Suped-Upman The Satire – Nireves (John Severin) (reprint from #160)

Page 92 – A Cracked Looks at Picture Phones – John Langton (reprint from #64)

Page 95 – The Completely Rebuilt Person – Vic Martin (reprint from #76)

Page 98 – Subscription ad – Rurik Tyler

Insert – Varoom! – Vic Martin (reprint from #248)

Back Cover – Great Moments in History Ice Age – Mike Ricigliano (reprint from #137)

Cracked Super #7, Summer 1993 (100 pages) ($2.95)

Cover – Superman Returns from the Dead – Walter Brogan (new)

Page 2 – *Cracked Spaced Out* #1 ad

Page 3 – Contents – Mike Ricigliano

Page 4 – Doggie Hoser M.D. – Walter Brogan / Tony Frank (Lou Silverstone) (reprint from #254)

Page 8 – One-Shots (Darth Vader) – Mike Ricigliano (reprint from #231)

Page 10 – Cracked's Superhero Section – O.O. Severin (John Severin) (reprint from #53)

Page 11 – Stupor-Hero Fanzine – Walter Brogan (reprint from #215)
Page 17 – Robot Wars (heh heh bbbzzz) – Steve Ditko / Mort Todd (reprint from #218)
Page 18 – The Incredible Hunk – Sigbjorn (John Severin) (reprint from #177)
Page 27 – Super Types in Ordinary Life – Warren Sattler (reprint from #183)
– Cracked Celebrates Spider Appreciation Month! – John Severin / Scott Thaler (reprint from #260) (full color)
Page 28 – The Confusing Spider-Dude – Frank Borth / Jerry De Fuccio, Lou Silverstone (reprint from #260)
Page 35 – The Day Batguy Almost Went Bats – John Severin (reprint from #73)
Page 37 – The Six Billion Dollar Man! – John Severin (reprint from #120)
Page 38 – The Six Billion Dollar Man – John Severin (reprint from #120)
Page 44 – Super Cracked Battyman – Mike Ricigliano (new)
Page 45 – 1993 Catalog for Costumed Heroes – John Severin (reprint from #190) (originally titled "1982 Catalog for Costumed Heroes")
Page 48 – Cracked's Very Own Superman Section – John Severin (reprint from #183)
Page 49 – Stuporman Back from the Dead! – Walter Brogan, Gary Fields / Lou Silverstone (full color) (new)
Page 53 – My Stupid Identity Supedupboy – Pete McDonnell (reprint from #253)
Page 57 – How the Movies Wrecked Supedupman – Rick Altergott / Mort Todd (reprint from #233)
Page 61 – One Day in Metropolitis – Don Orehek (reprint from #136)
Page 62 – What Christopher Reeve Will Be Like When He Gets Old – Samuel B. Whitehead (reprint from #183)
Page 65 – Ye Hang Ups (equal rights) – C.E. Severin (Catherine Severin) (reprint from #177)
Page 66 – Believe it or Not (reprint from #177)
Page 69 – Shut-Ups (put out the dog) – Don Orehek (reprint from #169)
Page 70 – If Professional Sports Were Played the Same Way as When We Were Kids – Val Mayerik (reprint from #177)
Page 73 – Subscription ad
Page 74 – Shut-Ups (slow down) – Don Orehek (reprint from #258) (full color)
Page 75 – The Inspection – Mike Ricigliano / Roger Brown (reprint from #252)
Page 76 – Last Words Before the Hang-Up – Sururi Gumen (reprint from #161)

Page 79 – TV Sets for Watching Specific TV Shows! – John Severin / Charles E. Hall (reprint from #254)

Page 83 – Spy and Saboteur in The Library – Mike Ricigliano (reprint from #252)

Page 84 – Cracked Action-Adventure Hero Sandwiches! – Milton Knight / Hilary Zatz (reprint from #225)

Page 87 – More Freak Outs from Back in the Future! – John Severin / George Gladir (reprint from #253)

Page 91 – Never Rent the Apartment if – Sururi Gumen (reprint from #177)

Page 93 – Jeoparty! – John Severin / Joe Catalano (reprint from #231)

Page 95 – Cracked Mini-TV Tube – Pete McDonnell / Vic Bianco (Lou Silverstone) (reprint from #254)

Page 99 – Tinoctin ad – John Severin (reprint from #258)

Back Cover – It Ain't Easy Being Ghost Rider – Gary Fields (new)

Cracked Super #8, Winter 1994-1995 (100 pages) ($2.95)

Cover – Exlax-Men – John Severin (new)

Page 2 and 51 – Cracked X-Lax Poster – Rurik Tyler (reprint from *Cracked Super* #5)

Page 3 – Contents – Mike Ricigliano

Page 4 – Welcome to our X-Rated Section (new)

Page 5, 7 – X-Mental Patients Comic Book –Rurik Tyler (reprint from *Cracked Super* #5)

Page 6 – Skata Curb (Skateboard Keyboard) – Phillips Studios (reprint from #247)

Page 15 – X-Mess the Movie – Bill Wray, Tony Salmons / Robert Loren Fleming (reprint from #243)

Page 18 – Dapperman! – O.O. Severin (John Severin) / George Gladir (reprint from #53)

Page 23 – Super Sylvester – Bob Fingerman, Bill Wray, O.O. Severin (John Severin), Steve Ditko / Mort Todd (reprint from *Super Cracked* #31)

Page 39 – Exercise Manual and Hot Dog Stunts for Super Heroes – Powers (John Severin) (reprint from #147)

Page 43 – Toon-Age Mutant Ninjerk Turtles – John Severin / Tony Frank (Lou Silverstone) (reprint from #256)

Page 49 – Stan Leak Presents: "The Fall of Rogue!" – Walter Brogan / Greg Grabianski (full color) (new)

Page 53 – Final Proof – John Severin / Don Edwing (reprint from #33)

Page 54 – Absolutely, Unquestionably, Positively, Undeniably, the Very, Very, Last of The Cracked Lens (and we really, really mean it this time, for sure!) Part XXVI (reprint from #207)

Page 58 – The Cracked Money Diet – LePoer (John Severin) (reprint from #210)

Page 61 – Spy and Saboteur at Echo Canyon – Mike Ricigliano (reprint from #256)

Page 62 – Cracked "You Know You're _____ When" – Don Orehek (reprint from #186)

Page 64 – G.I. Donut Boys – John Severin (reprint from #167)

Page 71 – A Cracked Catalog of Summer Survival Gear – Warren Sattler (reprint from #208)

Page 74 – Cracked's Uses for Used Computers – Mike Ricigliano / Roger Brown (reprint from #258)

Page 76 – The Cracked Soccer Question and Answer Booklet – Don Orehek (reprint from #191)

Page 80 – Cracked Looks at the T-Shirt Craze – Howard Nostrand (reprint from #143)

Page 84 – Subscription ad

Page 85 – A Cracked Western You'll Never See – John Severin (reprint from #211)

Page 86 – Cracked Tips for Improving Home Movies – Warren Sattler (reprint from #149)

Page 90 – Things You Hate So Much – Mike Ricigliano / Roger Brown (reprint from #257)

Page 92 – Germinator 2: Judgment Daze – Walter Brogan / Tony Frank (Lou Silverstone) (reprint from #268)

Back Cover – Stan Lee's Press-On Nails – John Severin / Gene Perone (reprint from #283)

Cracked Super #9, Summer 1995 (100 pages) ($2.95)

Cover – The New Mighty Moron Power Failures! – John Severin (new)

Page 2 – The Forest's Prime Evil! – John Severin (reprint from #84)

Page 3 – Contents – Mike Ricigliano

Page 4 – Blood Kicker – Walter Brogan / Tony Frank (Lou Silverstone) (reprint from #270)

Page 10 – The Perils of Edward Scissorhands – Rurik Tyler (reprint from #262)

Page 12 – The Cracked Guide to Determine if Someone Has Mailed You a Bomb – Frank Borth / Robert Hess (reprint from #274)

Page 14 – Shut-Ups (two cowpokes) – Don Orehek (reprint from #262)

Page 15 – The Scoreboard Kid – John Severin (reprint from #260)

Page 19 – Viering Off (Ye Olde Barber Shoppe) – Gary Fields / Jed Vier (reprint from #270)

Page 21 – The Replacement Shows – John Severin / Steve Strangio (reprint from #271)
Page 24 – A Fish Story – Milton Knight (reprint from #219)
Page 25 – Cracked's Comparative Guide to Learning Institutions – Pete Fitzgerald / Steve Strangio (reprint from #268)
Page 29 – Cracked's Plan for Converting Weapons for Civilian Use – John Severin / Fred Sahner (reprint from #267)
Page 32 – Absolutely, Unquestionably, Positively, Undeniably, the Very, Very, Last of The Cracked Lens (and we really, really mean it this time, for sure!) Part XXVII (reprint from #208)
Page 36 – The Cracked World of Toys and Games – Don Orehek (reprint from #148)
Page 40 – Barferly Hills-911 – John Severin / Lou Silverstone (reprint from #270)
Page 46 – Next Years' "Real Life" Shows – John Severin / Steve Glaser (reprint from #273)
Page 48 – Celebrity Guest Appearances on TV – Rurik Tyler – George Gladir (reprint from #263)
Page 50 – Cracked Celebrates Spider Appreciation Month! – John Severin / Scott Thaler (reprint from #260)
Insert – The New Mighty Moron Power Failures! – Walter Brogan (full color, glossy) (new)
Page 51 – Cracked Presents Superheroes of the Future – Willy Orwonte (John Severin) (reprint from #160)
Page 54 – Super Couple's Housewarming Party – Mike Ricigliano / Jerry De Fuccio (reprint from #269)
Page 57 – Superhero Long-Shots – Mike Ricigliano / Roger Brown (reprint from #257)
Page 60 – Robocop Ramblings – John Severin (reprint from #259)
Page 64 – Robocop-Out, Too! – Frank Borth (reprint from #259)
Page 70 – Up Close and Personal with the Rocketeer – Mike Ricigliano (reprint from #268)
Page 73 – The Crocketeer – John Severin / Lou Silverstone (reprint from #268)
Page 80 – Rocketeen! – Mike Ricigliano / Jerry De Fuccio (reprint from 3268)
Page 81 – Good News and Bad News for Teenage Mutated Ninjerk Turdles – Rurik Tyler (reprint from #255)
Page 84 – Cracked Interviews Donald Trumpet – Gary Fields (reprint from #259)
Page 87 – King Kong's Boyhood – Bill Ward (reprint from #141)
Page 91 – Bart's Catalogue for Conniving Underachievers – Frank Borth (reprint from #267)

Page 94 – Big Business of Little League – Tony Tallarico (reprint from #62)
Page 98 – Shut-Ups (pull them offside) – Don Orehek (reprint from #261)
Page 99 – Subscription ad – Frank Borth
Back Cover – Power Rangers Episode #1995 (Plus Tax) – Rurik Tyler / Todd Jackson (new)

***Cracked Super* #10, Winter 1995-1996 (68 pages) ($2.95)**
Cover – All-Batman Spectacular! – Walter Brogan (new)
Page 2 – The Emergency – Mike Ricigliano / Roger Brown (reprint from #243)
Page 3 – Contents – Mike Ricigliano
Page 4 – Barf, Man. Forever! – Walter Brogan / Lou Silverstone (new) Page 8 – A Cracked Look at Batman – Mike Ricigliano / Roger Brown (reprint from #248)
Page 10 – Batzman Meets the Green Horned Bee! – M & O.O. Severin (Marie Severin, John Severin) (reprint from #74)
Page 16 – Batman to the Rescue – Mike Ricigliano / Roger Brown (reprint from #248)
Page 17 – What if Bruise Payne Didn't Become Battyman?! – Ron Wagner / George Gladir (reprint from #248)
Page 21 – Shut-Ups (crummy issue of *Cracked*) – Don Orehek (reprint from #248)
Page 22 – Cracked Interview with Rabid the Wonder Boy! – John Severin / Rich Kriegel (Lou Silverstone) (reprint from #248)
Page 26 – The Cracked Lens Presents the Bat-Photo Scrapbook! (reprint from #248)
Page 28 – Battyman Return? – Walter Brogan / Lou Silverstone (reprint from #276)
Page 34 – Riddle Me This – Walter Brogan (new)
Insert – Riddle This! The Cracked Riddle Book – Walter Brogan, Mike Ricigliano, John Severin / Tom Bloomenfeld, Steve Strangio, Todd Jackson (full color and green color added, glossy covers, half size, 16 pages) (new)
Page 35 – Batty-Weapons that Didn't Quite Make it to the Utility Belt! – John Severin / George Gladir (reprint from #248)
Page 38 – Batastrophes! – Mike Ricigliano (reprint from #274)
Page 40 – Bat$man – John Severin / Mort Todd (reprint from #249)
Page 48 – Another Batastrophe – Mike Ricigliano (reprint from #274)
Page 49 – The Batzman Tapes – John Severin / Lou Silverstone (reprint from #274)
Page 54 – Battyman (Where's Dr. Freeze) – Rick Altergott (reprint from #257)

Page 59 – Them Battyman Sequels We're Sure to See! – John Severin / George Gladir (reprint from #248)

Page 62 – Bruce Waine's World – John Severin / Lou Silverstone (reprint from #288)

Page 67 – Subscription ad – Rurik Tyler (reprint from #248, 290, 291, 295

Back Cover – The Jerker – Bill Wray (reprint from #248)

Cracked Super #11, Summer 1996 (100 pages) ($2.99)

Cover – Showdown of the Century – Rurik Tyler (new)

Page 2 – Great Moments in History 1924 – Warren Sattler (reprint from #190)

Page 3 – Contents – Mike Ricigliano

Page 4 – Super Section – Walter Brogan (reprint from *Cracked Super* #7)

Page 5 – Teenage Mutant Ninjerk Turdles III The Sacred Sequel of Dumbness – Walter Brogan / Andy Simmons (reprint from #281)

Page 9 – The Robocop Crime-Fighters Catalogue – Frank Borth (reprint from #268)

Page 12 – Cashing in on the Man of Steel – Rurik Tyler / Eric Goldberg, Mark Howard (reprint from #280)

Page 14 – Spies and Saboteurs Hit the Superheroes – Mike Ricigliano / Jerry De Fuccio (reprint from #264)

Page 17 – Dork, Man! – Walter Brogan (reprint from #260)

Page 23 – Super Hurry-Ups! (Sure is romantic) – Rick Altergott (reprint from #243)

Page 24 – Super Heavies – Pete Fitzgerald / Steve Strangio (reprint from #264)

Page 26 – Cracked Form & Function The Batty-Wing – Rurik Tyler (reprint from #248)

Page 28 – U.S.A. Superforce – John Severin / E. Nelson Bridwell (reprint from #225)

Page 33 – Teenage Mutated Ninjerk Turdles Unfit Role Models for Our Children! – Rurik Tyler (reprint from #255)

Page 34 – Hazards of: Being a Superhero – Mike Ricigliano / Roger Brown (reprint from #243)

Page 36 – Shut-Ups (Dick, what's your pleasure) – Don Orehek (reprint from #258)

Page 37 – The Confusing Spider-Dude – Frank Borth / Jerry De Fuccio, Lou Silverstone (reprint from #260)

Page 44 – Supedupman's 50th Birthday! – John Severin / George Gladir (reprint from #235)

Page 49 – The Marvel Versus DC Battles! – Alan Kupperberg / Greg Grabianski (full color) (new)

Page 53 – And Now For the Rest of This Disaster (new)

Page 54 – Cracked's New Magazines for the New America – Pete Fitzgerald / Howie Mitchell (reprint from #261)

Page 56 – Reducing the Violence in Movies – Lugoze (reprint from #75)

Page 60 – The Replacement Shows – John Severin / Steve Strangio (reprint from #271)

Page 63 – Get Smarty – Walter Brogan / Tony Frank (Lou Silverstone) (reprint from #281)

Page 67 – Shut-Ups (can't seem to make out) – Don Orehek (reprint from #238)

Page 68 – How Cartoon Characters are Coping with the Recession – Gary Fields / Andy Simmons (reprint from #275)

Page 70 – Cracked's Guide to Good Eating – Pete Fitzgerald / Howie Mitchell (reprint from #263)

Page 72 – Socky V – Walter Brogan (reprint from *Cracked Collectors' Edition* #94)

Page 79 – Spies and Saboteurs Hit the Mob – Mike Ricigliano (reprint from #262)

Page 80 – You Know You're a VCR Freak if – Al Scaduto / George Gladir (reprint from #225)

Page 82 – One-Shots (surfing torpedo) – Mike Ricigliano / Roger Brown (reprint from #237)

Page 84 – Rangey Loner – John Severin (reprint from #236)

Page 89 – Cracked Interviews Mike Dyson the Boxing King! – Rob Orzechowski (reprint from #239)

Page 92 – If Television Censors Had Their Way – John Severin (reprint from #212)

Page 96 – Cracked Mini-Movie Theatre – Walter Brogan (reprint from #259)

Page 99 – Subscription ad – John Severin (reprint from #260)

Back Cover – The Uncanny Malcolm X, Man – Jim Lee Williams (reprint from #279)

Cracked Super #12, Winter 1996-1997 (100 pages) ($2.99)

Cover – Ex-Men The Final Mutation – John Severin (new)

Page 2 – Nicoduct ad – Tom Grimes / Andy Simmons (reprint from #274)

Page 3 – Contents – Mike Ricigliano

Page 4 – Slumming in America – Walter Brogan / Tony Frank (Lou Silverstone) (reprint from #242)

Page 9 – Modern Clowns (reprint from #285)

Page 12 – Grunge is Really Getting Out of Hand When – Jeff Wong / Gene Perone (reprint from #284)

Page 14 – Rasslin' Rowdies Magazine – John Severin / George Gladir (reprint from #223)

Page 18 – The Crusty Spoon Placemat – Bruce Bolinger / Lenore Skenazy (reprint from #279)

Page 20 – The Exam for the Presidency of the United States – Gary Fields / John Street (reprint from #276)

Page 24 – Familiar Ties – John Severin / Joe Catalano (reprint from #226)

Page 29 – To the Victors – Mike Ricigliano (reprint from #262)

Page 30 – Francho's Ark – Arnoldo Franchioni (reprint from #269)

Page 33 – Kenny the Cockroach's Toy Tenement Sale! – Frank Borth / Scott Franklin (reprint from #280)

Page 37 – The Billy Pluckett Story – John Severin (reprint from #169)

Page 43 – Mr. Wilson's Revenge – Gary Fields / Eric Goldberg, Mark Howard (reprint from #284)

Page 46 – Dangerous Toys – Ron Barrett (reprint from #279)

Page 48 – Cracked Super Section Dorkman – John Severin (reprint from #260)

Page 49 – Ex-Men of Lipgloss and Doom! – Alan Kupperberg / Greg Grabianski (full color) (new)

Page 53 – Future Turtlemania Product Tie-Ins – John Severin / George Gladir (reprint from #261)

Page 56 – Form & Function Looks at the New Bat Gear! – Rurik Tyler (reprint from #250)

Page 58 – Super Types in Ordinary Life – Warren Sattler (reprint from #183)

Page 62 – Still More Dick Tracy Bad Guys – John Severin (reprint from #258)

Page 64 – The True Story of The Lone Ranger – Brian Buniak (reprint from #198)

Page 67 – Super People Magazine – Sururi Gumen (reprint from #163)

Page 72 – Teenage Mutant Ninja Turtles in Japan – Mike Ricigliano (reprint from #281)

Page 74 – Cracked Interviews the Jerker – Walter Brogan / Rich Kriegel (Lou Silverstone) (reprint from #250)

Page 78 – Martial Art Weapons and Techniques – Bill Ward (reprint from #118)

Page 81 – 1996 Catalog for Costumed Heroes – John Severin (reprint from #190) (originally titled "1982 Catalog for Costumed Heroes")

Page 84 – Hudd & Dini (Batman) – Vic Martin (reprint from #248)

Page 86 – Yertle the Mutant Ninja Turtle! – Gary Fields (reprint from #256)

Page 90 – Comic Book Heroes – Bruce Bolinger / Dan DeBruin (reprint from #286)

Page 92 – The Six Billion Dollar Man – John Severin (reprint from #120)

Page 98 – One Day in Metropolitis – Don Orehek (reprint from #135)

Page 99 – Subscription ad – John Severin (reprint from #160)

Back Cover – Conan the Comedian is Victorious in the Talk Show Wars – Jeff Wong (reprint from #285)

Cracked Super #13, Summer 1997 (100 pages) ($2.99)

Cover – Lois Goes Batty! – Rurik Tyler (new)

Page 2 – It Ain't Easy Being Ghost Rider – Gary Fields (reprint from *Cracked Super* #7)

Page 3 – Contents – Mike Ricigliano

Page 4 – Beverly Hills Slop II – Walter Brogan / Joe Catalano (reprint from #233)

Page 9 – Cracked's New, Revamped (and Lots More Interesting) Olympic Events – Mike Ricigliano (reprint from #271)

Page 12 – Hazardous to Your Health! – Al Scaduto (reprint from #220)

Page 14 – Bart Goes to the Movies – John Severin (reprint from #284)

Page 19 – If We Had Designer Labels on Everything – Bruce Bolinger (reprint from #284)

Page 20 – Cut Out and Use These Sani-Strips – Ron Barrett (new)

Page 22 – Cracked Interviews the Game Show King – Bill Ward (reprint from #165)

Page 27 – If Romance Writers Wrote – Rurik Tyler / Jeff Wilson (reprint from #286)

Page 30 – The Icy Reception! – Dick Ayers (reprint from #243)

Page 31 – Beverly Hills High School Yearbook – Jim Bennett (reprint from #284)

Page 36 – Famous Last Laughs – Don Orehek / Andrew Osborne (reprint from #286)

Page 38 – Why is it That the Same People Who – Walter Brogan / Rich Kriegel (Lou Silverstone) (reprint from #284)

Page 40 – Super Section – John Severin (reprint from #160)

Page 41 – Superduperman – Walter Brogan / Andy Simmons (full color) (new)

Page 45 – From Bad to Worse – Mike Ricigliano / Roger Brown (reprint from #243)

Page 47 – My Stupid Identity Supedupboy – Pete McDonnell (reprint from #253)

Cracked Super #14, Winter 1997-1998 (84 pages) ($2.99)

Page 24 – The Cracked Lens Presents the Bat-Photo Scrapbook! (reprint from #248)

Page 26 – How the Movies Wrecked Supedupman – Rick Altergott / Mort Todd (reprint from #233)

Page 30 – Super Hero Ads – Bruce Day (reprint from #152)

Page 32 – The New and Sometimes Improved Robin Hood – Mike Ricigliano (reprint from #265)

Page 35 – The Toonage Mutant Ninja Turdles II – John Severin / Vic Bianco (Lou Silverstone) (reprint from #265)

Page 42 – Walter Brogan photo (new)

Insert – Batgirl vs. Poison Ivy Poster – Alan Kupperberg (full color, glossy) (new)

Insert – The Spawning of Spawn Poster – Rurik Tyler (full color, glossy) (new)

Page 44 – Magazines That Tried to Copy Cracked, But Failed – M.E. Tate (John Severin) (reprint from #212)

Page 48 – Spies and Saboteurs Hit an Amusement Park – Mike Ricigliano (reprint from #274)

Page 50 – The Walled-Ins – John Severin (reprint from #114)

Page 55 – Shut-Ups (two hours) – Don Orehek (reprint from #253)

Page 56 – The Cracked Guide to Golf – Bill Ward (reprint from #125)

Page 60 – Travel Ads Before and After – John Severin / Charles E. Hall (reprint from #246)

Page 63 – Cracked History of Skateboarding – Ron Wagner (reprint from #258)

Page 66 – A Dozen Things Never to Do at the Beach – John Langton (reprint from #173)

Page 68 – The Cracked Soccer Question and Answer Booklet – Don Orehek (reprint from #191)

Page 72 – Life's a Beach! – Mike Ricigliano (reprint from #293)

Page 74 – When All Businesses Go Automated – Sururi Gumen (reprint from #191)

Page 77 – Full of it House – John Severin / Greg Grabianski (reprint from #292)

Page 82 – Shut-Ups (101 Gourmet Ways Cookbook) – Don Orehek (reprint from #257)

Page 83 – Subscription ad – Rurik Tyler (reprint from #248, 290, 291, 295)

Back Cover – Tinoctin ad – John Severin (reprint from #258)

Cracked Super #15, Summer 1998 (68 pages) ($2.99)

Cover – Holy Spit! Full Color Super Stickers! – Walter Brogan (new)

Page 2 – Atlas Takes Recess – Rurik Tyler (reprint from *Cracked Collectors' Edition* #81)

Page 3 – Contents – Mike Ricigliano

Page 4 – Super Section – John Severin (reprint from *Pow!* #2)

Page 5, 7 – X-Mental Patients Comic Book –Rurik Tyler (reprint from *Cracked Super* #5)

Page 6 – Skata Curb (Skateboard Keyboard) – Phillips Studios (reprint from #247)

Page 15 – Rules and Regulations Regarding the Mask – Mike Ricigliano (reprint from #294)

Page 17 – Exercise Manual and Hot Dog Stunts for Super Heroes – Powers (John Severin) (reprint from #147)

Page 21 – Final Proof – John Severin / Don Edwing (reprint from #33)

Page 22 – SuperSylvester the Cracked Crusader! The Legend – John Severin / Mort Todd (reprint from #234)

Page 26 – You Know You're a Super Type – Warren Sattler (reprint from #211)

Page 28 – Toon-Age Mutant Ninjerk Turtles – John Severin / Tony Frank (Lou Silverstone) (reprint from #256)

Page 34 – Super Stickers – O.O. Severin (John Severin) (reprint from #53)

Insert – 12 Super Stickers – Walter Brogan (full color, sticky) (new)

Page 35 – Orehek at Large at a Comedy Club – Don Orehek / Steve Strangio (reprint from #268)

Page 38 – Cracked Guide to Behavior in Public Places – John Severin / Fred Sahner (reprint from #270)

Page 40 – Blood Kicker – Walter Brogan / Tony Frank (Lou Silverstone) (reprint from #270)

Page 46 – Cracked's Strategems and Weapons for Everyday Hostilities – Arnoldo Franchioni (reprint from #275)

Page 48 – Everyday Neuroses – Rurik Tyler / Steve Strangio (reprint from #270)

Page 51 – History Time Line – Mark Martin / Jeff Wilson (reprint from #281)

Page 54 – The Monkey Quotient – Bruce Bolinger / Arnie Bernstein (reprint from #281)

Page 58 – Sabotage in the 1990's – Mike Ricigliano (reprint from #254)

Page 60 – Viering Off (Ye Olde Barber Shoppe) – Gary Fields / Jed Vier (reprint from #270)

Page 62 – White Men Can't Dunk!! – Walter Brogan / Link Pershad (reprint from #274)

Page 67 – Subscription ad – John Severin (reprint from #260)

Back Cover – Stan Lee's Press-On Nails – John Severin / Gene Perone (reprint from #283)

Cracked Super #16, Summer 1999 (100 pages) ($2.99)

Cover – Xena & Hercules Can They Be-Headed to the Altar? – John Severin (new)

Page 2 – Under Siege The Cookbook for the Harried Chef! – Jeff Wong (reprint from #304)

Page 3 – Contents – Mike Ricigliano

Page 4 – Cracked Super Section – Rurik Tyler (reprint from *Cracked Super* #5)

Page 5 – Huncules Loves Eczema – Frank Cummings / Andy Simmons (full color) (new)

Page 9 – Superhero Services Guide – Brian Buniak / Steve Strangio (reprint from #305)

Page 12 – Shut-Ups (crummy issue of *Cracked*) – Don Orehek (reprint from #248)

Page 13 – Stan Leak Presents: "The Fall of Rogue!" – Walter Brogan / Greg Grabianski (reprint from *Cracked Super* #8) (full color)

Page 17 – Comic Book vs. Comic Strip Crossover Battles! – Alan Kupperberg / Judd Stomp (reprint from #307)

Page 21 – The Lost Batman Villains Files – Pete Fitzgerald / Rob Weske (reprint from #302)

Page 24 – Cracked Superhero Makeovers – Mike Ricigliano (reprint from #306)

Page 26 – Dapperman! – O.O. Severin (John Severin) / George Gladir (reprint from #53)

Page 31 – Super Ms Magazine – Warren Sattler (reprint from #161)

Page 36 – Things a Hero's Mom Could Never Get Used To! – Kurt Schaffenberger (reprint from #243)

Page 38 – Daddy-Long Legs-Man – Alan Kupperberg / Andy Simmons (reprint from #304)

Page 44 – Super Section's Over – Alan Kupperberg (new)

Page 45 – Cracked's "How-To" Video Clearance – Bruce Bolinger / Scott Franklin (reprint from #295)

Page 48 – Comic Con Confidential! – John Severin / George Gladir (reprint from #248)

Page 50 – Spies and Sabs Hit a Health Club – Mike Ricigliano (reprint from #290)

Page 52 – Clothing Ideas for the 90's – Don Orehek / Mike Mikula (reprint from #294)

Page 53 – The Big Book of Cracked Birthday Ideas! – Gary Fields / Lenore Skenazy (reprint from #294)

Page 57 – Aiming Gun Ads at Specific Groups – John Severin / George Gladir (reprint from #252)

Page 60 – Hazards of: (saying the wrong thing) – Mike Ricigliano / Roger Brown (reprint from #255)

Page 62 – Famous Missed Phone Calls that Changed History – Pete Fitzgerald / Mike Mikula (reprint from #295)

Page 64 – Cracked to the Future Part II – John Severin / Tony Frank (Lou Silverstone) (reprint from #254)

Page 69 – Ripper's Believe it or Bail! (Longest Railslide!) – Phillips Studios (reprint from #251)

Page 70 – Other Impact Tests – Mike Ricigliano / Jerry De Fuccio (reprint from #267)

Page 72 – Bart's Catalogue for Conniving Underachievers – Frank Borth (reprint from #267)

Page 75 – Travel Ads Before and After – John Severin / Charles E. Hall (reprint from #246)

Page 78 – Ill-Legal Weapons – Walter Brogan / Vic Bianco (Lou Silverstone) (reprint from #251)

Page 84 – Ye Hang Ups (Surf's up!) – John Severin (reprint from #256)

Page 85 – Cracked Toon Wanted Posters – Mike Ricigliano, Gary Fields / Daniel O'Keefe (reprint from *Cracked Collectors' Edition* #95) (full color)

Page 89 – Cracked Visits America's Grossest Kid – Bruce Bolinger / Barry Zeger (reprint from #293)

Page 92 – A TV Scene We're Dying to See – Jeff Wong (reprint from #293)

Page 93 – The Saturday Morning TV Show Awards – Walter Brogan / Andy Simmons (reprint from *Cracked Collectors' Edition* #106) (full color)

Page 97 – One Day in Africa – Mike Ricigliano / Roger Brown (reprint from *Cracked Blockbuster* #6)

Page 98 – Discovery: Inside the Pharaoh's Tomb – Don Orehek / Rob Weske (reprint from #294)

Page 99 – Subscription ad – John Severin (reprint from #260)

Back Cover – The Riddler Gets the Point! – Walter Brogan (reprint from #303)

Cracked Super #17, Summer 2000 (68 pages) ($2.99)

Cover – Fake-Out Puke-Mon Cards! – Rurik Tyler (new)

Page 2 – "B"-Movies of Cartoon Characters! – John Severin / Rob Weske (reprint from #301)

Page 3 – Contents – Mike Ricigliano

Page 4 – Batty, Man, Forever – Walter Brogan / Lou Silverstone (reprint from #301)

Page 11 – Jean Claude Van Damme: Serious Actor? – Don Orehek /
Rob Weske (reprint from #297)

Page 12 – Mighty Moviestar Power Rangers – Mike Ricigliano (reprint
from #301)

Page 14 – The Bunisher – Gary Fields (reprint from #254)

Page 16 – Cracked Health and Beauty Ads – John Severin / Steve
Strangio (reprint from #296)

Insert – 3 Puke-Mon cards – Gary Fields / Steve Strangio (full color
card stock) (new)

Page 20 – A to Z Chips We'd Really Like to See! – Jim Hunt / Dan
Birtcher (reprint from #305)

Page 23 – Superchumps – Rurik Tyler, Gary Fields / Steve Strangio
(reprint from #283)

Page 29 – At the Opera – Bruce Bolinger / Greg Grabianski (reprint
from #303)

Page 30 – The Growing Garbage Garble – John Severin (reprint from #69)

Page 34 – What Is Up With These Pokemon Cards? – Mike Ricigliano /
Todd Jackson (new)

Page 36 – If Other Magazines Had Swimsuit Issues...Like Cracked –
Bruce Bolinger / Barry Zeger (reprint from #298)

Page 38 – City Suckers II – John Severin / Andy Simmons (reprint from
#293)

Page 44 – Bad Professionals – Randy Jones / Randy Epley (reprint from #295)

Page 46 – X-Mess the Movie – Bill Wray, Tony Salmons / Robert Loren
Fleming (reprint from #243)

Page 49 – The NBA Bam Rulebook – Rurik Tyler / Steve Strangio
(reprint from #296)

Insert – 9 Puke-Mon cards – Gary Fields / Steve Strangio (full color,
card stock) (new)

Page 54 – New Rules of Thumb! – Pete Fitzgerald / Daniel Birtcher
(reprint from #289)

Page 56 – Pubescent Olympics World Records – Bruce Bolinger
(reprint from #310)

Page 59 – One Day in the Police Station – Don Orehek / Rob Weske
(reprint from #307)

Page 60 – The Mighty-Moron Chowder Rangers – John Severin / Greg
Grabianski (reprint from #290)

Page 66 – The Swimming Hole – Rurik Tyler / Rob Weske (reprint from
#310)

Page 67 – Subscription ad – Rurik Tyler (reprint from #248, 290, 291, 295)

Back Cover – Country Hits from Death Row – Rurik Tyler / Lenore
Skenazy (reprint from #297)

The First Annual Extra Special Cracked, 1976 (84 pages) ($1.00)

Cover – Cracking a Walnut – John Severin (reprint from #98)

Page 2 – The Cracked Bookstore ad – John Severin

Page 3 – Contents

Page 4 – Butch Cavity and the Sundrenched Kid – John Severin (reprint from #87)

Page 9 – Cracked Guide to Acupuncture – Dick Wright (reprint from #111)

Page 12 – Personalized Checks – Vic Martin (reprint from #114)

Page 16 – Take the Cracked Driving Test! – Tony Tallarico (reprint from #64)

Page 18 – Cracked's New Ways of Presenting the News – John Severin (reprint from #113)

Page 23 – The Information Clerk – Caracu (reprint from #114)

Page 24 – Hiss the Villains (reprint from #94)

Page 28 – You Know Your Stars Are All Screwed Up When – Don Orehek (reprint from #116)

Page 30 – Cracked Looks at An Apartment Building in the Big City – Bernard Baily (reprint from #112)

Page 32 – Dotty About Karate – Bill Ward (reprint from #112)

Page 36 – A Cracked Look at a Supermarket – John Severin (reprint from #115)

Page 38 – Success in Your Chosen Career – Bill McCartney (Bill Ward) (reprint from #96)

Page 41 – Cracked Interviews the Camp King – John Langton (reprint from #111)

Page 46 – Sports Smiles – John Severin (reprint from #56)

Page 48 – Monsterous Merriment (reprint from #98)

Page 50 – Specialized Magazines of the Future – Bill Ward (reprint from #112)

Page 52 – The World's First Psychedelic Janitor – John Severin (reprint from #71)

Page 55 – The Cracked Guide for First Aid – Bob Taylor (reprint from #82)

Page 57 – M*U*S*H (Dear Dad) – John Severin (reprint from #115)

Page 62 – Making Plain Ads Sensational – John Langton (reprint from #116)

Page 64 – How Easily are you Embarrassed? – Vic Martin (reprint from #112)

Page 66 – The Suicide – Caracu (reprint from #68)

Page 67 – The Game of Millionaire – John Severin (new)

Page 83 – Binders and Notebooks ad 2

Back Cover – Help Wanted – Charles Rodrigues (reprint from #113)

The Second Annual Extra Special Cracked, 1977 (84 pages) ($1.00) (This
issue actually came out in 1977 despite being dated 1976.)

Cover – Watering the Sidewalk Flower – John Severin (reprint from #97)

Page 2 – The Cracked Bookstore ad – John Severin

Page 3 – Contents

Page 4 – Murdering the Orient Express – John Severin (reprint from #126)

Page 10 – The Cracked Guide to Golf – Bill Ward (reprint from #125)

Page 14 – If People Switched from One Profession to Another – John Langton (reprint from #125)

Page 18 – Cat Gifts for Cats Who Have Everything – Mac Bush (Sururi Gumen) (reprint from #125)

Page 20 – The History of Early Flight – Tony Tallarico (reprint from #70)

Page 24 – Super Star Mementos – John Severin (reprint from #106)

Page 28 – A Cracked Look at a Crowded Beach – Don Orehek (reprint from #112)

Page 30 – If the Government Labeled All Products as Hazardous – Bernard Baily (reprint from #112)

Page 34 – Some Cracked Tips for Whipping Inflation – Bill Ward (reprint from #128)

Page 38 – Cracked Looks at a Summer Camp – Don Orehek (reprint from #128)

Page 41 – The Ridiculous Things of Life – Bill Ward (reprint from #124)

Page 44 – A Day at the Zoo – Charles Rodrigues (reprint from #108)

Page 47 – Cracked Guide to Magic – Bill Ward (reprint from #126)

Page 50 – Monopo-Oil – John Langton (reprint from #127)

Page 53 – When the World Runs Out of Space – Makbush (Sururi Gumen) (reprint from #127)

Page 57 – Cracked Methods of Staying Thin Forever – Bill Ward (reprint from #122)

Page 61 – Cracked Interviews the Newspaper King – Powers (John Severin) (reprint from #124)

Page 66 – Sagebrush #29 (beware!) – C.E. Severin (Catherine Severin) / John Severin (reprint from #122) / / Sagebrush #31 (this is war) – John Severin (reprint from #123)

Page 67 – The Newest Cracked "Flip the Faces" Book – John Severin (revised reprint from *Giant Cracked* #3)

Page 83 – The Jockey – Caracu (reprint from #96)

Back Cover – Great Moments in Science 1934 – Charles Rodrigues (reprint from #118)

***The Third Annual Extra Special Cracked*, Winter 1979 (84 pages)
($1.25)**

> Cover – Cracked Says Goodbye – John Severin (reprint from #133)
>
> Page 2 – The Cracked Bookstore ad – John Severin
>
> Page 3 – Contents
>
> Page 4 – Star-Warz – O.O. Severin (John Severin) / Joe Catalano (reprint from #146)
>
> Page 11 – The Cracked History of Art – John Langton (reprint from #117)
>
> Page 15 – How to Translate Travel Ads – Bob Taylor (reprint from #108)
>
> Page 18 – The Cracked Guide to Muscle Development – Howard Nostrand (reprint from #147)
>
> Page 22 – One Day in a Washington, D.C. School – Sururi Gumen (reprint from #142)
>
> Page 23 – Tarzan's Abdication – Bill Ward (reprint from #113)
>
> Page 28 – Guest Appearances by the World's Top Humor Artists – Charles Rodrigues (reprint from #107)
>
> Page 30 – How to Cover Up – John Severin (reprint from #113)
>
> Page 34 – A Cracked Look at New York City – Warren Sattler (reprint from #147)
>
> Page 36 – Dreamy Acres – John Severin (reprint from #133)
>
> Page 40 – A Cracked Look at a High School – Bill Ward (reprint from #116)
>
> Page 43 – Cracked Do-it-Yourself Divorce – Don Orehek (reprint from #119)
>
> Page 46 – When the World Runs Out of Food – Sururi Gumen (reprint from #122)
>
> Page 50 – The Day America Runs Out of Gas – John Severin (reprint from #113)
>
> Page 54 – Airplot '77 – Howard Nostrand (reprint from #145)
>
> Page 61 – Cracked Interviews the Writing King – Bill Ward (reprint from #147)
>
> Page 66 – Sagebrush #39 (thing on your back) – John Severin / Knights 'n' Daze #36 (hanging knight) – LePoer (John Severin) (reprint from #128)
>
> Page 67 – The Newest Cracked "Flip the Faces" Book – John Severin (revised reprint from *Giant Cracked* #3)
>
> Page 83 – Get Out the Vote! – John Severin (reprint from #51)
>
> Back Cover – Great Moments in Medicine 1882 – Charles Rodrigues (reprint from #122)

The Fourth Annual Extra Special Cracked, **Winter 1980 (84 pages) ($1.25)**

Cover – Cracking a Walnut – John Severin (reprint from #98)

Page 2 – The Cracked Bookstore ad – John Severin

Page 3 – Contents

Page 4 – If Hit Movies Were Combined – John Severin (reprint from #131)

Page 10 – If T.V. Commercials Were Honest – Warren Sattler (reprint from #143)

Page 14 – The Cracked Guide to Jogging – Howard Nostrand (reprint from #146)

Page 18 – A Cracked Look at America's Other Political Parties Running in November – Don Orehek (reprint from #138)

Page 21 – Sagebrush #51 (Injuns!) – John Severin / MF (reprint from #152)

Page 22 – What Goes on in a Monster's Mind – Don Orehek (reprint from #138)

Page 25 – The Art of Ventriloquism – Bob Taylor (reprint from #134)

Page 29 – Cracked's Inquiring Photographer Visits the Stars (reprint from #152)

Page 33 – Isn't it Rotten in School When – Warren Sattler (reprint from #152)

Page 36 – Super Hero Ads – Bruce Day (reprint from #152)

Page 38 – The Cracked World of Food – Don Orehek (reprint from #151)

Page 42 – A Gloomy Indian Story – Oskar Blotta (reprint from #147)

Page 43 – Disaster Movies You May Be Soon Seeing – John Severin (reprint from #128)

Page 46 – Redemption Coupons We'd Really Like to See – Howard Nostrand (reprint from #141)

Page 48 – The Campaign to Use Less Power – Bernard Baily (reprint from #109)

Page 52 – Accessories for the TV Football Freak – Bill Ward (reprint from #114)

Page 56 – The Starry-Eyed Astronomers – Don Orehek (reprint from #153)

Page 57 – Suggestions for Overcoming the School Crisis! – Bernard Baily (reprint from #110)

Page 61 – Cracked Interviews the Stunt King – Sururi Gumen (reprint from #128)

Page 66 – Shut-Ups (curtain about to go up) – Charles Rodrigues (reprint from #116)

Page 67 – Cracked's Road Race Game – John Severin (new)

Page 83 – Official Cracked Reporter T-Shirt ad

Back Cover – Great Moments in Games 1,057,649 B.C. – Howard Nostrand (reprint from #148)

The Fifth Annual Extra Special Cracked, Winter 1981 (84 pages) ($1.50)

Cover – M*U*S*H – John Severin (reprint from #115)

Page 2 – The Cracked Bookstore ad – John Severin

Page 3 – Contents

Page 4 – M*U*S*H (probably wondering why I called you) – John Severin (reprint from #168)

Page 11 – He's Really a Lone Ranger Now! – Bill Ward (reprint from #1)

Page 12 – Cracked Looks at Dating – Bill McCartney (Bill Ward) (reprint from #76)

Page 16 – "Whaddayacallits?" A New Cracked Game – Joe Mead (reprint from #77)

Page 19 – Why People Move to the Suburbs – Jack Davis (reprint from #14)

Page 23 – The Traffic Jam – Caracu (reprint from #70)

Page 24 – Cracked Suggestions for Improving Mail Service – Bill McCartney (Bill Ward) (reprint from #78)

Page 28 – The Funnies in the Flicks! (reprint from #72)

Page 30 – Cheeter, Tarzin's Faithful Chimp! (reprint from #71)

Page 33 – Moonwrecker – Sururi Gumen (reprint from #166)

Page 40 – Take the Cracked History Test – John Langton (reprint from #71)

Page 42 – The Cracked TV Sports Primer – Bill McCartney (Bill Ward) (reprint from #69)

Page 45 – Fly Me to the Moon – Oskar Blotta (reprint from #79)

Page 48 – Cat Gifts for Cats Who Have Everything – Mac Bush (Sururi Gumen) (reprint from #125)

Page 50 – The Parakeet – John Severin (reprint from #77)

Page 51 – Cracked's King Size Jigsaw Puzzle – Jack Davis, John Severin (reprint from *King-Sized Cracked* #3)

Page 67 – The Newest Cracked "Flip the Faces" Book – John Severin (revised reprint from *Giant Cracked* #3)

Page 83 – Official Cracked Reporter T-Shirt ad

Back Cover – Great Moments in War 1,000,007 B.C. – Howard Nostrand (reprint from #154)

The Sixth Annual Extra Special Cracked, Winter 1982 (84 pages) ($1.50)

Cover – Sweeping Up – John Severin (reprint from #87)

Page 2 – The Cracked Bookstore ad – John Severin

Page 3 – Contents

Page 4 – Cracked Space Encounters Game – Joe Banana (reprint from *Super Cracked* #11)

Page 20 – Leverne & Shirley (Thank you, whistle) – Sigbjorn (John Severin) (reprint from #136)

Page 26 – Are You a Dumb-Dumb? – Bill McCartney (Bill Ward) (reprint from #80)

Page 28 – Digital Instruments of the Future – Warren Sattler (reprint from #144)

Page 31 – A Swinging Good Time! (reprint from #71)

Page 32 – Behind Closed Doors – Don Orehek (reprint from #139)

Page 34 – Some Cracked Tips for Whipping Inflation – Bill Ward (reprint from #128)

Page 38 – Evolution Revolution – Howard Nostrand (reprint from #139)

Page 41 – The Magic Lamp – Don Orehek (reprint from #138)

Page 42 – Report Cards for Everybody – Lugoze (reprint from #77)

Page 44 – The Rhyme of the Thieving Sheik – John Langton (reprint from #165)

Page 48 – Movie Posters We'll Soon Be Seeing (reprint from #168)

Page 53 – The Pick-Up – John Severin (reprint from #34)

Page 54 – Discount Coupons of the Future – Bill Ward (reprint from #126)

Page 56 – You Know You're Nobody When – Bob Taylor (reprint from #131)

Page 58 – Rent-a-Person – John Langton (reprint from #72)

Page 61 – The Cracked Guide to Football – Howard Nostrand (reprint from #140)

Page 66 – The Pleasure is Ours! (reprint from #70)

Page 67 – The Newest Cracked "Flip the Faces" Book – John Severin (revised reprint from *Giant Cracked* #3)

Page 83 – Neveready Powercell ad (reprint from #165)

Back Cover – Training the Dog – Samuel B. Whitehead (reprint from #163)

The Seventh Annual Extra Special Cracked, Winter 1983 (84 pages) ($1.75)

Cover – Sylvester Paints Himself – Powers (John Severin) (reprint from #147)

Page 2 – Contents

Page 3 – Your Very Own Shut-Up Greeting Card Kit – Mike Ricigliano (new)

Page 19 – The Cracked Bookstore ad – John Severin

Page 20 – The Dorks of Hazzardous (kinda spongy Friday) – John Severin (reprint from #170)

Page 27 – Hudd & Dini (rocket) – Vic Martin (reprint from #87)

Page 28 – The Cracked World of Schooling – Bill Ward (reprint from #170)

Page 32 – Cracked Interviews the Stars (reprint from *Cracked Collectors' Edition* #24)

Page 37 – If All Violence Were Eliminated from TV – Howard Nostrand (reprint from #149)

Page 40 – Don't Believe a Word of it – John Severin (reprint from #82)

Page 42 – Ads from the Space Age – Warren Sattler (reprint from #171)

Page 46 – The Factors of Life – Samuel B. Whitehead (reprint from #181)

Page 53 – Destination Fun (reprint from #79)

Page 56 – Cracked's Charisma Test – John Langton (reprint from #121)

Page 58 – Isn't it Rotten in School When – Warren Sattler (reprint from #152)

Page 61 – Ye Hang Ups #4 (got a minute) – C.E. Severin (Catherine Severin) (reprint from #174)

Page 62 – Footboxhockbasetennbasketgolfpoly – John Severin (reprint from #97)

Page 66 – Shut-Ups (66...45...38) – Mike Ricigliano (reprint from #144)

Page 67 – The Game of Inflation – John Severin (reprint from *King-Sized Cracked* #8)

Page 83 – Mugging Minors (reprint from #98)

Back Cover – Happy-Daze Shut-Ups (I have a date) – Powers (John Severin) (reprint from #157)

The Eighth Annual Extra Special Cracked, Winter 1984 (84 pages) ($2.00)

Cover – Mechanical Horse and Indians – John Duillo (reprint from #79)

Page 2 – Contents

Page 3 – Make-Your-Own Newspaper Headlines (revised reprint from *Giant Cracked* #1)

Page 19 – The Jabbersons – Samuel B. Whitehead (reprint from #185)

Page 25 – How to Win a School Election – T. Severin (John Severin) (reprint from #174)

Page 29 – The Cracked Theory on the Relativity of Time – Howard Nostrand (reprint from #162)

Page 35 – Absolutely, Unquestionably, Positively, Undeniably, the Very, Very, Last of The Cracked Lens (and we really, really mean it this time, for sure!) Part VI (reprint from #181)

Page 36 – If Our Currency Truly Reflected Our Economy – Samuel B. Whitehead (reprint from #175)

Page 39 – New Detectors of the Future – Don Orehek (reprint from #171)

Page 42 – How Adults Drive Kids Nuts – Warren Sattler (reprint from #163)

Page 44 – How to Improve Your…ah…ah…Memory – Howard Nostrand (reprint from #163)

Page 47 – Super Ms Magazine – Warren Sattler (reprint from #161)

Page 52 – Crack Ups! Featuring Sagebrush #1 (Hay Nah-Nah!) – John Severin (reprint from #184)

Page 53 – Cracked Interviews the T.V. Ratings King – Bill Ward (reprint from #183)

Page 58 – Last Words Before the Hang-Up – Sururi Gumen (reprint from #161)

Page 61 – Blarney Miller (I want to report a crime) – John Severin (reprint from #176)

Page 66 – Shut-Ups (writing a book) – Don Orehek (reprint from #185)

Page 67 – The Cracked Flip-the-Faces Board Game – Mike Ricigliano, John Severin (new)

Page 83 – Hudd & Dini (Indu Magic) – Vic Martin (reprint from #89)

Back Cover – Great Moments in Sports 1,217,003 B.C. – Conky Nostrand (Howard Nostrand) (reprint from #171)

Extra Special Cracked #9, Winter 1985 (84 pages) ($2.00)

Cover – Monster Party – Bob Fingerman (new)

Page 2 – The Monster – Sururi Gumen (reprint from #130)

Page 3 – Contents

Page 4 – Monster Party! – John Severin (reprint from #31)

Page 6 – The Terror Trip – BOJ (reprint from #55)

Page 7 – Transylvanian TV – Bill McCartney (Bill Ward) (reprint from #36)

Page 11 – If Frankenstein's Monster Did Guest Appearances on T.V. – Howard Nostrand (reprint from #151)

Page 17 – A MonStar is Reborn – John Severin / George Gladir (reprint from _For Monsters Only_ #1)

Page 23 – The Cracked Monsters Lens (nuclear power) (reprint from _Cracked Collectors' Edition_ #61)

Page 28 – Hudd & Dini (inflatable man) – Vic Martin (reprint from #97)

Page 29 – School For Monsters – Nireves (John Severin) (reprint from #26)

Page 34 – Frankenstein the Untold Story (reprint from _Cracked Collectors' Edition_ #43)

Page 42 – The Desert Island Guest – John Severin (reprint from _For Monsters Only_ #3)

Page 43 – Cracked Puts the Bite on Dracula – Howard Nostrand (reprint from #155)

Page 47 – Who's Who at the Extra-Special Cracked Monster Party (new)

Page 48 – Horrible Humor (reprint from #97)

Page 50 – Modern Day Monsters – Joe Maneely (reprint from #5)

Page 52 – The Monster Howls' Baseball Team – John Severin (reprint from #37)

Page 57 – Vampires of the World – Bernard Baily (reprint from #108)

Page 61 – Cracked Monster Trading Cards – John Severin (reprint from *Cracked Collectors' Edition* #53)

Page 65 – The Movie Monsters Strike – John Severin (reprint from #32)

Page 71 – Mighty Monster Laughs!! (reprint from #45)

Page 73 – Monsters in the News – John Severin (reprint from #59)

Page 75 – A Little Off the Top! – BOJ (reprint from #53)

Page 76 – The Uggly Family "Melbin Goes to School" – Stosh Gillespie (Dan Clowes) / Eel O'Brian (Mort Todd) (1st *Uggly Family*) (new)

Page 83 – Black Magic – Bob Zahn (reprint from #37)

Back Cover – Monster House – John Severin (reprint from #43)

For Monsters Only #1, November 1965 (68 pages) (35¢) (Titled *Cracked's…* on cover of #1-8 and Annual #1.) (Many issues feature new material.)

Cover – Frankenstein

Page 2 – Our Founder

Page 3 – Contents

Page 4 – Post Mortem Office

Page 6 – Meet Our Staff

Page 7 – Transylvania Correspondence Schools ad

Page 8 – Like Father, Like Son

Page 14 – A MonStar is Reborn – John Severin / George Gladir

Page 20 – A Friend from Next Door

Page 21 – Transylvanian Tee Heeeeeees

Page 22 – Monster Mother Goose – Bill McCartney (Bill Ward)

Page 24 – Another Nice Neighbor

Page 25 – Orehek in Orbit – Don Orehek

Page 26 – A Transylvanian Family Album

Page 29 – Mucho Monsters from Mexico

Page 34 – Quick Quiz (Peter Lawford)

Page 36 – Art Gallery of Classic Chillers

Page 39 – Fetch! – John Severin

Page 40 – First Men in the Moon

Page 43 – ABC TV's The Addams Family

Page 44 – The Transylvanian TV Scene

Page 47 – Macabre Mirth

Page 48 – Chiller Dillers – John Severin, Joe Kiernan, Benson, Pete Wyma, Art Pottier, Lennie Herman, Norm Sutt, Bob

Page 50 – Stationery from Transylvania
Page 52 – The Annual Transylvania Census
Page 53-66 – (various real ads)
Page 67 – The First Lady of Transylvania
Back Cover – Transylvania Travel Stickers

For Monsters Only #2, September 1966 (68 pages) (35c)

Cover – Monster Fight – John Severin
Page 2 – (Nonchalant) *King Kong* photo
Page 3 – Contents
Page 4 – Post Mortem Office
Page 6 – Transylvania Mutual Insurance ad
Page 7 – A Fiend from Up the Street
Page 8 – The Bela Lugosi Story
Page 18 – The Addams Family Receives a Visitor
Page 19 – Transylvania's Montgomery & Morgue – John Severin
Page 25 – A Masterpiece of Horror – Hyde and Seek
Page 26 – Quick Quiz (Surprise dear)
Page 28 – Hercules and the Princess of Troy
Page 30 – A Grab Bag of Transylvania Monsters
Page 33 – Martin's Screams – Vic Martin
Page 34 – The Greatest Monster Battle of all Time! – John Severin
Page 36 – Transylvanian Cut-Out Signs
Page 38 – The Hunchback of Notre Dame Doesn't Score!
Page 39 – Clothes Don't Make the Man – Bob Schochet
Page 40 – Fight of the Century
Page 44 – Cartoons to Haunt a House By – Goodall, Ruth, Powers
    (John Severin), LePoer (John Severin), John Severin, Pete Wyma,
    Bara
Page 46 – Three Shrieks and You're Out!
Page 47 – Modern Witchcraft – Nireves (John Severin)
Page 50 – More Monster Mirth
Page 51 – Wacky Weirdos – Don Orehek, Joe Kiernan, Glover, Pete Wyma
Page 52 – The Munsters
Page 53-66 – (various real ads)
Page 67 – (acid indigestion) monster photo
Back Cover – Monster Diploma

For Monsters Only #3, November 1966 (68 pages) (35c)

Cover – Monsters in Haunted House – John Severin
Page 2 – ("Ugliest Student") *I Was a Teenage Werewolf* photo
Page 3 – Contents

Page 4 – Post Mortem Office
Page 6 – Transylvania's Man-Of-The-Month
Page 7 – Ugghh!!-Break - Bob Zahn
Page 8 – The Horror Worlds of Boris Karloff – Richard Bojarski
Page 13 – School For Monsters – Nireves (John Severin) (reprint from #26)
Page 23 – Transylvania's Handyman
Page 24 – Dungeon Dan-Dan-Dandies! – John Severin (The precursor to John's later *Ye Hang Ups.*)
Page 26 – Quick Quiz
Page 28 – Extra Special Terror Bonus
Page 29 – Addams and Evil (Lurch photo)
Page 30 – Mightiest Mad Monsters Strike Again!
Page 33 – Bill Ward's Chiller Dillers – Bill Ward
Page 34 – Our New Mayor
Page 35 – Son of Monster Mirth!!!
Page 36 – Bewitched Bothered and a Big Hit!
Page 38 – The Happy Birthday Boy!
Page 39 – Go By Subway – Bob Schochet
Page 40 – The Alligator People
Page 42 – Fun Time Monsters – Vic Martin
Page 43 – A Great, New Neighbor!
Page 44 – Transylvanian TV – Bill McCartney (Bill Ward) (reprint from #36)
Page 48 – Horror Hee-Haws
Page 50 – The Desert Island Guest – John Severin
Page 51 – Here Comes the Bride and Gloom!
Page 52 – Girls and Ghouls
Page 53-66 – (various real ads)
Page 67 – photo with gag quote ("One thing about Dean Martin")
Back Cover – Transylvanian Credit Cards

For Monsters Only #4, March 1967 (68 pages) (35c)
Cover – Female 2 Face (Miss Monster Contest)
Page 2 – ("sunken houses") (*Plague of the Zombies* photo)
Page 3 – Contents
Page 4 – Post Mortem Office
Page 6 – Transylvania's New Basketball Coach!
Page 7 – Transylvanian Artists Schools ad
Page 8 – Two Kings of Terror: Vincent Price Christopher Lee – Richard Bojarksi
Page 18 – He Went That-A-Way! – Bob Schochet
Page 19 – Boys and Ghouls Together!
Page 20 – Wincin Cigarette ad – Paul Reinman (reprint from #1)

Page 21 – Look Who Just Moved In!

Page 22 – Transylvania Go Go Football – Vic Martin

Page 25 – The Newly-Weds of Swamphollow Lane

Page 26 – Frankenstein Conquers The World!

Page 28 – Four Screaming Out Loud!

Page 29 – The Hall of Fiends

Page 30 – Cartoon Screams – Don Orehek

Page 31 – Home-Town Boy Makes Good!

Page 32 – A Transylvanian Family Album (reprint from *For Monsters Only* #1)

Page 35 – Is There A Wacky Doctor In The House? - Bob Schochet

Page 36 – TV Horror Listings (reprint from *Zany* #1)

Page 38 – Monster Mirth Rides Again

Page 40 – The Far Outers! - John Severin, George Kesner

Page 41 – The Lifeguard of the Month!

Page 42 – The Effects of Horror Movies! (reprint from *Zany* #1)

Page 44 – What Ever Happened To?

Page 45 – Vote Here for Miss Monster 1967

Page 46 – Quick Quiz ("Drop the Gun, Louie")

Page 48 – Modern Movie Monsters (reprint from #8)

Page 50 – Black Pit of Dr. M

Page 52 – Fun, Games and Monsters – Vic Martin

Page 53 – Ghoul Days!

Page 54-66 – (various real ads)

Page 67 – ("Hash for dinner") photo

Back Cover – For Monsters Only Car Bumper Stickers

For Monsters Only Annual, 1967 (92 pages) (50c)

Cover – Collage of Covers – John Severin (reprint from *For Monsters Only* #1-4 and *Monster Howls* #1)

Page 2 – (Nonchalant) "King Kong" photo (reprint from *For Monsters Only* #2)

Page 3 – Contents

Page 4 – The Monster's Advertising Agency – John Severin (reprint from #33)

Page 9 – Transylvania's Montgomery & Morgue – John Severin (reprint from *For Monsters Only* #2)

Page 15 – Orehek in Orbit - Don Orehek (reprint from *For Monsters Only* #1)

Page 16 – School For Monsters – Nireves (John Severin) (reprint from #26)

Page 21 – Transylvanian Artists Schools ad (reprint from *For Monsters Only* #4)

Page 22 – Mucho Monsters from Mexico (reprint from *For Monsters Only* #1)

Page 27 – Transylvania Correspondence Schools ad (reprint from *For Monsters Only* #1)

Page 28 – The Eerie World of Don Orehek - Don Orehek (reprint from *Monster Howls* #1)

Page 30 – Martin's Screams – Vic Martin (reprint from *For Monsters Only* #2)

Page 31 – A MonStar is Reborn – John Severin / George Gladir (reprint from *For Monsters Only* #1)

Page 37 – Bill Ward's Chiller Dillers – Bill Ward (reprint from *For Monsters Only* #3)

Page 38 – TV Horror Listings (reprint from *Zany* #1)

Page 40 – The Monster Baseball Team – John Severin (reprint from #37) (originally called "The Monster's Cracked Baseball Team")

Page 45 – Cartoon Screams – Don Orehek (reprint from *For Monsters Only* #4)

Page 46 – Modern Witchcraft – Nireves (John Severin) (reprint from *For Monsters Only* #2)

Page 50 – Monster Sandwich-Board Men – John Severin (reprint from #34)

Page 52 – Transylvanian Cut-Out-Signs (reprint from *For Monsters Only* #2)

Page 54 – Transylvania Go Go Football – Vic Martin (reprint from *For Monsters Only* #4)

Page 57 – Fun Time Monsters – Vic Martin (reprint from *For Monsters Only* #3)

Page 58 – Monster Party – John Severin (reprint from #43)

Page 60 – Mightiest Mad Monsters Strike Again! (reprint from *For Monsters Only* #3)

Page 63 – Transylvanian TV – Bill McCartney (Bill Ward) (reprint from #36)

Page 67 – The Desert Island Guest – John Severin (reprint from *For Monsters Only* #3)

Page 68-74 – (various real ads)

Page 75 – The Chamber of Horrors

Page 89 – Here Comes the Bride and Gloom! (reprint from *For Monsters Only* #3)

Page 90 – Fangmann's ad – John Severin (reprint from #36)

Page 91 – ("Ugliest Student") *I Was a Teenage Werewolf* photo (reprint from *For Monsters Only* #3)

Back Cover – Monster Diploma (reprint from *For Monsters Only* #2)

For Monsters Only #5, September 1967 (68 pages) (35c)
Cover – Ghoul, Vampire and Alien – John Severin
Page 2 – photo with gag quote ("My group didn't use any toothpaste")
Page 3 – Contents
Page 4 – Post Mortem Office
Page 6 – Transylvania's Man of Music
Page 7 – Directory of Transylvanian Clubs
Page 8 – The Man Behind the Monsters: The Story of Jack Pierce –
    Richard Bojarski
Page 18 – The Nightmares of Monsters – Bill McCartney (Bill Ward)
Page 20 – Werewolf In A Girl's Dormitory
Page 23 – Orehek's Funny Fiends! – Don Orehek
Page 24 – Monster Phrases – Vic Martin (Rip-off of *Mad's Horrifying Clichés*)
Page 26 – Transylvania's Airline Hostess of the Year!
Page 27 – It Came From Out of the Water!
Page 28 – Quick Quiz
Page 30 – Our New "Merry Mailman"
Page 31 – The Pick-Me-Up! – Schochet
Page 32 – The Horror Hits of Peter Lorre – Richard Bojarski
Page 36 – Our Readers' Want Ads
Page 38 – Transylvanian Rock 'n' Roll Monsters – Vic Martin
Page 40 – Mayhem Mirth
Page 41 – McCartney's Mighty Monsters – Bill McCartney (Bill Ward)
Page 42 – The Wacky Weirdos Howl Again!
Page 44 – The Screamers
Page 45 – Say Hello To Transylvania's Greatest Singer!
Page 46 – The Stone Age – Oscar Blotta
Page 48 – Greet and Meet a Neat Beat!
Page 49 – The Night Crawlers - Vic Martin
Page 50 – Gunspook – Don Orehek (reprint from *Zany* #2)
Page 53 – The One That Got Away!
Page 54-66 – (various real ads)
Page 67 – photo with gag quote ("Ugliest Student in Transylvanian
    High Award")
Back Cover – Terror Tour!

For Monsters Only #6, January 1969 (68 pages) (50c)
Cover – Strange Fanged Alien
Page 2 – *Frankenstein* photo with gag quote ("Let's call him Bruce!)
Page 3 – Contents
Page 4 – Post Mortem Office
Page 6 – The Life Story of Lionel Atwill – Richard Bojarski
Page 16 – The Colossus of New York

Page 18 – The Big Ones Scream Again!
Page 21 – The Neatest Trick Of The Year!
Page 22 – Quick Quiz
Page 24 – When Good Ghouls Get Together!
Page 25 – A Friend To One And All
Page 26 – John Carradine, the Master Villain – Richard Bojarski
Page 36 – The Wacky Weirdos
Page 38 – Horror Hee-Ho-Ho's!
Page 39 – A Collector's Item!
Page 40 – The Chiller-Dillers Swing Again!
Page 41 – Gags To Howl About
Page 42 – A Howling Good Time!
Page 43 – From Our Dusty Tomb Files!
Page 44 – Monster Mirth!
Page 46-58 – (various real ads)
Page 59 – The Secret Files of Marc Vangoro, Master of Horror! – Jerry
    Grandinetti
Page 67 – Gigantic Monster Mobile Bonus! – Vic Martin

For Monsters Only #7, April 1969 (76 pages) (50c)
Cover – Blue Monster with Orange Hair
Page 2 – (blemish) photo
Page 3 – Contents
Page 4 – Post Mortem Office
Page 6 – Peter Cushing: Monster Fighter – Richard Bojarski
Page 16 – The Wild Weirdos' Scream-In!
Page 18 – Step Right up and Meet the New President
Page 19 – Howls at Midnight
Page 20 – The Hunchback of Notre Dame
Page 23 – Just Good Fiends!
Page 24 – Quick Quiz (fell from his plane)
Page 26 – Karloff & Lugosi The Titans of Terror – Richard Bojarski
Page 36 – You'll Die Laughing!
Page 37 – Transylvania's Greatest P.O.E.T.
Page 38 – Ghouls and Giggles
Page 39 – The Face of the True Artist!
Page 40 – Something to Scream at!
Page 41 – A Really, Really Big Shew!
Page 42 – The Fright-Makers
Page 44 – The Woman who Stands Behind Our Mayor!
Page 45 – Big Things are Happening!
Page 46-58 – (various real ads)

Page 59 – The Secret Files of Marc Vangoro, Master of Horror! – Jerry Grandinetti (reprint from *For Monsters Only* #6)

Page 75 – (blind date) photo

Back Cover – Great Moments of Horror! – John Severin

For Monsters Only #8, July 1969 (68 pages) (50c)

Cover – Gravedigger and Ghouls – John Severin

Page 2 – *Invisible Man* photo with gag caption ("I DO want to marry you, Henry!")

Page 3 – Contents

Page 4 – Post Mortem Office

Page 6 – Fantasy Films of the Forties – Richard Bojarski

Page 16 – Screams from Land and Sea!

Page 18 – Where Are They Now?

Page 23 – Monster Madness!

Page 24 – Quick Quiz

Page 26 – Dwight Frye, The Mighty Midget Of Menace – Richard Bojarski

Page 36 – The Point Of The Matter!

Page 37 – Guess Who???

Page 38 – The Grand Winner Of The Good Citizen Award Of The Year!

Page 39 – The Fiendish Delights!

Page 40 – Creepy Chuckles!

Page 41 – A Salute To General Milton "Blood and Blood" Glibber!

Page 42 – The Fiends and the Females

Page 44 – That Wonderful Woman Of Swamp Murky has Another Birthday

Page 45 – Transylvania's Number One Hot Shot

Page 46-58 – (various real ads)

Page 59 – The Secret Files of Van Goro

Page 67 – Count Dracula photo with gag caption ("It's me the Count")

Back Cover – Transylvania Travel Stickers (reprint from *For Monsters Only* #1)

For Monsters Only #9, September 1971 (68 pages) (60c)

Cover – Trog

Page 2 – Barnabas Collins photo

Page 3 – Contents

Page 4 – Post Mortem Office

Page 6 – Trog!

Page 14 – Quick Quiz (Lawrence Zelk)

Page 16 – The Howls Are Here!

Page 17 – What Ever Happened To? (reprint from *For Monsters Only* #4)

Page 25 – Exhibit Six – Martin J. Arbunich

Page 32 – Let's Meet the Ladies

Page 34 – Monster Laughs!!!

Page 35 – More Fiendish Delights

Page 36 – Taste the Blood of Dracula!

Page 43 – Killer-Dillers!

Page 44 – The Big Things Do Their Thing!

Page 46 – John Carradine, the Master Villain – Richard Bojarski
    (reprint from *For Monsters Only* #6)

Page 56-66 – (various real ads)

Page 67 – Trog photo

Back Cover – Great Moments of Horror! – John Severin (reprint from
    For Monsters Only #7)

For Monsters Only #10, June 1972 (68 pages) (60c)

Cover – Scream and Scream Again – Gray Morrow

Page 2 – Transylvania's Top Tripper-In!

Page 3 – Contents

Page 4 – Post Mortem Office

Page 5 – Cry of the Banshee

Page 16 – Quick Quiz (two guys went on the wagon)

Page 18 – The Biggies Break it Up!

Page 20 – Scream and Scream Again

Page 30 – Howl Makers

Page 32 – Horror Hee-Haw

Page 34 – Demon of Distinction

Page 39 – Show Stoppers!

Page 40 – Fiendish for Fun!

Page 42 – Chilling Chuckles

Page 44 – Mad Mirth Makers!

Page 46 – Count Yorga, Vampire!

Page 49 – Blood Thirst! – Syd Shores / Terry Bisson

Page 56-66 – (various real ads)

Page 67 – Count Yorga photo

Back Cover – (scalp treatments) photo

**The Giant Cracked Annual, 1965 (92 pages) (50c) (This is the first
Cracked annual of any kind, all reprints except where indicated.)**

Cover – A Treasure Chest of Humor – John Severin

Page 2 – (Long Playing Records) dancing photo (new)

Page 3 – Contents

Page 4 – Throughout History with Home Movies – Ned Kelly (John
    Severin) (reprint from #38)

Page 10 – Perry Masonry – John Severin (reprint from #10)

Page 12 – Flashes from Outer Space – Basil Wolverton (reprint from #10)
Page 14 – When it all Started (Look at that) (reprint from #21)
Page 15 – It Could Be Verse – Richard Doxsee (reprint from #8)
Page 18 – Diplomas for the Man in the Street (reprint from #9)
Page 20 – Amateur Artists (reprint from #38)
Page 22 – Soupedupman (reprint from #2)
Page 23 – Polka Dot Toothpaste ad – Paul Reinman (reprint from #3)
Page 24 – Ancient Psychiatry – Bill Elder (reprint from #10)
Page 26 – The Home Life of a TV Moderator (reprint from #10)
Page 29 – Cracked Shut-Ups (Europe) – Bill McCartney (Bill Ward) (reprint from #2)
Page 30 – Directions – John Severin (reprint from #9)
Page 32 – Un-Togetherness (reprint from #9)
Page 35 – Maulbury Cigarette ad (reprint from #4)
Page 36 – It All Depends on the Point of View (snake) – Bill McCartney (Bill Ward) (reprint from #10)
Page 38 – To Tell the Truth (reprint from #9)
Page 40 – Whatever Happened to These Movie Scenes? (reprint from #10)
Page 41 – Cracked Shut-Ups (driving in the country) – Bill McCartney (Bill Ward) (reprint from #9)
Page 42 – Water Shortage (reprint from #38)
Page 46 – Interplanetary Magazines – Bill Everett (reprint from #8)
Page 48 – A Visit to the Beach – LePoer (John Severin) (reprint from #38)
Page 50 – Bridge on the River Kweer – John Severin (reprint from #2)
Page 53 – Orders – John Severin (reprint from #38)
Page 54 – Ya Pays Yer Money and Ya Takes Yer Cherce – Bill McCartney (Bill Ward) (reprint from #8)
Page 55 – Baseball Statisticiatic – John Severin (reprint from #10)
Page 58 – New Look Cigarette Packs (reprint from #7)
Page 60 – Huff and Puff – Bill McCartney (Bill Ward) (reprint from #9)
Page 61 – Sunshine Healthy – John Severin (reprint from #12)
Page 64 – Modern Art – John Severin (reprint from #9)
Page 66 – Restaurants to Make You Feel at Home! (reprint from #8)
Page 68 – American Grandstand – John Severin (reprint from #2)
Page 70 – Help! Wanted – Garry Owen (John Severin) (reprint from #38)
Page 71 – Push Button War – Bill Everett (reprint from #9)
Page 73 – Be a Movie Director (reprint from #10)
Page 74 – Cracked Shut-Ups (beastly hot) – Bill McCartney (Bill Ward) (reprint from #7)
Page 75 – Make your Own Headlines (new)
Page 91 – Breakodent ad – John Severin (reprint from #38)
Back Cover – Various Bonus Cut-Outs

The Second Giant Cracked Annual, 1966 (92 pages) (50c)

Cover – Signs – O.O. Severin (John Severin)

Page 2 – Cold ad – John Severin (reprint from #18)

Page 3 – Contents

Page 4 – Sports Go Show Biz – Sigbjorn (John Severin) (reprint from #45)

Page 8 – Modern Products for Modern Redskins – John Severin (reprint from #26)

Page 12 – Four Goodness Sakes (reprint from #45)

Page 13 – Famous Scenes from Great Broadway Movies – Vic Martin (reprint from #45)

Page 15 – College Coloring Book – John Severin (reprint from #26)

Page 19 – Ultra Realistic Motor Motoring Sets – John Severin (reprint from #45)

Page 23 – People Who Get on Our Nerves – John Severin (reprint from #16)

Page 26 – Beatlezania – John Severin (reprint from #42)

Page 31 – Panpm Airlines ad – Sigbjorn (John Severin) (reprint from #45)

Page 32 – Daily Times-News-Sun-Post-Globe – Bill McCartney (Bill Ward) (reprint from #45)

Page 36 – TV School – John Severin (reprint from #26)

Page 37 – Still Hanging in There (reprint from #42)

Page 42 – Architecture – Bill Elder (reprint from #12)

Page 44 – Gamble Gambol – John Severin (reprint from #42)

Page 48 – What Do TV Characters Do After the Show is Over – Bill McCartney (Bill Ward) (reprint from #45)

Page 50 – A Cracked Guide to Hand Language – John Severin (reprint from #26)

Page 54 – Cracked Takes a Look at 1897 – Vic Martin (reprint from #45)

Page 58 – Sing Along with Witch – John Severin (reprint from #43)

Page 59 – Shut-Ups (baseball) – Bill McCartney (Bill Ward) (reprint from #43)

Page 60 – Push-Buttons Unlimited – Bill McCartney (Bill Ward) (reprint from #43)

Page 61 – Bull Telephone System ad – Bill Elder (reprint from #11)

Page 62 – Canned Music – Bill McCartney (Bill Ward) (reprint from #43)

Page 67 – Shoot to Kill – John Severin (reprint from #33)

Page 68 – A Visit with Crosby and Hope (reprint from #38)

Page 70 – The Swordsman – Bill McCartney (Bill Ward) (reprint from #35)

Page 71 – Shut-Ups (Can I Stop?) – Vic Martin (reprint from #44)
Page 72 – Restaurants – Jack Davis (reprint from #11)
Page 74 – Great Moments in History – Oswaldo Laino (reprint from #23)
Page 75 – Cracked's Giant Crazy Kit! – O.O. Severin (John Severin)
Page 91 – Friends of the Family ad – John Severin (reprint from #29)
Back Cover – Reward Poster (reprint from #18)

The Third Giant Cracked Annual, 1967 (92 pages) (50c)
Cover – Gulliver Sylvester – John Severin
Page 2 – (Bull instead of turtle) bullfighting photo (reprint from #52)
Page 3 – Contents
Page 4 – Skydiving – Bill McCartney (Bill Ward) (reprint from #49)
Page 7 – That Wonderful Year 1032 BC – Bill McCartney (Bill Ward) (reprint from #36)
Page 8 – Auto Improvements – John Severin (reprint from #49)
Page 10 – For Laughing Out Loud (reprint from #44)
Page 11 – Montgomery Roebuck & Co. Mail Order Catalog – John Severin (reprint from #30)
Page 15 – Shut-Ups (don't need haircut) – Vic Martin (reprint from #49)
Page 16 – World War I – Bill McCartney (Bill Ward) (reprint from #46)
Page 20 – People Who Get on Our Nerves – John Severin (reprint from #16)
Page 21 – Instant Living – Oswaldo Laino (reprint from #22)
Page 24 – Rare Old Records (reprint from #46)
Page 26 – 3 Stories – Jerry Kirschen (reprint from #15)
Page 27 – Famous Scenes from Great Baseball Movies – Vic Martin (reprint from #46)
Page 29 – Charge it – John Severin (reprint from #10)
Page 30 – Dance Trend Graph – Bill McCartney (Bill Ward) (reprint from #30)
Page 31 – The Gals are Here (reprint from #46)
Page 32 – Neighborhood Confidential Magazine – John Severin (reprint from #22)
Page 41 – Cracked Cracks – Joe Kiernan, Ed Dahlin, Gene Myers, Lennie Herman, John Severin (reprint from #47)
Page 42 – Great Enemies of Fiction – Oswaldo Laino (reprint from #22)
Page 44 – There's One in Every Crowd – John Severin (reprint from #23)
Page 45 – Sylvester's Hobby Corner – Bill McCartney (Bill Ward) (reprint from #30)

Page 47 – Rodeo Riders – Bill McCartney (Bill Ward) (reprint from #49)

Page 51 – Guide for Job Hunting on Madison Avenue – McCarton (John Severin) (reprint from #47)

Page 55 – The Rationalizer – Stuart Sloves (reprint from #22)

Page 56 – Games, Hobbies and Sports (reprint from #47)

Page 58 – Autobiographies by the Man in the Street – John Severin (reprint from #26)

Page 60 – Handshakes of Different People – John Severin (reprint from #22)

Page 61 – Art Lesson – John Severin (reprint from #26)

Page 64 – Laugh it Up! (reprint from #47)

Page 65 – TV Sports of Tomorrow – John Severin (reprint from #49)

Page 70 – Lose Weight by Exercising Right on the Job – John Severin (reprint from #20)

Page 72 – Vegas Vignettes (reprint from #47)

Page 74 – Fun at Four! (reprint from #49)

Page 75 – "Flip the Faces" Book – John Severin

Page 91 – Four Annuals (*Biggest* 1, 2; *Giant* 1, 2) / Four Paperbacks / Back Issues ad (#54-61)

Back Cover – Chinese Paperback Book Cover – John Severin (reprint from #25)

The Fourth Giant Cracked Annual, 1968 (92 pages) (50c)

Cover – Cracked Newsstand – John Severin (reprint from #44)

Page 2 – Five Annuals (*Biggest* 2, 3; *Giant* 3; *King-Sized* 1; *Super* 1) / Three Paperbacks / Back Issues ad (#63-70)

Page 3 – Contents

Page 4 – More Beatlezania – John Severin (reprint from #50)

Page 9 – Towards Total Togetherness – Bill McCartney (Bill Ward) (reprint from #47)

Page 12 – Robert Booms ad – John Severin (reprint from #24)

Page 13 – Famous Scenes from Great Football Movies – Vic Martin (reprint from #51)

Page 15 – Civil War Facts – Jack Davis (reprint from #12)

Page 18 – The Silents Talk Back (reprint from #51)

Page 20 – At the Art Gallery – J. Lewis (John Severin) / Jay Lynch (reprint from #27)

Page 22 – On-the-Spot Test Commercials – John Severin (reprint from #21)

Page 26 – Draw Your Own Conclusion – John Severin (reprint from #19)

Page 29 – This is a Laughing Matter (reprint from #49)

Page 30 – Camp Kicey Doo-Bee – Bill McCartney (Bill Ward) (reprint from #55)

Page 32 – Picket Signs of the Future – John Severin (reprint from #48)

Page 34 – Lame ad – Bill McCartney (Bill Ward) (reprint from #33)

Page 35 – The Martian Report on Earth – Bill McCartney (Bill Ward) (reprint from #51)

Page 39 – Movie Mirth Matinee (reprint from #45)

Page 40 – Rexell ad (reprint from #3)

Page 42 – Flight 407 – Rory O'Moore (John Severin) (reprint from #51)

Page 46 – Home Sweet Home – John Severin (reprint from #24)

Page 48 – If Colleges Advertised – John Severin (reprint from #29)

Page 54 – Mighty Monster Laughs!! (reprint from #45)

Page 56 – Cracked Visits the N.Y. Mets – Charles Rodrigues (reprint from #39)

Page 58 – Things Are Tough All Over! – Bill McCartney (Bill Ward) (reprint from #7)

Page 59 – Horror House ad – John Severin

Page 60 – Creative Housekeeping – John Severin (reprint from #11)

Page 62 – Cracked Takes a Look at Basketball – Bill McCartney (Bill Ward) (reprint from #50)

Page 64 – The Bird House – John Severin (reprint from #36)

Page 65 – Cracked Fun Shoppe ad – John Severin

Page 66 – Banks Unlimited or (Money Does Grow on Trees) – McCarty (John Severin) (reprint from #51)

Page 69 – The Banana Man – Jerry Kirschen (reprint from #15)

Page 70 – Redesigning Ads to Appeal to Children – John Severin (reprint from #18)

Page 74 – Shut-Ups (20 cents) – Rodrigliani (Charles Rodrigues) (reprint from #46)

Page 75 – Make Your Own Personal Headlines

Page 76 – Bank of America Travelers Checks ad – John Severin (reprint from #28)

Back Cover – Insult Cards (reprint from #45)

The Fifth Giant Cracked Annual, 1969 (92 pages) (50c)

Cover – Everybody's Reading Cracked – John Severin

Page 2 – Five Annuals (*Biggest* 4; *Giant* 4; *King-Sized* 1, 2; *Super* 2) / Back Issues ad (#71-78)

Page 3 – Contents

Page 4 – Sunday Night Rating Battle – O.O. Severin (John Severin) (reprint from #65)

Page 8 – California Here I Went! – Bill McCartney (Bill Ward) (reprint from #57)
Page 12 – Memorial Tribute (reprint from #13)
Page 14 – Arrowed Shirts ad – Don Orehek (reprint from *Zany* #2)
Page 15 – Great Scenes from Great Horror Movies – John Severin (reprint from #42)
Page 17 – Pow Pix Strike Again! (reprint from *Pow!* #2)
Page 18 – Home Town Confidential (reprint from #8)
Page 20 – Commercials in Real Life – John Severin (reprint from #14)
Page 22 – Freezing People – Jack Davis (reprint from #13)
Page 27 – Cracked Space Shut-Ups! (most beautiful girl) – Bill McCartney (Bill Ward) (reprint from #8)
Page 28 – The Wide World of Laughs (reprint from #54)
Page 30 – The Establishment Goes Hippy – O.O. Severin (John Severin) (reprint from #67)
Page 32 – Fraternity Keys (reprint from #10)
Page 34 – Ignited Air Lines ad – John Severin (reprint from #13)
Page 38 – Lights Camera Action! – John Severin (reprint from #60)
Page 39 – The Nutty Traffic Jam Pickle – Bill McCartney (Bill Ward) (reprint from #62)
Page 43 – Believe it or Nuts!! – Jack Davis (reprint from #13)
Page 44 – A Sunday at Coney Island – Bill McCartney (Bill Ward) (reprint from #40)
Page 46 – The Last of the Hollywood "B" Pictures – Gray Morrow (reprint from #8)
Page 49 – Look Befour You Laugh! (reprint from #51)
Page 50 – If Some Famous Married Couples had Divorce Hearings – John Severin (reprint from #17)
Page 52 – Handshakes – John Severin (reprint from #11)
Page 56 – How Some of Our Customs Began – John Severin (reprint from #15)
Page 58 – Cracked's Intelligence Test (reprint from #15)
Page 61 – Stories of the Month (The Panhandler) – Jerry Kirschen (reprint from #18)
Page 62 – Sylvester P. Smythe As Seen by Different Artists (reprint from #14)
Page 64 – Cracked Fun Shoppe ad – John Severin
Page 65 – Romeo and Juliet – John Severin (reprint from #8)
Page 68 – Horror House ad – John Severin
Page 69 – Ultra Realistic Dolls – Bill McCartney (Bill Ward) (reprint from #28)
Page 73 – The Dungeon – Don Orehek (reprint from *Monster Howls* #1)

Page 74 – Shut-Ups! (Let's go home) – Charles Rodrigues (reprint from #42)

Page 75 – Do-it-Yourself Newspapers (revised reprint from *Giant Cracked* #1)

Page 91 – The Unsociables ad – John Severin (reprint from #16)

Back Cover – Batty Buttons (reprint from #61)

The Sixth Giant Cracked Annual, 1970 (92 pages) (50c)

Cover – Dingaling Bros. Circus – John Severin

Page 2 – Six Annuals ad (*Biggest* 4, 5; *Giant* 5; *King-Sized* 2, 3; *Super* 3)

Page 3 – Contents

Page 4 – Dapperman! – O.O. Severin (John Severin) / George Gladir (reprint from #53)

Page 9 – Farmer's Old Almanac – John Severin (reprint from #6)

Page 12 – Am I Really in Love? – John Severin (reprint from #11)

Page 14 – The Garbage Can – Caracu (reprint from #66)

Page 15 – Four for the Laugh Set (reprint from #54)

Page 16 – More People We Can Do Without – John Langton (reprint from #68)

Page 18 – The Day That Nothing Seemed to Go Right for the Ape Man – Fal Hoster (John Severin) (reprint from #55)

Page 21 – The Terror Trip – BOJ (reprint from #55)

Page 22 – Real Cracked Books – Vic Martin (reprint from #18)

Page 24 – Der Black Und Blue Max – O.O. Severin (John Severin) (reprint from #62)

Page 28 – The Fun Seekers! (reprint from #68)

Page 29 – A Little Off the Top! – BOJ (reprint from #53)

Page 30 – How to Make Vehicles Safer – John Severin (reprint from #58)

Page 33 – The Sports Fan – Bill McCartney (Bill Ward) (reprint from #54)

Page 34 – What Might Happen if all Civil Service & Federal Employees Resorted to Work Slowdowns – Vic Martin (reprint from #66)

Page 38 – Super Market Hospitals – Bill McCartney (Bill Ward) (reprint from #53)

Page 40 – Annoy Your Friends – John Severin (reprint from #28)

Page 43 – Blotta's Back Again! – Oskar Blotta (reprint from #59)

Page 44 – Big Business of Little League – Tony Tallarico (reprint from #62)

Page 48 – Products That Just Missed! – McCartin (John Severin) (reprint from #53)

Page 50 – Graffiti – Tony Tallarico (reprint from #66)

Page 53 – Bottoms Up (reprint from #48)

Page 54 – If Picture Postcards Told the Truth! – John Severin (reprint from #59)

Page 56 – Super Heroes A-Round the World – William Hoest / George Gladir (reprint from #59)

Page 60 – Cracked Takes you Back to When it All Started! – Jack Davis (reprint from #15)

Page 61 – Super Composites – Lugoze (reprint from #68)

Page 64 – Cracked Fun Shoppe ad – John Severin

Page 65 – Smiles from South of the Border – Oskar Blotta (reprint from #58)

Page 67 – Horror House ad – John Severin

Page 68 – Wonderful World of Wacky Laughs! (reprint from #58)

Page 69 – Throughout History with the Isolated Camera – John Severin (reprint from #48)

Page 73 – When it all Ended (The Science Fiction Movie) – John Severin (reprint from #24)

Page 74 – Shut-Ups (five pounds of tea) – Charles Rodrigues (reprint from #66)

Page 75 – 15 Hang-Up Posters and With-It Signs – John Severin

Page 91 – (hold your hand) Frankenstein photo (reprint from #38)

Back Cover – Travel Stickers – Tony Tallarico (reprint from #62)

The Seventh Giant Cracked Annual, 1971 (84 pages) (60c)

Cover – Strongman Sylvester – John Severin

Page 2 – Five Annuals ad (*Biggest* 5, 6; *Giant* 6; *Super* 3)

Page 3 – Contents

Page 4 – Goryson's Gorillas – John Severin (reprint from #71)

Page 10 – Up-Dated Mechanical Banks – Sigbjorn (John Severin) (reprint from #50)

Page 15 – Black Thoughts – Caracu (reprint from #69)

Page 16 – Lights Camera Action! – John Severin (reprint from #60)

Page 17 – A Cracked Looks at Picture Phones – John Langton (reprint from #64)

Page 20 – Sylvester P. Smythe Junior College Catalogue of Courses – John Langton (reprint from #75)

Page 25 – Four Fun Flicks! (reprint from #73)

Page 26 – State Posters to Lure the Hippies – John Severin (reprint from #64)

Page 28 – A Picture is Worth 1,000 Lies – Lugoze (reprint from #73)

Page 32 – Rowan and Martin's Laugh-In – John Severin (reprint from #73)

Page 34 – Fangmann's ad – John Severin (reprint from #36)

Page 35 – Crime on Prime Time – Vic Martin (reprint from #63)

Page 38 – ("Play bridge") Hollywood Bowl photo (reprint from #68)

Page 39 – Specialized Trading Stamps Catalogs – Tony Tallarico (reprint from #64)

Page 44 – The Superiority of TV Over Movies – John O'Hara (John Severin) (reprint from #63)

Page 48 – Horror House ad – John Severin

Page 49 – Sylvester, the Baseball Fan! – John Langton (reprint from #63)

Page 50 – 5 Fun Grabbers (reprint from #74)

Page 51 – Protest Signs Unlimited – Joe Mead (reprint from #73)

Page 54 – Rock 'n' Rook Record Albums – J.T. Dennett (reprint from #55)

Page 56 – Take the Cracked History Test – John Langton (reprint from #71)

Page 58 – Cracked Fun Shoppe ad – John Severin

Page 59 – Cue Cards for Everyone – Bill McCartney (Bill Ward) (reprint from #73)

Page 64 – Cracked's Gallery of Born Losers – Art Pottier (reprint from #69)

Page 66 – Shut-Ups (hang around) – Charles Rodrigues (reprint from #71)

Page 67 – The Cracked Complete Insult Guide – Bill McCartney (Bill Ward), Tony Tallarico (new)

Page 83 – (racked with pain, 3 months) photos (reprint from #70)

Back Cover – Crazy, Hip, Fun-Fad Bonus! – Tony Tallarico (reprint from #69)

The Eighth Giant Cracked Annual, 1972 (84 pages) (60c)

Cover – Earth Egg Hatching Monster – Nireves (John Severin)

Page 2 – Six Annuals ad (Biggest 5, 6, 7; Giant 7; King-Sized 5; Super 5)

Page 3 – Contents

Page 4 – Bonnie and Clyde! – O.O. Severin (John Severin) (reprint from #73)

Page 9 – The Growing Garbage Garble – John Severin (reprint from #69)

Page 13 – Commercializing the Moon – John Severin (reprint from #81)

Page 17 – Horror House ad – John Severin

Page 18 – The Big Guns! (reprint from #70)

Page 20 – Tall Story – John Severin (reprint from #77)

Page 25 – At Home with the Spiro T. Agnews – John Severin (reprint from #84)

Page 29 – Future Automated Devices – Nireves (John Severin) (reprint from #50)

Page 33 – Horror House ad – John Severin

Page 34 – As the Trend Towards Violence Increases – Lugoze (reprint from #69)

Page 40 – The Establishment Goes Hippy – O.O. Severin (John Severin) (reprint from #67)

Page 43 – Memorable Moments in Politics (reprint from #85)

Page 46 – Learning to Fly – John Severin (reprint from #80)

Page 52 – King of the Mafia – Art Pottier (reprint from #73)

Page 54 – Tom Jones – John Severin (reprint from #85)

Page 58 – Ironslide – John Severin (reprint from #82)

Page 63 – Go Fly a Kite – John Severin (reprint from #74)

Page 64 – Lights, Action, Camera! (reprint from #66)

Page 66 – Shut-Ups! (stick-in-the-mud) – Vito Montigliani (Charles Rodrigues) (reprint from #73)

Page 67 – Do-it-Yourself Newspapers (revised reprint from *Giant Cracked* #1)

Page 83 – Flicks that Click! (reprint from #56)

Back Cover – If at First You Don't Succeed Sign (reprint from #43)

The Ninth Giant Cracked Annual, 1973 (84 pages) (60c)

Cover – Vegetable Soup – John Severin (reprint from #73)

Page 2 – Five Annuals ad (*Biggest* 7, 8; *Giant* 8; *King-Sized* 5, 6)

Page 3 – Contents

Page 4 – Escape from the Boredom of the Apes – John Severin (reprint from #97)

Page 9 – The Awakening – John Severin (reprint from #97)

Page 10 – Cracked Looks at Mothers – Charles Rodrigues (reprint from #95)

Page 13 – The Future Computerized of Sports – Bill McCartney (Bill Ward) (reprint from #93)

Page 17 – If the Help-Wanted Ads Mirrored Today's Inefficient Business World (reprint from #94)

Page 20 – If Comic Strip Heroes Had Hang-Ups Like the Rest of Us – Lugoze (reprint from #96)

Page 24 – The Growing Cult of the Occult – Don Orehek (reprint from #96)

Page 27 – Hi! I'm Johnny Cashew! – John Severin (reprint from #93)

Page 32 – Cracked Visits a Restaurant –Vic Martin (reprint from #77)

Page 34 – Cracked Fun Shoppe ad – John Severin

Page 35 – Dogs Magazine – John Severin (reprint from #74)

Page 43 – The Man & the Fly – Oskar Blotta (reprint from #95)

Page 44 – The Cracked Annual Achievement Awards – Bill McCartney (Bill Ward) (reprint from #97)

Page 46 – Cracked's Crazy Comebacks – John Langton (reprint from #78)

Page 48 – What if They – John Severin (reprint from #94)

Page 52 – Sagebrush (Ah-Choo!) – John Severin (reprint from #85)

Page 54 – Guess Who…? – Bill McCartney (Bill Ward) (reprint from #76)

Page 56 – Hudd & Dini (cannon) – Vic Martin (reprint from #93)

Page 57 – Letters We'll Really Be Looking For (reprint from #95)

Page 60 – Horror House ad – John Severin

Page 61 – Snow Flake and the Seven Dwarfs – John Severin (reprint from #70)

Page 62 – Shut-Ups (only girl) – Carlos Gerdel (Charles Rodrigues) (reprint from #86)

Page 63 – Cracked Now Greeting Card Kit – Bill Ward, John Severin, John Langton, Bernard Baily (new)

Page 83 – W.C. Fields photos (new)

Back Cover – Modern Slumlord Magazine – John Severin (reprint from #101)

The Tenth Giant Cracked Annual, 1974 (84 pages) (75¢)

Cover – Green Giant Island – John Severin (reprint from #45)

Page 2 – Six Annuals ad (*Biggest* 8; *Collectors* 2, 3; *Giant* 9; *King-Sized* 6; *Super* 7)

Page 3 – Contents

Page 4 – Secretive Santa Victoria – John Severin (reprint from #88)

Page 8 – Cracked's Guide to Bicycling – Bob Taylor (reprint from #105)

Page 13 – Saturday Night in India – Oskar Blotta (reprint from #86)

Page 14 – Kings of Comedy (reprint from #57)

Page 16 – Cracked Looks at Hunting and Fishing – LePoer (John Severin) (reprint from #86)

Page 18 – Hudd & Dini (garbage can magnets) – Vic Martin (reprint from #92)

Page 19 – Popular Butterfingers Magazine – John Langton (reprint from #91)

Page 22 – Don Juan Lines That Just Don't Fit the Background – Joe Mead (reprint from #82)

Page 24 – Cracked Visits a Public Golf Course – Bill McCartney (Bill Ward) (reprint from #88)

Page 26 – Nightmares – Vic Martin (reprint from #102)

Page 28 – Fhive for the Fhun it! (reprint from #95)

Page 29 – Miss America Contest! – John Severin (reprint from #90)

Page 32 –First Prize, Man! – Joe Mead (reprint from #85)

Page 33 – Frontier Dude Magazine – John Severin (reprint from #84)

Page 38 – Horror House ad – John Severin

Page 39 – A Day at the Airport – Bernard Baily (reprint from #105)

Page 43 – Pix of the Flicks (reprint from #102)

Page 46 – Cracked Goes to the Hospital – John Severin (reprint from #94)

Page 48 – The Cracked Etiquette Quiz – John Langton (reprint from #82)

Page 50 – Ask a Silly Question, Get a – John Langton (reprint from #83)

Page 51 – The Yuch-hh Lawyers – John Severin (reprint from #92)

Page 56 – Cracked Looks at Hotels – Bill McCartney (Bill Ward) (reprint from #90)

Page 58 – A Swinging Good Time! (reprint from #71)

Page 59 – Cracked Interviews the Toy King – O.O. Severin (John Severin) (reprint from #103)

Page 64 – Shut-Ups (magnifique) – S. Gross Jr. (Charles Rodrigues) (reprint from #105)

Page 65 – Luck Is – Bob Taylor (reprint from #85)

Page 66 – Paperback Book Covers

Page 83 – Binders and notebooks ad

Back Cover – Attention People Born 1952-1962 (reprint from #103)

The Eleventh Giant Cracked Annual, 1975 (84 pages) ($1.00)

Cover – Raining Umbrella – John Severin (reprint from #95)

Page 2 – Binders and Notebooks ad 2

Page 3 – Contents

Page 4 – O'Meagre Man – John Severin (reprint from #100)

Page 9 – Psychologically Dangerous Toys – Vic Martin (reprint from #106)

Page 12 – Resort Brochure for Prison Living – John Langton (reprint from #109)

Page 16 – Famous Person's School Excuses (reprint from #108)

Page 18 – The Campaign to Use Less Power – Bernard Baily (reprint from #109)

Page 22 – A Cracked History of the Movies – Vic Martin (reprint from #109)

Page 26 – A Cracked Salute to Chicago – Russ Heath (reprint from #110)

Page 30 – Vampires of the World – Bernard Baily (reprint from #108)

Page 34 – Hudd & Dini (trampoline) – Vic Martin (reprint from #107)

Page 35 – Health Foods – Dick Wright (reprint from #109)

Page 37 – Cracked's Guide to Crime Prevention – Dick Wright (reprint from #110)

Page 41 – Fat Magazine – Bob Taylor (reprint from #104)

Page 48 – Cracked Goes to Las Vegas – Don Orehek (reprint from #108)

Page 50 – Cracked's Guide to Backpacking – John Severin (reprint from #108)

Page 55 – The Last of the 'Desert Island' Cartoons! – Irit Kajiij Jr. (Charles Rodrigues) (reprint from #109)

Page 58 – Upgrading the Female Image in Children's Books – Dick Wright

(reprint from #110)

Page 61 – Cracked Interviews the Music King – John Langton (reprint from #108)

Page 66 – Shut-Ups (what he sees in her) – Norman Rockwell (Charles Rodrigues) (reprint from #107)

Page 67 – 8 Posters (reprints from #75, 76, 77, 78, 107, 108, 109, 110)

Page 83 – The Cracked Bookstore ad – John Severin

Back Cover – Build Your Own Hi-Fi Stereo System (reprint from #107)

The Twelfth Giant Cracked Annual, 1976 (84 pages) ($1.00)

Cover – Stepping on a Bug – O.O. Severin (John Severin) (reprint from #103)

Page 2 – The Cracked Bookstore ad – John Severin

Page 3 – Contents

Page 4 – The Stinger – A. Shamed (John Severin) (reprint from #118)

Page 9 – Cracked's Pollution Solution – Bill Ward (reprint from #115)

Page 13 – The Telephone Call – Charles Rodrigues (reprint from #119)

Page 14 – It Happened at the Cemetery – Caracu (reprint from #69)

Page 16 – Cracked Interviews the Liberation Queen – John Severin, Joe Catalano (reprint from #115)

Page 21 – How Much Stress Can You Take? – Bill Ward (reprint from #118)

Page 24 – Daze & Knights (reprint from #82)

Page 26 – Cracked's Sure-Fire Guide to Weight Control – Don Orehek (reprint from #117)

Page 30 – Cracked Looks at Stock Car Racing – Don Orehek (reprint from #114)

Page 32 – Self-Praise in Government – John Severin (reprint from #115)

Page 35 – The Cracked History of Music – John Langton (reprint from #114)

Page 39 – Dogs Magazine – John Severin (reprint from #74)

Page 47 – Super Senses – Dick Wright (reprint from #111)

Page 50 – Horrible Humor (reprint from #97)

Page 53 – How to Stretch Your Dollar Getting the Most While Spending Less – Vic Martin (reprint from #112)

Page 56 – A Rodrigues Neighborhood – Charles Rodrigues (reprint from #117)

Page 58 – A Cracked Look at Little League Managers – Bill Ward (reprint from #119)

Page 61 – Silly Jack – Nireves (John Severin) (reprint from #116)

Page 66 – Shut-Ups (Tigers Bears) – Charles Rodrigues (reprint from #123)

Page 67 – 8 Posters (reprint from #79, 81, 96, 114, 115, 117, 118, 119)

Page 83 – If You're Cracked You're Happy! Iron-On – John Severin (reprint from #123)

Back Cover – It Happened on Main and First – Caracu (reprint from #103)

Giant Cracked #13, September 1977 (84 pages) ($1.00) (Title ceases to be an annual and in 1977-78 is actually published six times.)

Cover – Life Guard – John Severin (reprint from #88)

Page 2 – The Cracked Bookstore ad – John Severin

Page 3 – Contents

Page 4 – Papion – John Severin (reprint from #122)

Page 10 – A Cracked Look at Prizefighting – Don Orehek (reprint from #122)

Page 14 – A History of Fashion – Bill Ward (reprint from #121)

Page 18 – Celebrity Garage Sale – Bernard Baily (reprint from #116)

Page 22 – Programs for Non-Theatrical Events – John Langton (reprint from#115)

Page 26 – When America Runs Out of Electricity – Don Orehek (reprint from #116)

Page 29 – Ridiculous Renting Spaces – Bill Ward (reprint from #122)

Page 32 – A Cracked Look at Golf – Bill Ward (reprint from #123)

Page 36 – The Country Blues – John Langton (reprint from #123)

Page 40 – A Look at a UFO – Don Orehek (reprint from #116)

Page 42 – Are You a Loser? – Bernard Baily (reprint from #120)

Page 45 – The Far-Out Four – Polly Titian (John Severin) (reprint from #123)

Page 50 – How to Make Words Pictorial (reprint from #123)

Page 51 – Policeman Magazine – Don Orehek (reprint from #120)

Page 55 – Lights Camera Action! – John Severin (reprint from #60)

Page 56 – The Effect of the Energy Crisis on the Entertainment World – John Severin (reprint from #119)

Page 61 – Cracked Interviews the Oil King – Bill Ward (reprint from #120)

Page 66 – Shut-Ups (provide a blindfold) – Charles Rodrigues (reprint from #128)

Page 67 – 8 Posters (reprints from #85, 103, 120, 121, 122, 125, 126, 128)

Page 83 – Rocky's Sparring Partner Iron-On

Back Cover – Great Moments in Art 1705 – Charles Rodrigues (reprint from #119)

Giant Cracked Fun-Kit #14, January 1978 (84 pages) ($1.00) (1ˢᵗ Fun-Kit)

Cover – Signs – O.O. Severin (John Severin) (Partial reprint from *Giant Cracked* #2 with some minor changes to the artwork.)

Page 2 – The Cracked Bookstore ad – John Severin

Page 3 – Contents

Page 4 – Capony – John Severin (reprint from #128)

Page 10 – Cracked Looks at a Wedding Reception – Don Orehek (reprint from #111)

Page 12 – How Past Events Might Have Been Reported with a Government-Controlled Press – Sururi Gumen (reprint from #124)

Page 16 – Fighting Job Boredom – Bernard Baily (reprint from #118)

Page 20 – The Untold Story of How Betsy Ross Created the Flag (reprint from #128)

Page 23 – Cracked Interviews the Surveillance King – John Langton (reprint from #126)

Page 28 – The Superiority of TV Over Movies – John O'Hara (John Severin) (reprint from #63)

Page 32 – A Cracked Look at a Chinese Restaurant – Don Orehek (reprint from #117)

Page 34 – A Cracked Look at the Good Old Days? – John Langton (reprint from #120)

Page 37 – If Other Industries Gave Rebates – Bill Ward (reprint from #127)

Page 39 – Good Tymes – John Severin (reprint from #130)

Page 44 – Pre-Historic News – Don Orehek (reprint from #120)

Page 46 – Cracked Guide to Baseball – Bill Ward (reprint from #129)

Page 51 – Summer is – John Langton (reprint from #128)

Page 53 – Phone Services for Tots and Teens – John Severin (reprint from #28)

Page 58 – Where are they Now? – Don Orehek (reprint from #129)

Page 60 – Adolt Education! (reprint from #83)

Page 61 – If Real Life Were Like the Movies – Bill Ward (reprint from #116)

Page 64 – Magazine Covers from Planet of the Apes – John Severin (reprint from #124)

Page 66 – One Day in the Desert – Bill Ward (reprint from #132)

Page 67 – Space War Game – John Severin

Page 83 – Chickie, the Fuzz (reprint from #79)

Back Cover – Great Moments in History 1883 – Charles Rodrigues (reprint from #131)

Giant Cracked Fun-Kit #15, March 1978 (84 pages) ($1.00)

Cover – Christening the Ship – John Severin (reprint from #85)

Page 2 – The Cracked Bookstore ad – John Severin

Page 3 – Contents

Page 4 – The Godfodder, Part XXIII – Seymour Redley (John Severin) (reprint from #124)

Page 10 – A Teenager is – Don Orehek (reprint from #127)

Page 12 – A Cracked Look at Dentists (reprint from #81)

Page 16 – Why Does a Chicken Cross the Road? – Nellie Melba (Charles Rodrigues) (reprint from #76)

Page 18 – A Cracked Look at a Racetrack – Don Orehek (reprint from #127)

Page 20 – The Specialized Bionic Man – John Severin (reprint from #129)

Page 23 – Musical Strains for Brains - Bill McCartney (Bill Ward) (reprint from #47)

Page 26 – Fat is...Skinny is – Bob Taylor (reprint from #102)

Page 28 – Little Known Facts of the American Revolution? – Makbush (Sururi Gumen) (reprint from #128)

Page 30 – Cracked Goes to Las Vegas – Don Orehek (reprint from #108)

Page 32 – The First Dollar – Bernard Baily (reprint from #107)

Page 33 – The Future Computerized of Sports – Bill McCartney (Bill Ward) (reprint from #93)

Page 37 – Cracked's "Silent Pages" Spot – Larry Barth (reprint from #95)

Page 39 – New T.V. Game Shows for Next Season – Artie Choake (John Severin) (reprint from #126)

Page 44 – Getting There is All the Fun – LePoer (John Severin) (reprint from #29)

***Giant Cracked Fun-Kit* #16, May 1978 (84 pages) ($1.00)**

Page 42 – Yoga – John Severin (reprint from #9)

Page 45 – Cracked Interviews the Magic King – Bill Ward (reprint from #131)

Page 50 – Cracked's Fun and Puzzle Contests – Bob Taylor (reprint from #87)

Page 53 – The Status Symbol Rat Race – O.O. Severin (John Severin) (reprint from #62)

Page 57 – Ladie's Day (reprint from #98)

Page 58 – Cracked Takes a Look at Basketball – Bill McCartney (Bill Ward) (reprint from #50)

Page 60 – The Cracked Guide to Boating – Sailor Sam (John Severin) (reprint from #129)

Page 64 – Cracked Looks at Mothers – Charles Rodrigues (reprint from #95)

Page 67 – The U.F.O. Kit

Page 83 – (racked with pain, 3 months) photos (reprint from #70)

Back Cover – The Curious and the Modern Sculpture – Oskar Blotta (reprint from #127)

Giant Cracked Fun-Kit #17, July 1978 (84 pages) ($1.00)

Cover – Monk Painting Cracked Covers – John Severin (reprint from #33)

Page 2 – The Cracked Bookstore ad – John Severin

Page 3 – Contents

Page 4 – Jawz – John Severin (reprint from #129)

Page 10 – Cracked Goes to a Literary Cocktail Party – Don Orehek (reprint from #114)

Page 12 – The Non-People Population Explosion – Sururi Gumen (reprint from #130)

Page 16 – Trading Stamps – John Severin (reprint from #28)

Page 21 – The Day That Nothing Seemed to Go Right for the Ape Man – Fal Hoster (John Severin) (reprint from #55)

Page 24 – Past Predictions of the Future – Sururi Gumen (reprint from #121)

Page 28 – When the Super-Jets Take Over – John Severin (reprint from #86)

Page 32 – A Kook Look at Sports (reprint from #76)

Page 34 – Cracked Looks at Dining Out – Bill McCartney (Bill Ward) (reprint from #84)

Page 38 – A Note from the Teacher – Tony Tallarico (reprint from #165)

Page 40 – The Dream Came True – LePoer (John Severin) (reprint from #31)

Page 44 – The Cracked World of Automobiles – R. Khivez (John
   Severin) (reprint from #129)
Page 48 – Oops! Sorry! – Bruce Day (reprint from #102)
Page 50 – "Make Me a Deal" – Bill McCartney (Bill Ward) (reprint from
   #88)
Page 53 – Cracked Interviews the Lemonade King – John Langton
   (reprint from #129)
Page 58 – Cracked Takes a Look at Skiing – Bill McCartney (Bill Ward)
   (reprint from #48)
Page 60 – Bottoms Up (reprint from #48)
Page 61 – Pell-Mell with Mel – Mort Uarrie (John Severin) (reprint
   from #125)
Page 66 – One Morning in the Doctor's Office – Charles Rodrigues
   (reprint from #95)
Page 67 – The Newest Cracked Flip the Stars Book – John Severin
Page 83 – (TV dinners, big trouble, invite them, ice cubes, cheese,
   plastic) photos (new)
Back Cover – Great Moments in Journalism 1935 – Charles Rodrigues
   (reprint from #128)

Giant Cracked Fun-Kit #18, November 1978 (84 pages) ($1.00)

Cover – Sylvester's Crystal Ball – John Severin (reprint from #66)
Page 2 – The Cracked Bookstore ad – John Severin
Page 3 – Contents
Page 4 – Welcome Back, Kutter – John Severin (reprint from #133)
Page 10 – If Picture Postcards Told the Truth! – John Severin (reprint
   from #59)
Page 12 – The Cracked Guide to Skateboarding – Don Orehek (reprint
   from #134)
Page 16 – Ads and Animals! (reprint from #61)
Page 18 – Bullet Proof Car – John Severin (reprint from #35)
Page 19 – Annoy Your Friends – John Severin (reprint from #28)
Page 22 – California Here I Went! – Bill McCartney (Bill Ward) (reprint
   from #57)
Page 25 – Snow Flake and the Seven Dwarfs – John Severin (reprint
   from #70)
Page 30 – Cracked Looks at a Typical Savings Bank – Don Orehek
   (reprint from #132)
Page 32 – Story of the Month (Whoa, Bessie) – John Severin (reprint
   from #27)
Page 33 – A Guide to Modern Art – Bill McCartney (Bill Ward) (reprint
   from #37)

Page 38 – Some Cracked Tips for Whipping Inflation – Bill Ward (reprint from #128)

Page 42 – Don't Believe a Word of it – John Severin (reprint from #82)

Page 44 – The Bird House – John Severin (reprint from #36)

Page 45 – A Cracked Looks at Picture Phones – John Langton (reprint from #64)

Page 48 – Tall Story – John Severin (reprint from #77)

Page 53 – Exclamation!!! – Don Perlin (reprint from #50)

Page 54 – Camp Kicey Doo-Bee – Bill McCartney (Bill Ward) (reprint from #55)

Page 56 – The Generation Gap! (reprint from #78)

Page 57 – Cracked Interviews the Used Car King – Bill Ward (reprint from #133)

Page 62 – Realistic Toys and Games – Don Orehek (reprint from #134)

Page 65 – Look! Four Kooks! (reprint from #63)

Page 66 – The Banana Man – Jerry Kirschen (reprint from #15)

Page 67 – Cracked Greeting Cards – Warren Sattler (new)

Page 83 – The Information Clerk – Caracu (reprint from #114)

Back Cover – Chicken Soap label – John Severin (reprint from #108)

Giant Cracked Fun-Kit #19, March 1979 (84 pages) ($1.00)

Cover – Timber! – John Severin (reprint from #84)

Page 2 – The Cracked Bookstore ad – John Severin

Page 3 – Contents

Page 4 – Barfsky and Clutch – John Severin (reprint from #134)

Page 9 – Specialized Record Albums – John Langton (reprint from #84)

Page 11 – How to Tell If You Are An Adolescent – Howard Cruse (reprint from #97)

Page 13 – The American Revolution as Seen Through British Eyes – Sururi Gumen (reprint from #136)

Page 16 – One Evening in a Fancy Restaurant – Bob Taylor (reprint from #135)

Page 17 – The Cracked Guide to Plant Care – John Severin (reprint from #130)

Page 20 – Ballad of the Squeaky Voiced Cowboy – Joe Mead (reprint from #83)

Page 23 – Rule Changes in Sports that Reflect the Real World – John Langton (reprint from #131)

Page 27 – When All Competition is Eliminated – John Severin (reprint from #96)

Page 30 – Awards for School Kids – Bill McCartney (Bill Ward) (reprint from #77)

Page 34 – The Breaking Point – Bill McCartney (Bill Ward) (reprint from #2)

Page 35 – Why People Move to the Suburbs – Jack Davis (reprint from #14)

Page 39 – Specialized Parties That Fit a Magazine – John Severin (reprint from #87)

Page 43 – Now They're Hi-Jacking Everything! – Vic Martin (reprint from #78)

Page 46 – Cracked Methods for Repairing Your Car Inexpensively – Bill Dubay (reprint from #137)

Page 50 – A Cracked Look at a Picnic Area – Bill Ward (reprint from #138)

Page 52 – The Flipsides! – O.O. Severin (John Severin) / George Gladir (reprint from #52)

Page 56 – If the Fonze Guest Starred on Other Shows – Don Orehek (reprint from #137)

Page 60 – One Afternoon in a Local Stereo Store – Sururi Gumen (reprint from #138)

Page 61 – Cracked Interviews the Antique King – John Severin (reprint from #139)

Page 66 – Hilo Shampoo ad – Bill Everett (reprint from #9)

Page 67 – Battle of the Galaxy Game – John Severin

Page 83 – One Evening in Old Mexico – Bob Taylor (reprint from #133)

Back Cover – Great Moments in Science 495 B.C. – Mike Ricigliano (reprint from #136)

Giant Cracked Fun-Kit #20, July 1979 (84 pages) ($1.00)

Cover – Unfinished Sylvester a la Washington – John Severin (reprint from #23)

Page 2 – The Cracked Bookstore ad – John Severin

Page 3 – Contents

Page 4 – Churlie's Angels – John Severin (reprint from #141)

Page 10 – Fill-in-the-Blank Form Letters and Cards for Every Occasion – Sururi Gumen (reprint from #132)

Page 13 – How to Make Baseball More Interesting – Bill Ward (reprint from #137)

Page 17 – Celebrity Garbage – John Severin (reprint from #131)

Page 20 – Video Games We'll Soon Be Seeing – Howard Nostrand (reprint from #141)

Page 23 – The Wider World of Sports – John Severin (reprint from #139)

Page 28 – You Know You're Nobody When – Bob Taylor (reprint from #131)

Page 30 – Cracked Guide to Sky Diving – Sururi Gumen (reprint from #130)

Page 34 – If Different National Products Became the World Money Standard – John Severin (reprint from #133)

Page 38 – A Cracked Salute to the Olympics – Bill Ward (reprint from #135)

Page 43 – One Day in Metropolitis – Don Orehek (reprint from #136)

Page 44 – The Fonz Throughout History – Don Orehek (reprint from #136)

Page 48 – Guiness Book of Records – Howard Nostrand (reprint from #140)

Page 49 – Sagebrush #35 (cactus flowers) – John Severin / Knights 'n' Daze #37 (Klang) – LePoer (John Severin) (reprint from #127)

Page 51 – Poems to Cry By (reprint from #143)

Page 54 – A Cracked Look at a Newspaper – Don Orehek (reprint from #140)

Page 56 – Beach Blanket Party – John Severin (reprint from #137)

Page 61 – Cracked Interviews the Outdoor King – Bill Ward (reprint from #138)

Page 66 – Late One Evening – Howard Nostrand (reprint from #142)

Page 67 – The Cracked Puzzle Book – John Severin, Jack Davis, Bob Taylor

Page 83 – One Extremely Foggy Night in Minnesota – Howard Nostrand (reprint from #139)

Back Cover – The Lonely Convict and the Pet – Oskar Blotta (reprint from #141)

Giant Cracked Fun-Kit #21, October 1979 (84 pages) ($1.25)

Cover – Eskimo on an Ice Cube – John Severin (reprint from #40)

Page 2 – The Cracked Bookstore ad – John Severin

Page 3 – Contents

Page 4 – Rockey – John Severin (reprint from #143)

Page 10 – Exposing the Con in Contests – Howard Nostrand (reprint from #144)

Page 14 – A Cracked Look at CB Radios – Bob Taylor (reprint from #135)

Page 18 – Winners & Losers – Vic Martin (reprint from #133)

Page 21 – Romeo and Juliet – John Severin (reprint from #8)

Page 24 – If Comic Strip Characters Had Summer Replacements – Lugoze (reprint from #78)

Page 28 – Levenworth Mutual ad – John Severin (reprint from #19)

Page 29 – Tomorrow's Retirement Communities for the Now Generation – Bob Taylor (reprint from #134)

Page 33 – Cracked's Guide to Burglary Prevention – Vic Martin (reprint from #136)

Page 36 – How to Become a Comedy Writer – John Severin (reprint from #77)

Page 38 – A Cracked Look at Summer Camps – Howard Nostrand (reprint from #145)

Page 42 – Sagebrush (don't lag behind) – John Severin (reprint from *King-Sized Cracked* #5)

Page 44 – Digital Instruments of the Future – Warren Sattler (reprint from #144)

Page 47 – The Girl and the Butterfly – Oskar Blotta (reprint from #79)

Page 48 – Boretta – John Severin (reprint from #132)

Page 54 – Safari So Good (reprint from #104)

Page 56 – As the General, Young, and Restless Hospital Turns – Bill Ward (reprint from #137)

Page 61 – Cracked Interviews the Art King – John Severin (reprint from #137)

Page 66 – Sylvester, the Baseball Fan! – John Langton (reprint from #63)

Page 67 – Cracked Vampire Game – John Severin

Page 83 – One Day in Los Angeles – Bill Ward (reprint from #140)

Back Cover – Nader Raider Blasts Boss – Charles Rodrigues (reprint from #109)

Giant Cracked Fun-Kit #22, December 1979 (84 pages) ($1.25)

Cover – Your TV Favorites – John Severin (reprint from #138)

Page 2 – The Cracked Bookstore ad – John Severin

Page 3 – Contents

Page 4 – Havaii 5-0 – John Severin (reprint from #131)

Page 9 – If the American Revolution Happened Today – Don Orehek (reprint from #137)

Page 12 – The Cracked Guide to Soccer – Warren Sattler (reprint from #145)

Page 16 – Redoing the Evening News – John Severin (reprint from #142)

Page 20 – An Afternoon at an Artist's Studio – Howard Nostrand (reprint from #145)

Page 21 – Chatterbox Weekly Magazine (reprint from #147)

Page 27 – The Cracked Guide to Babysitting – Bill Ward (reprint from #145)

Page 31 – Crimedom's Mail Order Catalogue – Warren Sattler (reprint from #146)

Page 36 – Evolution Revolution – Howard Nostrand (reprint from #139)

Page 39 – Marathon Jam – John Severin (reprint from #141)

Page 45 – Cracked Interviews the Super Salesman King – Bill Ward (reprint from #132)

Page 50 – 5 Fun Grabbers (reprint from #74)

Page 51 – 4 Iron-Ons (1 new, reprints from #157, 172, 181), 1 small poster (new), Fly Me Model Plane Kit (partial reprint from *Biggest Greatest Cracked* #7), 8 Super-Size Posters (reprints from #96, 101, 118, 125, 127, 128, 131, 144) (new)

Page 83 – W.C. Fields Laff-In (reprint from #84)

Back Cover – Great Moments in Dentistry 1755 – Howard Nostrand (reprint from #143)

Giant *Cracked* Fun-Kit #23, March 1980 (84 pages) ($1.25)

Cover – Sylvester on Sylvester's Nose – John Severin (reprint from *Biggest Greatest Cracked* #7)

Page 2 – The Cracked Bookstore ad – John Severin

Page 3 – Your Official Cracked Holiday & Appointment Calendar for 1980 – John Severin (revised reprint from *Biggest Greatest Cracked* #5)

Page 19 – Contents

Page 20 – The Spy Who Snubbed Me – O.O. Severin (John Severin) (reprint from #148)

Page 26 – If Professional People Advertised – Howard Nostrand (reprint from #147)

Page 30 – Randolph the Reindeer – John Severin (reprint from #75)

Page 36 – Cracked Visits a Pro Football Locker Room – Bill Ward (reprint from #131)

Page 38 – The Cracked Guide to Basketball – Howard Nostrand (reprint from #142)

Page 43 – Cracked's Specially Tailored Birth Announcements (reprint from #149)

Page 46 – If Commercials Were Built Into TV Programs – John Severin (reprint from #144)

Page 51 – The 99,999 Mile Book – Warren Sattler (reprint from #148)

Page 55 – Open the Door, Seymour! – Larry Barth (reprint from #92)

Page 56 – Give it Back to the Indians – John Severin (reprint from #92)

Page 60 – You Know You're Rich When – Charles Rodrigues (reprint from #91)

Page 62 – Cracked Looks at Hotels – Bill McCartney (Bill Ward) (reprint from #90)

Page 65 – Saturday Night in India – Oskar Blotta (reprint from #86)
Page 66 – Cracked's Amazing Calculator Readouts (reprint from #147)
Page 67 – Poverty Game Kit (reprint from *Super Cracked* #5)
Page 83 – Official Cracked Reporter T-Shirt ad
Back Cover – Great Moments in History 974 A.D. – Howard Nostrand (reprint from #145)

Giant Cracked Fun-Kit #24, July 1980 (84 pages) ($1.25)

Cover – Sylvester Paints Himself – Powers (John Severin) (reprint from #147)
Page 2 – The Cracked Bookstore ad – John Severin
Page 3 – 14 Beautiful Full Color Double-Art Masterpieces
Page 19 – Contents
Page 20 – The Sappy Days – John Severin (reprint from #118)
Page 25 – When America Runs Out of Electricity – Don Orehek (reprint from #116)
Page 28 – The Cracked World of Movie Going – Sururi Gumen (reprint from #131)
Page 31 – Cracked's New Learn-At-Home Schools – LePoer (John Severin) (reprint from #141)
Page 34 – The Rock Craze Rolls On – John Langton (reprint from #135)
Page 37 – The Blue Night – John Severin (reprint from #140)
Page 43 – The Great Airline War – Howard Nostrand (John Severin) (reprint from #146)
Page 46 – One Minute TV Shows of the Future – Howard Nostrand (reprint from #148)
Page 50 – How to Run Your Home Using No Electrical Power – Don Orehek (reprint from #142)
Page 53 – If Other Actors Played the Parts Made Famous by Somebody Else – John Severin (reprint from #151)
Page 57 – Cracked Interviews the Olympic Training King – Bill Ward (reprint from #136)
Page 62 – The Check-Up – Don Orehek (reprint from #139)
Page 63 – If the Fonz Became Bionic – John Severin (reprint from #140)
Page 67 – The Game of Inflation – John Severin (reprint from *King-Sized Cracked* #8)
Page 83 – Official Cracked Reporter T-Shirt ad
Back Cover – Great Moments in Music 1,057,648 B.C. – Howard Nostrand (reprint from #144)

Giant Cracked Fun-Kit #25, October 1980 (84 pages) ($1.25)

Cover – Busted Hammer, Nails and Fingers – John Severin (reprint from #63)

Page 2 – The Cracked Bookstore ad – John Severin

Page 3 – Cracked's 1980 Moscow Olympics Game – John Severin

Page 19 – Contents

Page 20 – Fonzie's Presidential Platform – John Severin (reprint from *Cracked Collectors' Edition* #16)

Page 27 – The Class of 1932 – Bob Taylor (reprint from #103)

Page 30 – With-it Nursery Rhymes – Bill McCartney (Bill Ward) (reprint from #101)

Page 32 – Slums Can Be Made a Fun Thing! – John Severin (reprint from #74)

Page 36 – The World of Mr. Orehek – Don Orehek (reprint from #109)

Page 38 – The Cracked History of Humor – Bill Ward (reprint from #153)

Page 42 – How to Eat Better for Less Money – Warren Sattler (reprint from #151)

Page 47 – Cracked's Illustrated History – John Severin (reprint from #86)

Page 50 – Rodrigues' Side Show – Charles Rodrigues (reprint from #106)

Page 53 – Incurably Cracked (reprint from #153)

Page 56 – Cracked Interviews the Airline King – Bill Ward (reprint from #151)

Page 61 – High Noonish – John Severin / Joe Catalano (reprint from #152)

Page 67 – The Newest Cracked "Flip the Faces" Book – John Severin (revised reprint from *Giant Cracked* #3)

Page 83 – Official Cracked Reporter T-Shirt ad

Back Cover – Cracked's Energy Saving Guide – Charles Rodrigues (reprint from #117)

Giant Cracked Fun-Kit #26, December 1980 (84 pages) ($1.25)

Cover – Bionic Man in Star Wars – John Severin (reprint from #149)

Page 2 – The Cracked Bookstore ad – John Severin

Page 3 – Cracked's Oil Sheik Game – Bob Taylor (new)

Page 19 – Contents

Page 20 – The Six Billion Dollar Man – John Severin (reprint from #120)

Page 26 – When the World Runs Out of Food – Sururi Gumen (reprint from #122)

Page 30 – The Cracked Guide to Self-Recognition – Bill Ward (reprint from #127)

Page 32 – New T.V. Game Shows for Next Season – Artie Choake (John Severin) (reprint from #126)

Page 37 – Fun City Olympics – Warren Sattler (reprint from #156)

Page 40 – A Cracked Look at House Pets – Don Orehek (reprint from #153)

Page 44 – Cracked Visits the "Proverbs and Familiar Sayings" Museum – John Severin (reprint from #152)

Page 47 – A Modern Parent vs. Traditional Parent – Warren Sattler (reprint from #155)

Page 51 – Tyme Magazine (reprint from #154)

Page 57 – Cracked Interviews the Rock 'n' Roll King – Bill Ward (reprint from #153)

Page 62 – The Major Moose Show – John Severin (reprint from #125)

Page 66 – Sagebrush #25 (painting) – John Severin / Ye Hang Ups #4 (nice easy job) – Nireves (John Severin) (reprint from #117)

Page 67 – Cracked Mystery Cube Kit – John Severin (revised reprint from *King-Sized Cracked* #14)

Page 83 – Official Cracked Reporter T-Shirt ad

Back Cover – Help Wanted – Charles Rodrigues (reprint from #113)

Giant Cracked Fun-Kit #27, March 1981 (84 pages) ($1.25)

Cover – Sylvester In Case of Fire – John Severin / Bill Lederle (reprint from #70)

Page 2 – The Cracked Bookstore ad – John Severin

Page 3 – Cracked's Intelligence Test (revised reprint from #15)

Page 11 – Contents

Page 12 – Funniest Island – John Severin (reprint from #155)

Page 18 – Cracked's Detective Handbook – Bill Ward (reprint from #151)

Page 22 – The Telephone Call – Charles Rodrigues (reprint from #119)

Page 23 – Cowtown U.S.A. (reprint from #150)

Page 28 – Fringe Benefits Athletes Will Soon Be Demanding – Howard Nostrand (John Severin) (reprint from #146)

Page 31 – How Much Stress Can You Take? – Bill Ward (reprint from #118)

Page 34 – New Forms of Home Entertainment – Warren Sattler (reprint from #143)

Page 36 – Programs for Non-Theatrical Events – John Langton (reprint from #115)

Page 39 – If TV Characters Aged While Their Shows Stayed the Same – Sururi Gumen (reprint from #128)

Page 43 – Three's Crummier – John Severin (reprint from #156)
Page 49 – How to Buy a New Car – Bernard Baily (reprint from #119)
Page 53 – Cracked's Sure-Fire Guide to Weight Control – Don Orehek (reprint from #117)
Page 57 – The "How to Insult" Manual – Powers (John Severin) (reprint from #148)
Page 61 – Cracked Interviews the Oil King – Bill Ward (reprint from #120)
Page 66 – Shut-Ups (I remember) – Charles Rodrigues (reprint from #108)
Page 67 – Do-it-Yourself Newspapers (revised reprint from *Giant Cracked* #1)
Page 83 – Official Cracked Reporter T-Shirt ad
Back Cover – Silver Spoon Magazine – John Severin (reprint from #87)

Giant Cracked Fun-Kit #28, July 1981 (84 pages) ($1.25)

Cover – Formal Portrait of Sylvester P. Smythe – John Severin (reprint from #147)
Page 2 – The Cracked Bookstore ad – John Severin
Page 3 – 4 Cracked Posters (reprints from #75, 76, 108, 156)
Page 7 – Fly Me Model Plane Kit (partial reprint from *Biggest Greatest Cracked* #7)
Page 11 – Contents
Page 20 – M*U*S*H (Mail call!) – John Severin (reprint from #159)
Page 26 – The Cracked Investigation of the UFO Phenomenon – Howard Nostrand (reprint from #155)
Page 29 – The Cracked Book of Games and Puzzles That Anyone Can Solve – Warren Sattler (reprint from #159)
Page 34 – The Cracked World of Appliances – Don Orehek (reprint from #156)
Page 38 – Cloning: The Advantages and the Disadvantages – Howard Nostrand (reprint from #154)
Page 40 – And Still More from The Cracked Lens (reprint from #158)
Page 43 – Ad Campaigns for Unwanted Products – Bill Ward (reprint from #144)
Page 47 – "The Villain" – Val Mayerik (reprint from #158)
Page 48 – Cracked's I'm O.K. Test – Howard Nostrand (reprint from #157)
Page 51 – A Cracked Look at Phobias – Warren Sattler (reprint from #158)
Page 55 – Enough is Enough! – John Severin (reprint from #153)
Page 61 – Cracked Interviews the Radio King – Bill Ward (reprint from #145)

Page 66 – Shut-Ups (hit a tree) – S. Gross Jr. (Charles Rodrigues) (reprint from #102)

Page 67 – The Newest Cracked "Flip the Faces" Book – John Severin (revised reprint from *Giant Cracked* #3)

Page 83 – Official Cracked Reporter T-Shirt ad

Back Cover – Great Moments in Sports 1972 – Howard Nostrand (reprint from #150)

Giant Cracked Fun-Kit #29, October 1981 (84 pages) ($1.25)

Cover – "See Thru" Mirror Sandwich Board – John Severin (reprint from #76)

Page 2 – Contents

Page 3 – Cracked's Shut-Ups Game – John Severin, Charles Rodrigues, Bill Ward (new)

Page 19 – The Cracked Bookstore ad – John Severin

Page 20 – Space: 1998 – Sururi Gumen (reprint from #133)

Page 26 – Summer is – John Langton (reprint from #128)

Page 28 – The Big Budget Epic vs. The Low Budget Quickie – John Severin (reprint from #135)

Page 32 – The Cracked History of Television – Bill Ward (reprint from #124)

Page 36 – Cracked Exposes Detroit – Vic Martin (reprint from #132)

Page 40 – The Pirate Treasure Chest (reprint from #64)

Page 42 – Monopo-Oil – John Langton (reprint from #127)

Page 45 – Cracked Interviews the Lemonade King – John Langton (reprint from #129)

Page 50 – One Day in the Desert – Bill Ward (reprint from #132)

Page 51 – The Cracked Iron-On Kit – John Severin (revised from *King-Sized Cracked* #11 with reprint from #157)

Page 54 – 8 Posters (reprints from #115, 122, 125, 151, 156, 159, 162, 167)

Page 83 – Destination Fun (reprint from #79)

Back Cover – One Day in the Tropics – Val Mayerik (reprint from #159)

Giant Cracked Fun-Kit #30, December 1981 (84 pages) ($1.50)

Cover – The Fonze! – John Severin (reprint from #134)

Page 2 – Contents

Page 3 – The Cracked Insult Guide – John Severin, Mike Ricigliano (revised reprint from *Giant Cracked* #7)

Page 19 – The Cracked Bookstore ad – John Severin

Page 20 – Allien and How to Watch it – John Severin (reprint from #164)

Page 27 – Cracked's "Silent Pages" Spot – Larry Barth (reprint from #95)

Page 29 – Ridiculous Renting Spaces – Bill Ward (reprint from #122)

Page 32 – Are You a Loser? – Bernard Baily (reprint from #120)

Page 35 – Sagebrush (hmmmmmm) – Lor & John Severin (new)

Page 36 – The Put-Downers – Vic Martin (reprint from #106)

Page 38 – Cracked's Catchy First Lines For – Don Orehek (reprint from #111)

Page 40 – A Day at the Zoo – Charles Rodrigues (reprint from #108)

Page 43 – Ask a Silly Question, Get a – John Langton (reprint from #83)

Page 44 – How a Big City Can Prevent Bankruptcy – LePoer (John Severin) (reprint from #131)

Page 48 – Specialty Signs for Specialty Stores – Bill Ward (reprint from #143)

Page 50 – You Know You're Not a Kid Anymore When – Jared Lee (reprint from #99)

Page 52 – Silly Things We Do – John Severin (reprint from #101)

Page 54 – Training the Dog – Joe Mead (reprint from #98)

Page 55 – How to Stretch Your Dollar Getting the Most While Spending Less – Vic Martin (reprint from #112)

Page 58 – A Visit with Laurel and Hardy (reprint from #55)

Page 60 – You Know Your Stars Are All Screwed Up When – Don Orehek (reprint from #116)

Page 62 – I Don't Care Who You Are – John Severin (reprint from #96)

Page 64 – Luck Is – Bob Taylor (reprint from #85)

Page 66 – More Crazy Comebacks – Warren Sattler (reprint from #86)

Page 67 – Cracked Greeting Cards – Mike Ricigliano, John Severin (new)

Page 83 – Bull Telephone System ad – John Severin (reprint from #41)

Back Cover – Great Moments in Horsemanship 456 A.D. – Howard Nostrand (reprint from #151)

Giant Cracked Fun-Kit #31, March 1982 (84 pages) ($1.50)

Cover – Skiing – John Severin (reprint from #67)

Page 2 – Contents

Page 3 – The Cracked Familiar Sayings Photo Match Game (new)

Page 19 – The Cracked Bookstore ad – John Severin

Page 20 – Leverne and Shurley (what do you want for dinner) – John Severin (reprint from #166)

Page 27 – How to Stay Warm Without Wasting Energy – Bill Ward (reprint from #123)

Page 30 – A Look at Typical Family Gathering – Don Orehek (reprint from #119)

Page 33 – One Day at a Railroad Crossing – Howard Nostrand (reprint from #142)

Page 34 – The Quickest Fun in the West (reprint from #77)

Page 37 – Pet Plaza – Bill Ward (reprint from #118)

Page 42 – Simple Exercises for Simple People – Lugoze (reprint from #75)

Page 45 – Products and Ads Designed for the Arab Market – Mac Bush (Sururi Gumen) (reprint from #126)

Page 49 – The Talking Blob – John Severin / Joe Catalano (reprint from #149)

Page 55 – Late One Evening – Howard Nostrand (reprint from #142)

Page 56 – The Dumb-Dumb People! – Lugoze (reprint from #77)

Page 58 – Cracked Looks at Telephones – Bill McCartney (Bill Ward) (reprint from #87)

Page 61 – Cracked Interviews the Christmas King – Yul Tydde (John Severin) (reprint from #123)

Page 66 – Shut-Ups (66…45…38) – Mike Ricigliano (reprint from #144)

Page 67 – Your Official Cracked Holiday & Appointment Calendar for 1982 – John Severin (revised reprint from *Biggest Greatest Cracked* #5)

Page 83 – The Information Clerk – Caracu (reprint from #114)

Back Cover – The Curious and the Modern Sculpture – Oskar Blotta (reprint from #127)

Giant Cracked Fun-Kit #32, July 1982 (84 pages) ($1.75)

Cover – Sylvester, Court Jester – John Severin (reprint from *Biggest Greatest Cracked* #5)

Page 2 – Contents

Page 3 – The Cracked Losers Can Be Winners Game – Mike Ricigliano (new)

Page 19 – The Cracked Bookstore ad – John Severin

Page 20 – If Mork Appeared in Other TV Shows and Movies (Star Trek) – John Severin (reprint from #164)

Page 25 – The Ridiculous Things of Life – Bill Ward (reprint from #124)

Page 28 – Great Books at Great Prices When You Join the Book-a-Month Club (reprint from #157)

Page 30 – The Last of the 'Desert Island' Cartoons! – Irit Kajiij Jr. (Charles Rodrigues) (reprint from #109)

Page 33 – Policeman Magazine – Don Orehek (reprint from #120)

Page 37 – A Cracked History of the Movies – Vic Martin (reprint from #109)

426 If You're *Cracked*, You're Happy, Book Too

Page 41 – One Afternoon at a Stop Light – Howard Nostrand (reprint from #160)

Page 44 – Dotty About Karate – Bill Ward (reprint from #112)

Page 48 – One Morning on John Severin's Drawing Board – John Severin (reprint from #152)

Page 50 – Cracked's Guide for Spotting Self-Lovers – Howard Nostrand (reprint from #158)

Page 52 – If Real Life Operated Like TV Quiz Shows – Don Orehek (reprint from #125)

Page 57 – When Meat Becomes as Valuable as Money – John Langton (reprint from #112)

Page 61 – Cracked Interviews the Psychic King – Bill Ward (reprint from #156)

Page 66 – You Like to Live Dangerously When – LePoer (John Severin) (reprint from #157)

Page 67 – 8 Posters (reprints from #154, 157, 159, 164, 167, 168, 169, 172)

Page 83 – Snappy Answers! – John Langton (reprint from #86)

Back Cover – Karate Magazine – John Severin (reprint from #88)

Giant Cracked Fun-Kit #33, October 1982 (84 pages) ($1.75)

Cover – Trick Mirror – Jack Davis (reprint from #16)

Page 2 – Contents

Page 3 and 67 – Cracked Practical Joke Kit – John Severin (new)

Page 19 – The Cracked Bookstore ad – John Severin

Page 20 – Suped-Upman The Satire – Nireves (John Severin) (reprint from #160)

Page 27 – The Cracked Theory on the Relativity of Time – Howard Nostrand (reprint from #162)

Page 30 – The Cracked World of Teenagers – Don Orehek (reprint from #161)

Page 32 – Cracked Predictions for the 1980's – Sururi Gumen (reprint from #169)

Page 36 – What "Help Wanted" Ads Say and What They Really Mean – Howard Nostrand (reprint from #172)

Page 39 – One Afternoon in a Plastic Surgeon's Office – Bill Ward (reprint from #164)

Page 40 – The Coming Mini-Auto Age – John Langton (reprint from #169)

Page 44 – Famous Animal Celebrities – Nireves (John Severin) (reprint from #169)

Page 46 – Absolutely, Undeniably, Positively, Unquestionably, the Very Last of The Cracked Lens (reprint from #171)

Page 48 – Cracked Modernized Songs of Childhood – Bill Ward
   (reprint from #159)
Page 52 – What is a Fad Freak? – Sururi Gumen (reprint from #170)
Page 54 – How to Improve Your…ah…ah…Memory – Howard
   Nostrand (reprint from #163)
Page 57 – Cracked's Guide to Understanding Your Pet – Sururi Gumen
   (reprint from #165)
Page 61 – Cracked Interviews the Souvenir King – Bill Ward (reprint
   from #150)
Page 66 – Photoon (Kitchie-kitchie coo!) (reprint from #165)
Page 83 – 4 Out of 5 Dentists Surveyed (reprint from #170)
Back Cover – The Beanstalk – Conky Nostrand (Howard Nostrand)
   (reprint from #167)

Giant Cracked Fun-Kit #34, December 1982 (84 pages) ($1.75)

Cover – E.T. and Sylvester – John Severin (new)
Page 2 – Contents
Page 3 – 4 Cracked Posters (3 new, 1 reprint from *Cracked Collectors'
   Edition* #23)
Page 11 – 3 Iron-Ons (2 new, 1 reprint from #157)
Page 19 – The Cracked Bookstore ad – John Severin
Page 20 – EaTing – John Severin (new)
Page 27 – Colonel Jim Dandy's Guide to Good Manners for
   Discriminatin' Cowpokes 'n' Buckeroos – Samuel B. Whitehead
   (reprint from #163)
Page 31 – A Dog's Day Afternoon (reprint from #155)
Page 32 – Cracked's Playful Ways to Make Work Fun – Sururi Gumen
   (reprint from #162)
Page 34 – A Cracked Look at a High School – Bill Ward (reprint from #116)
Page 37 – How Different Magazines and Newspapers Would Caption
   the Same Picture (reprint from #132)
Page 41 – One Extremely Foggy Night in Minnesota – Howard
   Nostrand (reprint from #139)
Page 42 – Cracked's Inventory of Personal Spending Habits – Warren
   Sattler (reprint from #163)
Page 45 – Miss Weird – Bernard Baily (reprint from #107)
Page 48 – Winners & Losers – Vic Martin (reprint from #133)
Page 50 – The Cracked Guide to Fortune Telling – Don Orehek (reprint
   from #166)
Page 54 – Fat is…Skinny is – Bob Taylor (reprint from #102)
Page 56 – Why is it on T.V. You Never See – Bill Ward (reprint from #133)
Page 59 – The Piggy Bank – Caracu (reprint from #87)

Page 60 – Rodrigues' Hospital-ity – Charles Rodrigues (reprint from #110)

Page 63 – Chariots of the Clods? – John Severin (reprint from #122)

Page 66 – Lunch Time – Oskar Blotta (reprint from #89)

Page 67 – The Cracked Extra Terrestrial Game – Mike Ricigliano (new)

Page 83 – The Starry-Eyed Astronomers – Don Orehek (reprint from #153)

Back Cover – It Happened on Main and First – Caracu (reprint from #103)

Giant Cracked Fun-Kit #35, July 1983 (84 pages) ($1.75)

Cover – Thumb Painting – John Severin (reprint from #38)

Page 2 – Contents

Page 3 – Paperback Book Covers – John Severin (reprint from *Biggest Greatest Cracked* #13)

Page 19 – The Cracked Bookstore ad – John Severin

Page 20 – Happy Daze – John Severin (reprint from #144)

Page 26 – Fill-in-the-Blank Form Letters and Cards for Every Occasion – Sururi Gumen (reprint from #132)

Page 29 – Realistic Toys and Games – Don Orehek (reprint from #134)

Page 32 – Cracked Looks at the T-Shirt Craze – Howard Nostrand (reprint from #143)

Page 36 – Fields of Fun! (reprint from #71)

Page 38 – Cracked Looks at Mothers – Charles Rodrigues (reprint from #95)

Page 41 – Laff and Let Die – O.O. Severin (John Severin) (reprint from #116)

Page 47 – Poems to Cry By (reprint from #143)

Page 50 – Are you an Optimist or a Pessimist? – John Langton (reprint from #67)

Page 53 – Snap! Crackle! Flop! – Vic Martin (reprint from #93)

Page 56 – The Old Lady and the Laundromat – Bill McCartney (Bill Ward) (reprint from #28)

Page 58 – Cracked's Guide to Burglary Prevention – Vic Martin (reprint from #136)

Page 61 – The Academy Awards Show – John Severin (reprint from #134)

Page 66 – Unchained – Bob Zahn (reprint from *Monster Howls* #1)

Page 67 – Cracked Vampire Game – John Severin (reprint from *Giant Cracked Fun-Kit* #21)

Page 83 – The Train Robber – Bill McCartney (Bill Ward) (reprint from #34)

Back Cover – The Chicken Killer – Howard Nostrand / Jay Lynch (reprint from #168)

Giant Cracked Fun-Kit #36, October 1983 (84 pages) ($2.00)

Cover – Celebrities at the Beach – John Severin (reprint from *Cracked Collectors' Edition #38)*

Page 2 – Contents

Page 3 – The Cracked Shark Hunt Game – Sururi Gumen (reprint from *Super Cracked #9*)

Page 19 – The Cracked Bookstore ad – John Severin

Page 20 – The Dorks of Hazzardous With Chipps to go – John Severin (reprint from #172)

Page 27 – The Rescue? – Art Pottier (reprint from #100)

Page 28 – The Cracked World of Summer – Don Orehek (reprint from #155)

Page 32 – Cracked Frisbee Rating System – Bob Taylor (reprint from #133)

Page 35 – Postcard Collecting – Sururi Gumen (reprint from #132)

Page 39 – Hudd & Dini (painted wall) – Vic Martin (reprint from #76)

Page 41 – If Arnold Were Treated and Behaved Like a Real-Life Kid – John Severin (reprint from #171)

Page 46 – Take Me Out to the Old Cracked Ball Game – Charles Rodrigues (reprint from #53)

Page 48 – Cracked Looks at Hotels – Bill McCartney (Bill Ward) (reprint from #90)

Page 51 – Cracked's Guide to Bicycling – Bob Taylor (reprint from #105)

Page 55 – How the Airlines Can Save Money! – John Severin (reprint from #97)

Page 58 – Oh, Those Oh-So-Long Lines – John Langton (reprint from #77)

Page 62 – People Who Are Just Born Unlucky – Bill McCartney (Bill Ward) (reprint from #44)

Page 64 – I Don't Care Who You Are – John Severin (reprint from #56)

Page 66 – The Shade – Caracu (reprint from #65)

Page 67 – Summer Travel Fun-Kit – John Severin (new except reprints from #88 and #123)

Page 83 – Go Fly a Kite – John Severin (reprint from #74)

Back Cover – Greetings from Brooklyn Postcard – John Severin (reprint from #38)

Giant Cracked Fun-Kit #37, December 1983 (84 pages) ($2.00)

Cover – Four-Eyed Sylvester – John Severin (reprint from #24)

Page 2 – Contents

Page 3 – The Cracked Game of Videopoly – Mike Ricigliano, John Severin (new)

Page 35 – The Spy Who Snubbed Me – O.O. Severin (John Severin) (reprint from #148)

Page 41 – The Men Behind Kong – Bill Ward (reprint from *Cracked Collectors' Edition* #25)

Page 44 – Sagebrush (peace-pipe) – John Severin (reprint from #84)

Page 46 – Creating New Job Opportunities – John Severin (reprint from #96)

Page 49 – The Waiter and the Customers – Vic Martin (reprint from #98)

Page 50 – "Friends, Romans, Countrymen, Lend Me Your Laughs!" (reprint from #80)

Page 52 – Ten Tips on How to Become Rich – Vic Martin (reprint from #103)

Page 54 – Cracked Looks at Television Viewers – Bill McCartney (Bill Ward) (reprint from #85)

Page 58 – Small is Beautiful – John Langton (reprint from #143)

Page 61 – Cracked's Guide to Crime Prevention – Dick Wright (reprint from #110)

Page 65 – Sports Smiles – John Severin (reprint from #56)

Page 67 – Cracked Mystery Cube Kit – John Severin (revised reprint from *King-Sized Cracked* #14)

Page 83 – Ye Hang Ups (equal rights) – C.E. Severin (Catherine Severin) (reprint from #177)

Back Cover – The Angry Elephant and Tarzan's Son – Oskar Blotta (reprint from #147)

Giant Cracked Fun-Kit #38, March 1984 (84 pages) ($1.75)

Cover – In Case of Fire Break Glass – John Severin (reprint for #51)

Page 2 – Contents

Page 3 – Cracked's Oil Sheik Game – Bob Taylor (reprint from *Giant Cracked Fun-Kit* #26)

Page 19 – The Cracked Bookstore ad – John Severin

Page 20 – Diff'rent Strokes (two cups of wheat germ) – John Severin (reprint from #178)

Page 27 – Hudd & Dini (D.D.T.) – Vic Martin (reprint from #88)

Page 28 – Cracked Looks at Dining Out – Bill McCartney (Bill Ward) (reprint from #84)

Page 32 – You Know You're Rich When – Charles Rodrigues (reprint from #91)

Page 34 – If Comic Strip Heroes Had Hang-Ups Like the Rest of Us – Lugoze (reprint from #96)

Page 38 – Shaggies! – Larry Barth (reprint from #91)

Page 39 – Pow U. – Tony Tallarico (reprint from #65)

Page 43 – Famous Stars in Ads We'd Like to See (reprint from #95)

Page 46 – How Wise are Wise Old Proverbs? – Vic Martin (reprint from #98)

Page 50 – Battlestar Garlictica – John Severin (reprint from #159)

Page 56 – Cracked Looks at TV Commercials – Bill McCartney (Bill Ward) (reprint from #98)

Page 58 – Laurel and Hardy's Wacky World of Fun! (reprint from #59)

Page 60 – When We All Move to Alaska – John Severin (reprint from #91)

Page 64 – Status Symbols for Dogs! – John Severin (reprint from #86)

Page 66 – Cool-Its (take me out) – Mike Ricigliano (reprint from *Cracked Collectors' Edition* #16)

Page 67 – The Newest Cracked "Flip the Faces" Book – John Severin (revised reprint from *Giant Cracked* #3)

Page 83 – AT&TT ad – Vic Martin (reprint from #59)

Back Cover – Cadillack – John Severin (reprint from #85)

Giant Cracked Fun-Kit #39, October 1984 (84 pages) ($1.75)

Cover – Surfing Sylvester – John Severin (reprint from #86)

Page 2 – Contents

Page 3 – The Hollywood Game – John Severin, Samuel B. Whitehead, Howard Nostrand (reprint from *King-Sized Cracked* #15)

Page 19 – Star Drek the Moving Picture – John Severin (reprint from #169)

Page 27 – One Day at a Railroad Crossing – Howard Nostrand (reprint from #142)

Page 28 – The Cracked Guide to Babysitting – Bill Ward (reprint from #145)

Page 32 – Digital Instruments of the Future – Warren Sattler (reprint from #144)

Page 35 – The Awakening – John Severin (reprint from #97)

Page 36 – Cracked Fantasies – Sururi Gumen (reprint from #172)

Page 39 – Absolutely, Positively, Unquestionably, the Very Last of The Cracked Lens (reprint from #169)

Page 43 – Other "Self-Service" Businesses – Bruce Day (reprint from #150)

Page 46 – The Cracked World of Toys and Games – Don Orehek (reprint from #148)

Page 50 – Situations You Wish You Weren't In – Samuel B. Whitehead (reprint from #170)

Page 52 – Funniest Island – John Severin (reprint from #155)

Page 58 – Using Star Trek Logic and Technology to Solve Life's Everyday Problems – Don Orehek (reprint from #170)

Page 61 – Ye Hang Ups (mind closing the door) – C.E. Severin (Catherine Severin) (reprint from #170)

Page 62 – The Cracked Guide to Paddleball – Warren Sattler (reprint from #150)

Page 66 – Shut-Ups (I think I can K.O.) – Don Orehek (reprint from #145)

Page 67 – The Cracked Iron-On Kit – John Severin (revised from *King-Sized Cracked* #11)

Page 83 – A Gloomy Indian Story – Oskar Blotta (reprint from #147)

Back Cover – Great Moments in Auto Racing 1926 – Howard Nostrand (reprint from #149)

Giant *Cracked* Fun-Kit #40, March 1985 (84 pages) ($2.00)

Cover – Sylvesters on the Moon – John Severin (reprint from #68)

Page 2 – Contents

Page 3 – Cracked's 1985 Rock & Roll Calendar – Howard Nostrand (new with partial reprint from #144)

Page 19 – Magnumb Public Idiot – John Severin (reprint from #191)

Page 26 – Cracked's Method for Dealing with Traveling Salesman – Warren Sattler (reprint from #152)

Page 30 – Still More from The Cracked Lens (reprint from #157)

Page 33 – The Cracked History of Art – John Langton (reprint from #117)

Page 37 – Cracked Interviews the Garbage King – Sururi Gumen (reprint from #122)

Page 42 – The World of Kids – Don Orehek (reprint from #121)

Page 46 – What are the Old TV & Movie Detectives Doing Today? – John Severin (reprint from #121)

Page 50 – The Ridiculous Things of Life – Bill Ward (reprint from #124)

Page 54 – What to Do with Your Obsolete Gas Guzzler – Bill Ward (reprint from #120)

Page 56 – A Look at Typical Family Gathering – Don Orehek (reprint from #119)

Page 60 – The Starry-Eyed Astronomers – Don Orehek (reprint from #153)

Page 61 – If Newspapers Carried Pictures to Match Their Headlines – John Severin (reprint from #127)

Page 64 – The Cracked Guide to Self-Recognition – Bill Ward (reprint from #127)

Page 66 – Shut-Ups (Who goes there?) – Don Orehek (reprint from #152)

Page 67 – Cracked's Road Race Game – John Severin (reprint from *Extra Special Cracked* #4)

Page 83 – Dumb Questions That Don't Deserve an Answer – Don Orehek (reprint from #177)

Back Cover – Great Moments in Journalism 1935 – Charles Rodrigues (reprint from #128)

Giant Cracked Fun-Kit #41, July 1985 (84 pages) ($2.00)

Cover – We Need New Quarters – John Severin (reprint from #22)

Page 2 – Contents

Page 3 – The Cracked All-Star All-Pro All-American All-Everything Sports Game – John Severin, Mike Ricigliano, Don Orehek, Bill Ward, Warren Sattler, Bob Taylor, Sururi Gumen, Charles Rodrigues (reprint from *King-Sized Cracked* #16)

Page 19 – Cracked's Sequels to Classic Movies – John Severin (reprint from #180)

Page 25 – One Day at a Railroad Crossing – Howard Nostrand (reprint from #142)

Page 26 – The Cracked World of Snow – Sururi Gumen (reprint from #124)

Page 30 – Testimonial Ads, the Way They Should Be – Howard Nostrand (reprint from #158)

Page 32 – A Cracked Look at House Pets – Don Orehek (reprint from #153)

Page 36 – More Believe it or Not (Syrians) (reprint from #178)

Page 38 – Learning to Fly – John Severin (reprint from #80)

Page 44 – The Cracked World of Movie Going – Sururi Gumen (reprint from #131)

Page 47 – How a Rumor Gets Started – Al Jaffee (reprint from #7)

Page 49 – The Check-Up – Don Orehek (reprint from #139)

Page 50 – Exposing the Con in Contests – Howard Nostrand (reprint from #144)

Page 54 – The Cracked World of Hospitals – Don Orehek (reprint from #150)

Page 58 – Absolutely, Unquestionably, Positively, Undeniably, the Very, Very, Last of The Cracked Lens (and we really, really mean it this time, for sure!) Part V (reprint from #180)

Page 61 – Cracked's Cartoon Showcase Featuring Jeff Keate (camouflage experts) – Jeff Keate (reprint from #190)

Page 63 – The Layman's Guide to Hot and Cold Weather – Don Orehek (reprint from #160)

Page 66 – Shut-Ups (supreme court) – Charles Rodrigues (reprint from #180)

Page 67 – The Cracked Familiar Sayings Photo Match Game (reprint from *Giant Cracked Fun-Kit* #31)

Page 83 – Mod Fairy Tales (The Princess and the Frog) – C.E. Severin (Catherine Severin) (reprint from #192)

Back Cover – Great Moments in History 1561 – Warren Sattler (reprint from #183)

Giant *Cracked* Fun-Kit #42, October 1985 (84 pages) ($2.00)

Cover – We Ride Knight Rider! – John Severin (reprint from #193)

Page 2 – Contents

Page 3 – Bicycle Bumper Stickers (new)

Page 11 – Cracked Award Cards (new)

Page 19 – Tree's Company – John Severin (reprint from #201)

Page 26 – Isn't it Rotten in School When – Warren Sattler (reprint from #152)

Page 29 – Alaffin's Magic Lamp – Fran Matera (reprint from #204)

Page 30 – The Cracked World of Video Games – Samuel B. Whitehead (reprint from #184)

Page 34 – The Cracked Guide to Fortune Telling – Don Orehek (reprint from #166)

Page 38 – Collision Courses (Vote for Smith) – John Langton (reprint from #188)

Page 39 – When TV Goes Completely Sci Fi – Samuel B. Whitehead (reprint from #163)

Page 42 – A Cracked Look at the World's Worst "Knock Knock" Jokes – Don Orehek (reprint from #180)

Page 44 – War Gains – John Severin (reprint from #200)

Page 51 – Cracked's Specially Tailored Birth Announcements (reprint from #149)

Page 54 – What Your Mother/Father Would Say – Don Orehek (reprint from #197)

Page 57 – The Cracked Fix-It Yourself Manual – Bill Ward (reprint from #199)

Page 37 – Can You Pass the Teen-Age Drivers Test? – Warren Sattler (reprint from #200)

Page 64 – One Day at Tattoo School – Bill Ward (reprint from #193)

Page 65 – Family Ties – Vance Rodewalt (reprint from #202)

Page 72 – A Good Date vs. A Bad Date – Frank Fitzgerald (reprint from #187)

Page 75 – The Loser – John Severin (reprint from #131)

Page 77 – Cracked Interviews the Soap Opera King – Bill Ward (reprint from #186)

Page 82 – Shut-Ups (one more quarter) – Don Orehek (reprint from #198)

Page 83 – If You're Cracked You're Happy! Iron-On – John Severin (reprint from #123)

Back Cover – One Night at the Garden – Howard Nostrand (reprint from #165)

***Giant Cracked Sci-Fi Special* #43, March 1986 (84 pages) ($2.00)**

Cover – Star Trek – John Severin, More Star Wars – Powers (John
Severin) (reprints from #127 and 148)

Page 2 – Alien Shut-Ups! (most beautiful girl) – Bill McCartney (Bill
Ward) (reprint from #8) (originally called "Cracked Space Shut-
Ups)

Page 4 – EaTing – John Severin (reprint from *Giant Cracked Fun-Kit* #34)

Page 11 – Freezing People – Jack Davis (reprint from #13)

Page 16 – Star Yecch! – John Severin (reprint from #127) (originally
called "Star Tracks")

Page 21 – Cracked Space Lens (new)

Page 24 – Interplanetary Magazines – Bill Everett (reprint from #8)

Page 26 – Cracked Interviews Star Warts Creator George Lucre – John
Severin (reprint from #200)

Page 30 – Cloning: The Advantages and the Disadvantages – Howard
Nostrand (reprint from #154)

Page 32 – Star People Weekly and Creatures and Things Magazine –
John Severin (reprint from #148)

Page 37 – Hudd & Dini (rocket) – Vic Martin (reprint from #87)

Page 38 – Cracked Space Helmets – John Severin (reprint from #25)

Page 40 – Cracked Interviews the Trekker King – Bill Ward (reprint
from #169)

Page 45 – Vacation Guide to Outer Space – John Severin (reprint from
#39)

Page 49 – Cracked Alien Trading Cards – Basil Wolverton (new, but
reprints artwork from "Flashes from Outer Space" from #10)

Page 53 – The American Space Base on Mars – John Severin (reprint
from #32)

Page 55 – Allien and How to Watch it – John Severin (reprint from
#164)

Page 62 – The Uggly Family "My Real Weird Science Project" – Stosh
Gillespie (Dan Clowes) / Eel O'Brian (Mort Todd) (new)

Page 67 – The Cracked Extra Terrestrial Game – Mike Ricigliano
(reprint from *Giant Cracked Fun-Kit* #34)

Page 83 – It Happened on Main and First – Caracu (reprint from #103)

Back Cover – Sylvester P. Smythe Poster – John Severin (reprint from
#68)

***Giant Cracked TV Scream* #44, July 1986 (84 pages) ($2.00)**

Cover – TV Scream – Bob Fingerman (new)

Page 2 – Welcome to the Cracked TV Scream – John Severin (reprint
from #75)

Page 3 - Contents

Page 4 – Gunsmokes – Russ Heath (reprint from #1)

Page 7 – Highway Parole – Bill McCartney (Bill Ward) (reprint from #2)

Page 10 – Perry Masonry – John Severin (reprint from #10)

Page 12 – Peter Goon – Jack Davis (reprint from #12)

Page 15 – Television and Real Life – John Severin (reprint from #16)

Page 17 – Cracked Visits the Munsters (reprint from #52)

Page 18 – Batzman Meets the Green Horned Bee! – M & O.O. Severin (Marie Severin, John Severin) (reprint from #74)

Page 24 – It's a Weird, Weird, Weird, Weird, Weird World (reprint from #86)

Page 25 – "Make Me a Deal" – Bill McCartney (Bill Ward) (reprint from #88)

Page 28 – Rowan and Martin's Laugh-In – John Severin (reprint from #73)

Page 30 – The Brainy Bunch – John Severin (reprint from #89)

Page 35 – Kung-Phew – John Severin (reprint from #112)

Page 40 – Cracked Traces a Spinoff – John Severin (reprint from #127)

Page 44 – A Cracked History of the Bionic Man – Nireves (John Severin) (reprint from #136)

Page 48 – Leverne and Shurley (we have dates with men) – John Severin (reprint from #145)

Page 54 – M*U*S*H (Mail call!) – John Severin (reprint from #159)

Page 60 – The JR Family Photo Album – John Severin (reprint from #181)

Page 63 – The Wildest and Weirdest Love Boat Cruise of Them All – John Severin (reprint from #187)

Page 69 – Ye Hang Ups (Elric) – C.E. Severin (Catherine Severin) (reprint from #175)

Page 70 – The A-Team Way of Doing Things – O.O. Severin (John Severin) (reprint from #204)

Page 73 – The Silly Cosbey Show – John Severin (reprint from #212)

Page 76 – The Giant Cracked Television Trivia Test – John Severin, Jack Davis, John Reiner (new)

Page 83 – Happy-Daze Shut-Ups (I have a date) – Powers (John Severin) (reprint from #157)

Back Cover – Cracked TV Comedy Classics – John Severin, Jack Davis (partial reprints from #119, 145, 182, 201 among others)

Giant Cracked #45, October 1986 (84 pages) ($2.00)

Cover – Giant History of Cracked – Bill Wray (new)

Page 2 and 83 – Cracked Cover Gallery (new and reprints from #1, 2, 6, 12)

Page 3 – Contents

Page 4 – The Story Behind the Stories! (new)

Page 5 – Cracked Shut-Ups (Europe) – Bill McCartney (Bill Ward) (reprint from #2)

Page 6 – American Grandstand – John Severin (reprint from #2)

Page 8 – Psychological Predictions – Bill Elder (reprint from #6)

Page 10 – So You Think It's Easy to Buy Cracked? – John Severin (reprint from #6)

Page 13 – Cracked Brings You Greetings – Bill Everett (reprint from #1)

Page 14 – The Last of the Hollywood "B" Movies – Gray Morrow (reprint from #8)

Page 17 – A Beatnik Goes to a Party – Jack Davis (reprint from #12)

Page 19 – Those False Rumors About Cracked Magazine – John Severin / George Gladir (reprint from #25)

Page 23 – Big-John is Coming – LePoer (John Severin) (reprint from #31)

Page 27 – Shut-Ups (20 cents) – Rodrigliani (Charles Rodrigues) (reprint from #46)

Page 28 – The Flipsides! – C.O. Severin (John Severin) / George Gladir (reprint from #52)

Page 32 – The Cracked Office as it Would be Portrayed on TV – John Severin (new)

Page 34 – Sagebrush (don't lag behind) – John Severin (reprint from *King-Sized Cracked* #5)

Page 36 – Commercializing the Moon – John Severin (reprint from #81)

Page 40 – Hudd & Dini (garbage cans) – Vic Martin (reprint from #82)

Page 41 – Hawk – John Severin (reprint from #105)

Page 45 – The First Dollar – Bernard Baily (reprint from #107)

Page 46 – A Cracked History of the Movies – Vic Martin (reprint from #109)

Page 47 – Ye Hang Ups (Skrunch) – Nireves (John Severin) (reprint from #114) / Ye Hang Ups #3 (He hates to drink alone) – John Severin (reprint from #115)

Page 51 – If We Didn't Have Hair – John Severin (reprint from #115)

Page 54 – Cracked Interviews the Advertising King – Bill Ward (reprint from #117)

Page 59 – Late One Evening – Howard Nostrand (reprint from #142)

Page 60 – Cracked Looks at the T-Shirt Craze – Howard Nostrand (reprint from #143)

Page 62 – Shut-Ups (I think I can K.O.) – Don Orehek (reprint from #145)

Page 63 – Star-Warz – O.O. Severin (John Severin) / Joe Catalano (reprint from #146)

Page 70 – The Cracked Lens (reprint from #154)

Page 72 – King Author and the Knights of the Reserved Table – John Severin (reprint from #171)

Page 79 – Magazines That Tried to Copy Cracked, But Failed – M.E. Tate (John Severin) (reprint from #212)

Back Cover – A Giant History of Cracked – John Severin (reprint from #17)

Giant Cracked #46 (*John Severin*), January 1987 (84 pages) ($2.00)

Cover – Unfinished Sylvester a la Washington – John Severin (reprint from #23)

Page 2 – Story of the Month (Whoa, Bessie) – John Severin (reprint from #27)

Page 3 – Contents

Page 4 – The $64,000,000 Cracked-Pot Question – John Severin (reprint from #1)

Page 6 – It Shouldn't Happen to a Dog – LePoer (John Severin) (reprint from #4)

Page 7 – French Forlorn Legion – John Severin (reprint from #4)

Page 10 – 'Enry 'Iggins of Scotland Yard – John Severin (reprint from #5)

Page 13 – Romeo and Juliet – John Severin (reprint from #8)

Page 16 – Alaska – John Severin (reprint from #8)

Page 19 – Baseball Statisticiatic – John Severin (reprint from #10)

Page 22 – Rate Your Personality – LePoer (John Severin) (reprint from #12)

Page 24 – Do-it-Yourself Captions – John Severin (reprint from #15)

Page 26 – Shakespearean Shut-Ups (Romeo) – John Severin (reprint from #17)

Page 28 – De Queers Rhinestone Co. ad – John Severin (reprint from #66)

Page 29 – The Unsociables ad – John Severin (reprint from #16)

Page 30 – At the Art Gallery – J. Lewis (John Severin) / Jay Lynch (reprint from #27)

Page 32 – Curvy Sewer Cognac ad – John Severin (reprint from #28)

Page 33 – Clan Clinkers – John Severin (reprint from #28)

Page 38 – Mother Goose Confidential – John Severin (reprint from #29)

Page 40 – The Dream Came True – LePoer (John Severin) (reprint from #31)

Page 44 – Cracked Looks at Hunting and Fishing – LePoer (John Severin) (reprint from #86)

Page 46 – Hurry-Ups (house on fire) – John Severin (reprint from #32)

Page 47 – The Steve Allen Show! – John Severin (reprint from #34)

Page 53 – Beastyrust ad – John Severin (reprint from #39)

Page 54 – The Art of Kissing – LePoer – John Severin (reprint from #39)

Page 56 – A Martian Writes Home from Earth – John Severin (reprint from #40)

Page 58 – Get Out the Vote! – John Severin (reprint from #51)

Page 59 – Super Fan-Elan – John Severin (reprint from #51)

Page 63 – Room 5C – Sigbjorn (John Severin) (reprint from #59)

Page 67 – A Cracked Look at Photography – O.O. Severin (John Severin) (reprint from #63)

Page 72 – The Lone Rancher – O.O. Severin (John Severin) (reprint from #65)

Page 74 – Cracked's Snappy Comebacks! – John Severin (reprint from #75)

Page 76 – The Condemned Man – John Severin (reprint from #64)

Page 77 – Editor's Note – John Severin (new)

Page 78 – Help! I'm in the Pacific – Edvard Severin (John Severin) / Stu Schwartzberg (reprint from #79)

Page 83 – Ocean ad – John Severin (reprint from #15)

Back Cover – The Cracked Cover Art of John Severin (reprints from #8, 13, 22, 27, 28, 31, 40, 45, 53, 65, 69) (same images that were used for the stickers in #146)

Giant Cracked #47, Winter 1988 (100 pages) ($3.25)

Cover – The Giant Cracked Book of Shut-Ups (newlyweds) – Don Orehek (new)

Page 2 – Rare Olde Shut-Upf – Jack Davis (reprint from #16)

Page 3 – Contents Shut-Ups (hold my hand) – Don Orehek (new) (red color added)

Page 4 – Shut-Ups (prison reforms) – Noah Sark (Charles Rodrigues) (reprint from #106) (red color added)

Page 5 – Shut-Ups (what he sees in her) – Norman Rockwell (Charles Rodrigues) (reprint from #107) (red color added)

Page 6 – Shut-Ups (I remember) – Charles Rodrigues (reprint from #108) (red color added)

Page 7 – Shut-Ups (plastic surgery) – Charles Rodrigues (reprint from #109) (red color added)

Page 8 – Shut-Ups (bad luck to see bride) – Sam Gross Jr. (Charles Rodrigues) (reprint from #110) (red color added)

Page 9 – Shut-Ups (SHA-LLALA-KOO) – Charles Rodrigues (reprint from #111) (red color added)

Page 10 – Shut-Ups (fire escape) – Charles Rodrigues (reprint from #112) (red color added)

Page 11 – Shut-Ups (practice your violin) – Charles Rodrigues (reprint from #113)

Page 12 – Shut-Ups (shoplifting) – Charles Rodrigues (reprint from #114) (second page only)

Page 13 – Shut-Ups (difficult time) – Charles Rodrigues (reprint from #115)

Page 14 – Shut-Ups (curtain about to go up) – Charles Rodrigues (reprint from #116)

Page 15 – Shut-Ups (electronic calculator) – Charles Rodrigues (reprint from #117)

Page 16 – Shut-Ups (Here's his picture) – Charles Rodrigues (reprint from #118)

Page 17 – Shut-Ups (deadbeats) – Charles Rodrigues (reprint from #119)

Page 18 – Shut-Ups (grown man playing with a doll) – Charles Rodrigues (reprint from #120)

Page 19 – Shut-Ups (ain't got no horses) – Charles Rodrigues (reprint from #121)

Page 20 – Shut-Ups (new highway) – Charles Rodrigues (reprint from #122)

Page 21 – Shut-Ups (Helen doesn't mean anything) – Charles Rodrigues (reprint from #124)

Page 22 – Shut-Ups (KUH-RRRAK!) – Charles Rodrigues (reprint from #125)

Page 23 – Shut-Ups (good year) – Charles Rodrigues (reprint from #126)

Page 24 – Shut-Ups (manage our budget) – Charles Rodrigues (reprint from #127)

Page 25 – Shut-Ups (provide a blindfold) – Charles Rodrigues (reprint from #128)

Page 26 – Shut-Ups (black belt) – Charles Rodrigues (reprint from #129)

Page 27 – Shut-Ups (uncomfortable) – Charles Rodrigues (reprint from #130)

Page 28 – Shut-Ups (It's a mirage) – Charles Rodrigues (reprint from #131)

Page 29 – Shut-Ups (stopping the fight) – Charles Rodrigues (reprint from #132)

Page 30 – Shut-Ups (flight show movies) – Charles Rodrigues (reprint from #133)

Page 31 – Shut-Ups (good clean fight) – Mike Ricigliano (reprint from #134)

Page 32 – Shut-Ups (the score's tied) – Mike Ricigliano (reprint from #135)
Page 33 – Shut-Ups (let's go out dancing) – Mike Ricigliano (reprint from #136)
Page 34 – Shut-Ups (Have a good time!) – Mike Ricigliano (reprint from #138)
Page 35 – Shut-Ups (set up camp) – Mike Ricigliano (reprint from #139)
Page 36 – Shut-Ups (outlawing handguns) – Mike Ricigliano (reprint from #140)
Page 37 – Shut-Ups (Abra-kadabra) – Mike Ricigliano (reprint from #141)
Page 38 – Shut-Ups (put his footprints) – Mike Ricigliano (reprint from #142)
Page 39 – Shut-Ups (My debts) – Mike Ricigliano (reprint from #143)
Page 40 – Shut-Ups (66…45…38) – Mike Ricigliano (reprint from #144)
Page 41 – Shut-Ups (I think I can K.O.) – Don Orehek (reprint from #145)
Page 42 – Shut-Ups (Folkswagon Bunny) – Don Orehek (reprint from #146)
Page 43 – Shut-Ups (make up my mind) – Don Orehek (reprint from #147)
Page 44 – Shut-Ups (best nap) – Don Orehek (reprint from #148)
Page 45 – Shut-Ups (take it from the top) – Don Orehek (reprint from #149)
Page 46 – Shut-Ups (Hollywood contract) – Don Orehek (reprint from #150)
Page 47 – Shut-Ups (I like my new job) – Don Orehek (reprint from #151)
Page 48 – Shut-Ups (Who goes there?) – Don Orehek (reprint from #152)
Page 49 – Shut-Ups (losing your hair) – Don Orehek (reprint from #153)
Page 50 – Shut-Ups (I object) – Don Orehek (reprint from #155)
Page 51 – Shut-Ups (not going to forgive) – Don Orehek (reprint from #154)
Page 52 – Shut-Ups (Squeaky's breaking out) – Don Orehek (reprint from #156)
Page 53 – Shut-Ups (big game) – Don Orehek (reprint from #157)
Page 54 – Shut-Ups (start off this auction) – Don Orehek (reprint from #158)
Page 55 – Shut-Ups (best tattoo jobs) – Don Orehek (reprint from #159)

Page 56 – Shut-Ups (any other questions) – Don Orehek (reprint from #160)
Page 57 – Shut-Ups (play like you never played) – Don Orehek (reprint from #166)
Page 58 – Shut-Ups (married 25 years) – Don Orehek (reprint from #167)
Page 59 – Shut-Ups (big struggle) – Don Orehek (reprint from #168)
Page 60 – Shut-Ups (put out the dog) – Don Orehek (reprint from #169)
Page 61 – Shut-Ups (money and credit cards) – Don Orehek (reprint from #170)
Page 62 – Shut-Ups (our little diet) – Don Orehek (reprint from #161)
Page 63 – Shut-Ups (drive away your customers) – Don Orehek (reprint from #162)
Page 64 – Shut-Ups (I LOVE a parade) – Don Orehek (reprint from #163)
Page 65 – Shut-Ups (pastrami on rye) – Don Orehek (reprint from #164)
Page 66 – Shut-Ups (your eyes) – Don Orehek (reprint from #165)
Page 67 – Shut-Ups (flat tire) – Don Orehek (reprint from #173)
Page 68 – Shut-Ups (my greatest work of art) – Don Orehek (reprint from #174)
Page 69 – Shut-Ups (yellow-bellies) – Don Orehek (reprint from #175)
Page 70 – Shut-Ups (man trying to break down door) – Don Orehek (reprint from #176)
Page 71 – Shut-Ups (Our son, the graduate) – Don Orehek (reprint from #177)
Page 72 – Shut-Ups (2 voice lessons) – Don Orehek (reprint from #178)
Page 73 – Shut-Ups (horn section) – Don Orehek (reprint from #179)
Page 74 – Shut-Ups (supreme court) – Charles Rodrigues (reprint from #180)
Page 75 – Shut-Ups (To err is human) – Don Orehek (reprint from #181)
Page 76 – Shut-Ups (How do you address a king) – Charles Rodrigues (reprint from #183)
Page 77 – Shut-Ups (Mad Doctors' Monsters!) – Charles Rodrigues (reprint from #184)
Page 78 – Shut-Ups (writing a book) – Don Orehek (reprint from #185)
Page 79 – Shut-Ups (graduating class) – Charles Rodrigues (reprint from #186)
Page 80 – Shut-Ups (wanted a two wheeler) – Don Orehek (reprint from #187)
Page 81 – Shut-Ups (It takes a smart man) – Don Orehek (reprint from #188)

Page 82 – Shut-Ups (piece of my mind) – Don Orehek (reprint from #189)

Page 83 – Shut-Ups (wrap it up) – Don Orehek (reprint from #190)

Page 84 – Shut-Ups (road to Las Vegas) – Don Orehek (reprint from #192)

Page 85 – Shut-Ups (money out of the bank) – Don Orehek (reprint from #193)

Page 86 – Shut-Ups (pole-vaulting) – Don Orehek (reprint from #194)

Page 87 – Shut-Ups (aluminum siding) – Don Orehek (reprint from #195)

Page 88 – Shut-Ups (quick-acting remedy) – Don Orehek (reprint from #196)

Page 89 – Shut-Ups (bird imitations) – Don Orehek (reprint from #197)

Page 90 – Shut-Ups (one more quarter) – Don Orehek (reprint from #198)

Page 91 – Shut-Ups (man cannot live on bread) – Don Orehek (reprint from #199) (red color added)

Page 92 – Shut-Ups (Pate de Fois Gros) – Don Orehek (reprint from #200) (red color added)

Page 93 – Shut-Ups (start off this auction) – Don Orehek (reprint from #158) (red color added)

Page 94 – Shut-Ups (Checkmate!!) – Don Orehek (reprint from #203) (red color added)

Page 95 – Shut-Ups (cable, let's get it installed) – Don Orehek (reprint from #204) (red color added)

Page 96 – Shut-Ups (missing a great show) – Don Orehek (reprint from #205) (red color added)

Page 97 – Shut-Ups (such a dump) – Don Orehek (reprint from #206) (red color added)

Page 98 – Shut Up and Get it Over With! – Jared Lee (reprint from #101)

Page 99 – Shut-Ups! (tie clasps) – Rodrigliani (Charles Rodrigues) (reprint from #56)

Back Cover – Shut-Ups! (stick-in-the-mud) – Vito Montigliani (Charles Rodrigues) (reprint from #73) (color added)

Giant Cracked #48, Winter 1989 (100 pages) ($2.75)

Cover – Wild Weird Western Laughs & Thrills – John Severin (reprint from #39 and *Cracked Collectors' Edition* #9)

Page 2 and 99 – (wild west gags) – John Severin (originally called "OKKO Corral") (partial reprint from #4)

Page 3 – Contents

Page 4 – The Lone Ranger (reprint from #38)

Page 5 – Bat Masteyson – Jack Davis (reprint from #13)

Page 9 – Famous Scenes from Great Western Movies – John Severin (reprint from #43)

Page 11 – The Train Robber – Bill McCartney (Bill Ward) (reprint from #34)

Page 12 – When the West Was Fun! (reprint from #53)

Page 14 – Kung-Phew – John Severin (reprint from #112)

Page 19 – The Quickest Fun in the West (reprint from #77)

Page 21 – How to Become a Writer of Westerns – John Severin (reprint from #79)

Page 23 – Have Gun Won't Travel – Bill McCartney (Bill Ward) (reprint from #5)

Page 26 – The Owlhoots (reprint from #98)

Page 28 – McClod – Nireves (John Severin) (reprint from #111)

Page 33 – Famous Scenes from Great Indian-Type Movies! – Vic Martin (reprint from #59)

Page 34 – The Adventures of the Masked Bandito – John Severin (reprint from #157)

Page 40 – Gunsmokes – Russ Heath (reprint from #1)

Page 43 – Sagebrush (can't hold on) – John Severin (reprint from *Cracked Collectors' Edition* #5) (red color added)

Page 44 – Sagebrush (heavy pack) – John Severin (reprint from *Cracked Collectors' Edition* #9) (red color added)

Page 45 – Sagebrush (see them a-tumblin' down) – John Severin (reprint from *Cracked Collectors' Edition* #9) (red color added)

Page 46 – Sagebrush (think we can make it) – John Severin (reprint from *Cracked Collectors' Edition* #9) (red color added)

Page 47 – Sagebrush (barrel cactus) – John Severin (reprint from *Cracked Collectors' Edition* #9) (red color added)

Page 48 – Sagebrush (buffalo stampede) – John Severin (reprint from #91) (red color added)

Page 49 – Sagebrush (disguise yourself) – John Severin (reprint from *Cracked Collectors' Edition* #9) (red color added)

Page 50 – Sagebrush (YIPE!) – John Severin (reprint from *Cracked Collectors' Edition* #9) (red color added)

Page 51 – Sagebrush (SHMUNCH!) – John Severin (reprint from *Cracked Collectors' Edition* #9) (red color added)

Page 52 – Sagebrush (primitive arrows) – John Severin (reprint from *Cracked Collectors' Edition* #9) (red color added)

Page 53 – Sagebrush (Lil' Bear sends message) – John Severin (reprint from *Cracked Collectors' Edition* #9) (red color added)

Page 54 – Sagebrush (crossing the desert) – John Severin (reprint from #86) (red color added)

Page 55 – Sagebrush (Happy Anniversary) – John Severin (reprint from *Cracked Collectors' Edition* #9) (red color added)

Page 56 – Sagebrush (BOM-BIDDY) – John Severin (reprint from *Cracked Collectors' Edition* #9) (red color added)

Page 57 – Sagebrush (such a bad character) – John Severin (reprint from *Cracked Collectors' Edition* #9) (red color added)

Page 58 – Sagebrush (bubble-nose) – John Severin (reprint from *Cracked Collectors' Edition* #9) (red color added)

Page 59 – Civil War Facts – Jack Davis (reprint from #12)

Page 62 – Rollicking with Robert Redford (reprint from #92)

Page 64 – The True Story of The Lone Ranger – Brian Buniak (reprint from #198)

Page 67 – Hi! I'm Johnny Cashew! – John Severin (reprint from #93)

Page 72 – The Good Guys (reprint from #97)

Page 74 – Cracked Takes a Seat at Custer's Last Stand – Bill McCartney (Bill Ward) (reprint from #90)

Page 76 – Dan Coyote-Man of La Rancha – John Severin (reprint from #113)

Page 82 – Right from the Horse's Mouth (reprint from #46)

Page 84 – Rodeo Riders – Bill McCartney (Bill Ward) (reprint from #69)

Page 88 – Cracked Rides West! (reprint from #67)

Page 90 – He's Really a Lone Ranger Now! – Bill Ward (reprint from #1)

Page 91 – Silly Jack – Nireves (John Severin) (reprint from #116)

Page 96 – How the West was Lost (reprint from #39)

Page 98 – The Last Shot – Bob Zahn (reprint from #47)

Back Cover – Great Moments in Dentistry 1755 – Howard Nostrand (reprint from #143)

The First King-Sized Cracked Annual, 1967 (92 pages) (50c)

Cover – Celebrity Jalopy – O.O. Severin (John Severin) (new)

Page 2 – Ramington Shavers ad – John Severin (reprint from #24)

Page 3 – Contents

Page 4 – Cracked Takes a Look at Supermarkets – John Severin (reprint from #36)

Page 9 – The Sailing of the Vikings – John Severin (reprint from #18)

Page 11 – Beautyrester ad – John Severin (reprint from #18)

Page 12 – Their Dreams Almost Came True – Bill McCartney (Bill Ward) (reprint from #35)

Page 16 – McNasty's Great 3 Days Only Sale – Bill McCartney (Bill Ward) (reprint from #35)

Page 18 – There's One in Every Crowd – Bill McCartney (Bill Ward) (reprint from #9)

Page 20 – If – John Severin (reprint from #17)

Page 22 – Union Cards for Organized Crime – John Severin (reprint from #17)

Page 24 – A Cracked Alphabet Book for Home Owners – John Severin (reprint from #41)

Page 26 – Cracked Sympathy Cards (reprint from #20)

Page 30 – The Little World of Don Swanson (chinning hanger) – Don Swanson (reprint from #20)

Page 31 – Millionaire Magazine – John Severin (reprint from #34)

Page 37 – Board Her, Men! – Bill McCartney (Bill Ward) (reprint from #35)

Page 38 – Mixed Up Pocketbooks – Bill Elder (reprint from #12)

Page 40 – Nursery Rhymes (reprint from #15)

Page 42 – Cracked Fun Shoppe ad – John Severin / Horror House ad – John Severin

Page 43 – Occupational Calendars – John Severin (reprint from #16)

Page 44 – Boys and Girls Together (reprint from #44)

Page 48 – Cracked Looks at Old-Time Songs – Angel Martinez (reprint from #17)

Page 52 – Don't Throw Away Anything! – John Severin (reprint from #36)

Page 54 – Sylvester's Photo Album – John Severin (reprint from #35)

Page 58 – Mixed-Up Pocket Books – Vic Martin (reprint from #22)

Page 59 – Transylvania Life ad – John Severin (reprint from #35)

Page 60 – The Motel 40-Yard Line – John Severin (reprint from #41)

Page 64 – Wild Record Albums – Bill McCartney (Bill Ward) (reprint from #13)

Page 66 – American Commercials in Foreign Lands – Bill McCartney (Bill Ward) (reprint from #34)

Page 67 – How to Understand Sports Officials' Signals – Bill McCartney (Bill Ward) (reprint from #36)

Page 70 – Russian Magazines – Bill Elder (reprint from #13)

Page 72 – Television and Real Life – John Severin (reprint from #16)

Page 74 – Hurry-Ups (Sarge is pinned) – Bill McCartney (Bill Ward) (reprint from #36)

Page 75 – Cracked Gamesmanship for Sore Losers – Tony Tallarico (new)

Page 91 – Three Annuals (*Biggest* 2; *Giant* 2, 3) / Four Paperbacks / Back Issues ad (#56-63)

Back Cover – Brand X Cigarette Box Cut-Out (reprint from #12)

The Second King-Sized Cracked Annual, 1968 (92 pages) (50c)

Cover – Cracked Carnival of Fun – John Severin (new)

Page 2 – Six Annuals (*Biggest* 2, 3; *Giant* 3, 4; *King-Sized* 1; *Super* 1) ."
Three Paperbacks / Back Issues ad (#66-73)

Page 3 – Contents

Page 4 – Merry Old England Life ad (reprint from #47)

Page 5 – Age Rage Ad Fad – John Severin (reprint from #28)

Page 8 – Alaska – John Severin (reprint from #8)

Page 11 – The Horn – Bill McCartney (Bill Ward) (reprint from #32)

Page 13 – Screen Screams (reprint from #55)

Page 14 – Everybody's Got Something to Be Thankful For – Angelo
Torres (reprint from #7)

Page 16 – Cracked's Observation Test (reprint from #3)

Page 18 – Western Onion ad – John Severin (reprint from #17)

Page 19 – If Big League Business Takes Over Little League Baseball –
John Severin (reprint from #23)

Page 24 – The Breaking Point – Bill McCartney (Bill Ward) (reprint
from #2)

Page 25 – Famous Scenes from Great Monster Movies! – Vic Martin
(reprint from #56)

Page 27 – Believe it or No! – Jack Davis (reprint from #11)

Page 28 – Illustrated Limericks – Jack Davis (reprint from #15)

Page 30 – Six is the Number (reprint from #40)

Page 31 – If Different Personalities Played Tarzan – John Severin
(reprint from #60)

Page 35 – National Advertising – John Severin (reprint from #11)

Page 38 – Cracked Takes a Look at Skiing – Bill McCartney (Bill Ward)
(reprint from #48)

Page 40 – Cracked Brings You Greetings – Bill Everett (reprint from #_)

Page 42 – If Wedding Cakes Really Symbolized Marriages – Bill
McCartney (Bill Ward) (reprint from #55)

Page 44 – Audience Participation Programs of the Future – John
Severin (reprint from #30)

Page 49 – Four Film Swingers (reprint from #55)

Page 50 – Travlers Cheques ad (reprint from *Zany* #3)

Page 51 – Cracked's Footprint Forecourt of History – John Severin
(reprint from #55)

Page 54 – The Cracked World of Children's TV Shows – Bill McCartney
(Bill Ward) (reprint from #53)

Page 56 – Where the Action is!!! (reprint from #58)

Page 58 – A Cracked Gallery of New Artists – Oswaldo Laino, John
Severin (reprint from #21)

Page 62 – It Shouldn't Happen to a Dog – LePoer (John Severin) (reprint from #4)

Page 63 – Cracked Fun Shoppe ad – John Severin

Page 64 – How a Rumor Gets Started – Al Jaffee (reprint from #7)

Page 66 – So You Think It's Easy to Buy Cracked? – John Severin (reprint from #6)

Page 69 – Horror House ad – John Severin

Page 70 – Future Jet Set Fads – John Severin (reprint from #41)

Page 74 – Hip Shut-Ups (I'm floatin') – John Severin (reprint from #11)

Page 75 – Cracked's Funny Flips – Tony Tallarico

Page 76 – Cracked Fun and Activity Book (32 pages)

Page 91 – Bunt's Catsup ad (reprint from #49)

Back Cover – Cool-School Stickers (reprint from #58)

The Third King-Sized Cracked Annual, 1969 (92 pages) (50c)

Cover – Celebrities on Ice – John Severin

Page 2 – Five Annuals (*Biggest* 4; *Giant* 5; *King-Sized* 1, 2; *Super* 2) / Back Issues ad (#75-82)

Page 3 – Contents

Page 4 – Clan Clinkers – John Severin (reprint from #28)

Page 9 – If Other Jobs Had the Pressures of Baseball – Bill McCartney (Bill Ward) (reprint from #54)

Page 12 – Accessories for Your Car – John Severin (reprint from #23)

Page 14 – Jungle Gems (reprint from #63)

Page 16 – Hilo Shampoo ad – Bill Everett (reprint from #9)

Page 17 – Make Mine Well Done! – John Langton (reprint from #62)

Page 18 – The Daily Atlantis – John Langton (reprint from #68)

Page 22 – Do-it-Yourself Captions – John Severin (reprint from #15)

Page 24 – Psychological Predictions – Bill Elder (reprint from #6)

Page 26 – By the Numbers (reprint from #50)

Page 27 – The Steve Allen Show! – John Severin (reprint from #34)

Page 33 – Look! Four Kooks! (reprint from #63)

Page 34 – Cultural Exchange – Bill McCartney (Bill Ward) (reprint from #3)

Page 36 – Are Comics Ruining Our Children? – Bill Elder (reprint from #11)

Page 38 – Brigitte Bardot as Seen by Different Artists – John Severin (reprint from #12)

Page 41 – Stories of the Month (I don't mean to be nosey) – Jerry Kirschen (reprint from #16)

Page 42 – Shakespearean Shut-Ups (Romeo) – John Severin (reprint from #17)

Page 44 – Great War Heroes – Jack Davis (reprint from #15)

Page 46 – Traffic in the Supermarket (reprint from #7)

Page 48 – A Glossary of Cracked Definitions – LePeor (John Severin) (reprint from #29)

Page 51 – Why People Move to the Suburbs – Jack Davis (reprint from #14)

Page 55 – The Big Wig Gig – Bill McCartney (Bill Ward) (reprint from #35)

Page 58 – The Pirate Treasure Chest (reprint from #64)

Page 60 – Read the Fine Print – Bill McCartney (Bill Ward) (reprint from #30)

Page 65 – Cracked Fun Shoppe ad – John Severin

Page 66 – Specialized Buildings – Oskar Blotta (reprint from #61)

Page 69 – Horror House ad – John Severin

Page 70 – Those False Rumors About Cracked Magazine – John Severin / George Gladir (reprint from #25)

Page 74 – Shut-Ups (jump) – Rodrigliani (Charles Rodrigues) (reprint from #55)

Page 75 – Cracked's King Size Jigsaw Puzzle – Jack Davis, John Severin

Page 91 – Pink Horses ad – John Severin (reprint from #23) (All references to white horses were changed to pink horses.)

Back Cover – Cracked Proverb Stickers (reprint from #25)

The Fourth King-Sized Cracked Annual, 1970 (92 pages) (50c)

Cover – Welcome to Cracked U. – John Severin

Page 2 – Six Annuals ad (*Biggest* 4, 5; *Giant* 6; *King-Sized* 2, 3; *Super* 3)

Page 3 – Contents

Page 4 – Planets of the Creatures - John Severin (reprint from #72)

Page 10 – The Flipsides! – O.O. Severin (John Severin) / George Gladir (reprint from #52)

Page 14 – Cracked Visits the Munsters (reprint from #52)

Page 15 – 11 Sure-Fire, Far-Out, Cool, New, Neat Ways to be Popular in College! – Joe Mead (reprint from #72)

Page 17 – The Cracked Museum of Historical Trivia – Tony Tallarico (reprint from #69)

Page 20 – Rent-a-Person – John Langton (reprint from #72)

Page 24 – Square Buttons for Squares (reprint from #70)

Page 26 – If Comic Strip Characters Had to Face Simple But Realistic Problems! – John Severin (reprint from #69)

Page 29 – The Suntan – Caracu (reprint from #70)

Page 30 – Lowering the Mental Level of TV Programs – John Severin (reprint from #70)

Page 34 – It Happened at the Cemetery – Caracu (reprint from #69)

The Fifth King-Sized Cracked Annual, 1971 (84 pages) (60¢)

Page 23 – The Marx Brothers Ride Again! (reprint from #75)
Page 26 – Guess Who…? – Bill McCartney (Bill Ward) (reprint from #76)
Page 28 – School for Baby Sitters – Vic Martin (reprint from #78)
Page 31 – Horror House ad – John Severin
Page 32 – Cracked Looks at Fishing – Vic Martin (reprint from #76)
Page 34 – A Modern Family Primer – Vic Martin (reprint from #72)
Page 38 – Why Does a Chicken Cross the Road? – Nellie Melba (Charles Rodrigues) (reprint from #76)
Page 40 – Cracked Fun Shoppe ad – John Severin
Page 41 – Sagebrush (don't lag behind) – John Severin (new)
Page 43 – How to Make Soccer Our National Pastime – John Langton (reprint from #72)
Page 45 – The Evil Experiment! – John Langton (reprint from #75)
Page 46 – Phone Services for Tots and Teens – John Severin (reprint from #28)
Page 51 – Hudd & Dini (missing key) – Vic Martin (reprint from #77)
Page 52 – How to Become a Comedy Writer – John Severin (reprint from #77)
Page 54 – A Kook Look at Sports (reprint from #76)
Page 56 – Go Fly a Kite – John Severin (reprint from #74)
Page 57 – Cracked's Snappy Comebacks! – John Severin (reprint from #75)
Page 59 – The Generation Gap! (reprint from #78)
Page 60 – The College Entrance Rat Race – John Langton (reprint from #75)
Page 64 – G.I. Laugh-In! (reprint from #75)
Page 66 – Shut-Ups (Ladies first) – Rodrigliani (Charles Rodrigues) (reprint from #77)
Page 67 – My Own Family Album (new)
Page 83 – ("Play bridge") Hollywood Bowl photo (reprint from #68)
Back Cover – Emergency Flap (reprint from #63)

The Sixth King-Sized Cracked Annual, 1972 (84 pages) (60c)

Cover – We Need New Quarters – John Severin (reprint from #22)
Page 2 – Six Annuals ad (Biggest 6, 7; Giant 7, 8; King-Sized 5; Super 5)
Page 3 – Contents
Page 4 – A Cracked Look at Supermarkets – Bill McCartney (Bill Ward) (reprint from #83)
Page 8 – Costume Party Type-Casting (reprint from #72)
Page 10 – Cautionary Labels for Teenage Products – John Severin (reprint from #76)

Page 12 – Sports Oddities – Tony Tallarico (reprint from #72)

Page 13 – The Cracked World of the Arts Primer – John Langton (reprint from #80)

Page 16 – Cracked Visits a Track Meet – Bill McCartney (Bill Ward) (reprint from #87)

Page 18 – The Smythes – Losers Throughout History! – John Severin (reprint from #75)

Page 20 – Horror House ad – John Severin

Page 21 – Now They're Hi-Jacking Everything! – Vic Martin (reprint from #78)

Page 24 – Cracked Visits a Hollywood Motion Picture Studio – John Langton (reprint from #78)

Page 26 – Reel Gone! (reprint from #54)

Page 27 – Guess the Question – Bob Taylor (reprint from #83)

Page 29 – Hudd & Dini (mousetrap) – Vic Martin (reprint from #83)

Page 30 – Cracked's Illustrated History – John Severin (reprint from #86)

Page 33 – Jogging Throughout History – John Severin (reprint from #82)

Page 37 – Cracked Fun Shoppe ad – John Severin

Page 38 – The Dream Came True – LePoer (John Severin) (reprint from #31)

Page 42 – Cracked Takes You Back to the Year 1075 BC! – Bill McCartney (Bill Ward) (reprint from #74)

Page 44 – Tiny Tim in Everything – John Severin (reprint from #75)

Page 47 – Destination Fun (reprint from #79)

Page 50 – A Cracked Look at Typographical Errors – John Langton (reprint from #80)

Page 52 – Sagebrush (He sure hates rattlers) – John Severin (reprint from #80)

Page 54 – The Pick-Up – John Severin (reprint from #34)

Page 55 – Astrological Horoscopes – John Severin (reprint from #83)

Page 59 – Celebrity Cookbooks – John Severin (reprint from #76)

Page 61 – Specialized Parties That Fit a Magazine – John Severin (reprint from #87)

Page 65 – Hudd & Dini (kite) – Vic Martin (reprint from #86)

Page 66 – Shut-Ups! (stick-in-the-mud) – Vito Montigliani (Charles Rodrigues) (reprint from #73)

Page 67 – 8 Posters (reprint from #79, 80, 86, 90, 92, 94, 95, 96)

Page 83 – Adolt Education! (reprint from #83)

Back Cover – Aberican Bedical Association – John Severin (reprint from #90)

The Seventh King-Sized Cracked Annual, 1973 (84 pages) (60c)

Cover – Karate – John Severin (reprint from #65)

Page 2 – Five Annuals ad (*Collectors* 2; *Giant* 8, 9; *King-Sized* 6; *Super* 6)

Page 3 – Contents

Page 4 – Underneath the Planet of the Apes – John Severin (reprint from #90)

Page 8 – Don't Believe a Word of it – John Severin (reprint from #82)

Page 10 – Tom Jones – John Severin (reprint from #85)

Page 14 – Halls of Smaller Fame – Bill McCartney (Bill Ward) (reprint from #93)

Page 17 – Hudd & Dini (cannon) – Vic Martin (reprint from #93)

Page 18 – Daze & Knights (reprint from #82)

Page 20 – The Cornship of Oddie's Father – John Severin (reprint from #86)

Page 25 – Cracked Magazine Presents 65-Man Klonkball – Bill McCartney (Bill Ward) (reprint from #52)

Page 28 – Sagebrush (water) – John Severin (reprint from #82)

Page 30 – Ballad of the Squeaky Voiced Cowboy – Joe Mead (reprint from #83)

Page 33 – Snap! Crackle! Flop! – Vic Martin (reprint from #93)

Page 36 – The Future Computerized of Sports – Bill McCartney (Bill Ward) (reprint from #93)

Page 40 – Hi! I'm Johnny Cashew! – John Severin (reprint from #93)

Page 45 – Trimming the Fat off the Budget – Bill McCartney (Bill Ward) (reprint from #82)

Page 48 – Songs That Never Quite Made it – John Severin (reprint from #83)

Page 50 – Chip Shots (reprint from #83)

Page 53 – Butch Cavity and the Sundrenched Kid – John Severin (reprint from #87)

Page 58 – Horror House ad – John Severin

Page 59 – Awards to Unsung Heroes – John Severin (reprint from #85)

Page 61 – Cracked Fun Shoppe ad – John Severin

Page 62 – Cracked Looks at Television Viewers – Bill McCartney (Bill Ward) (reprint from #85)

Page 66 – Medicinal Mirth (reprint from #85)

Page 67 – The Way-Out Watergate Coloring Book – John Langton (new)

Page 83 – Uncover America (reprint from #84)

Back Cover – Cadillack – John Severin (reprint from #85)

454 If You're *Cracked*, You're Happy, Book Too

The Eighth King-Sized Cracked Annual, 1974 (84 pages) (75c)

Cover – Shoes on the Wrong Feet – John Severin (reprint from #89)

Page 2 – Seven Annuals ad (*Biggest* 8; *Collectors* 2, 3; *Giant* 9, 10; *King-Sized* 6; *Super* 7)

Page 3 – Contents

Page 4 – The Ghost and Mrs. Mire – John Severin (reprint from #83)

Page 9 – A Look at Correspondence Courses – John Langton (reprint from #79)

Page 13 – The Growing Garbage Garble – John Severin (reprint from #69)

Page 17 – Famous Stars in Ads We'd Like to See (reprint from #95)

Page 20 – The Put-Downers – Vic Martin (reprint from #106)

Page 22 – The Parakeet – John Severin (reprint from #77)

Page 23 – Rosemary's Baby Devlin – Lugoze (reprint from #76)

Page 26 – Cracked Looks at Vacations – Bill McCartney (Bill Ward) (reprint from #96)

Page 29 – Family Albums of Celebrities – John Severin (reprint from #14)

Page 32 – Rodrigues' Side Show – Charles Rodrigues (reprint from #106)

Page 35 – Hudd & Dini (prison bars) – Vic Martin (reprint from #81)

Page 37 – Great Scenes from Hollywood Movies if Shakespeare Had Written Them! – Bob Taylor (reprint from #95)

Page 40 – A Cracked Look at Desert Islands – Lugoze (reprint from #77)

Page 42 – The Day Comic Strip Characters Got up on the Wrong Side of Bed – John Severin (reprint from #76)

Page 45 – Cracked Interviews the Industrial King – John Langton (reprint from #106)

Page 50 – Cracked Looks at Dating – Bill McCartney (Bill Ward) (reprint from #76)

Page 54 – Status Symbols for Dogs! – John Severin (reprint from #86)

Page 56 – The Cracked Travel Primer – Tony Tallarico (reprint from #76)

Page 60 – Service-O-Mats of the Future – John Severin (reprint from #25)

Page 64 – Cracked Looks at Fishing – Vic Martin (reprint from #76)

Page 66 – Shut-Ups (prison reforms) – Noah Sark (Charles Rodrigues) (reprint from #106)

Page 67 – The Game of Inflation – John Severin

Page 83 – Binders and notebooks ad

Back Cover – Greetings from Brooklyn Postcard – John Severin (reprint from #38)

***The Ninth King-Sized Cracked Annual*, 1975 (84 pages) ($1.00)**

Cover – Shadow Boxing – John Severin (reprint from #94)

Page 2 – Binders and Notebooks ad 2

Page 3 – Contents

Page 4 – The Candidaze – John Severin (reprint from #107)

Page 9 – How to Translate Travel Ads – Bob Taylor (reprint from #108)

Page 12 – The Cracked School of Applied Nuttiness – Jack Barrett (reprint from #103)

Page 14 – If Other Civil Servants Tried to Hustle on the Side Like the Astronauts – Dick Wright (reprint from #110)

Page 18 – Cracked Looks at Drivers – Bill Ward (reprint from #111)

Page 22 – If Archie Bunker Took Over the Leads in Other TV Series – John Severin (reprint from #108)

Page 26 – Cracked's Catchy First Lines For – Don Orehek (reprint from #111)

Page 28 – Black Movie Monsters – LePoer (John Severin) (reprint from #111)

Page 33 – How to Reduce Wedding Costs – John Langton (reprint from #111)

Page 37 – Pop! Population Explosion – Jack Barrett / Ron Wiggins (reprint from #101)

Page 40 – Trouble at the Reducing Clinic or The Weighty Problem – Bernard Baily / Joe Catalano (reprint from #111)

Page 44 – A Cracked History of Gambling – Bill Ward (reprint from #110)

Page 48 – The World of Mr. Orehek – Don Orehek (reprint from #109)

Page 50 – Dickie Von Dork Show – Nireves (John Severin) (reprint from #109)

Page 55 – The Class of 1932 – Bob Taylor (reprint from #103)

Page 58 – With-it Nursery Rhymes – Bill McCartney (Bill Ward) (reprint from #101)

Page 60 – Cracked Interviews the Consumer King – Powers (John Severin) (reprint from #110)

Page 66 – Hudd & Dini (saint Bernard) – Vic Martin (reprint from #108)

Page 67 – The Newest Cracked "Flip the Faces" Book – John Severin (revised reprint from *Giant Cracked* #3)

Page 83 – The Cracked Bookstore ad – John Severin

Back Cover – Nader Raider Blasts Boss – Charles Rodrigues (reprint from #109)

The Tenth King-Sized Cracked Annual, 1976 (84 pages) ($1.00)
   Cover – Let's Make America Beautiful Again! – John Severin (reprint
      from #116)
   Page 2 – The Cracked Bookstore ad – John Severin
   Page 3 – Contents
   Page 4 – High Plains Shifter – John Severin (reprint from #117)
   Page 10 – A Look at Typical Family Gathering – Don Orehek (reprint
      from #119)
   Page 14 – Cracked's Solution for Solving the Energy Crisis – Bill Ward
      (reprint from #117)
   Page 19 – Understanding Hi-Fidelity – John Langton (reprint from
      #118)
   Page 23 – Cracked Interviews the Advertising King – Bill Ward (reprint
      from #117)
   Page 28 – The Big City Versus the Small Town – Bernard Baily (reprint
      from #117)
   Page 31 – The Cracked History of Art – John Langton (reprint from #117)
   Page 35 – Pet Plaza – Bill Ward (reprint from #118)
   Page 40 – The Cracked Manual for Good Photography – John Langton
      (reprint from #115)
   Page 45 – Cracked Do-it-Yourself Divorce – Don Orehek (reprint from
      #119)
   Page 48 – Magnificent Mae West (reprint from #89)
   Page 49 – How to Buy a New Car – Bernard Baily (reprint from #119)
   Page 53 – Martial Art Weapons and Techniques – Bill Ward (reprint
      from #118)
   Page 56 – New Methods Banks Can Use to Attract Customers – John
      Langton (reprint from #119)
   Page 60 – Cracked Interviews the Housing King – Sigbjorn (John
      Severin) (reprint from #116)
   Page 65 – Guest Appearances by the World's Top Humor Artists – Don
      Orehek (reprint from #106)
   Page 67 – Cracked's Fonz for President Game – John Severin
   Page 83 – T.V. Tally Ho Ho's (reprint from #65)
   Back Cover – Who'd She Expect…Richard Burton? – Bill McCartney
      (Bill Ward) (reprint from #4)

The Eleventh King-Sized Cracked Annual, 1977 (84 pages) ($1.00)
   Cover – Surfing Sylvester – John Severin (reprint from #86)
   Page 2 – The Cracked Bookstore ad – John Severin
   Page 3 – Contents
   Page 4 – Laff and Let Die – O.O. Severin (John Severin) (reprint from #116)

Page 10 – A Cracked Look at a High School – Bill Ward (reprint from #116)

Page 13 – The Seers Rubbish Catalog of Useless Items for 1974 – John Langton (reprint from #117)

Page 18 – A Rodrigues Wedding Reception – Charles Rodrigues (reprint from #118)

Page 20 – A Short Look at a Long Gas Line – Bill Ward (reprint from #118)

Page 23 – If We Didn't Have Hair – John Severin (reprint from #115)

Page 26 – The Thrill of the Flying Chartered – Bernard Baily / Joe Catalano (reprint from #115)

Page 30 – A Cracked Look at a Department Store – Don Orehek (reprint from #118)

Page 32 – New Methods Banks Can Use to Attract Customers – John Langton (reprint from #119)

Page 36 – If Comic Strip Characters Had to Face Simple But Realistic Problems! – John Severin (reprint from #69)

Page 39 – Just Bumming Around! – Tony Tallarico (reprint from #106)

Page 40 – The Cracked Guide to Tennis – Nat Ball (John Severin) (reprint from #120)

Page 45 – Tarzan's Abdication – Bill Ward (reprint from #113)

Page 50 – What Will Super K Do When He Leaves the Government? – Sururi Gumen (reprint from #124)

Page 53 – Cracked Interviews the Hospital King – John Severin (reprint from #112)

Page 58 – Rose Brawl Parade – Bob Taylor (reprint from #107)

Page 62 – The Cracked World of Snow – Sururi Gumen (reprint from #124)

Page 66 – The Monster – Sururi Gumen (reprint from #130)

Pave 67 – The Cracked Iron-On Kit – John Severin (reprint from #123)

Page 83 – Monster Laughs!!! (reprint from *For Monsters Only* #9)

Back Cover – The Man and the Beast – Oskar Blotta (reprint from #80)

The Twelfth King-Sized Cracked Annual, 1978 (84 pages) ($1.25)

Cover – Jawz – John Severin (reprint from #129)

Page 2 – The Cracked Bookstore ad – John Severin

Page 3 – Contents

Page 4 – Police Lady – John Severin (reprint from #128)

Page 9 – Cracked's Snide Guide to Motion Pictures – Bill McCartney (Bill Ward) (reprint from #80)

Page 11 – How a Rumor Gets Started – Al Jaffee (reprint from #7)

Page 13 – If the Help-Wanted Ads Mirrored Today's Inefficient Business World (reprint from #94)

Page 16 – Up-Dated Mechanical Banks – Sigbjorn (John Severin) (reprint from #50)

Page 20 – If Dolphin's Day Every Comes! – John Severin (reprint from #89)

Page 23 – Paranoia News Magazine – John Langton (reprint from #89)

Page 26 – Sincerely Yours, Sam Quarter – Bill McCartney (Bill Ward) (reprint from #95)

Page 30 – Learning to Fly – John Severin (reprint from #80)

Page 36 – Famous Events as Seen on the Isolated Camera – John Severin (reprint from #92)

Page 40 – The Dumb-Dumb People! – Lugoze (reprint from #77)

Page 42 – Non-Polluting Cars Auto Safety Devices – Jack Barrett (reprint from #101)

Page 46 – Cue Cards for Everyone – Bill McCartney (Bill Ward) (reprint from #73)

Page 51 – Ten Tips on How to Become Rich – Vic Martin (reprint from #103)

Page 53 – Cracked Interviews the Supermarket King – Sururi Gumen (reprint from #125)

Page 58 – Rent-a-Person – John Langton (reprint from #72)

Page 62 – Wild Wheels (reprint from #104)

Page 64 – Cracked Looks at a Doctor's Waiting Room – Don Orehek (reprint from #113)

Page 66 – Stories of the Month (My problem, Doctor) – Vic Martin (reprint from #19)

Page 67 – The Cracked Iron-On Kit – John Severin (revised from *King-Sized Cracked* #11 with reprint from #123)

Page 83 – Go Fly a Kite – John Severin (reprint from #74)

Back Cover – Great Moments in History 1656 – Charles Rodrigues (reprint from #132)

The 13th King-Sized Cracked Annual, Summer 1979 (84 pages) ($1.25)

Cover – We Need New Quarters – John Severin (reprint from #22)

Page 2 – The Cracked Bookstore ad – John Severin

Page 3 – Contents

Page 4 – Cracked Mazagine Presents the Great Nielson Airwave War – McTurk (John Severin) (reprint from #138)

Page 10 – Behind Closed Doors – Don Orehek (reprint from #139)

Page 12 – Some Garage Sales We'd Like to See – Howard Nostrand (reprint from #141)

Page 14 – The Snell Test – John Langton (reprint from #100)

Page 15 – Fat Magazine – Bob Taylor (reprint from #104)

Page 21 – Help Wanted – Bill Ward (reprint from #143)

The 14th King-Sized Cracked Annual, **Summer 1980 (84 pages) ($1.25)**

Page 48 – A Cracked Look at a Skateboard Park – Sururi Gumen (reprint from #145)

Page 50 – Papion – John Severin (reprint from #122)

Page 56 – A Teenager is – Don Orehek (reprint from #127)

Page 58 – Cracked Interviews the Pet Store King – Bill Ward (reprint from #144)

Page 63 – If Rockey Appeared in Other Movie and TV Spots – John Severin (reprint from #145)

Page 67 – Cracked Comic Cube Kit – John Severin (new)

Page 83 – Official Cracked Reporter T-Shirt ad

Back Cover – Great Moments in Industry 1889 – Charles Rodrigues (reprint from #126)

The 15th King-Sized Cracked Annual, **Summer 1981 (84 pages) ($1.25)**

Cover – Mechanical Horse and Indians – John Duillo (reprint from #79)

Page 2 – Contents

Page 3 – Cracked Stationery Kit – John Severin, Warren Sattler (new)

Page 19 – The Cracked Bookstore ad – John Severin

Page 20 – Jaws Too! – John Severin (reprint from #154)

Page 27 – A Brochure from P.T.U. (Prime Time University) – Bill Ward (reprint from #148)

Page 30 – Vermin Fight Back – Warren Sattler (reprint from #155)

Page 32 – The Cracked World of Hospitals – Don Orehek (reprint from #150)

Page 36 – Combination Sports of the Future – Bruce Day (reprint from #154)

Page 39 – When the World Runs Out of Space – Makbush (Sururi Gumen) (reprint from #127)

Page 43 – Sagebrush #52 (Keep up with me) – John Severin / MF (reprint from #153)

Page 44 – How Easily are you Embarrassed? – Vic Martin (reprint from #112)

Page 46 – The Deeep – Howard Nostrand (reprint from #146)

Page 52 – One Afternoon in Japan – Sururi Gumen (reprint from #134)

Page 53 – The Cracked Guide to Fishing – John Severin (reprint from #153)

Page 57 – Cracked's Method for Dealing with Traveling Salesman – Warren Sattler (reprint from #152)

Page 61 – Cracked Interviews the Hobo King – Bill Ward (reprint from #148)

Page 66 – Shut-Ups (ain't got no horses) – Charles Rodrigues (reprint from #121)

Page 67 – The Hollywood Game – John Severin, Samuel B. Whitehead, Howard Nostrand (new)

Page 83 – Pologloid No-Step ad (reprint from #161)

Back Cover – Great Moments in Auto Racing 1926 – Howard Nostrand (reprint from #149)

The 16th King-Sized Cracked Annual, **Summer 1982 (84 pages) ($1.50)**

Cover – Clean-up After the Anti-Pollution Parade – John Severin (reprint from *Super Cracked* #4)

Page 2 – Contents

Page 3 – Cracked's Travel Kit (new)

Page 19 – The Cracked Bookstore ad – John Severin

Page 20 – The Return of Mork and Mindy – John Severin (reprint from #163)

Page 27 – Airline Fares – Warren Sattler (reprint from #160)

Page 30 – Last Words Before the Hang-Up – Sururi Gumen (reprint from #161)

Page 33 – Cracked's Absurd Album of More Appropriate Acronyms (reprint from #159)

Page 34 – Clone Ads of the Future – Samuel B. Whitehead (reprint from #159)

Page 36 – Snide Guide to Camping – John Severin (reprint from #61)

Page 39 – The Blossoming Botany Business – Bill McCartney (Bill Ward) (reprint from #88)

Page 43 – The Layman's Guide to Hot and Cold Weather – Don Orehek (reprint from #160)

Page 46 – Testimonial Ads, the Way They Should Be – Howard Nostrand (reprint from #158)

Page 48 – The Cracked Guide to Gymnastics – John Langton (reprint from #167)

Page 52 – Daze & Knights (reprint from #82)

Page 54 – Trimming the Fat off the Budget – Bill McCartney (Bill Ward) (reprint from #82)

Page 57 – Cracked Looks at Racing – Samuel B. Whitehead (reprint from #160)

Page 61 – Cracked Interviews the Movie King – Bill Ward (reprint from #134)

Page 66 – The Explorer, the Dog & the Bone – Oskar Blotta (reprint from #84)

Page 67 – The Cracked All-Star All-Pro All-American All-Everything
Sports Game – John Severin, Mike Ricigliano, Don Orehek,
Bill Ward, Warren Sattler, Bob Taylor, Sururi Gumen, Charles
Rodrigues (new)
Page 83 – One Rustic Day Outside Tijuana, Mexico – John Severin
(reprint from #166)
Back Cover – Travel Stickers – Tony Tallarico (reprint from #62)

The 17th King-Sized Cracked Annual, **Summer 1983 (84 pages) ($2.00)**
Cover – "See Thru" Mirror Sandwich Board – John Severin (reprint
from #76)
Page 2 – Contents
Page 3 – The Cracked Complete Room Decorating Kit – Tony Tallarico
(reprint from *Super Cracked* #2)
Page 19 – The Cracked Bookstore ad – John Severin
Page 20 – Leverne and Shurley (we have dates with men) – John
Severin (reprint from #145)
Page 26 – Cracked's New Type Baseball Cards that Tell it Like it is –
Howard Nostrand (reprint from #138)
Page 29 – Super People Magazine – Sururi Gumen (reprint from #163)
Page 34 – The Cracked World of Vacations – Don Orehek (reprint from
#173)
Page 38 – Photoon (funniest looking person) (reprint from #156)
Page 39 – A Cracked Look at CB Radios – Bob Taylor (reprint from
#135)
Page 43 – The Cracked Guide to Muscle Development – Howard
Nostrand (reprint from #147)
Page 47 – Developing a New Product – Bill Ward (reprint from #130)
Page 51 – One Date at a Time – John Severin (reprint from #142)
Page 57 – Cracked Methods for Repairing Your Car Inexpensively – Bill
Dubay (reprint from #137)
Page 60 – The Truth You'll Never Hear – Warren Sattler (reprint from
#166)
Page 62 – Rule Changes in Sports that Reflect the Real World – John
Langton (reprint from #131)
Page 66 – The Mirage – Sururi Gumen (reprint from #140)
Page 67 – Make-Your-Own Newspaper Headlines (revised reprint from
Giant Cracked #1)
Page 83 – Ladie's Day (reprint from #98)
Back Cover – The Man and the Ink Spot – Oskar Blotta (reprint from
#146)

The 18th King-Sized Cracked Annual, **Summer 1984 (84 pages) ($1.75)**

Cover – Cracked Pot – John Severin (reprint from *Cracked Collectors' Edition* #24)

Page 2 – Contents

Page 3 – The Z Team Game – Mike Ricigliano, John Severin (new)

Page 19 – A Close Encounter with the Star Warz Gang – Howard Nostrand (John Severin) (reprint from #152)

Page 25 – One Evening in the McDuffy Home – Warren Sattler (reprint from #152)

Page 26 – The Cracked World of Travel – Don Orehek (reprint from #154)

Page 30 – Cracked's I'm O.K. Test – Howard Nostrand (reprint from #157)

Page 32 – The Cracked Guide to Sailing – Bill Ward (reprint from #156)

Page 37 – Cracked's Absurd Album of More Appropriate Acronyms (reprint from #159)

Page 38 – Fun City Olympics – Warren Sattler (reprint from #156)

Page 41 – Cracked Examines Telephone Answering Machines – Howard Nostrand (reprint from #157)

Page 44 – Cracked's new Soon-to-be-a-Fad Diets – Don Orehek (reprint from #158)

Page 46 – Diff'rent Strokes (Good morning, Mrs. Carrot) – John Severin (reprint from #162)

Page 52 – The Cracked Lens (reprint from #154)

Page 54 – The Cracked Guide to Fishing – John Severin (reprint from #153)

Page 58 – If the "Family Hour" Extended Into Our Everyday Lives – Warren Sattler (reprint from #153)

Page 60 – The Scuba Diver – Howard Nostrand (reprint from #159)

Page 61 – Cracked Interviews the Skateboard King – Bill Ward (reprint from #152)

Page 66 – "The Villain" – Val Mayerik (reprint from #158)

Page 67 – The Newest Cracked "Flip the Faces" Book – John Severin (revised reprint from *Giant Cracked* #3)

Page 83 – The Traffic Jam – Caracu (reprint from #70)

Back Cover – The Discovery – Stu Schwartzberg (reprint from #100)

The 19th King-Sized Cracked Annual, **Summer 1985 (84 pages) ($2.00)**

Cover – More Mork – John Severin (reprint from #167 with a *Frankenstein* head pasted over Mork's drawn by Aron Laikin.)

Page 2 – Contents

Page 3 – The Cracked Puzzle Book – John Langton (reprint from *Biggest Greatest Cracked* #9)

Page 19 – Knut Rider – John Severin (reprint from #193)

Page 26 – Real Kids Don't Eat Spinach – Warren Sattler (reprint from #197)

Page 30 – If Schools Patterned Themselves After TV – Samuel B. Whitehead (reprint from #168)

Page 34 – The Cracked Encyclopedia of Great Excuses! – Bull Dubay (reprint from #184)

Page 37 – Gift Catalogue for Teen-Agers – Don Orehek (reprint from #196)

Page 41 – One Evening in a Fancy Restaurant – Bob Taylor (reprint from #135)

Page 42 – A Cracked Look at a Supermarket – John Severin (reprint from #115)

Page 44 – Traitors of the Lost Ark – John Severin (reprint from #183)

Page 52 – A Cracked Look at Home Computers – Warren Sattler (reprint from #201)

Page 56 – If T.V. Commercials Were Forced to Tell the Truth – Samuel B. Whitehead (reprint from #186)

Page 60 – Talking Vending Machines – Sururi Gumen (reprint from #188)

Page 62 – The Cracked World of Toys and Games – Don Orehek (reprint from #148)

Page 66 – Too Dumb For Comfort – Samuel B. Whitehead (reprint from #187)

Page 73 – In the Electronic Game Room – Sururi Gumen (reprint from #181)

Page 74 – New Products to Make Kids Feel Even More Like Adults – Samuel B. Whitehead (reprint from #182)

Page 77 – Cracked Interviews the Saturday Morning Cartoon King – Bill Ward (reprint from #159)

Page 82 – Shut-Ups (flat tire) – Don Orehek (reprint from #173)

Page 83 – Marvin Manley Bodywrecking Club ad (reprint from #162)

Back Cover – The Swordsman – Bill McCartney (Bill Ward) (reprint from #35)

The King-Sized Cracked #20, Summer 1986 (84 pages) ($2.00)

Cover – Monster Movie – O.O. Severin (John Severin) (reprint from #105)

Page 2 – Sagebrush (crossing the desert) – John Severin (reprint from #86)

Page 3 – Contents

Page 4 – The Talking Blob – John Severin / Joe Catalano (reprint from #149)

Page 10 – High Noonish – John Severin / Joe Catalano (reprint from #152)
Page 16 – The Greatest Sequel Ever Made – John Severin / Joe Catalano
    (reprint from #155)
Page 23 – Shylock Homes and the Case of the Lifted Locket – Moe
    Riarty (John Severin) / Joe Catalano (reprint from #162)
Page 30 – The Cracked Movie – Nireves (John Severin) / Joe Catalano
    (reprint from #178)
Page 37 – The Cracked Movie II – Nireves (John Severin) / Joe Catalano
    (reprint from #183)
Page 44 – Star Drek – The Last Hurrah? – John Severin / Joe Catalano
    (reprint from #184)
Page 51 – Cracked Interviews the Cracked Mazagine King – Will Bored
    (John Severin) / Joe Catalano (reprint from #185)
Page 57 – A Press Conference with Ronald Reagan – John Severin / Joe
    Catalano (reprint from #186)
Page 62 – The Cracked Movie III – John Severin / Joe Catalano (reprint
    from #189)
Page 69 – The Cracked Movie IV – Nireves (John Severin) / Joe
    Catalano (reprint from #195)
Page 77 – The Cracked Movie V – John Severin / Joe Catalano (reprint
    from #211)
Page 83 – Sagebrush #25 (painting) – John Severin (reprint from #117)
    / Ye Hang Ups #28 (want to play a game?) – John Severin (reprint
    from #122)
Back Cover – Cracked Movie Marathon (reprint from #133)

***Monster Howls* #1, December 1966 (68 pages) (35c) (Some new material.)**
Cover – Mr. Sardonicus and Company – John Severin
Page 2, 4, 5, 11, 14, 15, 18, 19, 22, 23, 24, 32, 33, 43, 49, 53, 67 – Various
    Captioned Monster Photos
Page 3 – Contents
Page 6 – The Monster Howls' Baseball Team – John Severin (reprint
    from #37) (originally called "The Monster's Cracked Baseball Team')
Page 12 – The Eerie World of Don Orehek – Don Orehek
Page 16 – Modern Day Monsters – Joe Maneely (reprint from #5)
Page 20 – Monster Sandwich-Board Men – John Severin (reprint from #3)
Page 25 – Great Scenes from Great Horror Movies – John Severin
    (reprint from #42)
Page 27 – The Dungeon – Don Orehek
Page 28 – Fangmann's ad – John Severin (reprint from #36)
Page 29 – Frankenstein and Rock 'n Roll! – Joe Maneely (reprint from
    #2)

Page 34 – Monster Party! – John Severin (reprint from #31)

Page 36 – Do-it-Yourself Horror Cartoons

Page 37 – The Monster's Advertising Agency – John Severin (reprint from #33)

Page 42 – To the Top – Pete Wyma

Page 44 – Memorial Tribute (reprint from #13)

Page 46 – Interplanetary Magazines – Bill Everett (reprint from #8)

Page 48 – Unchained – Bob Zahn

Page 50 – The Stalk – Ned Kelly (John Severin) / Don Edwing (reprint from #30)

Page 52 – Hannibal the Horrible Cannibal – Pete Wyma

Pages 54-66 – (various real ads)

Back Cover – *Monster Howls* ad

Monsters Attack! #1, September 1989 (52 pages) ($1.49) (Many issues feature new material.)

Cover – Reading Monsters Attack! – John Severin

Page 2 and 51 – Reading Monsters Attack! Poster – John Severin

Page 3 – Contents

Page 4 – The Boneyard! (Mort Todd photo)

Page 5 – The Sex Vampires from Outer Space – Gray Morrow / Olivo Vincent

Page 11 – George Romero's Dead – Evan Michelson, Charles Victor, Johnny Zhivago

Page 14 – A Monster for All Seasons! – Pat Boyette

Page 21 – Return of the Golem! – John Severin / Mort Todd

Page 30 – Frankenstein: 1990 – Rick Altergott / Jon Loring

Page 36 – Pirate's Plunder – Mort Todd

Page 37 – In Solid! – Steve Ditko

Page 43 – Weirdbeard – Madman

Back Cover – The Werewolf – Walter Brogan

Monsters Attack! #2, October 1989 (52 pages) ($1.49)

Cover – The Claws that Refreshes (Freddy Krueger) – John Severin

Page 2 – Ride, Goblin, Ride! – Pat Boyette

Page 3 – Contents

Page 4 – The Boneyard! / Subscription ad

Page 5 – Aquacarnivora – Gray Morrow / Olivo Vincent

Page 13 – The Mars Attacks Chronicles: The Pulp Paintbrush of Norman Saunders – Norman Saunders / Bhob Stewart

Page 18 – The Cask of Amontillado! – Walter Brogan / Charles E. Hall

Page 25 – It's All in his Head! – Steve Ditko / Eel O'Brian (Mort Todd)

Page 30 – Radical New Pipe – Mort Todd
Page 31 – The Outsider – Steve Harper / Bhob Stewart
Page 37 – Are you Ready for Freddy? – Kevin McMahon
Page 43 – Abracadaver – Madman
Page 51 – The Claws that Refreshes (Freddy Krueger) – John Severin
Back Cover – I Want My Mummy – Walter Brogan

Monsters Attack! #3, July 1990 (52 pages) ($2.25)

Cover – Jason's Body Count – John Severin
Page 2 – Pin-Up – Gray Morrow
Page 3 – Contents
Page 4 and 20 – The Boneyard! (Mort Todd photo) / Subscription ad
Page 6 – Little Nemo Pin-Up – Pat Redding
Page 7 – A Boy's Life – John Severin / Mort Todd
Page 14 – Godzilla Pin-Up – Mort Todd
Page 15 – Face It – Steve Ditko
Page 21 – Jason's Body Count! – Kevin McMahon
Page 29 – Cells – Madman (Rurik Tyler)
Page 37 – The Wake of the Monster – Pat Boyette
Page 43 – The Daemon – Gene Colan
Page 51 – Jason' Body Count Pin-Up – John Severin
Back Cover – "Monsters Attack!" Reader Pin-Up – Madman (Rurik Tyler)

Monsters Attack! #4, September 1990 (52 pages) ($2.25)

Cover – Godzilla – John Severin
Page 2 – A Grave Shock – Walter Brogan
Page 3 – Contents
Page 4 and 20 – The Boneyard! (Mort Todd photo) / Subscription ad
Page 6 – Tag Yer Ded!! – John Severin / Mort Todd
Page 15 – Goribis – Pat Boyette
Page 16 – Neo-Tokyo is About to Explode Akira The Movie – Eel
    O'Brian (Mort Todd)
Page 20 – Monsters Attack! Bookworm – Mort Todd
Page 21 – Illusion – Steve Ditko
Page 26 – Godzilla: King of the Monsters! – Mort Todd
Page 33 – Circulation: Zero! – Gray Morrow / Charles E. Hall
Page 41 – Darman Rising! An Interview with Sam Raimi – Quelou
    Parente
Page 45 – Bookworm – Alex Toth / Nick Cuti
Page 51 – Squall – Rurik Tyler
Back Cover – Godzilla – John Severin

Monsters Attack! #5, December 1990 (52 pages) ($2.25)
Cover – Frankenstein – George A. Bush
Page 2 and 51 – Frankenstein Poster – George A. Bush
Page 3 – Contents
Page 4 – Letters/Subscription ad
Page 5 – A Job Well Done – Richard Meyers / Alex Toth
Page 12 – Monster Trucks – Pat Redding
Page 13 – The Trouble Was – Ron Goulart / Gray Morrow
Page 20 – The Frankenstein Legend – Kevin McMahon / Gene Colan
Page 27 – Freak Show – Mary Silverstone / Walter Brogan
Page 36 – Batcopter Attack – Pat Redding
Page 37 – The Creator – Steve Ditko
Page 43 – Cellar Jelly – Rurik Tyler
Back Cover – Final Resting Place – Frank Borth

Pow! #1, August 1966 (44 pages) (30c) (Many issues feature new material.)
Cover – Fighting Celebrities – John Severin
Page 2 – Sound Effects photos
Page 3 – Contents
Page 4 – Pow! Mail Call
Page 5 – Super Hero Confidential – Vic Martin
Page 10 – Pow! Puts You in the Laughing Seat
Page 11 – Advertising Combine Inc.
Page 12 – Arnold Hitchshnook Presents (reprint from *Zany* #1)
Page 15 – Arrowed Shirts ad – Don Orehek (reprint from *Zany* #2)
Page 16 – Play Pool – Bill McCartney (Bill Ward)
Page 20 – Wacky Inventions – Joe Sinnott (reprint from *Zany* #2) (originally called "Zany Inventions")
Page 22 – Ignited Air Lines – John Severin (reprint from #13)
Page 24 – Historical Telegrams That Never Got There (reprint from #17)
Page 26 – Remember! Forest Fires Can Prevent Bears! – Russ Heath (reprint from #13)
Page 27 – Pow's Pix!!
Page 28 – Digest Magazines – John Severin (reprint from #16)
Page 32 – Have Grunion Will Travel – George Peltz (reprint from *Zany* #4)
Page 35 – Nuts a Go-Go – Jack O'Brien, Joe Kiernan, Don Orehek, Pete Wyma
Page 36 – Quiz Time
Page 37 – Zwordo – Carl Burgos (reprint from *Zany* #2)
Page 40 – Grins That Won the West!

Page 42 – Stories of the Month (I don't mean to be nosey) – Jerry Kirschen (reprint from #16)

Page 43 – L&N Cigarette ad – Bill McCartney (Bill Ward) (reprint from *Zany* #1)

Back Cover – Pow Travel Stickers

Pow! #2, November 1966 (44 pages) (30c)

Cover – Godzilla and Pow-Man – John Severin

Page 2 – *Dr. Terror's House of Horrors* photos

Page 3 – Contents

Page 4 – Pow! Mail Call

Page 5 – Super Heros in Advertising – Bill McCartney (Bill Ward)

Page 9 – Like It's Happening Now!

Page 10 – Camping Out – Richard Doxsee (reprint from *Zany* #4)

Page 12 – Ultra Realistic Dolls – Bill McCartney (Bill Ward) (reprint from #28)

Page 16 – I Wake Up Screening – Golden

Page 20 – Pow's Pix Strike Again!

Page 21 – The Man on the Ledge – Bill McCartney (Bill Ward)

Page 22 – Handshakes – John Severin (reprint from #11)

Page 24 – Build This Beautiful Color TV Set in Your Spare Time!

Page 26 – Robbin Hood and his Band of Merrie Men (reprint from *Zany* #4)

Page 29 – Phone Services for Tots and Teens – John Severin (reprint from #28)

Page 34 – G.I. Remember Those Days!

Page 36 – Dinosaurs are Sweeping the Country – John Forte

Page 38 – More Nuts a-Go-Go! – Don Orehek, Jack O'Brien, George Kesner

Page 39 – Fresh, Fast & Funny!

Page 40 – Testimonial Dinner – Carl Burgos (reprint from *Zany* #2)

Page 42 – Stories of the Month (The Panhandler) – Jerry Kirschen (reprint from #18)

Page 43 – *Cat Ballou* and *Dr. Terror's* photos

Back Cover – Pow's Champ 'Camp' Certificate

Pow! #3 does not exist despite claims in *The Overstreet Comic Book Price Guide*.

The Super Cracked Annual, 1968 (92 pages) (50c)

Cover – Cracked Bookends – John Severin (reprint from #17)

Page 2 – Four Annuals (*Biggest* 2, 3; *Giant* 3; *King-Sized* 1) / Three Paperbacks / Back Issues ad (#61-68)

Page 3 – Contents
Page 4 – Russia Goes Madison Ave. – John Severin (reprint from #52)
Page 10 – Throw-Away Everything! – Bill McCartney (Bill Ward) (reprint from #56)
Page 13 – Famous Scenes from Great Western Movies – John Severin (reprint from #43)
Page 15 – Still Laughing (reprint from #48)
Page 16 – Cracked's Fast Cut Out Comebacks – John Severin (reprint from #52)
Page 18 – Office Objects Laughs! – Bill McCartney (Bill Ward) (reprint from #56)
Page 20 – The Little World of Don Swanson (poster) – Don Swanson (reprint from #21)
Page 21 – Modern Cliff-Hanging Situations – Bill McCartney (Bill Ward) (reprint from #48)
Page 24 – Shoverollit ad – John Severin (reprint from #32)
Page 25 – The American Space Base on Mars – John Severin (reprint from #32)
Page 27 – What if There Had Been Guidance Counselors Throughout History? – O.O. Severin (John Severin) (reprint from #53)
Page 30 – Cards to Get You of Jams – Charles Rodrigues (reprint from #55)
Page 32 – Cracked Takes a Look at Spring Training – Bill McCartney (Bill Ward) (reprint from #52)
Page 34 – The Swingers Set (reprint from #59)
Page 35 – Customized Career Cars – John Severin (reprint from #59)
Page 39 – Famous Scenes from Great Prison-Type Movies – Vic Martin (reprint from #55)
Page 41 – Oases Cigarette ad – John Severin (reprint from #12)
Page 42 – The Couples – John Severin (reprint from #60)
Page 44 – The Cracked Campaign Against Foreign Travel – Bill McCartney (Bill Ward) (reprint from #53)
Page 46 – Exclamation!!! – Don Perlin (reprint from #50)
Page 47 – School for T.V. Wrestlers – Sean Powers (John Severin) (reprint from #48)
Page 55 – Curvy Sewer Cognac ad – John Severin (reprint from #28)
Page 56 – New Designs for Business Cards (reprint from #20)
Page 58 – School Ties – Vic Martin (reprint from #48)
Page 60 – Of the Apes – Ned Kelly (John Severin) / Don Edwing (reprint from #29)
Page 61 – Ultra-Realistic Barbra & Ben Doll Accessories – Bill McCartney (Bill Ward) (reprint from #52)
Page 64 – Laurel and Hardy's Wacky World of Fun! (reprint from #59)

Page 66 – Proverbs Can Wreck Your Life – LePoer (John Severin)
(reprint from #28)

Page 68 – Cracked Trading Stamp Gift Catalog – Bill McCartney (Bill
Ward) (reprint from #52)

Page 70 – The Beach Balloon – John Severin (reprint from #27)

Page 71 – Cracked Fun Shoppe ad – John Severin / Horror House ac –
John Severin

Page 72 – Hurry-Ups (fly in soup) – Bill McCartney (Bill Ward)
(reprint from #41)

Page 73 – Cracked Fun and Activity Book – Tony Tallarico

Page 91 – Belnova Watch ad – John Severin (reprint from #50)

Back Cover – Cracked Cut-Out Paste-On Matchbook Covers – John
Severin (reprint from #22)

The Second Super Cracked Annual, 1969 (92 pages) (50c)

Cover – Cracked Celebrity Boat – John Severin

Page 2 – Eight Annuals (*Biggest* 2, 3, 4; *Giant* 3, 4; *King-Sized* 1, 2; *Super*
1) / Three Paperbacks / Back Issues ad (#69-76)

Page 3 – Contents

Page 4 – Tarzan Goes Around the World in 80 Pictures – John Severin
(reprint from #33)

Page 10 – The Cult of Culture Snobbery – Bill McCartney (Bill Ward)
(reprint from #46)

Page 13 – Famous Scenes from Great Lawyer-Type Movies! – Vic
Martin (reprint from #53)

Page 15 – Five Fun Flicks! (reprint from #58)

Page 16 – Male College Types to Be Wary Of – Bill McCartney (Bill
Ward) (reprint from #6)

Page 18 – A Beatnik Goes to a Party – Jack Davis (reprint from
#12)

Page 20 – I Got My Job Through The Daily Times ad – John Severin
(reprint from #15)

Page 21 – If Different Poets Had Read Cracked – John Severin (reprint
from #13)

Page 26 – Monster Party – John Severin (reprint from #43)

Page 28 – Have you Ever Noticed How Walking Advertisements Never
Match the Man? – John Severin (reprint from #27)

Page 30 – Sticks and Stitches – John Severin (reprint from #42)

Page 34 – Lucky Panther Cigarette ad – John Severin (reprint from
#27)

Page 35 – How I Saw Europe on Only 58c a Day – Bill McCartney (Bill
Ward) (reprint from #40)

Page 38 – When the West Was Fun! (reprint from #53)

Page 40 – When Doctors Advertise! – Jack Davis, John Severin (reprint from #24)

Page 42 – "Camp" Comic Heroland – John Severin (reprint from #58)

Page 47 – Ancient Egypt (reprint from #4)

Page 48 – Hypnotism – Richard Doxsee (reprint from #6)

Page 51 – A Guide to Modern Art – Bill McCartney (Bill Ward) (reprint from #37)

Page 56 – Cinema Chuckles (reprint from #57)

Page 57 – Julius Caesar in Modern Dress – John Severin (reprint from #6)

Page 60 – Rate Your Personality – LePoer (John Severin) (reprint from #12)

Page 62 – Guns and Gags for Hire! (reprint from #62)

Page 64 – The Flower – Bob Zahn (reprint from #37)

Page 65 – Cracked Fun Shoppe ad – John Severin

Page 66 – Merit Badges for Everyone – Tony Tallarico (reprint from #62)

Page 69 – Horror House ad – John Severin

Page 70 – Navy-Rated Wife – John Severin (reprint from #27)

Page 74 – Shut-Ups! (erector set) – Arthur Knockwurst (Charles Rodrigues) (reprint from #59)

Page 75 – The Cracked Complete Room Decorating Kit – Tony Tallarico (new)

Page 91 – Log Cabin Syrup ad – John Severin (reprint from #27)

Back Cover – The Cracked States of America? Flags – Tony Tallarico (new)

The Third Super Cracked Annual, 1970 (92 pages) (50c)

Cover – Wedding Cake – John Severin

Page 2 – Six Annuals (*Biggest* 4, 5; *Giant* 5; *King-Sized* 1, 2, 3) / Back Issues ad (#77-84)

Page 3 – Contents

Page 4 – Snow Flake and the Seven Dwarfs – John Severin (reprint from #70)

Page 9 – The Pleasure is Ours! (reprint from #70)

Page 10 – The History of Early Flight – Tony Tallarico (reprint from #70)

Page 14 – Graphic Speech – John Langton (reprint from #66)

Page 16 – The Old Lady and the Laundromat – Bill McCartney (Bill Ward) (reprint from #28)

Page 18 – If John Q. Public Hired a Press Agent – John Severin (reprint from #31)

The Fourth Super Cracked Annual, 1971 (92 pages) (60c)

Page 4 – Batzman Meets the Green Horned Bee! – M & O.O. Severin (Marie Severin, John Severin) (reprint from #74)

Page 10 – Life's Dropouts are Getting Younger and Younger – Bill McCartney (Bill Ward) (reprint from #66)

Page 14 – The Monsters Laugh it Up! (reprint from #56)

Page 16 – Cracked Form Telegrams – John Severin (reprint from #34)

Page 19 – A Cracked Look at Photography – O.O. Severin (John Severin) (reprint from #63)

Page 24 – Slums Can Be Made a Fun Thing! – John Severin (reprint from #74)

Page 28 – (Albert, Jerry) photos (reprint from #63)

Page 29 – Tales for Tots – Don Orehek (reprint from #66)

Page 32 – The TV Space Trend – Lugoze (reprint from #66) (originally titled "The Television Space Trend")

Page 36 – Cracked Map – John Langton (reprint from #63)

Page 38 – Dogs Magazine – John Severin (reprint from #74)

Page 46 – Metropolis the Slave – Arnoldo Franchioni (reprint from #63)

Page 48 – At the Barber Shop – Caracu (reprint from #67)

Page 49 – 4 Ever Funny (reprint from #57)

Page 51 – Horror House ad – John Severin

Page 52 – The Stones Keep Rollin! – John Severin (reprint from #57)

Page 56 – The Day Kosygin Came to New York – Lugoze (reprint from #68)

Page 58 – Marvin of the Apes! – O.O. Severin (John Severin) (reprint from #57)

Page 62 – Sylvester, the Blaw Son of Glock – Charles Rodrigues (reprint from #54)

Page 64 – Develop a Sense of Humor – Carl Burgos (reprint from #9)

Page 66 – Cracked Fun Shoppe ad – John Severin

Page 67 – The Cracked Hollywood First Read – Bill McCartney (Bill Ward) (reprint from #54)

Page 70 – A Funny Thing Happened to Me on the Way to the Happening – O.O. Severin (John Severin) (reprint from #66)

Page 74 – Shut-Ups (big crowd) – Philip Garbage (Charles Rodrigues) (reprint from #67)

Page 75 – Do-it-Yourself Newspapers (revised reprint from *Giant Cracked* #1)

Page 91 – Goodnight, Dick! Goodnight, Chet! (Dan Rowan and Dick Martin photo) (reprint from #73)

Back Cover – Crazy, Hip, Fun-Fad Bonus! – Tony Tallarico (reprint from #69)

The Fifth Super Cracked Annual, 1972 (84 pages) (60c)

Cover – Poiyoit Pants – John Severin (rip-off of *Mad* #93)

Page 2 – ("Keep Off the Grass") *The Good, The Bad & The Ugly* photo (reprint from #67)

Page 3 – Contents

Page 4 – The Fight Against Air & Water Pollution – John Severin (reprint from #87)

Page 8 – What's in a Name? – Art Pottier (reprint from #74)

Page 10 – Medallions with a Message – Tony Tallarico (reprint from #79)

Page 13 – The Status Symbol Rat Race – O.O. Severin (John Severin) (reprint from #62)

Page 17 – Cracked's Fractured Nursery Rhymes (reprint from #86)

Page 18 – If Comic Strip Characters Had Summer Replacements – Lugoze (reprint from #78)

Page 22 – Snow Flake and the Seven Dwarfs – John Severin (reprint from #70)

Page 27 – The Hippies' Coloring Book – Lugoze (reprint from #79)

Page 30 – Reducing the Violence in Movies – Lugoze (reprint from #75)

Page 34 – The Explorer, the Dog & the Bone – Oskar Blotta (reprint from #84)

Page 35 – Simulating the Thrills of Big-Time Sports at Home – Vic Martin (reprint from #83)

Page 38 – The History of Inflation – Vic Martin (reprint from #86)

Page 40 – Mission: Implausible – O.O. Severin (John Severin) (reprint from #80)

Page 46 – Read Any Good Trees Lately? – John Severin (reprint from #78)

Page 48 – The Cracked Travel Primer – Tony Tallarico (reprint from #75)

Page 52 – The Charlie Chan Caper (reprint from #71)

Page 54 – The Losingest Family in History! – John Severin (reprint from #77)

Page 57 – The Garbage Can – Caracu (reprint from #66)

Page 58 – The Celebrities' Flower Power – Lugoze (reprint from #70)

Page 60 – Cracked's Fun and Puzzle Contests – Bob Taylor (reprint from #87)

Page 63 – The Girl and the Butterfly – Oskar Blotta (reprint from #79)

Page 64 – Let's Travel Down Under…and Take a Cracked's-Eye View of Australia! – Bill McCartney (Bill Ward) (reprint from #86)

Page 66 – Shut-Ups (walking on air) – Vito Modigliani (Charles Rodrigues) (reprint from #75)

Page 67 – Poverty Game Kit

Page 83 – (hippies, Junior) photos (one from *Eight on the Lam*) (reprint from #66)

Back Cover – Karate Magazine – John Severin (reprint from #88)

The Sixth Super Cracked Annual, 1973 (84 pages) (60c)

Cover – Eskimo on an Ice Cube – John Severin (reprint from #40)

Page 2 – Five Annuals ad (*Biggest* 7, 8; *Giant* 8 ; *King-Sized* 5, 6)

Page 3 – Contents

Page 4 – Mockus Smellby, M.D. – John Severin (reprint from #90)

Page 9 – Magnificent Mae West (reprint from #89)

Page 10 – When the Super-Jets Take Over – John Severin (reprint from #86)

Page 14 – Simple Exercises for Simple People – Lugoze (reprint from #75)

Page 17 – Ruin 222 – John Severin (reprint from #84)

Page 22 – It Happened at the Cemetery – Caracu (reprint from #69)

Page 24 – Cracked Fun Shoppe ad – John Severin

Page 25 – Cue Cards for Everyone – Bill McCartney (Bill Ward) (reprint from #73)

Page 30 – Cracked Visits a Prison Yard – Lugoze (reprint from #75)

Page 32 – Rent-a-Person – John Langton (reprint from #72)

Page 36 – Horror House ad – John Severin

Page 37 – Cracked Specialized Books of Etiquette – Bill McCartney (Bill Ward) (reprint from #89)

Page 41 – Cowsmoopolitan Magazine – John Severin (reprint from #90)

Page 45 – Sagebrush (Z) – John Severin (reprint from #81)

Page 47 – The Johnny Dick Griffson Show – John Severin (reprint from #99)

Page 52 – Oh, Those Oh-So-Long Lines – John Langton (reprint from #77)

Page 56 – Baseball Hall of Shame – Bill McCartney (Bill Ward) (reprint from #89)

Page 59 – Famous Scenes from Great Lawyer-Type Movies! – Vic Martin (reprint from #53)

Page 61 – The Flower – Bob Zahn (reprint from #37)

Page 62 – When We All Move to Alaska – John Severin (reprint from #91)

Page 66 – Shut-Ups (the water's fine) – Vincent Van Stop (Charles Rodrigues) (reprint from #82)

Page 67 – The Game of Polluting – John Severin

Page 83 – It's a Weird, Weird, Weird, Weird, Weird World (reprint from #86)

Back Cover – Optimists Anonymous (Pat Paulsen photo) (reprint from #74)

The Seventh Super Cracked Annual, 1974 (84 pages) (75c)

Cover – Sylvester's Court – John Severin (reprint from *Biggest Greatest Cracked* #2)

Page 2 – Five Annuals ad (*Biggest* 8; *Collectors* 2; *Giant* 8 ; *King-Sized* 7; *Super* 6)

Page 3 – Contents

Page 4 – Airpot – John Severin (reprint from #91)

Page 9 – The Cracked Supermarket Primer – Don Orehek (reprint from #63)

Page 12 – Today's Swinger is Tomorrow's Square – John Severin (reprint from #96)

Page 16 – Cracked Looks at Hospitals – Bill McCartney (Bill Ward) (reprint from #86)

Page 19 – Paranoia News Magazine – John Langton (reprint from #89)

Page 22 – If Everyday People Were Stand-Up Comics – John Langton (reprint from #89)

Page 25 – The Electric Shave – Oskar Blotta (reprint from #86)

Page 26 – You Know There's a Generation Gap When – Jared Lee (reprint from #98)

Page 28 – Everybody is Doing the Don Rickles Bit – Noel Severin (John Severin) (reprint from #80)

Page 31 – The History of Sports – Don Orehek (reprint from #100)

Page 34 – Cracked Takes a Seat at Custer's Last Stand – Bill McCartney (Bill Ward) (reprint from #90)

Page 36 – Cracked Interviews the Hamburger King – John Severin (reprint from #99)

Page 40 – The Day When the Under-30 Set Takes Over the Nation! – Joe Mead (reprint from #75)

Page 43 – W.C. Fields Laff-In (reprint from #84)

Page 44 – Cracked's Travel Agency Tourist Attractions – John Langton (reprint from #85)

Page 46 – What's it Going to Cost in 1980? – John Severin (reprint from #98)

Page 48 – If T.V. Shows Were Combined to Make Hits – John Severin (reprint from #96)

Page 51 – Tense Moments in Sports (reprint from #90)

Page 52 – Initialists – Bill McCartney (Bill Ward) (reprint from #90)

Page 55 – The Man & the Fly – Oskar Blotta (reprint from #95)

Page 56 – Did You Ever Have One of Those Days? – Charles Rodrigues (reprint from #99)

Page 58 – A Visit to Transylvania – Bill McCartney (Bill Ward) (reprint from #55)

Page 61 – Will-Odd – John Severin (reprint from #99)
Page 66 – Shut-Ups (true or false) – Sue Sioux (Charles Rodrigues) (reprint from #91)
Page 67 – The Cracked Deck of Tarot Cards – John Langton
Page 83 – Mugging Minors (reprint from #98)
Back Cover – Leaving Hair ad – John Severin (reprint from #82)

The Eighth Super Cracked Annual, 1975 (84 pages) (75c)
Cover – Fruit Salad Jackpot – John Severin (reprint from #91)
Page 2 – Binders and Notebooks ad
Page 3 – Contents
Page 4 – The Brainy Bunch – John Severin (reprint from #89)
Page 9 – The Losingest Family in History! – John Severin (reprint from #77)
Page 12 – Los Angeles Balance – John Severin (reprint from #98)
Page 16 – The Fight Against Air & Water Pollution – John Severin (reprint from #87)
Page 20 – Those Old-Time Radio Serials or Ma Gherkins – She's Always in a Pickle – Vic Martin (reprint from #98)
Page 24 – Deceiving Movie Titles – Lugoze (reprint from #82)
Page 27 – Hudd & Dini (rocket) – Vic Martin (reprint from #87)
Page 28 – How Wise are Wise Old Proverbs? – Vic Martin (reprint from #98)
Page 32 – Let's Travel Down Under…and Take a Cracked's-Eye View of Australia! – Bill McCartney (Bill Ward) (reprint from #86)
Page 34 – Planets of the Creatures - John Severin (reprint from #72)
Page 40 – The Day We Have Our First Female President – Bill McCartney (Bill Ward) (reprint from #71)
Page 44 – Awards for School Kids – Bill McCartney (Bill Ward) (reprint from #77)
Page 48 – The French Commotion – John Severin (reprint from #102)
Page 53 – The Garbage Can – Caracu (reprint from #66)
Page 54 – Non-Polluting Cars Auto Safety Devices – Jack Barrett (reprint from #101)
Page 58 – When Prime Time Goes Gourmet – John Severin (reprint from #87)
Page 61 – The Blossoming Botany Business – Bill McCartney (Bill Ward) (reprint from #88)
Page 65 – Shut-Ups (sports car) – Charles Rodrigues (reprint from #87)
Page 66 – De Queers Rhinestone Co. ad – John Severin (reprint from #66)
Page 67 – Do-it-Yourself Newspapers (revised reprint from *Giant Cracked* #1)

Page 83 – The Cracked Bookstore ad – John Severin
Back Cover – Remember! Forest Fires Can Prevent Bears! – Russ Heath (reprint from #13)

The Ninth Super Cracked Annual, 1976 (84 pages) ($1.00)

Cover – Fishing for Sylvester – John Severin (reprint from #81 and partial reprint from #131)
Page 2 – The Cracked Bookstore ad – John Severin
Page 3 – Contents
Page 4 – Kung-Phew – John Severin (reprint from #112)
Page 9 – French Forlorn Legion – John Severin (reprint from #4)
Page 12 – The Daily Atlantis – John Langton (reprint from #68)
Page 16 – Reducing the Violence in Movies – Lugoze (reprint from #75)
Page 20 – Ballad of the Squeaky Voiced Cowboy – Joe Mead (reprint from #83)
Page 23 – Levenworth Mutual ad – John Severin (reprint from #19)
Page 24 – Cracked's Illustrated Quiz – Charles Rodrigues (reprint from #78)
Page 27 – Ploys Against Noise – Vic Martin (reprint from #65)
Page 31 – Blech Shampoo ad – LePoer (John Severin) (reprint from #21)
Page 32 – Cracked Visits a Skating Rink – John Langton (reprint from #70)
Page 34 – Underneath the Planet of the Apes – John Severin (reprint from #90)
Page 38 – The Explorer and the Snowman – Oskar Blotta (reprint from #90)
Page 39 – And the Defendant Answered – Bernard Baily (reprint from #110)
Page 40 – The College Entrance Rat Race – John Langton (reprint from #75)
Page 44 – What Might Happen if all Civil Service & Federal Employees Resorted to Work Slowdowns – Vic Martin (reprint from #66)
Page 48 – Destination Fun (reprint from #79)
Page 51 – Hudd & Dini (painted wall) – Vic Martin (reprint from #76)
Page 53 – Throughout History with the Isolated Camera – John Severin (reprint from #48)
Page 57 – The Pick-Up – John Severin (reprint from #34)
Page 58 – Cracked Suggestions for Improving Mail Service – Bill McCartney (Bill Ward) (reprint from #78)
Page 62 – A Modern Family Primer – Vic Martin (reprint from #72)
Page 66 – Shut-Ups (Peanuts) – Ellsworth A. Sap (Charles Rodrigues) (reprint from #69)

Page 67 – The Cracked Shark Hunt Game – Sururi Gumen (new)
Page 83 – Binders and Notebooks ad 2
Back Cover – Silver Spoon Magazine – John Severin (reprint from #87)

The Tenth Super Cracked Annual, 1977 (84 pages) ($1.00)
Cover – Sweeping Up – John Severin (reprint from #87)
Page 2 – The Cracked Bookstore ad – John Severin
Page 3 – Contents
Page 4 – Three Mascoteers – John Severin (reprint from #121)
Page 10 – When the World Runs Out of Food – Sururi Gumen (reprint from #122)
Page 14 – The World of Kids – Don Orehek (reprint from #121)
Page 18 – The Eech 80's – John Severin (reprint from #121)
Page 20 – Cracked's Charisma Test – John Langton (reprint from #121)
Page 22 – Cracked's New Look for the Post Office – Bill Ward (reprint from #112)
Page 26 – Boating – Don Orehek (reprint from #112)
Page 28 – Cracked Interviews the Restaurant King – John Langton (reprint from #121)
Page 33 – Miss Weird – Bernard Baily (reprint from #107)
Page 36 – You Know It's Not Your Day When – Bill Ward (reprint from #123)
Page 39 – If There Had Been Women's Lib Throughout History – Sururi Gumen (reprint from #123)
Page 42 – A Cracked Look at a Zoo – Don Orehek (reprint from #122)
Page 44 – What to Do with Your Obsolete Gas Guzzler – Bill Ward (reprint from #120)
Page 46 – If the Government Put a Tax on Our Sins – Bernard Baily (reprint from #114)
Page 50 – When Meat Becomes as Valuable as Money – John Langton (reprint from #112)
Page 54 – Nostalgic Amusement Parks – Bill Ward (reprint from #122)
Page 58 – Cracked Interviews the Garbage King – Sururi Gumen (reprint from #122)
Page 63 – Chariots of the Clods? – John Severin (reprint from #122)
Page 66 – The Garbage Can – Caracu (reprint from #66)
Page 67 – Make-Your-Own Newspaper Headlines (revised reprint from *Giant Cracked* #1)
Page 83 – Shut-Ups (prison reforms) – Noah Sark (Charles Rodrigues) (reprint from #106)
Back Cover – Great Moments in Medicine 1882 – Charles Rodrigues (reprint from #122)

The Eleventh Super Cracked Annual, 1978 (84 pages) ($1.00)

Cover – Mini-Sylvester's Help Note – John Severin (reprint from #50)

Page 2 – The Cracked Bookstore ad – John Severin

Page 3 – Contents

Page 4 – China Clown – Sururi Gumen (reprint from #123)

Page 10 – Discount Coupons of the Future – Bill Ward (reprint from #126)

Page 12 – Products and Ads Designed for the Arab Market – Mac Eush (Sururi Gumen) (reprint from #126)

Page 16 – Cracked Stars on the Moon – John Severin (reprint from #82)

Page 18 – More Cracked Solutions for Solving the Energy Crisis – John Langton (reprint from #120)

Page 22 – The Cracked History of Medicine – Doe Torr (John Severin) (reprint from #128)

Page 26 – Olympics for Non-Athletes – Bill Ward (reprint from #124)

Page 29 – Female Magazines of Tomorrow – Vic Martin (reprint from #103)

Page 33 – If Newspapers Carried Pictures to Match Their Headlines – John Severin (reprint from #127)

Page 36 – A Cracked Look at a Bowling Alley – Don Orehek (reprint from #124)

Page 38 – How Wise are Wise Old Proverbs? – Vic Martin (reprint from #98)

Page 42 – Life's Dropouts are Getting Younger and Younger – Bill McCartney (Bill Ward) (reprint from #66)

Page 46 – The Cracked Guide to Self-Recognition – Bill Ward (reprint from #127)

Page 48 – A Swinging Good Time! (reprint from #71)

Page 49 – Future Automated Devices – Nireves (John Severin) (reprint from #50)

Page 53 – Cracked's Guide to Bicycling – Bob Taylor (reprint from #105)

Page 57 – Cracked Interviews the Resort King – Bill Ward (reprint from #127)

Page 62 – When We All Move to Alaska – John Severin (reprint from #91)

Page 66 – The Flower – Bob Zahn (reprint from #37)

Page 67 – Cracked Space Encounters Game – Joe Banana (new)

Page 83 – Welcome to Marlboro Country – John Severin (reprint from #53)

Back Cover – The Man and the Mousey – Oskar Blotta (reprint from #124)

The Twelfth Super Cracked Annual, 1979 (84 pages) ($1.25)

Cover – Super-Sylvester – O.O. Severin (John Severin) (reprint from #53)

Page 2 – The Cracked Bookstore ad – John Severin

Page 3 – Contents

Page 4 – Blarney Miller (my husband is missing) – John Severin (reprint from #139)

Page 10 – Redemption Coupons We'd Really Like to See – Howard Nostrand (reprint from #141)

Page 12 – C.B. Mania – Bill Ward (reprint from #138)

Page 16 – Orehek on Wry – Don Orehek (reprint from #108)

Page 18 – Cracked Guide to Surfing – John Severin (reprint from #136)

Page 23 – How to Prepare a Job Resume (reprint from #19)

Page 26 – A Cracked Look at an Airport Terminal – Bob Taylor (reprint from #135)

Page 28 – Cracked's New Type Baseball Cards that Tell it Like it is – Howard Nostrand (reprint from #138)

Page 31 – Cracked Interviews the Traveling Carnival King – Bill Ward (reprint from #140)

Page 36 – Cowtown Gazette (reprint from #139)

Page 40 – Cracked Methods for Repairing Your Car Inexpensively – Bill Dubay (reprint from #137)

Page 44 – The Cracked Guide to Hang Gliding – John Severin (reprint from #140)

Page 48 – Cracked's Favorite TV Scenes from Last Season (reprint from #137)

Page 51 – At the Barber Shop – Caracu (reprint from #67)

Page 52 – Cracked Looks at the World of Superdom – Don Orehek (reprint from #139)

Page 56 – Senior Citizen – Lugoze (reprint from #82)

Page 60 – Cracked's Cheaper Methods for Powering Automobiles – John Langton

Page 62 – The Making of Silent Movie – McTurk (John Severin) (reprint from #138)

Page 67 – 8 Posters (reprints from #130, 131, 133, 136, 138, 139, 141, 143)

Page 83 – One Afternoon in Japan – Sururi Gumen (reprint from #134)

Back Cover – Great Moments in Gardening 1708 – Howard Nostrand (reprint from #140)

The 13th Super Cracked Annual, **Spring 1980 (84 pages) ($1.25)**

Cover – Cracked Carnival of Fun – John Severin (partial reprint from *King-Sized Cracked #2)*

Page 2 – The Cracked Bookstore ad – John Severin

Page 3 – Contents

Page 4 – The Six Billion Dollar Man vs. Dark Badar – O.O. Severin (John Severin) (reprint from #149)

Page 10 – The Machine Mania Monopolizes the Movies – Warren Sattler (reprint from #148)

Page 13 – Jerry Interviews the Stars – Howard Nostrand (reprint from #149)

Page 19 – The Cracked History of Ecology – Bill Ward (reprint from #144)

Page 23 – The Awakening – John Severin (reprint from #97)

Page 24 – The Cracked World of Toys and Games – Don Orehek (reprint from #148)

Page 28 – It's a Lot Worse in Buffalo – Warren Sattler (reprint from #149)

Page 31 – The Cracked Guide to Martial Arts – Sean Severin (John Severin) (reprint from #150)

Page 35 – When the Country Runs Out of Water – Bill Ward (reprint from #146)

Page 39 – Cracked Interviews the Garbage King – Sururi Gumen (reprint from #122)

Page 44 – A Rodrigues Wedding Reception – Charles Rodrigues (reprint from #118)

Page 46 – More Cracked Solutions for Solving the Energy Crisis – John Langton (reprint from #120)

Page 50 – Sylvester's Silly Strips – Ye Hang Ups (Skrunch) – Nireves (John Severin) / Your (Ugh) Ancestors? (stone TV) – Lo Linkert / Sagebrush (only the shadow knows) – John Severin / Sagebrush (Pikes Peak or Bust) – John Severin (reprint from #114)

Page 52 – Reconstructing the Remains of 20th Century Civilization – Bill Ward (reprint from #113)

Page 57 – If We Didn't Have Hair – John Severin (reprint from #115)

Page 60 – American Car-Daffy – Sururi Gumen (reprint from #121)

Page 66 – Hudd & Dini (trampoline) – Vic Martin (reprint from #107)

Page 67 – Paperback Book Covers – Howard Nostrand (new)

Page 83 – Official Cracked Reporter T-Shirt ad

Back Cover – The Man and the Ink Spot – Oskar Blotta (reprint from #146)

The 14th Super Cracked, Fall 1980 (84 pages) ($1.25)

Cover – Star Warz – John Severin (reprint from #146)

Page 2 – The Cracked Bookstore ad – John Severin

Page 3 – Contents

Page 4 – The Happy Dazes' Close Encounters of the Third Kind – John Severin (reprint from #153)

Page 10 – Cracked Interviews the Stars (reprint from *Cracked Collectors' Edition* #24)

Page 15 – The Cracked History of Art – John Langton (reprint from #117)

Page 19 – Martial Art Weapons and Techniques – Bill Ward (reprint from #118)

Page 22 – What are the Old TV & Movie Detectives Doing Today? – John Severin (reprint from #121)

Page 27 – A Dog's Day Afternoon (reprint from #155)

Page 28 – A Cracked Look at a State Pen – Don Orehek (reprint from #152)

Page 32 – A Short Look at a Long Gas Line – Bill Ward (reprint from #118)

Page 34 – The World of Kids – Don Orehek (reprint from #121)

Page 38 – Honesty on the Tube – Howard Nostrand (John Severin) (reprint from #152)

Page 40 – TV Guise Magazine (reprint from #151)

Page 46 – Other "Self-Service" Businesses – Bruce Day (reprint from #150)

Page 49 – Leverne and Shurley – John Severin (reprint from #145)

Page 55 – The Cracked Lens (reprint from #154)

Page 57 – Exercise Manual and Hot Dog Stunts for Super Heroes – Powers (John Severin) (reprint from #147)

Page 61 – Cracked Interviews the Skateboard King – Bill Ward (reprint from #152)

Page 66 – Shut-Ups (winning tickets) – S. Gross Jr. (Charles Rodrigues) (reprint from #103)

Page 67 – The Cracked Empire Strikes Out Puzzle Book – John Severin, Warren Sattler (new)

Page 83 – Official Cracked Reporter T-Shirt ad

Back Cover – It Happened on Main and First – Caracu (reprint from #103)

The 15th Super Cracked, Winter 1981 (84 pages) ($1.25)

Cover – The Descent of Man – Jack Davis (reprint from #14)

Page 2 – The Cracked Bookstore ad – John Severin

Page 3 – Contents

Page 4 – Paperback Book Covers – Samuel B. Whitehead (new)

Page 20 – Greased! – John Severin (reprint from #156)

Page 27 – The Cracked Guide to Skiing – Bill Ward (reprint from #115)

Page 32 – What to Do with Your Obsolete Gas Guzzler – Bill Ward (reprint from #120)

Page 34 – The Cracked World of Travel – Don Orehek (reprint from #154)

Page 38 – One Afternoon in the Park (reprint from #156)

Page 39 – The Cracked Almanac – Howard Nostrand (reprint from #153)

Page 44 – If the "Family Hour" Extended Into Our Everyday Lives – Warren Sattler (reprint from #153)

Page 46 – Cracked's Solution for Solving the Energy Crisis – Bill Ward (reprint from #117)

Page 51 – Still More from The Cracked Lens (reprint from #157)

Page 54 – The Cracked World of Snow – Sururi Gumen (reprint from #124)

Page 58 – Lue Grunt – Noel Powers (John Severin) (reprint from #158)

Page 64 – The Cracked Etiquette Quiz – John Langton (reprint from #32)

Page 66 – Shut-Ups (flight show movies) – Charles Rodrigues (reprint from #133)

Page 67 – Cracked's Unemployment Game – Warren Sattler (new)

Page 83 – Official Cracked Reporter T-Shirt ad

Back Cover – Great Moments in Psychiatry 1227 – Howard Nostrand (reprint from #152)

The 16th Super Cracked, Fall 1981 (84 pages) ($1.25)

Cover – Close Encounters of the Worst Kind! – John Severin (reprint from #150)

Page 2 – Contents

Page 3 – My Family Album (reprint from *King-Sized Cracked* #5)

Page 19 – Caption the Photo Contest ad

Page 20 – M*U*S*H (Dear Dad) – John Severin (reprint from #115)

Page 25 – Cracked Guide to Magic – Bill Ward (reprint from #126)

Page 28 – The Non-People Population Explosion – Sururi Gumen (reprint from #130)

Page 32 – You Know You're a Skateboard Freak When – Warren Sattler (reprint from #154)

Page 34 – Popular Songs for Everyday Working People – Howard Nostrand (reprint from #156)

Page 38 – The Cracked Guide to Sailing – Bill Ward (reprint from #155)

Page 42 – The Eech 80's – John Severin (reprint from #121)

Page 44 – It's a Weird, Weird, Weird, Weird, Weird World (reprint from #86)

Page 45 – Postcard Collecting – Sururi Gumen (reprint from #132)

Page 49 – Family's Feud – Howard Nostrand (reprint from #154)

Page 55 – The Cracked Guide to Paddleball – Warren Sattler (reprint from #150)

Page 59 – The Cracked Guide for First Aid – Bob Taylor (reprint from #82)

Page 61 – Cracked Interviews the Publicity King – Bill Ward (reprint from #154)

Page 66 – Shut-Ups! (exit slowly) – Charles Rodrigues (reprint from #89)

Page 67 – Cracked's Make it Rich Game – John Severin (revised reprint from *Extra Special Cracked* #1 originally called "The Game of Millionaire")

Page 83 – The Cracked Bookstore ad – John Severin

Back Cover – Great Moments in Science 1600 – Mike Ricigliano (reprint from #139)

The 17th Super Cracked, **Spring 1982 (84 pages) ($1.50)**

Cover – Jawz Too! – John Severin (reprint from #154)

Page 2 – Contents

Page 3 – The Cracked TV Coloring Book – John Langton (new)

Page 19 – The Cracked Bookstore ad – John Severin

Page 20 – Everything You Should Know About Sharks (Before It's Too Late) (reprint from *Cracked Collectors' Edition* #26)

Page 23 – How a Shark Attacks (reprint from *Cracked Collectors' Edition* #26)

Page 25 – Cracked's New Look for the Post Office – Bill Ward (reprint from #112)

Page 29 – Cracked's Illustrated Quiz – Charles Rodrigues (reprint from #78)

Page 32 – You Know You're in a Tacky Bank When – Warren Sattler (reprint from #155)

Page 34 – The Great White's Boyhood – John Severin (reprint from *Cracked Collectors' Edition* #26)

Page 37 – As the General, Young, and Restless Hospital Turns – Bill Ward (reprint from #137)

Page 42 – Are you a Hypochondriac? – John Langton (reprint from #106)

Page 44 – The Effect of the Energy Crisis on the Entertainment World – John Severin (reprint from #119)

Page 48 – Everything You Should Know About Sharks-Part II (reprint from *Cracked Collectors' Edition* #26)

Page 53 – Cracked Guide to Acupuncture – Dick Wright (reprint from #111)

Page 56 – Understanding Hi-Fidelity – John Langton (reprint from #118)
Page 60 – More Whaddaya Callits – Joe Mead (reprint from #81)
Page 62 – Cracked Interviews the Magic King – Bill Ward (reprint from #131)
Page 67 – The Cracked Game of Saboteurs and Investigators – Mike Ricigliano, John Severin, Don Orehek, Bill Ward, Catherine Severin, Warren Sattler, Sururi Gumen (new)
Page 39 – Just Bumming Around! – Tony Tallarico (reprint from #106)
Back Cover – Great Moments in Science 1934 – Charles Rodrigues (reprint from #118)

The 18th Super Cracked, Fall 1982 (84 pages) ($1.75)
Cover – We Wreck Star Trek – John Severin (reprint from #169)
Page 2 – Contents
Page 3 – The Cracked TV Coloring Book – John Langton (new)
Page 4 – Make-Your-Own Newspaper Headlines (revised reprint from *Giant Cracked* #1)
Page 19 – Caption the Photo Contest
Page 20 – Star Drek the Moving Picture – John Severin (reprint from #159)
Page 28 – Did You Ever Have One of Those Days? – Charles Rodrigues (reprint from #99)
Page 30 – Using Star Trek Logic and Technology to Solve Life's Everyday Problems – Don Orehek (reprint from #170)
Page 33 – You're Really Overdoing it a Little When – LePoer (John Severin) (reprint from #165)
Page 34 – Goofed-Up Genes – Vic Martin (reprint from #86)
Page 36 – Cowtown Gazette (reprint from #139)
Page 40 – Read Any Good Trees Lately? – John Severin (reprint from #78)
Page 42 – Reducing the Violence in Movies – Lugoze (reprint from #75)
Page 46 – Goldie Oldie Rock Yocks (reprint from #91)
Page 48 – A Cracked Look at Little League Managers – Bill Ward (reprint from #119)
Page 51 – Photoon (Haven't I seen you) (reprint from #160)
Page 52 – How Adults Drive Kids Nuts – Warren Sattler (reprint from #163)
Page 54 – The Cracked Guide to Frizbee – Howard Nostrand (reprint from #142)
Page 58 – Take the Cracked Driving Test! – Tony Tallarico (reprint from #64)
Page 60 – One Afternoon in a Local Stereo Store – Sururi Gumen (reprint from #138)
Page 61 – Cracked Interviews the Orkan King – Bill Ward (reprint from #168)

Page 66 – Magnificent Mae West (reprint from #89)

Page 67 – Star Track Game – John Severin, Sururi Gumen (new)

Page 83 – Auntie Dinger's ad (reprint from #164)

Back Cover – Oh, Those Long Lines – Howard Nostrand (reprint from #164)

The 19th Super Cracked, Winter 1983 (84 pages) ($1.75)

Cover – Your TV Favorites – John Severin (reprint from #138)

Page 2 – Contents

Page 3 – The Cracked Magazine Game – Mike Ricigliano, John Severin (new)

Page 19 – Everything You've Ever Wanted to Know About "The Fonze" and More – John Severin (reprint from #134)

Page 25 – The Cracked Guide to Canoeing – Warren Sattler (reprint from #146)

Page 29 – Popular Butterfingers Magazine – John Langton (reprint from #91)

Page 32 – A Cracked Look at Desert Islands – Lugoze (reprint from #77)

Page 34 – Absolutely, Unquestionably, Positively, Undeniably, the Very, Very, Last of The Cracked Lens (reprint from #172)

Page 37 – Service-O-Mats of the Future – John Severin (reprint from #25)

Page 40 – Cracked Looks at Fishing – Vic Martin (reprint from #76)

Page 42 – Sagebrush (only the shadow knows) – John Severin / Sagebrush (Pikes Peak or Bust) – John Severin (reprint from #114)

Page 43 – Products Designed for Overweight Americans – Warren Sattler (reprint from #162)

Page 47 – The Billy Pluckett Story – John Severin (reprint from #169)

Page 53 – Cracked Interviews the Apartment King – Bill Ward (reprint from #157)

Page 58 – If Picture Postcards Told the Truth! – John Severin (reprint from #59)

Page 60 – If Mork Appeared in Other T.V. Shows and Movies (Fantasy Island) – John Severin (reprint from #167)

Page 66 – Shut-Ups (flat tire) – Don Orehek (reprint from #173)

Page 67 – Cracked Greeting Cards (new)

Page 83 – The Cracked Bookstore ad – John Severin

Back Cover – Great Moments in Gardening 1708 – Howard Nostrand (reprint from #140)

The 20th Super Cracked, Spring 1983 (84 pages) ($1.75)

Cover – More M*A*S*H – John Severin (reprint from #168)

Page 2 – Contents

Page 3 – The Cracked Night Rider Game – Mike Ricigliano (new)

Page 19 – The Cracked Bookstore ad – John Severin

Page 20 – M*U*S*H (millions of clocks) – John Severin (reprint from #142)

Page 26 – Cracked Looks at the World of Superdom – Don Orehek (reprint from #139)

Page 30 – Exciting Games for Daredevils – Zackary Taylor (Bob Taylor) (reprint from #94)

Page 32 – Ten Little Drivers – Warren Sattler (reprint from #164)

Page 34 – The Cracked Guide to Bowling – Bill Dubay (reprint from #141)

Page 39 – One Evening in Old Mexico – Bob Taylor (reprint from #133)

Page 40 – The Fonz Throughout History – Don Orehek (reprint from #136)

Page 43 – Shylock Homes and the Case of the Lifted Locket – Moe Riarty (John Severin) / Joe Catalano (reprint from #162)

Page 50 – On Capitol Hill – Howard Nostrand (reprint from #146)

Page 51 – When TV Goes Completely Sci Fi – Samuel B. Whitehead (reprint from #163)

Page 54 – The Moon Ate a Big Pink Kumquat (reprint from #87)

Page 56 – Your Dentist is Your Friend – Don Orehek (reprint from #158)

Page 58 – Cracked's Fun and Puzzle Contests – Bob Taylor (reprint from #87)

Page 61 – Cracked Interviews the Game Show King – Bill Ward (reprint from #165)

Page 66 – The Man and the Bird – Oskar Blotta (reprint from #87)

Page 67 – The Cracked Video IQ Test – Mike Ricigliano (new)

Page 83 – Cracked's Fractured Nursery Rhymes (reprint from #86)

Back Cover – Landing On Mars – Howard Nostrand / Murad Gumen (reprint from #156)

The 21st Super Cracked, Summer 1983 (84 pages) ($1.75)

Cover – Green Giant Island – John Severin (reprint from #45)

Page 2 – Contents

Page 3 – Cracked Practical Joke Kit – John Severin (reprint from *Giant Cracked Fun-Kit* #33)

Page 19 – The Cracked Bookstore ad – John Severin

Page 20 – Real Incredible People – John Severin (reprint from #174)

Page 26 – You're Going a Little Too Far When – Sururi Gumen (reprint from #164)

Page 28 – Miracle Workers the World has Never Heard of ('Til Now) – Samuel B. Whitehead (reprint from #165)

Page 31 – Crimedom's Mail Order Catalogue – Warren Sattler (reprint from #146)

Page 36 – Weather Forecasting Kit ad – Howard Nostrand (reprint from #165)

Page 37 – Why Today Will Seem like the Good Old Days 20 Years from Now – Bill Ward (reprint from #139)

Page 41 – Cracked Tips for Economizing – Samuel B. Whitehead (reprint from #164)

Page 44 – The Cracked World of Lines – Don Orehek (reprint from #165)

Page 48 – Safari So Good (reprint from #104)

Page 50 – Fonzerella! – Sigbjorn (John Severin) (reprint from #135)

Page 55 – When Gambling Becomes Legal in Everyday Life – Warren Sattler (reprint from #164)

Page 58 – Success in Your Chosen Career – Bill McCartney (Bill Ward) (reprint from #96)

Page 61 – Sport Sillystrated Magazine (reprint from #165)

Page 66 – One Day in the North Woods – Howard Nostrand (reprint from #163)

Page 67 – The Cracked Pollution Game – John Severin (new)

Page 83 – Bunt's Catsup ad (reprint from #49)

Back Cover – Chicken Soap label – John Severin (reprint from #108)

The 22nd Super Cracked, Fall 1983 (84 pages) ($1.75)

Cover – Fishing for Sylvester – John Severin (reprint from #81)

Page 2 – Contents

Page 3 – Battle of the Galaxy Game – John Severin (reprint from *Giant Cracked Fun-Kit* #19)

Page 19 – The Cracked Bookstore ad – John Severin

Page 20 – If Other Actors Played the Parts Made Famous by Somebody Else – John Severin (reprint from #151)

Page 24 – The Cracked History of Boating? – Bill Ward (reprint from #126)

Page 27 – Incurably Cracked (reprint from #153)

Page 30 – A Cracked Look at Indirect Messages – Don Orehek (reprint from #159)

Page 32 – Super Skateboard Stunts – Howard Nostrand (reprint from #144)

Page 36 – If Comic Strip Characters Had to Face Simple But Realistic Problems! – John Severin (reprint from #69)

Page 39 – Blech Shampoo ad – LePoer (John Severin) (reprint from #21)

Page 40 – Beach Blanket Party – John Severin (reprint from #137)

Page 45 – Luck Is – Bob Taylor (reprint from #85)
Page 47 – A Modern Parent vs. Traditional Parent – Warren Sattler
(reprint from #155)
Page 51 – The Cracked Guide to Golf – Bill Ward (reprint from #125)
Page 55 – Hudd & Dini (lifeguards) – Vic Martin (reprint from #100)
Page 56 – Keystone Komedy Kapers (reprint from #96)
Page 58 – How to Make Money in Your Spare Time – John Severin
(reprint from #168)
Page 62 – Cracked Looks at Vacations – Bill McCartney (Bill Ward)
(reprint from #96)
Page 65 – Cracked Investigates I.F.O.'s – Samuel B. Whitehead (reprint
from #161)
Page 69 – The History of Advertising – Howard Nostrand (reprint from
#166)
Page 73 – When the Country Runs Out of Water – Bill Ward (reprint
from #146)
Page 77 – Cracked Fishing Game Kit – Don Orehek (reprint from
Biggest Greatest Cracked #16)
Page 83 – Ye Hang Ups #2 (castle) – C.E. Severin (Catherine Severin)
(reprint from #173)
Back Cover – Freezca ad – John Severin (reprint from #81)

The 23rd Super Cracked, **Summer 1984 (84 pages) ($2.00) (Says "24th"**
inside.)
Cover – Earthshake – John Severin (reprint from #125)
Page 2 – Contents Page 3 – Make-Your-Own Newspaper Headlines
(revised reprint from *Giant Cracked* #1)
Page 19 – The Dorks of Hazzardous (Rub his roof) – John Severin
(reprint from #179)
Page 26 – A Teenager is – Don Orehek (reprint from #127)
Page 28 – Cracked's Inquiring Photographer Visits the Stars (reprint
from #152)
Page 32 – The Put-Downers – Vic Martin (reprint from #106)
Page 34 – The Telephone Call – Charles Rodrigues (reprint from #119)
Page 35 – The Cracked Almanac – Howard Nostrand (reprint from
#153)
Page 40 – The World of Mr. Orehek – Don Orehek (reprint from #109)
Page 42 – The Cracked Handbook of Acting – Warren Sattler (reprint
from #159)
Page 46 – Moonwrecker – Sururi Gumen (reprint from #166)
Page 53 – Olympics for Non-Athletes – Bill Ward (reprint from #124)
Page 56 – How Easily are you Embarrassed? – Vic Martin (reprint from
#112)

Page 58 – All At Sea (reprint from #104)

Page 61 – Cracked Interviews the Resort King – Bill Ward (reprint from #127)

Page 66 – Shut-Ups (new highway) – Charles Rodrigues (reprint from #122)

Page 67 – Cracked's Strike it Rich Game – John Severin (revised reprint from *Extra Special Cracked* #1 originally called "The Game of Millionaire")

Page 83 – The Quick Quippers! (reprint from #69)

Back Cover – Great Moments in Sports 1958 – Warren Sattler (reprint from #176)

The 24ᵗʰ *Super Cracked*, Fall 1984 (84 pages) ($1.75) Cover – Life Guard – John Severin (reprint from #88)

Page 2 – Contents

Page 3 – Cracked's 1984 Los Angeles Olympics Game – Mike Ricigliano (new)

Page 19 – The Greatest TV Show Ever Made – John Severin (reprint from #161)

Page 26 – Cracked Looks at Dating – Bill McCartney (Bill Ward) (reprint from #76)

Page 30 – How to Translate Travel Ads – Bob Taylor (reprint from #108)

Page 33 – Cracked's New Sidewalk, Street and Playground Games – Warren Sattler (reprint from #173)

Page 37 – Sagebrush (such a bad character) – John Severin (reprint from *Cracked Collectors' Edition* #9)

Page 38 – You Know There's a Generation Gap When – Jared Lee (reprint from #98)

Page 40 – A Cracked Salute to the Olympics – Bill Ward (reprint from #135)

Page 45 – Absolutely, Positively the Very Last of Those Cracked Monsters (reprint from #168)

Page 48 – A Cracked Look at the Beach – Don Orehek (reprint from #97)

Page 51 – Family's Feud – Howard Nostrand (reprint from #154)

Page 57 – Airline Fares – Warren Sattler (reprint from #160)

Page 60 – Cracked's All-Purpose, Time-Saving "Denial of Charges" Speech for Politicians – John Severin (reprint from #172)

Page 62 – Cracked Interviews the Trekker King – Bill Ward (reprint from #169)

Page 67 – The Cracked Puzzler of Puzzle Books – Jack Davis, Bob Taylor (reprint from *Biggest Greatest Cracked* #11)

Page 44 – Ye Hang Ups #3 (screams) – C.E. Severin (Catherine Severin) (reprint from #172)

Back Cover – Great Moments in Technology 1029 – Howard Nostrand (reprint from #170)

The 25th Super Cracked, Winter 1985 (84 pages) ($1.75)

Cover – Old Time Movie Stars – John Severin (reprint from #93 with Michael Jackson thrown in)

Page 2 – One Evening in a Posh Midwestern Restaurant – Sururi Gumen (reprint from #182)

Page 3 – Contents

Page 4 – Diff'rent Strokes (You can have the bathroom) – John Severin (reprint from #184)

Page 10 – The Cracked World of Disco – Don Orehek (reprint from #164)

Page 14 – The Last of The Cracked Lens (reprint from #164)

Page 20 – Career Dreams That Came True – Sururi Gumen (reprint from #167)

Page 23 – Crack Ups! Featuring The Child Psychiatrist – Powers (John Severin) (reprint from #185)

Page 24 – Cracked Look at Teacher Types – John Severin (reprint from #136)

Page 26 – Combination Sports of the Future – Bruce Day (reprint from #154)

Page 29 – The JR Family Photo Album – John Severin (reprint from #181)

Page 32 – Cracked Looks at Parent-Teacher Conferences – Sururi Gumen (reprint from #184)

Page 33 – Jock State University Bulletin – Warren Sattler (reprint from #183)

Page 36 – Press Mistakes! (avant-garde artist) – John Langton (reprint from #180)

Page 38 – Ye Hang Ups #5 (lil' hug and kiss) – C.E. Severin (Catherine Severin) (reprint from #182)

Page 39 – If Gary Coleman Played Other Parts – R. McGeddon (John Severin) (reprint from #161)

Page 43 – Cracked's Unusual Gift Catalog (reprint from #179)

Page 46 – Three'sa Company – Samuel B. Whitehead (reprint from #185)

Page 52 – Cracked's Cartoon Showcase Featuring Bill Maul – Bill Maul (reprint from #184)

Page 54 – Gag Lines for Every Profession – Warren Sattler (reprint from #165)

Page 57 – Still More Believe it or Not (reprint from #181)

Page 60 – Ye Hang Ups #10 (He can't be serious) – C.E. Severin (Catherine Severin) (reprint from #190)

Page 61 – The Cracked Guide to Football – Howard Nostrand (reprint from #140)

Page 66 – Shut-Ups (big struggle) – Don Orehek (reprint from #168)

Page 67 – The Cracked Entertainment Trivia Game – John Severin (new)

Page 83 – 4 Out of 5 Dentists Surveyed (reprint from #170)

Back Cover – Great Moments in Entertainment 200 B.C. – Warren Sattler (reprint from #181)

The 26th Super Cracked, Spring 1985 (84 pages) ($2.00)

Cover – Monk Painting Cracked Covers – John Severin (reprint from #33)

Page 2 – Contents

Page 3 – 14 Posters (reprints from #177-191)

Page 19 – Cracked's Intelligence Test (revised reprint from #15)

Page 27 – The Adventures of the Masked Bandito – John Severin (reprint from #157)

Page 33 – Iffy U.F.O. Info Magazine – Howard Nostrand (reprint from #156)

Page 38 – Sagebrush #50 (There's gold here) – John Severin (reprint from #159)

Page 39 – And Still More from The Cracked Lens (reprint from #158)

Page 42 – A Cracked Look at a State Pen – Don Orehek (reprint from #152)

Page 46 – Cracked Visits the "Proverbs and Familiar Sayings" Museum – John Severin (reprint from #152)

Page 49 – One Afternoon at a Stop Light – Howard Nostrand (reprint from #160)

Page 50 – You Know You're in a Tacky Bank When – Warren Sattler (reprint from #155)

Page 52 – The Cracked World of Appliances – Don Orehek (reprint from #156)

Page 56 – Great Books at Great Prices When You Join the Book-a-Month Club (reprint from #157)

Page 58 – A Cracked Look at Phobias – Warren Sattler (reprint from #158)

Page 62 – How to be a Salesman – John Severin (reprint from #175)

Page 50 – Shut-Ups (yellow-bellies) – Don Orehek (reprint from #175)

Page 67 – Cracked Greeting Cards – Mike Ricigliano, John Severin (reprint from "Cracked Fun-Kit" #30)

Page 83 – Hudd & Dini (caveman) – Vic Martin (reprint from #96)

Back Cover – Canadian Crud ad – John Severin (reprint from #97)

The 27ᵗʰ Super Cracked does not exist!!!

The 28ᵗʰ Super Cracked, Fall 1985 (84 pages) ($2.25)

Cover – Super-Sylvester – O.O. Severin (John Severin) (reprint from #53)

Page 2 – Contents

Page 3 – Travel Stickers for People Who Hated the Trip and Cracked Hangups (new)

Page 19 – Webfoot – O.O. Severin (John Severin) (reprint from #203)

Page 26 – Signs That It's a Computer Age – Warren Sattler (reprint from #199)

Page 28 – What You'll Really Miss After you Graduate – Don Orehek (reprint from #198)

Page 32 – Loser Magazine – John Severin (reprint from #172)

Page 37 – Cracked Methods for Repairing Your Car Inexpensively – Bill Dubay (reprint from #137)

Page 41 – One Afternoon in a Plastic Surgeon's Office – Bill Ward (reprint from #164)

Page 42 – A Cracked Look at an Airport Terminal – Bob Taylor (reprint from #135)

Page 44 – Acnnie – John Severin (reprint from #191)

Page 52 – The Translator & the Duel – Mike Ricigliano (reprint from #189)

Page 53 – Cracked's New Sidewalk, Street and Playground Games – Warren Sattler (reprint from #173)

Page 57 – How Gullible Are You? – Ron Zalme (reprint from #188)

Page 60 – Cracked's First (and Probably Last) Annual Soap Opera Awards – Warren Sattler (reprint from #176)

Page 64 – Read Between the Lines! – John Langton (reprint from #196)

Page 65 – The Factors of Life – Samuel B. Whitehead (reprint from #181)

Page 72 – I.F.C. Pencil Sharpener Repair School – Samuel B. Whitehead (new)

Page 73 – Kids vs. Adults – Ron Zalme (reprint from #190)

Page 77 – Cracked Interviews the Olympic Training King – Bill Ward (reprint from #136)

Page 82 – Shut-Ups (quick-acting remedy) – Don Orehek (reprint from #196)

Page 83 – "Money Making" Iron-On (reprint from #181)

Back Cover – Insult Cards (reprint from #45)

The 29ᵗʰ *Super Cracked*, Winter 1986 (84 pages) ($2.00)

Cover – The Chicken or Sylvester – John Severin (reprint from #80)

Page 2 – Contents

Page 3 – Cracked Book Covers (new)

Page 11 – Cracked Plaques (new)

Page 19 – The A-a-a-y-y Team (Let's go men) – John Severin (reprint from #206)

Page 26 – If Kids Took Over Completely – Vance Rodewalt (reprint from #206)

Page 29 – Robot Report Magazine – John Severin (reprint from #194)

Page 33 – The ABC's of Video – Warren Sattler (reprint from #206)

Page 37 – One Day in Metropolitis – Don Orehek (reprint from #136)

Page 38 – A Cracked Look at Cable TV – Don Orehek (reprint from #193)

Page 42 – Cracked Visits a Hollywood Movie Set – Sururi Gumen (reprint from #178)

Page 44 – Star Drek III: The Search for Spook – John Severin (reprint from #208)

Page 51 – The True Meaning of Art – Rurik Tyler (reprint from #212)

Page 52 – The Cracked World of Teenagers – Don Orehek (reprint from #161)

Page 56 – New Uses for Televisions – Sururi Gumen (reprint from #190)

Page 58 – The Cracked Guide to Jogging – Howard Nostrand (reprint from #146)

Page 62 – Wishful Thinking – Bob Taylor (reprint from #212)

Page 64 – The Day Mr. Smyth Saved Knut Rider – John Severin (reprint from #202)

Page 71 – The Jay Walk – Sururi Gumen (reprint from #184)

Page 72 – New Tamper-Resistant Packaging – Sururi Gumen (reprint from #201)

Page 74 – Kids, You Know You Really Have to Worry When – Don Orehek (reprint from #188)

Page 77 – Cracked Interviews the Music Video King – Vance Rodewalt (reprint from #209)

Page 82 – Shut-Ups (man trying to break down door) – Don Orehek (reprint from #176)

Page 83 – Scratch 'n' Sniff Poster – Cracked Poster (reprint from #191)

Back Cover – Great Moments in Aviation 1947 – Samuel B. Whitehead (reprint from #173)

The 30ᵗʰ *Super Cracked*, Spring 1986 (84 pages) ($2.00)

Cover – We Attack the A-Team – John Severin (reprint from #201)

Page 2 – Contents

Page 3 – The Official Cracked Calendar for 1986 (revised reprint from *Biggest Greatest Cracked* #5)

Page 19 – The Awakening – John Severin (reprint from #97)

Page 20 – If the A-a-ayy Team Was Made Less Violent – John Severin (reprint from #210)

Page 27 – How to Have a Fun Time on Earth – Don Orehek (reprint from #196)

Page 32 – Past, Present and Future Changes in Sports – Don Orehek (reprint from #199)

Page 36 – A Teenager is – Don Orehek (reprint from #127)

Page 38 – The Cracked Guide to Martial Arts – Sean Severin (John Severin) (reprint from #150)

Page 42 – A Cracked Look at a Big City Office – Don Orehek (reprint from #173)

Page 44 – Grumblins – John Severin (reprint from #209)

Page 51 – Another Cracked Look at a Video Arcade – Sururi Gumen (reprint from #208)

Page 54 – The Cracked World of Disco – Don Orehek (reprint from #164)

Page 58 – Cracked's Early Warning Signs of "No Respect" – John Langton (reprint from #198)

Page 60 – When All Businesses Go Automated – Sururi Gumen (reprint from #191)

Page 63 – One Day in the North Woods – Howard Nostrand (reprint from #163)

Page 64 – Cracked's New Type Baseball Cards that Tell it Like it is – Howard Nostrand (reprint from #138)

Page 67 – Tootsie Roll – John Severin (reprint from #196)

Page 74 – Future Ultra Realistic Electronic Games – Val Mayerik (reprint from #174)

Page 77 – Ye Hang Ups #4 (got a minute) – C.E. Severin (Catherine Severin) (reprint from #174)

Page 78 – Cracked Interviews the Hamburger King – John Severin (reprint from #99)

Page 82 – Shut-Ups (haven't had this much fun) – Don Orehek (reprint from #210)

Page 83 – 4 Out of 5 Dentists Surveyed (reprint from #170)

Back Cover – Chicken Soap label – John Severin (reprint from #108)

Super Cracked #31, Summer 1986 (84 pages) ($2.00)

Cover – Super Sylvester – Bob Fingerman (new)

Page 2 – The REAL Ape Man! – Ned Kelly (John Severin) / Don Edwing (reprint from #29) (originally called "Of the Apes")

Page 3 – Contents (reprint from #53)

Page 4 – "Camp" Comic Heroland – John Severin (reprint from #58)

Page 6 – Are Comics Ruining Our Children? – Bill Elder (reprint from #11)

Page 8 – What Today's Strips Would Look Like if They Were Drawn by Ronald Reagan – John Severin (reprint from #194)

Page 12 – The Funnies in the Flicks! (reprint from #72)

Page 14 – Cracked Heroes A-Round the World – William Hoest / George Gladir (reprint from #59) (originally called "Super Heroes A-Round the World")

Page 18 – Dapperman! – O.O. Severin (John Severin) / George Gladir (reprint from #53)

Page 23 – Help! Wanted – Garry Owen (John Severin) (reprint from #38)

Page 24 – Merged Comic Strips – Bill McCartney (Bill Ward) (reprint from #37)

Page 28 – Exercise Manual and Hot Dog Stunts for Super Heroes – Powers (John Severin) (reprint from #147)

Page 32 – Soupedupman (reprint from #2)

Page 33 – The Day Batguy Almost Went Bats – John Severin (reprint from #73) (originally called "The Day Bazman Almost Went Bats")

Page 35 – The Lone Ranger (reprint from #38)

Page 36 – If the Comics Were Drawn by Famous Movie Directors – Bill McCartney (Bill Ward) (reprint from #51)

Page 40 – Yellow Pearl – John Severin (reprint from #114)

Page 44 – What Christopher Reeve Will Be Like When He Gets Old – Samuel B. Whitehead (reprint from #183)

Page 47 – Get the Energizer! – John Severin (reprint) (originally called something else)

Page 48 – You Know You're a Super Type – Warren Sattler (reprint from #211)

Page 50 – Cracked Looks at the World of Superdom – Don Orehek (reprint from #139)

Page 53 – Cracked Presents Superheroes of the Future – Willy Orwonte (John Severin) (reprint from #160)

Page 56 – Super Hero Ads – Bruce Day (reprint from #152)

Page 58 – If Comic Strip Characters Had to Face Simple But Realistic Problems! – John Severin (reprint from #69)

Page 61 – The Adventures of the Masked Bandito – John Severin (reprint from #157)

Page 67 – Super Sylvester – Bob Fingerman, Bill Wray, O.O. Severin (John Severin), Steve Ditko / Mort Todd (new)

Page 83 – Final Proof – John Severin / Don Edwing (reprint from #33)

Back Cover – Super-Powered Laughs (reprints from #53, 183, 194)

Super Cracked #32, Fall 1986 (84 pages) ($2.00) (Series starts over with #1 next issue and becomes *Cracked Super* with #5.)

Cover – Super Sylvester, G.I. Joke and the Ape Man – Bob Fingerman, Shawn Kerri, John Severin (new, with partial reprint from #58)

Page 2 – Charlie Weakling ad – Bill McCartney (Bill Ward) (reprint from #54)

Page 3 – Contents

Page 4 – Canine the Barbarian (The Coming of Canine) – Gary Fields (1st appearance of "Canine the Barbarian") (new)

Page 9 – G.I. Joke in Worry Warts – Shawn Kerri / Stu Schwartzberg (new)

Page 14 – Another Origin of the Super Sylvester Cracked Crusader – Bob Fingerman, Bill Wray (new)

Page 19 – Marvin of the Apes! – O.O. Severin (John Severin) (reprint from #57)

Page 23 – Modern Cliff-Hanging Situations – Bill McCartney (Bill Ward) (reprint from #48)

Page 26 – Judo – Jack Davis (reprint from #11)

Page 29 – Catalog for Costumed Heroes – John Severin (reprint from #190) (originally titled "1982 Catalog for Costumed Heroes")

Page 32 – Tarzan Goes Around the World in 80 Pictures – John Severin (reprint from #33)

Page 38 – Jungle Gems (reprint from #63)

Page 40 – Draw Your Own Conclusion – John Severin (reprint from #19)

Page 43 – A Guide to Modern Art – Bill McCartney (Bill Ward) (reprint from #37)

Page 48 – The Day Comic Strip Characters Got up on the Wrong Side of Bed – John Severin (reprint from #76)

Page 51 – 20th Century Coat-of-Arms – John Severin (reprint from #55)

Page 54 – Tarzan's Abdication – Bill Ward (reprint from #113)

Page 59 – Pow U. – Tony Tallarico (reprint from #65)

Page 63 – Safari So Good (reprint from #104)

Page 65 – The Day That Nothing Seemed to Go Right for the Ape Man – Fal Hoster (John Severin) (reprint from #55)

Page 68 – Updated Torture Devices for Catching the Witches of Today – John Severin (reprint from #58) (the dates in the article were removed)

Page 71 – Cracked Interviews the Psychic King – Bill Ward (reprint from #156)

Page 76 – G.I. Donut Boys – John Severin (reprint from #167)

Page 83 – ("Don't shoot me, Batman") (Batman, Flash Gordon, Superman) (new)

Back Cover – Karate Magazine – John Severin (reprint from #88)

Super Cracked #1, Summer 1987 (100 pages) ($2.75) (Series starts over with #1 due to the numbering mistakes of the prior series. This series becomes *Cracked Super* with #5.)

Cover – Super Sylvester – Bill Wray (new)

Page 2 – The Uggly Family (give this bone) – Stosh Gillespie (Dan Clowes) / Eel O'Brian (Mort Todd) (reprint from #221)

Page 3 – Contents

Page 4 – Soupedupman (reprint from #2) (red color added)

Page 5 – Super Sylvester – Bob Fingerman, Bill Wray, O.O. Severin (John Severin), Steve Ditko / Mort Todd (reprint from *Super Cracked* #31) (red color added)

Page 10 – Exclamation!!! – Don Perlin (reprint from #50) (red color added)

Page 11 – Rockey: 2001 – John Severin / Eel O'Brian (Mort Todd) (reprint from #219)

Page 15 – Super Types in Ordinary Life – Warren Sattler (reprint from #183)

Page 19 – Fhive for the Fhun it! (reprint from #95)

Page 20 – The Real Secrets Behind Agent 0007 – O.O. Severin (John Severin) (reprint from #56)

Page 24 – Buggy – John Severin (reprint from #40)

Page 27 – What Christopher Reeve Will Be Like When He Gets Old – Samuel B. Whitehead (reprint from #183)

Page 30 – Showbiz-Type Election Ads – John Severin (reprint from #209)

Page 33 – Axis Sallies – John Severin (reprint from #26)

Page 36 – The Spy Who Snubbed Me – O.O. Severin (John Severin) (reprint from #148)

Page 42 – The Machine Gun Nest – Ned Kelly (John Severin) / Don Edwing (reprint from #30)

Page 43 – Man's Best Friend? – Jack Davis (reprint from #11)

Page 44 – What Today's Strips Would Look Like if They Were Drawn by Ronald Reagan – John Severin (reprint from #194)

Page 48 – Death Wishy-Washy 3! – Bob Fingerman (reprint from #220)

Page 52 – Are Comics Ruining Our Children? – Bill Elder (reprint from #11)

Page 54 – Russia Goes Madison Ave. – John Severin (reprint from #52)

Page 60 – The Moon Ate a Big Pink Kumquat (reprint from #87)

Page 62 – When the Woman's Lib Movement Spreads to the Comics! – John Severin (reprint from #92)

Page 66 – Cracked Look at Young Schlock Holmes! – Walter Brogan / Joe Catalano (reprint from #220)

Page 70 – Super People Magazine – Sururi Gumen (reprint from #163)

Page 74 – Cracked Interviews the Saturday Morning Cartoon King –
Bill Ward (reprint from #159)

Page 79 – The Swingers Set (reprint from #59)

Page 80 – If Different Cartoonists had Painted the Mona Lisa – John
Severin (reprint from #25)

Page 82 – Russian Magazines – Bill Elder (reprint from #13)

Page 84 – Soupedupman The Satire – Nireves (John Severin) (reprint
from #160) (originally called "Suped-Upman The Satire")

Page 91 – G.I. Joke in Worry Warts – Shawn Kerri / Stu Schwartzberg
(reprint from Super Cracked #32) (red color added)

Page 99 – Robot Wars (Whirrrrrrrr) – Steve Ditko / Mort Todd (reprint
from #219)

Back Cover – Godzilla and Pow-Man – John Severin, Bob Fingerman
(reprint from Pow! #2 and Super Cracked #32)

Super Cracked #2, Summer 1988 (100 pages) ($2.75)

Cover – Bad Guys vs. Good Guys – Bill Wray (new)

Page 2 – Ya Pays Yer Money and Ya Takes Yer Cherce – Bill McCartney
(Bill Ward) (reprint from #8)

Page 3 – Contents (red color added)

Page 4 – Bullet Proof Car – John Severin (reprint from #35) (red color
added)

Page 5 – Powerhouse Pepper in "The Bank Book with Blank Look" –
Basil Wolverton (new to Cracked) (red color added)

Page 11 – Reel Gone Goodies (reprint from #75)

Page 12 – Moonwrecker – Sururi Gumen (reprint from #166)

Page 19 – How a Rumor Gets Started – Al Jaffee (reprint from #7)

Page 21 – Cobrat – Bill Wray / Mort Todd (reprint from #225)

Page 27 – The Sailing of the Vikings – John Severin (reprint from #18)

Page 30 – Hudd & Dini (painted wall) – Vic Martin (reprint from #76)

Page 31 – Cracked Looks at World War I Sky Fighters – John Severin
(reprint from #107)

Page 35 – Shut-Ups (Who goes there?) – Don Orehek (reprint from #152)

Page 36 – Wild Wheels (reprint from #104)

Page 38 – Another Origin of the Super Sylvester Cracked Crusader –
Bob Fingerman, Bill Wray (reprint from Super Cracked #32)

Page 43 – One Rustic Day Outside Tijuana, Mexico – John Severin
(reprint from #166)

Page 44 – Awards from the Syndicate – Bill Elder (reprint from #12)

Page 47 – The Loser – John Severin (reprint from #131)

Page 49 – China Clown – Sururi Gumen (reprint from #123)

Page 55 – Hiss the Villains (reprint from #94)

Page 59 – The Magic Lamp – Don Orehek (reprint from #138)

Page 60 – High Plains Shifter – John Severin (reprint from #117)

Page 66 – Illustrated Limericks – Jack Davis (reprint from #15)

Page 68 – The Pirate Treasure Chest (reprint from #64)

Page 70 – Julius "Little" Caesar – John Severin (reprint from #6)

Page 73 – Way Out West! – Jack Davis (reprint from #11)

Page 75 – Batzman Meets the Green Horned Bee! – M & O.O. Severin (Marie Severin, John Severin) (reprint from #74)

Page 81 – Hudd & Dini (Vacancy) – Vic Martin (reprint from #79)

Page 82 – Returns of the Jed Eye – John Severin (reprint from #199)

Page 90 – The Way They Should Have Filmed it – John Severin (reprint from #29)

Page 91 – The Freakniks Meet the Wreckin' Crew (new) (red color added)

Page 98 – Shut-Ups (let's go out dancing) – Mike Ricigliano (reprint from #136) (red color added)

Page 99 – Sagebrush (hmmmmmm) – Lor & John Severin (reprint from *Giant Cracked Fun-Kit* #30)

Back Cover – Who'd She Expect...Super Sylvester? – Bill McCartney (Bill Ward) (reprint from #4) (originally called "Who'd She Expect...Elvis?")

Super Cracked #3, Summer 1989 (100 pages) ($2.75)

Cover – Good Guys vs. Bad Guys – Rick Altergott (new)

Page 2 and 99 – Gross Busters – Walter Brogan (new)

Page 3 – Contents – Batman – Mike Ricigliano (new)

Page 4 – Traitors of the Lost Ark – John Severin (reprint from #183)

Page 12 – The Moon Ate a Big Pink Kumquat (reprint from #87)

Page 14 – Star Drek the Moving Picture – John Severin (reprint from #169)

Page 22 – Tardzan the Apish Man – John Clayton (John Severin) / Joe Catalano, Mort Todd (reprint from #226)

Page 27 – The Lone Ranger (reprint from #38)

Page 28 – The Real Secrets Behind Agent 0007 – O.O. Severin (John Severin) (reprint from #56)

Page 32 – Poopeye – Nireves (John Severin) (reprint from #179)

Page 39 – The Day Batguy Almost Went Bats – John Severin (reprint from #73)

Page 41 – Star Drek – The Last Hurrah? – John Severin / Joe Catalano (reprint from #184)

Page 48 – YuckTales – Gary Fields / John Arcudi (reprint from #236)

Page 51 – Battyman – Rick Altergott / Charles E. Hall (reprint from #234)

Page 55 – Indianapolis Bones and the Temple of Gloom – John Severin (reprint from #208)

Page 62 – Cracked Interviews Clint Beastwood – Rob Orzechowsk: / Joe Catalano (reprint from #234)

Page 65 – The Uggly Family Uglystoppers Textbook – Stosh Gillespie (Dan Clowes) / Eel O'Brian (Mort Todd) (reprint from #234)

Page 69 – Fhive for the Fhun it! (reprint from #95)

Page 70 – SuperSylvester the Cracked Crusader! The Legend – John Severin / Mort Todd (reprint from #234)

Page 74 – Rangey Loner – John Severin (reprint from #236)

Page 79 – How the Movies Wrecked Supedupman – Rick Altergott / Mort Todd (reprint from #233)

Page 83 – Man's Best Friend? – Jack Davis (reprint from #11)

Page 84 – Star Drek III: The Search for Spook – John Severin (reprint from #208)

Page 91 – Modern Cliff-Hanging Situations – Bill McCartney (Bill Ward) (reprint from #43)

Page 94 – Are Comics Ruining Our Children? – Bill Elder (reprint from #11)

Page 96 – .007 Devices that Bombed! – Rob Orzechowski / Eel O'Brian (Mort Todd) (reprint from #233)

Back Cover – Slopeye – Bill Wray (new)

Super Cracked #4, Summer 1990 (100 pages) ($3.50) (Series continues as Cracked Super with #5.)

Cover – Super Guys vs. Super Scoundrels – Rurik Tyler (gatefold cover) (new)

Page 2, 3 and 99 – Super Guys vs. Super Scoundrels – Rick Altergott (inside gatefold cover) (new)

Page 3 – Contents

Page 4 – Columbum – Walter Brogan / Tony Frank (Lou Silverstone) (reprint from #247)

Page 8 – Chariots of the Clocs? – John Severin (reprint from #122)

Page 11 – Batman to the Rescue – Mike Ricigliano / Roger Brown (reprint from #248)

Page 12 – Beaujack – John Severin / Charles Rodrigues (reprint from #122)

Page 17 – Twits – Walter Brogan (reprint from #245)

Page 21 – Shut-Ups (crummy issue of Cracked) – Don Orehek (reprint from #248)

Page 22 – The True Story of The Lone Ranger – Brian Buniak (reprint from #198)

Page 25 – Batty-Weapons that Didn't Quite Make it to the Utility Belt! – John Severin / George Gladir (reprint from #248)
Page 28 – Hazards of: Being a Superhero – Mike Ricigliano / Roger Brown (reprint from #243)
Page 30 – Ill-Legal Weapons – Walter Brogan / Vic Bianco (Lou Silverstone) (reprint from #251)
Page 36 – Things a Hero's Mom Could Never Get Used To! – Kurt Schaffenberger (reprint from #243)
Page 38 – Cracked Songs from Outer Space – John Langton (reprint from #172)
Page 40 – Young Bums – Rick Altergott (reprint from #243)
Page 44 – Comic Con Confidential! – John Severin / George Gladir (reprint from #248)
Page 46 – Kung-Phew – John Severin (reprint from #112)
Page 51 – The Musketeers – Mike Ricigliano / Roger Brown (reprint from #247)
Page 52 – What are the Old TV & Movie Detectives Doing Today? – John Severin (reprint from #121)
Page 57 – Hazards of: (Dating) – Mike Ricigliano / Roger Brown (reprint from #250)
Page 59 – Them Battyman Sequels We're Sure to See! – John Severin / George Gladir (reprint from #248)
Page 62 – Shut-Ups (shell fragment) – Don Orehek (reprint from #247)
Page 63 – The Rodfather – O.O. Severino (John Severin) (reprint from #104)
Page 69 – From Bad to Worse – Mike Ricigliano / Roger Brown (reprint from #243)
Page 71 – Shut-Ups (who does the dishes) – Don Orehek (reprint from #245)
Page 72 – What if Bruise Payne Didn't Become Battyman?! – Ron Wagner / George Gladir (reprint from #248)
Page 76 – Hudd & Dini (Vic Martin) – Vic Martin (reprint from #250)
Page 82 – The War on Law – John Severin (reprint from #57)
Page 84 – The Cracked Lens Presents the Bat-Photo Scrapbook! (reprint from #248)
Page 87 – Fairy Tale Characters – Mike Ricigliano / Roger Brown (reprint from #247)
Page 88 – Sagebrush #27 (reptiles are better) – John Severin (reprint from #119) / Ye Hang Ups #27 (fishing) – Nireves (John Severin) (reprint from #119)
Page 90 – Cracked Form & Function The Batty-Wing – Rurik Tyler (reprint from #248)
Page 92 – Things You Don't See – Mike Ricigliano / Roger Brown (reprint from #245)

Page 94 – The Real Secrets Behind Agent 0007 – O.O. Severin (John Severin) (reprint from #56)

Page 98 – Martial Art Weapons and Techniques – Bill Ward (reprint from #118)

Back Cover – Subscription ad / Cracked Hat / Severin Cracked T-Shirt / Black Cracked T-Shirt / Sylvester Doll ad (reprint from #66)

Zany #1, September 1958 (52 pages) (25c)

Cover – The Sky is Falling Down

Page 2 – L&N Cigarette ad – Bill McCartney (Bill Ward)

Page 3 – Contents

Page 4 – What'll You Have?

Page 5 – Lil Dabner

Page 6 – Arnold Hitchshnook Presents

Page 9 – Bazeball Then and Now

Page 11 – Trick Dacy

Page 13 – The Underworld of Sports Skin Diving

Page 16 – Stranger Than Strange (1st *Stranger Than Strange*)

Page 17 – The Buzinezz Card Craze Page 18 – An Afternoon With the Stars – Don Orehek Page 23 – The Western Gangster Horror Show

Page 24 – Keep Kool

Page 26 – Vacation Time

Page 28 – It Could Happen

Page 29 – Mail This Risky Coupon Now!

Page 30 – Win.... Place and Oh! – Don Orehek

Page 32 – La Trivia Lotta

Page 34 – TV Horror Listings

Page 36 – The Effects of Horror Movies!

Page 38 – They'll Rue It Every Time – Don Orehek

Page 39 – See America First The Raving Boys

Page 42 – The Cowboy

Page 46 – Does The Moon Really Rhyme With June?

Page 48 – TV Or Not TV ? ? ? ?

Page 50 – Sports Slants

Page 51 – Beerdon's New Half and Half – Don Orehek

Back Cover – Subscription ad

Zany #2, December 1958 (52 pages) (25c)

Cover – Firemen – Bill Everett

Page 2 – Arrowed Shirts ad – Don Orehek

Page 3 – Contents

Page 4 – Time to Check your Witch and Voodoo Supplies
Page 5 – Stranger Than Strange
Page 6 – Letters
Page 7 – Maggee and Jizz
Page 8 – Zany Inventions – Joe Sinnott
Page 10 – I Am Who? – Carl Burgos
Page 11 – Prince Val Runt – Don Orehek
Page 12 – Pogoo
Page 13 – Gunspook – Don Orehek
Page 16 – Women Wrestlers
Page 18 – Testimonial Dinner – Carl Burgos
Page 20 – The Answer Man – Tim Roth
Page 22 – The Grapevine
Page 23 – Zwordo – Carl Burgos
Page 26 – The Robots Take Over
Page 28 – A Day in the Life of Gassie!
Page 30 – Henri – Carl Burgos
Page 32 – The Dilemma of Doreen Dior – Joe Sinnott
Page 34 – The Fantom – Tim Roth
Page 35 – A Day in the Life of Mr. Adman
Page 37 – Flush Gordon
Page 38 – Dean Lewis & Jerry Martin Make Up
Page 40 – Horror House ad
Page 42 – Crime Wave by Kids From Good Homes – Stan Goldberg
Page 44 – Rum'ple Room
Page 46 – Around Mars
Page 48 – Joe Bazooka Retires
Page 49 – Cazee at the Bat
Page 51 – Subscription ad – Carl Burgos
Back Cover – Back To School Zany Book Labels

Zany #3, March 1959 (52 pages) (25c)

Cover – Sputnik Monsters – Bill Everett
Page 2 – Look Mommy.. I Don't Have Cavities! – Don Orehek
Page 3 – Contents
Page 4 – Stranger Than Strange
Page 5 – Smilin' Mac – Don Orehek
Page 7 – Mike Monster – Private Eye
Page 10 – Ally Oops
Page 11 – The Truth About People
Page 13 – Ahchee
Page 16 – Your Snoopin' Reporter

Page 18 – Horror House ad
Page 20 – The Katzenpajama Kids
Page 22 – Buck Dogers
Page 23 – Louella Persons in Hollywood
Page 25 – Steve Canyou
Page 26 – Picture Puzzles to go Zany by... Zany Brainbusters
Page 28 – Abbie 'n Splats
Page 30 – Big Ben Built
Page 32 – Sure-Fire-7-Day-Reducing-Diet
Page 34 – Maulbury Cigarette ad (reprint from #4)
Page 35 – Angel Touche Page 36 – Travlers Checques ad
Page 37 – Polka Dot Toothpaste ad – Paul Reinman (reprint from #3)
Page 38 – Mavertrick
Page 41 – Daddy-O and Me
Page 43 – Steve Canyou
Page 44 – Limited Warfare
Page 46 – People Are Humorous
Page 48 – Letters
Page 49 – Mansnake the Magician
Page 51 – Subscription ad Back Cover – Zany Greeting Cards

Zany #4, May 1959 (52 pages) (25c)

Cover – Gunsmoke – Bill Everett
Page 2 – Nitoil ad – Don Orehek
Page 3 – Contents
Page 4 – Camping Out – Richard Doxsee
Page 6 – Robbin Hood and his Band of Merrie Men
Page 9 – Seeing Hams – Carl Burgos
Page 10 – Fashion
Page 12 – Have Grunion Will Travel – George Peltz
Page 15 – Vitamin "X" – Stan Goldberg
Page 16 – What's Brand New in Science? – John Forte
Page 18 – Zany Illustrated
Page 20 – How to Avoid Borrowers – Carl Burgos
Page 22 – How to Win Friends While Under the Influence – Richard
    Doxsee
Page 24 – Big Cars – John Forte
Page 26 – Russian Bubble-Gum Cards – Richard Doxsee
Page 28 – Housewrecking Made Easy – John Severin
Page 30 – Inside a Cauliflower Ear
Page 32 – Dinosaurs are Sweeping the Country – John Forte
Page 34 – Horror House ad – John Severin

Page 36 – Wigs, Mops and Tousle-Heads
Page 38 – Good, Clean, Fun Novelty Practical Jokes
Page 44 – Torn Tremor
Page 48 – Chinese Records
Back Cover – Zany Satellite Cards

Paperback Books:

***The Cracked Reader*, 1960 (Ace Books) (160 pages + covers) (35c) (1ˢᵗ ad appearance in *Cracked* #15. The old *Cracked* logo appears on the covers of this and the next two paperback collections, yet no material was reprinted from those first nine issues.)**

Cover – Broken Glasses – John Severin (new)
Page 1 – Title page
Page 2 – Copyright page
Page 3 – From the Cracked Publisher – Robert C. Sproul (new)
Page 4 – Brigitte Bardot as Seen by Different Artists – John Severin
    (reprint from #12)
Page 11 – Russian Shut-Ups (Russia) – Bill McCartney (Bill Ward)
    (reprint from #12)
Page 14 – Believe it or Nuts!! – Jack Davis (reprint from #13)
Page 16 – Judo – Jack Davis (reprint from #11)
Page 24 – When it all Started (First World War) – John Severin (reprint
    from #13)
Page 27 – Bat Masteyson – Jack Davis (reprint from #13)
Page 38 – Are Comics Ruining Our Children? – Bill Elder (reprint from
    #11)
Page 42 – HIP Alphabet Book – Vic Martin (reprint from #13)
Page 51 – Illustrated Little Willies – LePoer (John Severin) (reprint
    from #12)
Page 55 – A Beatnik Goes to a Party – Jack Davis (reprint from #12)
Page 62 – Rate Your Personality – LePoer (John Severin) (reprint from
    #12)
Page 71 – Fraternity Keys (reprint from #10)
Page 76 – Believe it or No! – Jack Davis (reprint from #11)
Page 78 – How Different Nationalities Make Marriage Proposals – Bill
    McCartney (Bill Ward) (reprint from #12)
Page 82 – If Different Poets Had Read Cracked – John Severin (reprint
    from #13)
Page 89 – Do-it-Yourself Cartoons (reprint from #12)
Page 91 – The Casual Format – Angelo Torres (reprint from #10)

Page 100 – Are We Civilized? – Russ Heath (reprint from #13)

Page 106 – Story of the Year (I'm afraid) – Jack Davis (reprint from #11) (originally called "Story of the Month")

Page 110 – Freezing People – Jack Davis (reprint from #13)

Page 124 – Cartoons of the Year – Jack Davis (reprint from #13)

Page 128 – When it all Started (take the nice gun) – Jack Davis (reprint from #11)

Page 131 – TV and Real Life Western Heroes – John Severin (reprint from #14)

Page 137 – Celebrity Shut-Ups (shampoo) – John Severin (reprint from #14)

Page 143 – Sea Haunt – Jack Davis (reprint from #14)

Page 153 – Band-Aides for Weird Color Skin – Jack Davis (reprint from #14)

Page 156 – Sylvester P. Smythe As Seen by Different Artists (reprint from #14)

Back Cover – text

More Cracked, 1961 (Ace Books) (144 pages + covers) (35c) (1ˢᵗ ad appearance in Cracked #21.)

Cover – Drawing Guns in the Mirror – John Severin (new)

Page 1 – Title page

Page 2 – Copyright page

Page 3 – The Cracked People – Robert C. Sproul (new)

Page 4 – Hollywood Life Stories from the Pages of History – John Severin (reprint from #15)

Page 12 – Commercials in Real Life – John Severin (reprint from #14)

Page 22 – If Literature Were Written in the Gossip Columns (reprint from #15)

Page 31 – Endings for Old TV Shows – Jack Davis (reprint from #11)

Page 40 – Historical Headlines (reprint from #18)

Page 44 – How Family Life Would be if the Sexes Changed Places – John Severin (reprint from #15)

Page 53 – Sports Oddities (Hank Luckeezi) – Jack Davis (reprint from #15)

Page 55 – A Cracked Hip Primer – John Severin (reprint from #18)

Page 63 – Trade School for Misfits (reprint from #11)

Page 67 – Cracked's Applied Psychology – Angel Martinez (reprint from #17)

Page 74 – If TV Shows Weren't Rigged – John Severin (reprint from #17)

Page 83 – Modern Appliances Have Overshot Their Function! – John Severin (reprint from #13)

Page 89 – Why People Move to the Suburbs – Jack Davis (reprint from #14)

Page 101 – Rare Olde Shut-Upf – Jack Davis (originally titled "Ye Olde Shut-Upf") (reprint from #16)

Page 104 – Magazine Covers – Jack Davis (reprint from #16)

Page 110 – What They're Really Saying? – John Severin (reprint from #16)

Page 116 – How Some of Our Customs Began – John Severin (reprint from #15)

Page 122 – When It All Ended (go to the police) – John Severin (reprint from #14)

Page 125 – The Searcher – Jack Davis (reprint from #14)

Page 127 – Cracked's Handy Guide to Self-Analysis – John Severin (reprint from #16)

Page 133 – Sports Oddities (Fullback Arnold) – Jack Davis (reprint from #15)

Page 135 – If Some Famous Married Couples had Divorce Hearings – John Severin (reprint from #17)

Back Cover – text

Completely Cracked, 1962 (Ace Books) (144 pages + covers) (35c) (1ˢᵗ ad appearance in Cracked #24.)

Cover – Napoleon Sylvester – John Severin (new)

Page 1 – Title page

Page 2 – Copyright page

Page 3 – Dear Reader – Robert C. Sproul (new)

Page 4 – How Madison Avenue Can Make Unpopular Subjects Popular – John Severin (reprint from #20)

Page 9 – How to Break Bad Habits – John Severin (reprint from #14)

Page 16 – If Racketeers Took Over the Children's World – Jack Davis (reprint from #11)

Page 28 – Send Out Your Own Greeting Cards (reprint from #13)

Page 35 – Ads You Never Get to See – John Severin (reprint from #19)

Page 44 – If Political Figures Did TV Guest Shots – John Severin (reprint from #20)

Page 54 – Real Wildlife Nature's Oddities (reprint from #20)

Page 56 – They Shoulda Listened – Jack Davis (reprint from #15)

Page 62 – Educational Motion Pictures – John Severin (reprint from #19)

Page 71 – Handwriting Analysis – John Severin (reprint from #20)

Page 78 – If Different Comedians Played Shakespeare – John Severin (reprint from #20)

Page 84 – Specialized Eye Charts (reprint from #19)
Page 88 – How Infantile Are You? – John Severin (reprint from #16)
Page 98 – Awards from the Syndicate – Bill Elder (reprint from #12)
Page 104 – Future on the Spot Reporting – John Severin (reprint from #18)
Page 116 – Madison Avenue Shut-Ups (no cavities) – Vic Martin (reprint from #20)
Page 124 – Great Women of History – Oswaldo Laino (reprint from #20)
Page 130 – Things We Shoulda Done – Jack Davis (reprint from #17)
Page 140 – Real Wildlife Nature's Oddities (reprint from #20)
Page 142 – When it all Ended – George Peltz (reprint from #18)
Back Cover – text

Cracked Again, 1966 (Ace Books) (128 pages + covers) (45c) (1st ad appearance in Cracked #58.)
Cover – Sylvester Joker Card Hand – John Severin (reprint from #13)
Page 1 – Title page
Page 2 – Copyright page
Page 3 – Something Funny is Going on Here! – Robert C. Sproul (new)
Page 4 – Historical Scoops – John Severin (reprint from #32)
Page 8 – Trading Stamps Updated – Pete Wyma (reprint from #33)
Page 14 – The TV Strike – John Severin (reprint from #35)
Page 21 – Personalized Wrist Watches! – John Severin (reprint from #36)
Page 26 – If Different Cartoonists had Painted the Mona Lisa – John Severin (reprint from #25)
Page 30 – Cracked Space Helmets – John Severin (reprint from #25)
Page 34 – Hip Talk Taken Literally – Chic Stone (reprint from #16)
Page 45 – G.I. Jr. – John Severin (reprint from #33)
Page 51 – Typical Graduates – John Severin (reprint from #27)
Page 61 – The Rescue – John Severin / Don Edwing (reprint from #32)
Page 64 – The Unsociables ad – John Severin (reprint from #16)
Page 65 – TV Medical Symbols – John Severin (reprint from #34)
Page 73 – Story of the Month (Hi, mom) – John Severin (reprint from #25)
Page 75 – ("tipped the waiters") "Some Like it Hot" photo
Page 76 – There's One in Every Crowd – John Severin (reprint from #16)
Page 85 – Farmer's Old Almanac – John Severin (reprint from #6)
Page 92 – Letters, We Have Letters – John Severin (reprint from #33)
Page 101 – The Revels of Ancient Rome – John Severin (reprint from #20)
Page 103 – Fine Art Shut-Ups (lopsided hat) – John Severin (reprint from #19)

Page 105 – A Cracked Guide to Footwear – Bill McCartney (Bill Ward) (reprint from #42)

Page 112 – Is the Ink Blot Test Reliable? (reprint from #20)

Page 114 – The Shooting of Dan McGrew – John Severin (reprint from #18)

Page 120 – Cracked Headlines (reprint from #15)

Page 122 – Little League Everything – Bill McCartney (Bill Ward) (reprint from #37)

Page 128 – (14-year-old girl) *West Side Story* photo (reprint from #40)

Back Cover – Reviews

Get Me Cracked, March 1973 (Dell Books) (128 pages + covers) (75c) (1ˢᵗ ad appearance in *Cracked* #112.)

Cover – Shattered Fun House Mirror – John Severin (new)

Page 1 – How This Book Came Into Being (new)

Page 2 – Oh, That Henny Youngman! – John Severin (reprint from #78)

Page 3 – Title page

Page 4 – Copyright page

Page 5 – Famous Events as Seen on the Isolated Camera – John Severin (reprint from #92)

Page 15 – Alice's Toy – Joe Mead (reprint from #84)

Page 18 – When the Woman's Lib Movement Spreads to the Comics! – John Severin (reprint from #92)

Page 32 – Great Scenes from Hollywood Movies if Shakespeare Had Written Them! – Bob Taylor (reprint from #95)

Page 38 – Mockus Smellby, M.D. – John Severin (reprint from #90)

Page 52 – What Really Happened to General Custer – Larry Barth (reprint from #88)

Page 54 – If Modern Personalities Had Written the Great Classics! – John Severin (reprint from #89)

Page 62 – Open the Door, Seymour! – Larry Barth (reprint from #92)

Page 63 – The Man and the Bird – Oskar Blotta (reprint from #87)

Page 66 – The War on Law – John Severin (reprint from #57)

Page 77 – Consecutive Translation – Art Pottier (reprint from #86)

Page 81 – The Status Symbol Rat Race – O.O. Severin (John Severin) (reprint from #62)

Page 87 – Shut-Ups – Charles Rodrigues (reprints from #78, 79, 95)

Page 90 – The Selling of the Department of Defense – Bill McCartney (Bill Ward) (reprint from #88)

Page 98 – The Girl and the Butterfly – Oskar Blotta (reprint from #79)

Page 101 – Pow U. – Tony Tallarico (reprint from #65)

Page 111 – Give it Back to the Indians – John Severin (reprint from #92)

Page 119 – Shut-Ups – Sam Gross (Charles Rodrigues) (reprints from #95, 81, 86)

Page 122 – At Home with the Spiro T. Agnews – John Severin (reprint from #84)

Back Cover – text about book – John Severin

Half-Cracked, April 1974 (Dell Books) (128 pages + covers) (75c) (1st ad appearance in Cracked #120.)

Cover – Split Picture – Basil Gogos (new)

Page 1 – This Book is Being Published in Response to an Enormous Demand! (new)

Page 3 – Title Page

Page 4 – Copyright Page

Page 5 – Those False Rumors About Cracked Magazine – John Severin / George Gladir (reprint from #25)

Page 15 – Why Does a Chicken Cross the Road? – Nellie Melba (Charles Rodrigues) (reprint from #76)

Page 19 – Krakaknuckle East of Hoboken! – John Severin (reprint from #85)

Page 33 – Make Mine Well Done! – John Langton (reprint from #62)

Page 36 – A Glossary of Cracked Definitions – LePoer (John Severin) (reprint from #29)

Page 44 – Churly – Vic Martin (reprint from #81)

Page 59 – "Whaddayacallits?" A New Cracked Game – Joe Mead (reprint from #77)

Page 68 – Fruity Tunes – Vic Martin (reprint from #88)

Page 74 – Batzman Meets the Green Horned Bee! – M & O.O. Severin (Marie Severin, John Severin) (reprint from #74)

Page 91 – The Electric Shave – Oskar Blotta (reprint from #86)

Page 94 – Initialists – Bill McCartney (Bill Ward) (reprint from #90)

Page 100 – That'll Be the Day! ($30 a week raise) – John Langton (reprint from #81)

Page 103 – Sagebrush (what heat) – John Severin (reprint from #89)

Page 107 – Handufactured Products – John Severin (reprint from #31)

Page 115 – Rollicking with Robert Redford (reprint from #92)

Page 120 – Yoga – John Severin (reprint from #9)

Back Cover – text about book – Basil Gogos

Cracked Up, June 1974 (Dell Books) (192 pages + covers) (95c) (1st ad appearance in Cracked #122.)

Cover – Split Crystal Ball – Basil Gogos (new)

Page 1 – It's Not Simply Because You're an Idiot That You're Paying More for This Book! (new)

Your Cracked, July 1974 (Dell Books) (192 pages + covers) (95c) (1ˢᵗ ad appearance in *Cracked* #125.)

Cover – Shaking a Finger – Basil Gogos (new)

Page 1 – The Cracked Tapes (new)

Page 3 – Title Page

Page 4 – Copyright Page

Page 5 – Cracked Looks at Department Stores – Bob Taylor (reprint from #99)

Page 11 – Commercializing the Moon – John Severin (reprint from #81)

Page 21 – If Famous Lines Were Said in Different Situations – John Severin (reprint from #101)

Page 26 – The Jockey – Caracu (reprint from #96)

Page 29 – The Chicken Killer – Bill McCartney (Bill Ward) / Jay Lynch (reprint from #30)

Page 33 – A Cracked Look at Desert Islands – Lugoze (reprint from #77)

Page 39 – What Really Happens During the Filming of Television Commercials! – Arnoldo Franchioni (reprint from #69)

Page 52 – The Emergency Landing – O.O. Severin (John Severin) (reprint from #63)

Page 61 – The Man with the Sign – Caracu (reprint from #68)

Page 63 – Merged Comic Strips – Bill McCartney (Bill Ward) (reprint from #37)

Page 74 – Get Out the Vote! – John Severin (reprint from #51)

Page 77 – Marx Brothers' Laff-In! (reprint from #73)

Page 83 – Would Columbus Have Discovered America Etc.? – O.O. Severin (John Severin) (reprint from #64)

Page 97 – The Shade – Caracu (reprint from #65)

Page 100 – Cracked's Double-Take Signs (reprint from #71)

Page 106 – Help! I'm in the Pacific – Edvard Severin (John Severin) / Stu Schwartzberg (reprint from #79)

Page 121 – G.I. Laugh-In! (reprint from #75)

Page 125 – It All Depends Upon the Point of View – Bill McCartney (Bill Ward) (reprint from #51)

Page 131 – Hudd & Dini (foot race) – Vic Martin (reprint from #104)

Page 134 – Exciting Games for Daredevils – Zackary Taylor (Bob Taylor) (reprint from #94)

Page 140 – Fields of Fun! (reprint from #71)

Page 146 – The Day Bazman Almost Went Bats – John Severin (reprint from #73)

Page 152 – Cracked Looks at Telephones – Bill McCartney (Bill Ward) (reprint from #87)

Page 163 – The Traffic Jam – Caracu (reprint from #70)

Page 166 – The Luckless League – Lugoze (reprint from #74)

Page 171 – Always a Rookie (reprint from #65)

Page 180 – How Different T.V. Cowboys Get Their Man – John Severin (reprint from #27)

Page 188 – Wedding Announcements We'd like to See (reprint from #104)

Back Cover – text about book – Basil Gogos

Cracked in the Saddle, June 1975 (Dell Books) (192 pages + covers) (95c) (1st ad appearance in *Cracked* #128.)

Cover – Horse Ride – Basil Gogos (new)

Page 1 – The Cracked Pledge to Our Readers (new)

Page 3 – Title Page

Page 4 – Copyright Page

Page 5 – A Cracked Alphabet Book About Politicians – John Langton (reprint from #70)

Page 19 – Tall Story – John Severin (reprint from #77)

Page 33 – The Hippies' Coloring Book – Lugoze (reprint from #79)

Page 39 – Stories of the Month (The Panhandler) – Jerry Kirschen (reprint from #18)

Page 42 – Develop a Sense of Humor – Carl Burgos (reprint from #9)

Page 49 – Black Thoughts – Caracu (reprint from #69)

Page 52 – Celebrity Childhoods – William Hoest (reprint from #57)

Page 64 – The New Mod Army – Bill McCartney (Bill Ward) (reprint from #100)

Page 76 – Marvin of the Apes! – O.O. Severin (John Severin) (reprint from #57)

Page 88 – Believe it or Nuts!! – Jack Davis (reprint from #13)

Page 90 – The Art of Kissing – LePoer – John Severin (reprint from #39)

Page 98 – A Cracked Look at Photography – O.O. Severin (John Severin) (reprint from #63)

Page 112 – It Happened at the Cemetery – Caracu (reprint from #69)

Page 117 – Cracked's Think Tank Solutions (reprint from #71)

Page 131 – When It All Ended (go to the police) – John Severin (reprint from #14)

Page 134 – Cue Cards for Everything – Bill McCartney (Bill Ward) (reprint from #73)

Page 144 – Nutty Nicknames – John Langton (reprint from #81)

Page 152 – How to Tell If You Are An Adolescent – Howard Cruse (reprint from #97)

Page 155 – Cracked Looks at Old-Time Songs – Oswaldo Laino (reprint from #21)

Page 158 – The Dream Came True – LePoer (John Severin) (reprint from #31)

Page 169 – Cracked Visits a U.S. Army Camp – Lugoze (reprint from #79)
Page 174 – Insult Cards for All Occasions – Bill McCartney (Bill Ward) (reprint from #78)
Page 181 – Cracked Form Telegrams – John Severin (reprint from #34)
Page 186 – Am I Really in Love? – John Severin (reprint from #11)
Back Cover – text about book – Basil Gogos

***It's a Cracked World*, July 1975 (Dell Books) (192 pages + covers) (95¢)
(1st ad appearance in *Cracked* #130.)**
Cover – Sylvester in a Globe – Basil Gogos (new)
Page 1 – We Guarantee This Collection (new)
Page 3 – Title Page
Page 4 – Copyright Page
Page 5 – What if They – John Severin (reprint from #94)
Page 14 – Medallions with a Message – Tony Tallarico (reprint from #79)
Page 22 – That'll Be the Day! – John Severin (reprint from #80)
Page 25 – A Visit to Transylvania – Bill McCartney (Bill Ward) (reprint from #55)
Page 34 – Cracked's 8 Great Ways to Beat the Heat – Vic Martin (reprint from #54)
Page 40 – Accessories for Your Car – John Severin (reprint from #23)
Page 45 – What's in a Name? – Art Pottier (reprint from #74)
Page 50 – A Cracked Look at Supermarkets – Bill McCartney (Bill Ward) (reprint from #83)
Page 65 – Metropolis the Slave – Arnoldo Franchioni (reprint from #63)
Page 71 – Sea Haunt – Jack Davis (reprint from #14)
Page 81 – Tales for Tots – Don Orehek (reprint from #66)
Page 86 – A Swinging Good Time! (reprint from #71)
Page 89 – Brigitte Bardot as Seen by Different Artists – John Severin (reprint from #12)
Page 95 – Nobody Knows I'm Chicken! – Art Pottier (reprint from #74) (for some reason the title got reversed so it reads "I'm Chicken! Nobody Knows")
Page 100 – The Comparison Test – Vic Martin (reprint from #55)
Page 103 – Cracked's Gallery of Born Losers – Art Pottier (reprint from #69)
Page 109 – Old, Old Fashions for the New Generation – Johnny Langston (reprint from #79)
Page 114 – Cracked's Snappy Comebacks! – John Severin (reprint from #75)
Page 120 – What They Really Mean – Vic Martin (reprint from #80)

Page 123 – How to Make an "X" Movie Out of a Classic Film – Bob Taylor (reprint from #87)

Page 129 – Three for the Price of One (reprint from #53)

Page 130 – Psychological Predictions – Bill Elder (reprint from #6)

Page 140 – What if Mae West Were a High School Principal (partial reprint)

Page 143 – Try This Cracked 5-Day Diet (reprint from #4)

Page 150 – Welcome to the Strange World of Rodrigues – Charles Rodrigues (reprint from #54)

Page 155 – When All Competition is Eliminated – John Severin (reprint from #96)

Page 163 – Cracked Cracks – Don Orehek, Lennie Herman, Jack O'Brien, Art Pottier, Pete Wyma (reprint from #54)

Page 168 – Fly Me to the Moon – Oskar Blotta (reprint from #79)

Page 177 – A Kook Look at Sports (reprint from #76)

Page 181 – The Breaking Point! – Vic Martin (reprint from #56)

Page 184 – Musical Strains for Brains – Bill McCartney (Bill Ward) (reprint from #47)

Back Cover – text about book – Basil Gogos

***Don Martin's Droll Book*, November 1992 (Dark Horse Comics) (128 pages + covers) ($9.95 paperback / $19.95 hardback) (Not a *Cracked* publication, but it reprints a number of Don Martin strips that originally appeared in *Cracked*.)**

Cover – Don Martin's Droll Book – Don Martin (new)

Page 1 – Title page – Don Martin

Page 2 – Copyright and Dedication page – Don Martin

Page 3 – Introduction – John Callahan (new)

Page 5 – Part 1: Short Takes – Don Martin

Page 6 – Don Martin's One Fine Day in Florence – Don Martin (reprint from #253)

Page 7 – Don Martin's One Fine Day on the Great American Plains – Don Martin (reprint from #262)

Page 8 – Don Martin's Robin Hood – Don Martin (reprint from #266)

Page 13 – Don Martin's One Fine Day Whilst Walking – Don Martin (reprint from #254)

Page 14 – Don Martin's One Especially Fine Day this Winter – Don Martin (reprint from #235)

Page 15 – Don Martin's Crime-Thwarters Handbook – Don Martin (reprint from #260)

Page 16 – Don Martin's One Fine Evening in Manhattan – Don Martin (reprint from #242)

Page 17 – Don Martin's One Fine African Afternoon – Don Martin (reprint from #238)

Page 19 – Don Martin's One Fine Day in the Outback – Don Martin
(reprint from #255)
Page 20 – Don Martin's One Fine Day in Your Typical Cave Dwelling –
Don Martin (reprint from #249)
Page 22 – Don Martin's The Evolution of the Movie Kiss! – Don Martin
(reprint from #236)
Page 24 – Don Martin's One Fine Day in Nantucket – Don Martin
(reprint from #252)
Page 25 – Don Martin's The Half-Time Show! – Don Martin (reprint
from #234)
Page 26 – Don Martin's One Fine Day in Holland – Don Martin
(reprint from #254)
Page 27 – Don Martin's Late One Night in the City – Don Martin
(reprint from #270)
Page 29 – Don Martin's One Summer's Day in Bayonne – Don Martin
(reprint from #247)
Page 30 – Don Martin's One August Day in the Nursing Home – Don
Martin (reprint from #252)
Page 31 – Don Martin Does Quasimodo – Don Martin (reprint from
#241)
Page 34 – Don Martin's One Fine Day in the Great Outdoors – Don
Martin (reprint from #238)
Page 35 – Part 2: The Nutheads – Don Martin (reprints from Martin's
short-lived syndicated newspaper strip)
Page 65 – Part 3: More Nonsense – Don Martin (reprints from Martin's
Mad paperbacks with new dialogue written by Mort Todd.)
Page 127 – The End – Don Martin
Back Cover – Don Martin and Friend – Don Martin

***The Cracked Guide to the Movies*, 2001 (NBM Publishing, Inc.) (96 pages
+ covers) ($9.95 paperback)**
Cover – Sylvester's Film Reel – Dick Kulpa (new)
Page 1 – Title Page
Page 3 – Title Page with Captioned Photo (new)
Page 4 – Copyright Page
Page 5 – Bart Goes to the Movies – John Severin (reprint from #284)
Page 10 – Austin Poopers: The Spy Who Gagged Me – Frank
Cummings / Andy Simmons (reprint from *Cracked Summer Special*
#9)
Page 15 – Gourde O' Th' Bungle – John Severin / Lou Silverstone
(reprint from #324)
Page 21 – Cracked Interviews Leonardo – Bruce Bolinger / Lou
Silverstone (reprint from #329)

Page 26 – Tipanic! – John Severin / Andy Simmons (reprint from #325)
Page 32 – Snore Wars Epic-Dud 1 The Phantom Cuteness – John Severin / Lou Silverstone (reprint from #338)
Page 38 – Tarzan – Walter Brogan / Lou Silverstone (reprint from #339)
Page 43 – The Tatooine 500 – Bruce Bolinger / Rob Weske (reprint from #338)
Page 46 – Galaxy Queasy – Walter Brogan / Andy Simmons (reprint from #341)
Page 52 – Toy Borey, Too – John Severin / Lou Silverstone (reprint from #341)
Page 57 – Rocker and Bullwanker – Frank Cummings / Bobbie Bender (reprint from #346)
Page 62 – EXcreMENt! – Tom Richmond / Barry Dutter (reprint from #346)
Page 68 – Spies and Sabs Hit the X-Men – Mike Ricigliano (reprint from #346)
Page 70 – Me, Myself & Ireek – Walter Brogan / Barry Dutter (reprint from #347)
Page 72 – The Patridiot – John Severin / Peet Janes (reprint from #347)
Page 74 – Graft – Dick Ayers / Robbie Bender (reprint from #347)
Page 76 – Done in 60 Seconds! – Dick Kulpa / Suzie Estridge (reprint from #347)
Page 78 – Gladidiot! – Tom Richmond / Barry Dutter (reprint from #347)
Page 83 – From the Cracked Lens! (elevator operator) (new)
Page 84 – From the Cracked Lens! (Do you like 'em) (reprint from #350)
Page 86 – Cracked Lens (lay off the hot sauce) (reprint from #351)
Page 88 – Charlie's Hotties – Frank Cummings / Barry Dutter (reprint from #351)
Page 92 – The Grunch Who Repossessed Christmas – Rich Hedden / Barry Dutter (reprint from #351)
Back Cover – Hollywood Through the Blender! – John Severin, Frank Cummings, Jeff Wong, Bruce Bolinger (reprint from #325, 329, 338, 351, *Cracked Summer Special* #9)

***You Might Be a Zombie and Other Bad News* From the Editors of Cracked.com, January 2011 (Plume Books) (120 pages + covers) ($14.00 paperback) (The material for this book was cobbled together from various postings on the Cracked.com website. As the book falls outside the scope of this book and the writers and artists are not connected to the magazine, its contents are not described in detail.)**

THE CRACKED WHO'S WHO

PEOPLE who worked at *Cracked* in issues #1-365 (1958-2004): the REAL *Cracked*! (every attempt was made to list people by their real name: the proofreader name excepted)

Editors:
Sol Brodsky – 1-10
No Editor listed – 11-13, 198-199
Paul Laikin – 14-23, 213-218
Robert C. Sproul – 24-35, 63-83, 102-161
Joe Kiernan – 36-62
Arlene Newman – 84-85
Jimm J. Grady – 86-95
Duane Morse – 96-99
Stephen H. Snow – 100-101
Bill Sproul – 162-181, 207-212
Marion Sproul – 182-197
Elaine Ozimok – 200-207
Mort Todd – 219-257
Lou Silverstone – 258-343
Jerry De Fuccio – 258-272
Andy Simmons – 273-343
Dick Kulpa – 344-351
Barry Dutter – 352-361
Scott Gosar – 362-365
Marten Jallad – 362-365

Managing Editor:
Peet Janes – 344-351
Suzie Estridge – 352-354
David Berns – 359-361

Roving Editor:
Dan Fiorella – 354-356

Publisher:
No Publisher listed – 1, 213-253, 255-262, 344-354
Robert C. Sproul – 2-212
Kenneth Baratto – 254 (Actual publisher with Larry Levine from 213-262)
Barry Rosenbloom – 263-343
Dick Kulpa – 344-363
Rick Nielsen – 364-365

Chief Operating Officer:
David Pecker – 344-351

General Manager:
Jean Fornasieri – 344-345
Larry Bornstein – 346-351

Chief Executive Officer:
Kevin Hyson – 344-351
Dick Kulpa – 352-365

Chief Financial Officer:
John Miley – 344-351
Jon Bates – 363-365

General Counsel:
Scott Price – 344-351
Mark Shoemaker – 352-355, 361
Donna M. Friedah – 357-358
Howard Enrique – 359-360
Ron W. Methvin – 362-365

VP Direct Response Marketing:
Bette Rockmore – 344-351

VP / Editorial Director:
Eddie Clontz – 344-347

Executive VP Publishing:
Richard Amann – 346-351

Internet Boss:
Bobbie Bender – 352-358

Webmaster / Promotions Editor:
Mark Van Woert – 356-365

Business / Advertising Manager:
Charles Novinskie – 355-356
Janet P. McGill – 357-358

Business Consultant:
Howard Enrique – 357

Business Analyst:
Leonelly Moreno Lara – 357

Customer Care / Systems Analyst:
Elizabeth Semple – 359-361
Hara Bender – 362-365

Administration / Bookkeeper:
Fern Parks – 357-365

Production:
Rex Roman – 2
Harry Chester – 9-19, 100
George Peltz – 20
Charles Foster – 21-80
Shirley Otey – 98
Allan Kurzrok – 125-128

Art Director:
William Clark – 2
Aron Mayer – 213-216
Mel Unger – 217-218
Barry Shapiro – 219-236
Cliff Mott – 237-343
Steph Ramsay – 345-353

Assistant Art Director:
Lewis Hamilton – 217-219

Production Associate / Assistant:
Tom Walsh – 2
Roberta Vandermolen – 44
Elaine Ozimok – 183-199

Roving Correspondent:
R.L. Flynn – 2

Script Editor:
Paul Laikin – 7

Assoc. / Assist. / Managing Editor:
Jane M. Thaler – 24-25
Bette Martin – 26-32
Joe Kiernan – 33-35, 80-83
Arlene Newman – 73-83
Steve Hollis – 125-126
Mike Ricigliano – 136-138
Bill Sproul – 145-161
Marion Sproul – 178-181
Eden Laikin – 213-217
Mort Todd – 218, 221
Jerry De Fuccio – 242-257
Don Crosby – 246-253
Cliff Mott – 258-343
Daniel O'Keefe – 275-288
Greg Grabianski – 289-295
Todd Jackson – 297-312, 314-343
Barry Dutter – 344-351
Susie Estridge – 344-351
Bobbie Bender – 346-351

Contributing / Consulting Editor:
Joe Catalano – 154-212
Mort Todd – 217
Dave Berns – 358

Assistant Troublemaker:
Deborah Klein – 220

Missing-in-Action:
Walter Brogan – 222

Press and Publicity:
Diana Rickard – 260-262

Intern:
Eric Finkelstein – 324-330
Igor – 332-338
Adam Marlowe – 339-340

Jr. Editor:
Michele Marie Kaye – 358

Contributing Writer:
Peter I. Sosa – 357

Travel Consultant:
Adam Bender – 364-365

Artists:
John Severin – 1-334, 336-355, 360, 362-363
Paul Reinman – 1-4
Ed Winiarski – 1
Russ Heath – 1-3, 6, 13-14, 17, 95, 110, 117
Joe Maneely – 1-5, 12, 77
Bill Everett – 1-10, 23-25, 40, 61
Carl Burgos – 1-10, 54, 356
Al Williamson – 1
Joe Kiernan – 1, 37, 42, 52, 56
Don Orehek – 1, 8, 13-14, 33-40, 42, 46, 52-54, 56-58, 60-71, 95-97, 99, 104-106, 108-132, 134-212, 218, 220-279, 281-289, 291-298, 300-302, 304-308, 310-315, 317-334, 336-337, 339-345, 347, 3490350, 352-353, 364
Bill Ward – 2-10, 12-14, 22-71, 73-102, 110-195, 197-205, 215, 242, 244, 246-247, 250-251, 253-257, 351-353, 355, 360

D.A. Vinci – 2
Bernard Baily – 3-8, 22, 105-121
Syd Shores – 3-7
Pete Costanza – 3
Jack Davis – 5, 11-18, 36, 39, 42-44, 47, 51, 53, 55-57, 66, 78, 80, 215, 238-240, 262, 352, 354
Bill Elder – 5-6, 10-13, 15, 26, 37, 260, 270
Al Jaffee – 5-7, 36
Jerry Behar – 5
Richard Doxsee – 6-10, 38
Dick Richards – 6-10
Angelo Torres – 7-10, 12, 361
Gray Morrow – 8-10, 228-229, 238, 241, 249, 252, 288, 294, 296-297, 299
Stan Quinnley – 9-10
Basil Wolverton – 10, 254
Vic Martin – 13-14, 18-23, 37, 39, 41, 44-61, 63-66, 72-109, 112, 115, 132-133, 136, 206, 213-223, 226-231, 235-240, 242, 246-252, 254, 256-257, 262, 265-270, 363
Jack Kirby – 14
Jerry Kirschen – 15-18, 46
Chic Stone – 16-17, 81
Angel Martinez – 17-18
George Peltz – 18-19
Don Swanson – 19-23
Oswaldo Laino – 20-25, 27, 59, 61
Sam Hayle – 20-21
Betty Silon – 20
Stuart Sloves – 22
Bayon – 23
Brutus – 23
Pete Wyma – 30-33, 37-38, 41-46, 54
Milton Fenster – 34
Melvin Z. Fenton – 35
Edward Freen – 36
Jack Totten – 37
Noel Klineman – 37
Bob Zahn – 37-38, 47
Bud Carter – 38-40
Art Pottier – 38-39, 41-44, 49, 51-58, 69, 73-74, 86, 100, 103
Charles Rodrigues – 39, 42, 51, 53-134, 180, 182-186, 206, 208

Writers:

Proofreader:

If You're *Cracked*, You're Happy, Book Too

Janitor / Chief Maintenance Engineer:

World's Most Hated Man:

Chief Bully:

Cover-up Editor:

Addresses:
218 West 48th Street, New York 36, NY – 1-19
45 West 45th Street, New York 36, NY – 20-66
1585 Broadway, New York, NY 10036 – 67-92
235 Park Avenue South, New York, NY 10003 – 93-189
239 Park Avenue South, Suite 5D, New York, NY 10003 – 190-212
   (Bob Sproul published from Florida – 93-212)
535 Fifth Avenue, New York, NY 10017 – 213-214
441 Lexington Avenue, Suite 505, New York, NY 10017 – 215-261
441 Lexington Avenue, 2nd Floor, New York, NY 10017 – 262-303
3 East 54th Street, New York, NY 10022 – 304-343
5401 N.W. Broken Sound Blvd., Boca Raton, FL 33487 – 344-353
2500 Quantum Lakes Drive, Suite 203, Boynton Beach, FL 33426 – 354-357
6146 Terra Rosa Circle, Boynton Beach, FL 33437 – 358-362
P.O. Box 3098, Rockford, IL 61104 – 363-365

Major Magazines, a division of Candar Publishing – 1-212
Larken Communications – 213-214
   Distributed by Ace – 1-87
Distributed by Dell – 88-126
Distributed by Select Magazines – 127-214
Globe Communications Corporation – 215-341
   Distributed by F – 215-240
Distributed by Globe – 241-341
American Media Corporation – 342-343
American Media Consumer Entertainment – 344-351
Mega Media Corporation – 352-357, 362-365
Mega Media Entertainment, Inc. – 358-361

19, April 1961, Average number of copies sold: 140,676
24, April 1962, Average number of copies sold: 159,113
29, May 1963, Average number of copies sold: 135,632
30, July 1963, Average number of copies sold: 145,438
36, June 1964, Average number of copies sold: 138,463
43, May 1965, Average number of copies sold: 263,612
50, March 1966, Average number of copies sold: 266,338
60, May 1967, Average number of copies sold: 264,459
68, May 1968, Average number of copies sold: 132,401
75, March 1969, Average number of copies sold: 143,413
83, March 1970, Average number of copies sold: 137,676
92, May 1971, Average number of copies sold: 138,005
100, May 1972, Average number of copies sold: 133,997
108, May 1973, Average number of copies sold: 148,750
116, May 1974, Average number of copies sold: 203,330
123, March 1975, Average number of copies sold: 366,800
131, March 1976, Average number of copies sold: 413,481

140, March 1977, Average number of copies sold: 441,245
149, March 1978, Average number of copies sold: 473,801
158, March 1979, Average number of copies sold: 463,085
167, March 1980, Average number of copies sold: 434,946
176, March 1981, Average number of copies sold: 388,863
185, March 1982, Average number of copies sold: 341,762
193, March 1983, Average number of copies sold: 309,406
202, March 1984, Average number of copies sold: 272,581
210, March 1985, Average number of copies sold: 238,595
223, October 1986, Average number of copies sold: 190,100
226, March 1987, Average number of copies sold: 197,047
235, May 1988, Average number of copies sold: 182,654

VARIOUS CRACKED MERCHANDISE PRODUCED OVER THE YEARS

"Who's *Cracked*?" T-Shirt

"Horror House" and "Joke Shop" novelty items

Cracked Blow-Up Poster

6 Binders and 6 Notepads featuring cover images from #80, 86, 93, 97, 98, 105

"If You're *Cracked*, You're Happy" Iron-On

56 Card Set and 10 Stickers "Best of *Cracked*" Wax Packs 1978

"Perfect 10" Iron-On

"Official *Cracked* Reporter" T-Shirt

Cracked Fan Club Kit: Flying Disc, Membership Card, Secret Message Decoder

Square Egg Maker

1988 *Cracked* T-Shirt

Intergalactic Wrestling Cards

Sylvester P. Smythe Plush Doll

Don Martin T-Shirt

1988 *Cracked* Convention

Black *Cracked* T-Shirt

12 *Cracked* Monster Cards

56 *Cracked* Phloggs/Caps

Cracked Flying Saucer

Cracked Water Bottles

Cracked Sunglasses

White *Cracked* T-Shirt

6 *Cracked* Signs

Cracked Millennium Lithograph

4 T-Shirts: "Bite Me," "Cracked Millennium," "Hangin' On," "Sylvester"

Cracked Button

Various Cracked.com merchandise

BiBLiOGRAPHY

Comic Book Comics #4 (November 2009)

Crime Illustrated volume of the Picto-Fiction box set published by Gemstone

Gerber Goes Crazy! By Mark Arnold

Comics Journal #215, August 1999

The Krantz Connection, by Curt Ladnier

Mad Cover to Cover

The Mad World of William M. Gaines by Frank Jacobs, 1972

Marvel Bullpen

Men's Adventure Magazines

David A. Roach's and Jon B. Cooke's *The Warren Companion*

Wikipedia

…and of course, the 758 issues of *Cracked* and their related titles as listed in the index.

INDEX

ABOUT THE AUTHOR

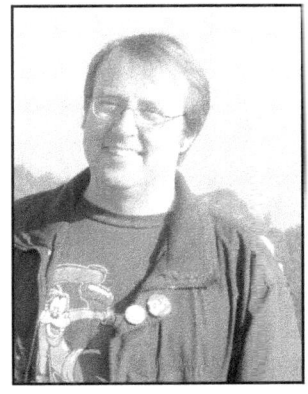

MARK ARNOLD (born December 15, 1966 in San Jose, California) is an American writer who grew up in Saratoga, California. He has contributed to several publications in the United States, including *The Comics Journal*, *Hogan's Alley*, *Back Issue* and *Comic Buyer's Guide*. Arnold also worked with Jerry Beck and Leslie Cabarga on their *Harvey Comics Classics* series for Dark Horse Comics.

Here's what working on a *Cracked* book for over a year does to you. Before...

Arnold has written two books about comic books and animation. The first, *The Best of The Harveyville Fun Times!*, focused on the comic book publisher Harvey Comics. The second was *Created and Produced by Total TeleVision productions: The Story of Underdog, Tennessee Tuxedo and the Rest.*

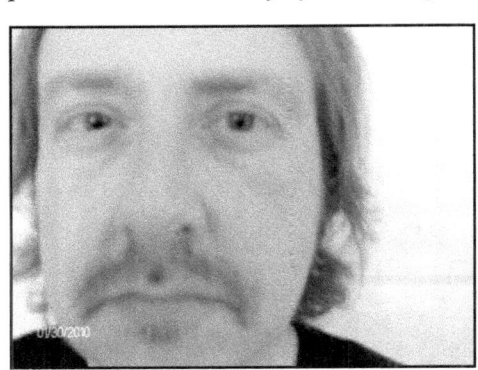

... and after!

Arnold also compiled the traveling original art show entitled *From Richie Rich to Wendy the Witch: The Art of Harvey Comics* which debuted in June 2008 at San Francisco's Cartoon Art Museum, moving to New York City's Museum of Comic and Cartoon Art in December 2008 and traveling again to Pittsburgh, Pennsylvania, in May 2009. The show ended in Pittsburgh in July 2009.

The Saratoga History Museum honored Arnold by including him in a display of famous Saratogans, which ran from November 2009 through January 2010.

Arnold has a BA degree in Broadcast Communication Arts from San Francisco State University, and has studied art through Art Instruction Schools. He currently resides in Saratoga, California, and is working on a book about The Beatles.

If you didn't like this book, you surely won't enjoy:

The Best of the Harveyville Fun Times!

Created and Produced by Total TeleVision productions:
The Story of Underdog, Tennessee Tuxedo and the Rest